THE COMPUTER FURNITURE PLAN & PROJECT BOOK

JACK WILEY

Other TAB Books by the Author

No. 1242 *How To Fix Up An Old Boat On A Small Budget*
No. 1297 *The Fiberglass Repair & Construction Handbook*
No. 1639 *Wood Carving, with Projects*
No. 1669 *The Kite Building & Kite Flying Handbook with 42 Kite Plans*
No. 1779 *Make Your Own Exercise Equipment*

FIRST EDITION

FIRST PRINTING

Copyright © 1985 by TAB BOOKS Inc.

Printed in the United States of America

Reproduction or publication of the content in any manner, without express permission of the publisher, is prohibited. No liability is assumed with respect to the use of the information herein.

Library of Congress Cataloging in Publication Data

Wiley, Jack.
The computer furniture plan and project book.

Includes index.
1. Computer furniture. 2. Woodworking. I. Title.
TT197.5.C65W55 1985 684.1 85-14775
ISBN 0-8306-0949-0
ISBN 0-8306-1949-6 (pbk.)

Contents

	Introduction	iv
1	**Design, Planning, and Basic Concepts of Computer Furniture**	1
2	**Basic Construction Techniques**	15
	Tools—Basic Techniques	
3	**Plans and Patterns for Basic Computer Tables**	38
	Basic Budget Computer Table—Basic Computer Table with Full Sides—Basic Computer Table with Half Sides—Basic Budget Computer Table with Video and Storage Rack—Basic Computer Table with Full Sides and Video and Storage Rack—Basic Computer Table with Half Sides and Video and Storage Rack	
4	**Plans and Patterns for Basic Printer Stands**	167
	Basic Budget Printer Stand—Basic Printer Stand with Full Sides—Basic Printer Stand with Half Sides	
5	**Plans and Patterns for Modular Units**	222
	Basic Computer Table for Modular Units—Construction of Extenders	
6	**Built-In Wall Units**	253
	Construction—Variations	
7	**Plans and Patterns for Miscellaneous Projects**	269
	Printer Platform—Storage Rack—Kneeling Chair	
	Index	282

Introduction

Computers have invaded our lives, at our places of business and in our homes. This has resulted in a tremendous demand for computer furniture, essentially, office furniture designed especially for computers, computer printers, and other devices used with computers.

Manufacturers are trying to keep up with the growing demand for all types of computer furniture. To date, however, the demand has kept ahead of the supply. Thus, the price of manufactured furniture is high, unlike that of most popular computers, which are dropping in price. Many computer owners, finding that they cannot get exactly what they want in manufactured computer furniture, are going to custom computer furniture builders to meet their specific needs.

One alternative that has been largely overlooked until now is to make your own computer furniture. This, to my knowledge, is the first complete handbook devoted to the subject of making your own computer furniture. Although many books cover furniture building, I do not know of any that focus on computer furniture.

The material presented in this book is intended for all levels of skill, from the complete beginner to the advanced do-it-yourselfer. Your reasons for making your own computer furniture can range from a desire to save money or get exactly what you want, to setting up a business making custom computer furniture to sell to others.

This book is project-oriented. The basics necessary to get you started are covered in the opening chapters. Then you move on to the actual projects, where the real art and craft of building computer furniture is learned.

The art and craft of building computer furniture can be just about anything you want to make it. You can devote very little time and effort to it, or you can make it a full-time endeavor.

The assumption is made that you are investing in this book to actually learn how to make functional and attractive computer furniture, so to get your money's worth, you must not only read this book, but get involved in the actual construction processes. Many projects are included in this book to help you learn how to make your own computer furniture; you must actually try them, not just read about them. In order to learn to swim, you will need to get wet.

Complete instructions are given for budget designs of computer furniture that are not only functional and attractive, but can be built for very little money, and custom furniture that will be of interest to more advanced do-it-yourselfers.

Chapter 1

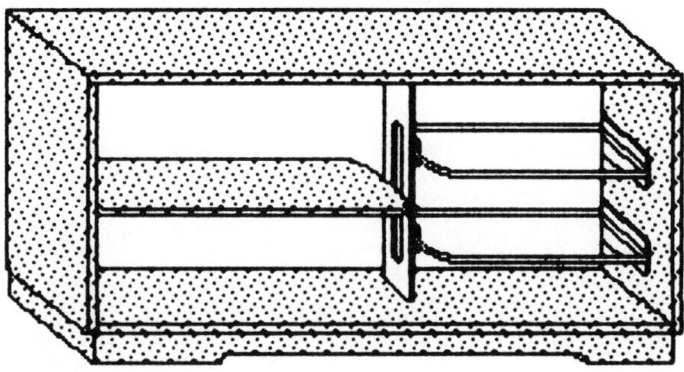

Design, Planning, and Basic Concepts of Computer Furniture

Computer furniture should be, first of all, functional (Fig. 1-1). It should be designed for convenient use of computers and peripheral equipment (printers, communication equipment, external disk drives, mouse input devices, etc.). Optimum design takes many factors into consideration, most importantly, operator fatigue, which should be reduced to a minimum by proper position of video displays, keyboard home-row heights, and other ergonomic considerations (Fig. 1-2).

Although the design of most manufactured furniture is getting better, some, especially low-cost furniture designed for home use, leaves much to be desired. Many computer tables, for example, have no place for an open book, as though computers have eliminated the need for books. In practice, this is usually not the case. Even if you don't use books for your actual computer work, which is unlikely, you will still need a place for open computer manuals so that you can see them while you work at the keyboard (Figs. 1-3 and 1-4). In many cases, the novice computer owner starts out with a basic computer with a cassette tape recorder, and he has ample space to work on a typical small manufactured computer table. Then a printer is purchased, and all the work space adjacent to the computer is used up (Fig. 1-5).

At this point, there are several options available. You can get a separate table or stand for the printer (Fig. 1-6) that can be positioned as a workspace beside your computer, or you can get a larger table. In most cases, however, it would have been better to have started with a larger table in the first place.

Besides being functional, durable, and easy to maintain, most people want their computer furniture to be attractive and of modern design (Fig. 1-7). Although antique and old-style furniture can and is being used for computers, this does not seem to fit in with the modern design of the computers themselves. (I haven't yet seen a computer manufactured with an antique-style cabinets.) In any case, most computer furniture is made of either natural wood or plastic laminate finishes (Fig.

Fig. 1-1. Basic computer table is simple yet very functional.

1-8). Metal furniture can cause many possible electrical problems with computers and thus has for the most part been avoided as computer furniture.

The basic starting unit is the single-table computer work station (Fig. 1-9). This is a table that has space for a computer and some peripheral equipment and, usually, some storage space, often in the form of a shelf below (Figs. 1-10 and 1-11) the table and/or a rack above the table top at the back (Fig. 1-12). In Chapter 3, construction of a variety of tables, both with and without racks, is detailed. Designs are provided for both computers with keyboards and monitors as a unit and those with separate monitors and keyboards. These computer tables can be modified to fit your particular needs. You may, for example, only have a certain limited space in to which to put your computer table. You will want the most functional computer table possible that will fit in that space. If you have adequate space, a table larger than your present needs is recommended, because you will probably add equipment as you go along.

The second main class of computer furniture is printer tables or stands (Fig. 1-13). These are usually separate tables or stands that are placed next to, either in line or perpendicular, the basic computer table. The computer printers are then placed on these small tables or stands. This has a number of advantages. It frees work space on the main computer table, and if the printer shakes (many of the daisy wheel printers do), this does not cause problems with the main computer. If your system allows you to do other computer work while you are printing out hard copy, the separate printer table or stand makes it convenient for you to do this (Fig. 1-14). Computer printers are often best positioned lower than the computer table. The separate printer stand or table allows you to have two different table heights. Printer stands are detailed in Chapter 4.

The modular concept (Fig. 1-15) has a lot going for it. These are essentially separate pieces of furniture that can be connected together to form complete units. You can arrange these in a variety of patterns that allow you to start with one or two pieces and then add to these as your needs grow— and for many computer enthusiasts they do grow (Fig. 1-16). First, it's a simple computer, then a printer is added, then an external disk drive, a second printer, a second computer, and so on. That's what happened with me. Modular units can be arranged in a variety of patterns, including L- and U-shapes, to accommodate these add-ons (Fig. 1-17). Modular units can also be arranged for use by more than one person at a time. Plans and patterns for modular units are given in Chapter 5.

Still another possibility is to build your computer furniture into wall units (Fig. 1-18) as detailed

Fig. 1-2. Computer table with top and shelves conveniently placed reduces operator fatigue.

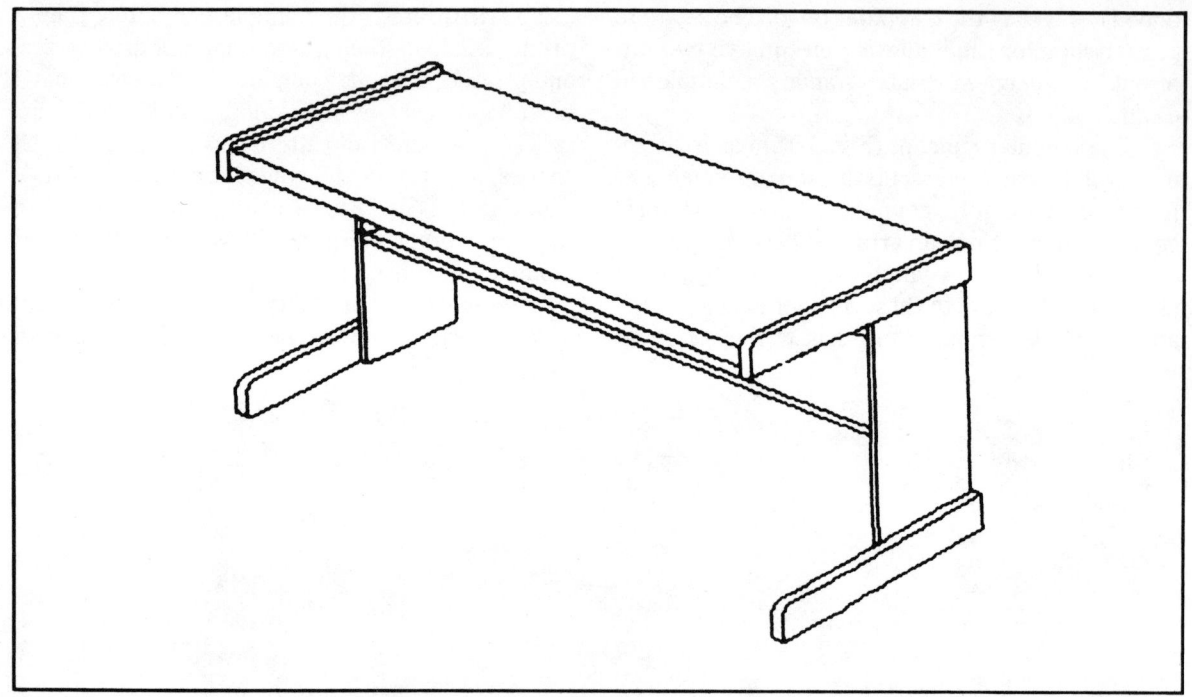

Fig. 1-3. Although simple, this basic table has lots of room for computer, manuals, and work.

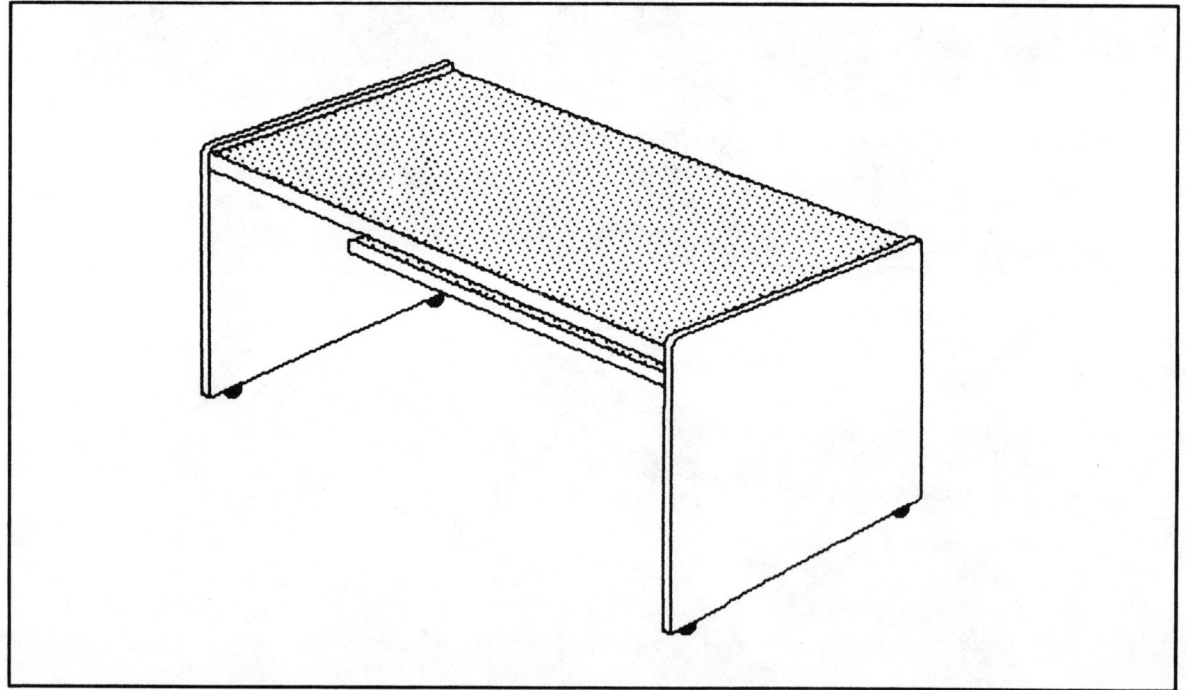

Fig. 1-4. A table with storage shelf provides even more work room.

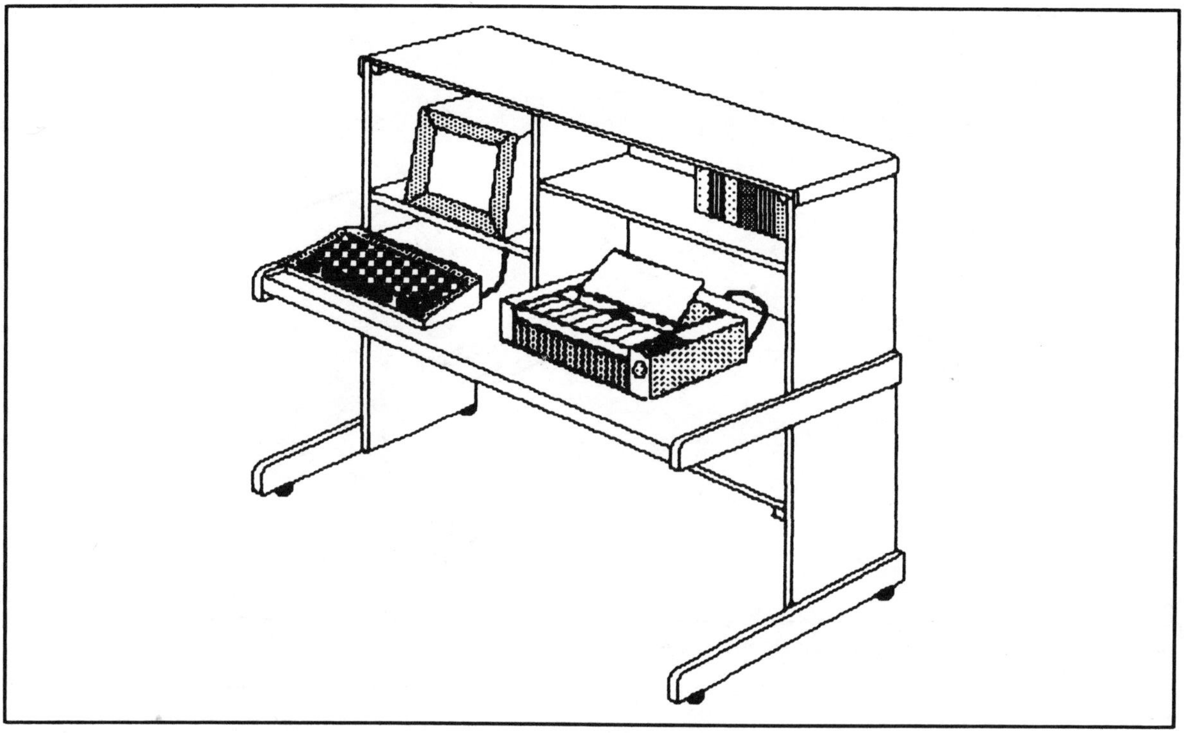

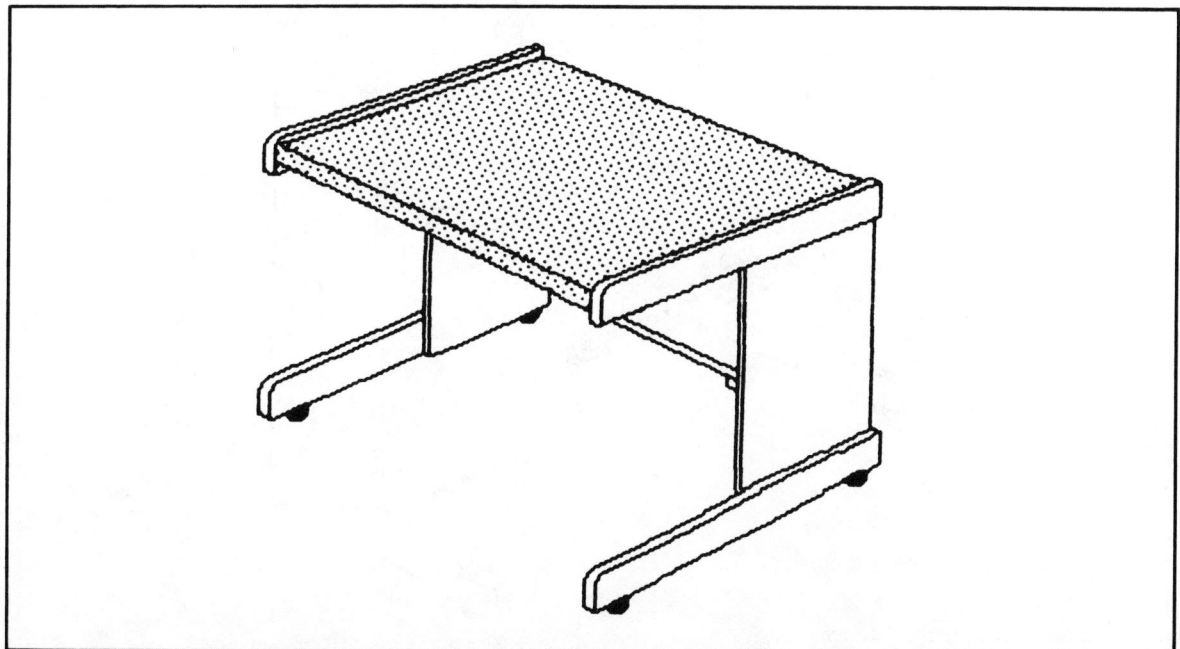

Fig. 1-5. This design has ample space for computer and printer.

Fig. 1-6. Separate printer stand can expand workspace.

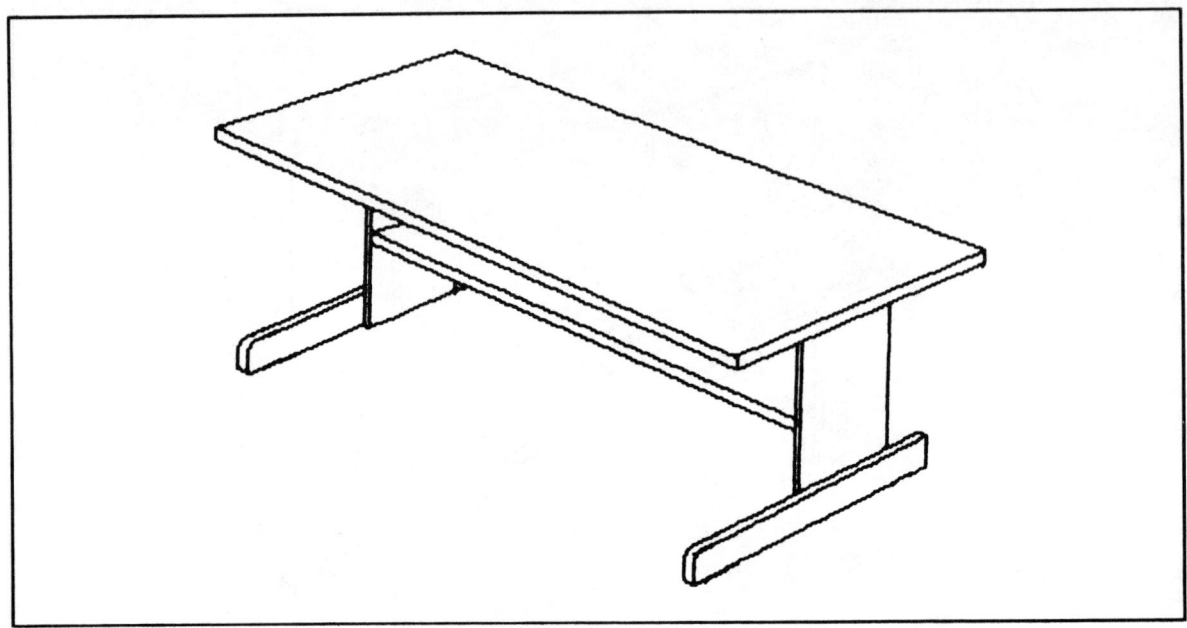

Fig. 1-7. This table is durable, functional, and sleekly modern.

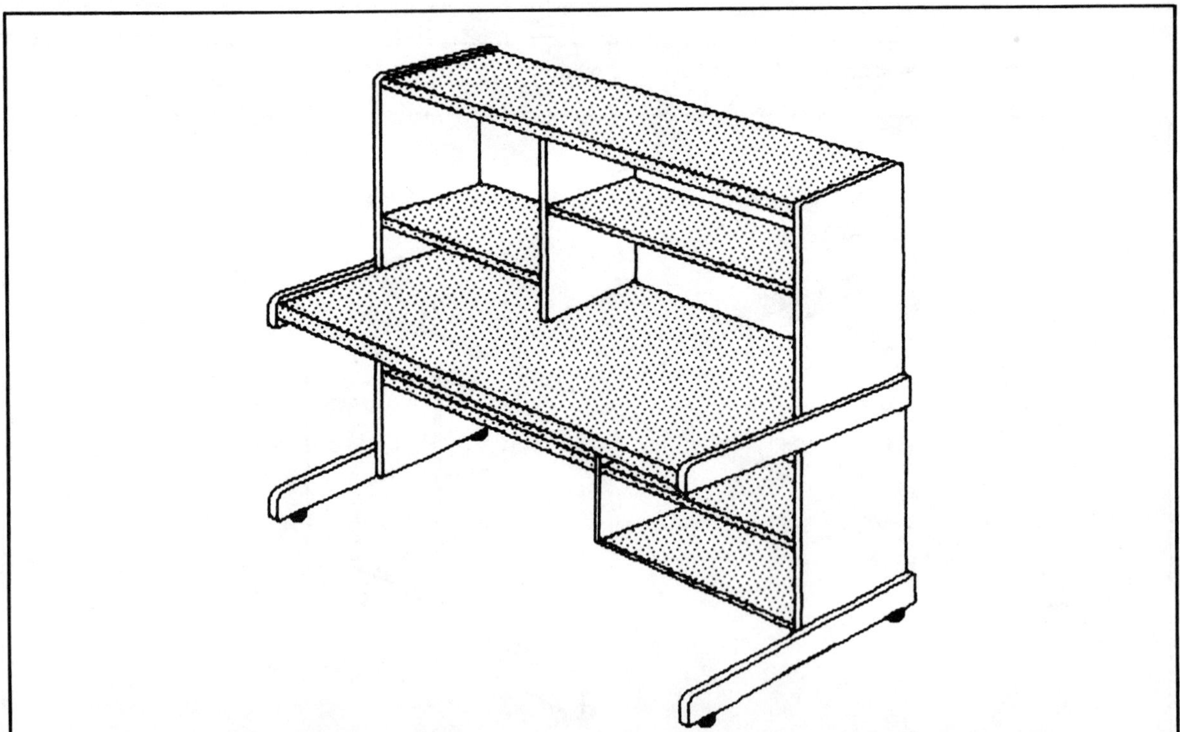

Fig. 1-8. Plastic laminates cover all table and shelf tops in this highly organized table.

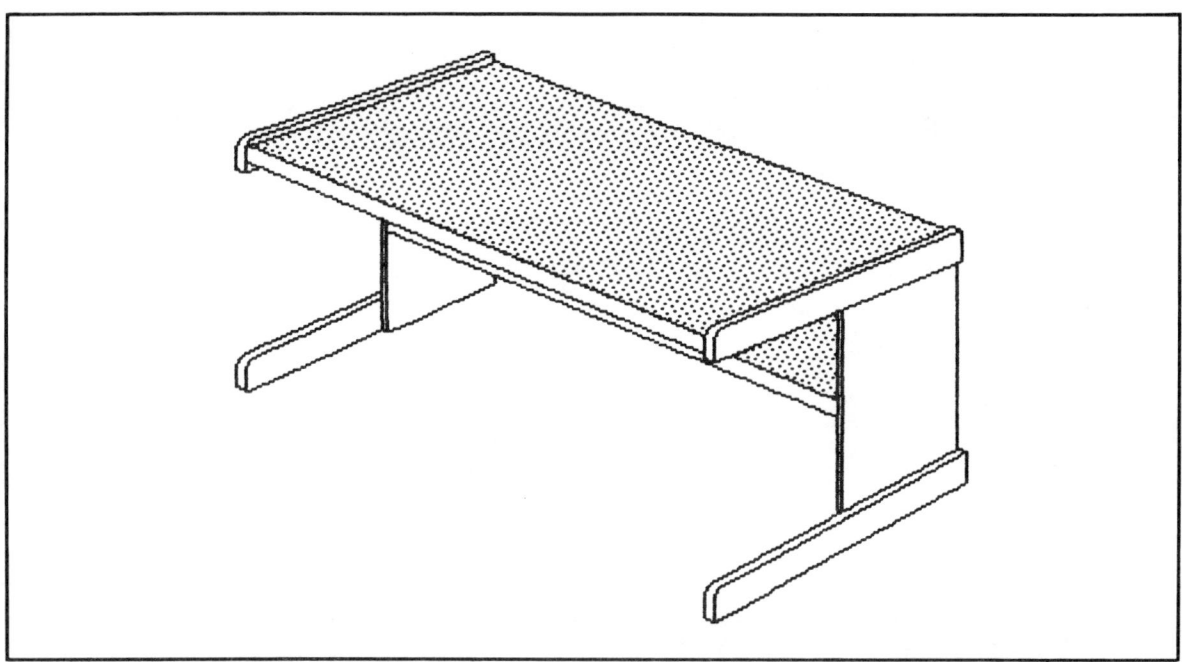

Fig. 1-9. Basic computer table with half sides.

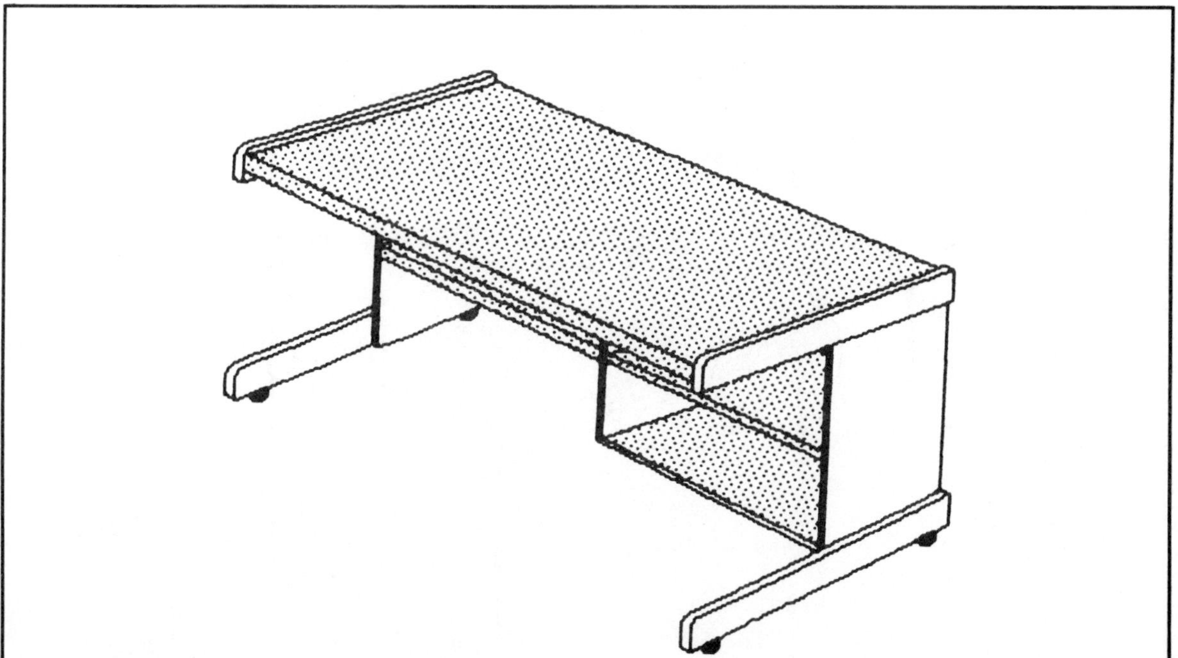

Fig. 1-10. Shelves under table provide storage.

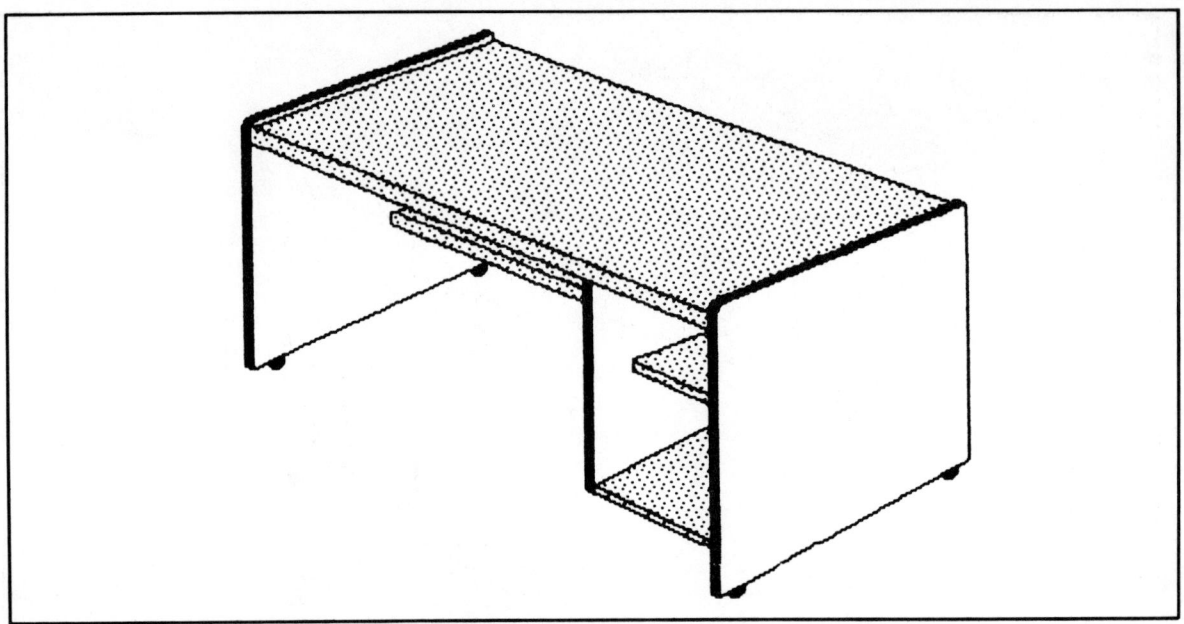

Fig. 1-11. Alternate arrangement of storage shelves.

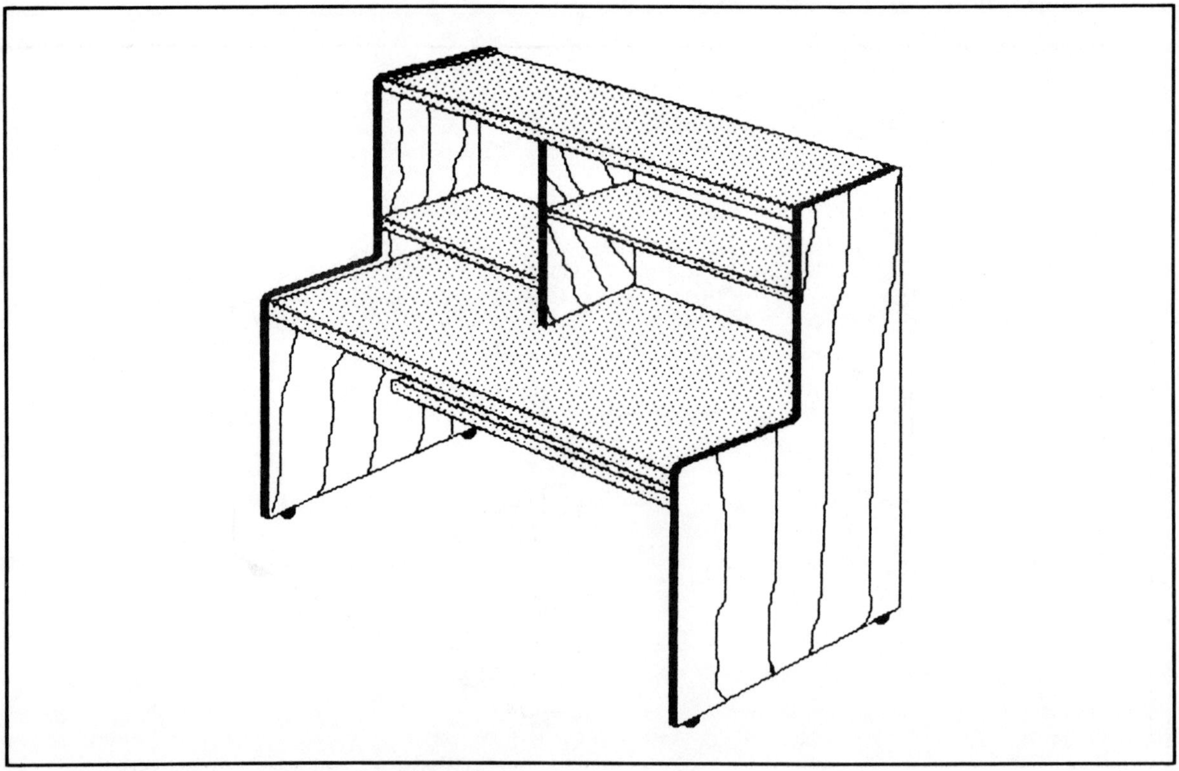

Fig. 1-12. Racks above table expand storage capacity.

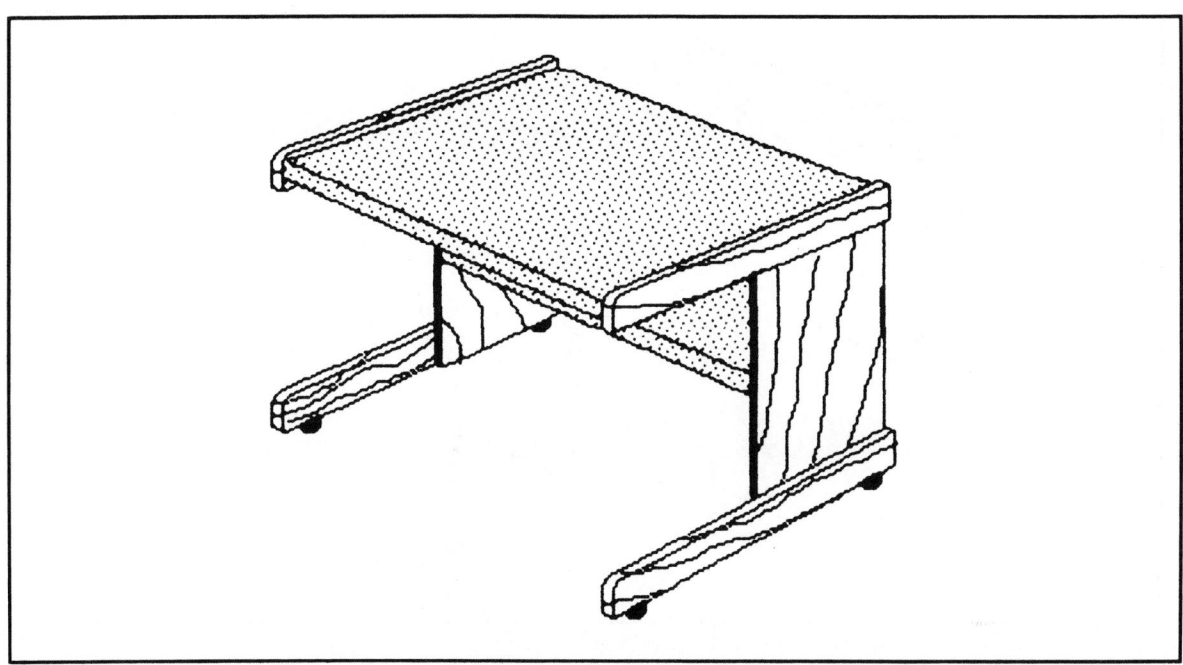

Fig. 1-13. Basic printer stand with plastic laminate on shelf and top.

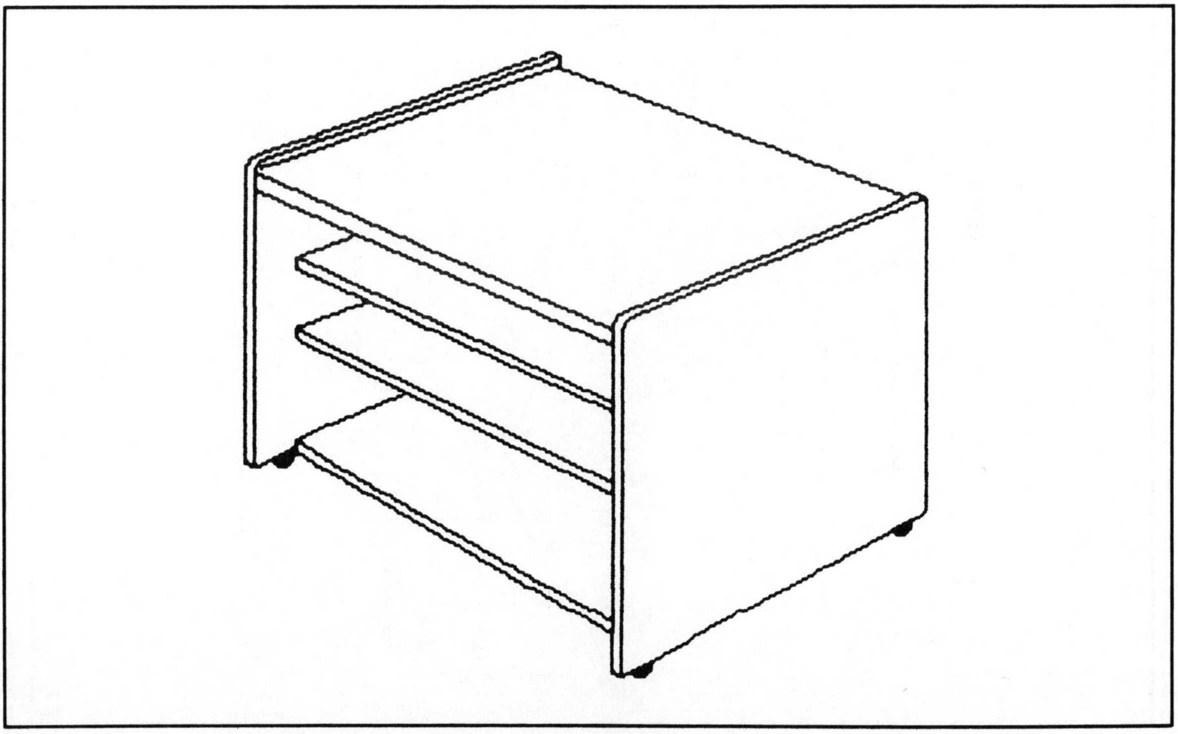

Fig. 1-14. Basic printer stand with shelves and full sides for extra storage.

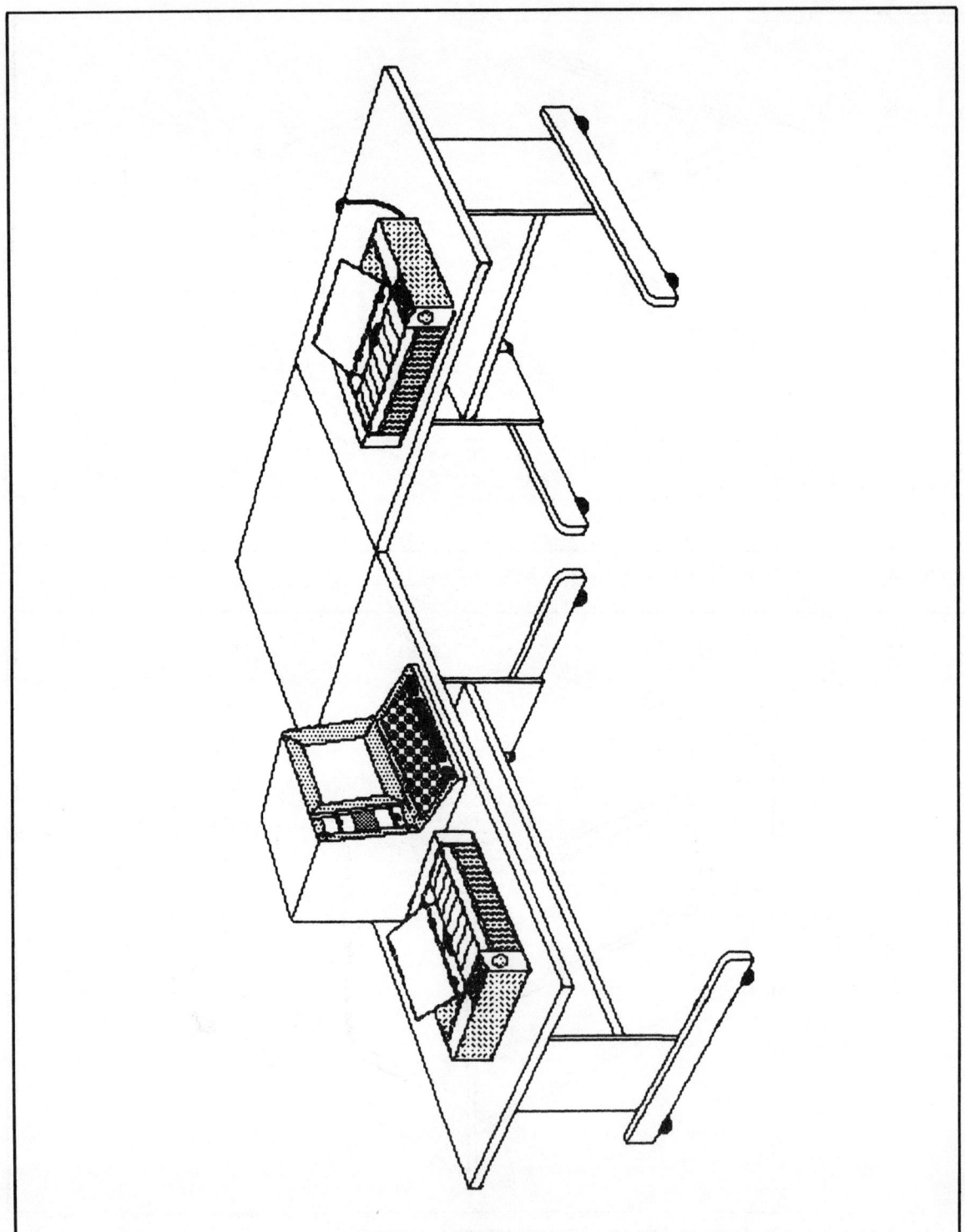

Fig. 1-15. Modular arrangement of basic tables.

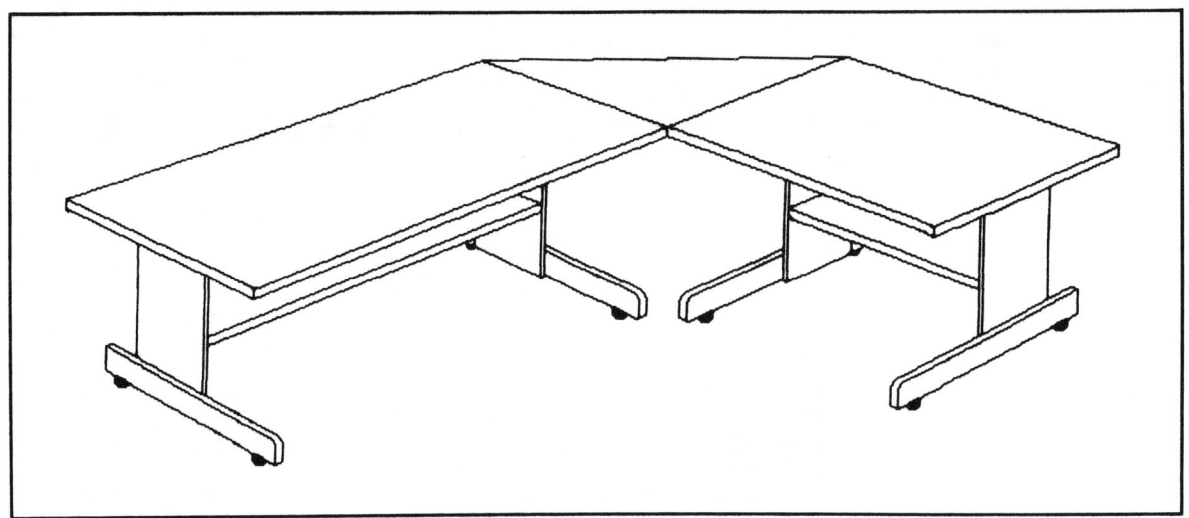

Fig. 1-16. Long and short tables connected with 90-degree extender.

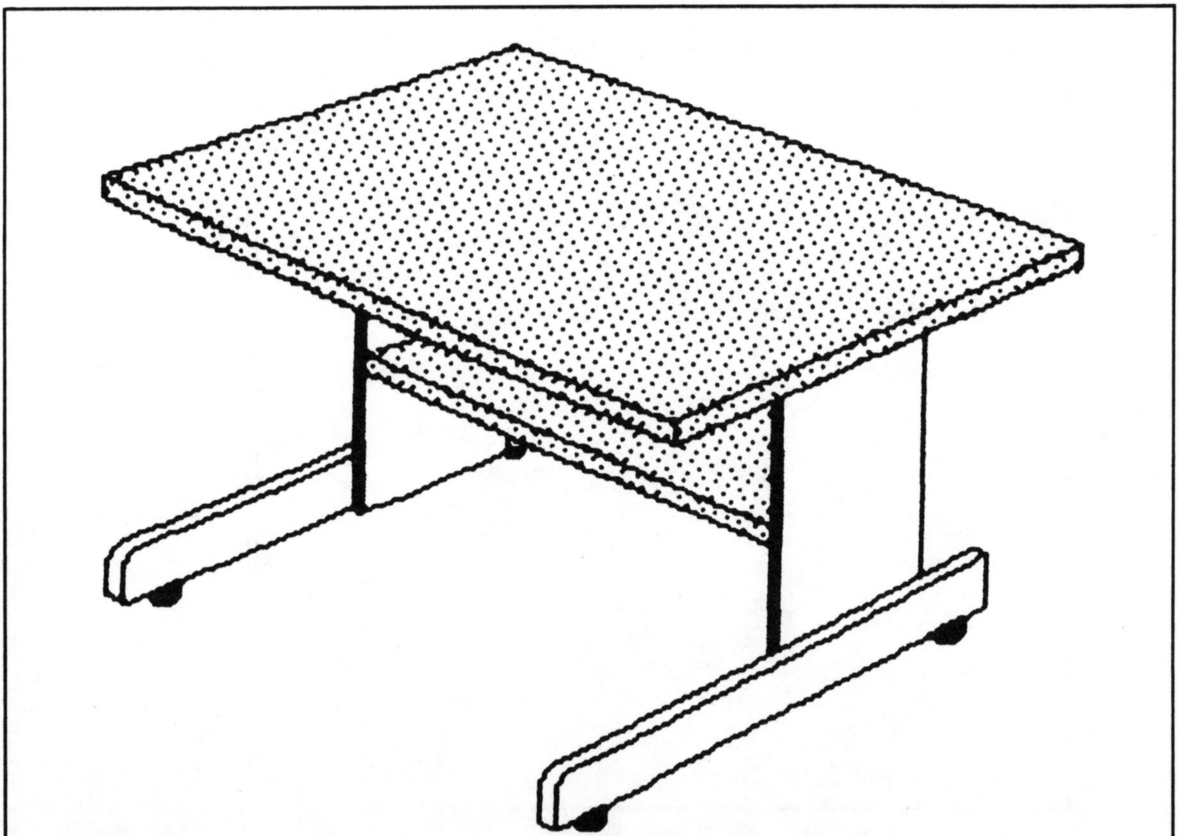

Fig. 1-17. Shorter version of modular table, covered in laminate.

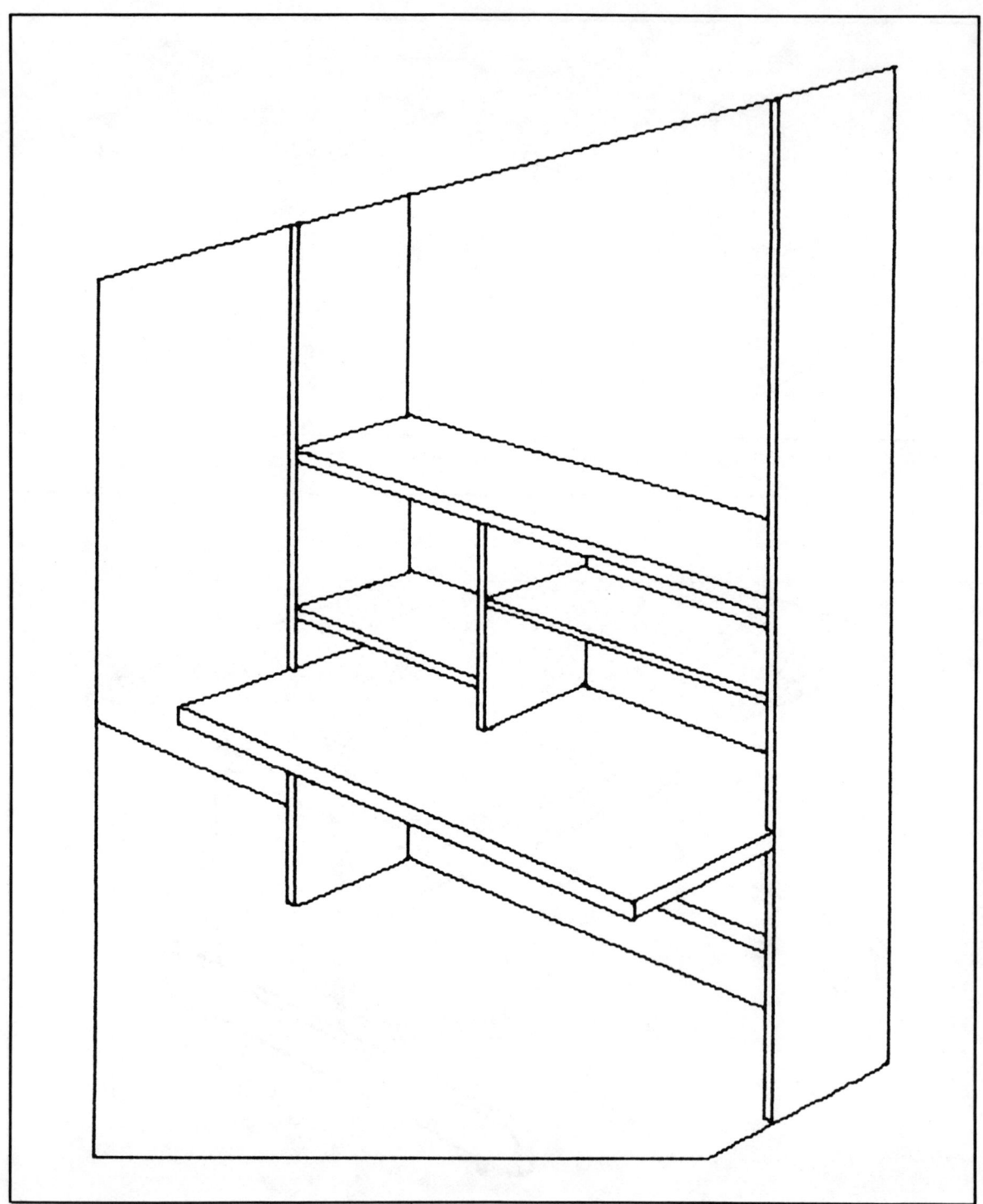

Fig. 1-18. Built-in wall unit.

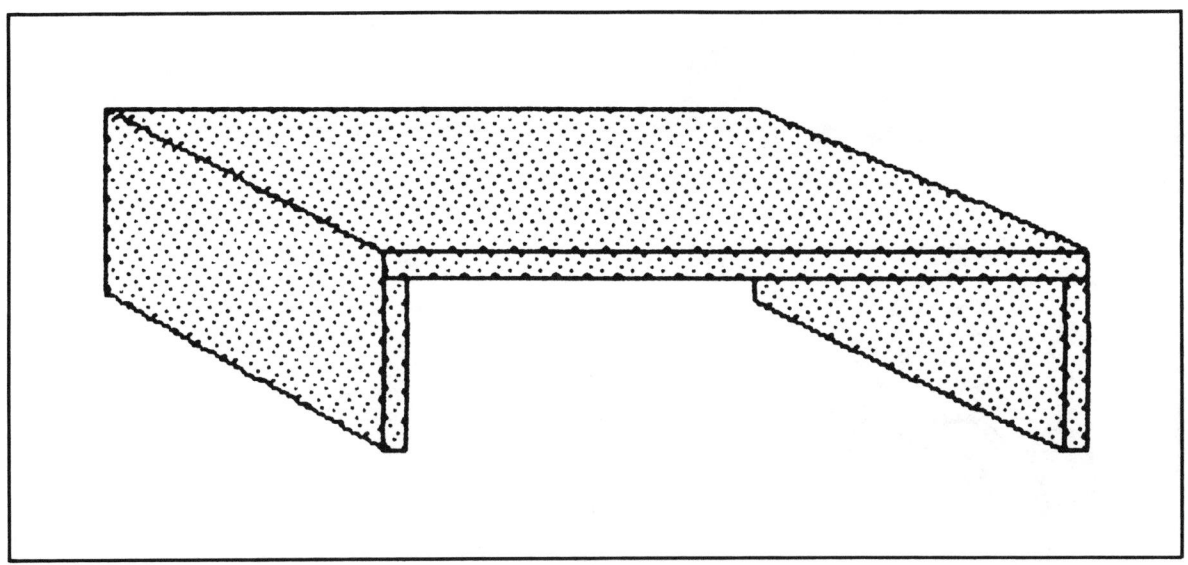

Fig. 1-19. Printer platform with plastic laminate.

in Chapter 6. If you are planning construction of a wall unit anyway, or already have one in your house, the addition of a computer table and storage rack into the unit may be a practical idea.

Miscellaneous small projects covered in Chapter 7 include a printer platform (Fig. 1-19), storage racks (Fig. 1-20), and a kneeling chair (Fig. 1-21).

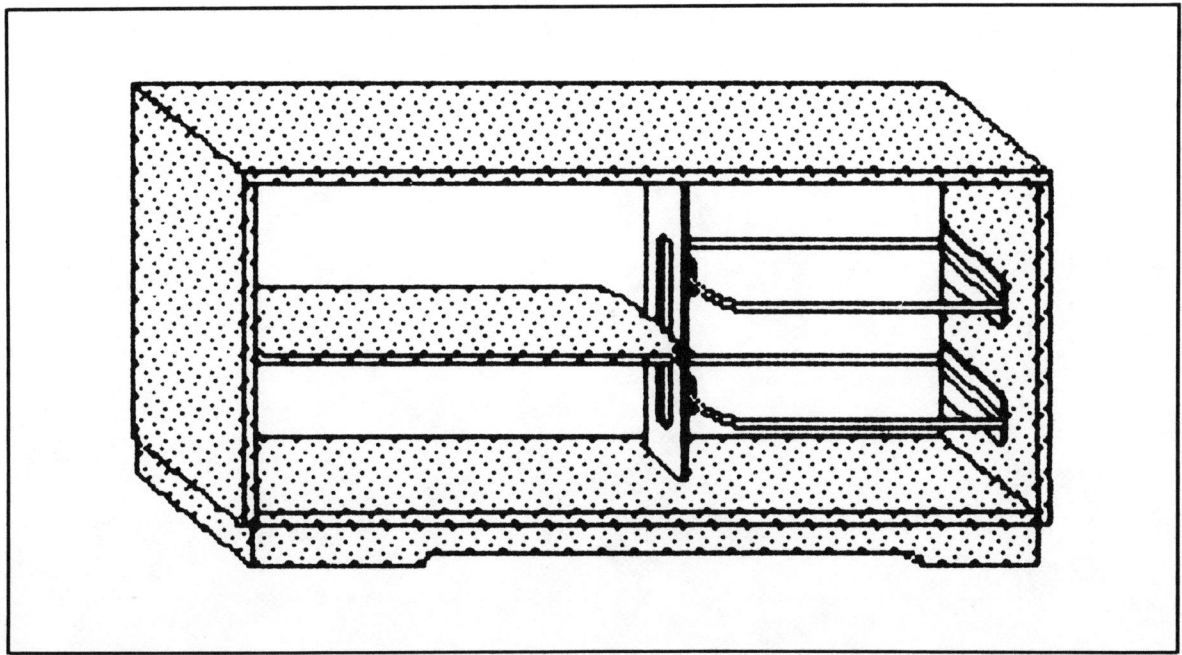

Fig. 1-20. Storage rack.

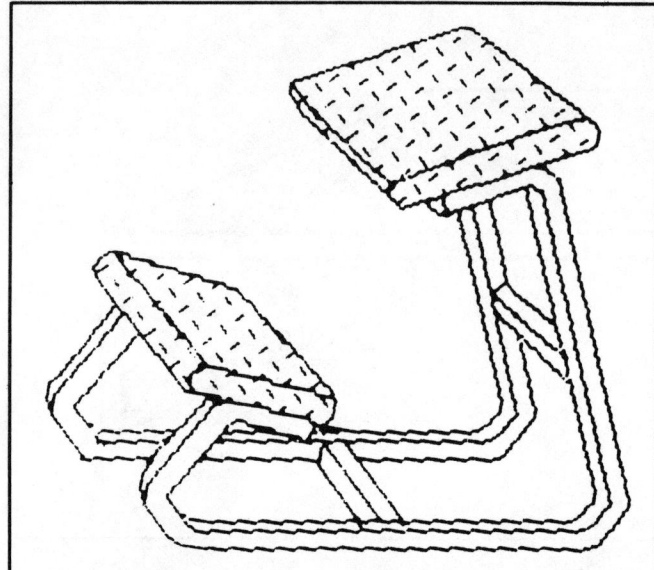

Fig. 1-21. Kneeling chair.

Regardless of the type of computer furniture that you build, it must have adequate strength and good appearance. You will also need to consider available materials, the cost of materials, and the tools, experience, and workshop that you have available for making the computer furniture.

Chapter 2

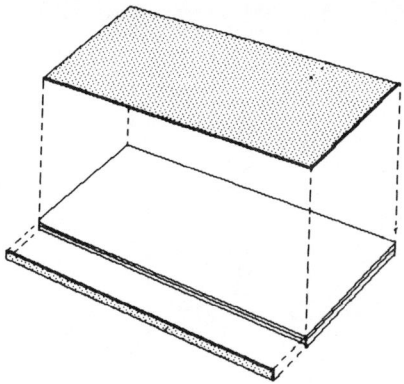

Basic Construction Techniques

This chapter covers tools, materials, and construction techniques for making computer furniture.

TOOLS

Having the right tools is extremely important for quality computer furniture construction work. Even if you have never done any computer furniture construction before, you probably have at least some suitable tools. Most households do.

The size and nature of the particular project will dictate what tools are needed. Most constructions will require basic hand tools and a few power tools (Fig. 2-1). Of course, you can do without any power tools, but they will allow you to do some jobs better—or at least faster.

A basic set of tools will do for a start. Then you can select additional tools as special needs arise. Tools can be purchased new or used. I recommend tools of at least medium quality. Cheap tools are often false economy, because they tend to wear out quickly or break easily.

Saws

A variety of handsaws is available for woodcutting. A common feature of most types is a blade with a handle at one end.

Generally speaking, you get what you pay for in saws. In addition to conventional steel blades, there are now Teflon coated steel blades that provide a self-lubricating quality that makes cutting easier and adds rust resistance.

Although there are multipurpose saws for crosscutting (sawing across the grain) and ripping (cutting with the grain), these tend not to do either job well. It is generally much better to have both a *crosscut saw* and *ripsaw*. The difference is in the size, shape, and set of the teeth. A general purpose ripsaw might have four-and-one-half teeth per inch, and a crosscut might have seven teeth per inch. The ripsaw teeth are set so that they cut chips; the crosscut teeth are set so that they cut two parallel grooves.

In addition to a crosscut saw and a ripsaw, you

Fig. 2-1. Basic construction techniques are used to build computer furniture.

will probably want to have one or more of the following: a coping saw, a keyhole saw, a compass saw, a backsaw, and a dovetail saw.

A *coping* saw is used to cut curves and make interior cutouts. The *keyhole saw*, as the name implies, is used to cut holes for locks in doors and to make other similar small cuts. The *compass saw* is similar to the keyhole saw, but with a wider blade. The compass saw is designed for sawing curves. A single handle often fits interchangeable blades for keyhole and compass saws.

The *backsaw* is designed so that perfectly straight cuts can be made across the wood cleanly without splintering. The backsaw is frequently used with a miter box or gauge. The backsaw has many uses for computer furniture construction work and other cabinet work.

A *dovetail saw* is designed for fine cutting, as when making dovetails. It's similar to a backsaw except that it has a thinner blade. This saw is useful when very accurate cutting without chipping and leaving burred areas is desired.

If you do any quantity of computer furniture construction work, you will probably want to add one or more portable or stationary power saws. Power *circular saws,* both portable and stationary types, are useful for making straight cuts. As with all power tools, you should have a blade guard and other necessary safety features. Other useful power saws include *saber saws, jigsaws, radial arm saws,* and *band saws.*

Hole Making Tools

A carpenter's *brace* with about a medium swing

will serve for most general hole boring work. To go along with this, you will need an *auger bit* for each hole size you intend to drill, or an expansive auger bit that covers the range of hole sizes.

Twist drills, which have a hand crank and either a handle or breast plate, and *push drills* can also be used for drilling holes in wood.

A portable electric drill, however, will make most hand braces and drills unnecessary. Although a 1/4-inch drill is adequate for most general work, 3/8-inch model can be advantageous. Variable speed features are also useful.

Stationary *power drill presses* are important shop tools for the more advanced worker. Many types and sizes are available, ranging from presses that hold portable electric drills to heavy duty self-contained units. A variety of attachments is available for drill presses that make possible carving, shaping, sanding, and many other jobs that you may find useful for computer furniture construction work.

Chisels, Gouges, and Planes

A variety of chisels, gouges, and planes is useful for computer furniture construction work.

Chisels come in various shapes and sizes. For many jobs, especially with softer woods, they can be operated by hand pressure only. For hardwoods, soft-face hammers or mallets are often used to strike the end of the handle of the chisel to force the beveled end of the blade down into the wood.

Gouges are a special form of chisels with rounded and curved cutting ends. They are useful for a variety of wood shaping and curving tasks and are available in many shapes and sizes.

Planes are used for smoothing and shaping tasks. Most people who construct computer furniture will want to have at least a bench plane in their tool kits. Other types can be added as a need develops. A *drawknife* is another useful woodworking tool.

More advanced do-it-yourselfers might want to use related power tools, such as electric planes, routers, jointers, and shapers for computer furniture construction work.

Surform Tools, Files, and Rasps

Surform tools come in a variety of sizes and shapes. These are relatively new tools and, as such, some traditional craftsmen don't like them. They are, however, rapidly replacing older types of files and rasps for many woodworking tasks. Some are held like a block plane and others are held like a file; both flat and curved blades are available.

Many shapes and sizes of *files* and *rasps* are available. Typical shapes are flat, half round, and round. You will probably want to have a number of files and rasps in your tool kit.

Sanding Papers and Tools

Abrasive papers are frequently called "sandpaper" although sand is not actually used. The main types available are garnet paper, aluminum oxide, and silicon carbide. Abrasive papers are graded: the larger the number, the finer the grit. Most sanding is accomplished by starting with coarser grits (smaller grade numbers) and gradually working down to finer grits (larger grade numbers). Selection of abrasive papers will depend on the particular sanding job at hand.

The abrasive paper can be held around a small block of wood, or special sanding blocks that clamp the abrasive paper in place can be used.

Power sanders are useful tools for large sanding jobs. There are three basic types: pad, disk, and belt. The *pad sanders* are made with orbital, straight line, and combination orbital and straight line actions. They are designed for finishing and light duty work, making them ideal for sanding computer furniture.

Disk sanders have disks mounted at right angles to the drive spindle. These are not useful for typical computer furniture sanding.

Belt sanders have a belt of abrasive paper traveling over two drums. These are useful for many types of sanding, especially for large computer furniture sanding tasks.

Measuring and Marking Tools

Tools for measuring and marking accurately

17

are important for quality computer furniture construction work. Two measuring systems are still in use in the United States: American standard and metric. The United States is supposedly in the process of converting to the metric system. You can convert measurements from one system to the other (for example, 1 inch equals about 25.4 millimeters), but this can be confusing. If you are only familiar with one system, you will probably want to work mainly with that system and have your measuring tools in that system.

Many types and sizes of rules and tapes are available. For general use, I suggest at least a *steel rule* a yard or meter long, a zigzag *folding rule*, and a *power tape* rule.

You will probably want at least a basic *try square*. This is useful for checking squareness and laying out lines on the materials with which you are working. A carpenter's square with 45- and 90-degree angles is also useful in computer furniture construction work. *Shop protractors* can be used for marking and measuring any angles.

Pencils, awls, and scribers are all useful marking devices. Other possibilities include pens, crayons, and chalk.

Vises and Clamps

Vises are important tools in computer furniture construction work. A woodworking bench vise or one of the work tables with a vise arrangement built in provides a convenient method for clamping and holding a variety of wood sizes and shapes. A metalworking vise will also find many uses.

Many different clamps are available to hold parts together while gluing or performing other tasks in computer furniture construction. A common and extremely useful type is the C-clamp, which comes in sizes of up to about 1- foot long. Other types of clamps, such as bar and pipe clamps that allow wide openings, are also useful.

Hammers

Many types and sizes of hammers are available, each intended for a specific range of uses. Using them for other purposes can damage the hammer or the materials you are working on and may present a safety hazard.

Claw hammers are frequently called nail or carpenters' hammers. Their purpose is to drive and pull or draw out nails. They are available with either curved or straight claws. The nail driving face of the hammer might be flat, slightly rounded, or even convex. The plain flat face is recommended as a general purpose hammer for computer furniture construction work. Some hammers have a wooden handle attached to the steel head, others have a steel handle that is one piece with the head and a rubber or plastic grip. Fiberglass handles are also being manufactured. Although claw hammers come in a variety of weights, one with a 16-ounce head is recommended for general use. Because a hammer is a frequently used tool, I suggest that you buy one or more of at least medium quality.

Ball-peen hammers are available with wood, steel, and fiberglass handles. The ball-peen end can be used to strike in areas where the face will not fit. They are useful for striking punches and other metalworking tasks that may be required in some computer furniture constructions.

Mallets are hammers with soft materials for the heads. They are used in situations where a steel hammer would cause damage, as when striking wood and plastic. Mallet faces are made from wood, plastic, rawhide, and rubber.

Screwdrivers

The standard *screwdriver* is a basic tool designed for driving and removing screws. A screwdriver also makes a handy pry bar for removing lids from paint cans and other similar tasks, but because these jobs can ruin a good screwdriver by rounding the corners of the tip and distorting its shape, only old screwdrivers no longer suitable for driving and removing screws should be used as pry bars.

Most screws have ordinary slotted heads. Screws are made in gauge sizes, and each size has a specific slot width and depth. The tip of the screwdriver used should fit the slot closely. Screwdrivers come with tips designed to fit specific screw gauge sizes. Ideally, a different size screwdriver is used for each screw gauge, but it is usually possible to use a screwdriver for a screw of one gauge smaller and larger than the screwdriver was designed for. Three or four screwdriver sizes will take care of the screw sizes typically used in computer furniture construction work.

A screwdriver for slotted heads should have a straight end on the tip. If the corners are rounded, even slightly, the tip will tend to slip out of the screw slot.

There are also recessed-head screwdrivers. While there are a variety of screwhead types in use, the Phillips (with cross-slots) is the only one of these that will ordinarily be used (besides the slotted screw) for computer furniture construction work. As with standard screwdrivers, always use a Phillips screwdriver that is the correct size for the screw.

Screwdrivers come in various lengths. More leverage can generally be applied to the screw with a long screwdriver, but restricted working spaces necessitate short screwdrivers for some jobs.

Handles should feel comfortable and give a good grip. Plastic, wood, and metal handles can all be satisfactory, and flutes are often used on hard smooth surfaces to give a good grip.

Much of the price variation in screwdrivers is due to the quality and treatment of the steel used for the shank. The shank must withstand considerable twisting force and yet must not crumble or break.

Other Useful Tools

Other tools that may be required or useful for specific computer furniture construction work include pliers, wrenches, power bench grinders, metal snips and cutters, metal files, and safety clothing and equipment.

BASIC TECHNIQUES

The primary skill required for building the projects detailed in this book is working with wood, and there has to be a starting point. What is your present ability at using tools and working with wood? This might be very little or a whole lot. If your primary experience has been as a handyman around your house or as a house carpenter, your skills and techniques can easily be transferred to computer furniture making.

Each woodworking job is basically a problem (Fig. 2-2). How can you best use your skills and available tools and materials to accomplish the job at hand? To achieve professional results, divide each project into small steps. Then spend some time thinking about how these steps can best be done. Try to do each step right. Don't let sloppy work get by, because it can accumulate. By the same token, if you do each step—each little job—right, the result will be workmanship of which you can be proud.

If your woodworking experience is limited, a good starting point is to take a class in woodworking. Many adult education programs offer classes that will allow you to learn with supervision. You may even be able to build some of the computer furniture detailed in this book as a class project.

Types of Wood

Before going into the actual woodworking skills, it is important to consider woods that are suitable for making computer furniture.

Douglas fir is a wood of medium hardness that is popular for making wood furniture. Although far from ideal, it's available in most areas of the United States. It is fairly easy to work with this wood, and it makes attractive computer furniture.

Both *white* and *yellow pine* are suitable woods for making computer furniture. Knots in the wood often add character to the construction, and knotty pine furniture is now known as a special type. Cedar, including Western Red, Port Orford, and Alaska, are other possible softwood choices.

For custom constructions, oak is perhaps the first choice because of its outstanding strength and longevity. Both white and red oak can be used. Mahogany is another popular choice for custom constructions.

Many other woods can also be used. As a general rule, any wood that is suitable for constructing household tables will probably also work for computer furniture.

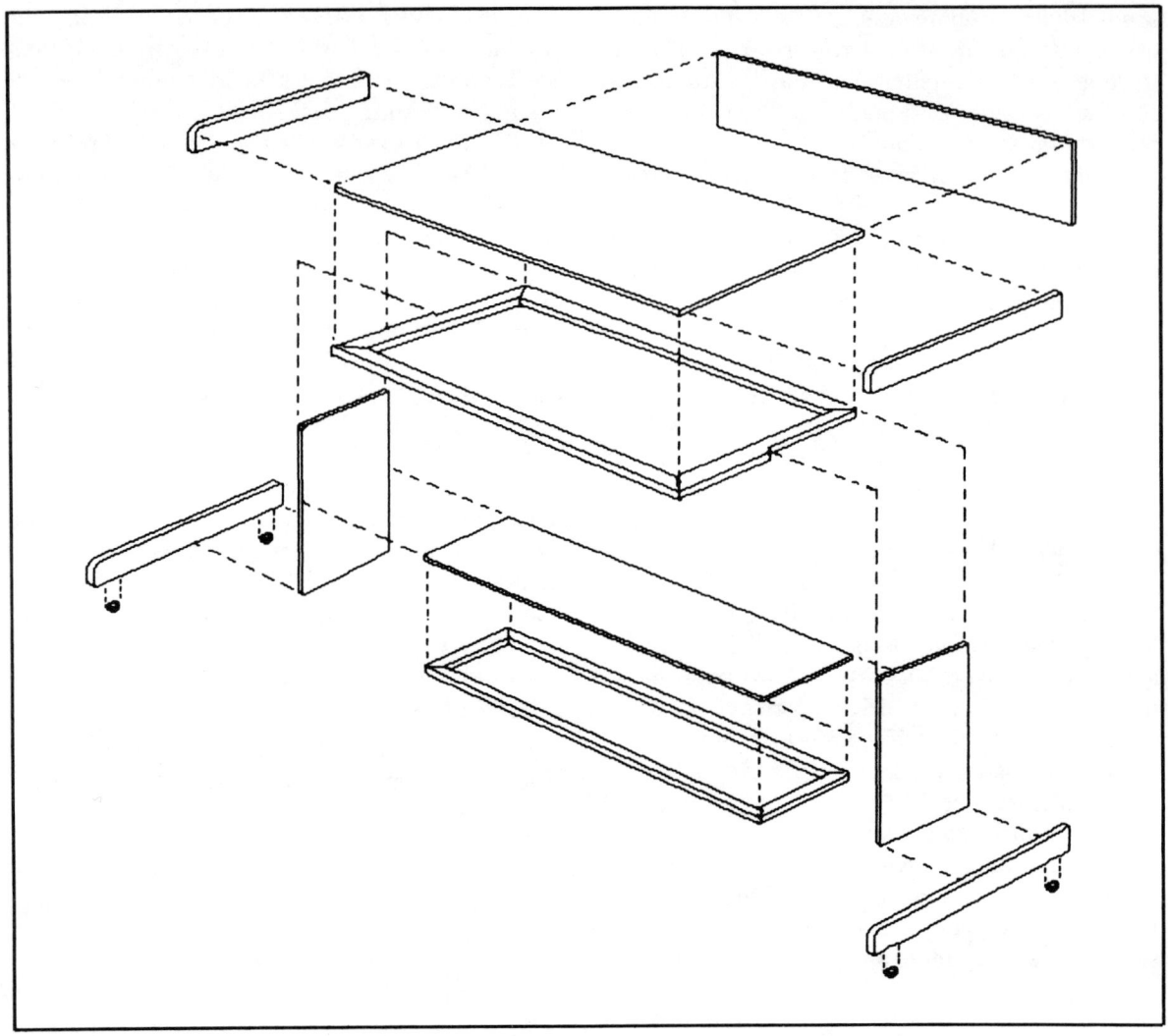

Fig. 2-2. Taken step by step, even complicated constructions can be reduced to a series of minor jobs.

Plywood

Plywood is used extensively for the projects detailed in this book (Fig. 2-3). Plywood is made of veneers that are laminated together, with Douglas fir by far the most common wood used for making plywood. Plywood is also available with one or both outside veneers of another wood, such as birch, mahogany, or oak and the inner layers of Douglas fir or other similar woods. This is ideal for making custom computer furniture at a much lower cost than if solid wood construction were used.

It is extremely important, I believe, to avoid interior grade plywood. Even though the computer furniture will be used indoors, there will usually be enough moisture to delaminate this type of plywood. Use only exterior grades. If the plywood is to be covered with a plastic laminate, shop grade, as long as it is exterior plywood, will do. If you want to finish in natural wood, get the best grade that you can afford.

Plywood usually comes in standard 4-feet-by-8-feet sheets, but is sometimes available in both smaller and larger sizes, such as 2 feet by 4 feet and 4 feet by 16 feet. Plywood is commonly available in 1/4-inch, 3/8-inch, 1/2-inch, and 3/4-inch thickness. Also manufactured are 1/8-inch and 1-inch thickness.

Shaping Wood Parts

A fundamental woodworking skill is shaping wood parts. Measuring and marking patterns on wood is extremely important, and is done preliminary to cutting and shaping the wood to the

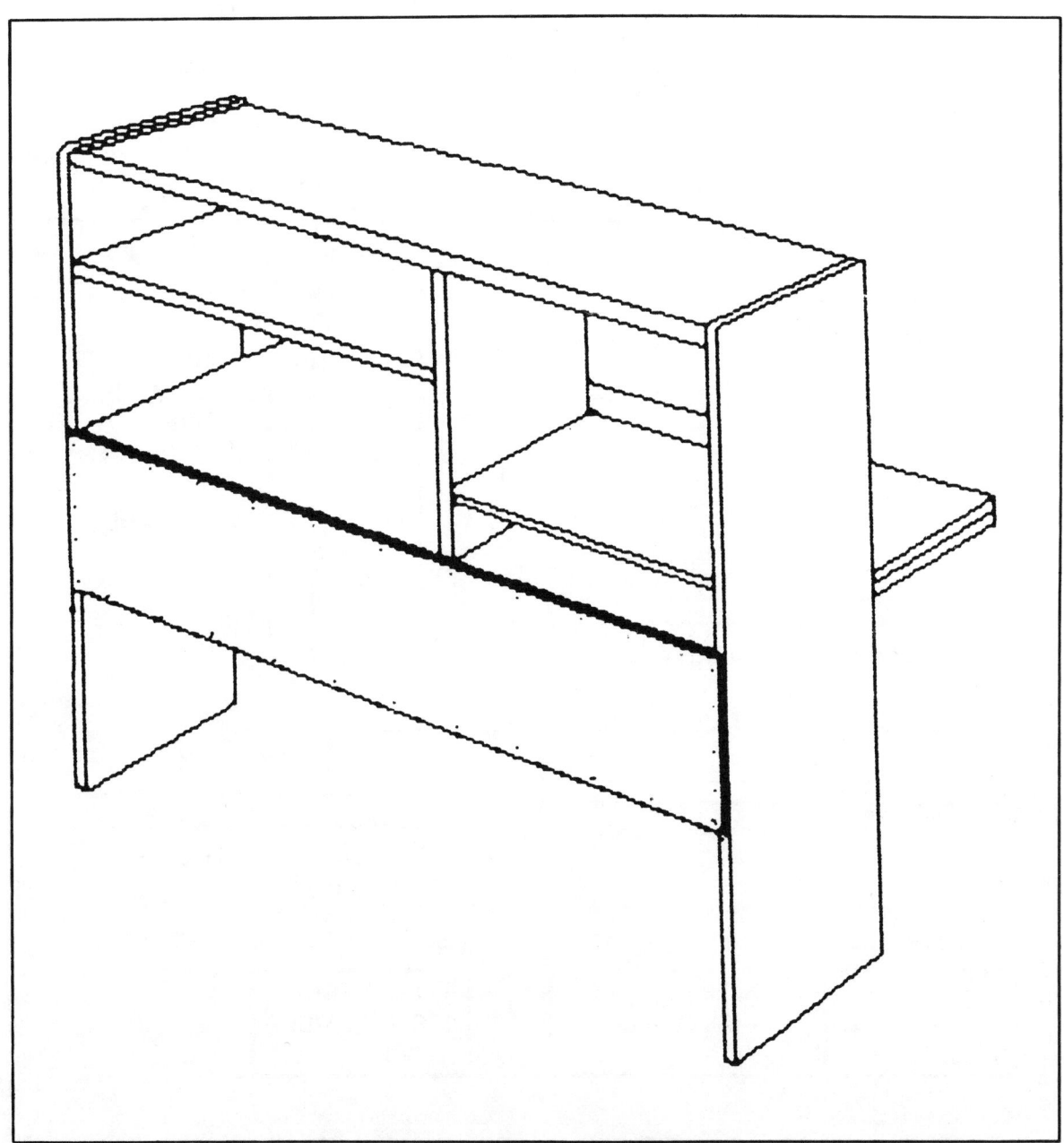

Fig. 2-3. Made entirely of natural finish plywood, this table is sturdy and attractive.

desired size. Make certain that the wood is suitable for the job in which it is being used. Use wood so that there will be the least possible waste. If, for example, a certain part requires only part of a piece of wood, pattern it on the wood in such a way that waste will be at a minimum and that the remaining wood will be of a size and shape that can be used later (Fig. 2-4). This will require looking ahead to future work, but it's worth it because reducing waste can result in considerable savings. Remember, it's what ends up as part of the computer furniture that counts.

Buying wood, in turn, is an important consideration. You will want to purchase the wood in sizes that will result in the least waste. In most cases, you will buy lumber by the *board foot*. This is 144 cubic inches of wood and is equal to a piece of wood 12 inches long, 12 inches wide, and 1 inch thick. For example, a piece of wood 2 feet long, 3 inches wide, and 2 inches thick is a board foot because it totals 144 cubic inches.

In most cases, however, you will actually get less wood than this. You pay for the wood on the basis of the size it was in rough form before the mill-

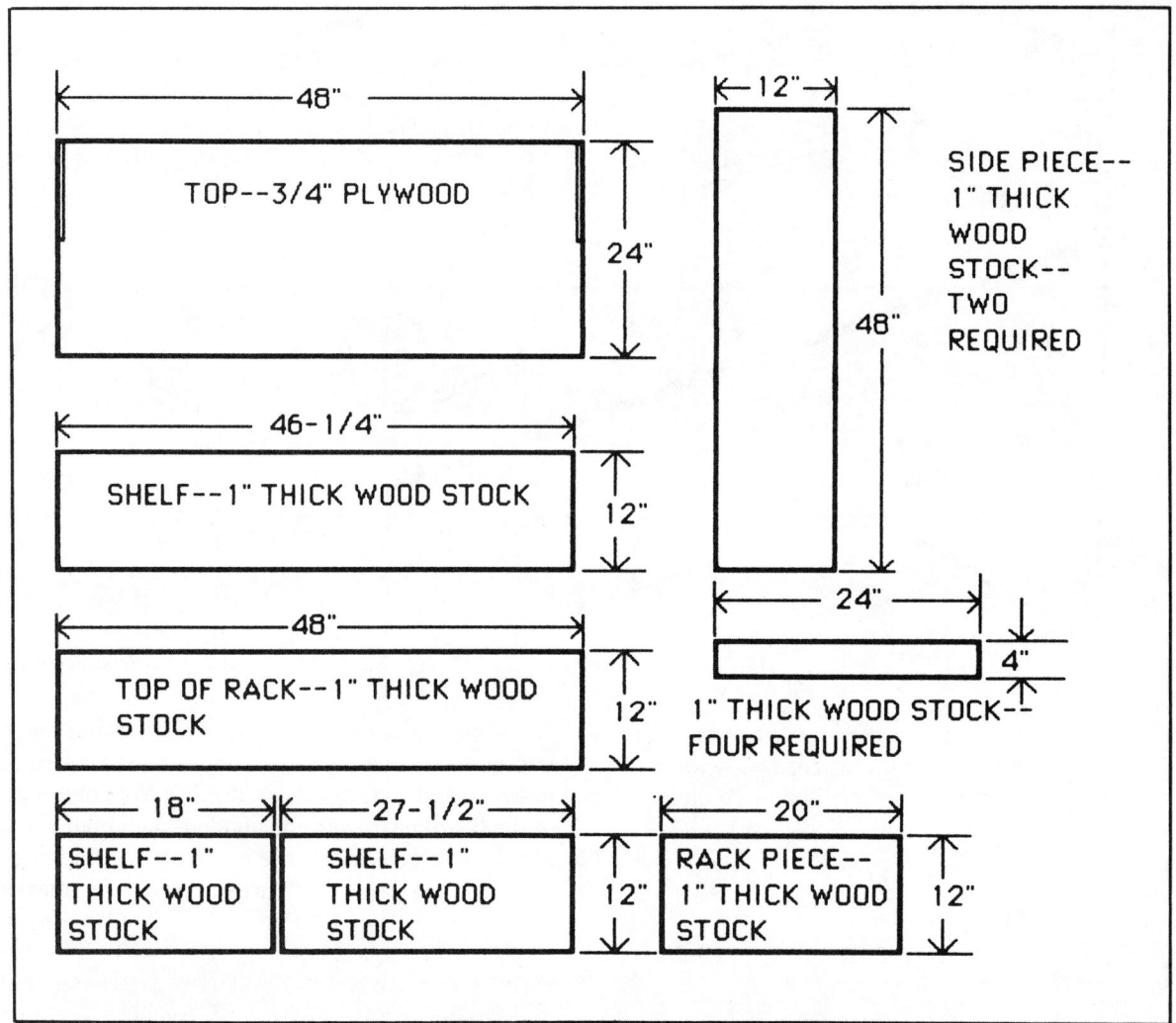

Fig. 2-4. Cut wood stock to avoid waste.

ing process. That is why what is called a two by four (2 inches by 4 inches) is actually less than 2 inches by 4 inches. Usually, about 1/8 to 1/4 inch is removed from a board in the milling process. This ends up as sawdust, but you still are paying for it in the board-foot pricing scheme. It's important to take this into account when purchasing wood for building computer furniture.

A recent trend is to sell wood by the running foot rather than the board foot. This method is used by many do-it-yourself and handyman supply stores and is less confusing to the person unfamiliar with the board foot system.

Plywood is usually sold as sheets that are of a certain thickness. As a general rule, plywood that is marked 1/2-inch plywood will be a full 1/2 inch in thickness.

In some cases, you may want to have the lumberyard or store saw a larger piece of wood into smaller pieces and do the milling or surfacing work on the rough sawn edges for you. There is usually a charge for this, but it can be well worth it if you do not have the tools to do this work yourself. There may be times when you will want a piece of plywood cut into two or more pieces, and some lumberyards and stores will do this for you. There will usually be a service charge, especially if more than one or two simple cuts are made. Also, some lumberyards and stores will cut and sell just part of a full sheet of plywood.

Take care in laying out and marking the pattern on the wood to be used. Use a sharp pencil or fine scribe for marking. In critical areas, a wide line might cause enough error in cutting and shaping that the piece will not fit properly.

There are many situations where you have a length of wood that is the desired width and thickness and all that is necessary is to cut it the correct length with square ends. First, select a suitable board. If some pieces of your lumber have more checks and cracks than others, you will want to make your selection on the basis of where the particular piece of wood is going to be used in the computer furniture project.

Because lumber frequently has checks or cracks near the ends when it comes from the lumberyard, you will probably want to mark a square line near one end of the board and later saw away this section. This wastes a small amount of lumber, but it is necessary for quality work in many situations. The blade of the square is positioned firmly against the edge of the board with the outside edge of the tongue of the square lined up where marks and cuts are to be made.

With a sharp pencil, make a line on the board, following the tongue of the square. A fine line should follow as close to the edge of the square as possible. Using a suitable measuring rule, lay out the desired length from the first line along one edge of the wood.

As a double check, you might want to lay out the length and make a mark a second time on the other side of the board. Use a square as described above. With the blade against the edge of the board, the tongue should line up with both marks. If it doesn't, the original end of the board was not marked off square, the edges of the board are not straight and parallel or, most likely, laying out the lengths was not done accurately. When everything looks okay, mark the line.

There are three systems for where the final cut is to be made: the line will be cut away, half the line will be cut away, and the cut will be made at the outside edge of the line so that the line will be visible after the cut is made. In situations where a good fit is critical, the system to be used must be taken into consideration. I suggest that you select one system and then stick to it; always cut the lines away, or half away, or leave the line. Learn to lay out and mark your work for the system you are using.

Frequently, you will need to lay out and mark widths for later cutting. Using a measuring rule, measure and mark the desired width from one edge of the board near each end and in the middle. Then place a straightedge on the board so that one edge lines up with the three marks. If the three marks do not line up, an error was made in the measuring and marking of the board or the edge of the board is not straight. Once you have the marks lined up, use a sharp pencil to mark the line for later cutting.

An alternate method that can be used on fairly wide boards is to use a square in the same way as for laying out and marking squared off lines across a board for length cuts. For this to be accurate, the end of the board must be fairly wide to give adequate distance for placing the blade of the square. The end of the board must be perfectly square.

There are situations where you will want to lay out angles. A shop protractor can be used for this, or you can use a carpenters' adjusting bevel and a protractor. Use the protractor for adjusting the bevel to the desired angle. Position the handle of the bevel firmly against the edge of the board and mark along the blade.

The same methods can be used for laying out and marking lines on plywood. A large square, long measuring rule, and straightedge are handy for this. There is some danger of making an error when extending a line. An example would be when the tongue of the square does not extend far enough, and you have to add to the line.

Sawing

After the pattern has been marked on the wood, the next step is usually sawing it to shape. A variety of hand and power saws can be used.

Crosscutting means making a straight cut across the grain of the wood. If a handsaw is used, it should have a crosscutting blade. Fasten the board to be cut in a woodworking vise so that the line where the cut is to be made extends an inch or so beyond the vise. Long or wide boards that cannot be placed conveniently in the vise can be placed across two or more sawhorses.

Because the saw actually cuts out a narrow section of wood, which ends up as sawdust, be sure to take this into account when positioning the saw to start the cut. Begin sawing with several short strokes. Use a small square to make certain that the saw is at a right angle to the wood. Begin cutting again, and this time use long strokes.

Stop periodically and check the angle of the saw with the square. With experience, you will probably be able to saw through the board without any twisting. When you are close to sawing through the board, hold the end of the part that is being cut off in your left hand and finish the cut with short easy strokes to keep the wood from breaking off or splitting from its own weight. If the wood is not too wide, a miter box and a backsaw can be used to make the same cut with even greater accuracy.

A portable power circular saw with a crosscutting or general purpose blade can also be used for crosscutting the board—even better are stationary power table saws and radial arm saws. When using power tools, or any tools for that matter, follow good safety practices: dress properly, follow all safety instructions for the safe operation of the particular tool, and use all necessary safety devices such as blade guards and shields.

Crosscuts can also be made at angles other than 90 degrees to the edge of the board. It takes considerable practice to do this accurately with just a handsaw. Some miter boxes can be adjusted for performing these operations with a backsaw, and the blades in most power saws can be angled as desired to the wood to be cut, making these jobs simple and accurate.

Ripping is making a cut with the grain of the wood. If a handsaw is used, it should have a ripping blade. Depending on the size of the board, it can be held in a woodworking bench vise or placed on sawhorses. Position the saw and start the sawing in a manner similar to crosscutting, as described above. Make sure that the cut is on the waste side of the wood. While sawing, the cutting edge of the blade should be at about a 60-degree angle to the board. A try square can be used to check the angle of the saw cut. For ripping, use short easy strokes. When you are close to sawing through the wood, hold the part you are cutting off or have it positioned over the sawhorse so that it will not break off.

Ripping can also be done with portable power circular saws, stationary table saws, and stationary radial arm saws. Use a ripping or general purpose blade.

Sawing curved patterns presents additional problems. Compass, keyhole, and coping saws can be used, but a portable electric saber saw is generally better. Stationary power jigsaws or band saws are other possibilities; the band saw is ideal for extensive work.

Sawing plywood requires special considerations. Special care must be taken to avoid chipping and splintering along the cut edge. Although the sawing methods described above apply in general also to plywood, handsaws and power saws with special fine-toothed blades designed especially for plywood should be used. Even better are special carbide-tipped blades. Applying a strip of masking tape over the area to be cut on both sides of the plywood, especially the underside, is also helpful, or clamp a solid piece of wood to the underside and saw through both plywood and the wood underneath.

Planing and Surfacing

Various hand planes and other surfacing tools are useful in computer furniture construction work. A frequent job is to plane the edge of a board where a saw cut has been made. Although a number of types and sizes of planes can be used, a jointer plane is most often used for long boards. Practice on scrap wood, and use a try square to test for squareness. It takes considerable practice to do a good job, and it also involves having the right plane for the job, keeping it sharp, and adjusting it properly. Hand planes can also be used for making chamfers, bevels, and rounded edges on boards.

Special care should be taken when planing end grain. A block plane, which has the blade at a more acute angle to the bottom of the plane than a jack plane, is ideal for this.

Power tools, such as a jointer and shaper, can also be used for these jobs. They make quick and easy work of them.

A variety of hand tools can be used for dressing and shaping curved edges on wood. Drawknives, spokeshaves, files, and surface forming tools are frequently used. The general method is to begin with coarse cutting tools and work down to finer ones until the surface is properly shaped and ready for sanding and finishing.

Many beginners partially shape a piece of wood for a computer furniture construction and then install it with the idea that they can finish shaping it later. This usually isn't good idea. As a general rule, it's easier to work on a piece of wood before it is installed. This varies, of course, depending on the particular construction.

Many chisels are available for cutting, shaping, and fitting wood pieces. Chisels are also used for woodcarving and surface decorating—jobs that are sometimes used for constructing computer furniture. For many jobs, especially with soft woods, the chisels can be worked by hand. For some jobs, especially on hard woods, a soft-faced mallet is used to strike the head of the chisel.

Scraping tools, such as cabinet scrapers, can be used to remove irregular surfaces left by planes and other rough surfacing tools.

Boring and Drilling Holes

Holes are frequently bored or drilled in wood for screws, bolts, and various fittings and a variety of other purposes in computer furniture constructions. Different hand tools are available for boring and drilling holes.

A typical hole making job begins by marking the position where the hole is to be drilled. Often this is done by measuring from two directions and making lines. The point where the lines intersect is where the hole will be drilled. An awl or other sharp pointed device is used to start the hole. Select the correct size drill or bit. (I assume that a brace will be used, but a hand crank or push drill can also be used, especially when making small diameter holes.)

Fasten the auger bit in the chuck, making sure that it is held securely. Place the feed screw in the starting hole and begin turning the brace to start boring the hole. After the hole has been started, use a try square to make sure that the hole is being bored at right angles to the surface of the wood. Resume boring until the tip of the feed screw goes through the wood. Then remove the bit, turn the wood over, and finish boring the hole from the opposite side. This will help to prevent splintering.

I find it much more convenient to use a portable electric drill for most computer furniture construction work. Although I have hand braces and drills in my tool collection, I seldom use them.

A variety of bits and drills can be used to make

holes in wood with an electric drill. Ordinary twist drills from about 1/16 inch to 1/2 inch in diameter can be used to make holes. A typical drilling job with one of these is as follows:

Install the desired size twist drill in the chuck of the electric drill and secure it with the chuck key. Immediately remove the chuck key. (The chuck key is frequently fastened to the cord of the drill with a special holder or plastic tape.) The drill should always be unplugged when changing twists drills or other types of drills or bits. Do not plug the drill back in until the chuck key has been removed from the chuck.

Make a starting hole with an awl in the position desired for the hole. The place the point of the twist drill over the hole.

Hold the drill by the grip in your right hand. Start the drill and apply pressure with your right hand. Use your left hand to guide the drill. Control the drilling so that the chuck does not contact the wood when the twist drill goes through. Hold the drill steady so that you do not break the twist drill. This is especially important when using small sizes of twist drills.

For drilling larger holes in wood (up to about 1 1/2 inches in diameter), spade-type bits are useful. For drilling all the way through a piece of wood, reverse the drill after the point has gone through and finish the hole from the other side.

A hole saw is another useful attachment. These are available in sizes from about 1/2 inch all the way up to about 6 inches. It takes a heavy duty drill to handle the larger sizes: around 2 inches is about maximum for a standard 1/4-inch drill. Start drilling the pilot drill with the drill held at right angles to the surface of the wood. The drill must be kept at this angle so that the saw bit will cut all the way around and the hole will be vertical to the surface. To avoid splintering when the saw cuts through, clamp a piece of scrap wood underneath the board.

One problem with hole saws is that you are limited to set sizes. If you need a hole in an in-between size, cut the size smaller and then file the hole out to the desired size.

Adjustable *fly cutters* are available for making holes from about 1/2 inch up to about 8 inches in diameter, but most cutters have a smaller range of adjustment. The advantage of the fly cutter over hole saws is that you can make any desired size of hole within the range of the cutter. The disadvantage is that it is more difficult to get a clean hole. Use a scrap piece of lumber clamped underneath the wood being drilled or drill from one side to the point where the pilot drill goes through. Then, using the hole made by the pilot drill as a guide hole, finish drilling the hole from the other side.

Another useful attachment for computer furniture construction is a combination wood drill and *countersink bit*. These make the hole for the screw threads and screw shank and a countersink for the flat-head screw all in one operation. A different bit is required for each screw size and length.

A similar bit also has a *counterbore section*. This means that in addition to the pilot hole and countersink, a counterbore for a wood plug is also made in the same drilling operation.

A *plug cutter* is another useful tool. Although you can buy precut wood plugs at hardware stores, it is often better to make your own so you can cut the plugs from the same stock of wood and get a closer match on the wood color. You will need a different size plug cutter for each diameter plug you want to make.

To cut a plug, install the plug cutter in the chuck of the drill. Position the drill at right angles to the surface of the wood. Start the drill, cut through the wood, and cut out the plug.

Drill presses can be used for even greater precision in drilling. These will largely eliminate problems of drilling at the desired angles.

Joining, Gluing, and Fastening

Joining wood pieces together is an operation frequently required in computer furniture constructions. Two pieces of wood can be fastened together with nails, screws, bolts, wood dowels, splines, various glues, or some combination of these. Glue should be used for joining pieces that you do not intend to take apart again (Fig. 2-5).

Many kinds of joints (Fig. 2-6) can be used in computer furniture constructions, including *angle butt* joint, *T-butt* joint, *angle butt* joint with corner

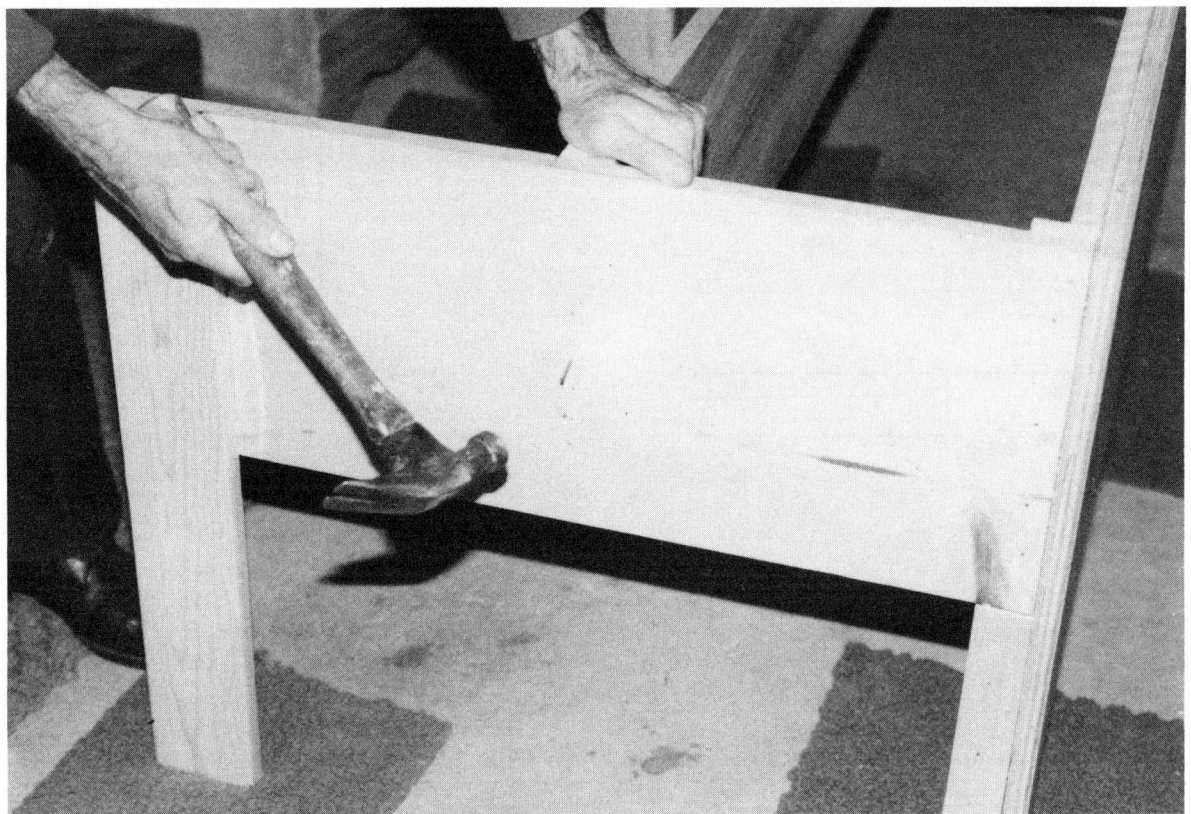
Fig. 2-5. Both glue and nails are used to join most pieces.

post, *rabbet joint*, *T-rabbet* joint, and *miter* joint.

Finishing nails are frequently used in computer furniture constructions. These are usually set below the surface of the wood with a set punch and the holes filled flush with wood filler to the surface of the wood (Fig. 2-7).

Screws and bolts are another fastener commonly used in computer furniture construction (Fig. 2-8). In most cases, a pilot hole is drilled for the screw. While ordinary twist drills can be used, special wood drills for shank and pilot holes are generally better. If a flat-head screw is used, you will also need to bore a countersink for the screw head (Fig. 2-9). A separate countersink bit can be used, but it is better to use a combination wood drill and countersink bit. If you intend to cap the screw head with a wood plug (Fig. 2-10) then use a combination wood drill, countersink, and counterbore bit.

A typical fastening is installed as follows:

- Clamp or otherwise hold the two pieces of wood in position.
- Mark the location for the screw with an awl and make the center hole in the wood for starting the drilling of the pilot hole.
- Drill the pilot hole and, if you prefer, countersink and counterbore. A combination bit that does all the operations in one drilling is convenient, especially if a large number of screws of the same size and length are to be used. The pilot bit used must be the correct size for the screw size and length that is to be used.
- Using a screwdriver, drive the screw. Hold the screwdriver firmly so that it will not slip out of the slot. In many cases, glue will be applied to the contact area of the two pieces of wood before the screws are installed.

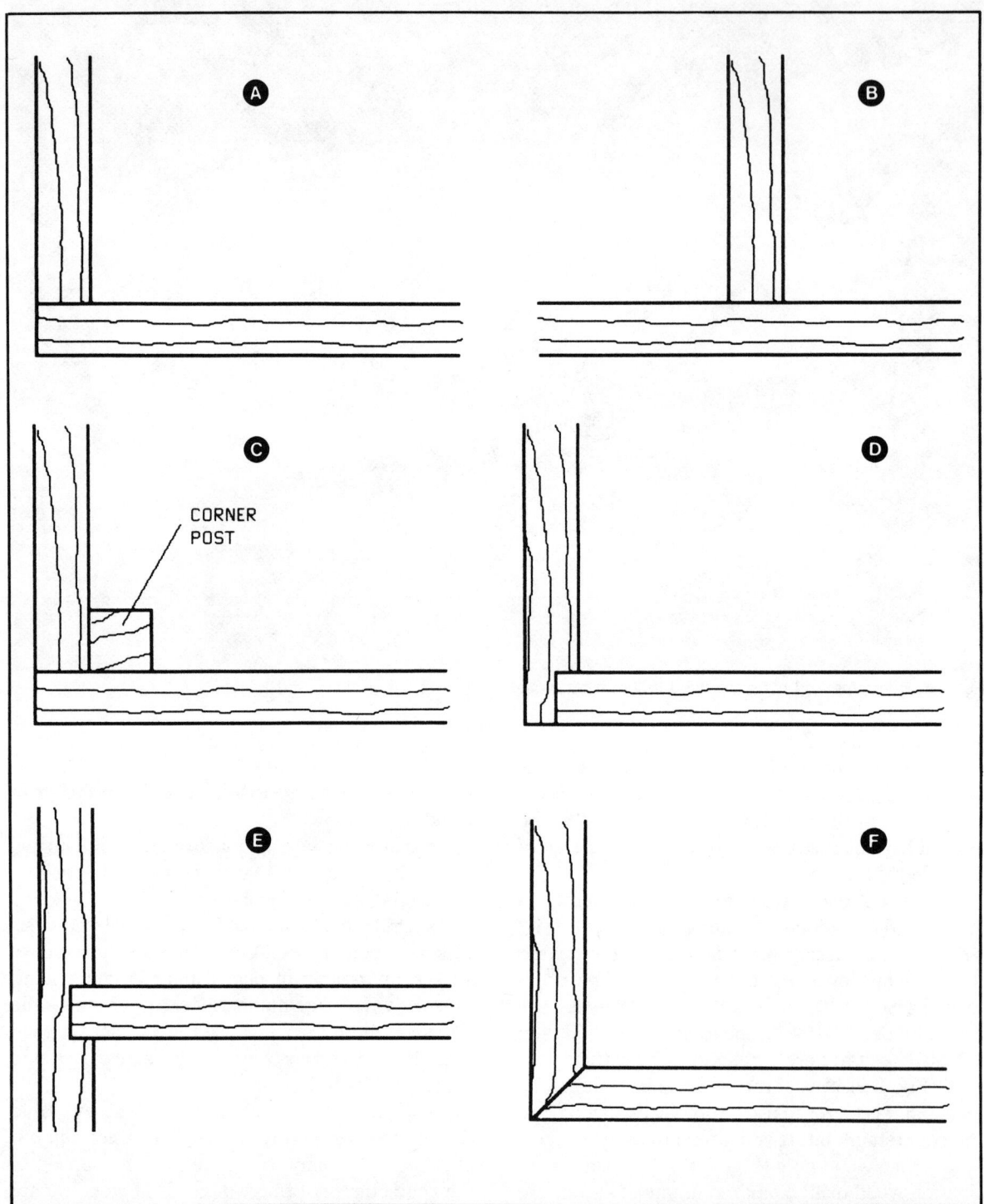

Fig. 2-6. Woodworking joints: (A) angle butt, (B) T-butt, (C) angle butt with corner post, (D) rabbet, (E) T-rabbet, and (F) miter.

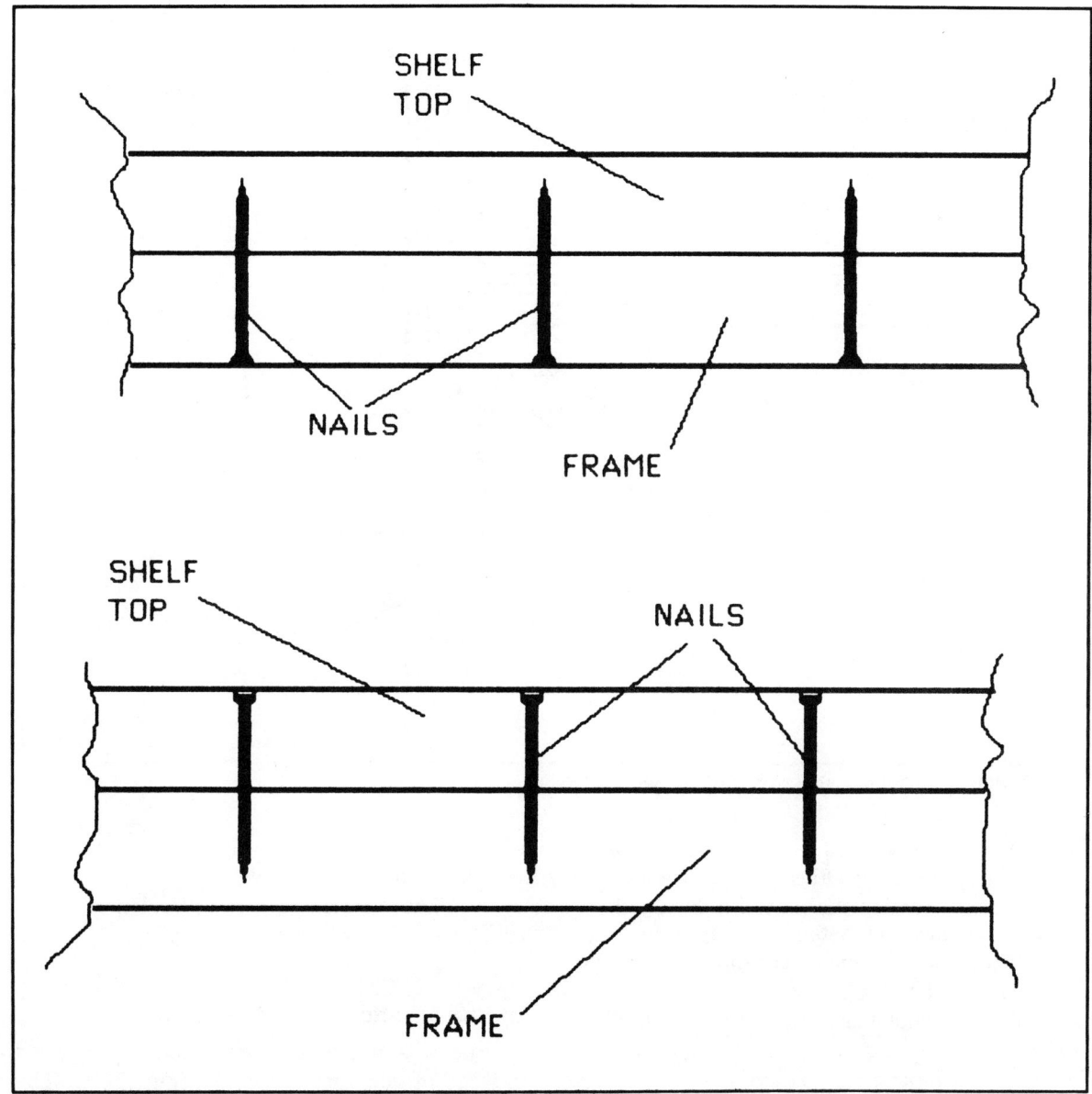

Fig. 2-7. Assembly of shelf top to frame when using a natural wood top (top) and plastic laminate (bottom).

Bolts are another popular fastener for computer furniture. Many types of bolts, including flat head machine screw, machine, round head, oval head, and carriage, can be used.

Numerous glues are suitable for joining wood computer furniture parts. I have found acrylic and epoxy glues to work especially well. Most glues will require clamping for a good bond to take place.

The steps for a typical gluing job are as follows:

• The two pieces of wood to be joined are shaped so that there will be a perfectly fitted joint.
• If fasteners are to be used, pilot holes for screws and holes for bolts are sometimes predrilled.

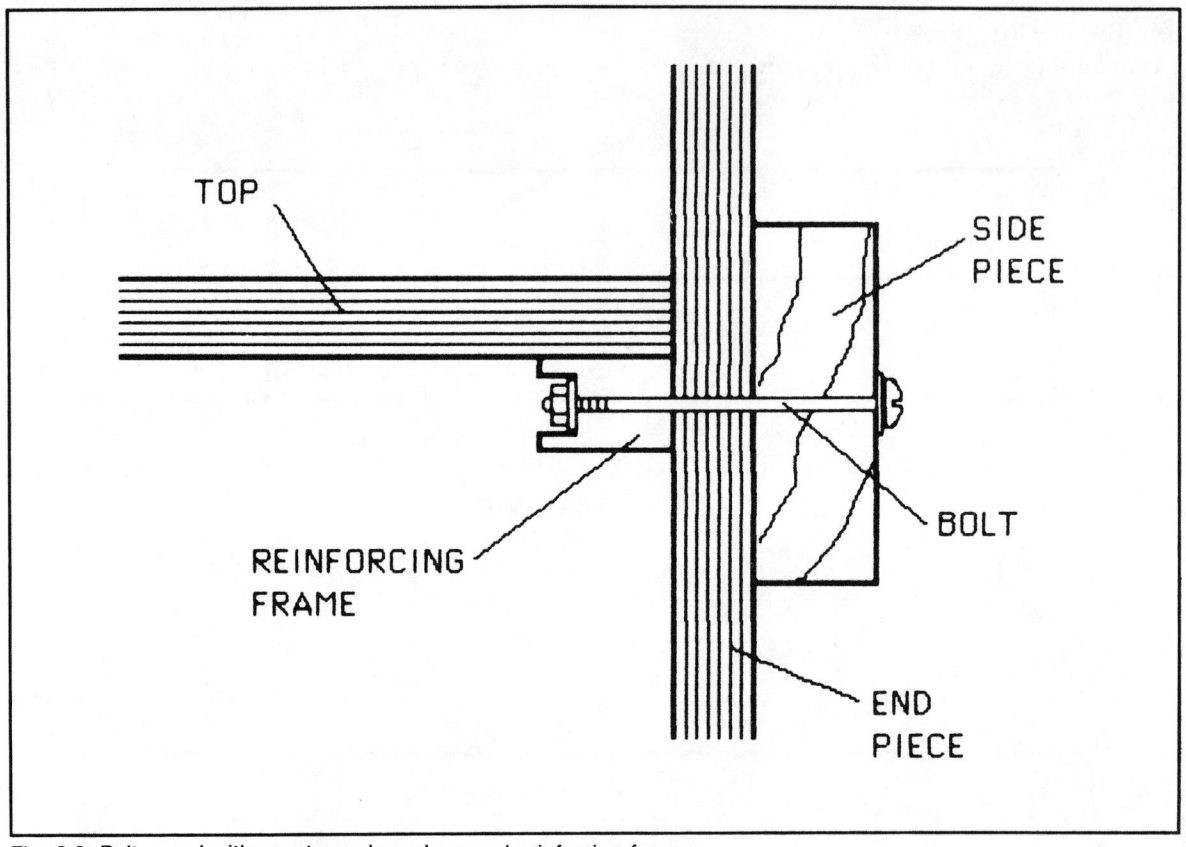

Fig. 2-8. Bolts used with countersunk washers and reinforcing frames.

In this way, the fasteners can be used as a clamp while the glue is setting. Otherwise, prepare clamps or wedges for holding the parts firmly together.

- Have tools and fasteners ready to use.
- Place wood for convenient spreading of glue on areas to be bonded.
- Follow manufacturer's directions for application of the particular glue used. Some glues require you to mix two parts.
- Using a brush or knife, spread a thin layer of glue evenly over both surfaces to be joined.
- Follow manufacturer's instructions regarding waiting time before bringing parts together. Place parts together and check the positioning.
- Secure the parts together with clamps, wedges, fasteners, or some combination of these.
- Wipe off excess glue with a rag. This step is important, because once the glue the sets, it will be more difficult to remove.
- Allow the glue to dry as directed in the instructions that come with the particular glue.

Adding Plastic Laminates to Wood

Plastic laminates are often applied to the wood surfaces of computer furniture (Fig. 2-11). The plastic laminate is installed as follows:

- All holes and defects in the surface of the wood should be filled with putty or wood filler.
- Sand the surface to be covered. This will help ensure good adhesion.
- Mark the plastic laminate to a pattern slightly larger than the area to be covered (Fig. 2-12). Use a straightedge and draw the pattern lines

on the finished or pattern side of the laminate. Leave 1/4 inch to 1/2 inch on all sides. This will be trimmed off later.

• Cut the plastic laminate to the pattern marked (Figs. 2-13 and 2-14). Even though the plastic laminate is extremely durable once applied, it is vulnerable to cracking and splitting before it is cemented in place. Fine-tooth handsaws or power saws with fine-tooth blades can be used. A rotary power saw with a 14 to 16 teeth per inch blade is ideal. Place the plastic laminate face up when cutting. Care should be taken so that the plastic laminate is not chipped or broken. You can use a carbide tip knife to score the plastic by drawing the knife

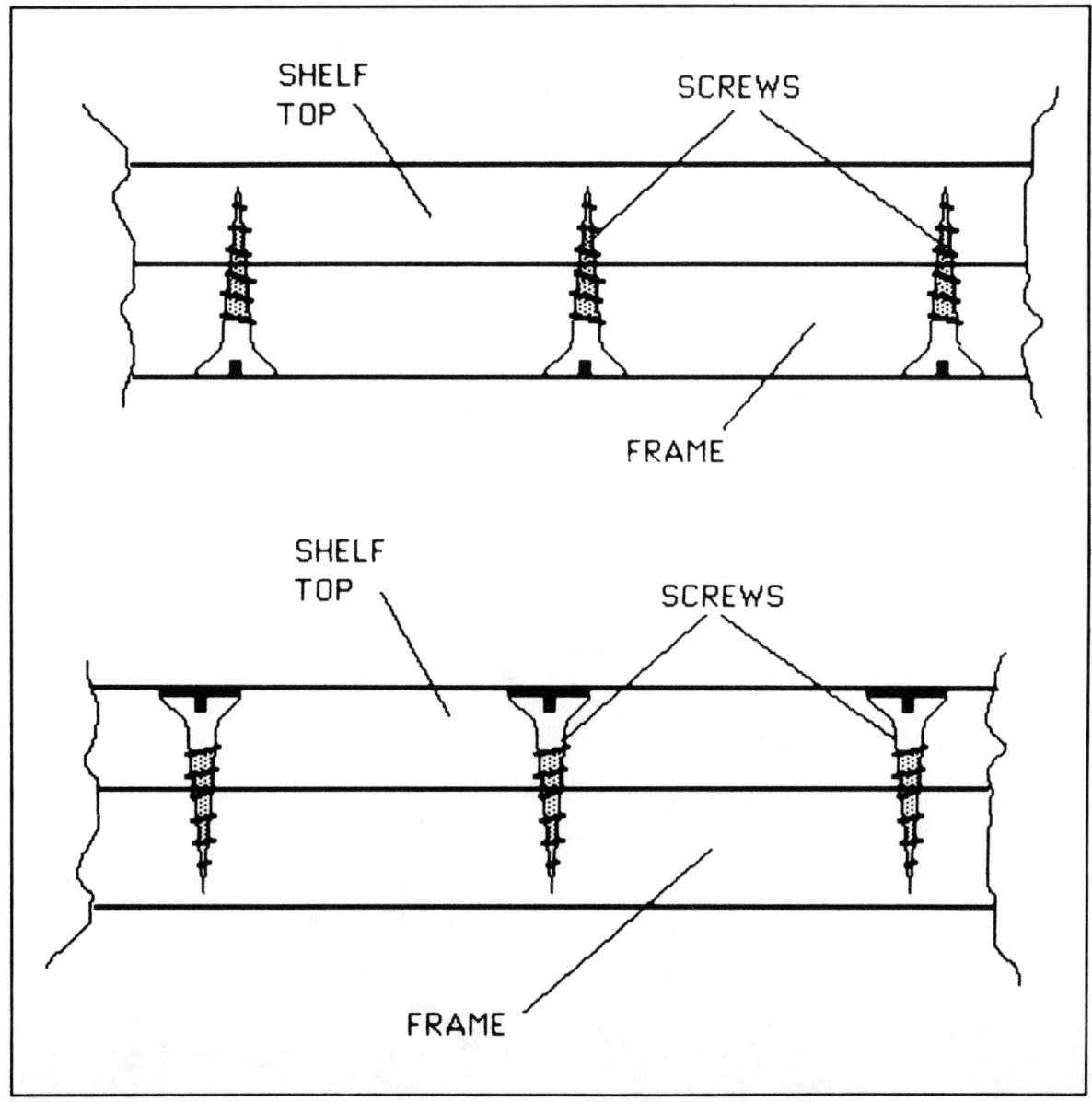

Fig. 2-9. Assembly of table top to frame when using natural wood (top) and laminate (bottom).

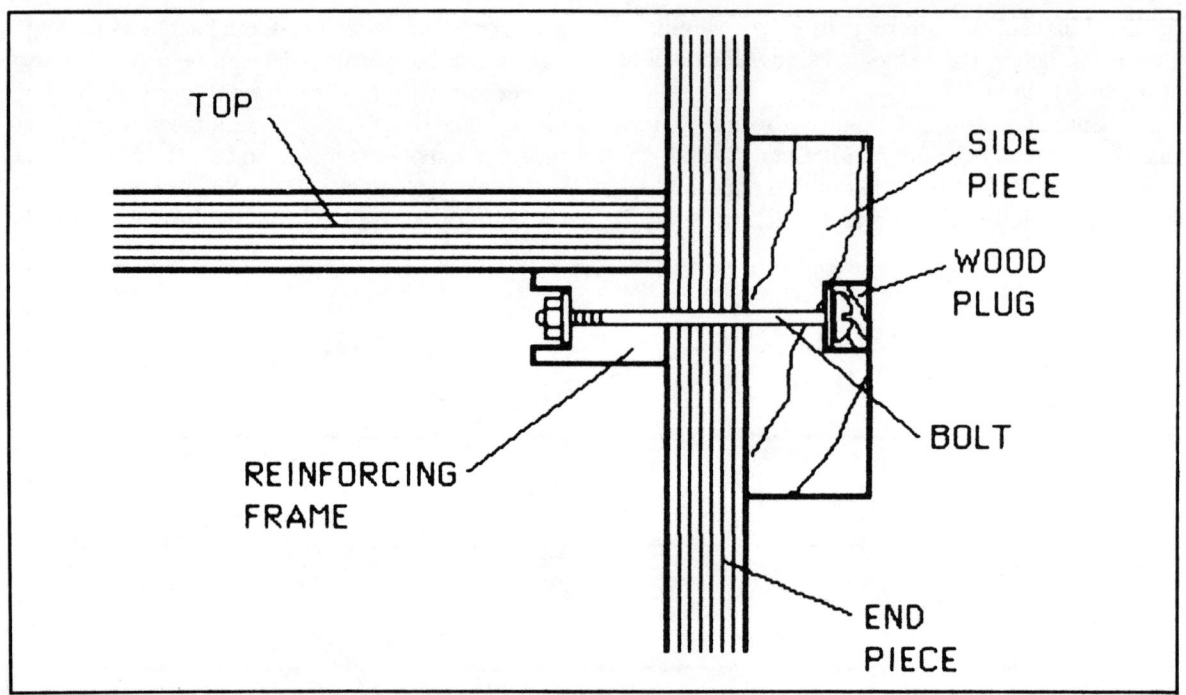

Fig. 2-10. Bolt head is countersunk and hole plugged.

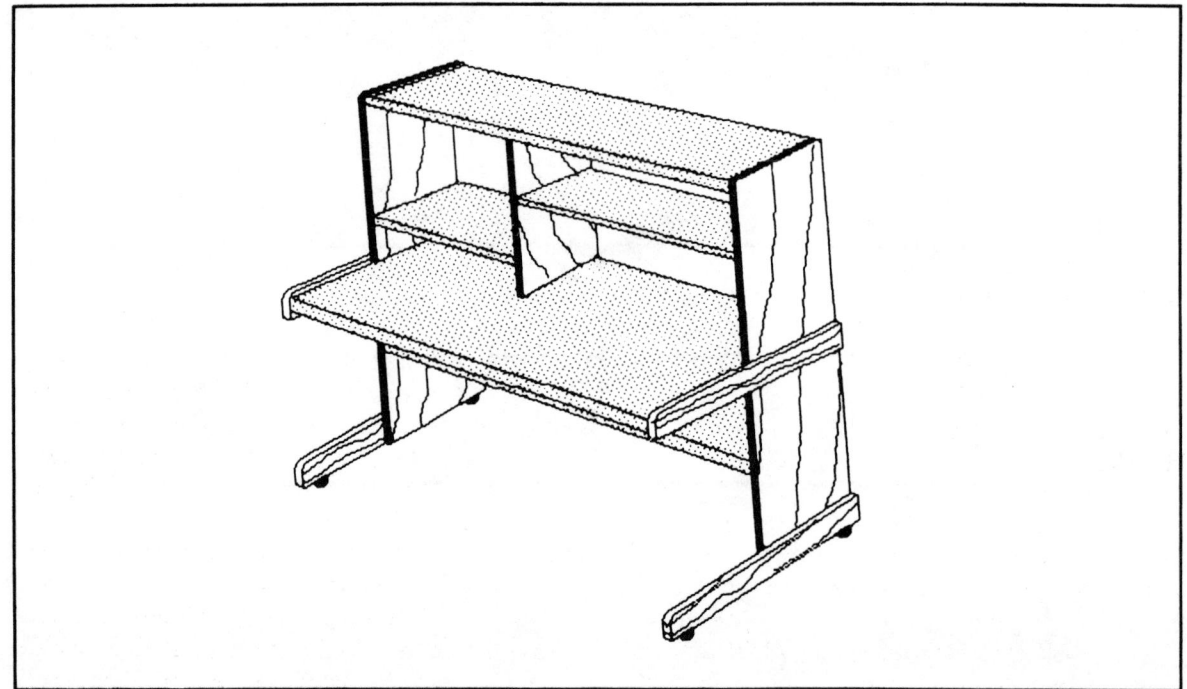

Fig. 2-11. Plastic laminates on tops and sides are attractive and durable.

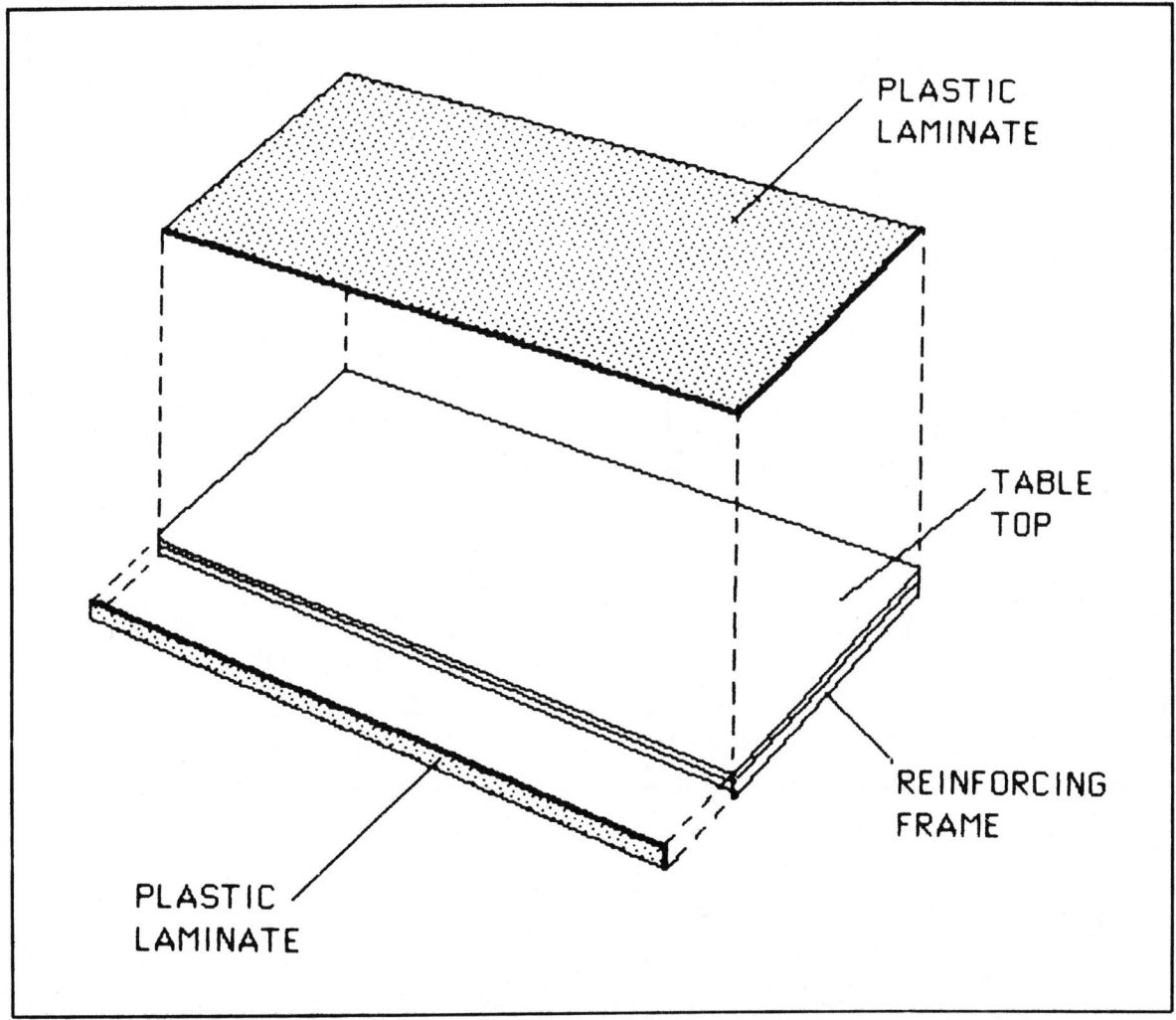

Fig. 2-12. Cut laminate with a 1/4-to-1/2-inch overhang on all sides.

point along a metal straightedge. Cut through the decorative surface. The laminate can then be broken by bending it toward the decorative surface side over the edge of a table or workbench.

• Apply contact cement to the surface of the wood to be covered and the back side of the plastic laminate. A brush, roller, or metal spreader with a serrated edge can be used to spread the contact cement. A thin, even application is important.

• Follow the manufacturer's instructions regarding drying time. Usually, this takes about 20 to 30 minutes.

• Place a sheet of heavy wrapping paper over the wood surface to be covered. Then position the laminate on the wood surface with the paper in between. The contact cement will not stick to the paper if it has been allowed to dry properly. Make certain that the laminate is positioned correctly. Once the two surfaces of contact cement touch, the laminate sheet cannot be moved again. When everything is lined up properly, pull the paper out from between the wood and the plastic laminate.

• Using a small block of wood and a hammer, lightly tap the laminate in place. An alternate

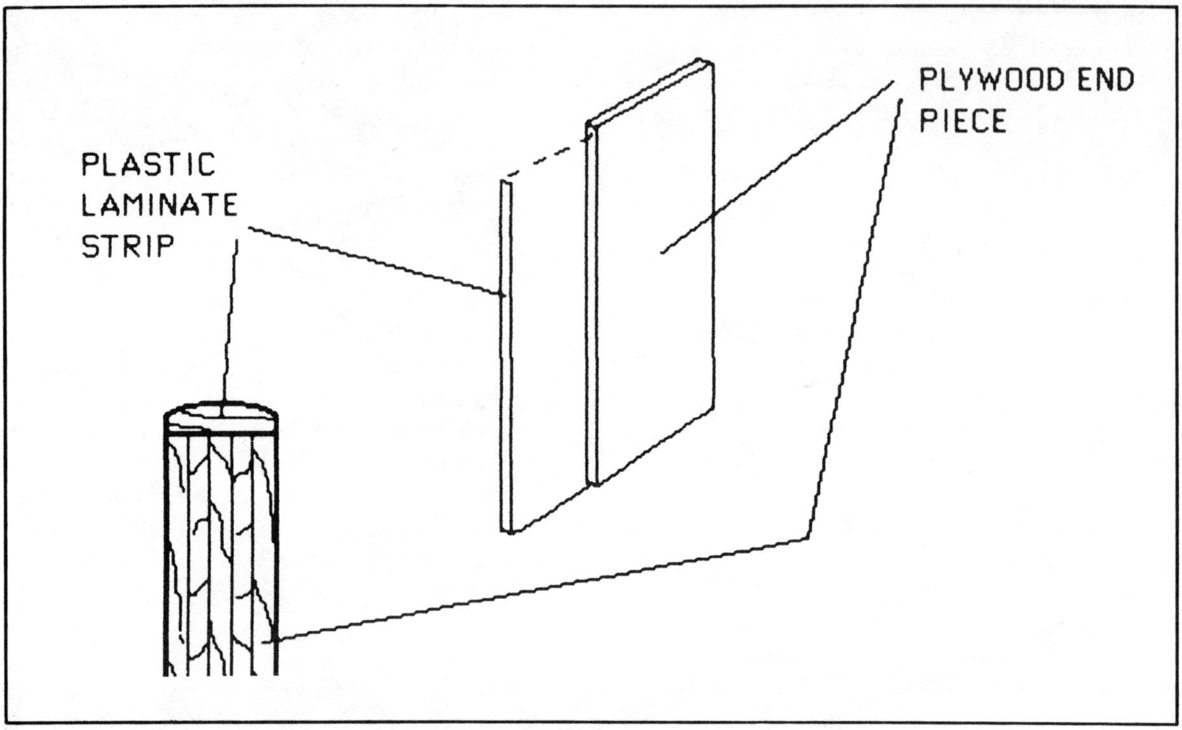

Fig. 2-13. Applying plastic laminate trim strip to forward edge of end piece.

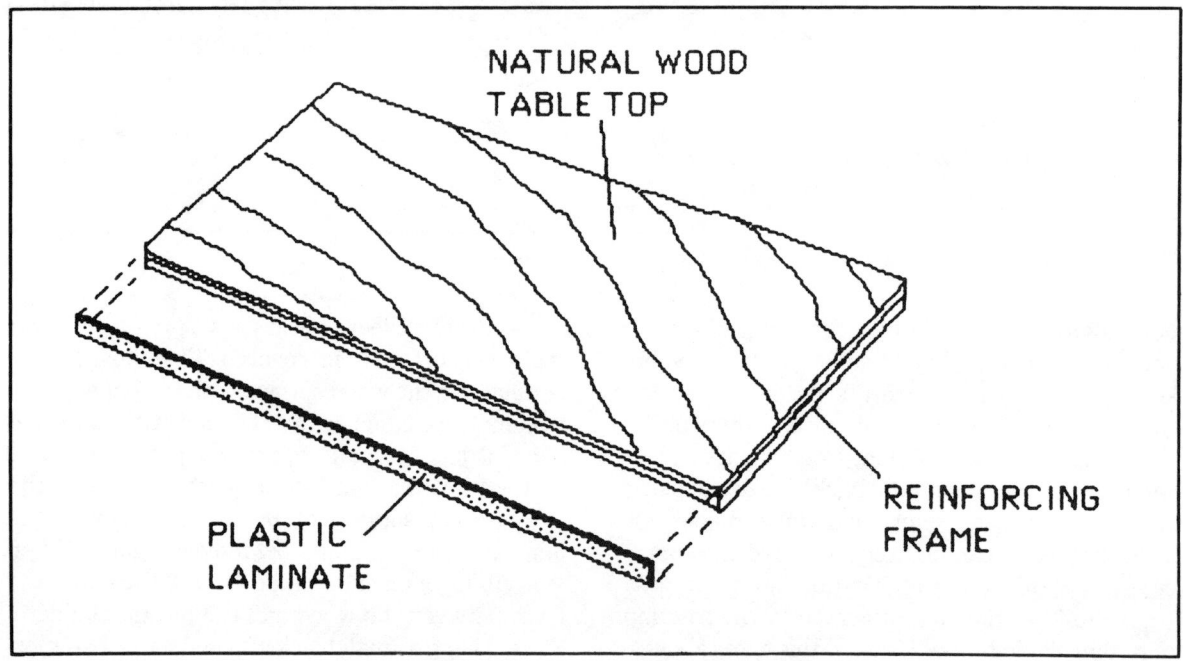

Fig. 2-14. If plastic laminate will be used as both top and trim pieces, apply trim pieces first.

method is to use a rolling pin (Fig. 2-15).

• Use a file to remove the surplus plastic laminate from the edges, or use a special cutter with a router that allows convenient trimming of excess plastic laminate to flush with the plywood edges.

• The thinner recommended for the contact cement can be used to clean contact cement from wood, plastic laminate, and tools.

Sanding and Finishing

Sanding and applying a finish are important steps in the construction process. Many beginners do a good job constructing computer furniture up to this point, only to give the unit a very amateur appearance by sloppy application of a finish. By taking care and a little time, however, even a beginner can give computer furniture a professional-looking finish.

Sanding is an important operation in preparing the wood for varnishing or painting. Small holes, checks, and other open defects in the wood should be filled in before sanding. If a clear finish is to be applied, use a wood filler that matches the color of the wood.

A sanding sealer should be applied to the plywood before doing any sanding on the surfaces.

The general principle to follow for sanding is to work from coarse grits to progressively finer grits, but don't start with a grit that is coarser than necessary for the particular sanding. The condition of the surface might be such that you can start with a medium or even fine grit. Coarser grits tend to leave scratches that need to be sanded away with finer grits.

Wood sanding is primarily done parallel to the grain. Across the grain sanding leaves scratches and tends to tear and roughen the wood surface. A scratch free surface is especially important if you are going to finish with oil or varnish.

For most hand sanding, especially on flat surfaces, use a sanding block rather than holding the sandpaper in your hand. Holding the sandpaper in your hand tends to leave a wavy surface on the wood because pressure is not applied evenly to all areas. A carpet or felt pad between the block and the sandpaper also helps.

At the final stages of sanding, most craftsmen use their fingertips to judge the smoothness of the

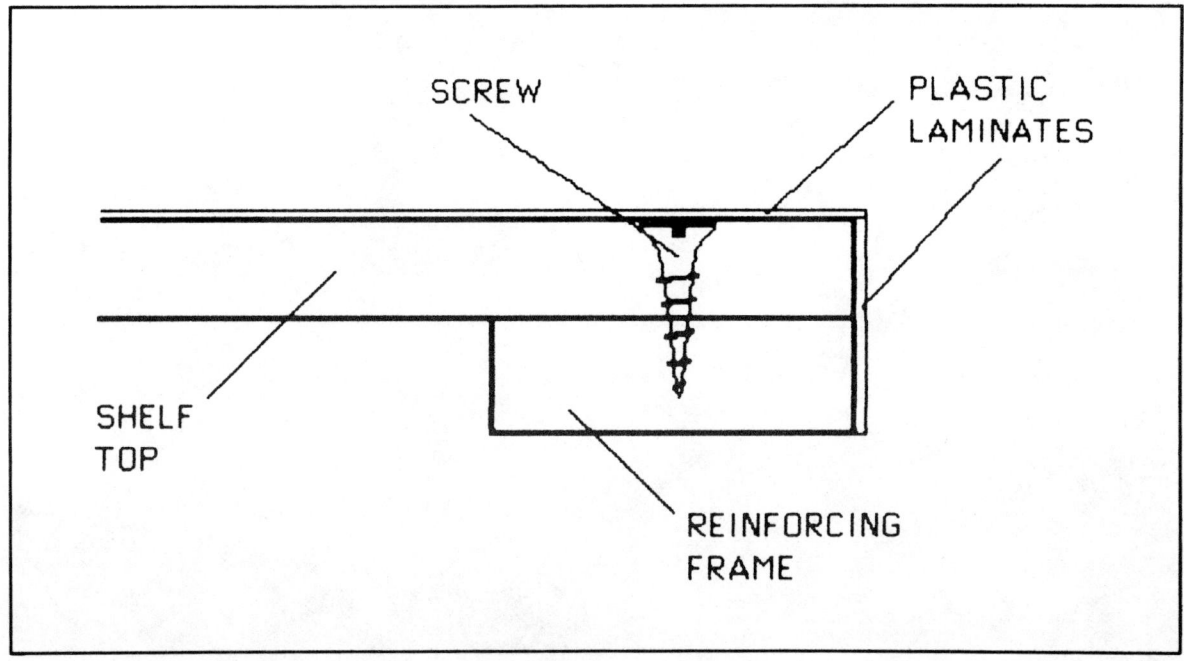

Fig. 2-15. Screws and nails should be countersunk when used under laminate.

surface. You can also judge by looking if you use a light held at a low angle to the wood surface. Taking special care with the sanding is an important step if a fine finish that you will be proud of is to be achieved.

If desired, a power sander can be used. A pad sander is the easiest to use without damaging the wood surface; belt sanders can be used by experienced operators.

A clear finish (Fig. 2-16) can be applied directly to natural wood, or you can first stain the wood to give it another color. Staining can enhance the natural grains of the wood and enrich relatively lifeless woods.

Before applying stain, first test color on a scrap piece of similar wood. Clean the surface area where stain is to be applied. Use a cloth to eliminate as much dust as possible. The stain can then be applied with a brush, foam brush applicator, or cloth. Apply a smooth, even coat of stain. Allow the stain to penetrate the wood; depending on the humidity, temperature, and particular stain used, this usually takes from 5 to 15 minutes. While the stain is still wet, wipe off the excess stain with a clean cloth. Be careful not to remove too much from corners and edges. Wipe across the grain first so that you work the stain into the wood pores, then give a final wipe with the grain. Allow the stain to dry. This

Fig. 2-16. Careful construction, sanding, and finishing produce professional quality results.

usually takes at least 8 hours. The finish can then be applied.

It is usually best to apply a series of light, even coats of clear finish rather than one thick coat. This will minimize possible drips and wrinkles as the finish dries.

Apply finish in brush-width strokes in direction of wood grain. Turn the table so that finish is applied to wood surface in a horizontal position whenever possible.

A minimum of two coats is recommended. Allow 6 to 8 hours for the first coat to dry before applying second coat. Sand lightly and use a tack cloth to remove sanded finish dust before applying next coat of finish.

Clear or stained finishes are usually applied to natural wood furniture but, if desired, color paint finishes can also be applied.

Chapter 3

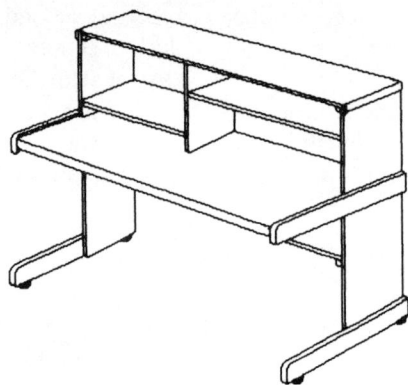

Plans and Patterns for Basic Computer Tables

In this chapter, various basic computer tables, both with and without video and storage racks, are detailed. A basic budget computer table that is easy to build from lumber and plywood available at discount stores is presented first as an ideal starting project. This table is very functional and can be built for a very low price. This project is followed by more difficult constructions. Tables without video and storage racks above the table top are detailed first, followed by a series of tables with racks. In most cases, measurements are given, but you can vary these to fit your special needs. The same applies to construction materials. For most uses, I recommend plywood rather than particle board, but particle board can be used if you want to make the furniture on the lowest possible budget.

BASIC BUDGET COMPUTER TABLE

I call this a basic budget computer table because it can be built from standard size pieces of plywood and lumber available from discount home building supply stores for a very low materials cost. I purchased the materials to build the one shown in Figs. 3-1 and 3-2 for $21 (in 1984). This table is similar to a model available in kit form that sells for about $100 and to one in ready-to-finish form that retails for about $150. From this, it is easy to see that large savings are possible by building your own. This computer table is of attractive and modern design and presents a good appearance even when built from low cost wood. You can give a custom appearance, however, by making the same design from more expensive woods, such as birch or oak.

The basic budget computer table is shown again in Fig. 3-3. The top has space for both a computer and printer. The table can have a natural wood top or plastic laminates (Fig. 3-4) can be added. The table features a shelf underneath that provides storage space and gives the table added strength. The half sides give a modern appearance.

Materials

The patterns for the wood parts are shown in

Fig. 3-1. Basic budget computer table.

Fig. 3-5. The top of the table is a 2-foot-by-4-foot piece of 3/4-inch thick plywood. If you intend to use the wood surface as the finished table top, without adding a plastic laminate, plywood with an upper layer of a hardwood, such as oak, is recommended. If a laminate is to be added, even an exterior grade of shop plywood will suffice. Although plywood is normally sold in standard 4-foot-by-8-foot sheets, many home building and discount stores also offer 2-foot-by-4-foot cuts. If this size is purchased, no additional cutting will be necessary, making this project ideal for a beginner.

Although 1/2-inch thick plywood could also be used, I don't recommend this. The savings are small, and a less sturdy table will result. Particle board can be substituted for the plywood if you are on an absolute minimum budget. Considerable numbers of low-grade high-priced manufactured computer furniture are made from particle board covered by plastic laminates. Particle board can be difficult to work with, however, and it is very difficult to get plastic laminates to bond properly to this material without special equipment. (It must be difficult even with special machinery, because laminates on manufactured furniture always seem to come loose at the edges.)

The side pieces and shelf are 1-inch thick by 12 inches wide wood stock. These are the dimensions before the wood was surfaced, so the wood that you purchase will have dimensions slightly less than these. When fitting parts, make certain that you take this into account. The shelf should be two wood thicknesses less than 48 inches, which will be about 46 1/4 inches, but you will want to be as exact as possible so that the shelf will fit properly between the end pieces.

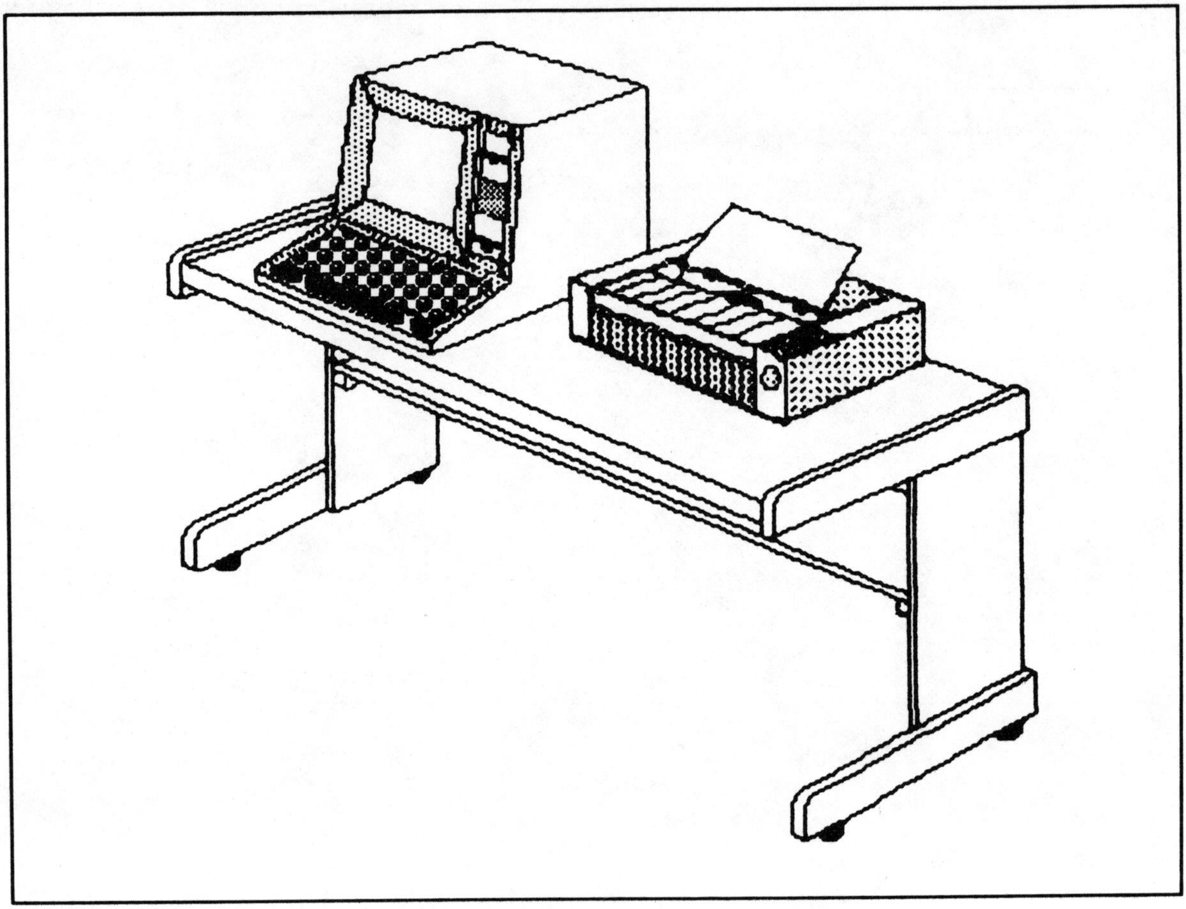

Fig. 3-2. Basic budget computer table with computer and printer.

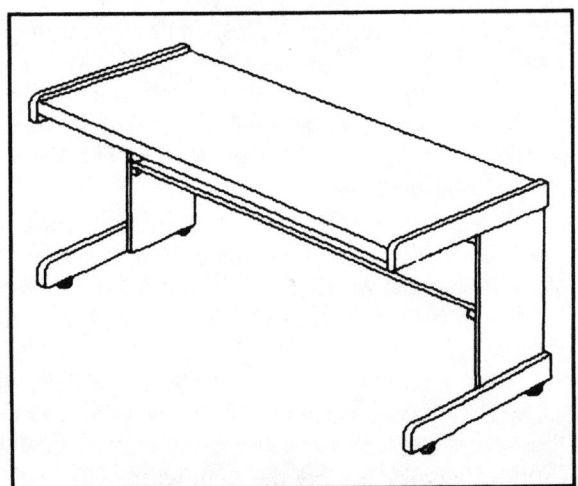

Fig. 3-3. Basic budget computer table.

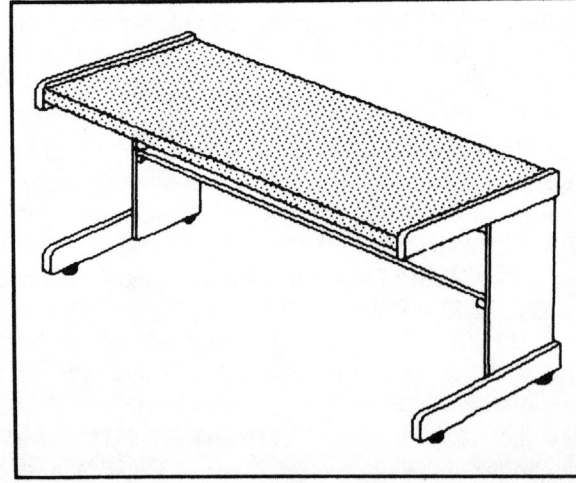

Fig. 3-4. Basic budget computer table with plastic laminates.

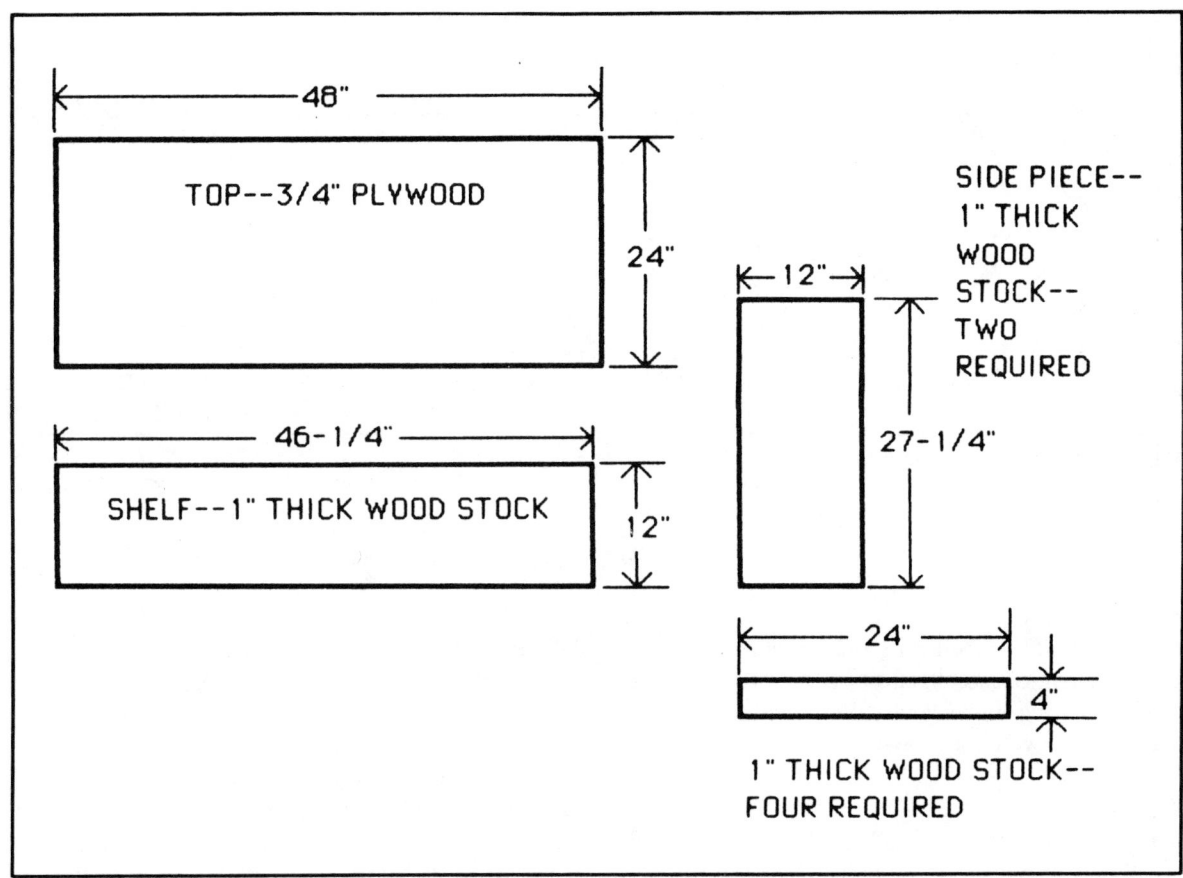

Fig. 3-5. Patterns for wood parts for basic budget computer table.

A height of 27 1/4 inches is shown for the side pieces. With the addition of the 3/4 inch thick table top, this will give a height of 28 inches before floor guides are added, which will increase the height somewhat, the exact distance depending on the type of floor guides used. You may want to have your table higher or lower than this. When using a computer keyboard, it is very important to have the height from the floor to the top of the keys correct for the user. Because table to keyboard heights vary from computer to computer, the proper table height for a particular user will vary depending on the computer used. Adjustable floor guides that allow you to adjust the height of the table within a limited range are available. Many typing tables are only about 26 inches high, and you may prefer to have your computer table this low to the floor.

You may want to do some experimenting before you decide on the final height of your computer table.

When selecting the wood stock, you can use a variety of woods, including pine, fir, and birch, but try to select wood that is as straight as possible and without cracks or other defects.

The end pieces or beams are 1-inch thick by 4-inch wide wood stock (dimensions before the wood was surfaced; the measurements of the wood you buy will be slightly less than these). You will need four of these, 24 inches long. The beams form a base of support for the table, add strength, and give a decorative appearance.

The backing piece (Fig. 3-6) can be either plywood or fiberboard. The backing piece is used to strengthen the table base and hold the frame in

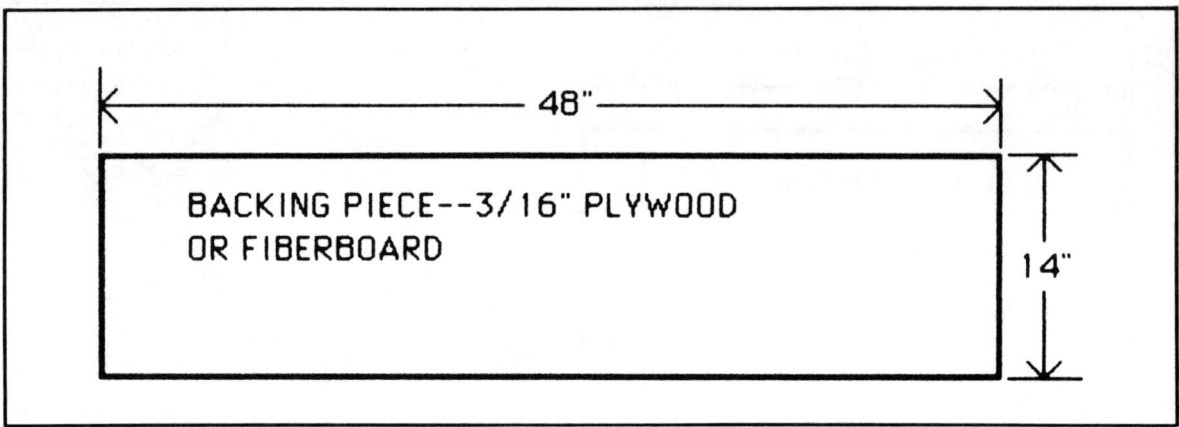

Fig. 3-6. Pattern for backing piece.

rectangular form. A 14-inch height is shown for the backing piece, but this will vary depending on how far below the top you wish to place the shelf. A minimum distance of 12 inches between the top plywood and the shelf is recommended to give the table base adequate strength. Notice that the top, shelf, backing piece, and side pieces form a box with the forward side open.

You will also need 1-inch-by-2-inch or larger framing stock for use under the plywood table top and as cleats under the ends of the shelf. A wood or plastic trim strip is used to cover the forward edge of the table top. This piece is 48 inches long and about 1 3/4 inches wide (the minimum width should be such that it will completely cover the widths of the plywood top (3/4 inch) and the framing (approximately 7/8 inch). It can be slightly wider than this, however.

Four floor pods or guides are used on the floor beams. A variety of suitable types are available from hardware stores. These can be of a fixed or adjustable type, as desired.

Finishing nails and other fasteners are required for assembly, as detailed below in this section. You will also need a suitable wood glue. The finish can be clear urethane or other type, as desired.

The top can be left natural or a plastic laminate can be added. If a plastic laminate is to be added, you will need a 2-foot-by-4-foot piece of suitable plastic laminate and contact cement for attaching it to the plywood.

Construction

Overviews of the complete assembly are shown in Figs. 3-7 and 3-8. Begin by constructing the table top. If you purchased a piece of plywood that was already cut to the 2-foot-by-4-foot size, no additional cutting will be required, assuming that it was cut accurately and is a true rectangular form. You might want to check this with a square.

If you purchased a larger piece of plywood, such as a standard 4-foot-by-8-foot sheet, you will need to cut out a section for the table top. In most cases, you will want to have the grain of the top layer running lengthwise, although this is not essential if you are going to add a plastic laminate. Use two factory cut edges for your table top and cut the other two. Use a ruler and square to make the pattern, marking the lines with a sharp pencil or scribing tool.

Sawing plywood requires special considerations. Special care must be taken to avoid chipping and splintering along the cut edge. Handsaws or power saws with special fine-toothed blades designed especially for plywood should be used. Even better are special carbide-tipped blades. Applying a strip of masking tape over the area to be cut on both sides of the plywood, but especially on the side opposite the one from which you are cutting, is also helpful. Another possibility is to clamp a solid piece of wood to the underside and make the cut through both the plywood and the piece of wood.

Be extremely careful when sanding plywood edges. Use a sanding block, and avoid sanding the surfaces of plywood until a wood sealer has been applied.

The next step is to add the reinforcing frame to the plywood, as shown in Fig. 3-9. Use a ruler and a square to make the patterns on the framing wood, marking the lines with a sharp pencil or other marking device. Then make the necessary saw cuts, as detailed in Chapter 2. The frame pieces should be glued and nailed or screwed in position (Fig. 3-10). If the plywood top is to be left natural wood (without a plastic laminate being added), the fasteners should go through the framing and into the plywood, but care should be taken so that the fasteners do not pass all the way through the plywood or leave a bulge in the upper surface. If a good glue is used, such as acrylic or epoxy, the glue alone should give adequate strength. The fasteners are mainly used as a clamping device for the gluing. Fasteners will not have much holding power in the plywood. To give greater holding power, the fasteners can be passed through the plywood and into the framing if a plastic laminate is to be added.

Next, cut the shelf wood to length. The shelf should be 48 inches long, minus the combined widths of the two side pieces. You will need to measure and cut this accurately so that the side pieces will be exactly perpendicular to the top when the table is assembled. The ends of the shelf should be perpendicular to the sides of the wood. Use a square as a guide for marking pattern lines.

Next, cut 1-inch-by-2-inch wood cleats to length, as shown in Fig. 3-11. These should match the depth of the shelf, as shown. Glue and nail these

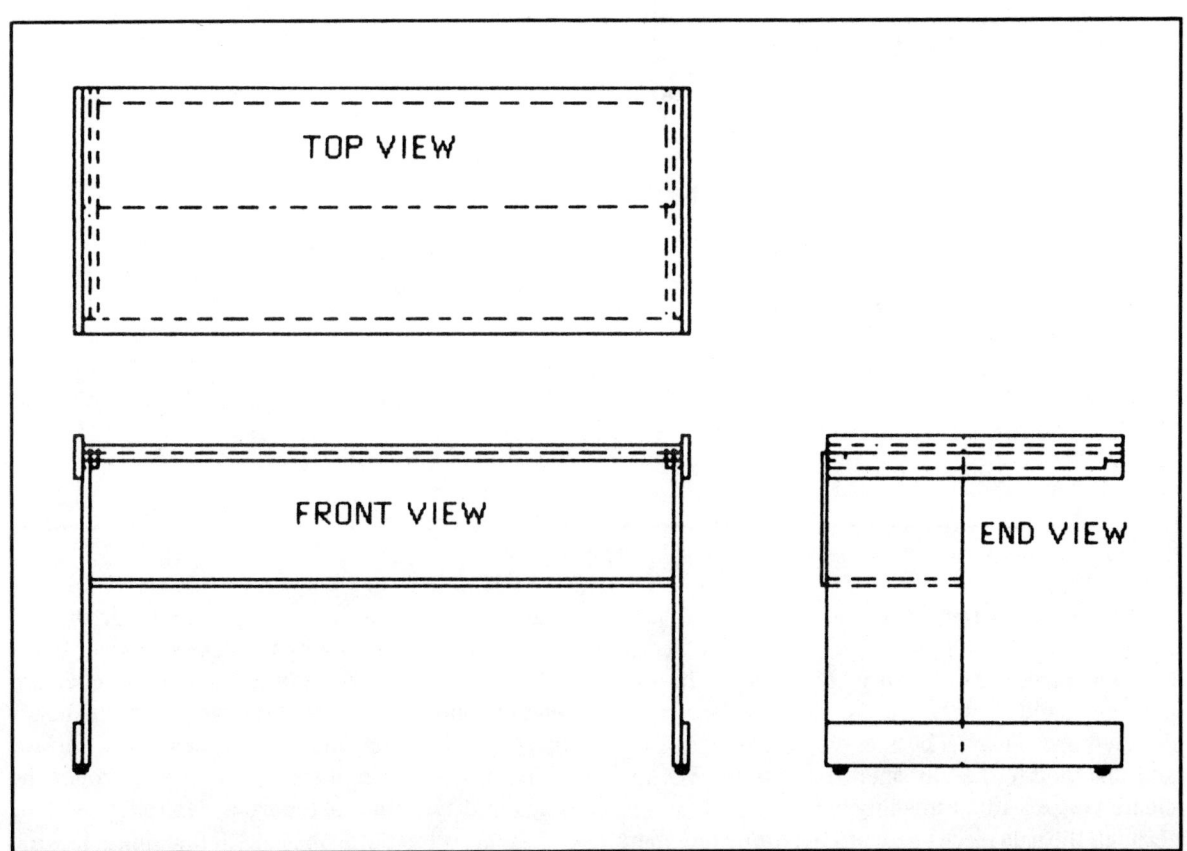

Fig. 3-7. Assembly of basic budget computer table.

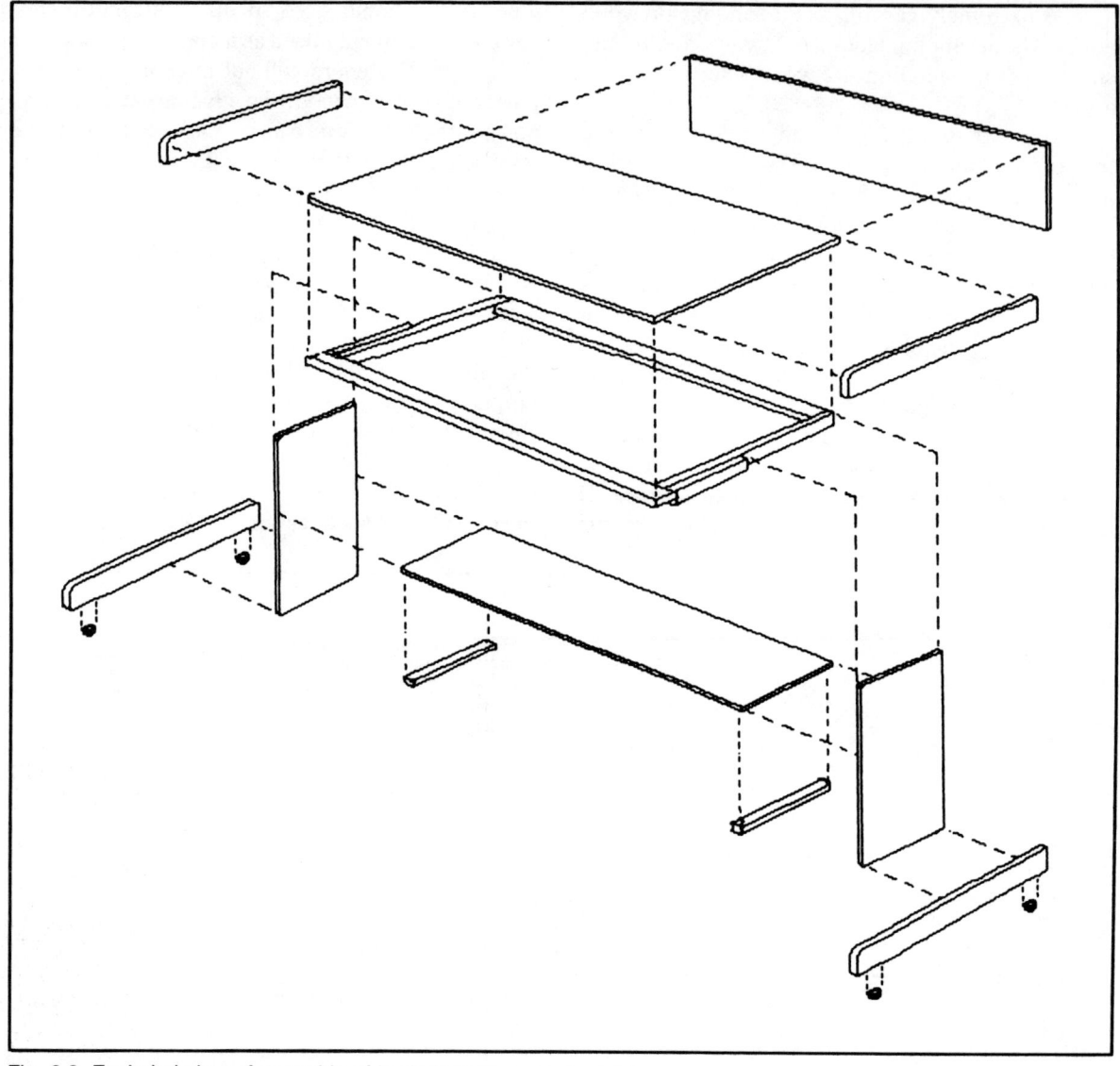

Fig. 3-8. Exploded view of assembly of basic budget computer table.

to the bottom of the shelf.

The table top and shelf are then assembled to the side pieces, as shown in Fig. 3-12. The end pieces should first be cut to desired length, as detailed previously. The side pieces are then glued and fastened to the top, shelf frame members and cleats (Fig. 3-13). Finishing nails can be driven through the side pieces and into the frame members and cleats. These can be set below the wood surface and wood filler used to cover and hide the nail heads. Another possibility is to use screws or bolts. Washers can be used, and heads and nuts can extend beyond the surface of the wood. Or, the heads and/or nuts can be countersunk below the surface of the wood. Wood plugs can be used to cover the holes and hide the fasteners if desired.

Regardless of the method of fastening, it is extremely important to install the side pieces perpen-

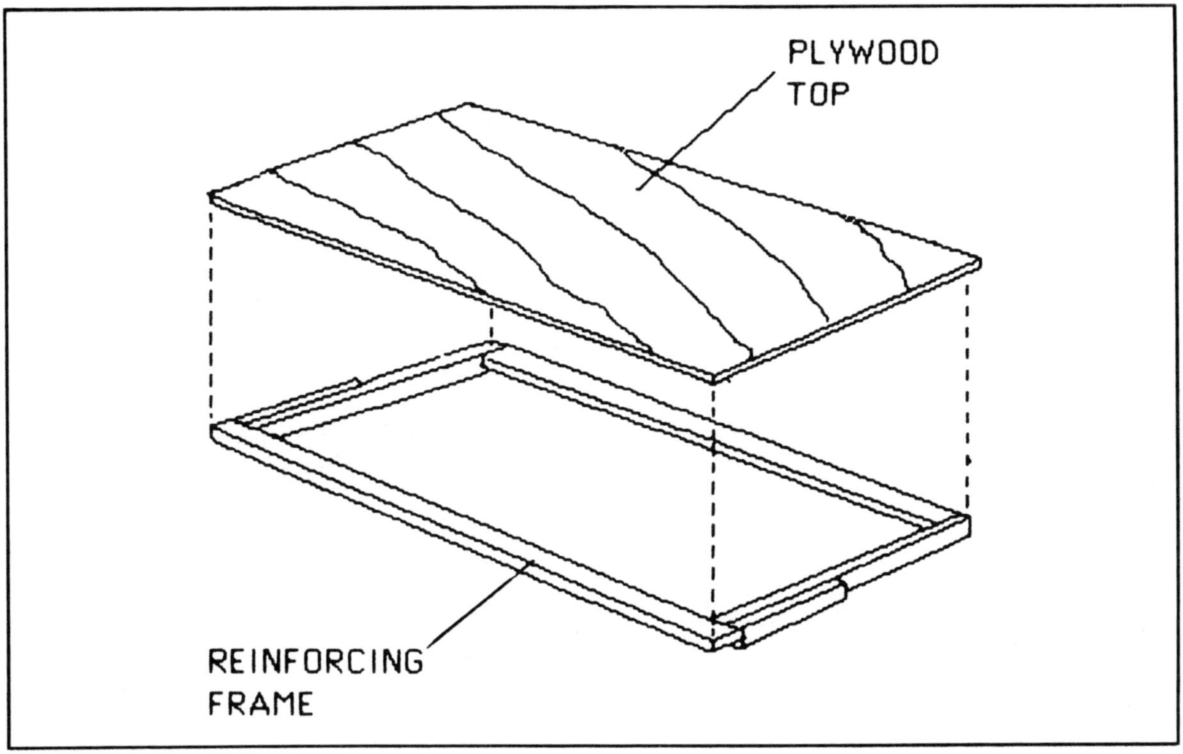

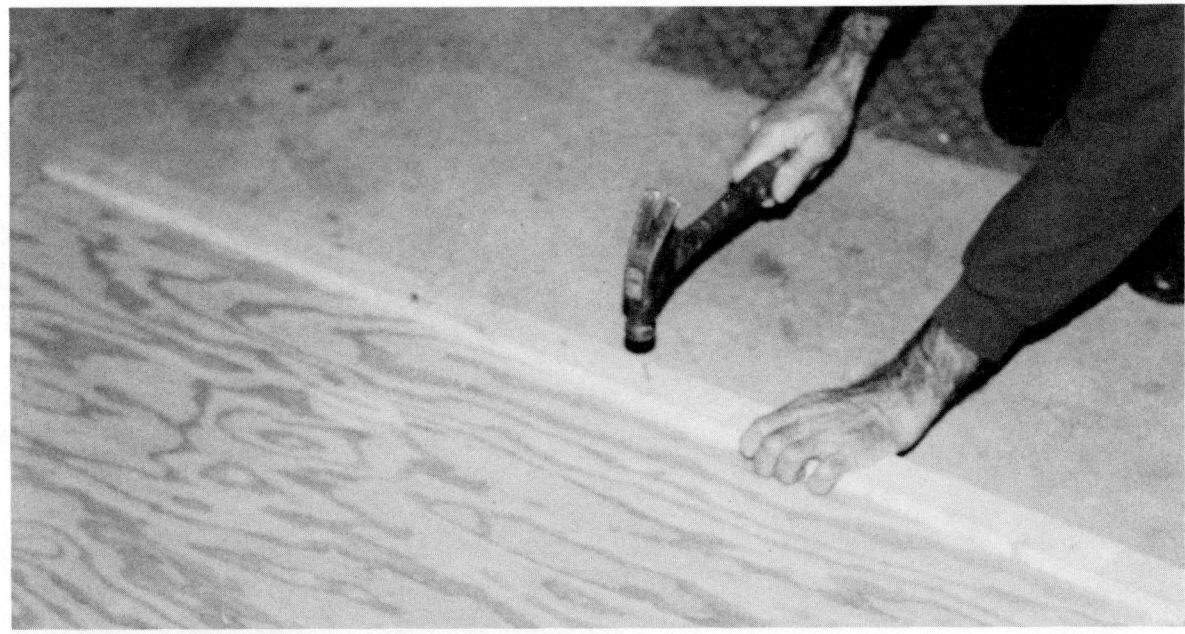

Fig. 3-9. Assembly of table top to reinforcing frame.

Fig. 3-10. Framing wood is glued and nailed to plywood top.

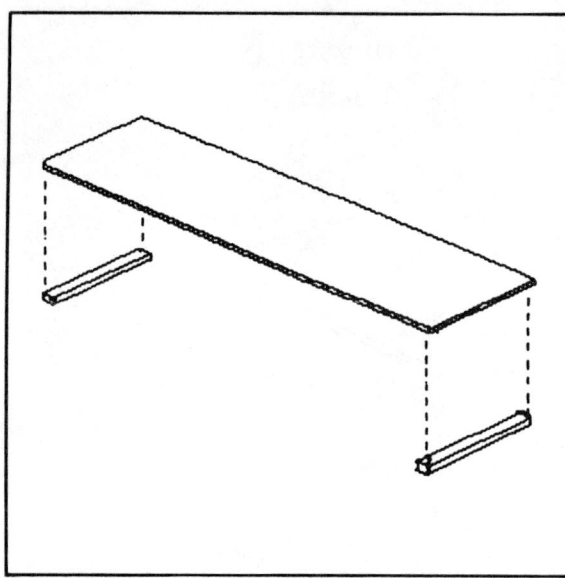

Fig. 3-11. Assembly of cleats to shelf.

dicular to the table top and shelf in a crosswise direction. Use a square to make pattern lines on the side pieces. It is also important to have exactly the same distance between the top and shelf on both sides. This distance can be as desired, but a minimum of 12 inches is required to give the table adequate strength.

Figure 3-14 shows the shelf and top assembled to the end pieces. The next step is to add the backing piece, as shown in Fig. 3-15. The backing piece forms a box with the top, shelf, and side pieces. It is important that the backing piece be attached securely to the wood members all the way around the edges. The backing piece is glued and nailed into position (Fig. 3-16). It is extremely important to make certain that the backing piece is a true rectangular form and that the side pieces are perpendicular to the table top and shelf before the backing piece is attached and the glue allowed to set. Fig-

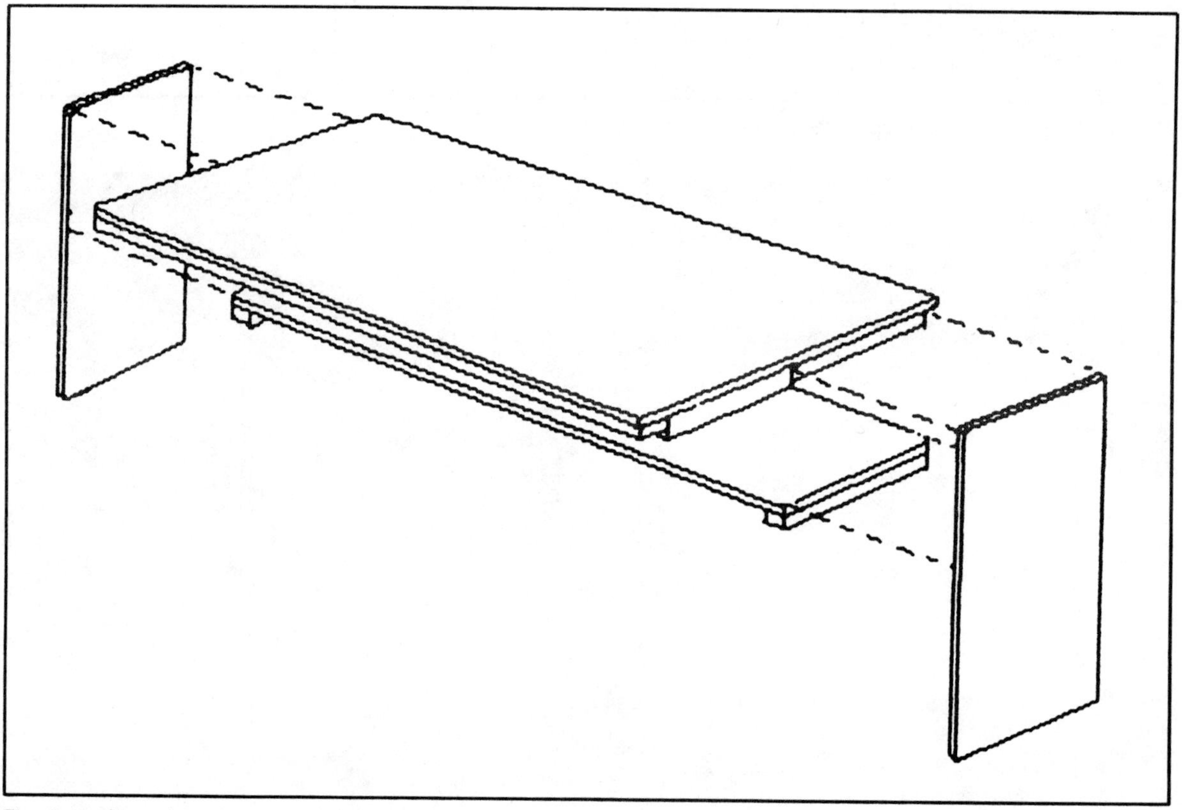

Fig. 3-12. Assembly of top and shelf to end pieces.

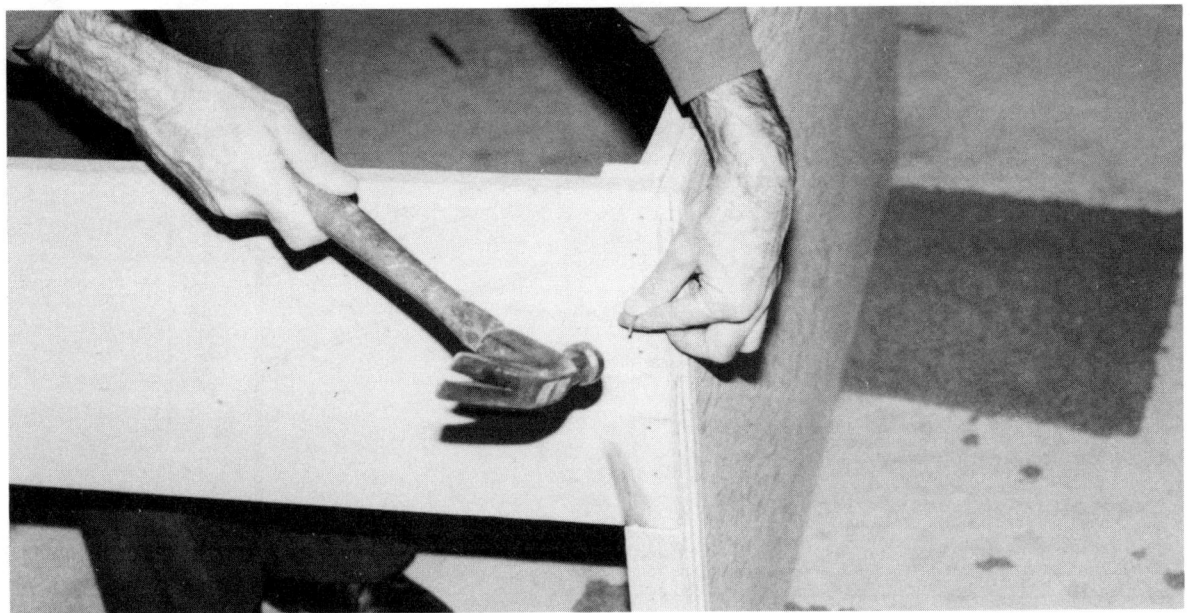

Fig. 3-13. End piece is glued and nailed to top frame.

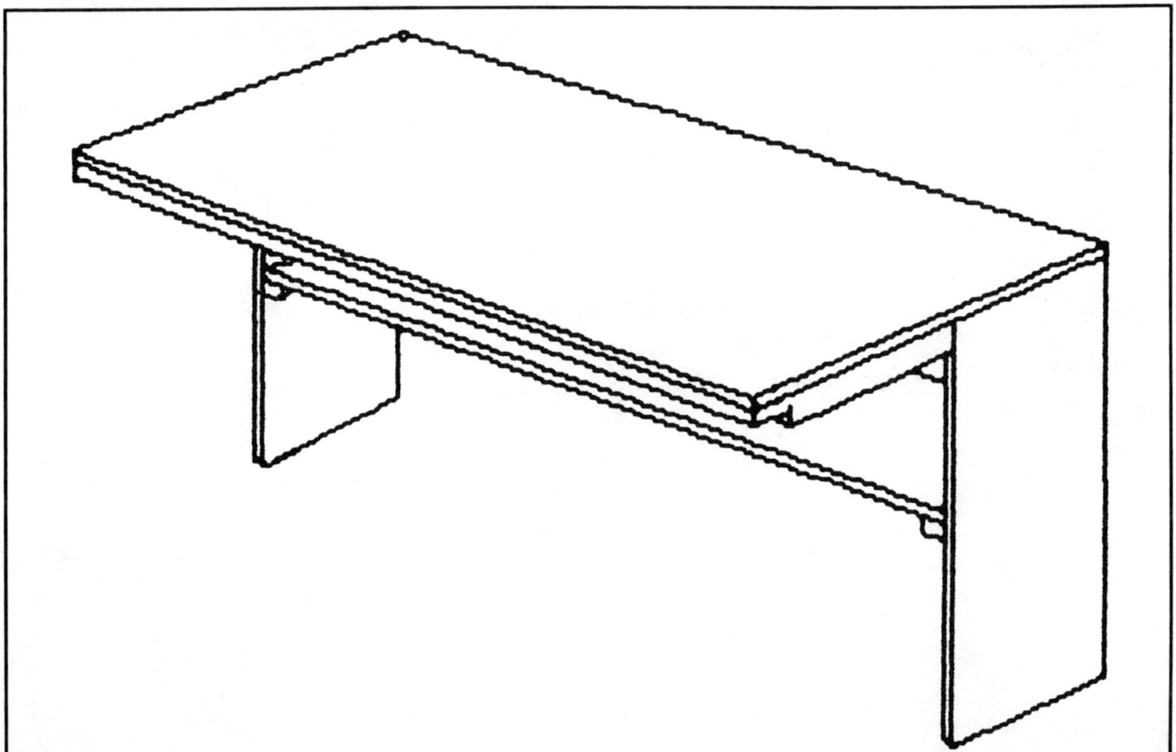

Fig. 3-14. Shelf and top assembled to end pieces.

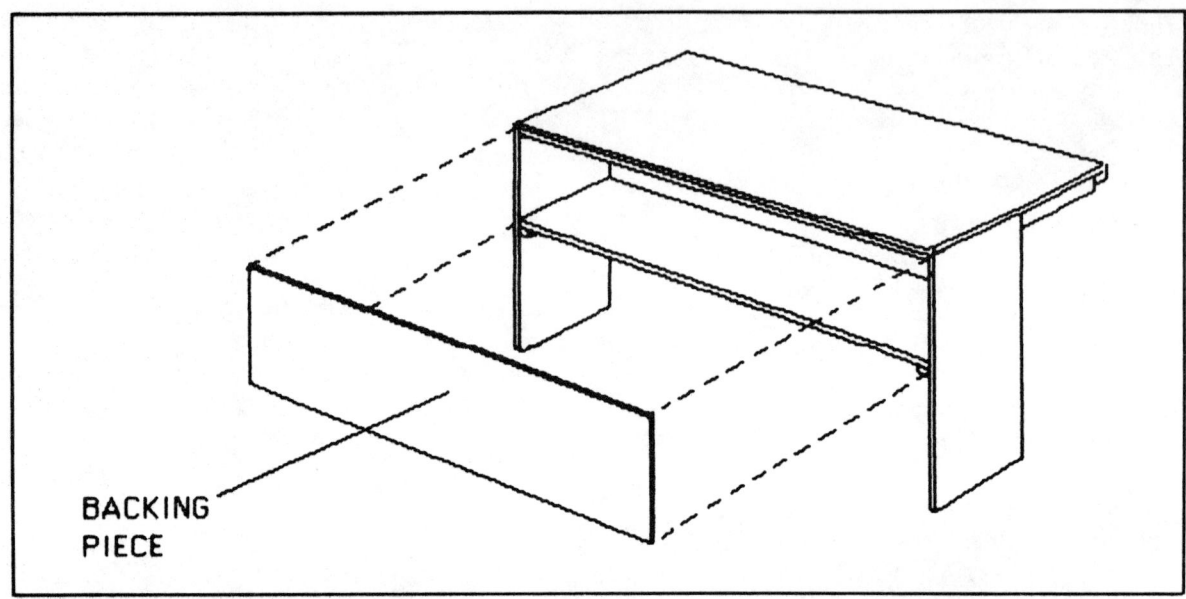

Fig. 3-15. Assembly of backing piece.

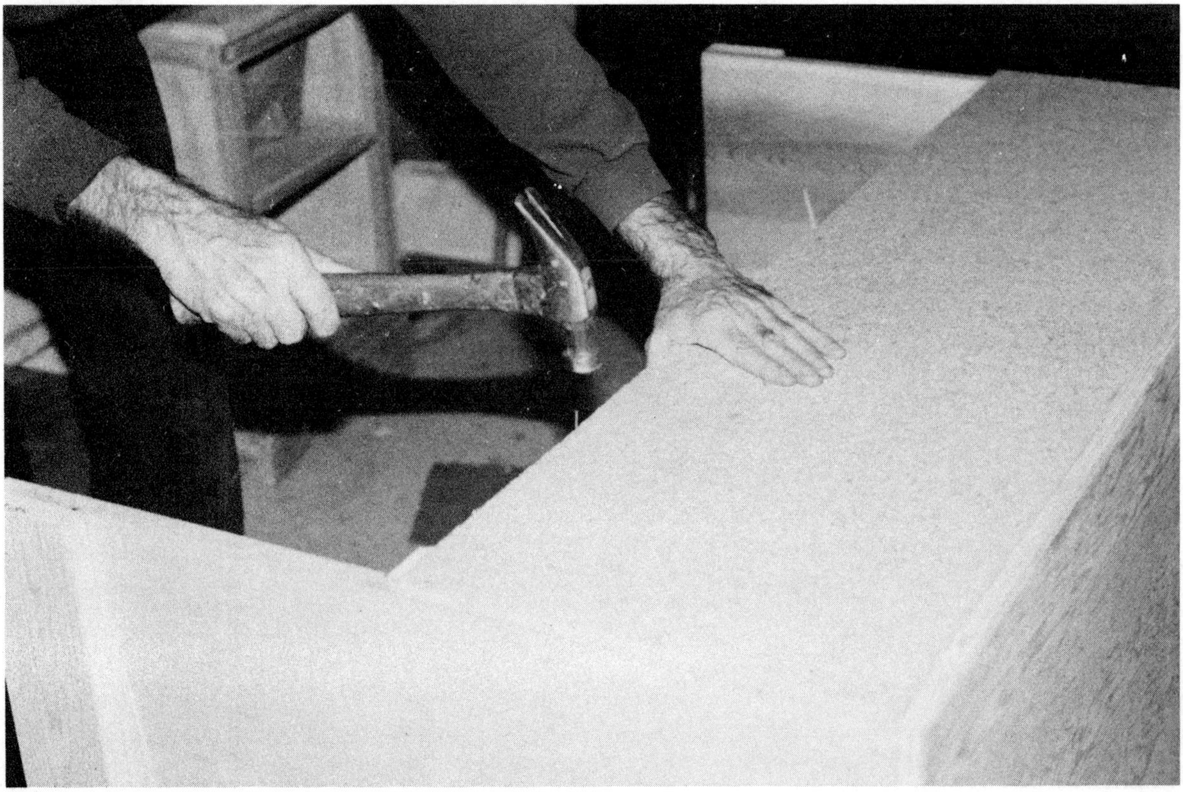

Fig. 3-16. Backing piece is glued and nailed in position.

ure 3-17 shows the backing piece installed.

If a plastic laminate is to be added to the plywood table top, it can be installed at this time. Plastic laminates are often applied to plywood for computer table tops. A large selection of plastic laminates are on the market, but I suggest using high quality plastic laminates.

If a plastic laminate is to also be applied to the forward edge of the table top, it should be applied first. This is then finished flush with the table top. The top laminate is then applied so that the edge overlaps the top edge of the laminate on the forward edge of the table.

The plastic laminate is installed as follows:

- All holes and defects in the surface of the plywood should be filled with putty or wood filler.
- Sand the surface to be covered. This will help ensure good adhesion.
- Mark the plastic laminate to a pattern slightly larger than the area to be covered. Use a straightedge and draw the pattern lines on the finished or pattern side of the laminate. Leave 1/4 inch to 1/2 inch on all sides. This will be trimmed off later.
- If a laminate is to be applied to the forward edge of the table, apply this first. After installation, as detailed below, trim and file the upper edge of the plastic laminate flush with the upper edge of the plywood table top before installing the plastic laminate to upper surface of the table top.
- Cut the plastic laminate to the pattern marked. Even though the plastic laminate is extremely durable once applied, it is vulnerable to cracking and splitting before it is cemented in place. Fine-tooth handsaws or power saws with fine-tooth blades can be used. A rotary power saw with a 14 to 16 teeth per inch blade is ideal. Place the plastic laminate face up when cutting, taking care that the plastic laminate is not chipped or broken. An alternate method is to use a carbide tip knife to score the plastic by drawing the knife point along a metal straight-edge. Cut through the decorative surface. The laminate can then be broken by bending it toward the decorative surface side over the edge of a table or workbench.

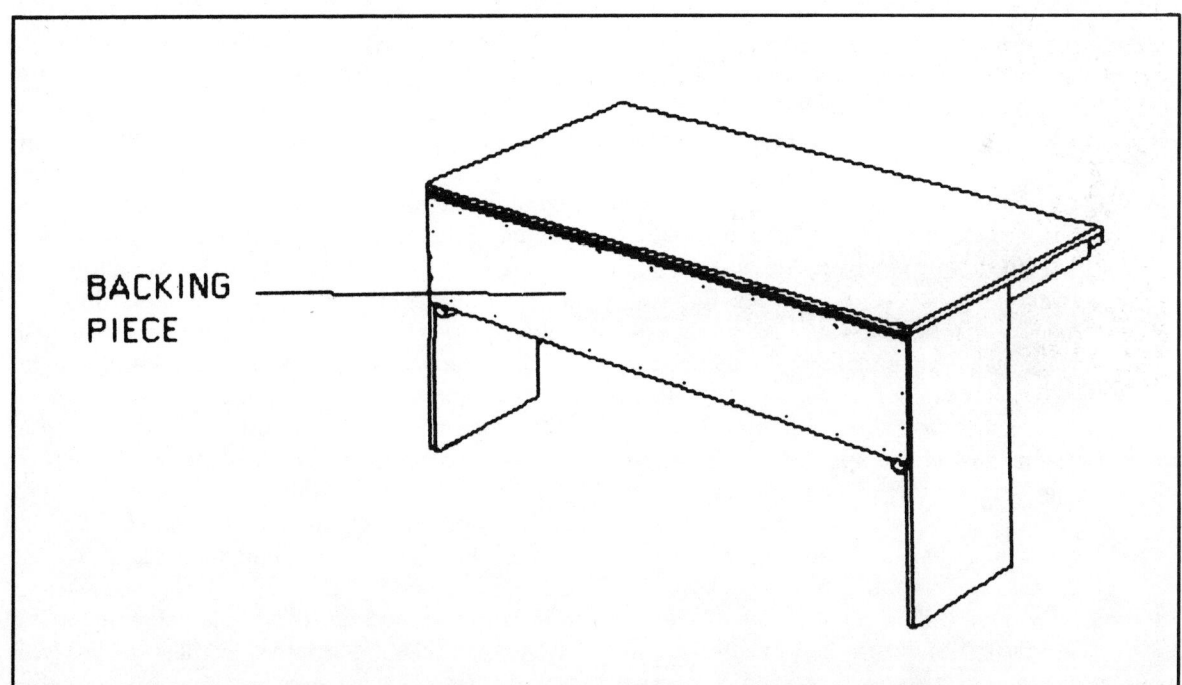

Fig. 3-17. Backing piece installed.

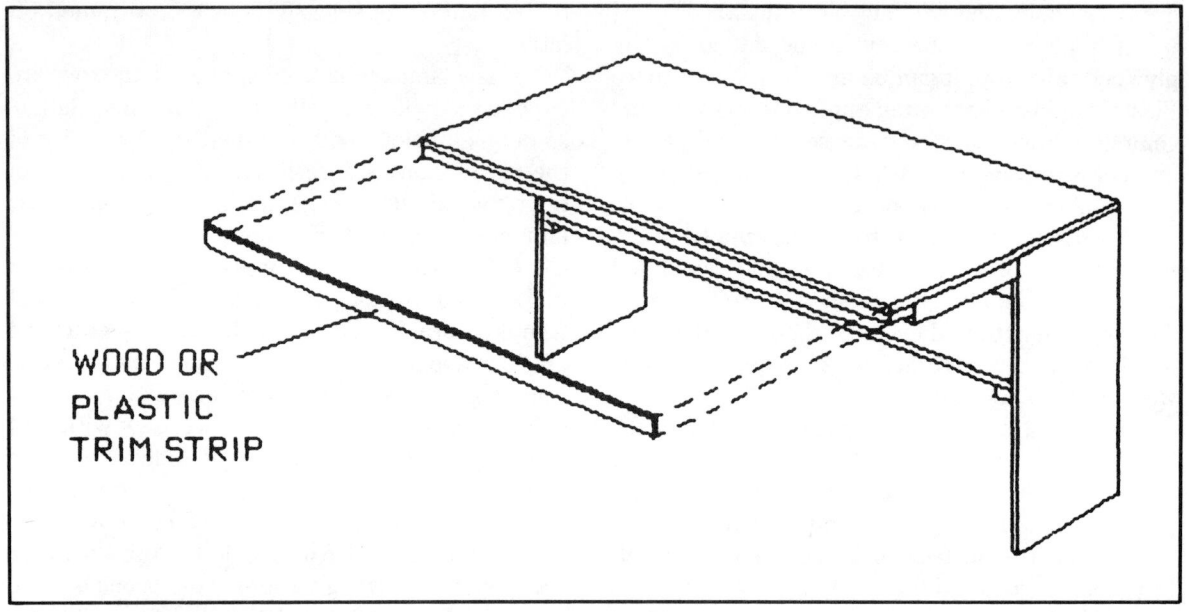

Fig. 3-18. Adding wood or plastic trim strip to front edge of table.

- Apply contact cement to the surface of the plywood to be covered and the back side of the plastic laminate. A brush, roller, or metal spreader with a serrated edge can be used to spread the contact cement. A thin, even application is important.
- Follow the manufacturer's instructions regarding drying time. Usually, this takes about 20 to 30 minutes.
- Place a sheet of heavy wrapping paper over the plywood surface to be covered. Then position the laminate on the plywood surface with the paper in between. The contact cement will not stick to the paper if it has been allowed to dry properly. Make certain that the laminate is positioned correctly. Once the two surfaces of contact cement touch, the laminate sheet cannot be moved again. When everything is lined up properly, pull the paper out from between the plywood and the plastic laminate.
- Using a small block of wood and a hammer, lightly tap the laminate in place. An alternate method is to use a rolling pin.
- Use a file to remove the surplus plastic laminate from the edges. Another method is to use a special cutter with a router, which allows convenient trimming of excess plastic laminate to flush with the plywood edges.
- The thinner recommended for the contact cement can be used to clean contact cement from wood and plastic laminate and tools.

If a plastic laminate was not added to the forward edge of the table previously, regardless of whether the top is natural wood or covered with a plastic laminate, the next step is to add a wood or plastic trim strip to the forward edge of the table top (Fig. 3-18). If plastic is used, it can be glued in place and/or installed with fasteners. A wood trim strip can be attached with glue and finishing nails. Set the heads below the wood surface and fill holes in with wood filler to flush with the wood surface.

The wood end pieces or beams are installed next, as shown in Fig. 3-19. Glue and use mechanical fasteners to make the joint (Fig. 3-20). One method is to use finishing nails that first pass through the end pieces and into the side pieces or reinforcing frame. Set the heads below the wood surface and fill holes in with wood filler to flush with the wood surface.

An alternate method is to fasten the end pieces

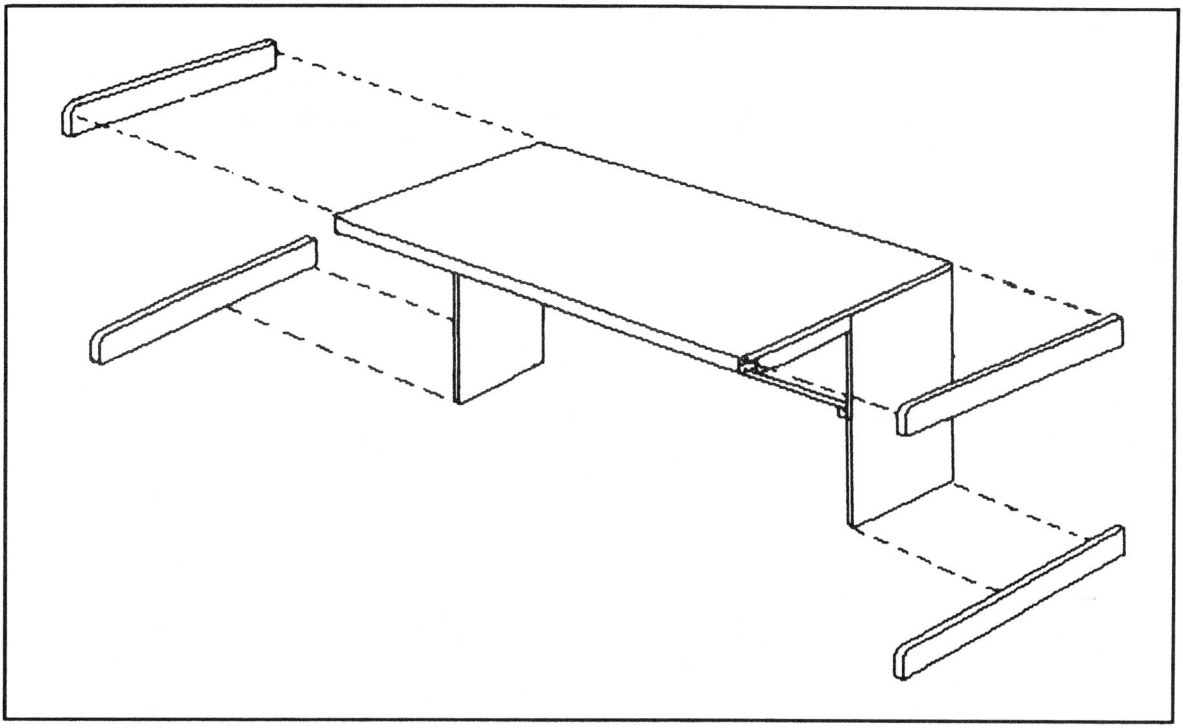

Fig. 3-19. Assembly of end pieces.

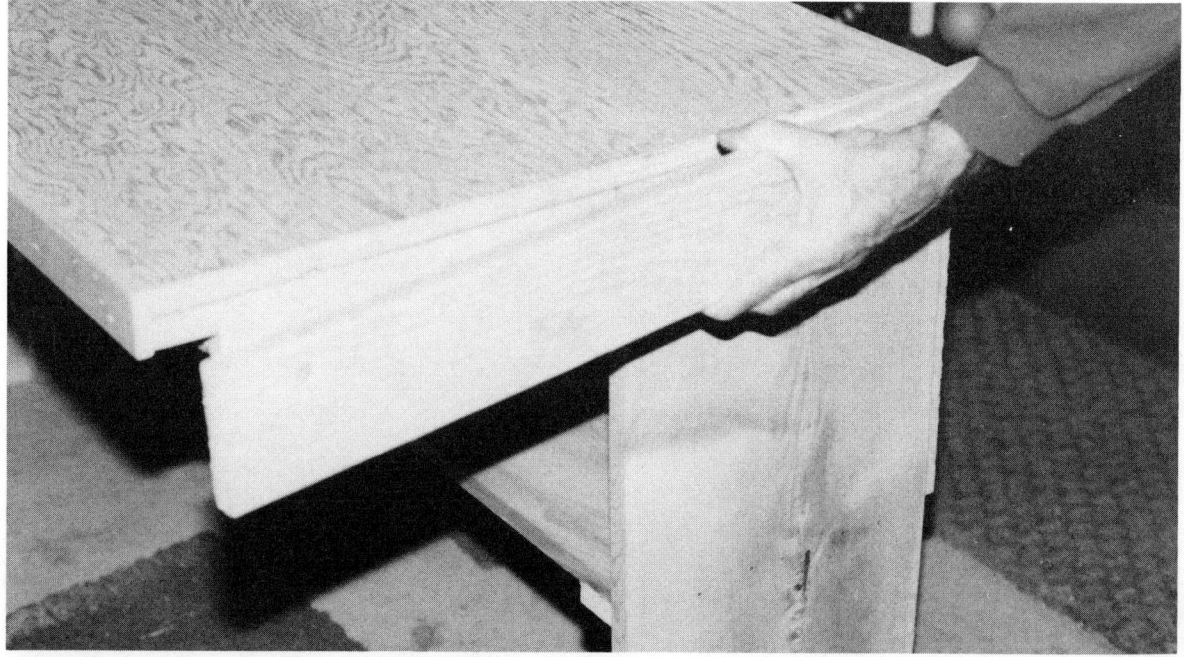

Fig. 3-20. End piece is glued and nailed in position.

with wood screws or through bolts. Figure 3-21 shows installed end pieces.

The floor guides are installed to the floor beams as shown in Fig. 3-21. Attachment varies depending on the type of floor guides selected; some fit in a mounting drilled in the wood beam, others are driven or screwed into the wood. Still others have separate screw fasteners to hold them in place.

Sanding and Finishing

Sanding and applying a finish are important steps in the construction process. Many beginners do a good job constructing the table up to this point, only to give the table a very amateur appearance by sloppy application of a finish. By taking care and a little time, however, even a beginner can give the table a professional finish.

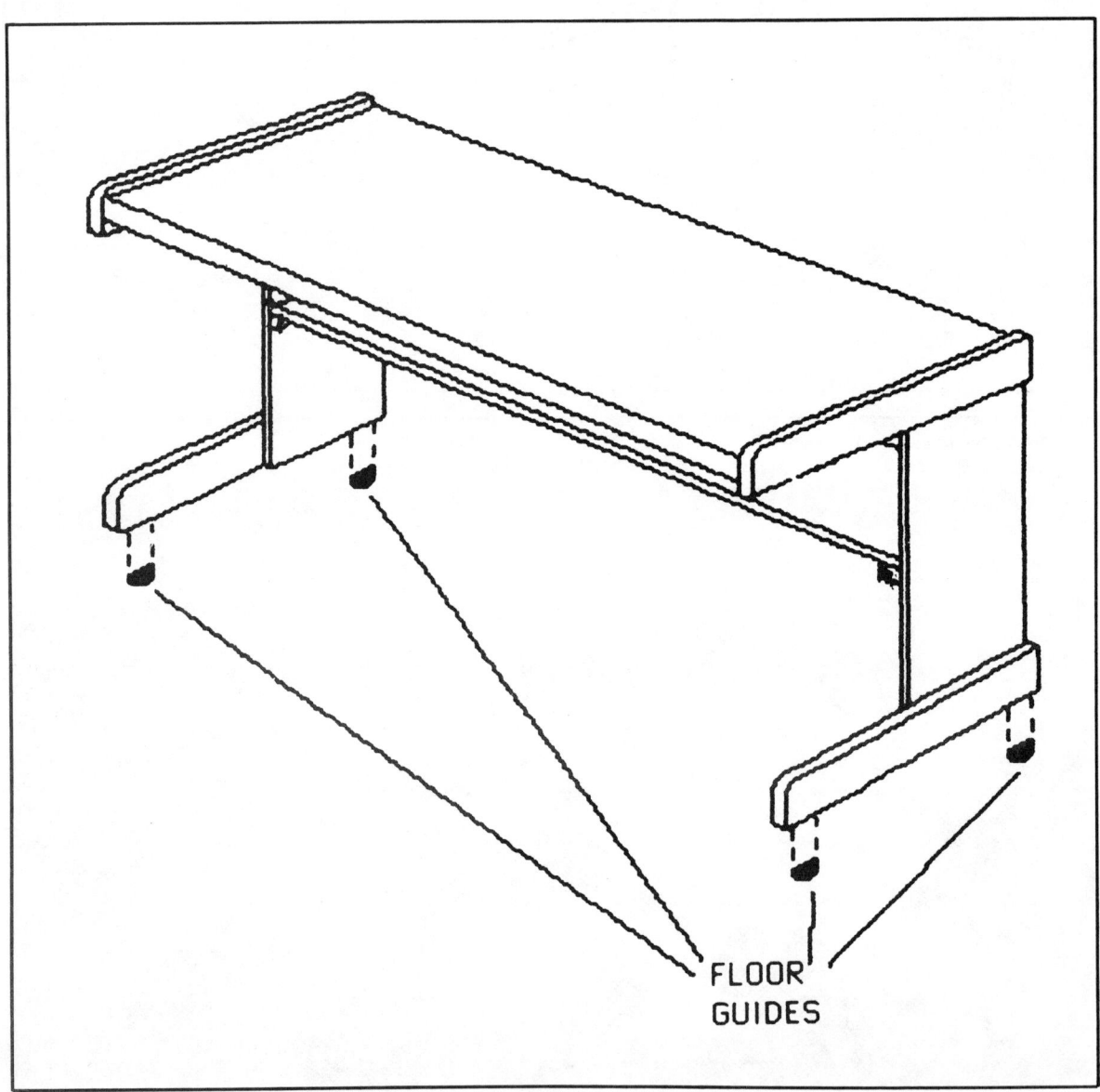

Fig. 3-21. Table with end pieces and floor guides installed.

Fig. 3-22. Finishing nail heads are set below surface of wood and holes filled with wood filler.

Sanding is an important operation in preparing the wood for varnishing or painting. Small holes, checks, and other open defects in the wood should be filled in (Fig. 3-22). If a clear finish is to be applied, use a wood filler that matches the color of the wood. Apply a sanding sealer to the plywood before doing any sanding.

The general principle to follow for sanding is to work from coarse grits progressively to finer grits, but don't start with a grit that is coarser than necessary. The condition of the surface might be such that you can start with a medium or even fine grit. Coarser grits tend to leave scratches that need to be sanded away with finer grits.

Wood sanding is done primarily parallel to the grain (Fig. 3-23). Across the grain sanding leaves scratches and tends to tear and roughen the wood surface. A scratch free surface is especially important if you are going to finish with oil or varnish.

For most hand sanding, especially on flat surfaces, use a sanding block rather than holding the sandpaper in your hand. Holding the sandpaper in your hand tends to leave a wavy surface on the wood, because pressure is not applied evenly to all areas. A carpet or felt pad between the block and the sandpaper also helps.

At the final stages of sanding, most craftsmen use their fingertips to judge the smoothness of the surface. You can also use a light held at a low angle to the wood surface, to judge the smoothness. Taking special care with the sanding is an important step if a fine finish is to be achieved.

If desired, a power sander can be used. A pad sander is the easiest to use without damaging the wood surface; belt sanders can be used by experienced operators.

A clear finish (polyurethane plastic is ideal) can be applied directly to natural wood, or you can first stain the wood to give it another color. Staining can enhance the natural grains of the wood and enrich unattractive woods.

Before applying stain, first test color on a scrap piece. Clean the surface area where stain will be applied, and use a cloth to eliminate as much dust

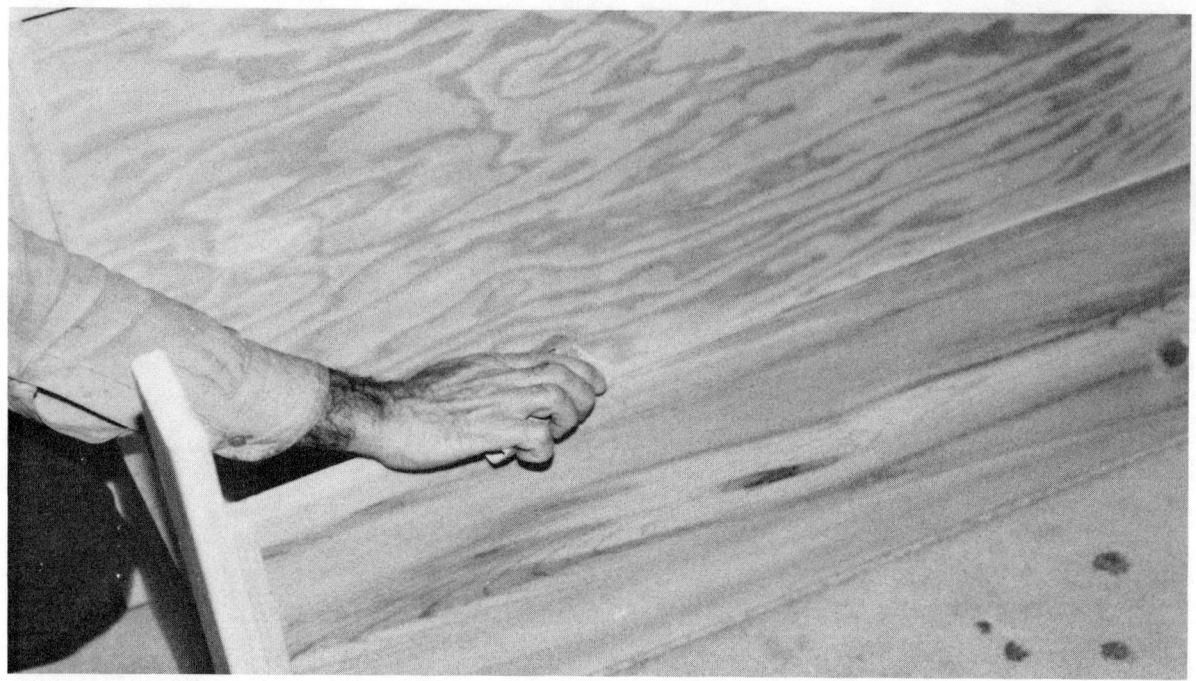
Fig. 3-23. Sanding with sanding block.

as possible. The stain can then be applied with a brush, foam brush applicator, or cloth. Apply a smooth, even coat of stain, allowing the stain to penetrate the wood. Depending on the humidity, temperature, and particular stain used, this usually takes from 5 to 15 minutes. While the stain is still wet, wipe off the excess with a clean cloth. Be careful not to remove too much from corners and edges. Wipe across the grain first so that you work the stain into the wood pores. Then give a final wipe with the grain. Allow the stain to dry. This usually takes at least 8 hours. The finish can then be applied.

It is usually best to apply a series of light, even coats of clear finish rather than one thick coat. This will minimize possible drips and wrinkles as the finish dries.

Apply finish in brush-width strokes in direction of wood grain (Fig. 3-24). Turn table so that finish is applied to wood surface in a horizontal position whenever possible.

A minimum of two coats is recommended. Allow 6 to 8 hours for the first coat to dry before applying second coat. Sand lightly and use a tack cloth to remove sanded finish dust before applying next coat of finish.

Clear or stained finishes are usually applied to natural wood furniture but, if desired, color paint finishes can also be applied.

Variations

Variations are possible for the basic budget computer table. One possibility is to substitute materials, such as to use particle board instead of plywood for the top. Another common variation is to construct the table with a different size top. For example, the top can be made longer or shorter. It is important, however, not to have the width of the top wider than about twice the length of the width of the side boards.

You can also add additional storage shelves below the table and/or a drawer immediately below the table top. Construction of a similar table with a video and storage rack is detailed later in this chapter.

The basic budget computer table makes a functional and attractive computer table even when built from inexpensive woods. This design is ideal for anyone who wants to build computer tables to sell to others. The table can be sold either unfinished or with finish applied. By using more expensive woods, such as oak, you can give the table a custom appearance. The plans given here show simple butt joints, but if you have the cabinet-making skills and know-how, you can also use more difficult joints.

BASIC COMPUTER TABLE WITH FULL SIDES

This table is slightly more difficult to construct than the basic budget computer table described above. It is constructed mainly from plywood, which presents more difficulties in cutting and covering edges than the stock wood used on the basic budget table. The materials are also more expensive, but this table gives more of a custom appearance than the basic budget table. By using hardwood faced plywood, you can construct an expensive-looking table for a fraction of the cost of making it out of solid hardwood. I suggest that a beginner build a basic budget computer table first. The basic computer table with full sides makes a good second project. This table is similar to a model available in ready-to-finish form that retails for about $180. Materials to build this table vary in cost, but would run around $35 (at 1984 prices) using Douglas fir plywood and a plastic laminate top, and around $80 using oak-faced plywood. These prices will vary, however, depending on where you purchase your wood, the area where you live, and other factors. In any case, large savings are possible by building your own. This computer table is attractive and modern even when built from standard plywood. You can produce a custom ap-

Fig. 3-24. Applying clear plastic finish.

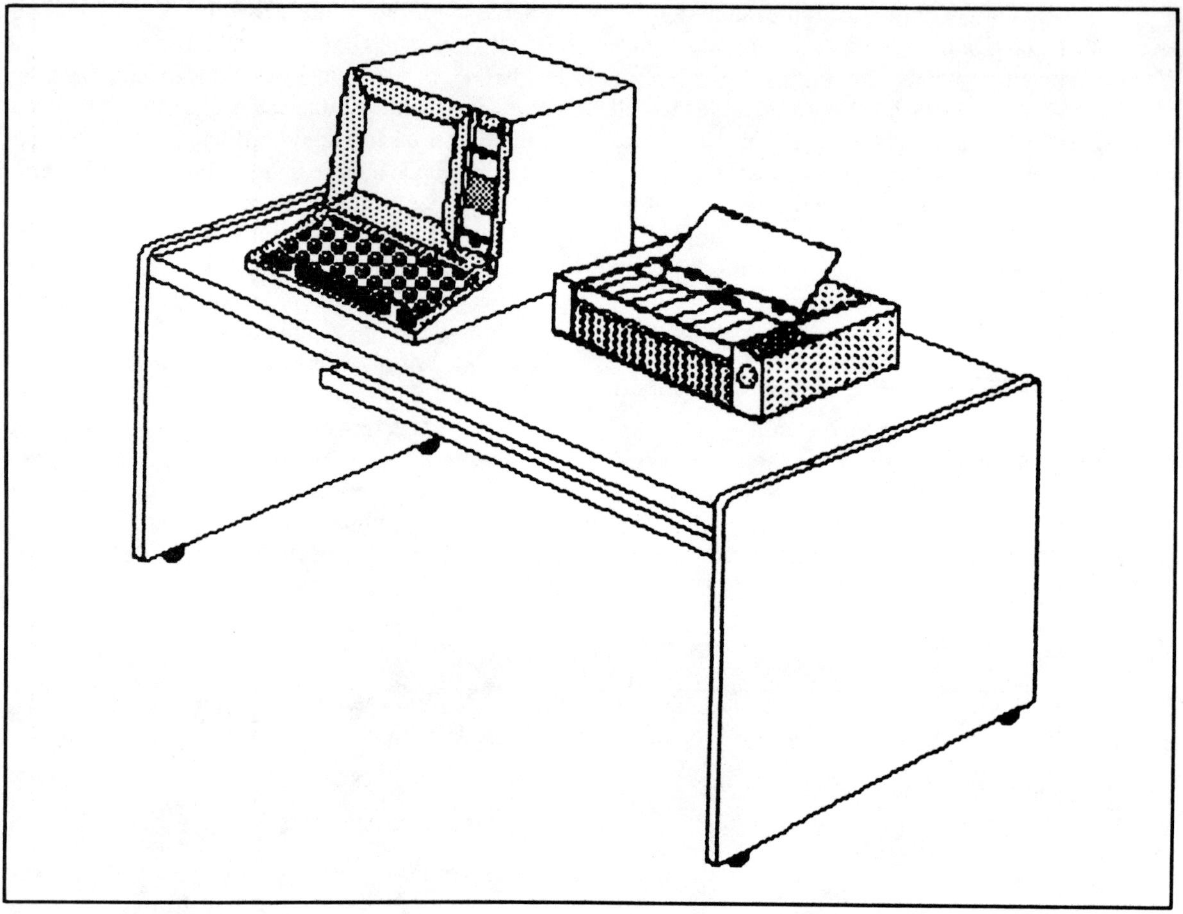

Fig. 3-25. Basic computer table with full sides. There is plenty of room for a computer and printer.

pearance by making the same design from more expensive plywoods, such as those faced with oak or other hardwoods.

The basic computer table with full sides is shown in Figs. 3-25 and 3-26. The top has space for both a computer and printer. The table can have a natural wood top or plastic laminates can be added. The table features a shelf underneath that provides storage space and gives the table added strength.

Materials

The patterns for the wood parts are shown in Fig. 3-27. The top of the table is a 26-inch-by-4-foot piece of 3/4-inch thick plywood. If you intend to use

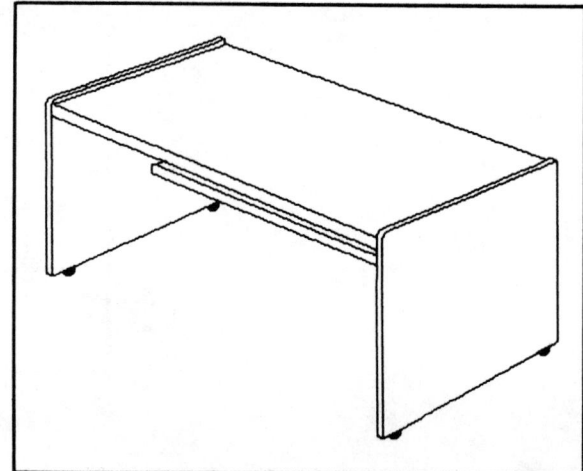

Fig. 3-26. Basic computer table with full sides.

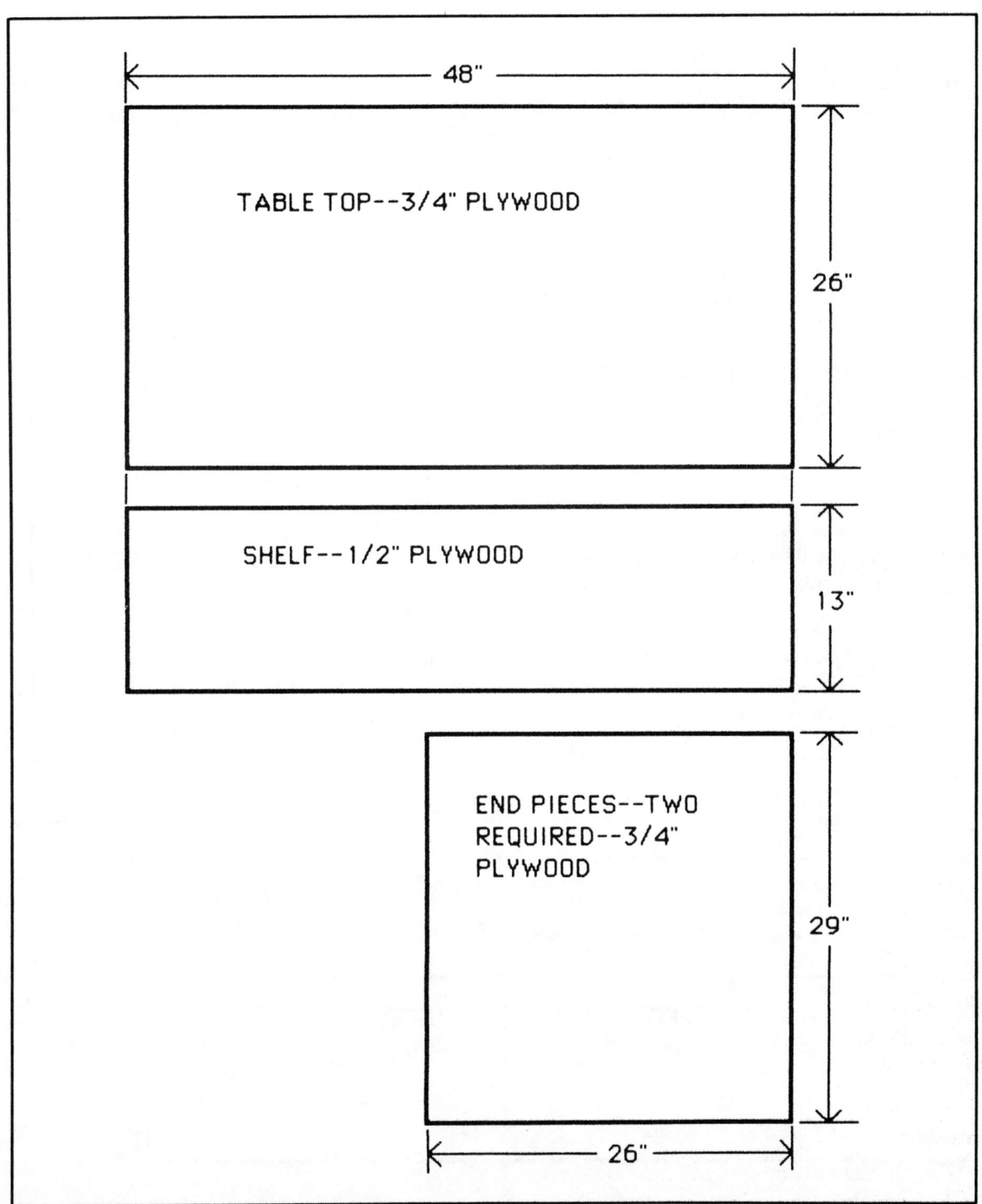

Fig. 3-27. Patterns for plywood parts for basic computer table with full sides.

the wood surface as the finished table top, without adding a plastic laminate, plywood with the upper layer of a hardwood is recommended. If a laminate is to be added, an exterior grade of shop plywood will suffice.

The shelf is plywood with a minimum thickness of 1/2 inch, but 3/4 inch is better. The shelf measures 48 inches by 13 inches. If desired, you can make the shelf wider than this.

The end pieces are 3/4-inch thick plywood and measure 26 inches by 29 inches. The 29-inch dimension gives a table that is 28 1/4 inches high, not counting the height added by whatever floor guides are used, so you may want to change the 29-inch dimension if you want your table a different height. Two end pieces are required.

Plywood is normally sold in standard 4-foot-by-8-foot sheets. Lay out the patterns to take advantage of this standard size and arrange them to keep waste to a minimum. Some lumberyards and plywood stores will cut plywood sheets for you to desired size, usually at additional cost. This can be worth it if you don't need full sheets, don't have room to carry full sheets in your car, or don't have a saw to accurately cut plywood.

Although 1/2-inch thick plywood could also be used, I don't recommend this. The savings are small, and a less sturdy table will result. Particle board can be substituted for the plywood if you are on an absolute minimum budget. It can be difficult to work with, however, and it is very difficult to get plastic laminates to bond properly to this material without special equipment. Even laminates on manufactured furniture seem to come loose at the edges.

The backing piece (Fig. 3-28) can be either plywood or fiberboard. The backing piece is used to strengthen the table base and hold the frame in rectangular form. The length of the backing piece is 49 1/2 inches. A 13-inch height is shown for the backing piece, which is about the minimum required to give this table adequate strength. The shelf can be installed a greater distance below the top, which will require changing the height of the backing piece. Notice that the top, shelf, backing piece, and side pieces form a box with the forward side open.

You will also need 1-inch-by-2-inch or larger framing stock for use under the plywood table top and the shelf.

Various wood and plastic trim strips can be used to cover the exposed edges of the plywood, as detailed later in this section. A wood or plastic trim strip is used to cover the forward edge of the table top and shelf. These pieces are 48 inches long and about 1 3/4 inches wide (the minimum width should be such that it will completely cover the widths of the plywood (3/4 inch for the top and 1/2 inch or 3/4 inch for the shelf) and the framing (approximately 7/8 inch). The trim strips can be slightly wider than this, however.

Four floor pods or guides are used on the side

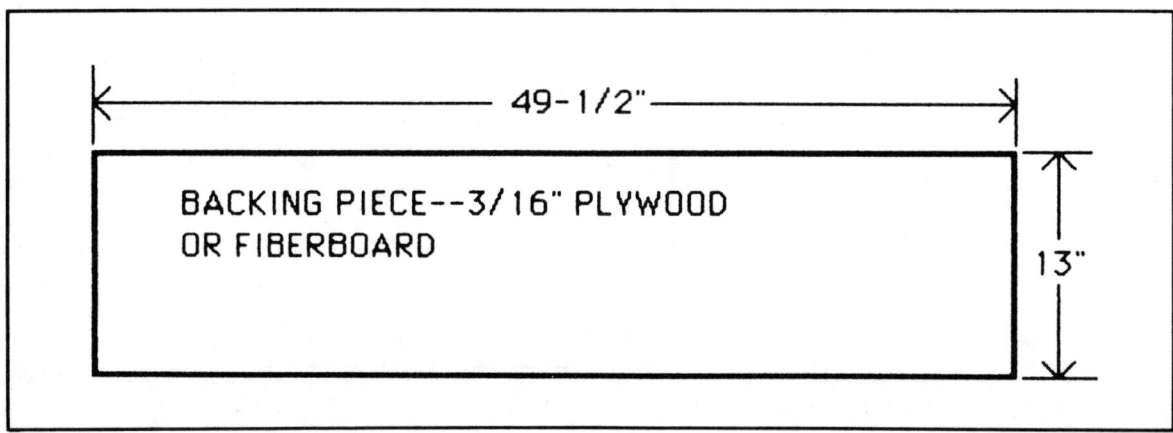

Fig. 3-28. Pattern for backing piece.

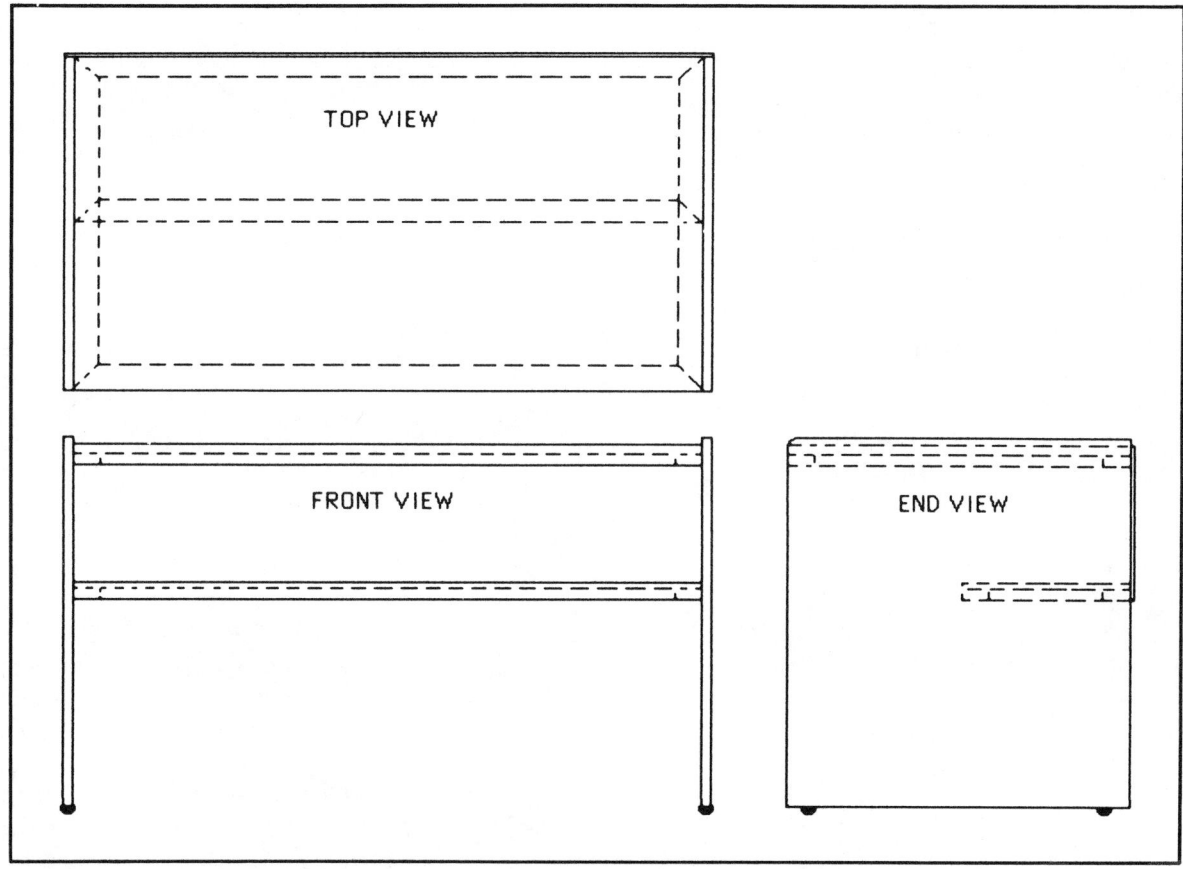

Fig. 3-29. Basic computer table with full sides.

pieces. Suitable fixed or adjustable types are available from hardware stores.

Several different fasteners can be used for assembly, as detailed below in this section. You will also need a suitable wood glue. The finish can be clear urethane or any other type, as desired.

The top can be left natural or a plastic laminate can be added. If a plastic laminate is to be added, you will need a 26-inch-by-4-foot piece of suitable plastic laminate and contact cement for attaching it to the plywood.

Construction

Overviews of the complete assembly are shown in Figs. 3-29 and 3-30.

Begin by constructing the table top, as detailed in Fig. 3-31. If you purchased a piece of plywood that was already cut to the 26-inch-by-4-foot size, no additional cutting will be required if it was cut accurately and is a true rectangle. You might want to check this with a square.

If you purchased a larger piece of plywood, such as a standard 4-foot-by-8-foot sheet, you will need to cut out a section for the table top. In most cases, you will want to have the grain of the top layer running lengthwise, although this is not essential if you are going to add a plastic laminate. In most cases, you will use two factory cut edges for your table top and cut the other two. Use a ruler and square to make the pattern, marking the lines with a sharp pencil or scribing tool.

Sawing plywood requires special considera-

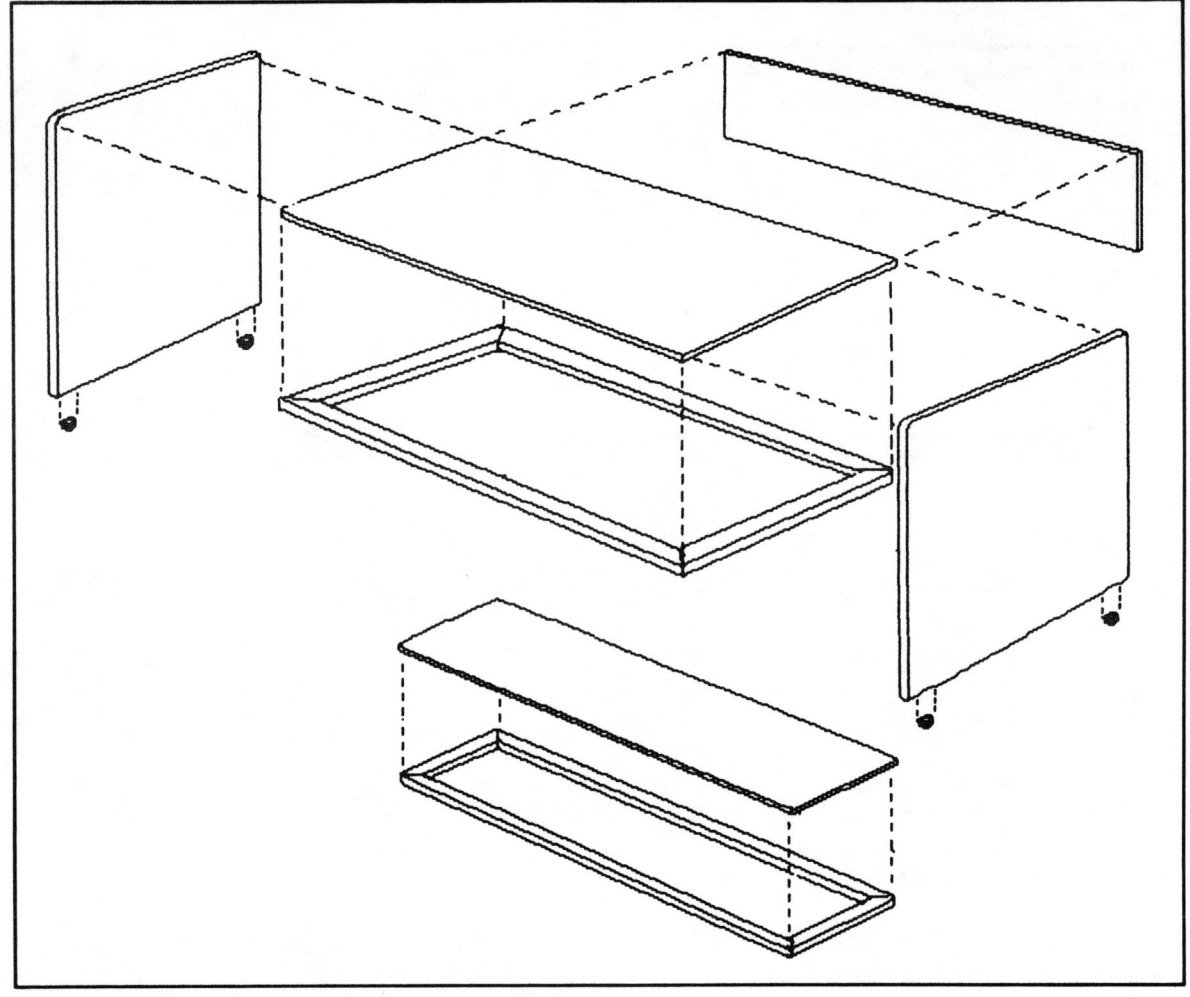

Fig. 3-30. Assembly of basic computer table with full sides.

tions; special care must be taken to avoid chipping and splintering along the cut edge. Handsaws or power saws with special fine-toothed or carbide tipped blades designed especially for plywood should be used. Applying a strip of masking tape over the area to be cut on both sides of the plywood, especially on the underside, is also helpful. You can also clamp a solid piece of wood to the underside and make the cut through both the plywood and the piece of wood.

Be extremely careful when sanding edges. Use a sanding block and do not sand the surfaces of plywood until a wood sealer has been applied.

The next step is to add the reinforcing frame to the table top, as shown in Fig. 3-31. Use a ruler and a square to make the patterns on the framing wood, marking the lines with a sharp pencil or other marking device. Then make the necessary saw cuts, as detailed in Chapter 2. The frame pieces should be glued and nailed or screwed in position (see Figs. 3-32 and 3-33). If the plywood top is to be left natural wood (without a plastic laminate being added), the fasteners should go through the framing and into the plywood. Take care that the fasteners do not pass all the way through the plywood or leave a bulge in the upper surface. If

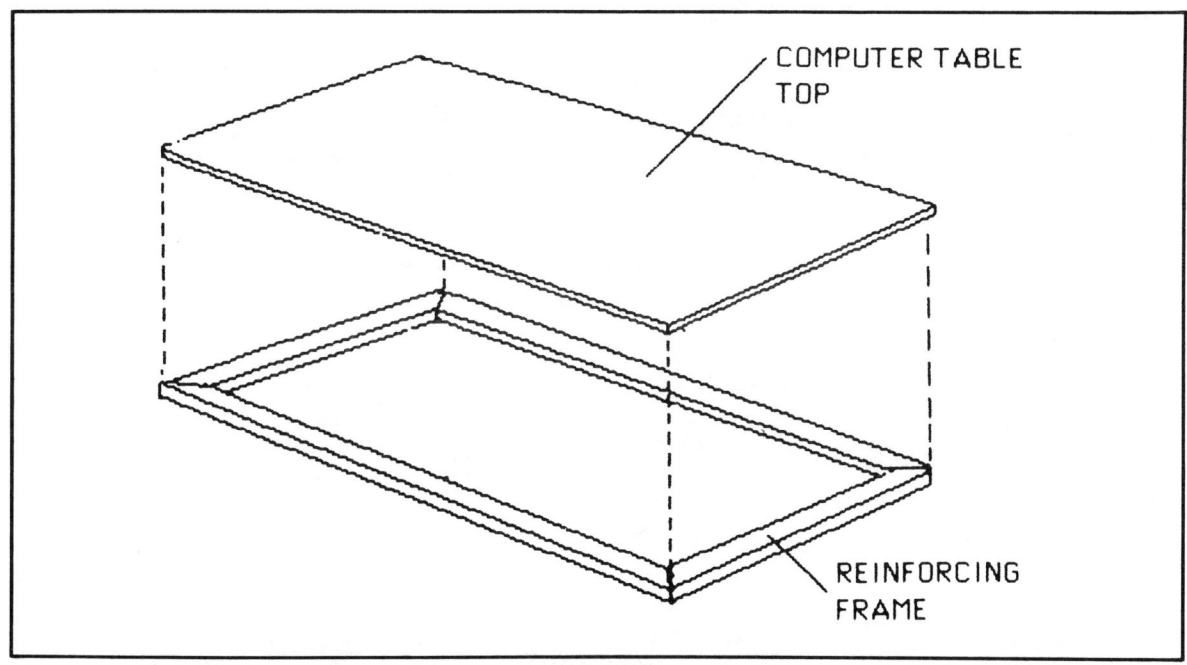

Fig. 3-31. Assembly of basic computer table top to reinforcing frame underneath.

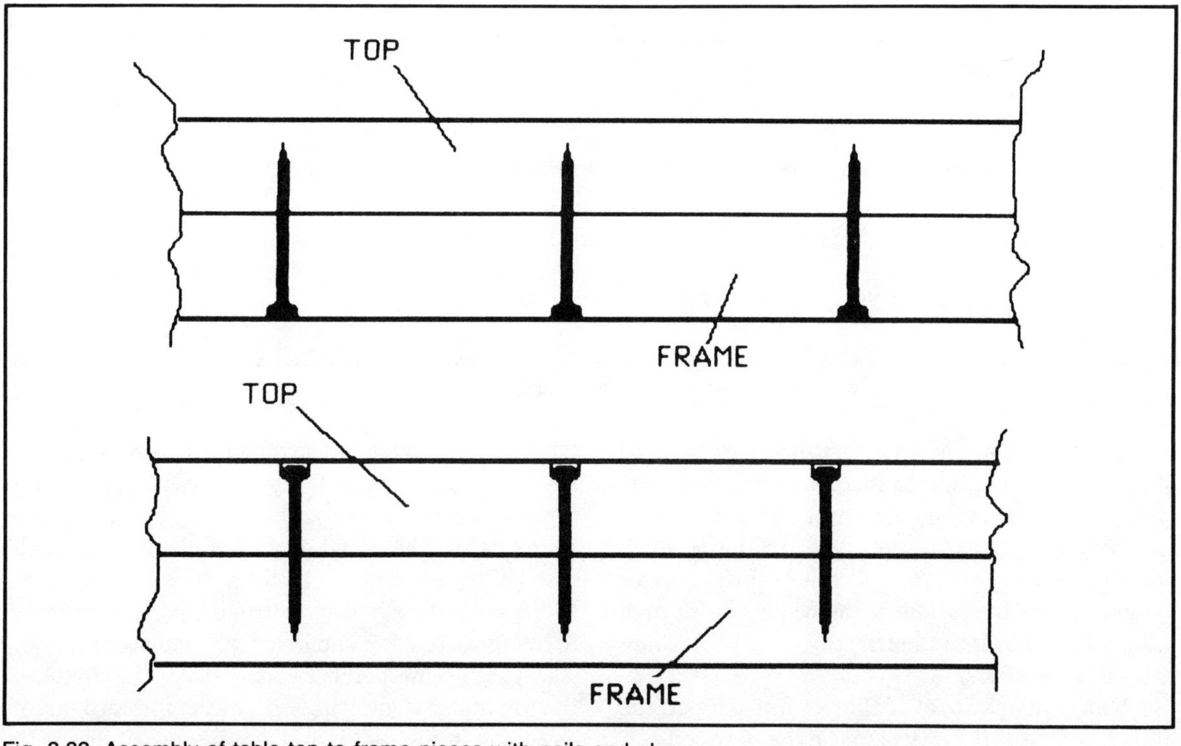

Fig. 3-32. Assembly of table top to frame pieces with nails and glue.

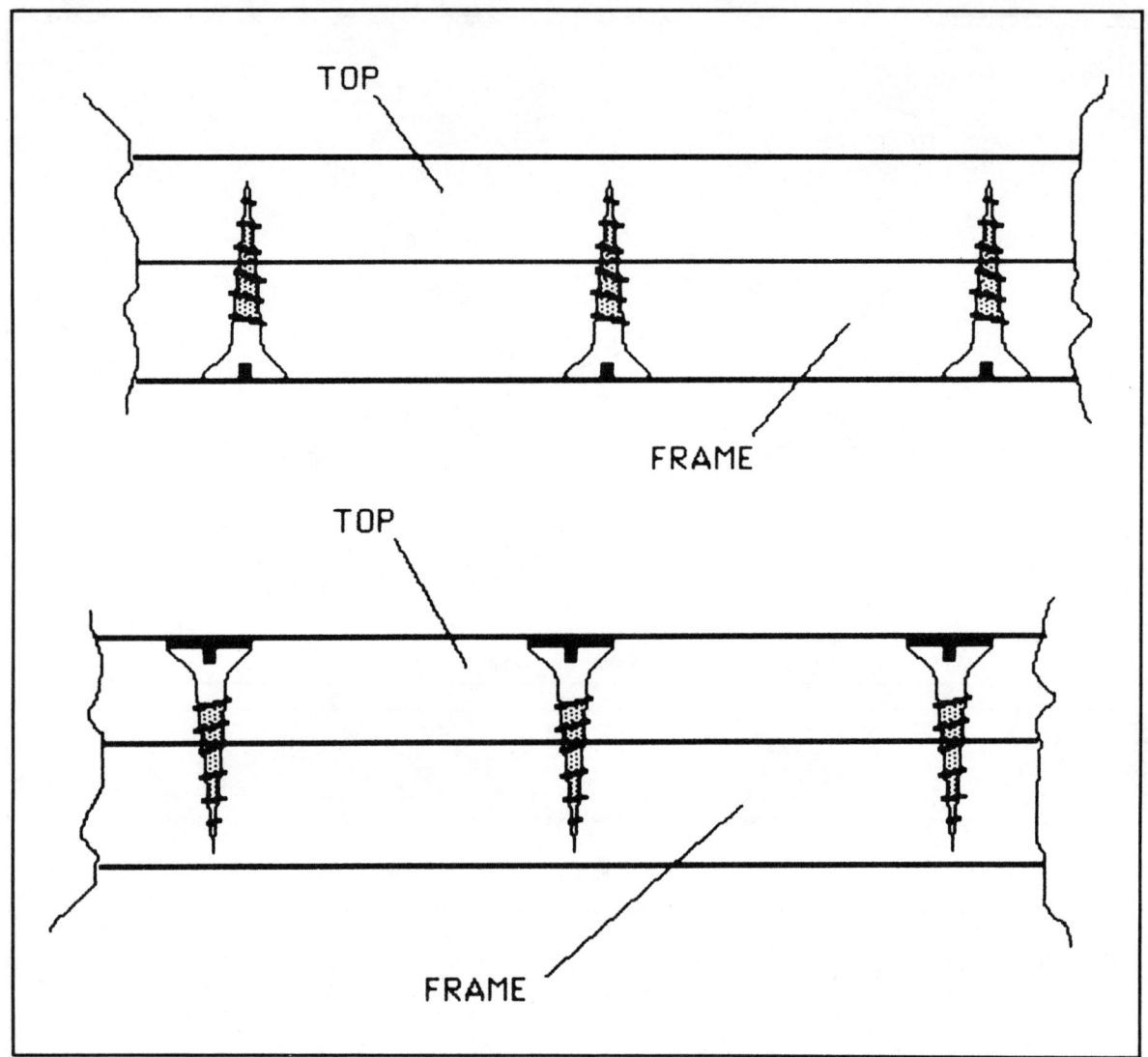

Fig. 3-33. Assembly of table top to frame pieces with screws and glue.

a good glue is used, such as acrylic or epoxy, the glue alone should give adequate strength; the fasteners will be mainly used as a clamping device for the gluing because they will not have much holding power into the plywood. For greater holding power, the fasteners can be passed through the plywood and into the framing if a plastic laminate is to be added.

Many options are available for finishing off the table top. One possibility is to use the plywood surface as the top and add a wood trim strip to the forward edge, as shown in Fig. 3-34. Glue and fasten the trim strip in place with finishing nails. Set the heads below the wood surface and fill holes with wood filler to flush with the wood surface.

A second possibility is to add a plastic laminate to the forward edge and leave the top natural wood.

Another method is to add a plastic laminate to the top and a wood trim strip to the forward edge, as shown in Fig. 3-35. Still another possibility is to

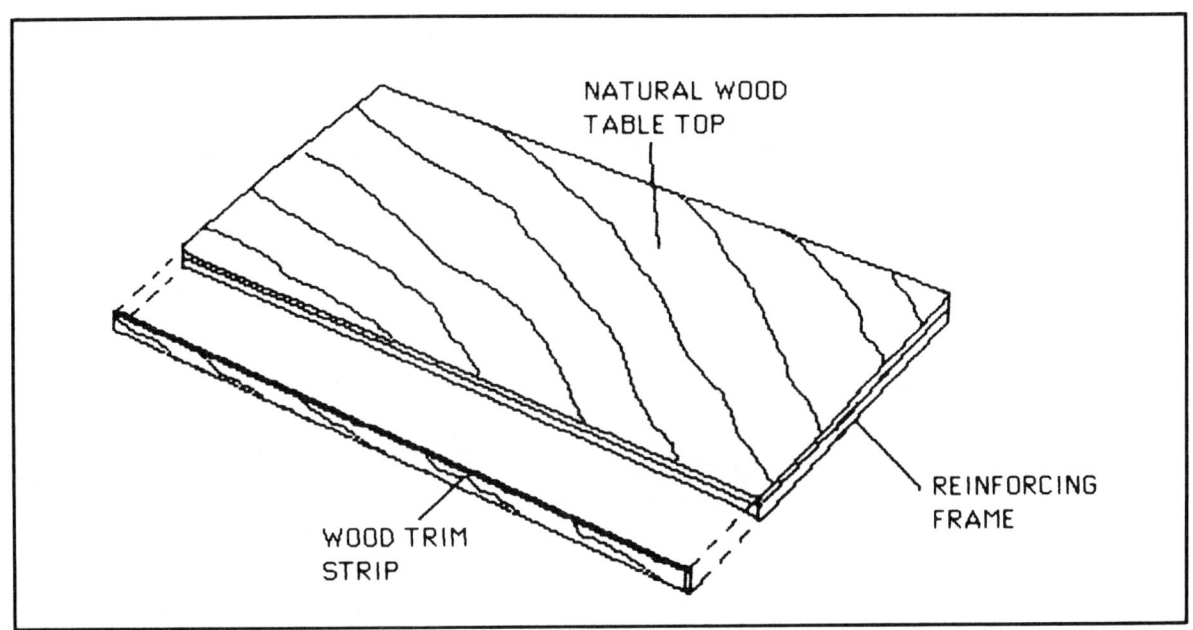

Fig. 3-34. Adding wood trim strip to forward edge of computer table top.

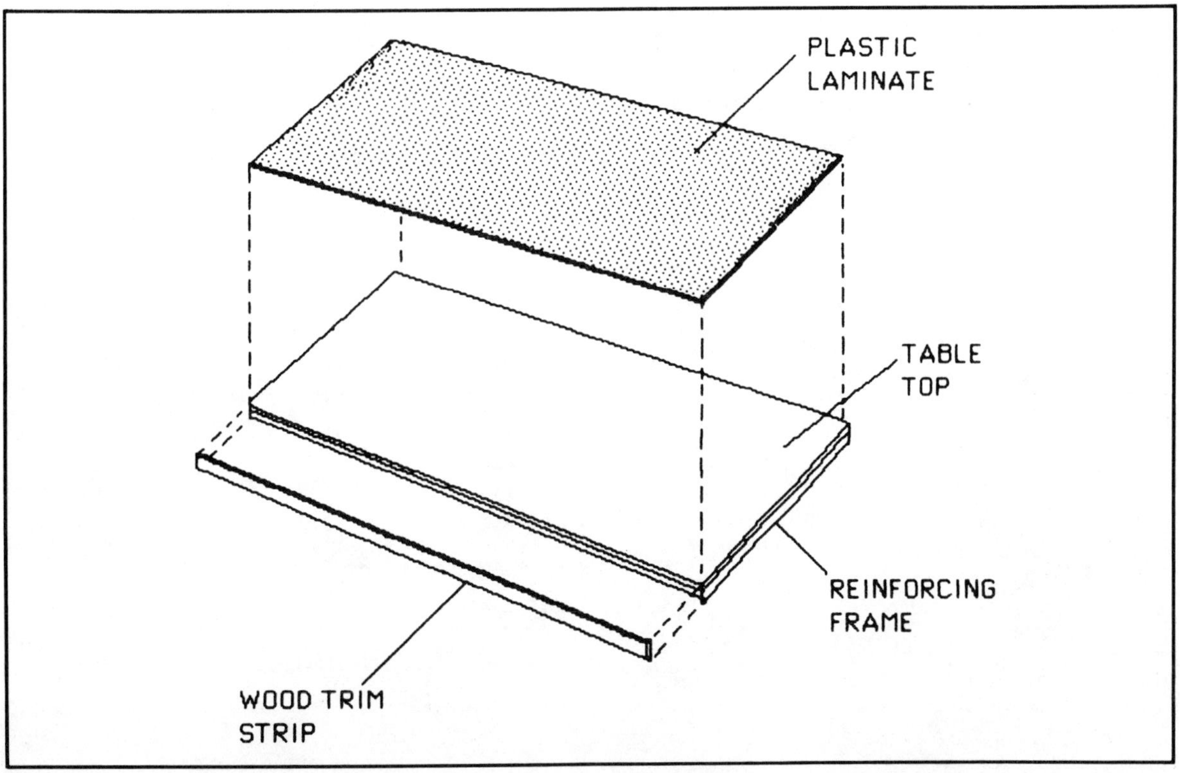

Fig. 3-35. Adding plastic laminate to top and wood trim strip to forward edge of computer table top.

add plastic laminates to both the top and forward edge, as shown in Fig. 3-36.

If a plastic laminate is added to the plywood table top and/or the forward edge, these pieces can be installed at this time. I suggest using only high quality plastic laminates for computer table tops.

If a plastic laminate is to also be applied to the forward edge of the table top, it should be applied first and finished flush with the table top. The top laminate is then applied so that the edge overlaps the top edge of the laminate on the forward edge of the table.

The plastic laminate is installed as follows:

• All holes and defects in the surface of the plywood should be filled with putty or wood filler.
• Sand the surface to be covered to ensure good adhesion.
• Mark the plastic laminate to a pattern slightly larger than the area to be covered. Use a straightedge and draw the pattern lines on the finished or pattern side of the laminate. Leave 1/4 inch to 1/2 inch on all sides, to be trimmed off later.
• If a laminate is to be applied to the forward edge of the table, apply this first. After installation, as detailed below, trim and file the upper edge of the plastic laminate flush with the upper edge of the plywood top before installing the plastic laminate to upper surface of the table top.
• Cut the plastic laminate to the pattern marked. Even though the plastic laminate is extremely durable once applied, it is vulnerable to cracking and splitting before it is cemented in place. Fine-tooth handsaws or power saws with fine-tooth blades can be used. A rotary power saw with a 14 to 16 teeth per inch blade is ideal. Place the plastic laminate face up when cutting. Care should be taken so that the plastic laminate is not chipped or broken. An alternate method is to use a carbide tip knife for scoring the plastic by drawing the knife point along a metal straightedge and cutting through the decorative surface. The laminate can then be broken by bending it toward the decorative surface side over the edge of a table or workbench.
• Apply contact cement to the surface of the plywood to be covered and the back side of the plastic laminate. A brush, roller, or metal spreader with a serrated edge can be used to spread the contact cement. A thin even application is important.
• Follow the manufacturer's instructions

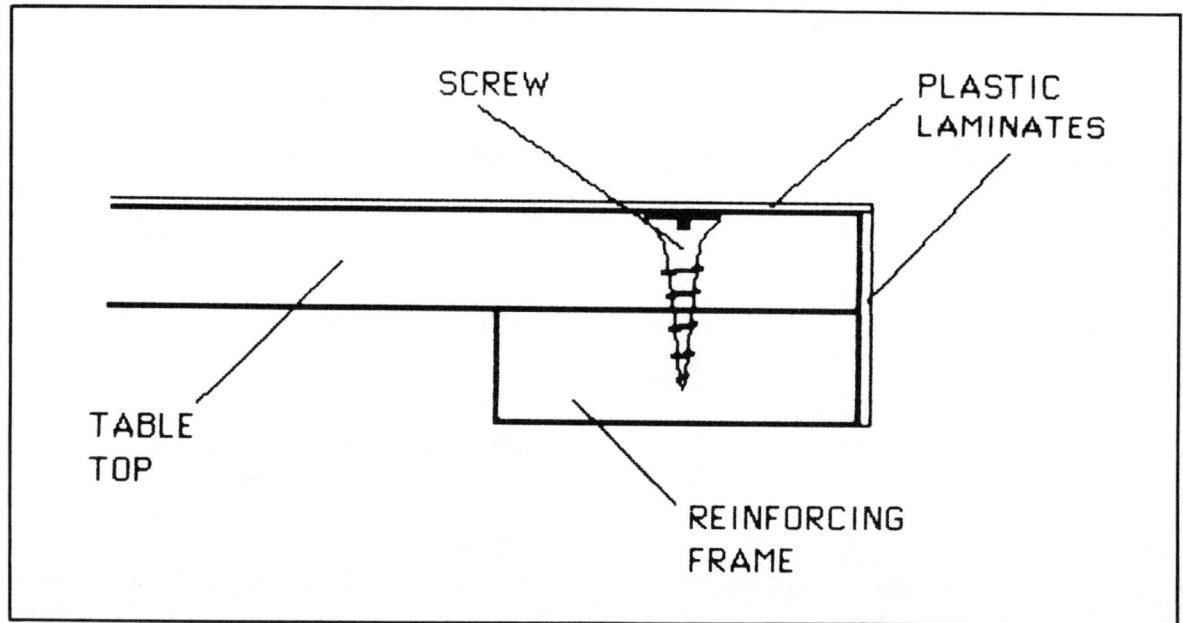

Fig. 3-36. Adding plastic laminate to top and forward edge of computer table top.

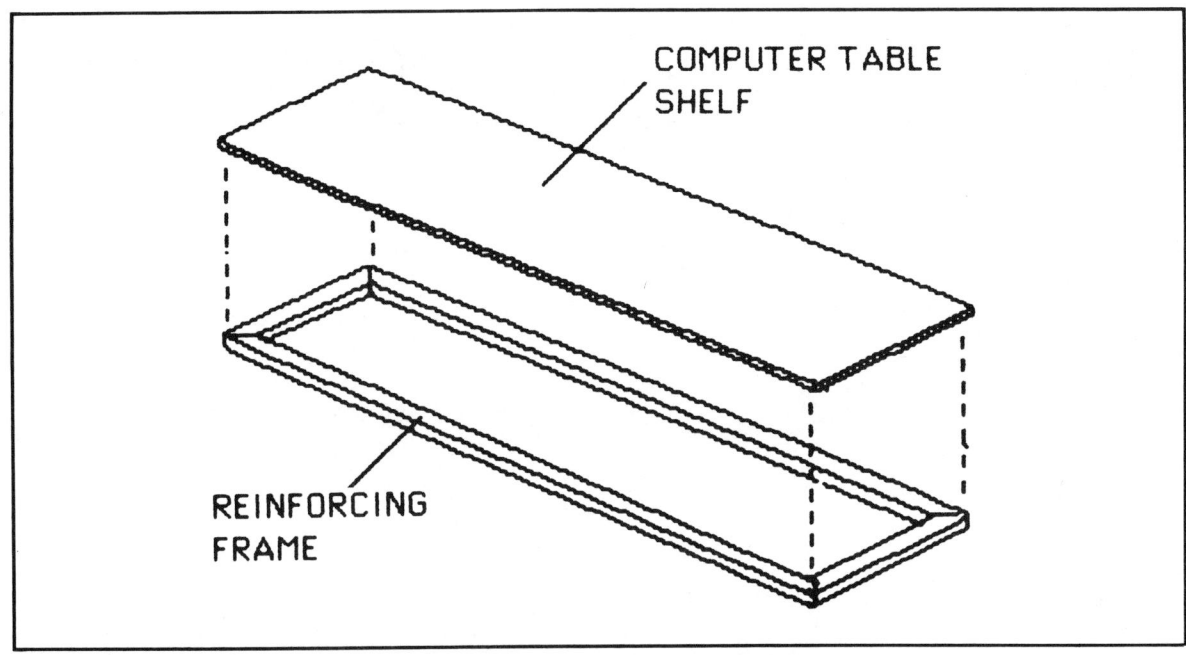

Fig. 3-37. Assembly of basic computer table shelf to reinforcing frame underneath.

regarding drying time. Usually, this takes about 20 to 30 minutes.

- Place a sheet of heavy wrapping paper over the plywood surface to be covered. Then position the laminate on the plywood surface with the paper between. The contact cement will not stick to the paper if it has been allowed to dry properly. Make certain that the laminate is positioned correctly. Once the two surfaces of contact cement touch, the laminate sheet cannot be moved again. When everything is lined up properly, pull the paper out from between the plywood and the plastic laminate.
- Using a small block of wood and a hammer, lightly tap the laminate in place. An alternate method is to use a rolling pin.
- Use a file to remove the surplus plastic laminate from the edges. Another method is to use a special cutter with a router, which allows convenient trimming of excess plastic laminate to flush with the plywood edges.
- The thinner recommended for the contact cement can be used for cleaning contact cement from wood and plastic laminate and tools.

The next step is to construct the shelf, as detailed in Fig. 3-37. If you purchased a piece of plywood that was already cut to the 13-inch-by-4-foot size, no additional cutting will be required, assuming that it was cut accurately and is a true rectangular form. Check this with a square.

If you purchased a larger piece of plywood, you will need to cut out a section for the shelf top. In most cases, you will want to have the grain of the top layer running lengthwise, although this is not essential if you are going to add a plastic laminate. In most cases, you will use two factory cut edges for your shelf top and cut the other two. Use a ruler and square to make the pattern, marking the lines with a sharp pencil or scribing tool. Sand cut edges carefully.

The next step is to add the reinforcing frame to the plywood shelf as shown in Fig. 3-37. Using a ruler and a square, make the patterns on the shelf framing wood, marking the lines with a sharp pencil. Make the necessary saw cuts, as detailed in Chapter 2. The shelf frame pieces should be glued and nailed or screwed in position. If the plywood shelf top will not be covered with a plastic laminate,

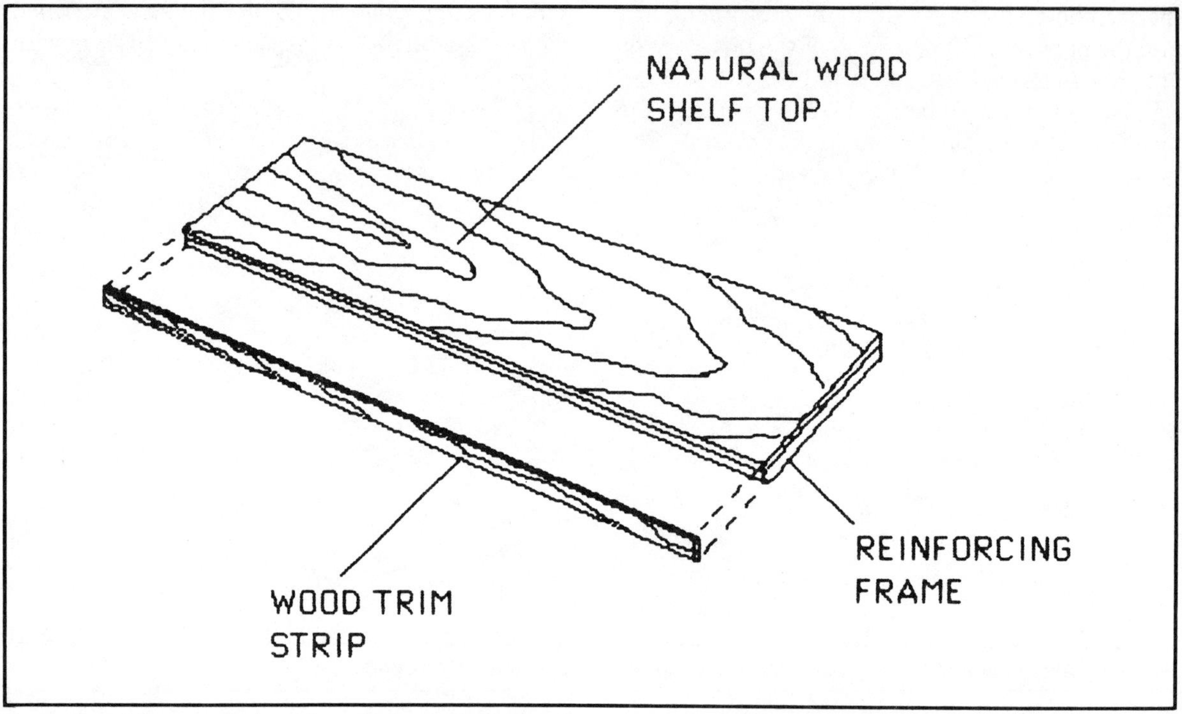

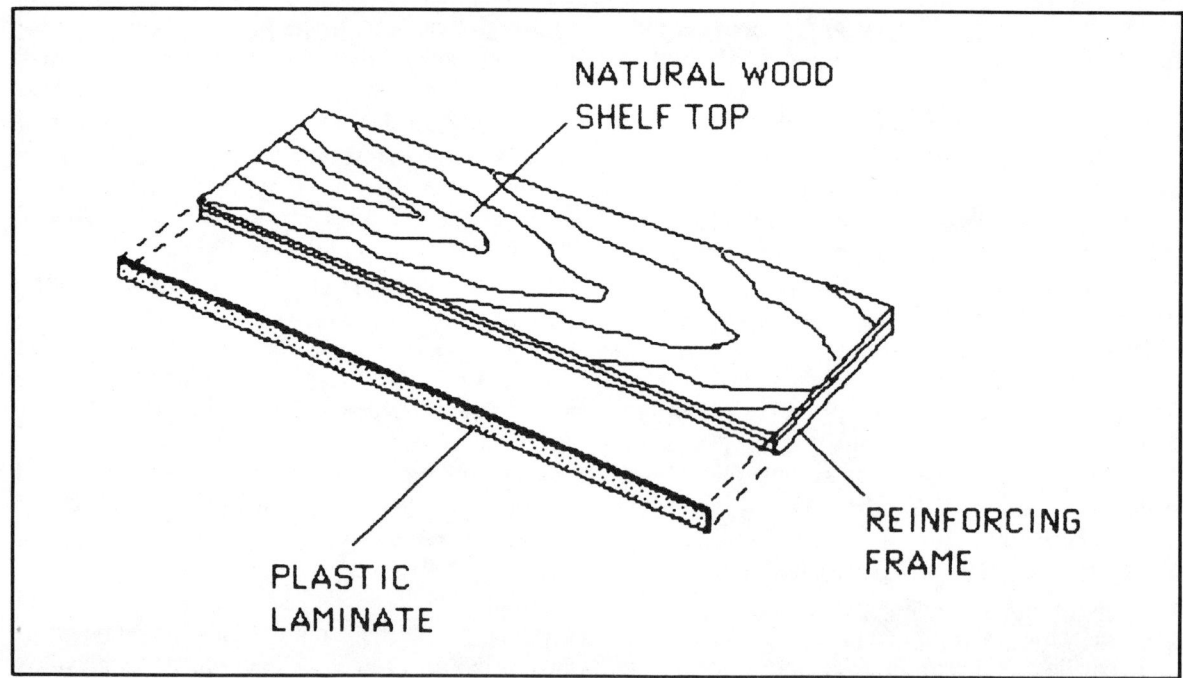

Fig. 3-38. Adding wood trim strip to forward edge of shelf.

Fig. 3-39. Adding plastic laminate to forward edge of shelf.

the fasteners should go through the framing and into the plywood, taking care that the fasteners do not pass all the way through the plywood or leave a bulge in the upper surface. Good acrylic or epoxy glue alone should give adequate strength. The fasteners are mainly used as a clamping device for the gluing and will not have much holding power into the plywood. If laminate is applied, the fasteners can be passed through the plywood and into the shelf framing.

As with the table top, a variety of options are available for finishing off the shelf. One possibility is to use the plywood surface as the shelf top and add a wood trim strip to the forward edge, as shown in Fig. 3-38. Glue and fasten the trim strip in place with finishing nails. Set the heads below the wood surface and fill holes with wood filler to flush with the wood surface.

A second possibility is to add a plastic laminate to the forward edge and leave the shelf top natural wood, as detailed in Fig. 3-39.

Another method is to add a plastic laminate to the shelf top and a wood trim strip to the forward edge, as shown in Fig. 3-40, or add plastic laminates to both the top and forward edge, as shown in Fig. 3-41.

If a plastic laminate is applied to the plywood shelf top and/or the forward edge, install them at this time. If a plastic laminate is to also be applied to the forward edge of the shelf top, it should be

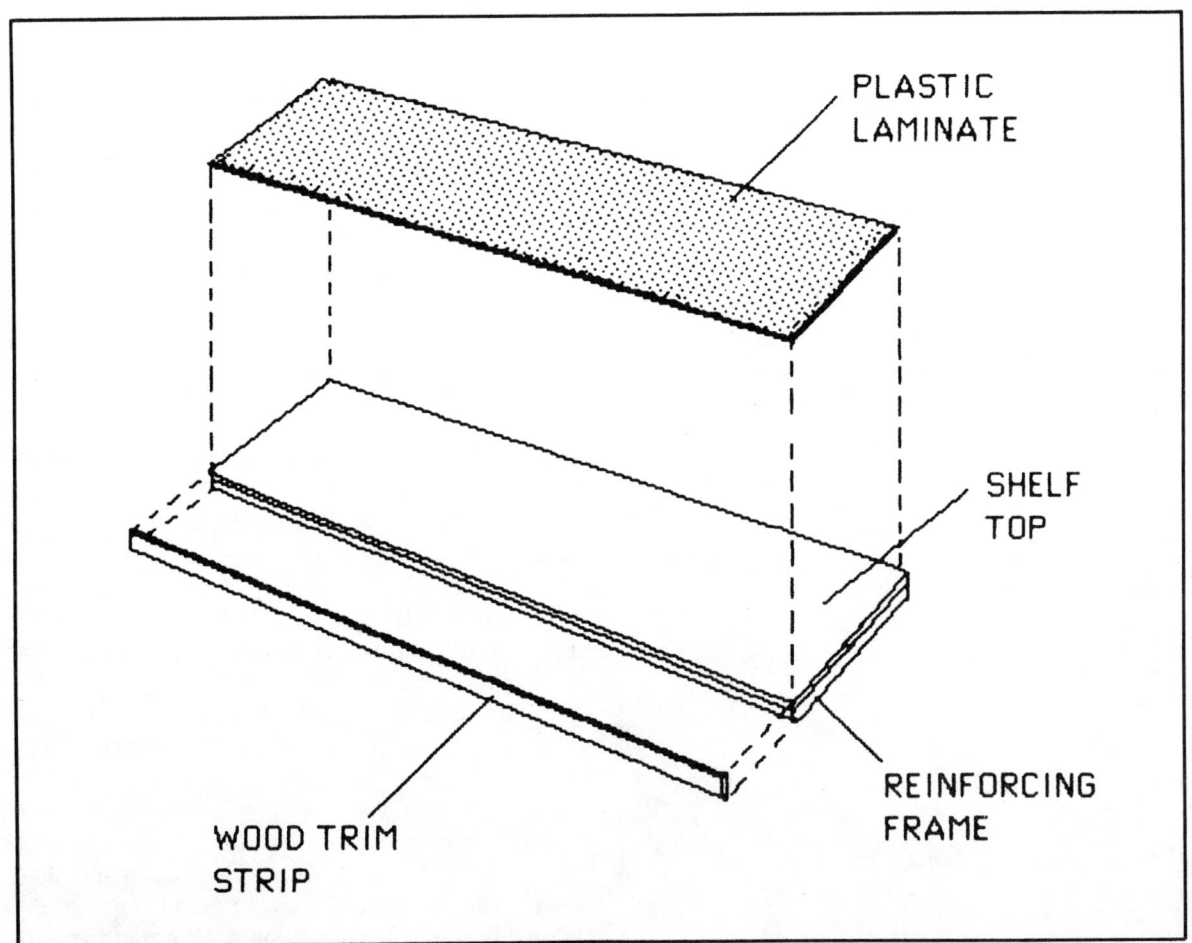

Fig. 3-40. Adding plastic laminate to top and wood trim strip to forward edge of computer shelf.

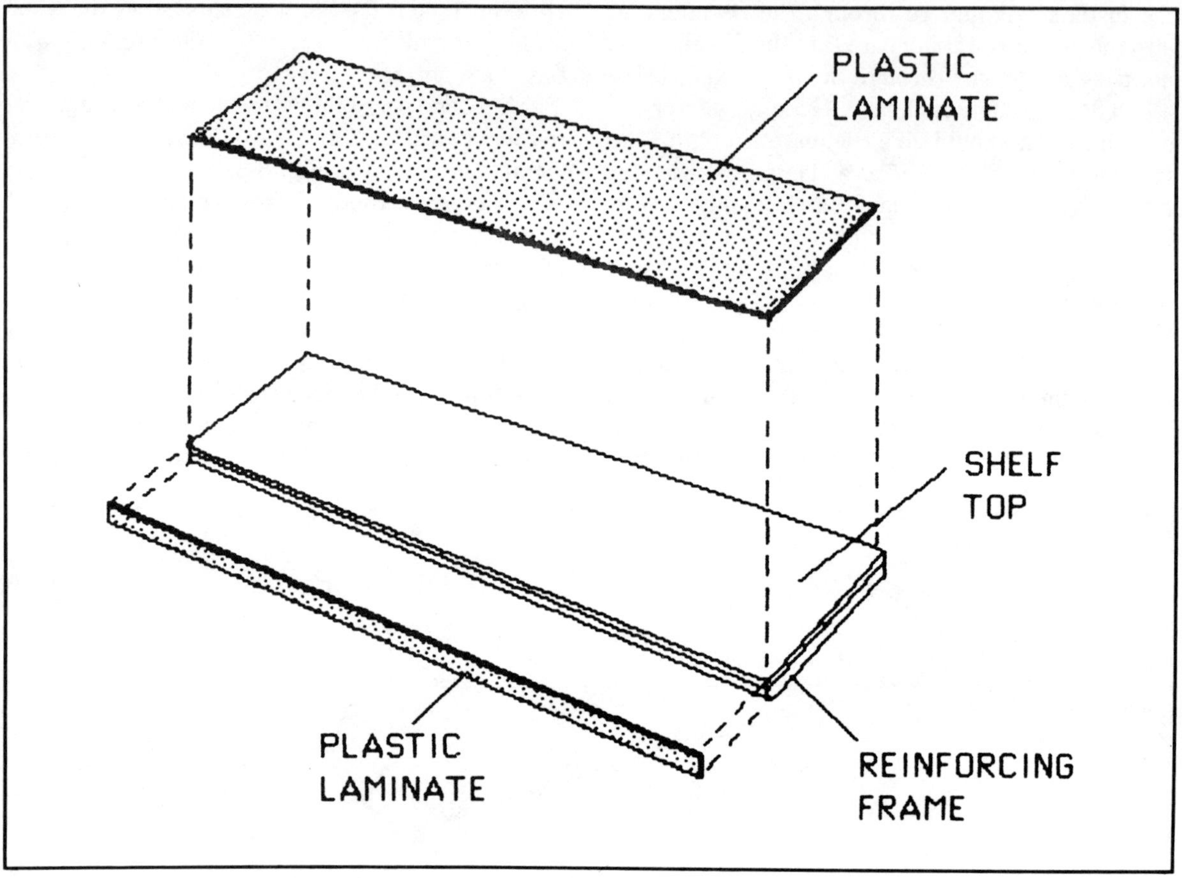

Fig. 3-41. Adding plastic laminate to top and forward edge of shelf.

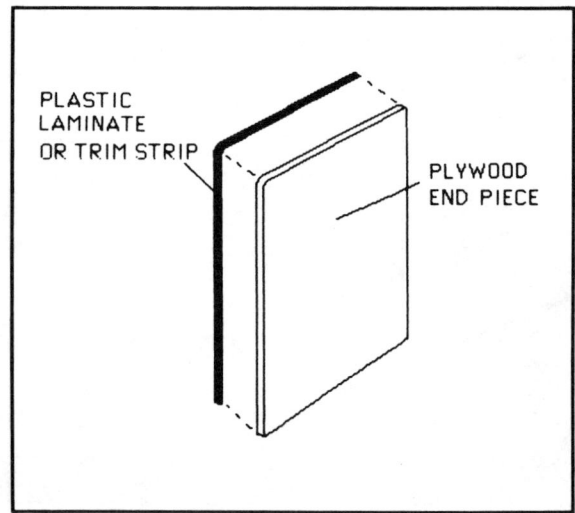

Fig. 3-42. Adding plastic laminate or trim strip to end pieces.

applied first, then finished flush with the shelf top. The top laminate is applied so that the edge overlaps the top edge of the laminate on the forward edge of the shelf.

Next, cut the end pieces to rectangular size and round off the upper forward corners. The curve can be on a 1/2-inch radius or as desired to fit a particular molding corner piece.

The next step is to add plastic (Fig. 3-42) or wood (Fig. 3-43) trim to the forward and top edges of the end pieces. This will protect the laminated edges of the plywood and give a neat appearance.

An overview of the remainder of the assembly is shown in Fig. 3-44. Assemble the top and shelf to the side pieces, as shown in Fig. 3-45, using both glue and mechanical fasteners. One method is to use finishing nails, passing them through the end

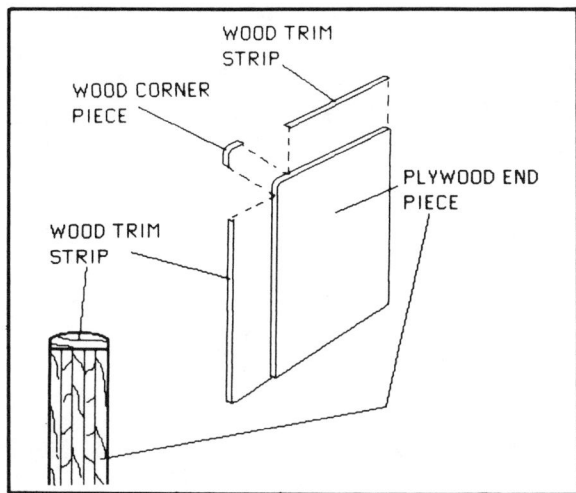

Fig. 3-43. Adding wood trim strips and corner piece to end pieces.

pieces and into the framing wood of the top and shelf. Set the heads below the wood surface and fill with wood filler to flush with the wood surface. Another method uses through bolts, as detailed in Fig. 3-46.

Regardless of the method, it is extremely important to install the side pieces perpendicular to the table top and shelf in a crosswise direction. Use a square to make pattern lines on the side pieces. It is also important to have exactly the same distance between the top and shelf on both sides. This distance can be any desired, but a minimum of 12 inches is required to give the table adequate strength.

After the shelf and top have been assembled to the side pieces, add the backing piece, as shown in Fig. 3-47. The backing piece forms a box with the top, shelf, and side pieces. It is important that the backing piece be attached securely to the wood members all the way around the edges, both glued and nailed into position. Make certain that the backing piece is a true rectangle and that the side pieces are perpendicular to the table top and shelf before the backing piece is attached and the glue allowed to set. Figure 3-48 shows the backing piece installed.

The floor guides are installed next (see Fig. 3-49). Attachment varies depending on the type of floor guides selected. Some fit in a mounting drilled in the wood beam. Others are driven or screwed into the wood. Still others have separate screw fasteners to hold them in place.

Sanding and Finishing

Sanding and applying a finish are important steps in the construction process. Many beginners do a good job constructing the table up to this point, but give the table a very amateur appearance by sloppy application of a finish. By taking care and a little time, however, even a beginner can give the table a professional finish.

Sanding is an important operation in preparing the wood for varnishing or painting. Small holes, checks, and other open defects in the wood should be filled in before sanding. If a clear finish is to be applied, use a wood filler that matches the color of the wood. A sanding sealer should be applied to the plywood before doing any sanding on the surface.

The general principle to follow for sanding is to work from coarse grits progressively to finer grits. Don't start with a grit that is coarser than necessary for the particular sanding; the surface might be such that you can start with a medium or even fine grit. Coarser grits leave scratches that must be sanded away with finer grits.

Sand wood parallel to the grain. Across the grain sanding leaves scratches and tears and roughens the wood surface. A scratch free surface is especially important if you are going to finish with oil or varnish.

For most hand sanding, especially on flat surfaces, use a sanding block. Holding the sandpaper in your hand tends to leave a wavy surface on the wood because pressure is not applied evenly to all areas. A carpet or felt pad between the block and the sandpaper also helps.

At the final stages of sanding, most craftsmen use their fingertips to judge the smoothness of the surface or by looking across the surface at a light held at a low angle to the wood surface. Special care with the sanding is important if a fine finish is to be achieved.

If desired, a power sander can be used. A pad sander is the easiest to use without damaging the

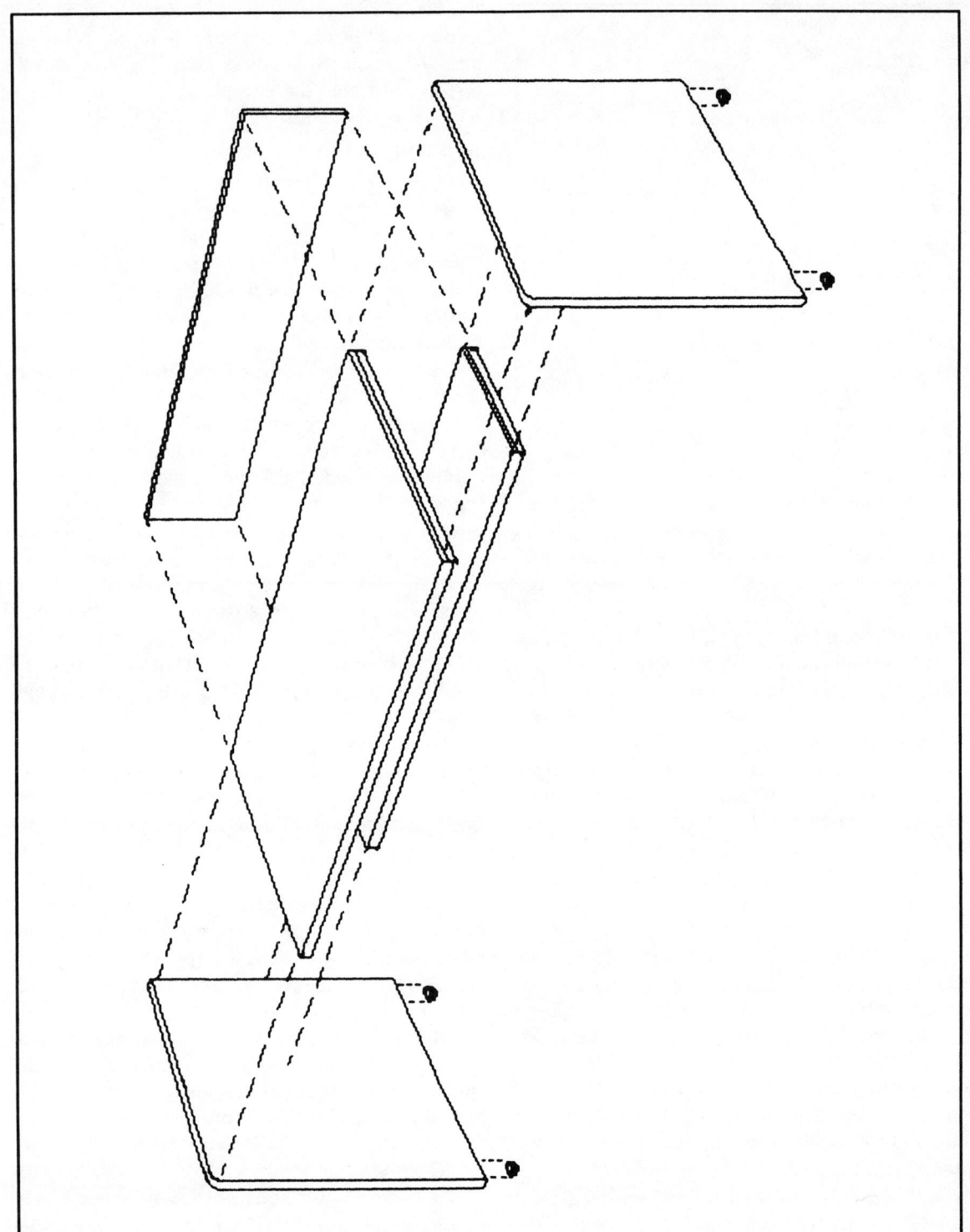

Fig. 3-44. Assembly of basic computer table with full sides.

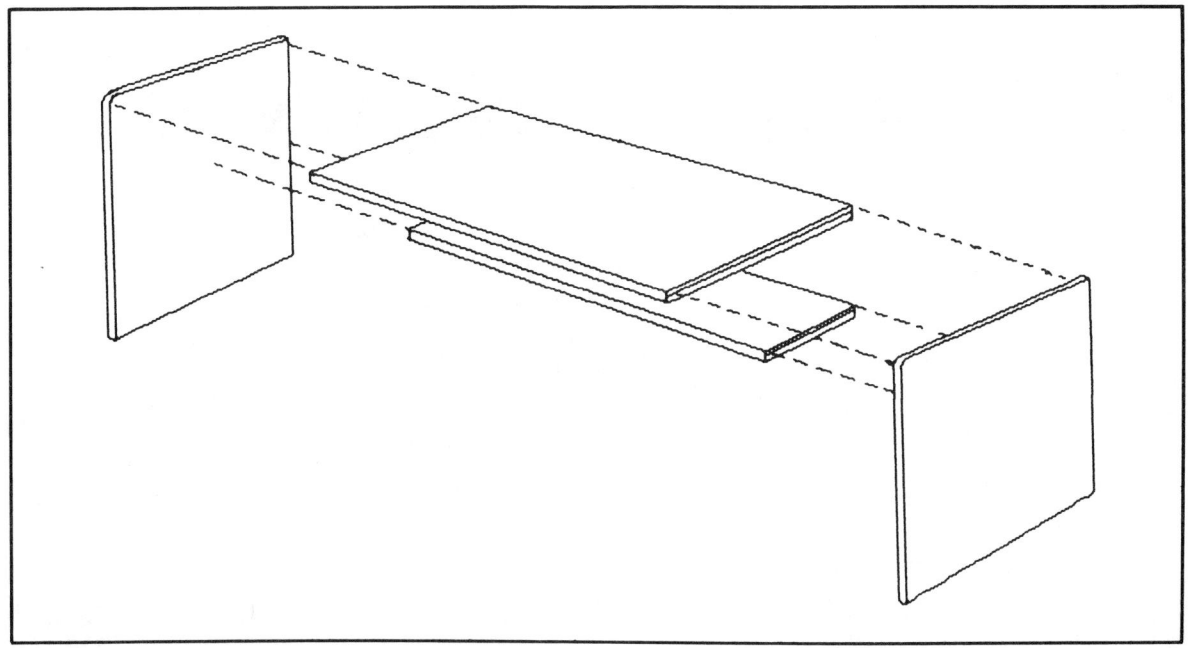

Fig. 3-45. Assembly of shelf and top to side pieces.

wood surface. Belt sanders can be used by experienced operators.

A clear finish (polyurethane plastic is ideal) can be applied directly to natural wood, or you can first stain the wood to another color. Staining can enhance the natural grains of the wood and enrich relatively lifeless woods.

Before applying stain, first test color on a scrap piece of similar wood. Clean the surface area where stain is to be applied. Use a cloth to eliminate as much dust as possible. Apply stain with a brush, foam brush applicator, or cloth. Apply a smooth, even coat of stain, allowing the stain to penetrate the wood. Depending on the humidity, temperature, and particular stain used, this usually takes from 5 to 15 minutes. While the stain is still wet, wipe off the excess stain with a clean cloth, being careful not to remove too much from corners and edges. Wipe across the grain first so that you work the stain into the wood pores, then give a final wipe with the grain. Allow the stain to dry, usually at least 8 hours. The finish can then be applied.

It is usually best to apply a series of light, even coats of clear finish rather than one thick coat. This minimizes possible drips and wrinkles as the finish dries.

Apply finish in brush-width strokes in direction of wood grain. Turn the table so that finish is applied to a horizontal wood surface whenever possible.

A minimum of two coats is recommended. Allow 6 to 8 hours for the first coat to dry before applying second coat. Sand lightly and use a tack cloth to remove sanded finish dust before applying next coat of finish.

Clear or stained finishes are usually applied to natural wood furniture, but a color paint finish can also be applied.

Variations

Variations are possible for the basic computer table with full sides. One possibility is to substitute materials, such as particle board instead of plywood for the top and/or other components. Another common variation is to construct the table with a different size top.

You can also add additional storage shelves

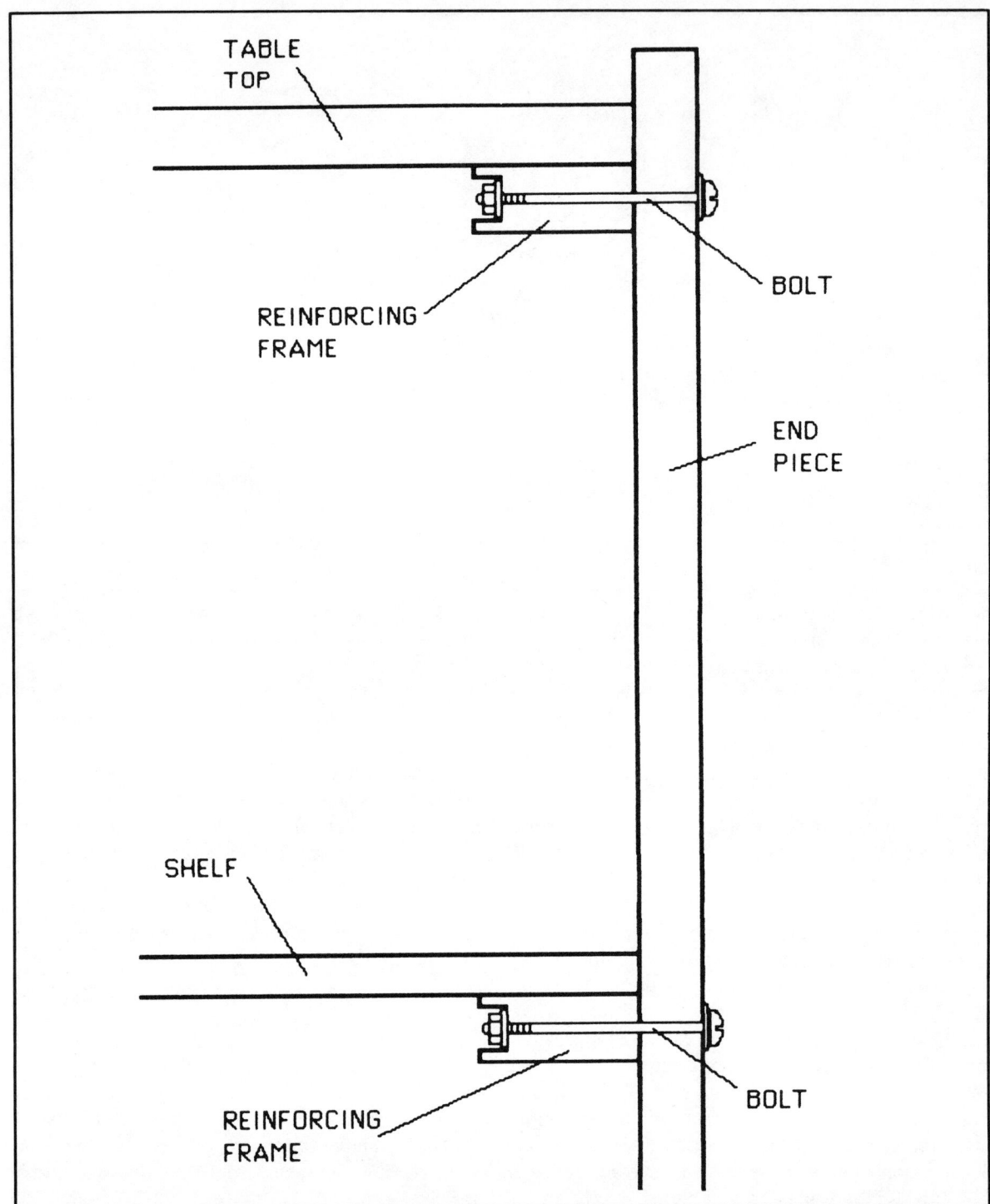
Fig. 3-46. Assembly of top and shelf to side pieces with bolts.

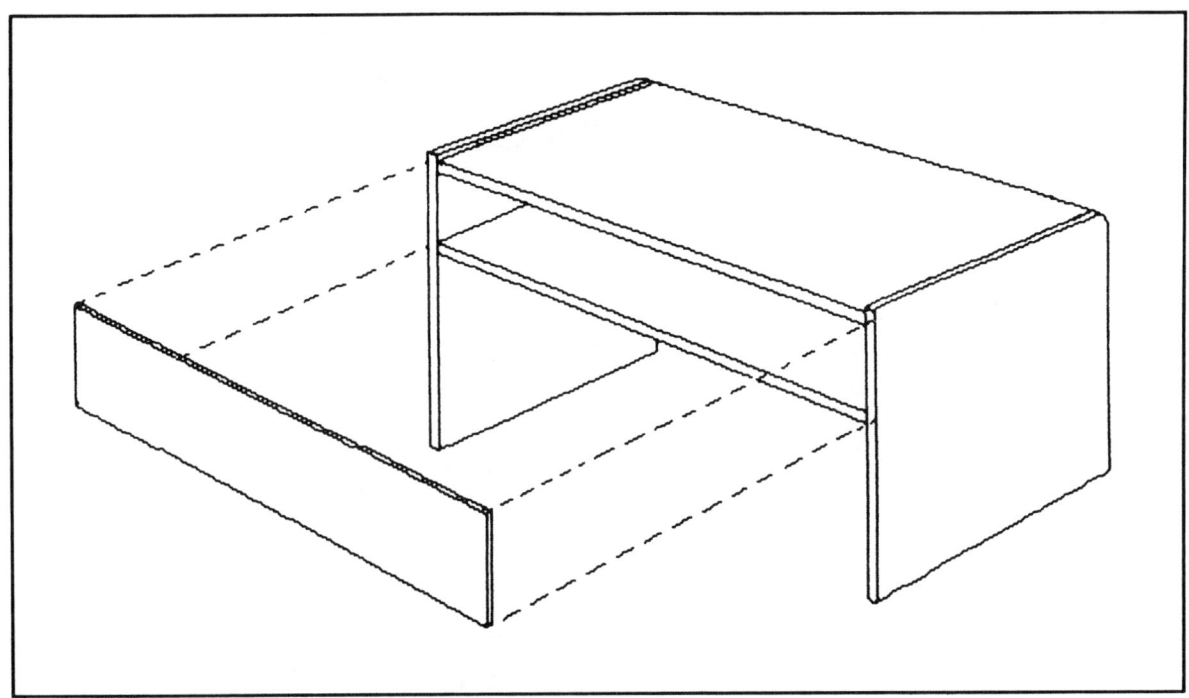

Fig. 3-47. Installing backing piece to basic computer table with full sides.

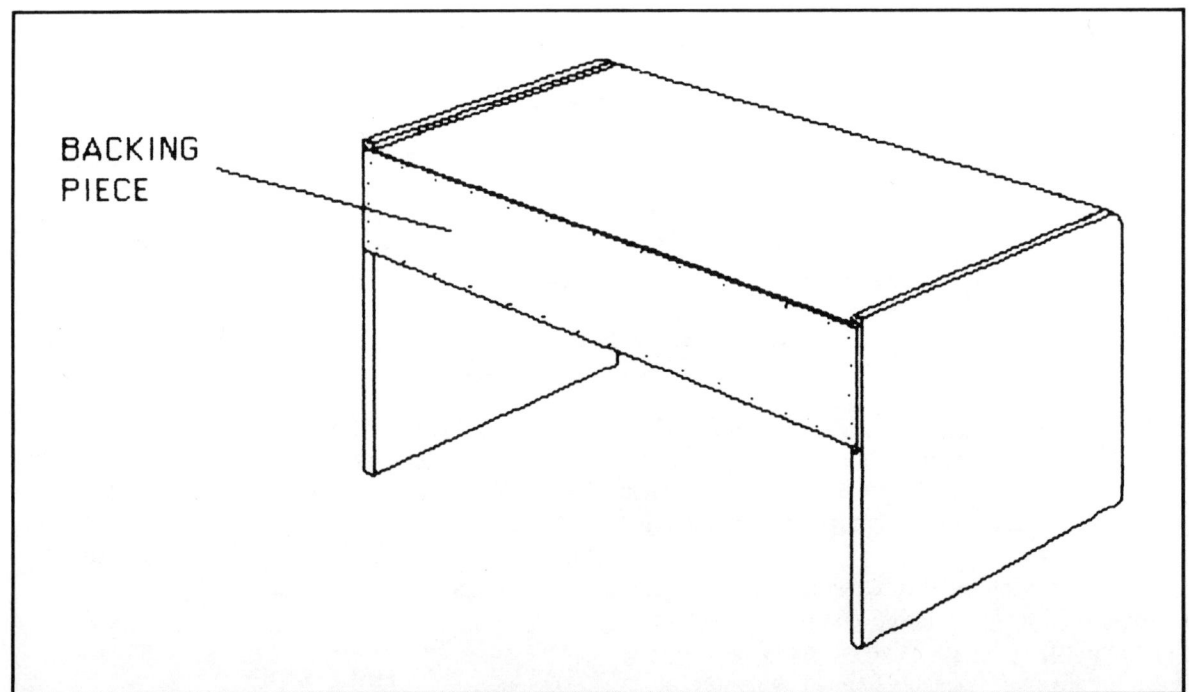

Fig. 3-48. Backing piece installed to basic computer table with full sides.

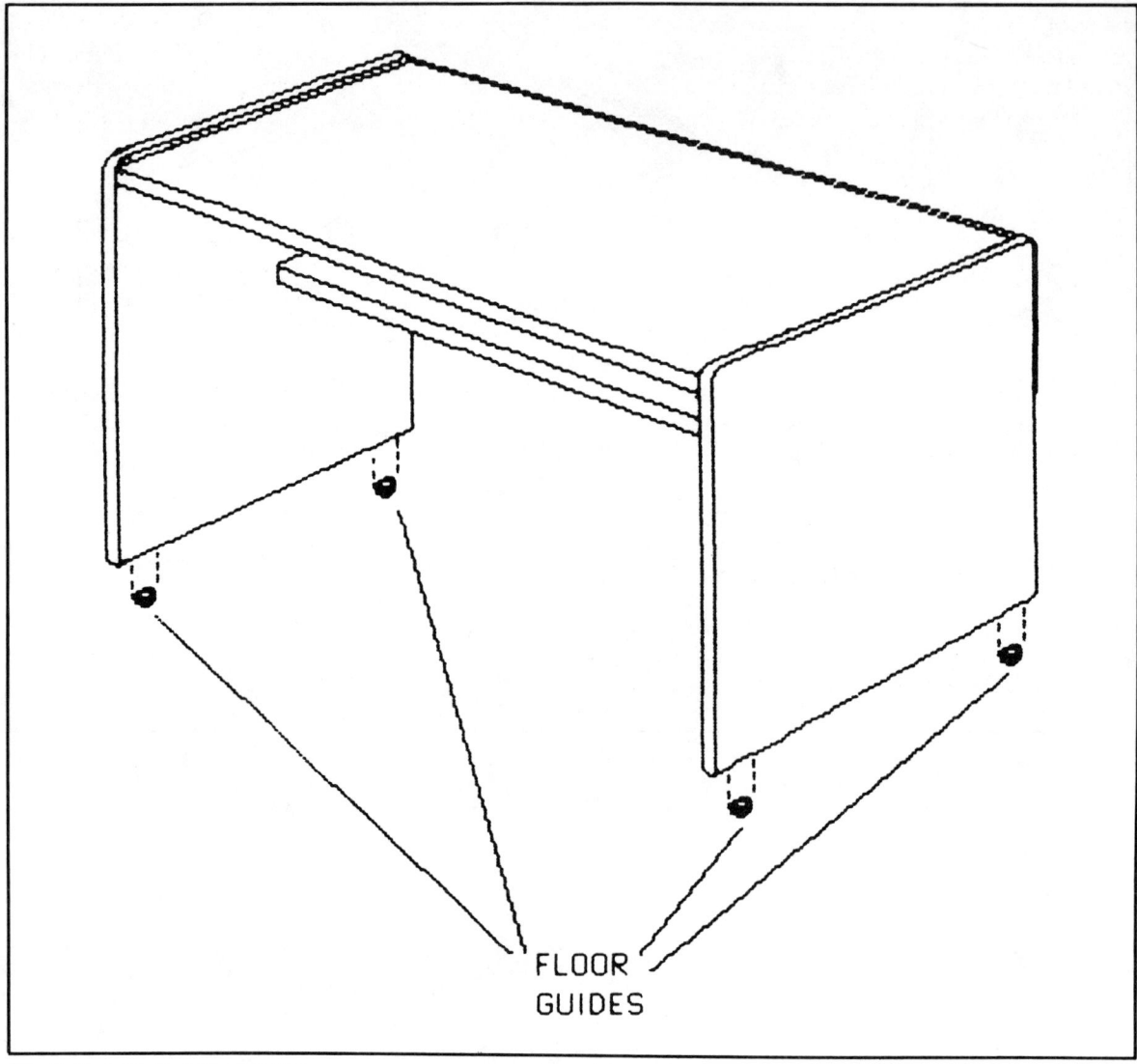

Fig. 3-49. Installing floor guides.

below the table and/or a drawer immediately below the table top. A popular shelf and storage arrangement is shown in Fig. 3-50. Construction of a similar table with a video and storage rack is detailed later in this chapter.

The basic computer table with full sides makes a functional and attractive computer table even when built from inexpensive woods. This design is ideal for anyone who wants to build computer tables to sell to others. The table can be sold either unfinished or with finish applied. By using more expensive woods, such as oak, you can give the table a custom appearance. The plans given here show simple butt joints, but if you have the cabinetmaking skills and know-how, you can also use rabbet, t-rabbet, mitre, or other joints.

BASIC COMPUTER
TABLE WITH HALF SIDES

This table is slightly more difficult to make than

the basic budget computer table and of about equal difficulty to the basic computer table with full sides described above. It is constructed mainly from plywood, and materials to build this table vary in cost—$35 (1984 prices), using Douglas fir plywood and a plastic laminate top; around $80 using oak-faced plywood. Prices will vary, depending on where you purchase your wood, your area, and other factors. In any case, large savings are possible when you build your own. This computer table presents an attractive and modern appearance even when built from standard plywood. A custom look can be achieved by making the same design from more expensive plywoods, such as those faced with oak or other hardwoods.

The basic computer table with half sides is shown in Figs. 3-51 and 3-52. The top has space for both a computer and printer. The table can have a natural wood top or a plastic laminated one. The table features a shelf underneath that provides storage space and gives the table added strength.

Materials

The patterns for the wood parts are shown in Fig. 3-53. The top of the table is a 26-inch-by-4-foot piece of 3/4-inch thick plywood. If you intend to use the wood surface as the finished table top, without adding a plastic laminate, plywood with the upper layer of a hardwood, such as oak, is recommended. If a laminate is to be added, exterior grade shop plywood will suffice.

The shelf is plywood with a minimum thickness of 1/2 inch; 3/4 inch is better. The shelf measures

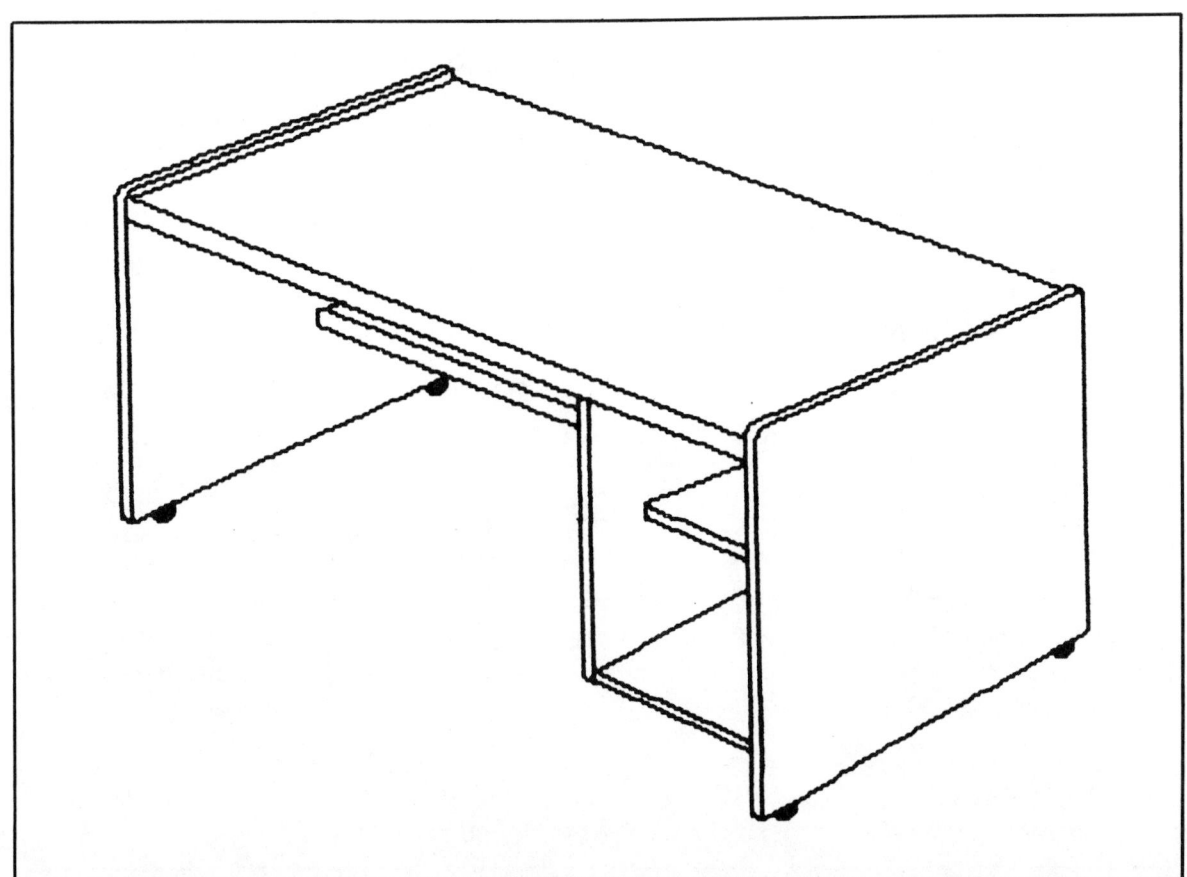

Fig. 3-50. Basic computer table with full sides with alternate shelf arrangement.

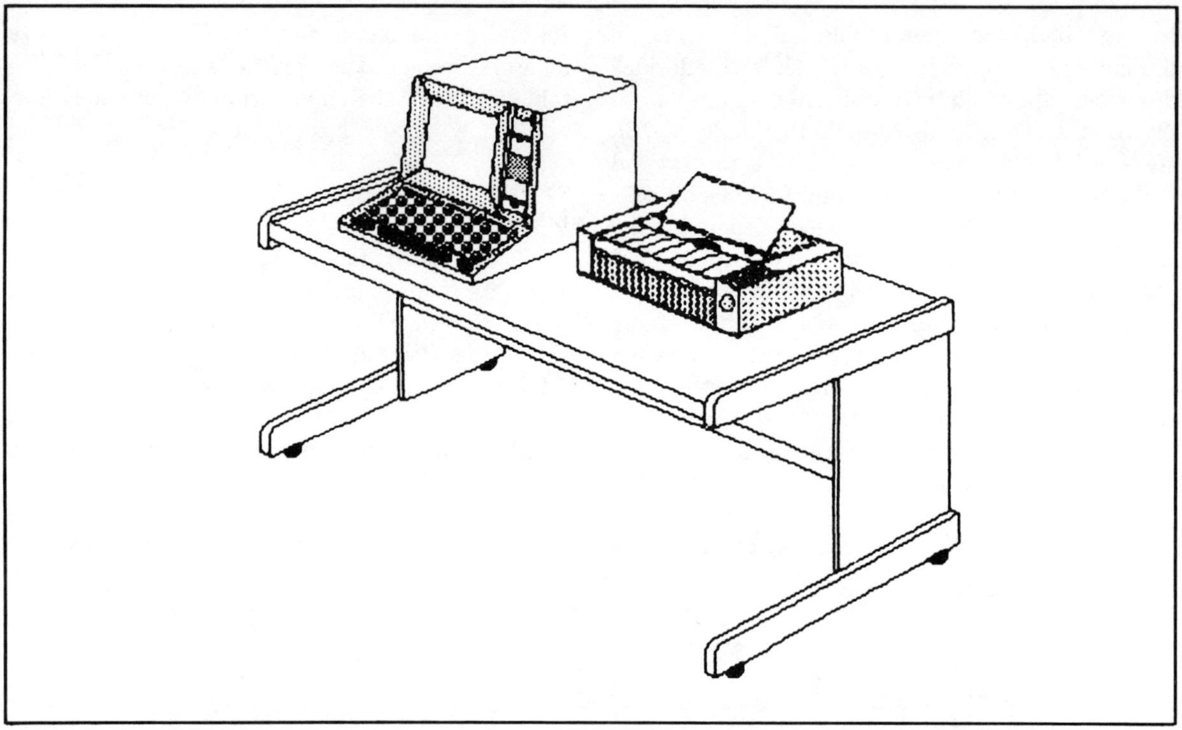

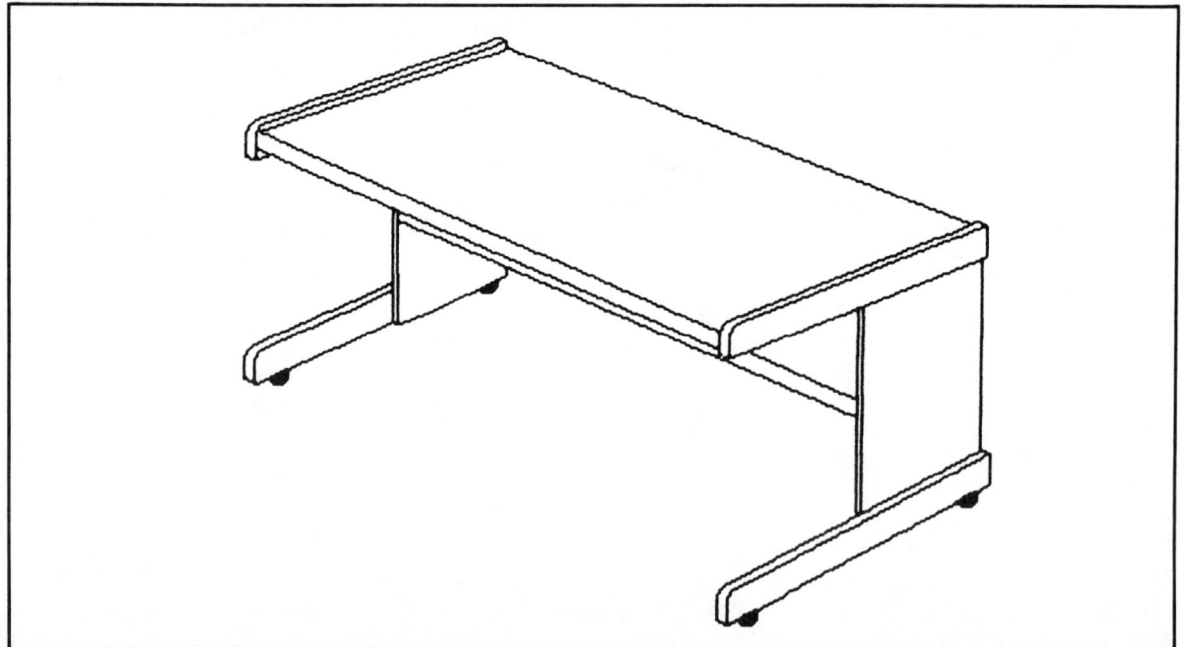

Fig. 3-51. Basic computer table with half sides, including computer and printer.

Fig. 3-52. Basic computer table with half sides.

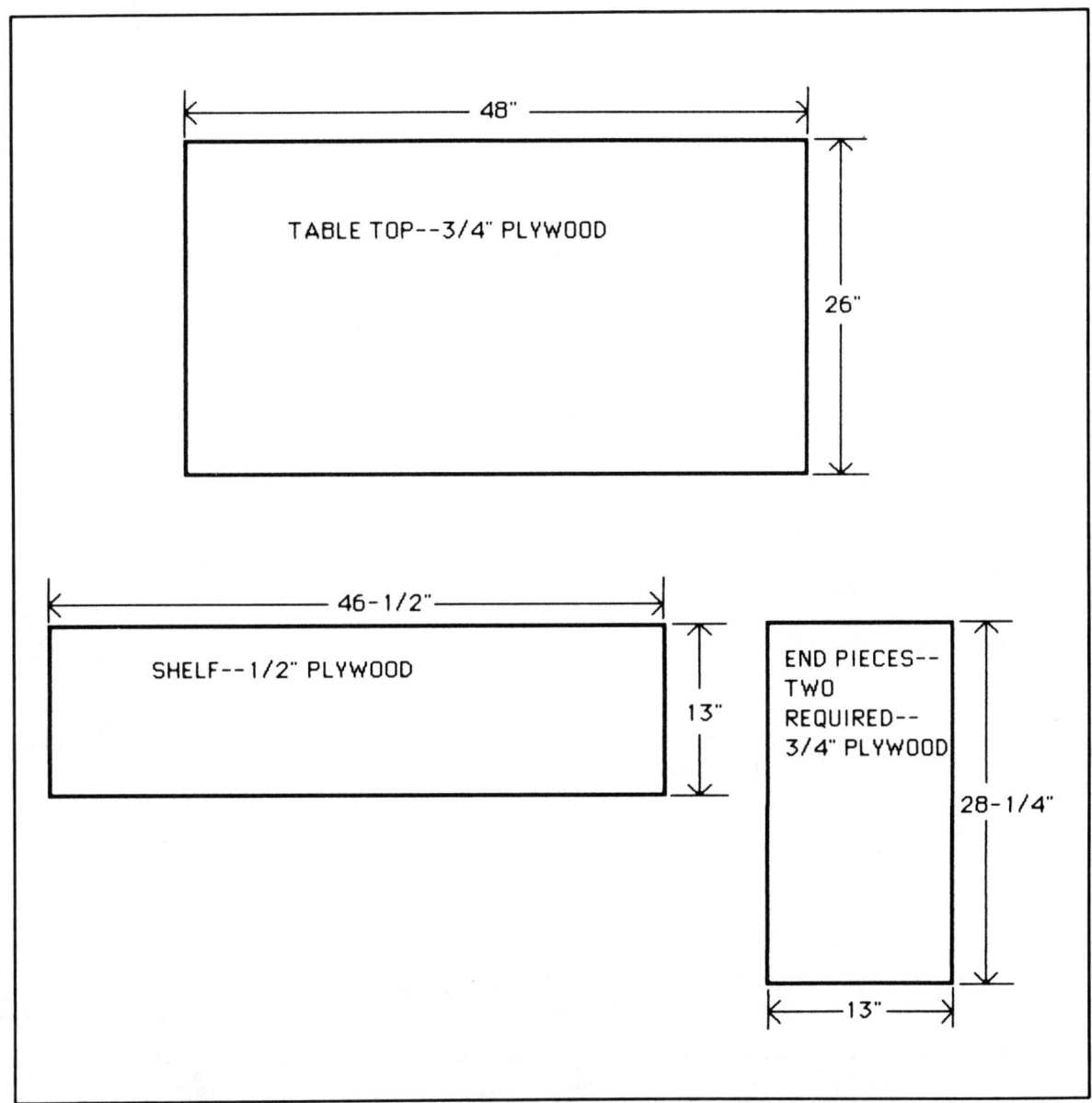

Fig. 3-53. Patterns for plywood parts for basic computer table with half sides.

46 1/2 inches by 13 inches. The end pieces are 3/4-inch thick plywood and measure 13 inches by 28 1/4 inches, giving the table a 29 inch height, not counting the height added by whatever floor guides are used. You may want to change the 29-inch dimension if you want your table a different height. Two end pieces are required.

Plywood is normally sold in standard 4-foot-by-8-foot sheets, so lay out the patterns to take advantage of this standard size and arrange them to keep waste to a minimum. Some lumberyards and plywood stores will cut plywood sheets to size for you, usually at additional cost. It can be worth the cost if you don't need full sheets, don't have room

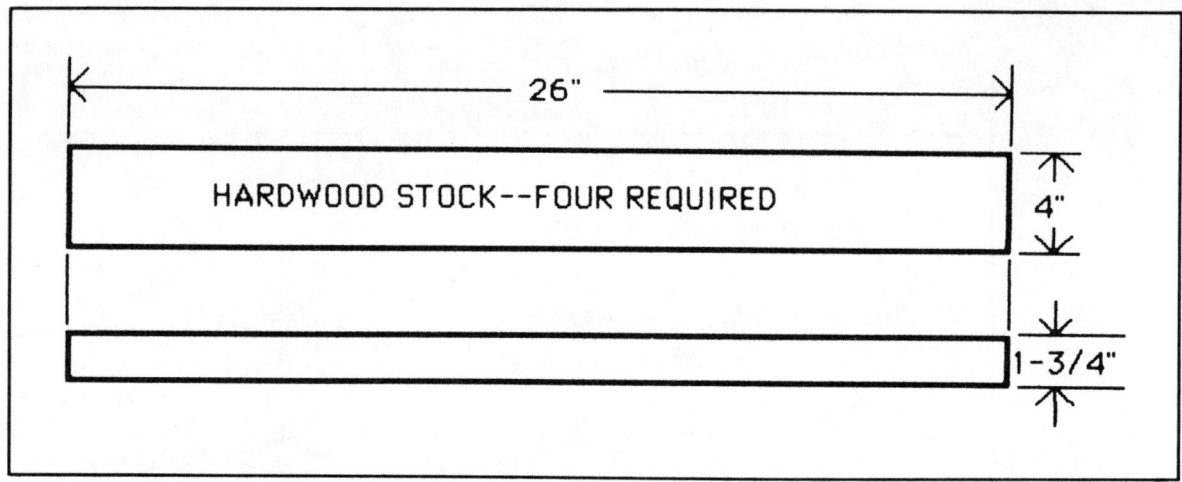

Fig. 3-54. Pattern for side pieces.

to carry full sheets in your car, or don't have a saw to accurately cut plywood.

Half-inch thick plywood could also be used, but I don't recommend this, because the savings are negligible and a less sturdy table will result. Particle board can be substituted for the plywood if you are on an absolute minimum budget. Some manufactured computer furniture is made from particle board covered by plastic laminates. Particle board can be difficult to work with, however, and it is very difficult to get plastic laminates to bond properly to this material without special equipment.

Four end pieces, 26 inches long, of 2-inch-by-4-inch hardwood stock are required for the side pieces (Fig. 3-54).

The backing piece (Fig. 3-55) can be either plywood or fiberboard. It is used to strengthen the table base and hold the frame in rectangular form. The length of the backing piece is 48 inches. A 13-inch height is shown for the backing piece, which is about the minimum required to give this table adequate strength. The shelf can be installed a greater distance below the top, which will require changing the height of the backing piece. Notice that the top, shelf, backing piece, and side pieces form a box with the forward side open.

You will also need 1-inch-by-2-inch or larger framing stock for use under the plywood table top and the shelf.

A variety of wood and plastic trim strips can

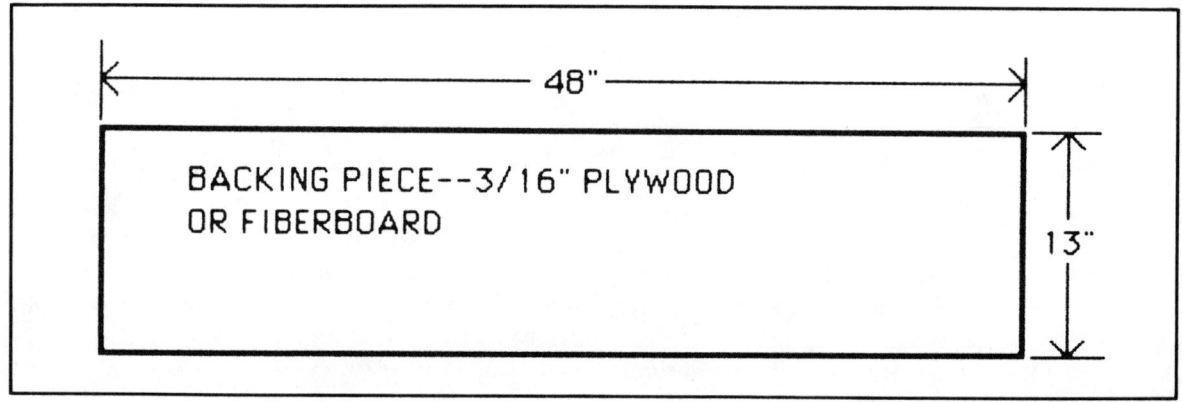

Fig. 3-55. Pattern for backing piece.

be used to cover the exposed edges of the plywood. A wood or plastic trim strip is used to cover the forward edge of the table top and shelf. These pieces are 48 inches and 46 1/2 inches long respectively and about 1 3/4 inches wide (the minimum width should be such that it will completely cover the widths of the plywood—3/4-inch for the top and 1/2-inch or 3/4-inch for the shelf, and approximately 7/8-inch for the framing. The trim strips can be slightly wider than this, however.

Four floor pods or guides are used on the floor beams (see Fig. 3-56). A variety of suitable types are available from hardware stores, of either a fixed or adjustable type, as desired.

Various fasteners can be used for assembly. You will also need a suitable wood glue. The finish can be clear urethane or other type, as desired.

The top can be left natural or a plastic laminate can be added. If a plastic laminate is to be added, you will need a 26-inch-by-4-foot piece of suitable laminate and contact cement for attaching it to the plywood.

Construction

Overviews of the complete assembly are shown in Figs. 3-56 and 3-57. Begin by building the table top, as detailed in Fig. 3-58. If you purchased a piece of plywood that was already cut to the 26-inch-by-4-foot size, no additional cutting will be required, assuming it was cut accurately and is a true rectangle. You might want to check this with a square.

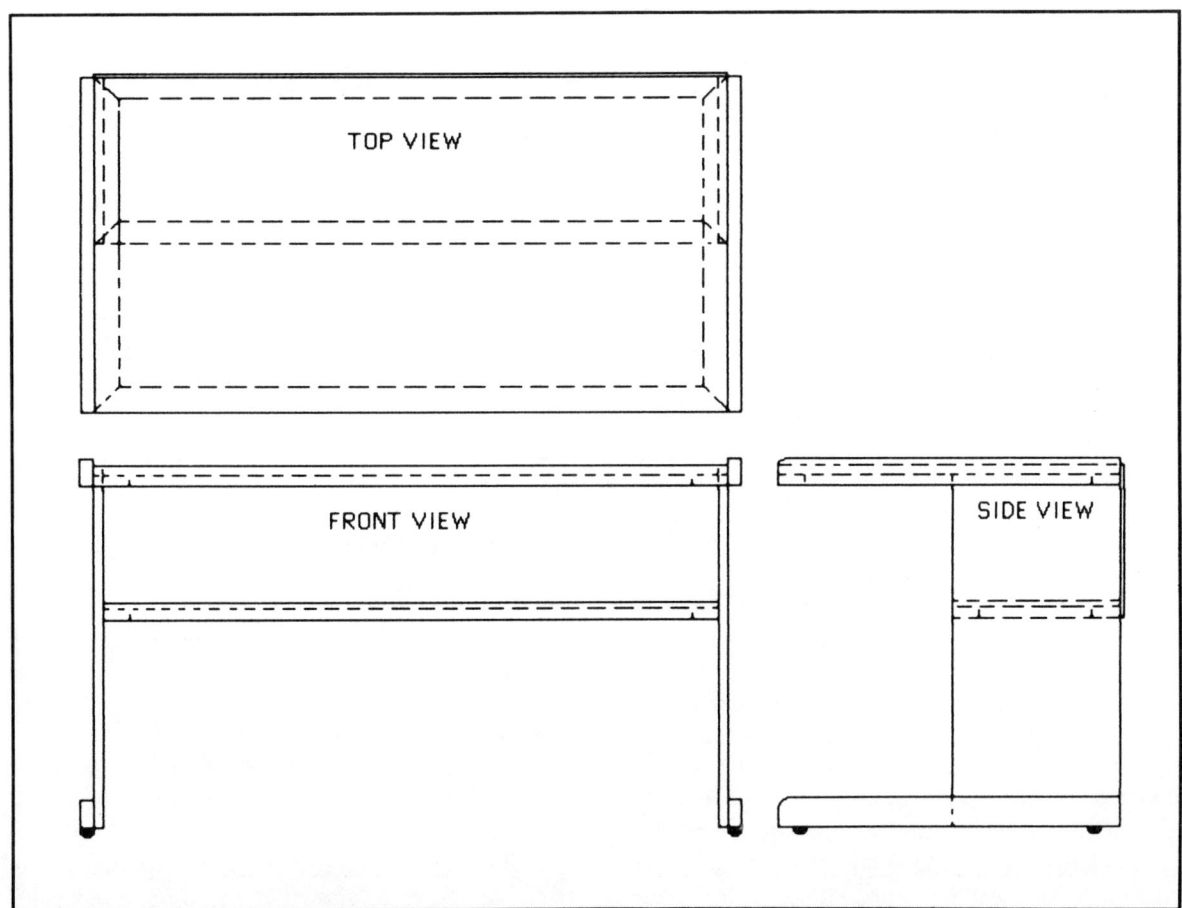

Fig. 3-56. Basic computer table with half sides.

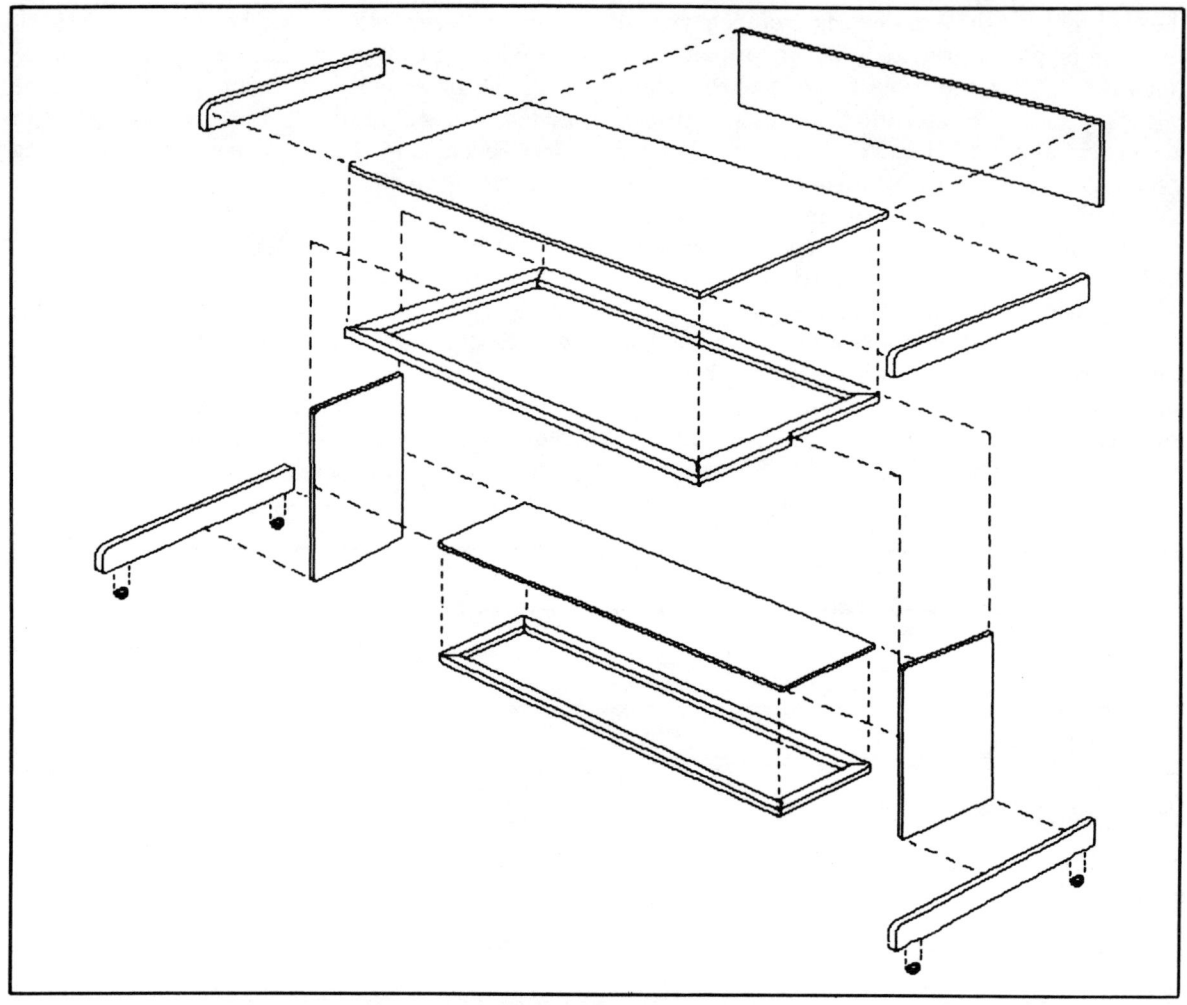

Fig. 3-57. Assembly of basic computer table with half sides.

If you purchased a larger piece of plywood, such as a standard 4-foot-by-8-foot sheet, you will need to cut out a section for the table top. Have the grain of the top layer running lengthwise, although this is not essential if you are going to add a plastic laminate. Try to use two factory cut edges for your table top and cut the other two. Use a ruler and square to make the pattern and mark the lines with a sharp pencil or scribing tool.

Sawing plywood requires special care to avoid chipping and splintering along the cut edge. Handsaws or power saws with special fine-toothed blades designed especially for plywood should be used; carbide-tipped blades are even better. Apply a strip of masking tape over the area to be cut on both sides of the plywood, but especially on the side opposite the one you are cutting, to prevent chipping. Another possibility is to clamp a solid piece of wood to the underside and make the cut through both plywood and scrap wood.

Be extremely careful when sanding edges and use a sanding block. Avoid sanding plywood until a wood sealer has been applied.

The next step is to add the reinforcing frame to the table top, as shown in Fig. 3-58. Use a ruler and a square to make the patterns on the framing

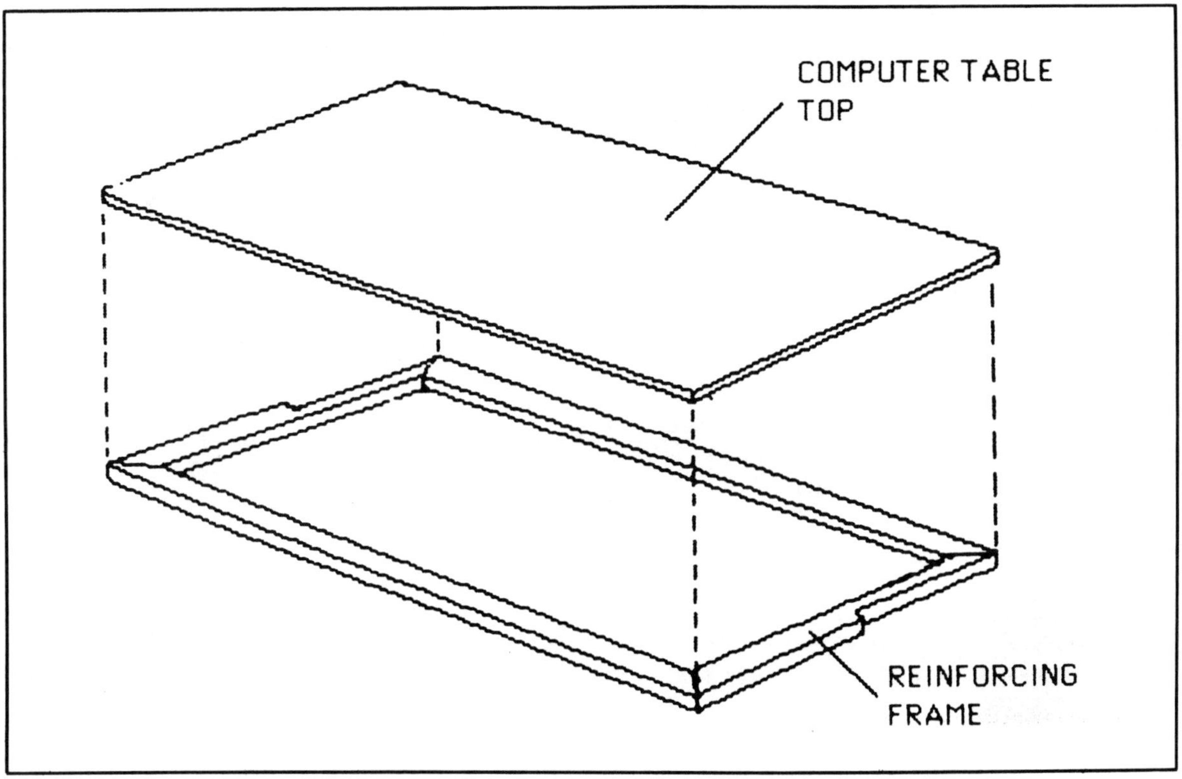

Fig. 3-58. Assembly of top and reinforcing frame.

wood, marking the lines with a sharp pencil or other marking device. Then make the necessary saw cuts, as detailed in Chapter 2. The frame pieces should be glued and nailed or screwed in position (see Figs. 3-59 and 3-60). If the plywood top is to be left natural wood (without a plastic laminate being added), the fasteners should go through the framing and into the plywood. Take care they do not pass all the way through the plywood or leave a bulge in the upper surface. If a good glue is used, such as acrylic or epoxy, the glue alone should give adequate strength; the fasteners are mainly used as a clamping device for the gluing and will not have much holding power. For greater holding power, the fasteners can be passed through the plywood and into the framing if a plastic laminate is to be added.

You can finish the table top in different ways. One possibility is to use the plywood surface as the top and add a wood trim strip to the forward edge,

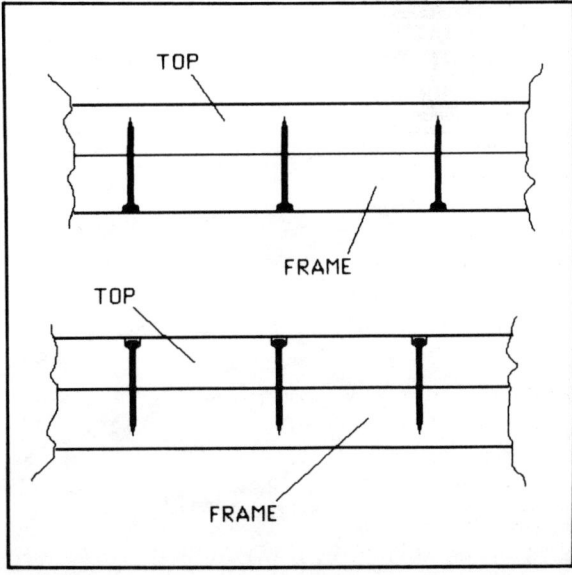

Fig. 3-59. Assembly of table top to frame pieces with nails and glue.

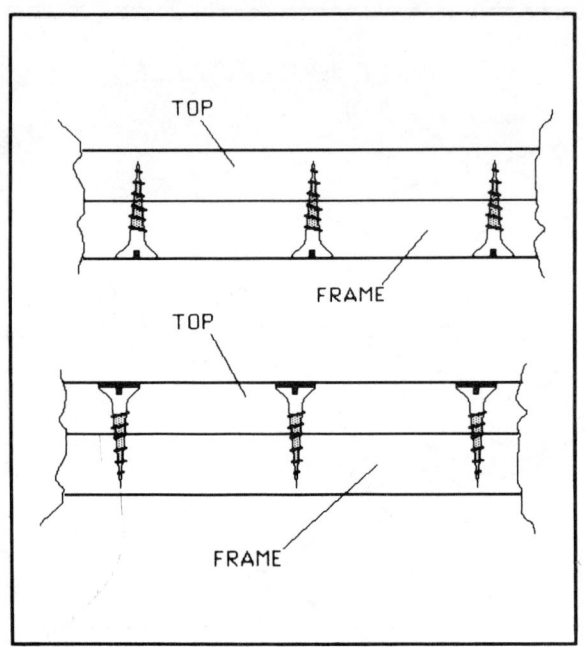

Fig. 3-60. Assembly of table top to frame pieces with screws and glue.

as shown in Fig. 3-61. Glue and fasten the trim strip in place with finishing nails. Set the heads below the wood surface and fill holes with wood filler to flush with the wood surface.

A second possibility is to add a plastic laminate to the forward edge and leave the top natural wood, as detailed in Fig. 3-62. Or, add a plastic laminate to the top and a wood trim strip to the forward edge, as shown in Fig. 3-63. Plastic laminates can also be applied to both the top and forward edge, as shown in Figs. 3-64 and 3-65.

If a plastic laminate is added to the plywood table top and/or the forward edge, these can be installed now. A large selection of plastic laminates are on the market, but I suggest using only high quality plastic laminates for computer table tops.

If a plastic laminate is going to be applied to the forward edge of the table top, it should be applied first and finished flush with the table top. The top laminate is then applied so that the edge overlaps the top edge of the laminate on the forward edge of the table, as shown in Fig. 3-65.

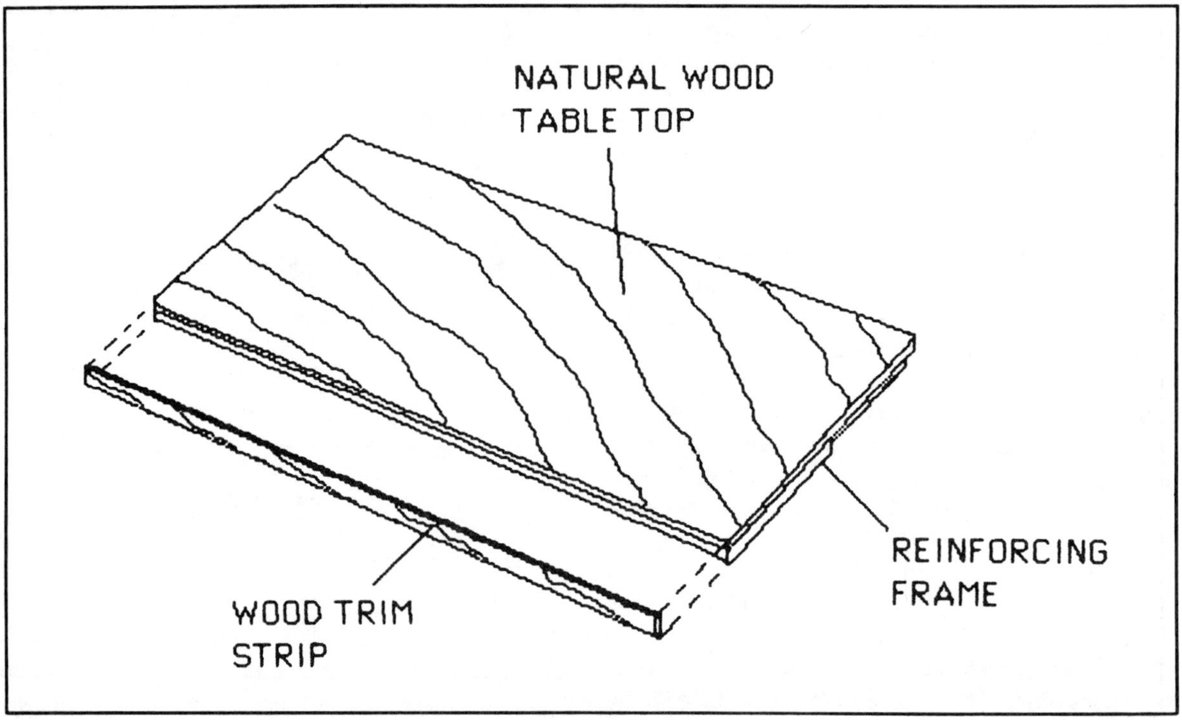

Fig. 3-61. Adding wood trim strip to forward edge of computer table top.

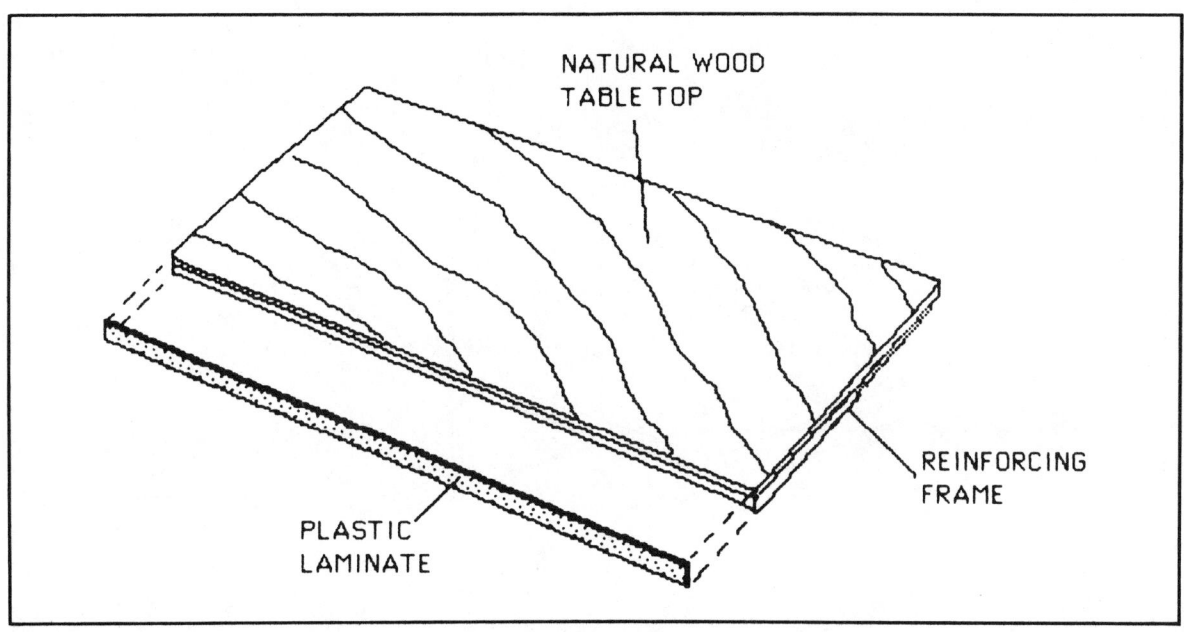

Fig. 3-62. Adding plastic laminate to forward edge of computer table top.

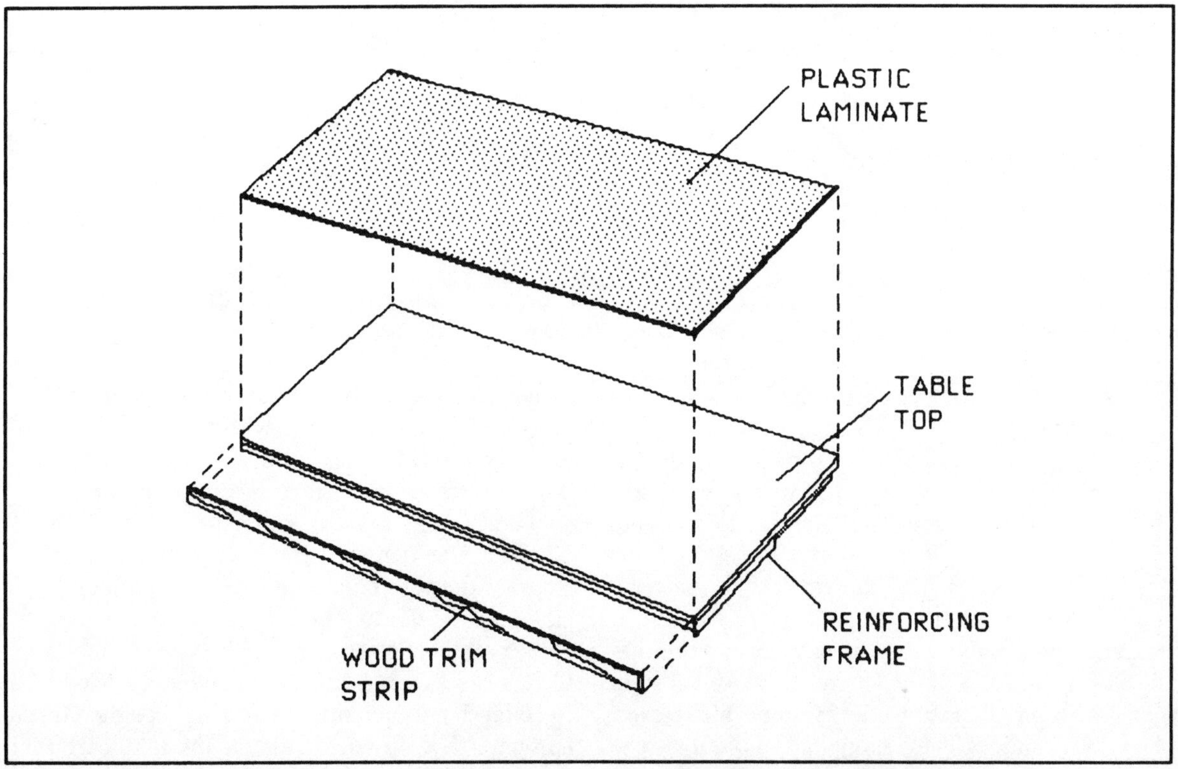

Fig. 3-63. Adding plastic laminate to top and wood trim strip to forward edge of computer table top.

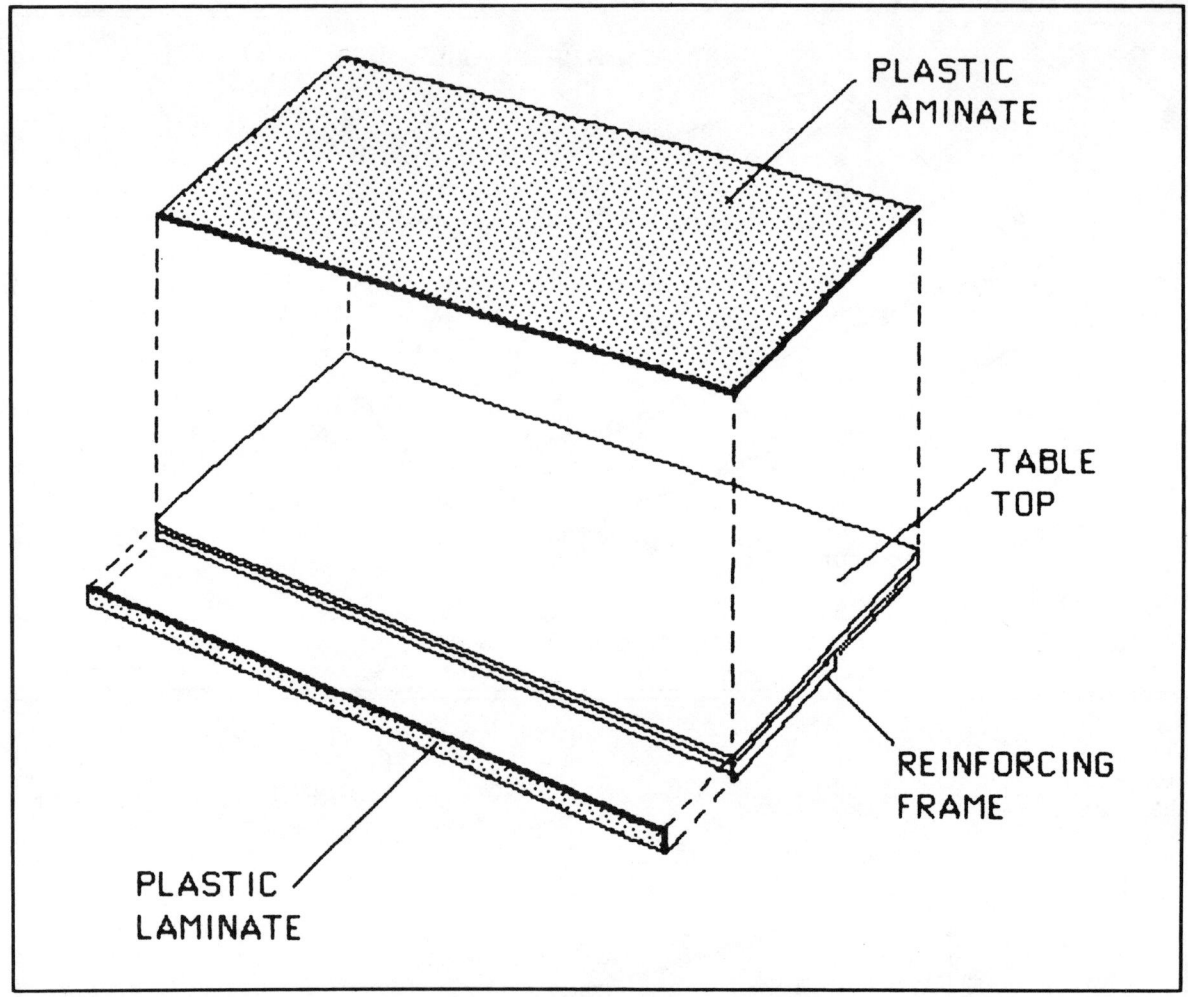

Fig. 3-64. Adding plastic laminate to top and forward edge of computer table top.

The plastic laminate is installed as follows:

• All holes and defects in the surface of the plywood should be filled with putty or wood filler.

• Sand the surface to be covered for good adhesion.

• Mark the plastic laminate to a pattern slightly larger than the area to be covered. Use a straightedge and draw the pattern lines on the finished or pattern side of the laminate. Leave 1/4 inch to 1/2 inch on all sides to be trimmed off later.

• If a laminate is to be applied to the forward edge of the table, apply this first. After installation, as detailed below, trim and file the upper edge of the plastic laminate flush with the upper edge of the plywood table top before installing the plastic laminate to upper surface of the table top.

• Cut the plastic laminate to the pattern marked. Even though the plastic laminate is extremely durable once applied, it is vulnerable to cracking and splitting before it is cemented in place. Fine-tooth handsaws or power saws with fine-tooth blades can be used; a rotary power saw with a 14 to 16 teeth per inch blade is ideal. Place the plastic laminate face up when cutting and take care that the laminate is not chipped or broken. An alternate

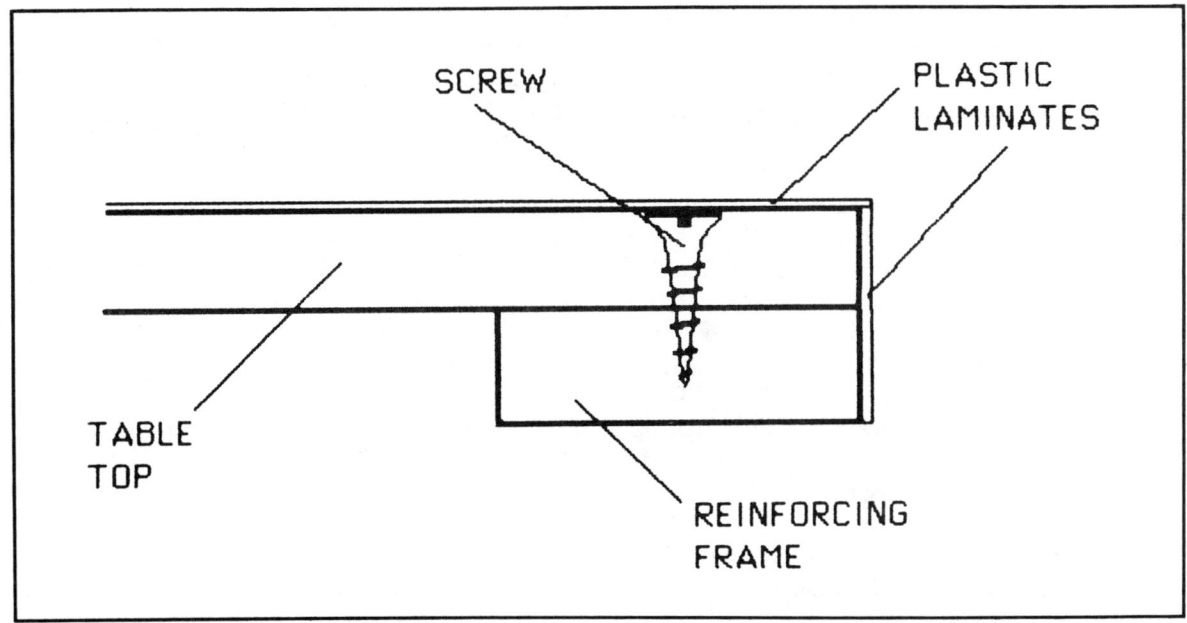

Fig. 3-65. Adding plastic laminate to top.

method is to use a carbide tip knife for scoring the plastic by drawing the knife point along a metal straightedge. Cut through the decorative surface; the laminate can then be broken by bending it toward the decorative surface side over the edge of a table or workbench.

• Apply contact cement to the surface of the plywood to be covered and the back side of the

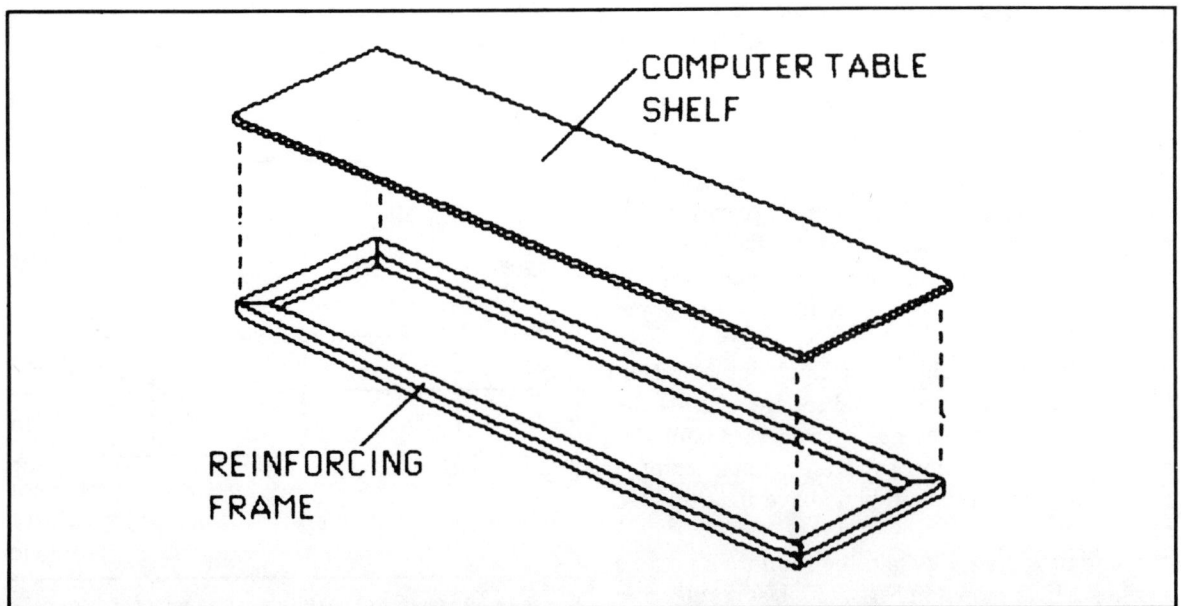

Fig. 3-66. Assembly of shelf top to reinforcing frame.

plastic laminate. A brush, roller, or metal spreader with a serrated edge can be used to spread the contact cement. A thin, even application is important.

- Follow the manufacturer's instructions regarding drying time—about 20 to 30 minutes.
- Place a sheet of heavy wrapping paper over the plywood surface to be covered and position the laminate on the plywood surface with the paper in between. The contact cement will not stick to the paper if it has been allowed to dry properly. Make certain that the laminate is positioned correctly. Once the two surfaces of contact cement touch, the laminate sheet cannot be moved again. When everything is lined up properly, pull the paper out from between the plywood and the plastic laminate.
- Using a small block of wood and a hammer, lightly tap the laminate in place or use a rolling pin.
- Use a file to remove the surplus plastic laminate from the edges. You can also use a special cutter with a router, which allows you to conveniently trim excess plastic laminate flush with the plywood edges.
- The thinner recommended for the contact cement can be used to clean contact cement from wood and plastic laminate and tools.
- The next step is to construct the shelf, as detailed in Fig. 3-66. If you purchased a piece of plywood that was already cut to the 13-inch-by-46 1/2-inch size, no additional cutting of the plywood will be required, if it was cut accurately and is true. Check this with a square.

If you purchased a larger piece of plywood, you will need to cut out a section for the shelf top. Try to have the grain of the top layer running lengthwise. (This is not essential if you are going to add a plastic laminate.) In most cases, you will use two factory cut edges for your shelf top and cut the other two. Use a ruler and square to draw the pattern, and mark the lines with a sharp pencil or scribing tool. Saw and sand the shelf carefully, following procedures outlined above for the table top.

The next step is to add the reinforcing frame to the shelf as shown in Fig. 3-66. Use a ruler and a square to draw the patterns on the framing wood, marking the lines with a sharp marking device. Then make the necessary saw cuts, as detailed in Chapter 2. The frame pieces should be glued and nailed or screwed in position (see Figs. 3-67 and 3-68). If the plywood shelf top will not be covered with plastic laminate, the fasteners should go through the framing and into the plywood, but care should be taken so that the fasteners do not pass all the way through the plywood or leave a bulge in the upper surface. If a good glue is used, such as acrylic or epoxy, the glue alone should give adequate strength. Here, the fasteners are mainly used as a clamp for the gluing. They will not have much holding power in the plywood. To give greater holding power, the fasteners can be passed through the plywood and into the framing, but only if a plastic laminate is to be added.

A variety of options are available for finishing off the shelf. Your choice will depend on how you finish the table top. One possibility is to use the plywood surface as the shelf top and add a wood trim strip to the forward edge, as shown in Fig. 3-69. Glue and fasten the trim strip in place with

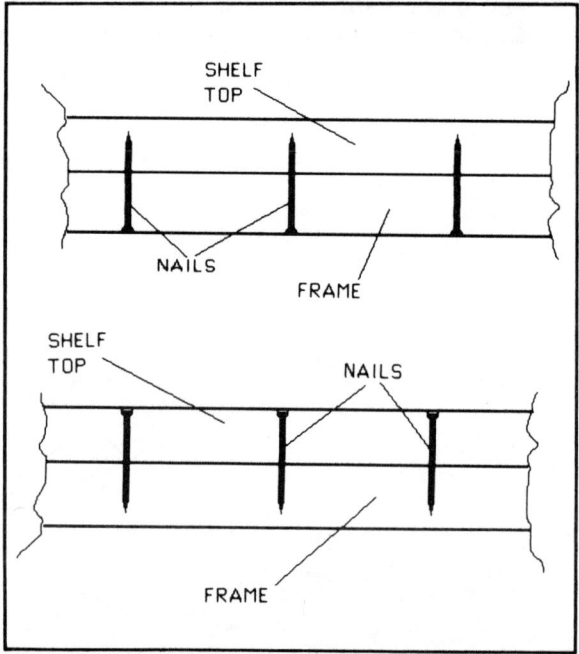

Fig. 3-67. Assembly of shelf top to frame pieces with nails and glue.

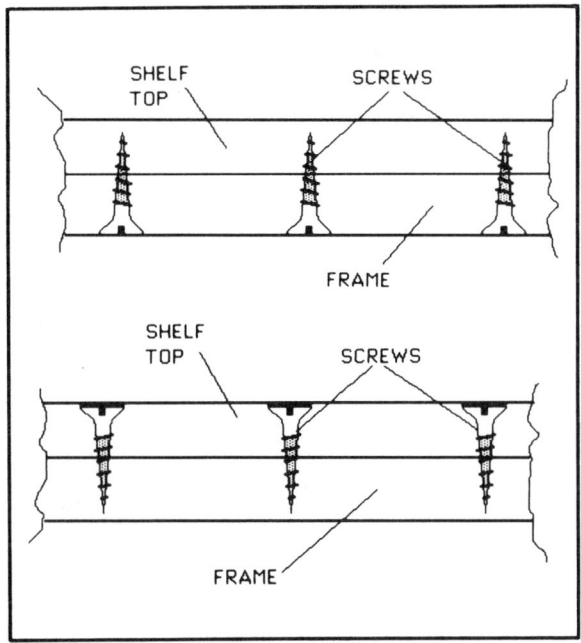

Fig. 3-68. Assembly of shelf top to frame pieces with screws and glue.

finishing nails. Set the heads below the wood surface and fill holes with wood filler to flush with the wood surface.

A second possibility is to add a plastic laminate to the forward edge and leave the shelf top natural wood, as detailed in Fig. 3-70. Another method is to add a plastic laminate to the shelf top and a wood trim strip to the forward edge, as shown in Fig. 3-71, or add plastic laminates to both the top and forward edge, as shown in Figs. 3-72 and 3-73.

If a plastic laminate will be applied to the plywood shelf top and/or the forward edge, install these pieces now. Apply plastic laminate to the forward edge of the shelf top first. Finish it flush with the shelf top; the top laminate is then applied so that its edge overlaps the top edge of the forward edge laminate, as shown in Fig. 3-73.

Next, cut the end pieces to rectangular size, using cutting procedures described above. A power circular saw is ideal for making straight cuts.

Next, add plastic (Fig. 3-74) or wood (Fig. 3-75) trim to the forward edges of the end pieces. This

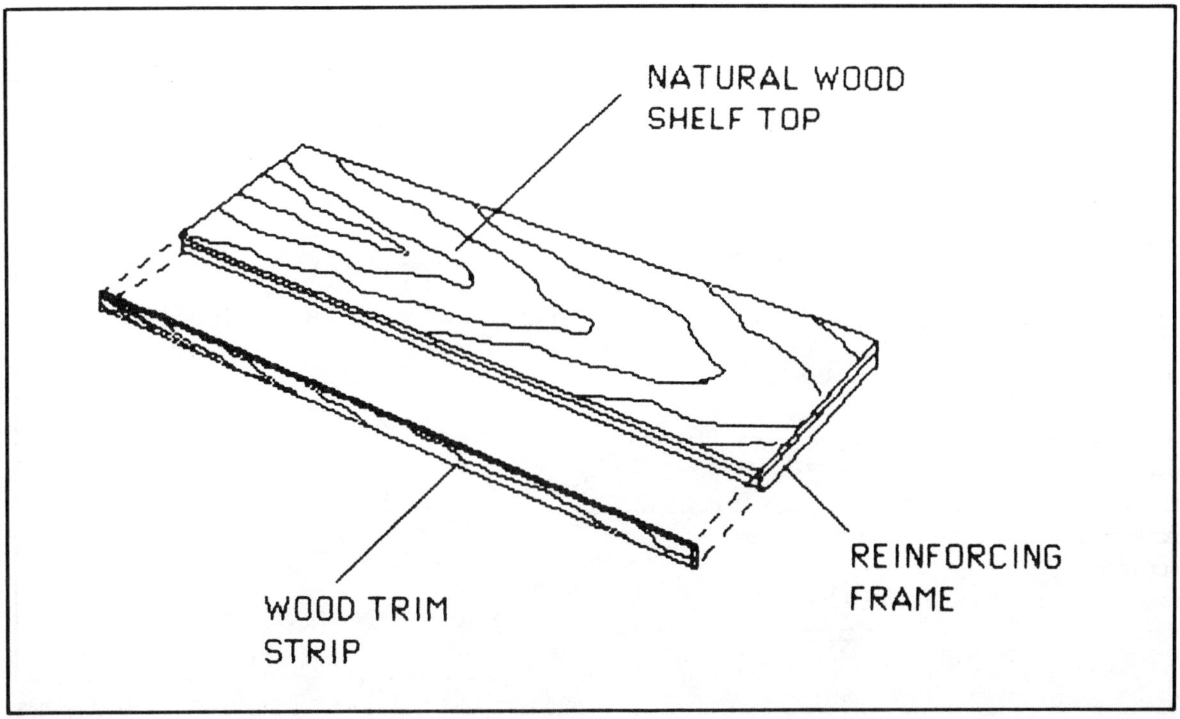

Fig. 3-69. Adding wood trim strip to forward edge of shelf.

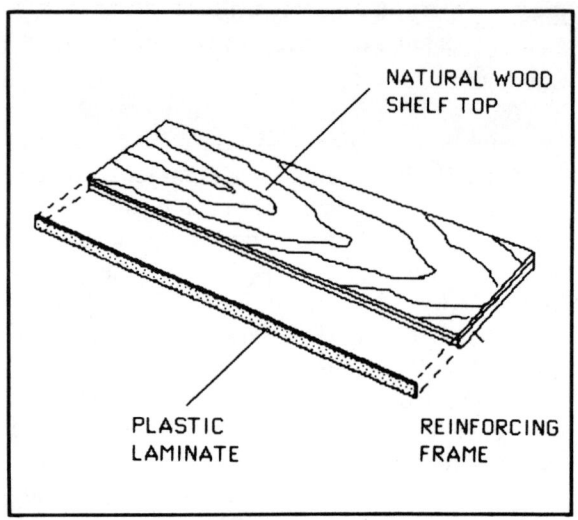

Fig. 3-70. Adding plastic laminate to forward edge of shelf.

protects the laminated edges of the plywood and gives them a neat appearance.

An overview of the remainder of the assembly is shown in Fig. 3-76. The next step is to assemble the top and shelf to the side pieces, as shown in Fig. 3-77. This is accomplished by both glue and mechanical fasteners. One method is to use finishing nails, passing them through the end pieces and into the framing wood of the top and shelf. Set the heads below the wood surface and fill with wood filler flush with the surface. Another method uses through bolts, as detailed in Fig. 3-78. The bolts for the top will also pass through the beam pieces, as detailed later.

Regardless of the method, it is extremely important to install the side pieces perpendicular to the table top and shelf in a crosswise direction. Use

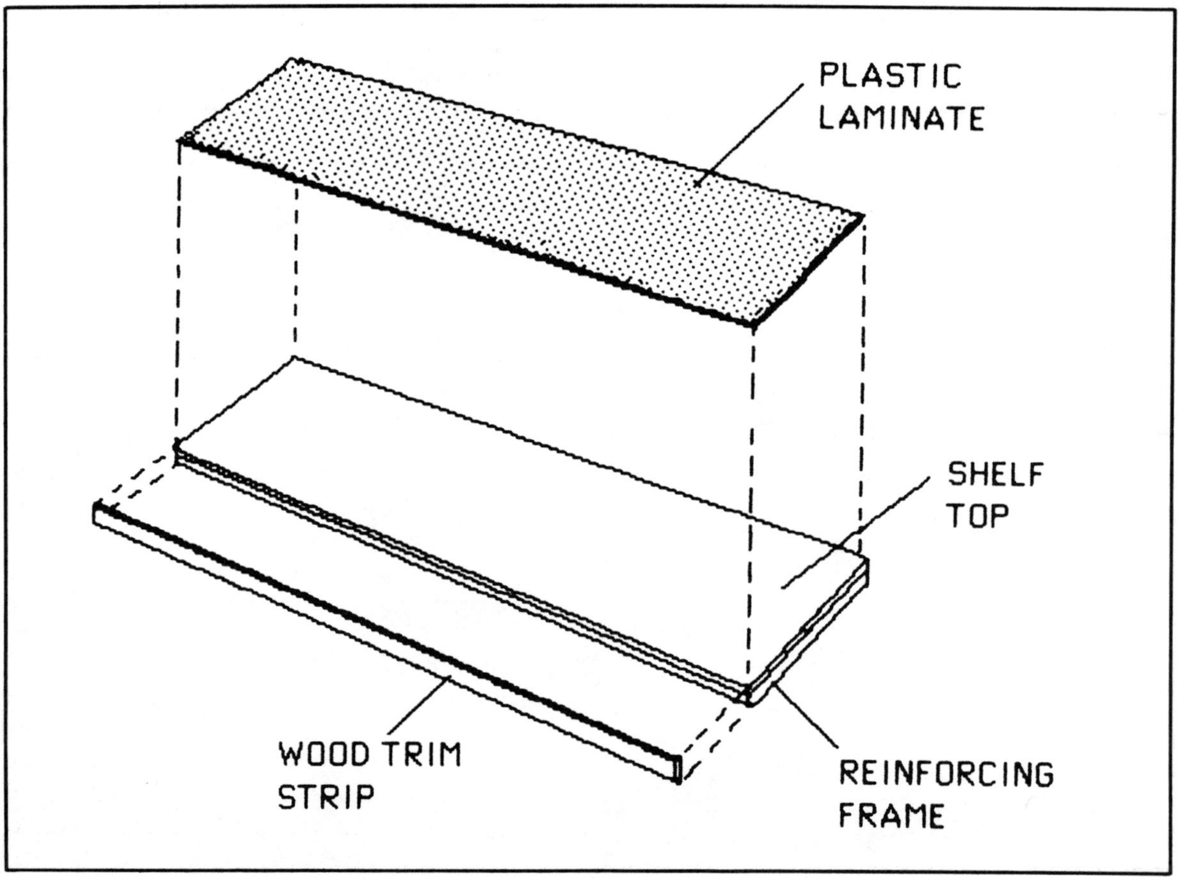

Fig. 3-71. Adding plastic laminate to top and wood trim strip to forward edge of shelf.

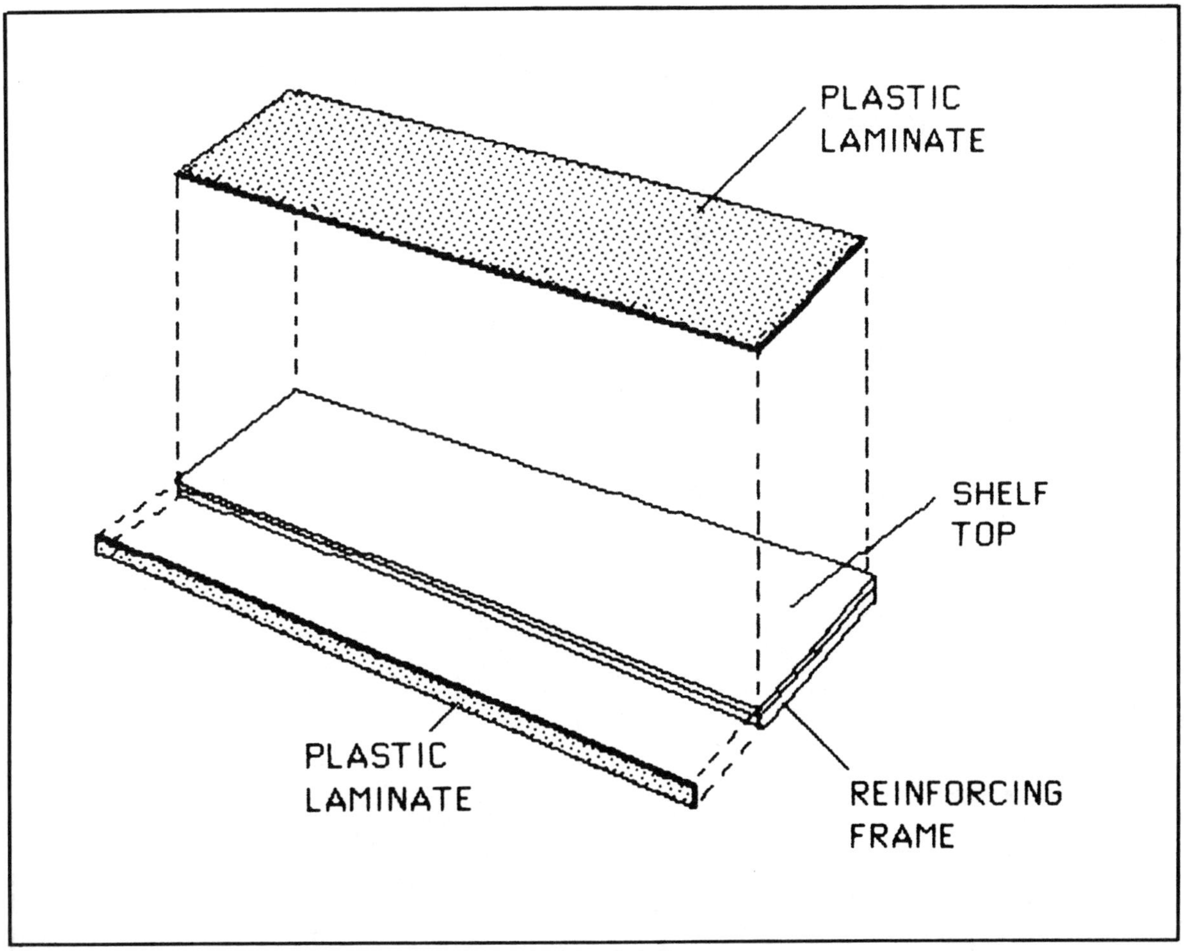

Fig. 3-72. Adding plastic laminate to top and forward edge of shelf.

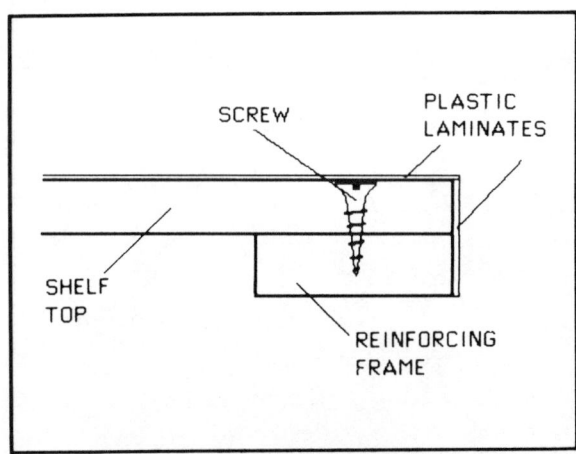

Fig. 3-73. Adding plastic laminate to top.

a square to make pattern lines on the side pieces. It is also important to have exactly the same distance between the top and shelf on both sides. This can be any distance, but a minimum of 12 inches is required for adequate strength. Figure 3-79 shows the top and shelf assembled to the end pieces.

After the shelf and top have been assembled to the side pieces, add the backing piece, as shown in Fig. 3-80. The backing piece forms a box with the top, shelf, and side pieces, so it is important that the backing piece be attached securely to the wood members all the way around the edges. The backing piece is glued and nailed into position. It is extremely important to make certain that the backing

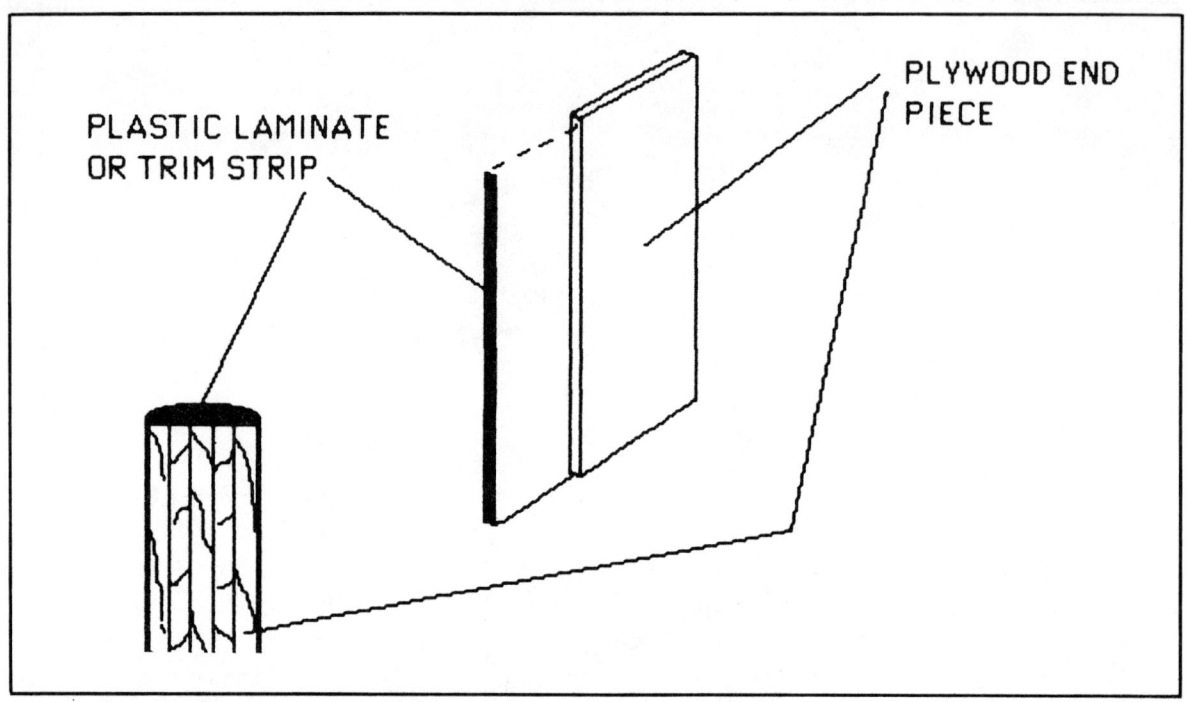

Fig. 3-74. Adding plastic laminate or trim strip to forward edge of plywood end piece.

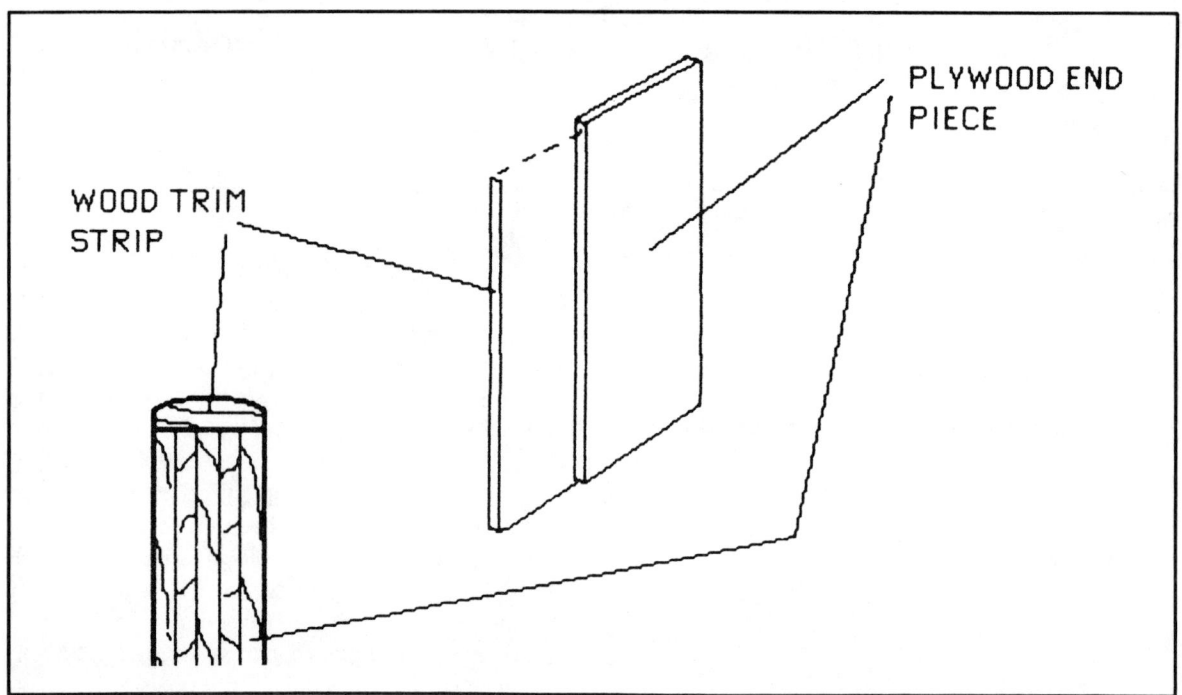

Fig. 3-75. Adding wood trim strip to forward edge of end piece.

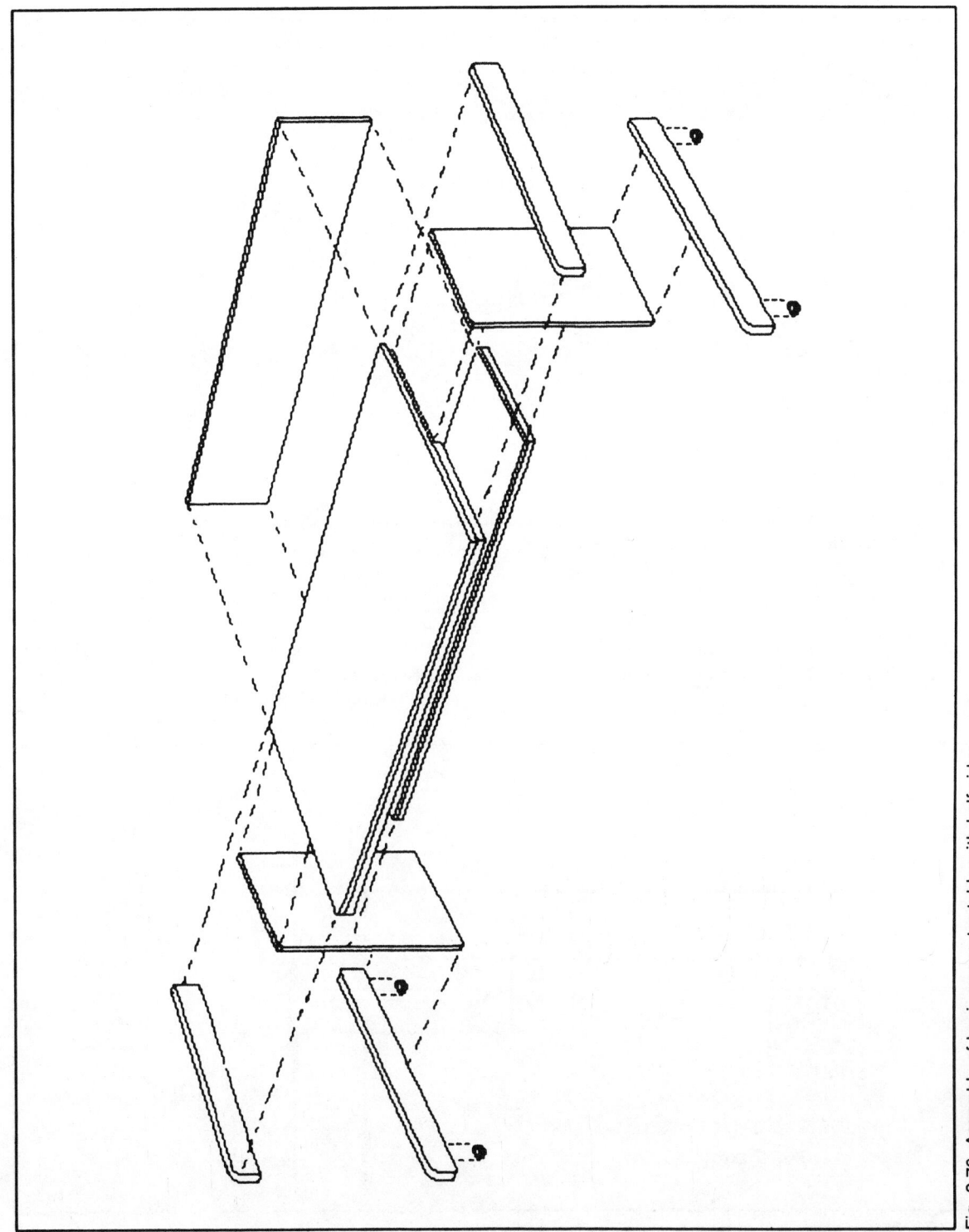
Fig. 3-76. Assembly of basic computer table with half sides.

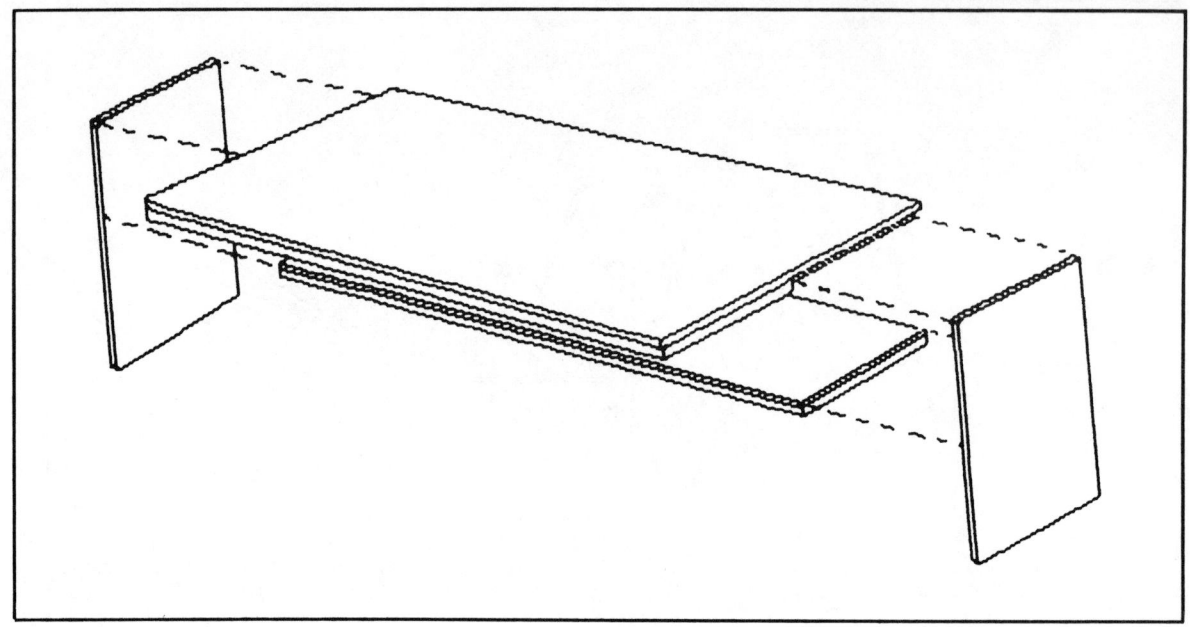

Fig. 3-77. Assembly of top and shelf to end pieces.

piece is truly rectangular and that the side pieces are perpendicular to the table top and shelf before the backing piece is attached and the glue allowed to set. Figure 3-81 shows the backing piece installed.

The side and floor beams are added next, as shown in Figure 3-82. These should be glued and through-bolted, as shown in Figs. 3-83, 3-84, 3-85, and 3-86. Figure 3-87 shows the side and floor beams installed on the table.

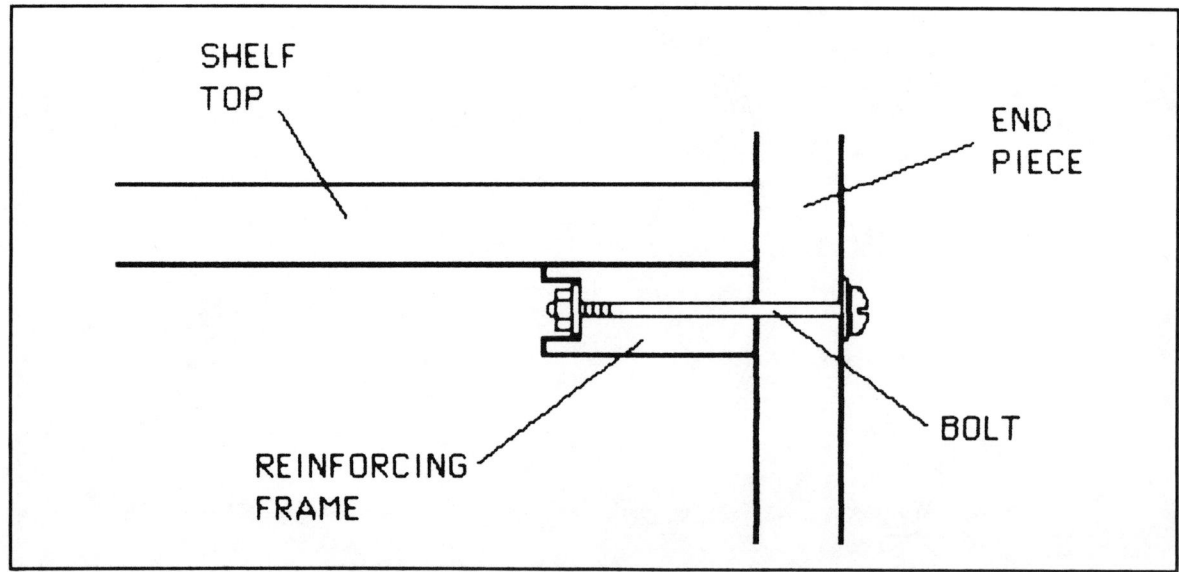

Fig. 3-78. Assembly of shelf to side pieces with bolts.

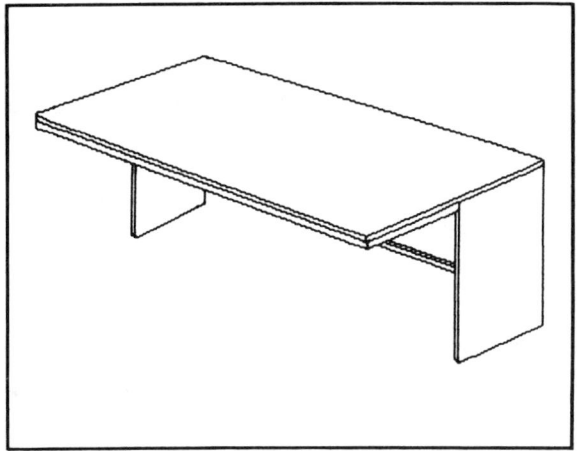

Fig. 3-79. Top and shelf assembled to end pieces.

The floor guides are installed next (see Fig. 3-88), depending on the type of floor guides selected. Some fit in a mounting drilled in the wood beam, others are driven or screwed into the wood, and still others have separate screw fasteners to hold them in place.

Sanding and Finishing

Sanding and finishing are important steps in the construction process. By taking care and a little time, even a beginner can give the table a professional finish.

Sanding is an important operation in preparing the wood for varnishing or painting. Small holes, checks, and open defects should be filled in before sanding. If a clear finish is to be applied, use a wood filler that matches the color of the wood. Always apply a sanding sealer to the plywood before sanding.

When sanding, work from coarse grits progressively to finer grits. Don't start with a grit that is coarser than necessary for the particular sanding, however. The condition of the surface might be such that you can start with a medium or even fine grit. Coarser grits tend to leave scratches that need to be sanded away with finer grits.

Wood sanding is done primarily parallel to the grain. Across the grain sanding leaves scratches and tends to tear and roughen the wood surface.

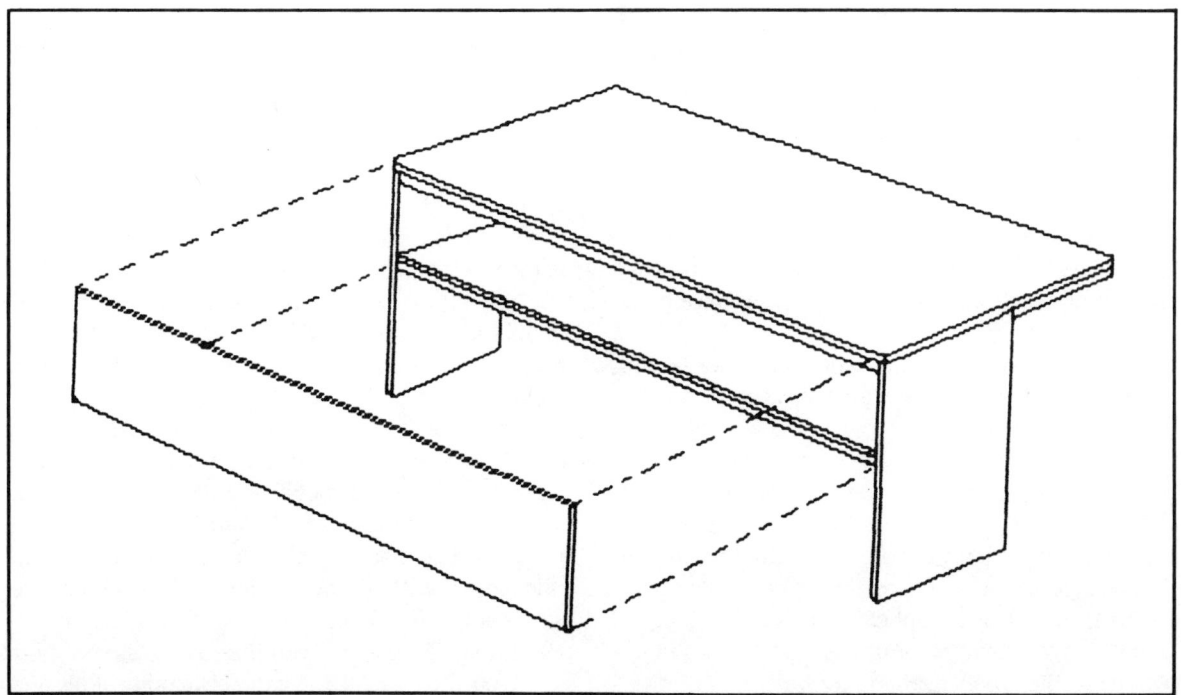

Fig. 3-80. Assembly of backing piece.

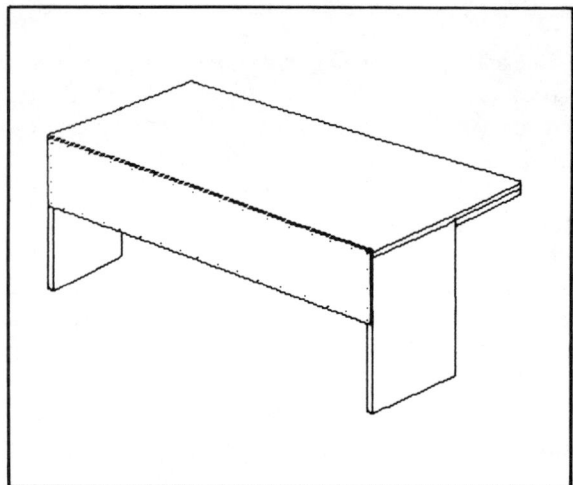

Fig. 3-81. Backing piece installed.

A scratch free surface is especially important if you are going to finish with oil or varnish.

For most hand sanding, especially on flat surfaces, use a sanding block rather than hold the sandpaper in your hand. Holding the sandpaper in your hand leaves a wavy surface on the wood because pressure is not applied evenly to all areas. A carpet or felt pad between the block and the sandpaper also helps.

At the final stages of sanding, use your eyes and fingertips to judge the smoothness of the surface. Taking special care with the sanding is an important step to a fine finish.

A power sander can be used. A pad sander is the easiest to use without damaging the wood surface. Belt sanders can be used by experienced operators.

A clear polyurethane plastic finish can be applied directly to natural wood, or you can first stain the wood to give it another color. Staining enhances and enriches the natural grains of wood.

Before applying stain, first test color on a scrap of similar wood. Clean the surface area where stain is to be applied, using a cloth to eliminate as much dust as possible. The stain can then be applied with a brush, foam brush applicator, or cloth. Apply a smooth, even coat of stain. Allow the stain to penetrate the wood. Depending on the humidity, temperature, and particular stain used, this usually takes from 5 to 15 minutes. While the stain is still wet, wipe off the excess stain with a clean cloth. Be careful not to remove too much from corners and edges. Wipe across the grain first so that you work the stain into the wood pores. Then give a final wipe with the grain. Allow the stain to dry. This usually takes at least 8 hours. The finish can then be applied.

It is usually best to apply a series of light, even coats of clear finish rather than one thick coat. This will minimize possible drips and wrinkles as the finish dries. Apply finish in brush-width strokes in the direction of wood grain. Turn table so that finish is applied to horizontal wood surfaces whenever possible.

A minimum of two coats is recommended. Allow 6 to 8 hours for the first coat to dry before applying second coat. Sand lightly and use a tack cloth to remove sanded finish dust before applying next coat of finish. Clear or stained finishes are usually applied to natural wood furniture, but paint finishes can also be applied.

Variations

Variations are possible for the basic computer table with half sides. One possibility is to substitute materials, using particle board instead of plywood for the top and/or other components. Another common variation is to construct the table with a different size of top.

You can also add additional storage shelves below the table and/or a drawer immediately below the table top. A popular shelf and storage arrangement is shown in Fig. 3-89. Construction of a similar table with a video and storage rack is detailed later in this chapter.

The basic computer table with half sides makes a functional and attractive computer table even when built from inexpensive woods. It's ideal for anyone who wants to build computer tables to sell to others, because the table can be sold either unfinished or with finish applied. More expensive woods, such as oak, can give the table a custom appearance. The plans given here show simple butt joints, but if you have the cabinet-making skills and know-how, you can also use more difficult joints.

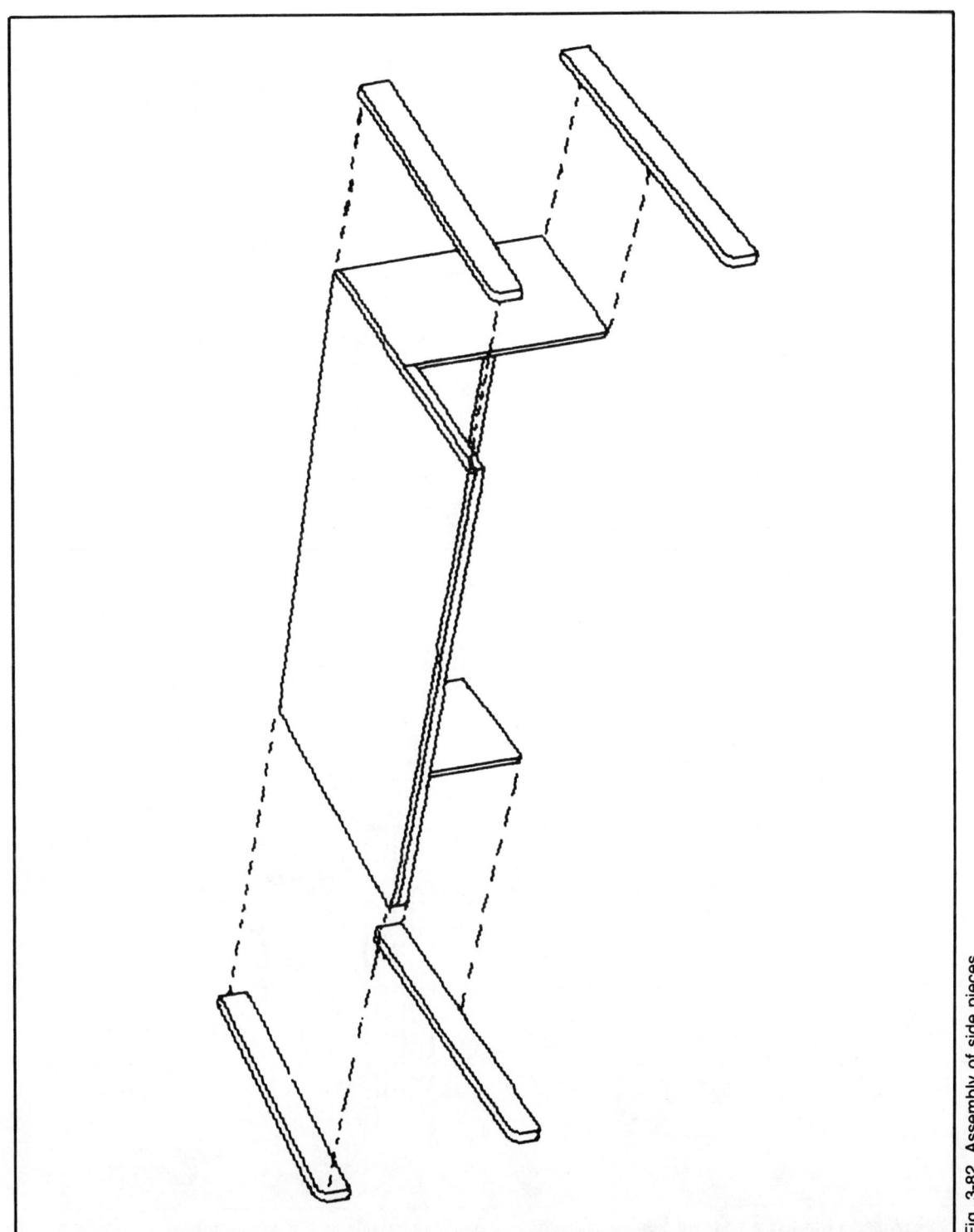

Fig. 3-82. Assembly of side pieces.

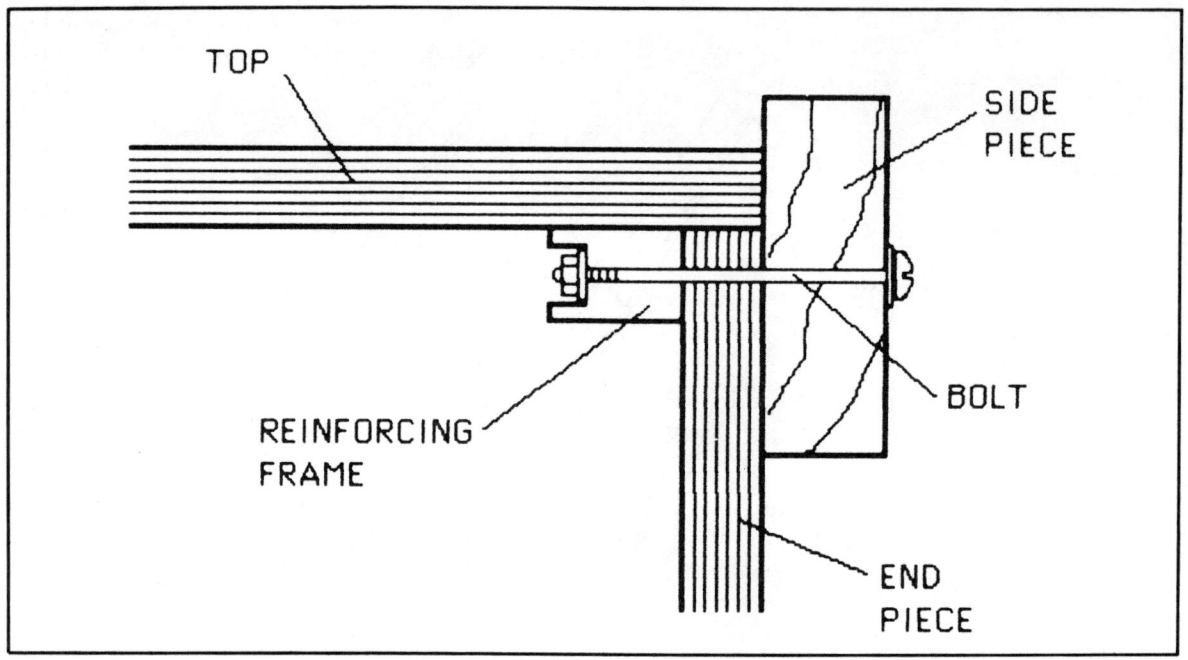

Fig. 3-83. Assembly of top to end and side pieces with bolts.

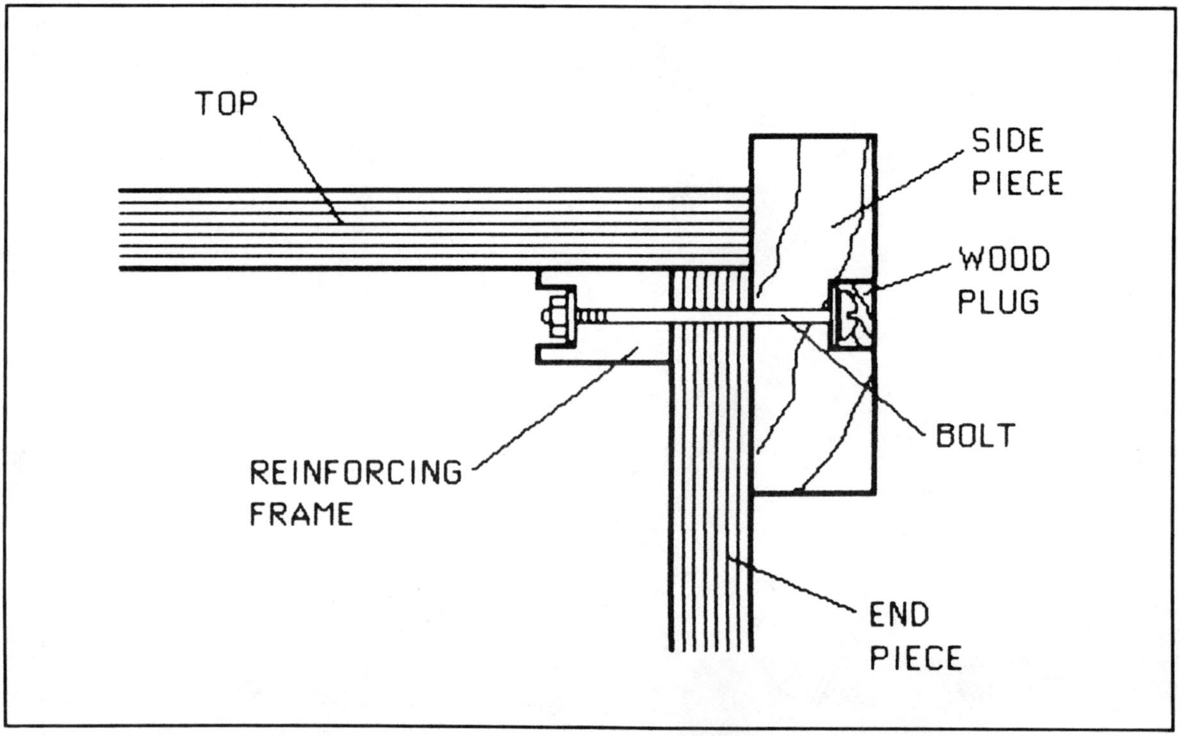

Fig. 3-84. Assembly of top to end and side pieces with bolt head countersunk and hole plugged.

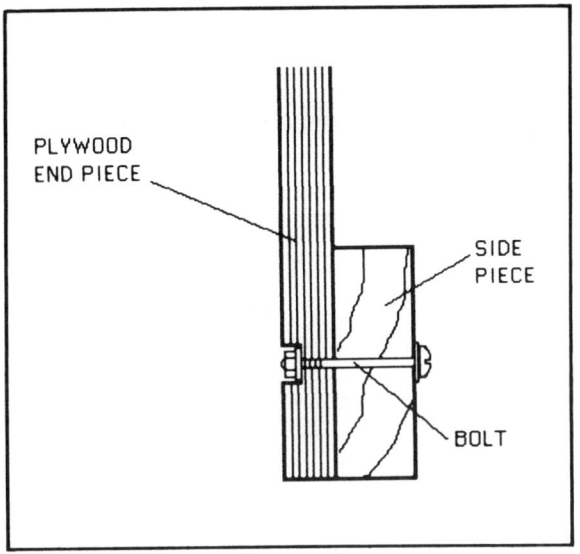

Fig. 3-85. Assembly of end and side pieces with bolts.

BASIC BUDGET COMPUTER TABLE WITH VIDEO AND STORAGE RACK

This is a basic budget computer table because it can be built from standard size pieces of plywood and lumber available from discount home building supply stores for a very low materials cost. I purchased the materials to build the one shown in Figs. 3-90 and 3-91 for $28 (in 1984). This table is similar to a model in ready-to-finish form that retails for about $150. From this, it is easy to see that large savings are possible by building your own. This computer table is attractive and modern even when built from low cost wood, but you can give it a custom appearance by making the same design from more expensive woods, such as birch or even better, oak.

The basic budget computer table with a video and storage rack is shown in Fig. 3-92. The top has space for both a computer and printer. The rack has a shelf for a video monitor and space to store computer disks, reference manuals, and so on. The table can have a natural wood top or a plastic laminate (Fig. 3-93) can be added. The table features a shelf underneath that provides storage space and gives the table added strength.

Materials

The patterns for the wood parts are shown in Fig. 3-94. The top of the table is a 2-foot-by-4-foot piece of 3/4-inch thick plywood. If you intend to use the wood surface as the finished table top, without a plastic laminate, hardwood faced plywood is recommended. If a laminate is to be added, even

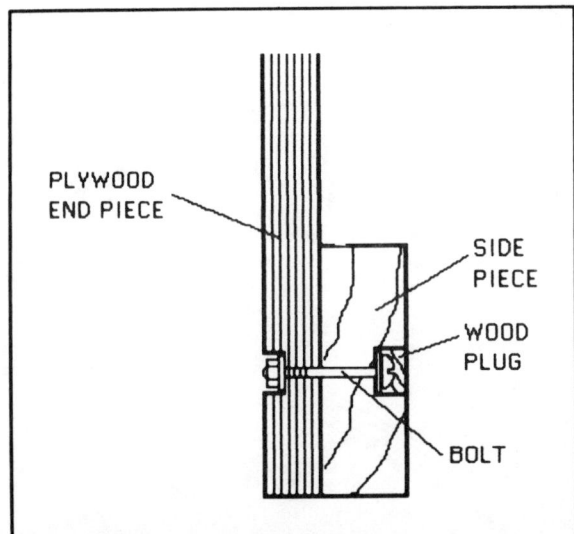

Fig. 3-86. Assembly of end and side pieces with bolt head countersunk and hole plugged.

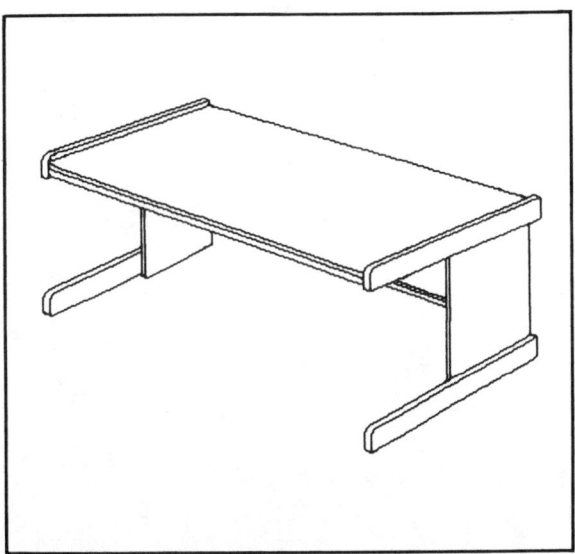

Fig. 3-87. Side pieces installed.

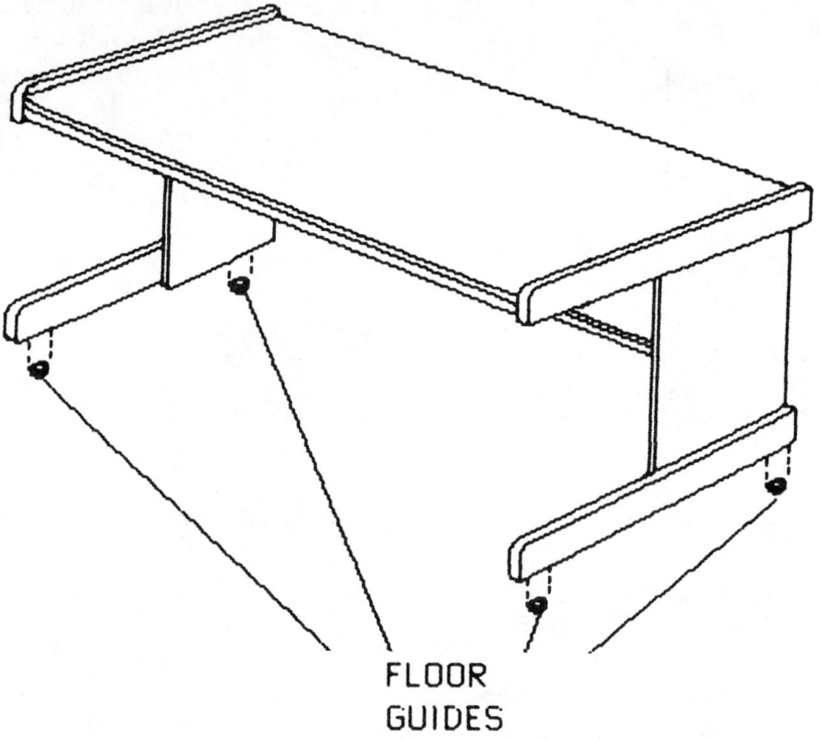

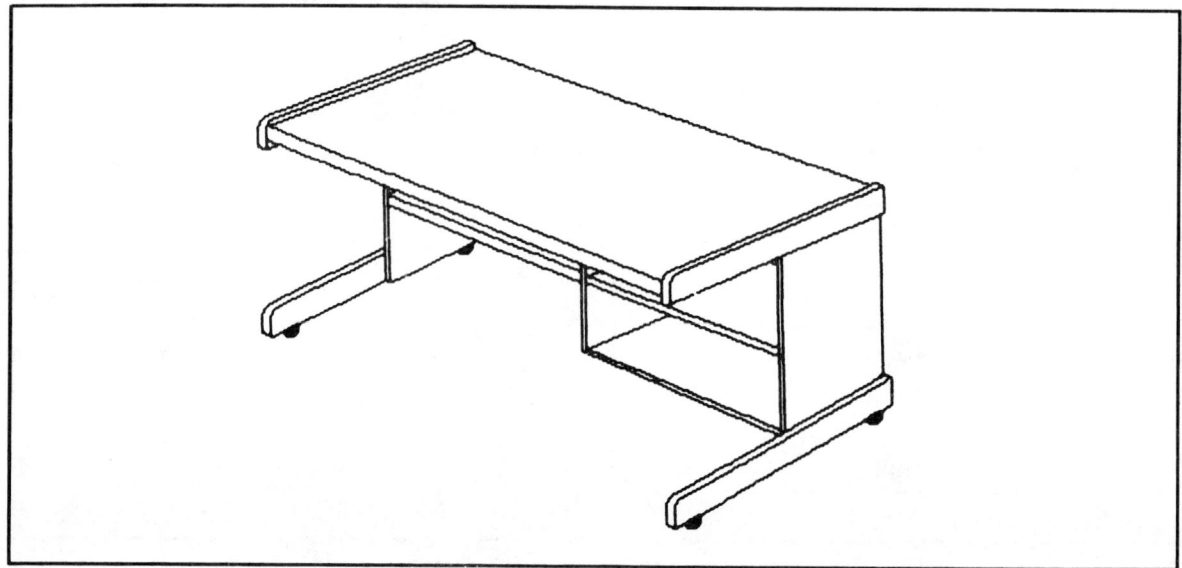

Fig. 3-88. Installing floor guides.

Fig. 3-89. Basic computer table with half sides with alternate shelf arrangement.

Fig. 3-90. Front view of the basic budget computer table with video and storage rack.

an exterior grade of shop plywood will suffice. Although plywood is normally sold in standard 4-foot-by-8-foot sheets, many home building and discount stores also offer 2-foot-by-4-foot cuts. If this size is purchased, no additional cutting will be necessary, thus making this project ideal for a beginner.

Although 1/2-inch thick plywood could also be used, I don't recommend this. The savings are small, and the table won't be as sturdy. Particle board can be substituted for the plywood if you are on an absolute minimum budget. Considerable numbers of low grade manufactured computer furniture are made from particle board covered by plastic laminates. Particle board can be difficult to work with, however, and it is very difficult to get plastic laminates to bond properly to this material without special equipment. (It seems difficult even with special machinery, because laminates on manufactured furniture always seem to come loose at the edges.)

The side pieces and shelf are 1-inch thick by 12-inch wide wood stock. These are the dimensions before the wood was surfaced, so the wood that you purchase will have slightly smaller dimensions. When fitting parts, make certain that you take this

Fig. 3-91. Another view of the basic budget computer table with video and storage rack.

into account. The length of the lower shelf should measure two wood thicknesses (1 3/4 inches) less than 48 inches, equalling about 46 1/4 inches. Be as exact as possible so that the shelf will fit properly between the end pieces. The top of the rack is the same wood stock cut 48 inches long. The shelf pieces for the rack are detailed in Fig. 3-94.

A height of 40 inches is shown for the side pieces. With the addition of the 3/4-inch thick table top, this will give a desk top height of 28 inches before floor guides are added, which will increase the height somewhat. The exact distance will depend on the type of floor guides used. You may want to have your table higher or lower than this because it is very important to have the height from the floor to the top of the keyboard correct for the user. Because table to keyboard heights vary from computer to computer, the proper table height for a user will vary depending on the particular computer used. Adjustable floor guides are available to adjust the height of the table within a limited range. Many typing tables are only about 26 inches high, and you may prefer to have your computer table this low, or you may want to do some experimenting before you decide on the height to build your computer table.

When selecting the wood stock, you can use a variety of woods, including pine, fir, and birch, but try to select wood that is as straight as possible and without cracks or other defects.

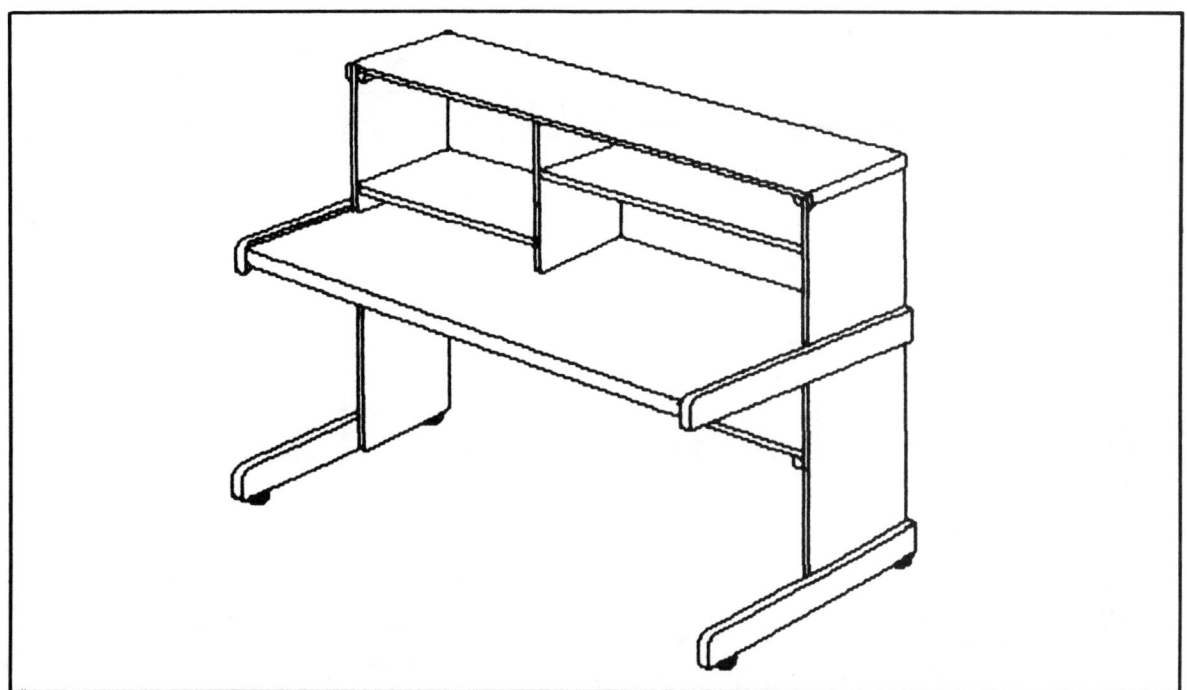

Fig. 3-92. Diagram of the basic budget computer table with video and storage rack.

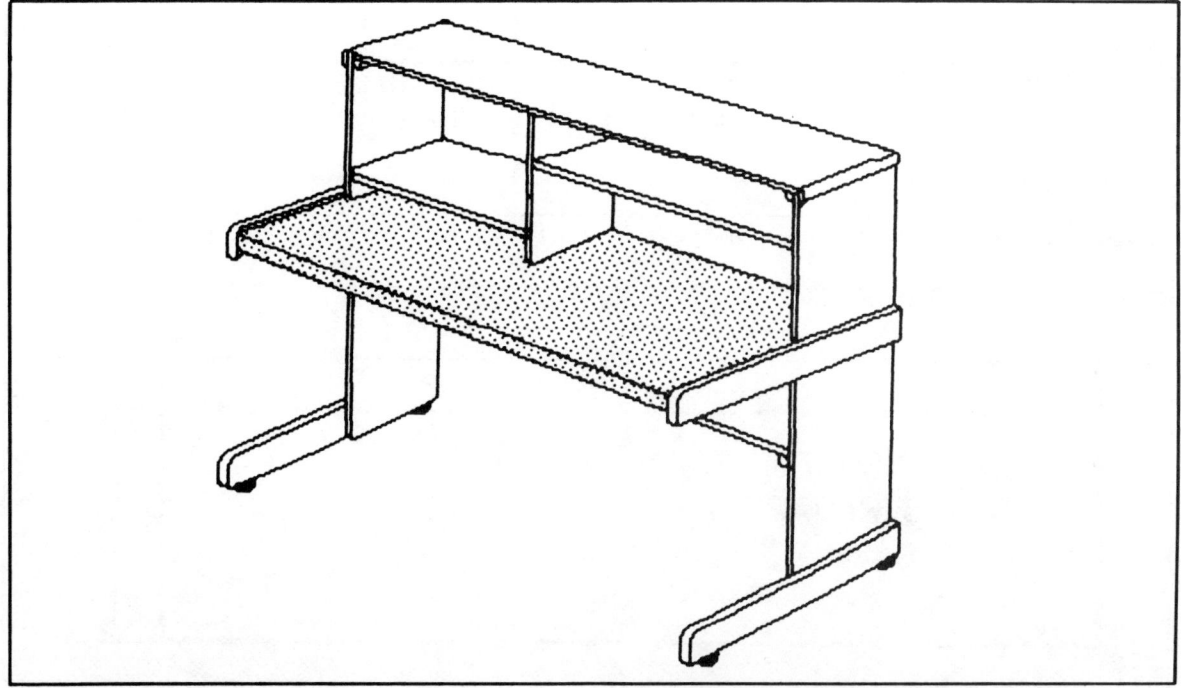

Fig. 3-93. Basic budget computer table with video and storage rack with plastic laminate.

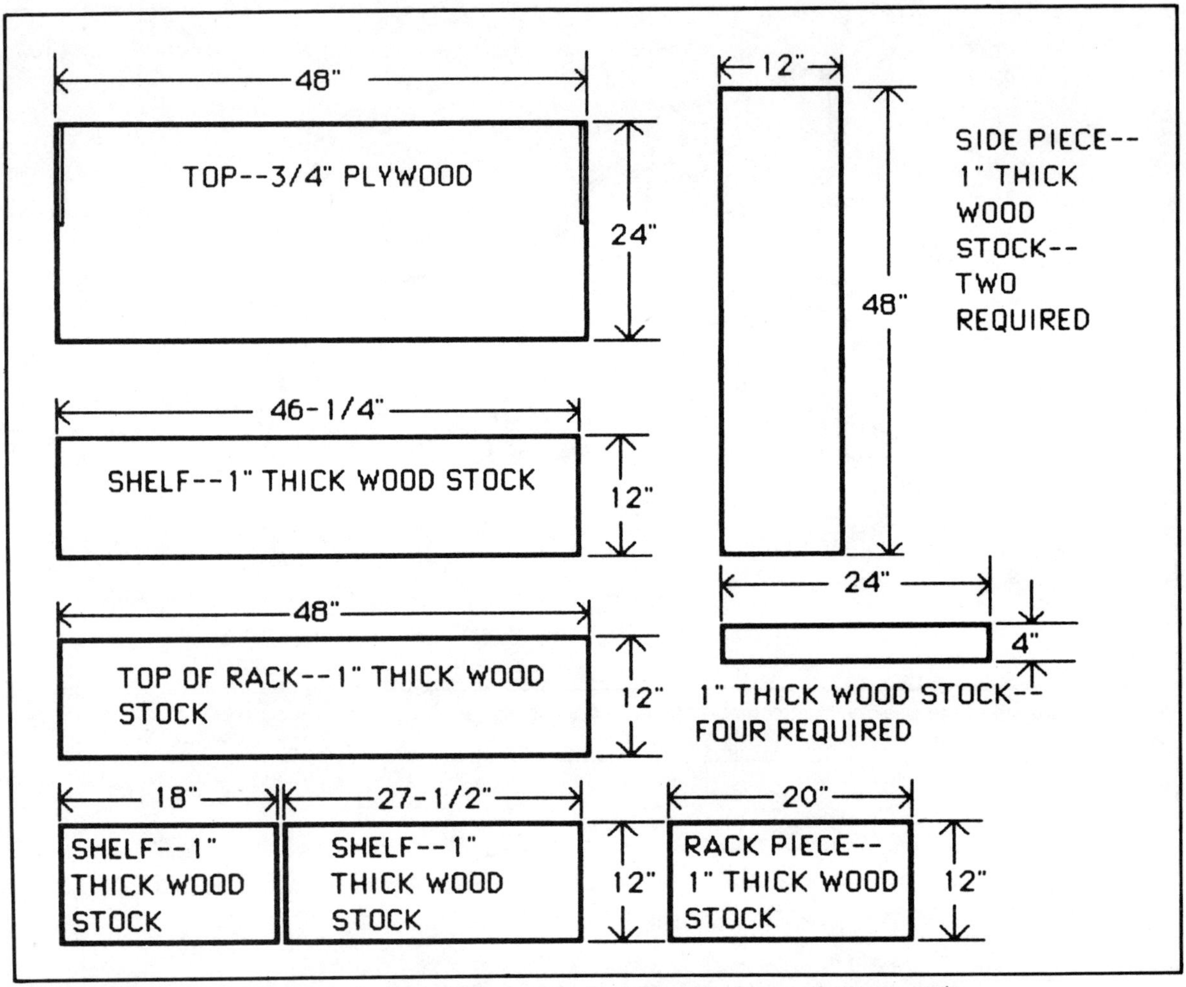

Fig. 3-94. Patterns for wood parts for basic budget computer table with video and storage rack.

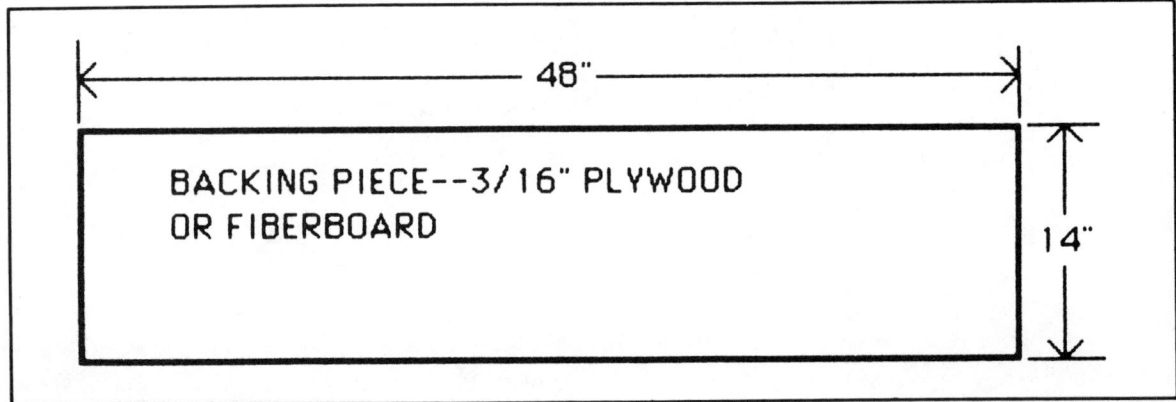

Fig. 3-95. Pattern for backing piece.

The end pieces or beams are 1-inch thick by 4-inch wide wood stock (dimensions before the wood was surfaced; the measurements of the wood you buy will be slightly less than these). You will need four of these, 24 inches long. The beams form a base of support for the table, add strength, and give a decorative appearance.

The backing piece (Fig. 3-95) can be either plywood or fiberboard. The backing piece is used to strengthen the table base and hold the frame in rectangular form. A 14-inch height is shown for the backing piece, but this will vary depending on how far below the top you wish to place the shelf. A minimum distance of 12 inches between the top plywood and the shelf is recommended to give the table base adequate strength. Notice that the top, shelf, backing piece, and side pieces form a box with the forward side open.

You will also need 1-inch-by-2-inch or larger framing stock for use under the plywood table top and as cleats under the ends of the shelf. Cleats of 1-inch-by-1-inch wood stock are used at the ends of the top piece for the rack. A wood or plastic trim strip is used to cover the forward edge of the table top. This piece is 48 inches long and about 1 3/4 inches wide (the minimum width should be such that it will completely cover the widths of the plywood top (3/4 inch) and the framing (approximately 7/8 inch). It can be slightly wider than this. Trim strips are also added to the sides of the top section of the rack, as detailed later in this section.

Four fixed or adjustable floor pods or guides are used on the floor beams. Many good types are available from hardware stores.

Finishing nails and other fasteners are required for assembly. You will also need a good wood glue. Finish the table with clear urethane, varnish, or paint.

The top can be left natural or a plastic laminate can be added. If a plastic laminate is applied, you will need a 2-foot-by-4-foot piece and contact cement.

Construction

An overview of the complete assembly is shown in Fig. 3-96. Begin by constructing the table top. If the plywood was already cut to the 2-foot-by-4-foot size, no additional cutting will be required, assuming that it was cut accurately and is a true rectangle. You might want to check this with a square.

If you purchased a larger piece of plywood, cut out a section for the table top. It is usually best to have the grain of the top layer running lengthwise, but this is not essential if you are going to add a plastic laminate. In most cases, you will use two factory cut edges for your table top and cut the other two. Use a ruler and square to make the pattern, marking the lines with a sharp pencil or scribing tool. Also mark the pattern for the side board cutouts.

Sawing plywood requires special considerations: special care must be taken to avoid chipping and splintering along the cut edge. Handsaws or power saws with special fine-toothed or carbide-tipped blades designed especially for plywood should be used. A strip of masking tape applied over the area to be cut, especially the underside, will prevent chipping. Or, clamp a solid piece of wood to the underside and make the cut through both the plywood and the piece of wood.

Be extremely careful when sanding plywood edges. Use a sanding block and avoid sanding the surfaces until a wood sealer has been applied.

The next step is to add the reinforcing frame to the plywood table top, as shown in Fig. 3-97. Use a ruler and a square to mark the patterns on the framing wood, drawing the lines with a sharp pencil or marking tool. Then make the necessary saw cuts. The frame pieces should be glued and nailed or screwed in position. In a natural wood plywood top (without a plastic laminate), the fasteners should go through the framing and into the plywood, being careful that they do not pass all the way through the plywood or leave a bulge in the upper surface. If a good acrylic or epoxy glue is used, the glue alone should give adequate strength. In this instance, the fasteners are mainly used as clamping devices for the gluing. Fasteners will not have much holding power; to give greater holding power, the fasteners can be passed through the plywood

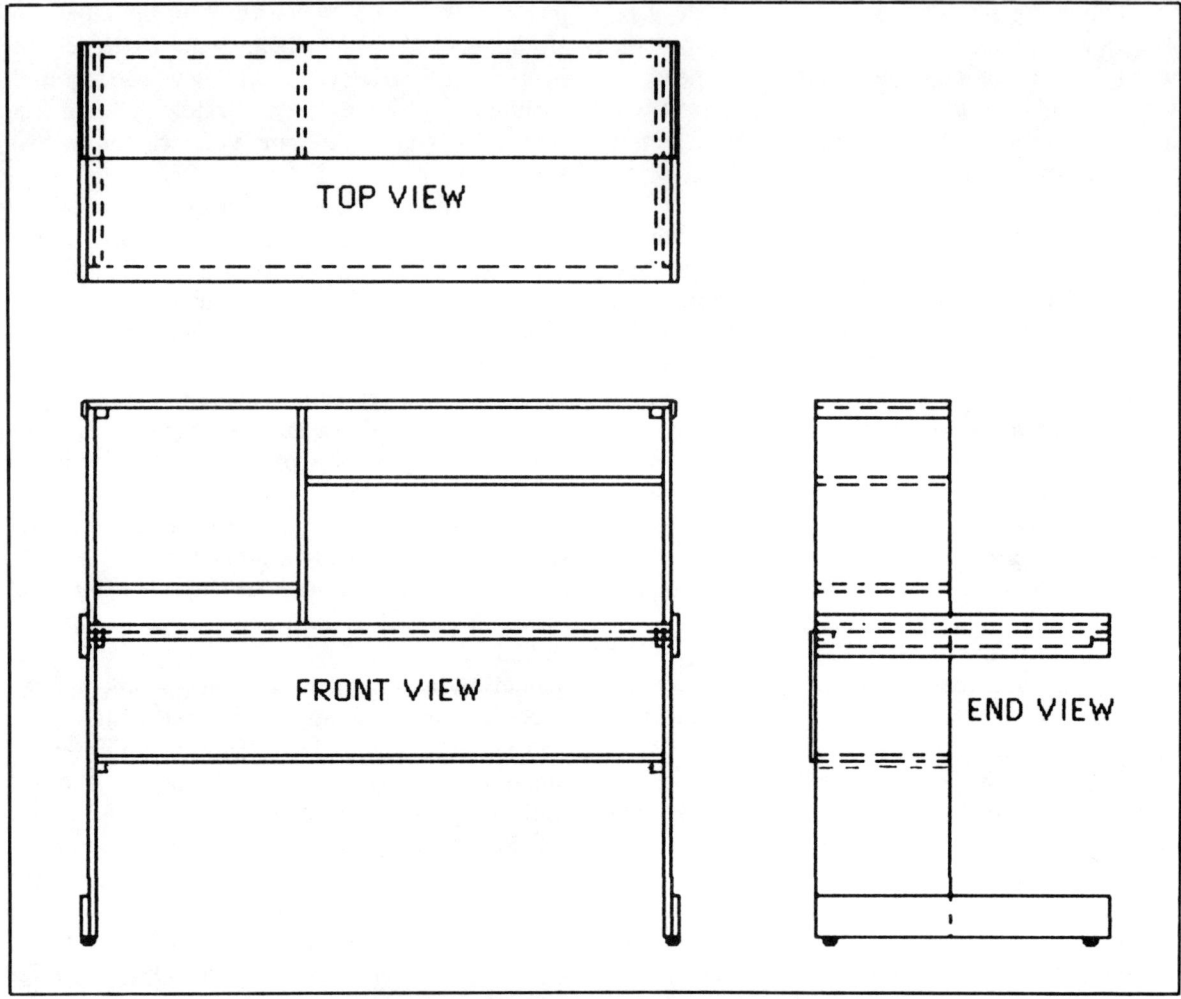

Fig. 3-96. Assembly of basic budget computer table with video and storage rack.

and into the framing if a plastic laminate will be added.

If you want a plastic laminate table top, it is installed at this time. Despite the large selection, I suggest using only high quality plastic laminates for computer table tops.

If a plastic laminate is to also be applied to the forward edge of the table top, it should be applied first, then finished flush with the table top. The top laminate is then applied so that the edge overlaps the top edge of the laminate on the forward edge of the table.

The plastic laminate is installed as follows:

• All holes and defects in the surface of the plywood should be filled with putty or wood filler.

• Sand the surface to be covered. This will help ensure good adhesion.

• Mark the plastic laminate to a pattern slightly larger than the area to be covered. Use a straightedge and draw the pattern lines on the finished or pattern side of the laminate. Leave 1/4 inch to 1/2 inch on all sides. This will be trimmed off later.

• If a laminate will be applied to the forward edge of the table, apply this first. After installation, as detailed below, trim and file the upper edge of

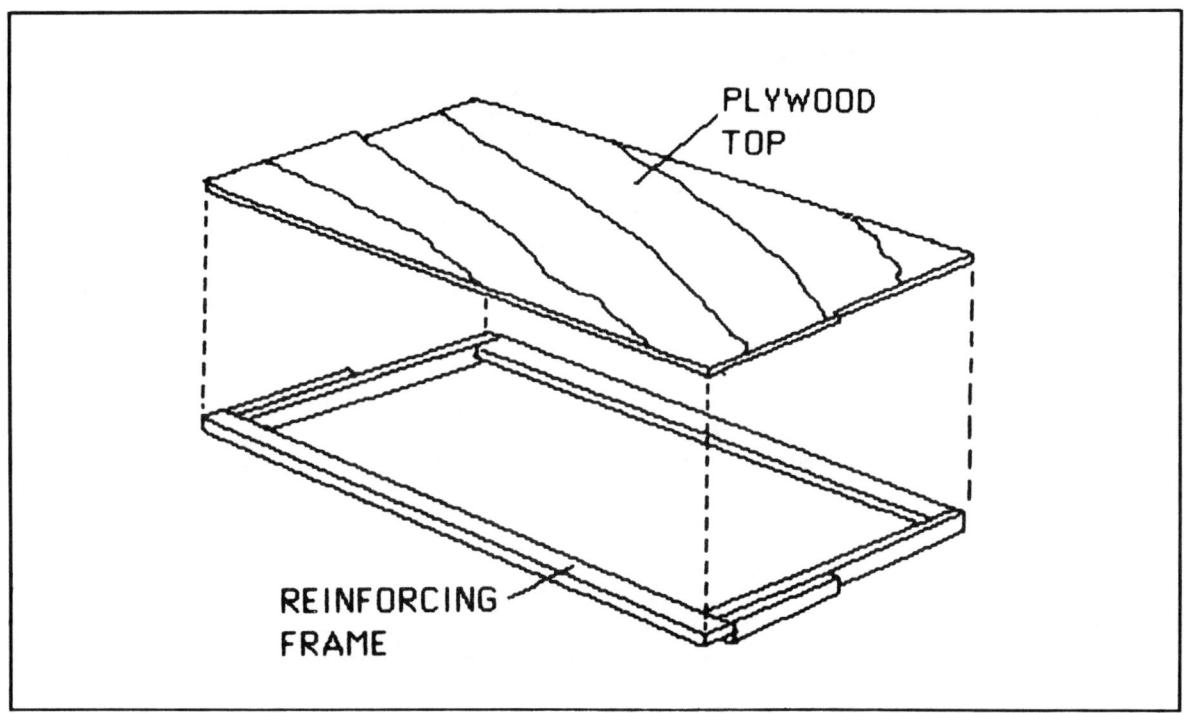

Fig. 3-97. Assembly of table top to reinforcing frame.

the plastic laminate flush with the upper edge of the plywood table top before installing the plastic laminate to upper surface of the table top.

- Cut the plastic laminate to the pattern marked. Even though the plastic laminate is extremely durable once applied, it is vulnerable to cracking and splitting before it is cemented in place. Fine-tooth handsaws or power saws with fine-tooth blades can be used; a rotary power saw with a 14 to 16 teeth per inch blade is ideal. Place the plastic laminate face up when cutting. Care should be taken so that the plastic laminate is not chipped or broken. An alternate method is to use a carbide tip knife for scoring the plastic by drawing the knife point along a metal straightedge. Cut through the decorative surface. The laminate can be broken by bending it toward the decorative surface side over the edge of a table or workbench.
- Apply contact cement to the surface of the plywood to be covered and the back side of the plastic laminate with a brush, roller, or metal spreader with a serrated edge. A thin even application is important.
- Follow the manufacturer's instructions regarding drying time, usually about 20 to 30 minutes.
- Place a sheet of heavy wrapping paper over the plywood surface to be covered. Then position the laminate on the plywood surface with the paper between. The contact cement will not stick to the paper if it has been allowed to dry properly. Make certain that the laminate is positioned correctly. Once the two surfaces of contact cement touch, the laminate sheet cannot be moved again. When everything is lined up properly, pull the paper out from between the plywood and the plastic laminate.
- Using a small block of wood and a hammer, lightly tap the laminate in place. An alternate method is to use a rolling pin.
- Use a file to remove the surplus plastic laminate from the edges. Another method is to use a special cutter/router that allows you to trim excess plastic laminate to flush with the plywood edges.

• The thinner recommended for the contact cement can be used to clean contact cement from wood, plastic laminate, and tools.

Next, cut the wood for the shelf to length. It should be 48 inches long, minus the combined widths of the two side pieces. You will need to measure and cut this accurately so that the side pieces will be exactly perpendicular to the top when the table is assembled. The ends of the shelf should be perpendicular to the sides of the wood. Use a square as a guide for marking pattern lines.

Next, cut 1-inch-by-2-inch wood cleats to length, as shown in Fig. 3-98. These should match the depth of the shelf, as shown. Glue and nail these to the bottom of the shelf.

The wood piece for the top of the rack is 48 inches long. This should match the length of the plywood table top exactly. The end cuts should be perpendicular to the sides of the wood. Use a square as a guide for marking pattern lines. Next, cut two 1-inch-by-1-inch cleats to length. Glue and nail these to the top of the rack at a distance equal to the width of the end piece from the end of the top piece.

The table top, shelf, and top of the rack are then assembled to the side pieces, as shown in Fig. 3-99. The end pieces should first be cut to desired length. The side pieces are then glued and fastened to the top, shelf, and top of rack frame members and cleats. Different fasteners can be used. If using finishing nails, drive them through the side pieces and into the frame members and cleats. These can be set below the wood surface and wood filler used to cover and hide the nail heads. If you use screws or bolts, washers can be used and heads and nuts can extend beyond the surface of the wood. Or the heads and/or nuts can be countersunk below the surface of the wood. Wood plugs can be

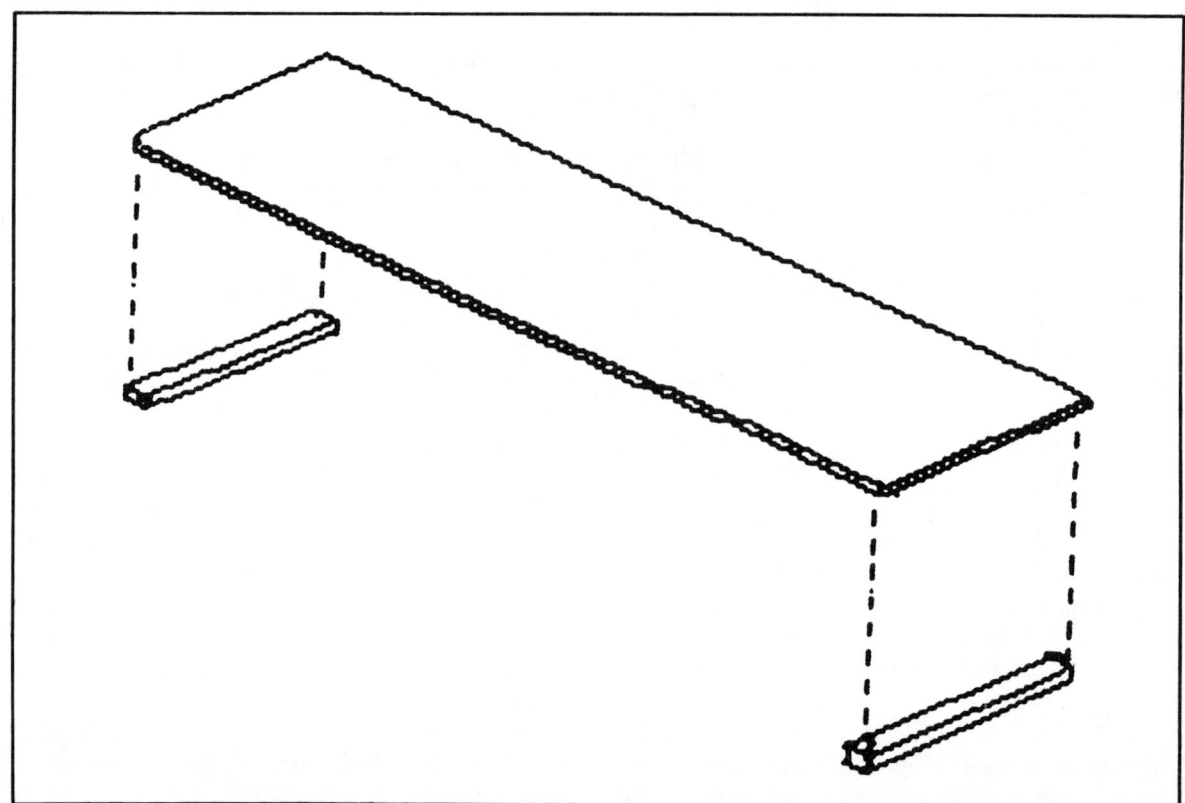

Fig. 3-98. Assembly of cleats to shelf.

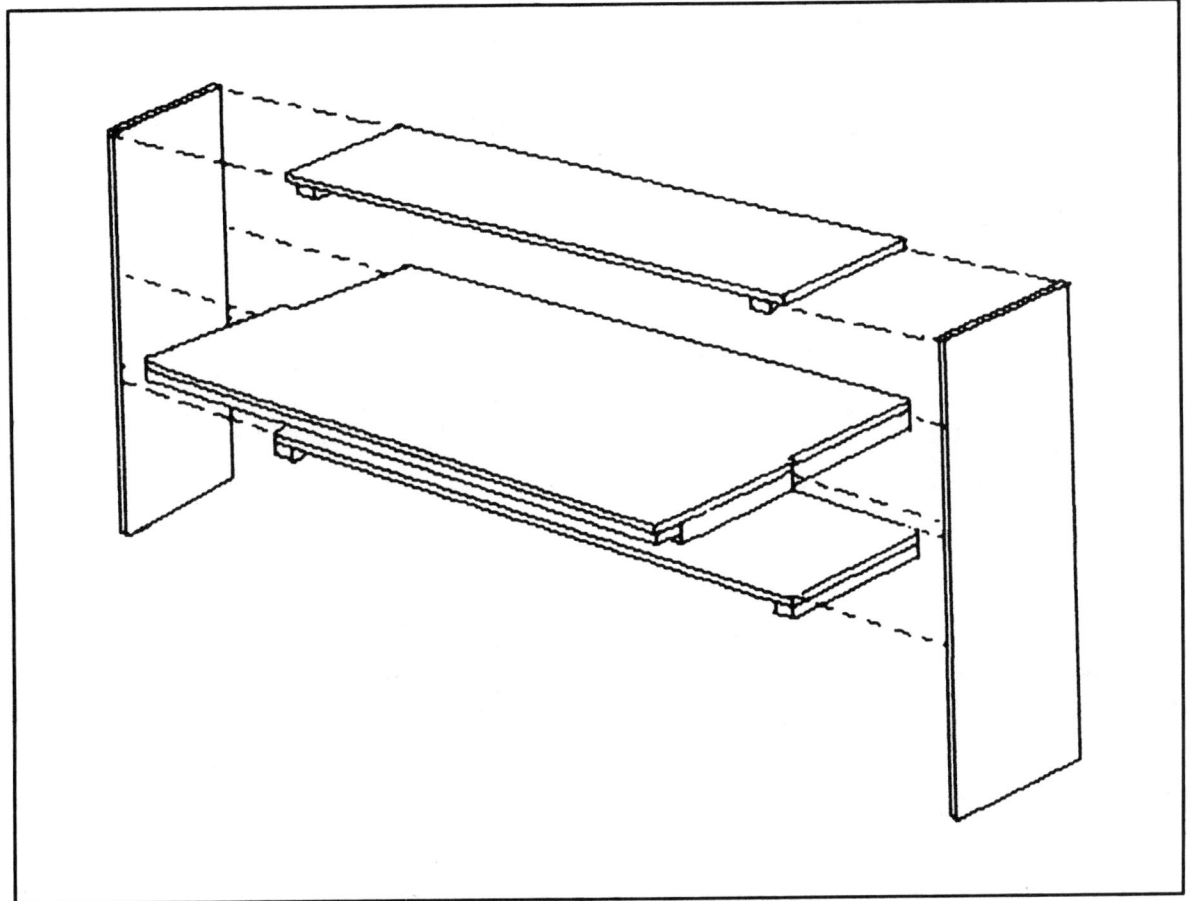

Fig. 3-99. Assembly of top and shelves to end pieces.

used to cover the holes and hide the fasteners, if desired.

Regardless of how you fasten, it is extremely important to install the side pieces perpendicular to the table top, shelf, and top of rack in a crosswise direction. Use a square to make pattern lines on the side pieces. It is also important to have exactly the same distance between the top and shelf on both sides and the table top and rack top on both sides. The distance between the table top and shelf can be whatever you like, but a minimum of 12 inches is required for adequate strength.

Figure 3-100 shows the shelf, table top, and rack top assembled to the end pieces. The next step is to add the backing piece, as shown in Fig. 3-101. The backing piece forms a box with the top, shelf, and side pieces, and it is important that the backing piece be attached securely to the wood members all the way around the edges. The backing piece is glued and nailed into position (Fig. 3-102). It is extremely important to make certain that the backing piece is true and that the side pieces are perpendicular to the table top and shelf before the backing piece is attached and the glue allowed to set.

If a plastic laminate was not added to the forward edge of the table previously, regardless of whether the top is natural wood or covered with a plastic laminate, the next step is to add a wood or plastic trim strip to the forward edge of the table top (Fig. 3-103). If plastic is used, it can be glued in place and/or installed with fasteners. A wood trim strip can be attached with glue and finishing

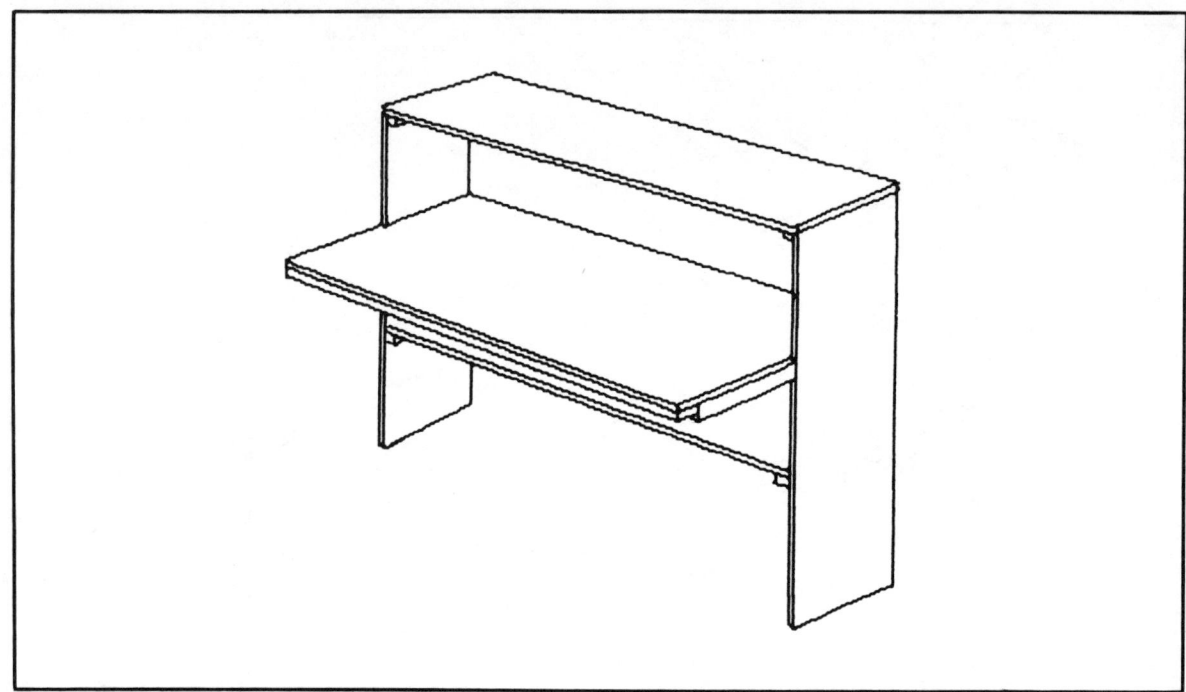

Fig. 3-100. Top and shelves assembled to end pieces.

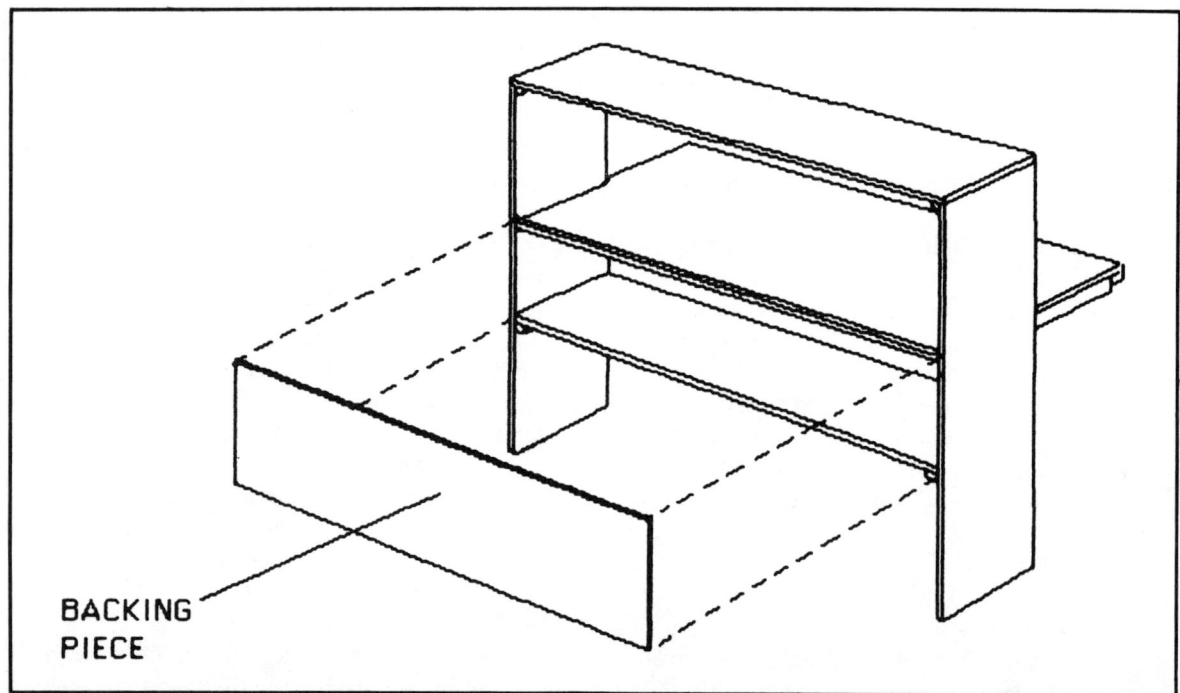

BACKING PIECE

Fig. 3-101. Assembly of backing piece.

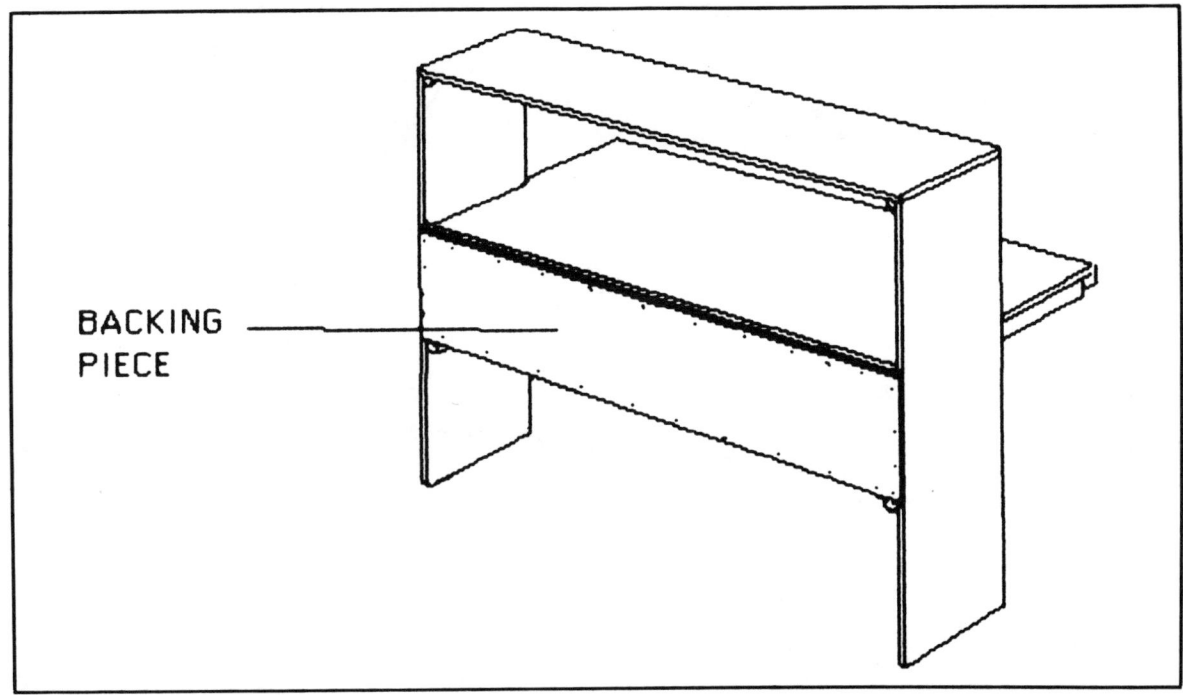
Fig. 3-102. Backing piece installed.

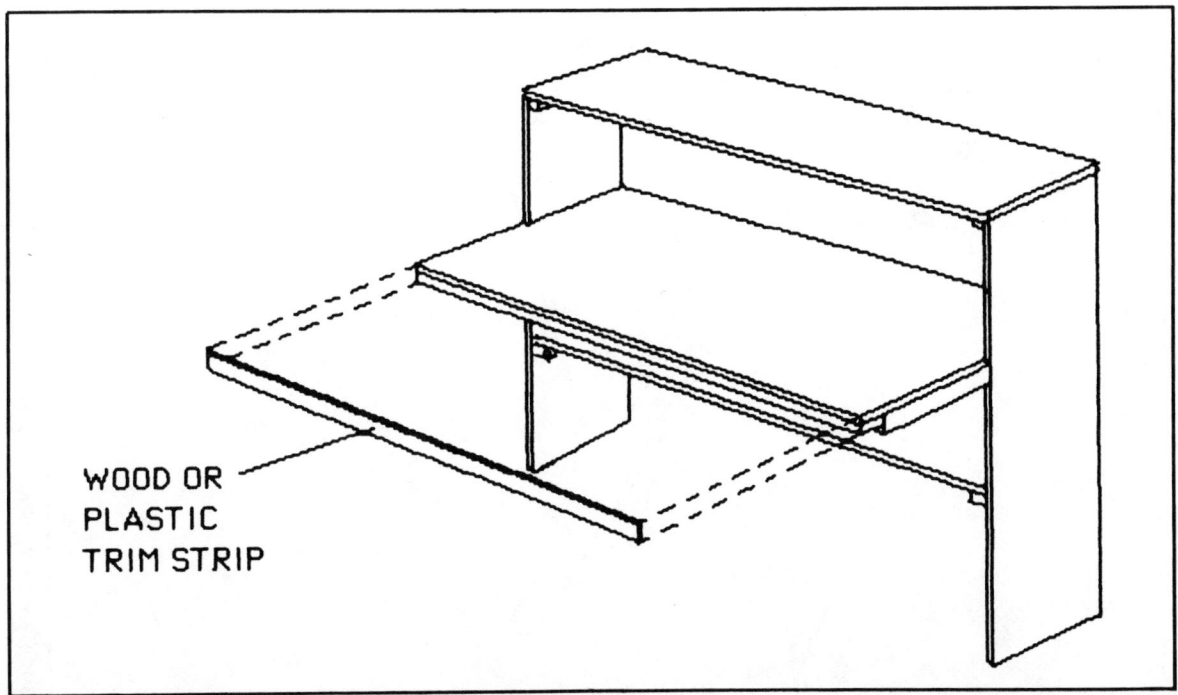
Fig. 3-103. Adding wood or plastic trim strip to front edge of table.

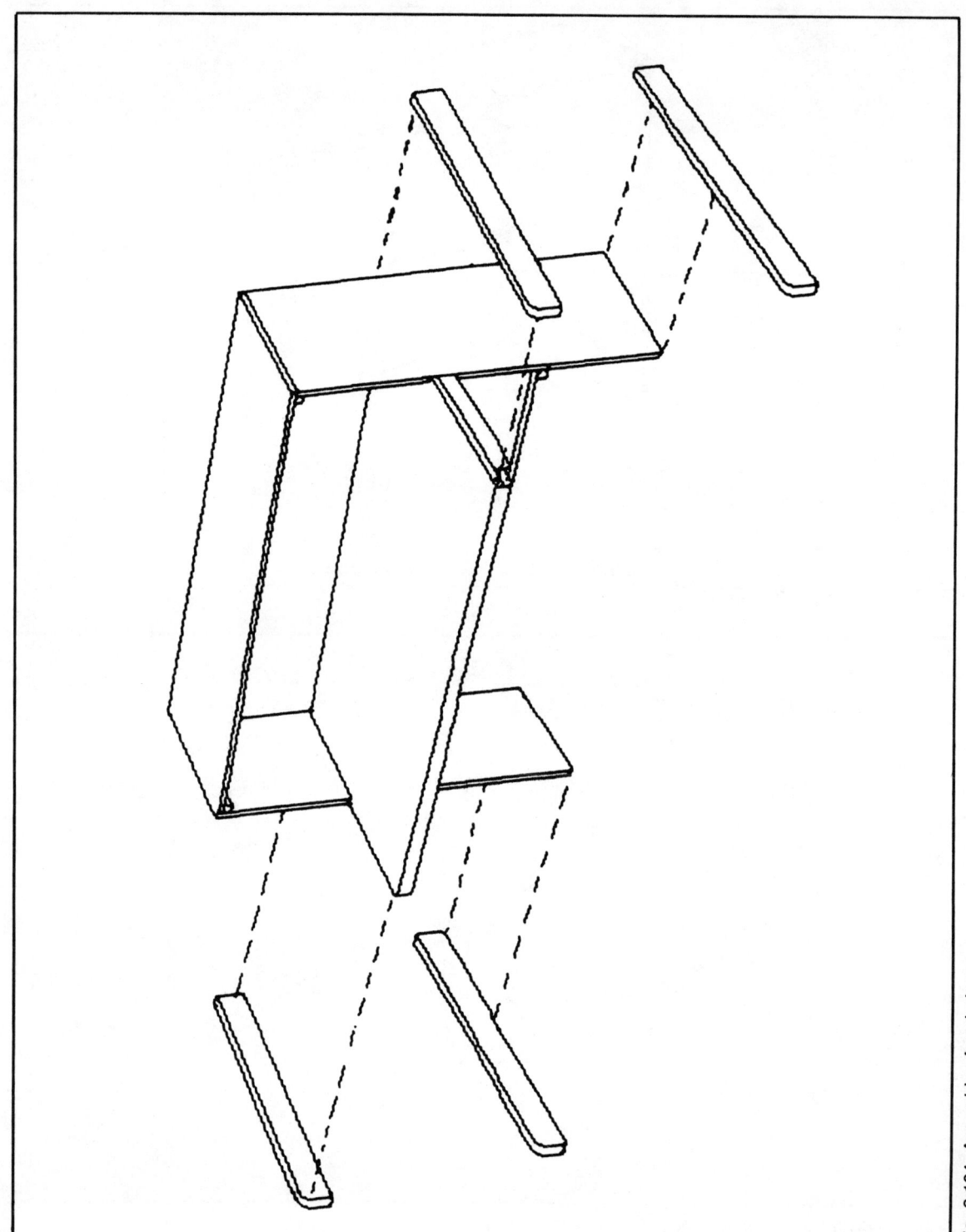

Fig. 3-104. Assembly of end pieces.

nails. Set the heads below the wood surface and fill holes in with wood filler to flush with the wood surface.

The wood end pieces or beams are installed next, as shown in Fig. 3-104. Glue and use mechanical fasteners to make the joint (Fig. 3-105). One method is to use finishing nails that first pass through the end pieces and into the side pieces or reinforcing frame. Set the heads below the wood surface and fill holes in flush with wood filler. An alternate method is to fasten the end pieces with wood screws or through bolts.

Figure 3-106 shows the end pieces assembled to the sides.

The next step is to install the vertical piece and shelves in the rack, as shown in Figs. 3-107 and 3-108.

Trim pieces are installed at the top ends of the rack as shown in Fig. 3-109. Glue and fasten with finishing nails, setting the heads below the surface of the wood. Fill the holes with wood filler. The table is shown in Fig. 3-110 with the rack and end and trim pieces installed.

The floor guides are installed to the floor beams as shown in Fig. 3-111. This installation will depend on the type of floor guides selected, whether mounted in the wood beam, driven or screwed into the wood, or with separate screw fasteners holding them in place.

Sanding and Finishing

Sanding and applying a finish are important steps in the construction process. Many beginners do a good job constructing the table up to this point,

Fig. 3-105. End piece is glued and nailed in place.

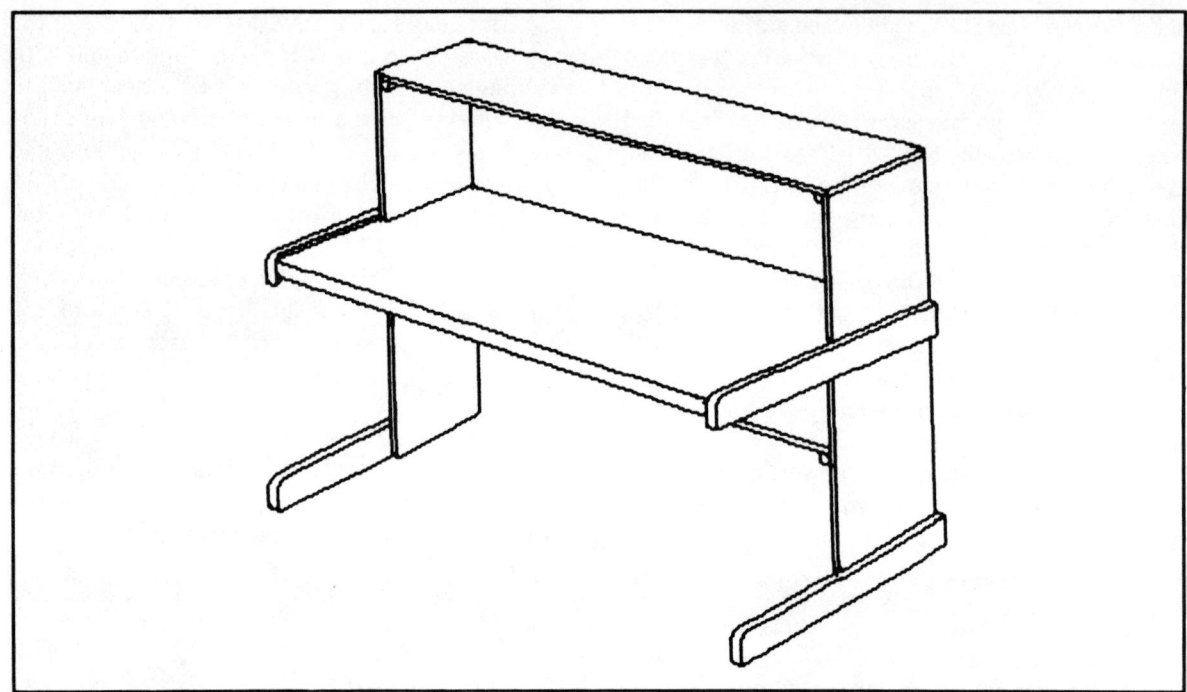

Fig. 3-106. End pieces assembled to sides.

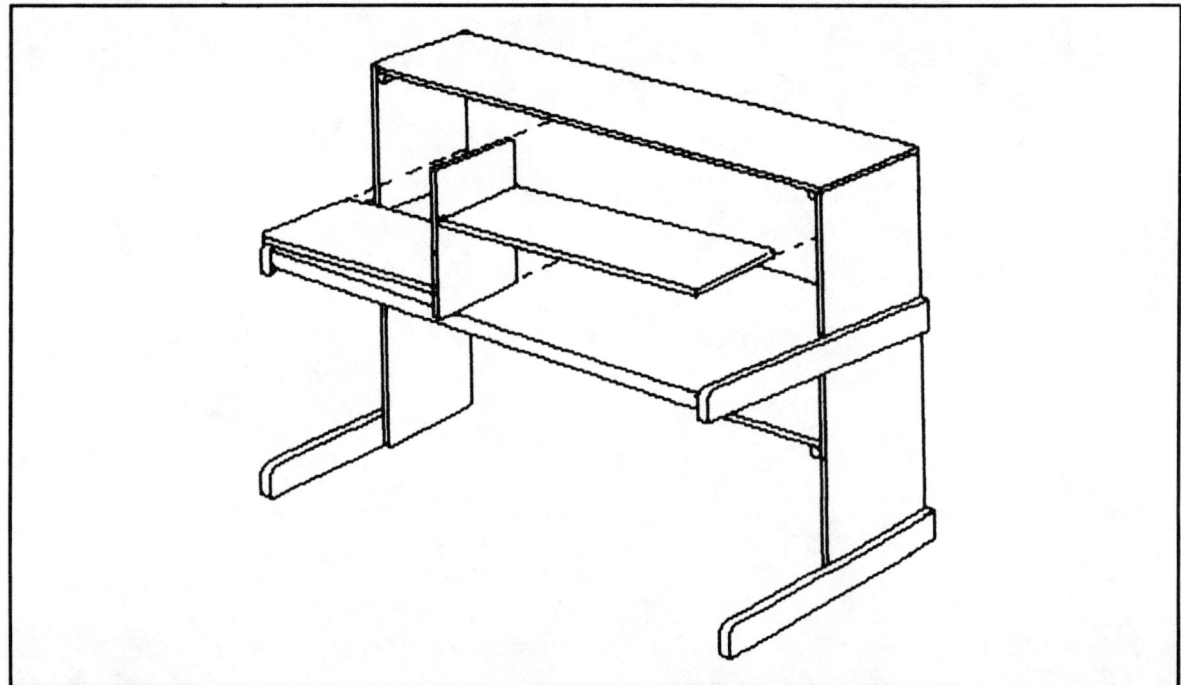

Fig. 3-107. Installing shelves in rack.

Fig. 3-108. Shelves installed in rack.

but give the table a very amateur appearance by sloppy application of a finish. With care and a little time, however, even a beginner can give the table a professional finish.

Sanding is an important operation in preparing the wood for varnishing or painting. Small holes, checks, and other open defects in the wood should be filled. If a clear finish is to be applied, use a wood filler that matches the color of the wood. A sanding sealer should be applied before doing any sanding on the surface.

The general principle to follow for sanding is to work from coarse grits progressively to finer grits. Don't start with a grit that is coarser than necessary for the particular sanding; the condition of the surface might be such that you can start with a medium or even fine grit. Coarser grits leave scratches that must be sanded away with finer grits.

Sand wood parallel to the grain. Across the grain sanding leaves scratches and tends to tear and roughen the wood surface. A scratch free surface is especially important if you are going to finish with oil or varnish.

For most hand sanding, especially on flat surfaces, use a sanding block. Holding the sandpaper in your hand tends to leave a wavy surface on the wood because pressure is not applied evenly to all areas. A carpet or felt pad between the block and the sandpaper also helps.

At the final stages of sanding, most craftsmen use their fingertips to judge the smoothness of the surface. You can also judge by looking if you use

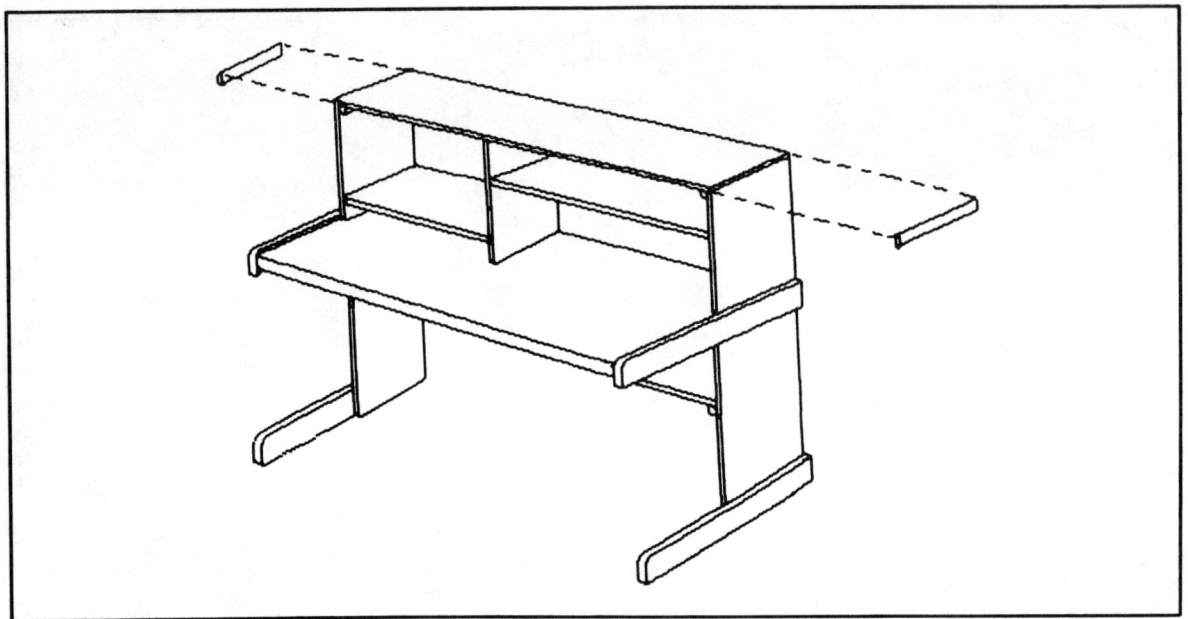

Fig. 3-109. Installing rack trim pieces.

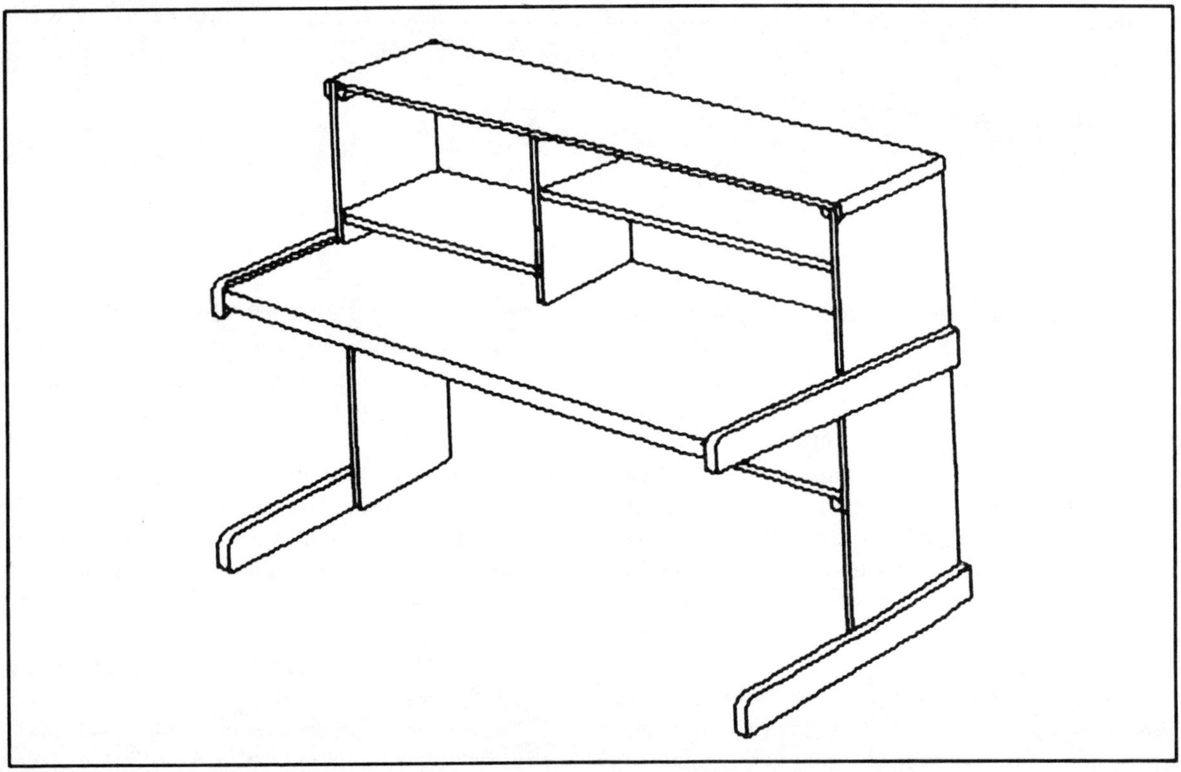

Fig. 3-110. Basic budget computer table with video and storage rack with end pieces installed.

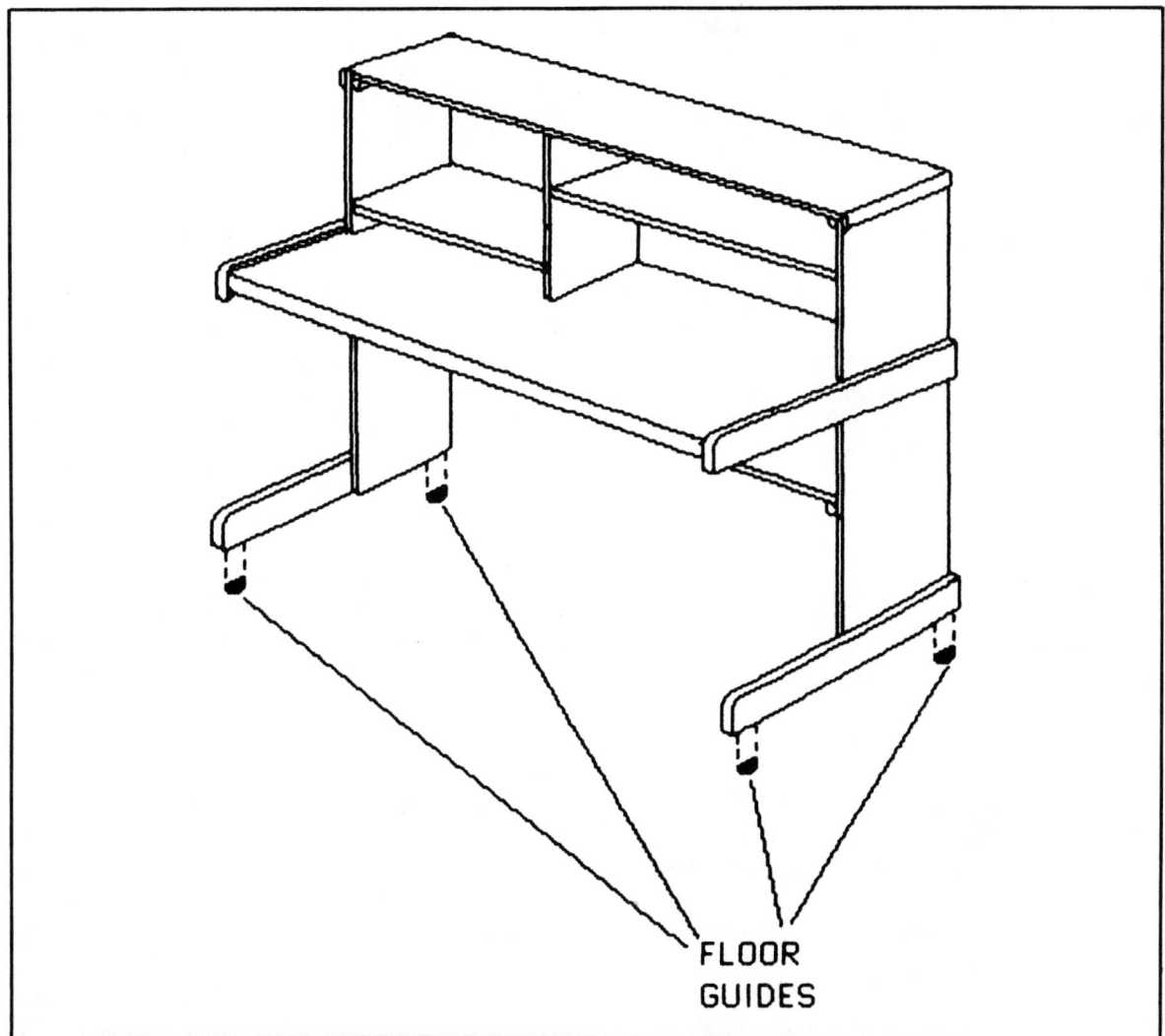

Fig. 3-111. Installing floor guides.

a light held at a low angle to the wood surface. Taking special care with the sanding is an important step to a fine finish of which you will be proud.

If desired, a power sander can be used. A pad sander is the easiest to use without damaging the wood surface. Belt sanders can be used by experienced operators.

A clear finish (polyurethane plastic is ideal) can be applied directly to natural wood, or you can first stain the wood another color to enhance the natural grains or enrich relatively lifeless woods.

Before applying stain, test color on a scrap piece. Clean the surface area where stain is to be applied and use a cloth to eliminate as much dust as possible. The stain is applied with a brush, foam brush applicator, or cloth in a smooth, even coat. Allow the stain to penetrate the wood. Depending on the humidity, temperature, and particular stain used, penetration takes from 5 to 15 minutes. While the stain is still wet, wipe off the excess stain with a clean cloth, being careful not to remove too much from corners and edges. Wipe across the grain first so that the stain works into the wood pores. Then give a final wipe with the grain. Allow the stain to dry. This usually takes at least 8 hours. The finish can then be applied.

It is usually best to apply a series of light, even coats of clear finish rather than one thick coat. This will minimize drips and wrinkles as the finish dries. Apply finish in brush-width strokes in direction of wood grain. Turn table so that finish is applied to wood surface in a horizontal position whenever possible.

A minimum of two coats is recommended. Allow 6 to 8 hours for the first coat to dry before applying second coat. Sand lightly and use a tack cloth to remove sanded finish dust before applying next coat of finish. Clear or stained finishes are usually applied to natural wood furniture, but if you like color, paint finishes can also be applied.

Variations

A number of variations are possible for the basic budget computer table with video and storage rack. One possibility is to substitute particle board instead of plywood for the top. Another common variation is to construct the table with a different size of top. The top can be made longer or shorter, but it is important not to have the width of the top wider than about twice the length of the width of the side boards.

You can also install additional storage shelves to the rack or change their arrangement.

The basic budget computer table with video and storage rack makes a functional and attractive computer table even when built from inexpensive woods. This design is ideal for building to sell to others. The table can be sold either unfinished or with finish applied. By using more expensive woods, such as oak, you can give the table a custom appearance. The plans given here show simple butt joints, but if you have the cabinet-making skills and know-how, you can use any cabinetry joints.

BASIC COMPUTER TABLE WITH FULL SIDES AND VIDEO AND STORAGE RACK

This table is slightly more difficult to construct than the basic budget computer table with video and storage rack described above. It is built mainly from plywood, which presents more difficulties in cutting and covering edges than the stock wood used on the basic budget table. The materials are also more expensive, but this table gives more of a custom appearance than the basic budget table. By using hardwood faced plywood, you can construct an expensive-looking table for a fraction of the cost of making it out of solid hardwood. Materials to build this table vary in cost, but would run around $40 (at 1984 prices) using Douglas fir plywood and a plastic laminate top, and around $90 using oak-faced plywood. These prices will vary, however, depending on where you purchase your wood, the area where you live, and other factors. This attractively modern design gives a good appearance even when built from standard plywood.

The basic computer table with full sides and video and storage rack is shown in Figs. 3-112 and 3-113. The top has space for both a computer and printer. The table can have a natural wood or plastic laminate top. The table features a shelf underneath that provides storage space and gives the table added strength. The design of the full sides give a modern appearance.

Materials

The patterns for the wood parts are shown in Fig. 3-114. The top of the table is a 26-inch-by-4-foot piece of 3/4-inch thick plywood. If you intend to use the wood surface as the finished table top, without adding a plastic laminate, plywood with a hardwood upper layer is recommended. If a laminate is to be added, exterior grade shop plywood will suffice.

The shelves are 3/4-inch thick plywood. The shelves measures 48 inches by 13 inches. You can make the lower shelf deeper than this.

The two end pieces are 3/4-inch thick plywood and measure 26 inches by 49 inches. The 49-inch dimension gives a table that is 28 1/4 inches high, not counting the height added by whatever floor guides are used. You may want to change the 29-inch dimension if you want your table a different height.

The patterns for the shelf parts used inside the

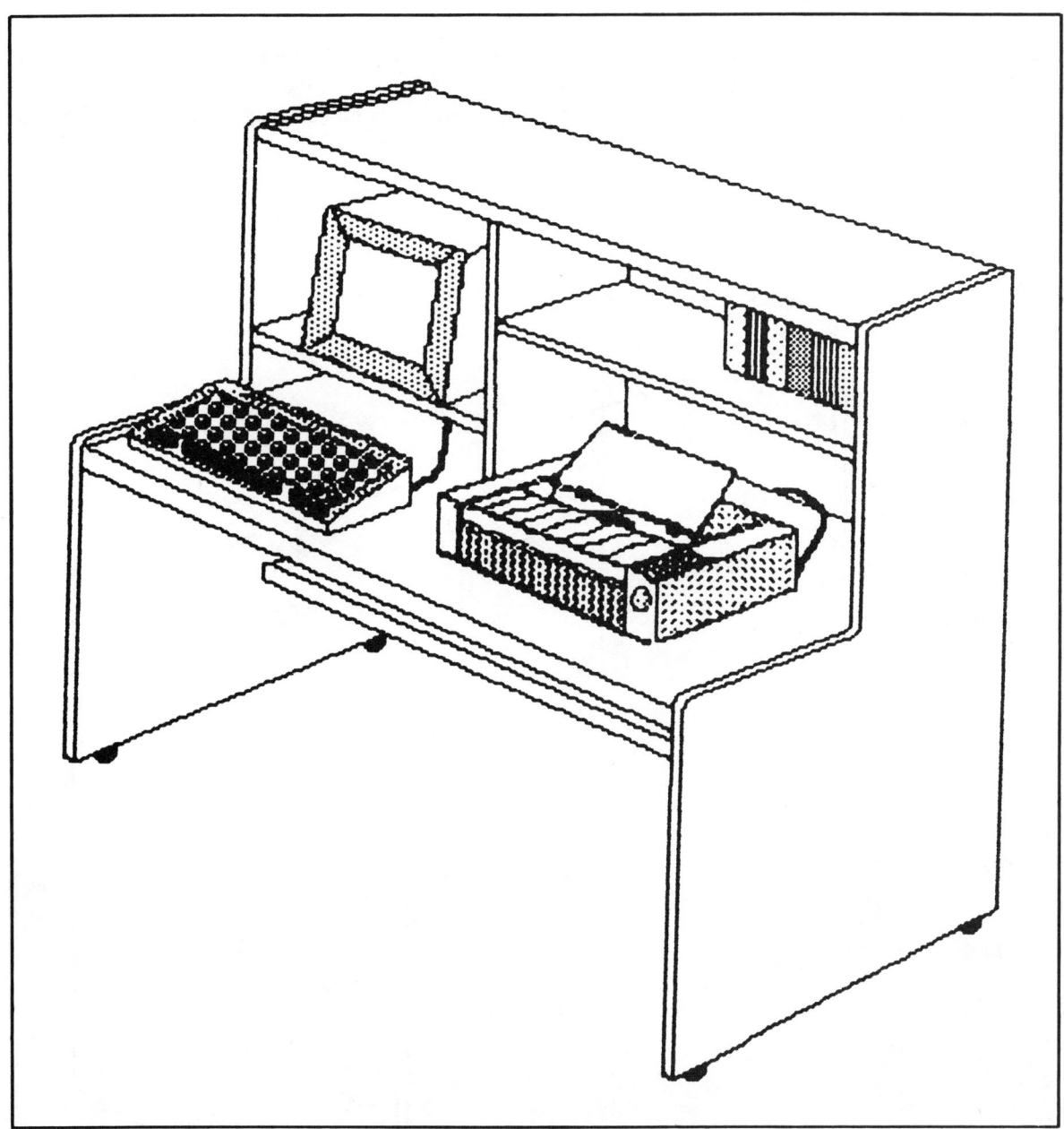

Fig. 3-112. Basic computer table with full sides and video and storage rack.

rack are shown in Fig. 3-114.

Plywood is usually sold in standard 4-foot-by-8-foot sheets. Lay out the patterns to take advantage of this standard size and arrange them to keep waste to a minimum. Some lumberyards and plywood stores will cut plywood sheets for you to desired size, usually at additional cost. This can be worth it if you don't need full sheets, don't have room to carry full sheets in your car, or don't have a saw to accurately cut plywood.

Half-inch thick plywood could also be used, but I don't recommend it: the savings are small, and you'll end with a less sturdy table. Particle board can be substituted for the plywood if you are on an absolute minimum budget. A lot of computer furniture is made from particle board covered by plastic laminates. It can be difficult to work with, however, and it is very difficult to get plastic laminates to bond properly without special equipment. Even the laminates on manufactured fur-

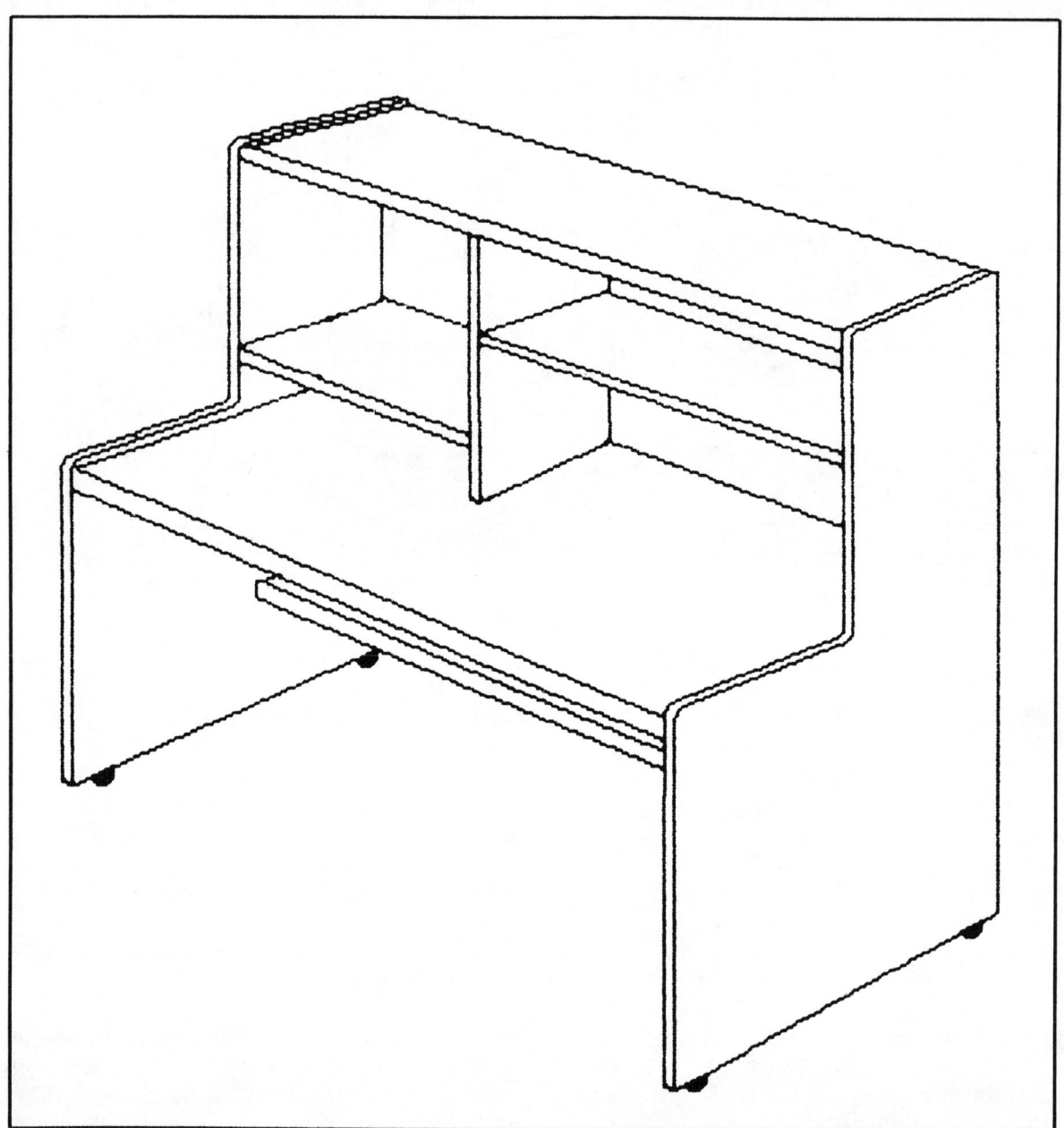

Fig. 3-113. Another view of the basic computer table with full sides and video and storage rack.

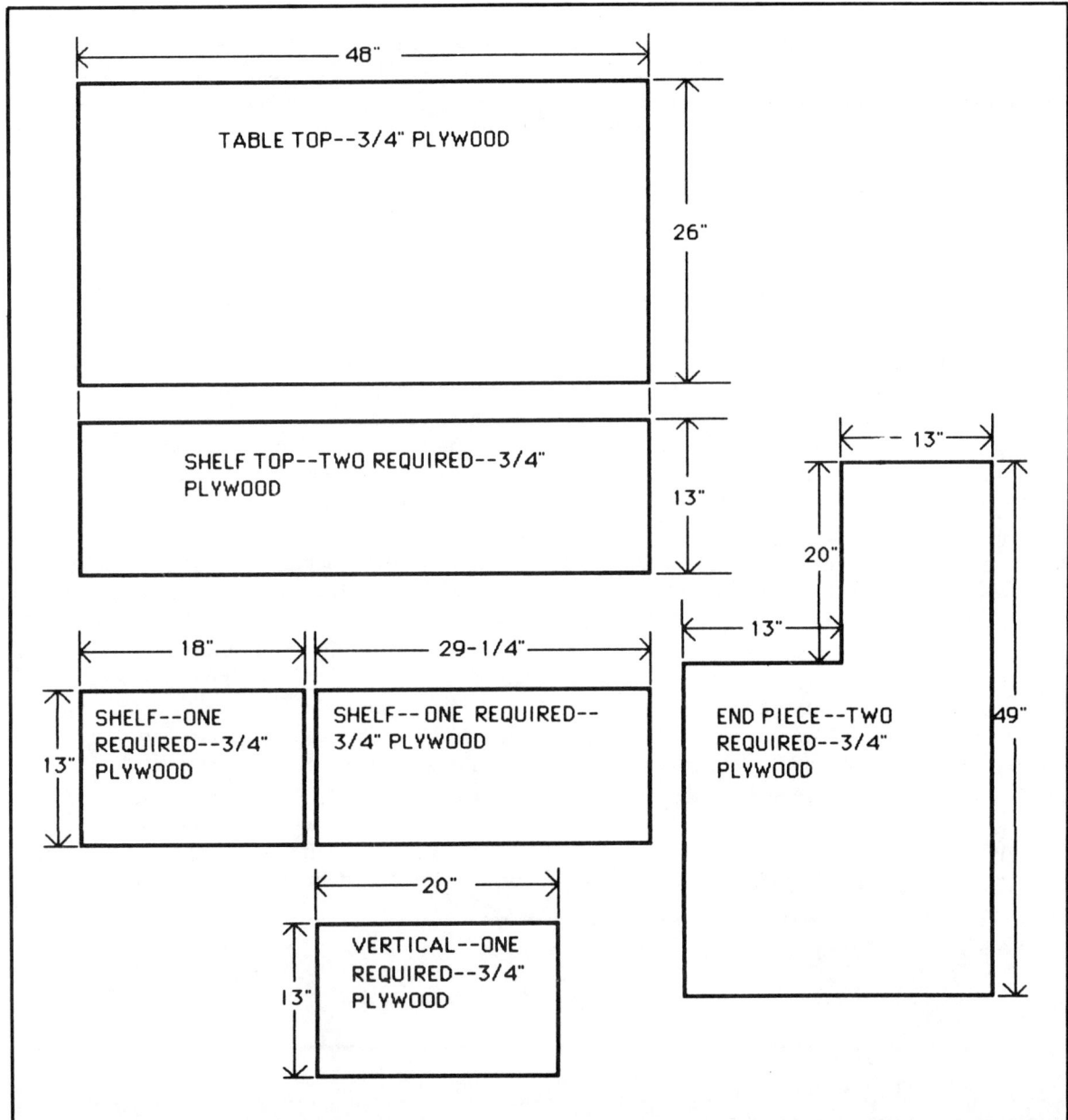

Fig. 3-114. Patterns for plywood parts.

niture often seem to come loose at the edges.

The backing piece (Fig. 3-115) can be either plywood or fiberboard. The backing piece is used to strengthen the table base and hold the frame in rectangular form. The length of the backing piece is 49 1/2 inches. A 13-inch height is shown for the backing piece, which is about the minimum required to give this table adequate strength. The shelf can be installed a greater distance below the top, which will require changing the height of the backing piece. Notice that the top, shelf, backing piece, and side pieces form a box with the forward side open.

You will also need 1-inch-by-2-inch or larger framing stock for use under the plywood table top and the shelves.

Wood or plastic trim strips can be used to cover the exposed edges of the plywood, as detailed later in this section. A wood or plastic trim strip is used to cover the forward edge of the table top and shelves; these pieces are 48 inches long and about 1 3/4 inches wide. The minimum width should be such that it will completely cover the widths of the plywood (3/4 inch for the top) and the framing (approximately 7/8 inch). The trim strips can be slightly wider than this, however.

Four suitable floor pods or guides are used on the floor beams. These can be either the fixed or adjustable type, as desired.

A variety of fasteners can be used for assembly (nails, bolts, screws, etc.). You will also need a suitable wood glue. The finish can be clear urethane, paint, or any other.

The top can be left natural or a plastic laminate can be added. If a plastic laminate is added, you will need a 26-inch-by-4-foot piece and suitable contact cement for attaching it to the plywood. Plastic laminates can also be added to the shelf tops.

Construction

An overview of the complete assembly is shown in Fig. 3-116. Begin by constructing the table top, as detailed in Fig. 3-117. If you purchased a piece of plywood that was already cut to the 26-inch-by-4-foot size, no additional cutting is required, if it was cut accurately. You might want to check for true corners with a square.

If you purchased a larger piece of plywood, such as a standard 4-foot-by-8-foot sheet, cut out a section for the table top. In most cases, the grain of the top layer should run lengthwise, although this is not essential if you are going to add a plastic laminate. Use two factory cut edges for your table top and cut the other two. With a ruler and square to make the pattern, mark the lines with a sharp pencil or scribing tool.

When sawing plywood, you must take special care to avoid chipping and splintering along the cut edge. Handsaws or power saws with special fine-toothed blades designed especially for plywood should be used; special carbide-tipped blades are even better. Applying a strip of masking tape over the area to be cut on both sides of the plywood, but especially on the underside, is also helpful. Another possibility is to clamp a solid piece of wood to the underside and make the cut through both the plywood and the piece of wood.

Be extremely careful when sanding edges; always use a sanding block. Avoid sanding plywood surfaces until a wood sealer has been applied.

Next, add the reinforcing frame to the table top plywood, as shown in Fig. 3-117. Again, use a ruler

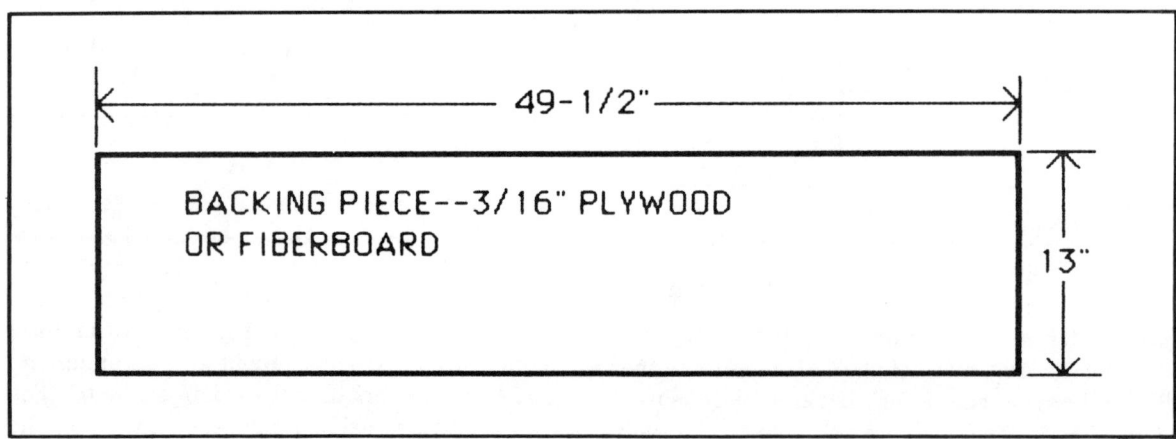

Fig. 3-115. Pattern for backing piece.

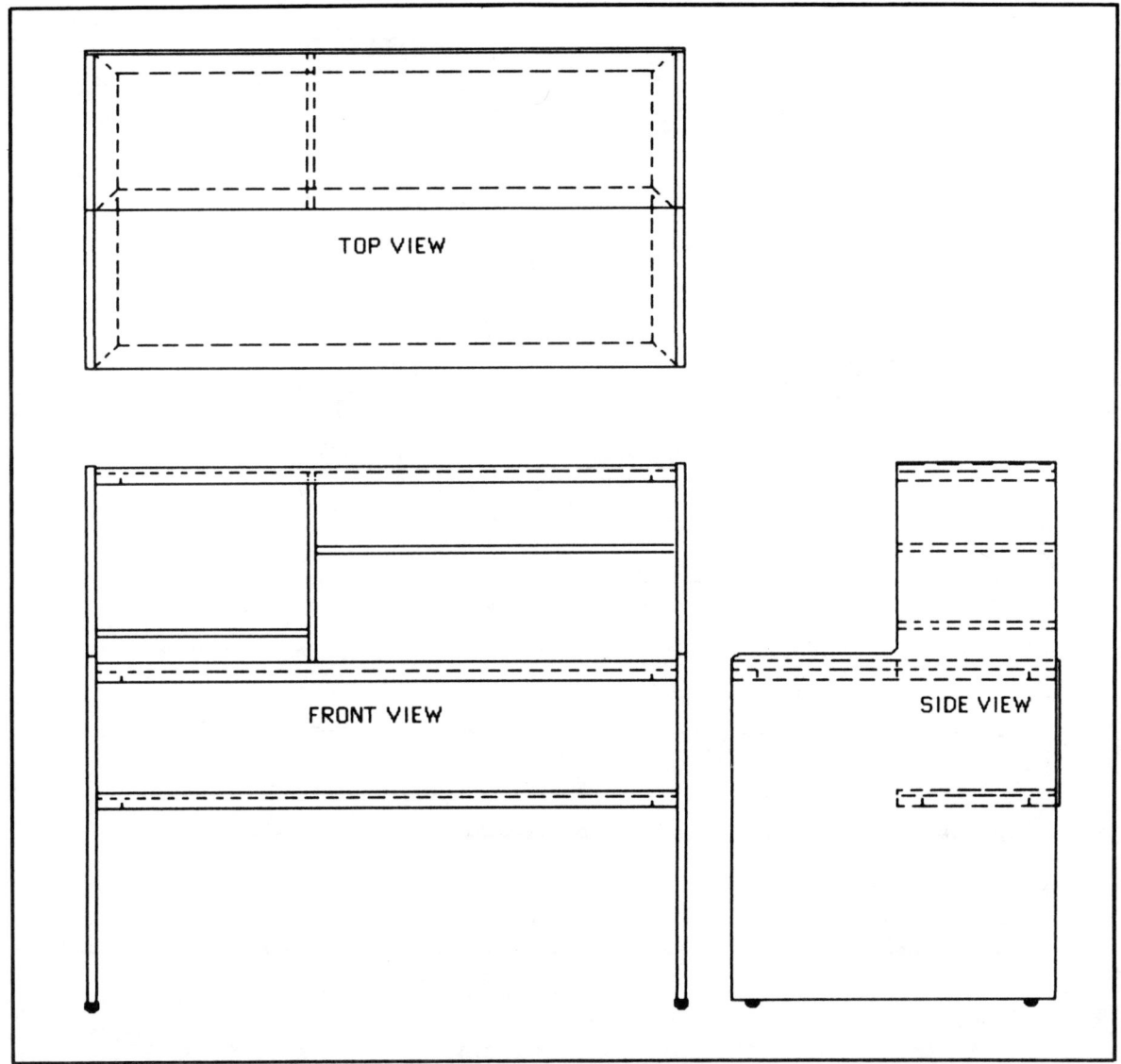

Fig. 3-116. Basic computer table with full sides and video and storage rack.

and a square to draw the patterns on the framing wood, and mark the lines with a sharp pencil. Then make the necessary saw cuts, as detailed in Chapter 2. The frame pieces should be glued and nailed or screwed in position (see Figs. 3-118 and 3-119). If the plywood top is to be left unlaminated, the fasteners should go through the framing and into the plywood. Be sure that the fasteners do not pass all the way through the plywood or leave a bulge in the upper surface. If a good glue is used, such as acrylic or epoxy, the glue alone should give adequate strength, with fasteners mainly used as a clamping device. Fasteners will not have much holding power in plywood. For greater holding power, the fasteners can be passed through the plywood and into the framing if a plastic laminate is to be added.

Several options are open for finishing off the

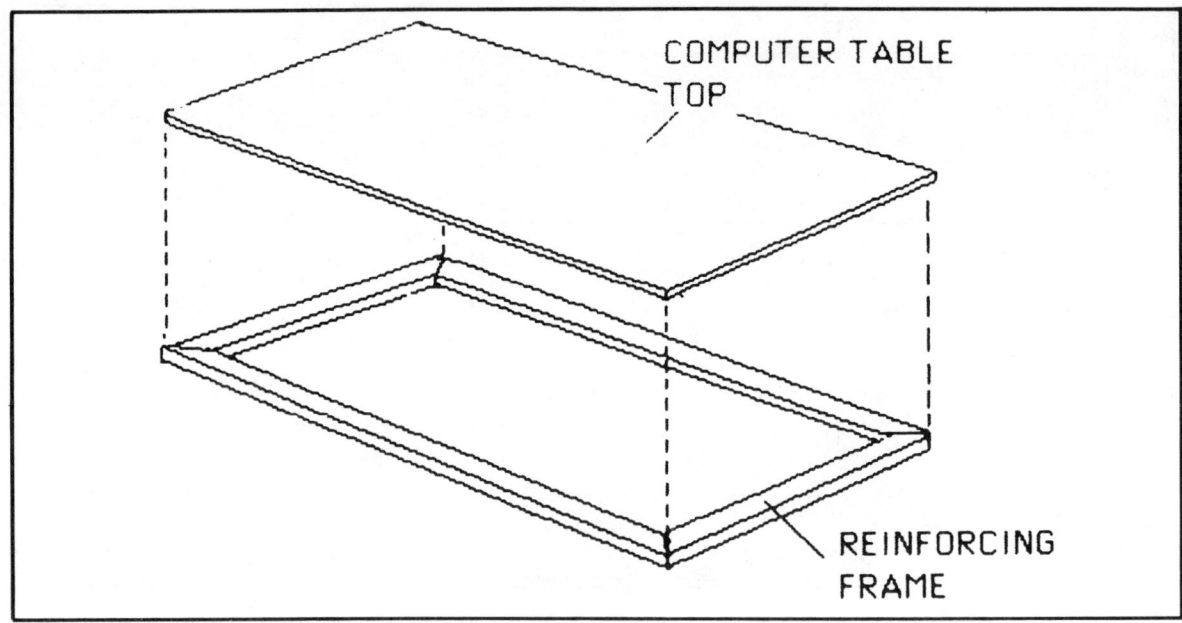

Fig. 3-117. Assembly of table top and reinforcing frame.

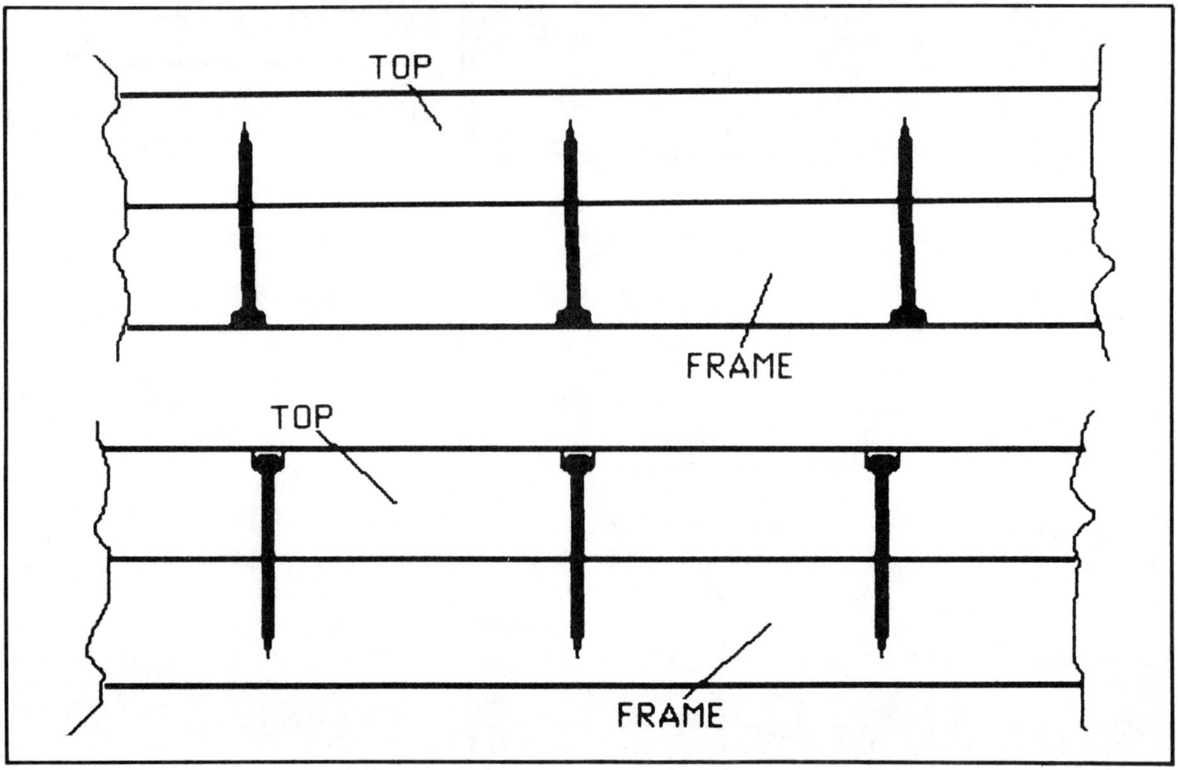

Fig. 3-118. Assembly of table top to frame pieces with nails and glue.

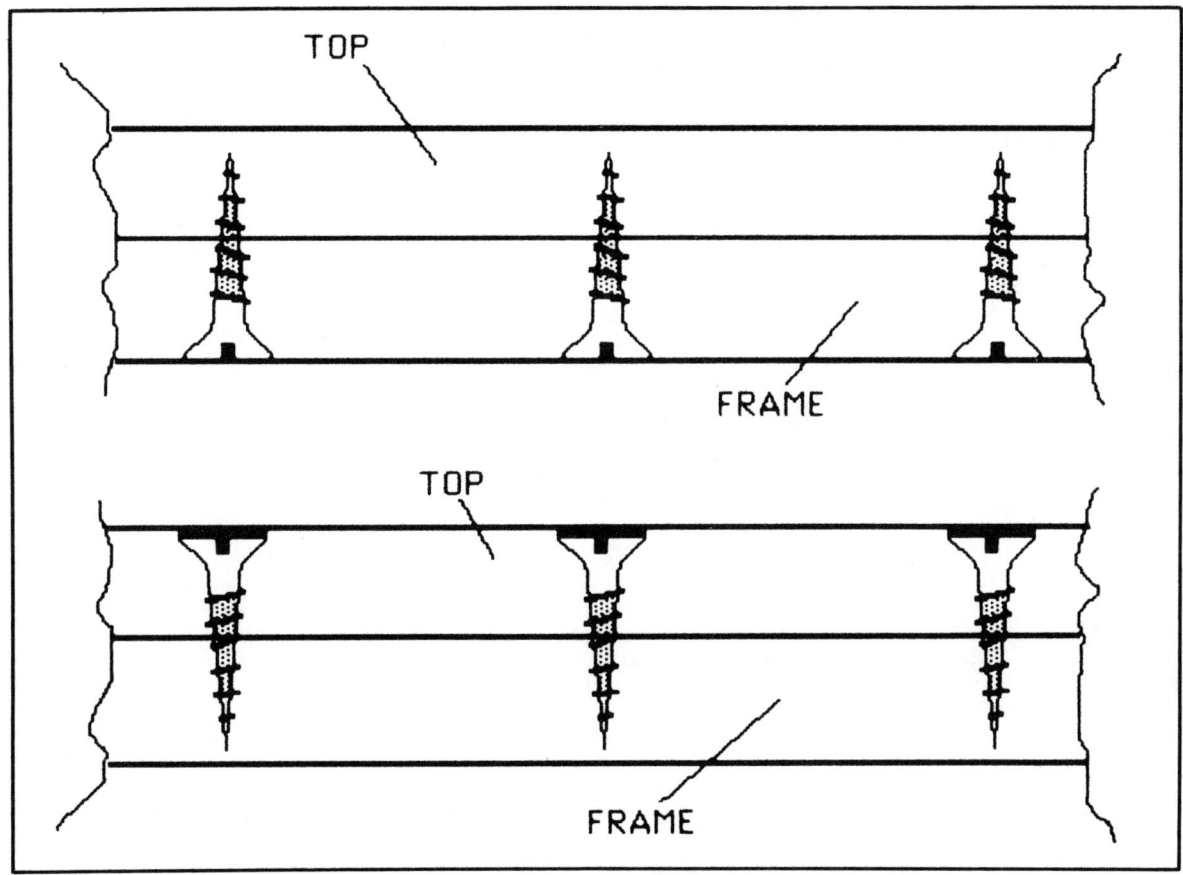

Fig. 3-119. Assembly of table top to frame pieces with screws and glue.

table top. One possibility is to use the natural plywood surface as the top and add a wood trim strip to the forward edge, as shown in Fig. 3-120. Glue and fasten the trim strip in place with finishing nails. Set the heads below the wood surface and fill holes with wood filler to flush with the wood surface.

You can also add a plastic laminate to the forward edge and leave the top natural wood, as detailed in Fig. 3-121. Or, add a plastic laminate to the top and a wood trim strip to the forward edge, as shown in Fig. 3-122. Still another possibility is to add plastic laminates to both the top and forward edge, as shown in Figs. 3-123 and 3-124.

If a plastic laminate is to be added to the plywood table top and/or the forward edge, they can be installed at this time. Plastic laminates are often applied to plywood for computer table tops and large selections are on the market. I suggest you use high quality plastic laminates for your computer table top.

If a plastic laminate is to also be applied to the forward edge of the table top, it should be applied first. This is then finished flush with the table top. The top laminate is then applied so that the edge overlaps the top edge of the laminate on the forward edge of the table, as shown in Fig. 3-124.

The plastic laminate is installed as follows:

• All holes and defects in the surface of the plywood should be filled with putty or wood filler.
• Sand the surface to be covered to help ensure good adhesion.
• Mark the plastic laminate to a pattern

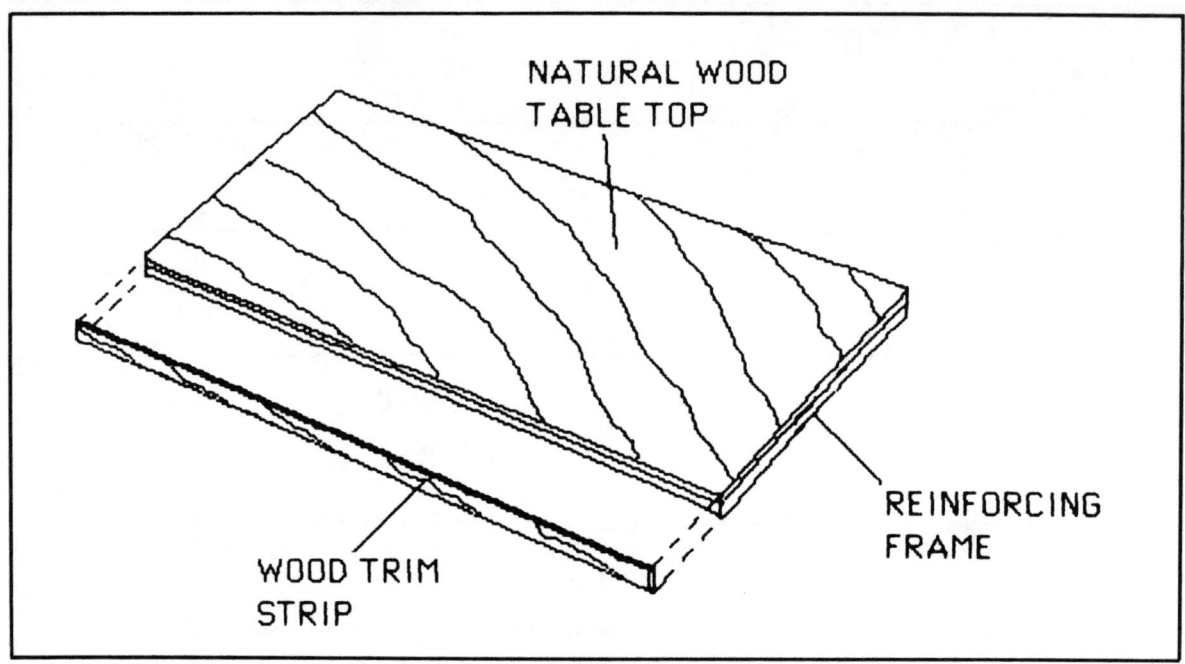

Fig. 3-120. Adding wood trim strip to forward edge of computer table top.

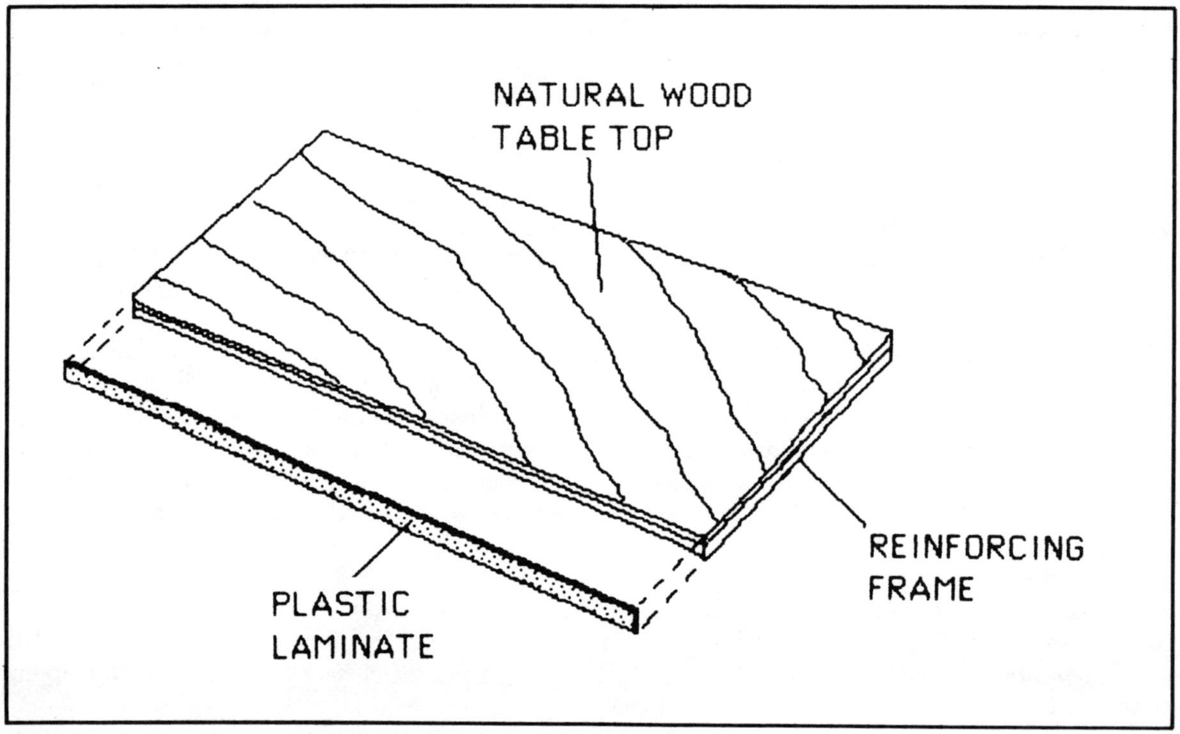

Fig. 3-121. Adding plastic laminate to forward edge of computer table top.

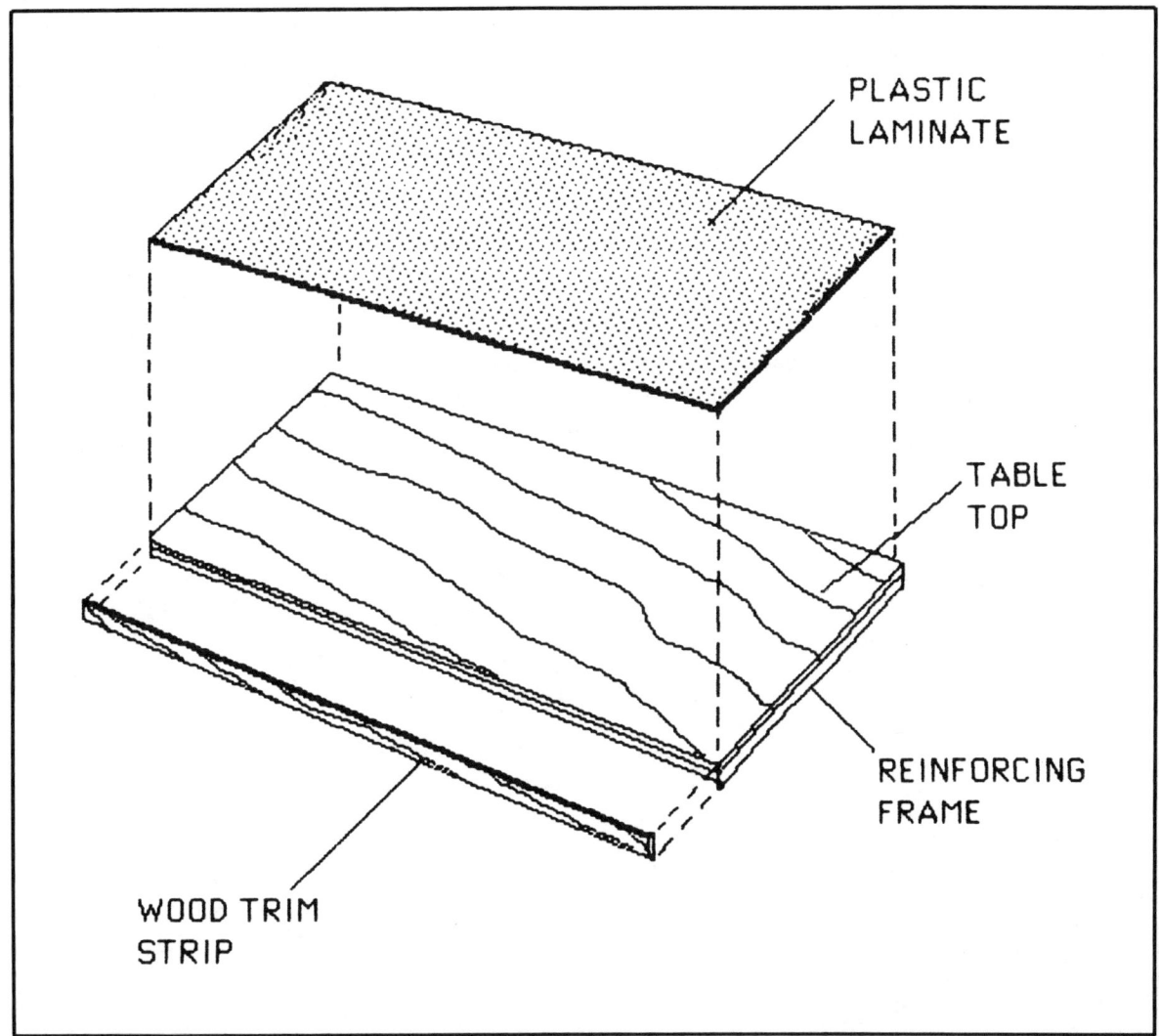

Fig. 3-122. Adding plastic laminate to top and wood trim strip to forward edge of table top.

slightly larger than the area to be covered. Use a straightedge and draw the pattern lines on the finished or pattern side of the laminate. Leave 1/4 inch to 1/2 inch on all sides. This will be trimmed off later.

- If a laminate is to be applied to the forward edge of the table, apply this first. After installation, as detailed below, trim and file the upper edge of the plastic laminate flush with the upper edge of the plywood table top before installing the plastic laminate to upper surface of the table top.

- Cut the plastic laminate to the pattern marked. Even though the plastic laminate is extremely durable once applied, it is vulnerable to cracking and splitting before it is cemented in place. Fine-tooth handsaws or power saws with fine-tooth blades can be used—a rotary power saw with a 14 to 16 teeth per inch blade is ideal. Place the plastic laminate face up when cutting, taking care that the plastic laminate is not chipped or broken. You can use a carbide tip knife to score the plastic by drawing the knife point along a metal straightedge. Cut through the decorative surface. The laminate can then be broken by bending it toward the decorative surface side over the edge of a table or workbench.

• Apply contact cement to the surface of the plywood to be covered and the back side of the plastic laminate. A brush, roller, or metal spreader with a serrated edge can be used to spread the contact cement. A thin, even application is important.

• Follow the manufacturer's instructions regarding drying time. Usually, this takes about 20 to 30 minutes.

• Place a sheet of heavy wrapping paper over the plywood surface to be covered. Then position the laminate on the plywood surface with the paper between. The contact cement will not stick to the paper if it has been allowed to dry properly. Make certain that the laminate is positioned correctly. Once the two surfaces of contact cement touch, the laminate sheet cannot be moved again. When everything is lined up properly, pull the paper out from between the plywood and the plastic laminate.

• Using a small block of wood and a hammer, lightly tap the laminate in place. An alternate method is to use a rolling pin.

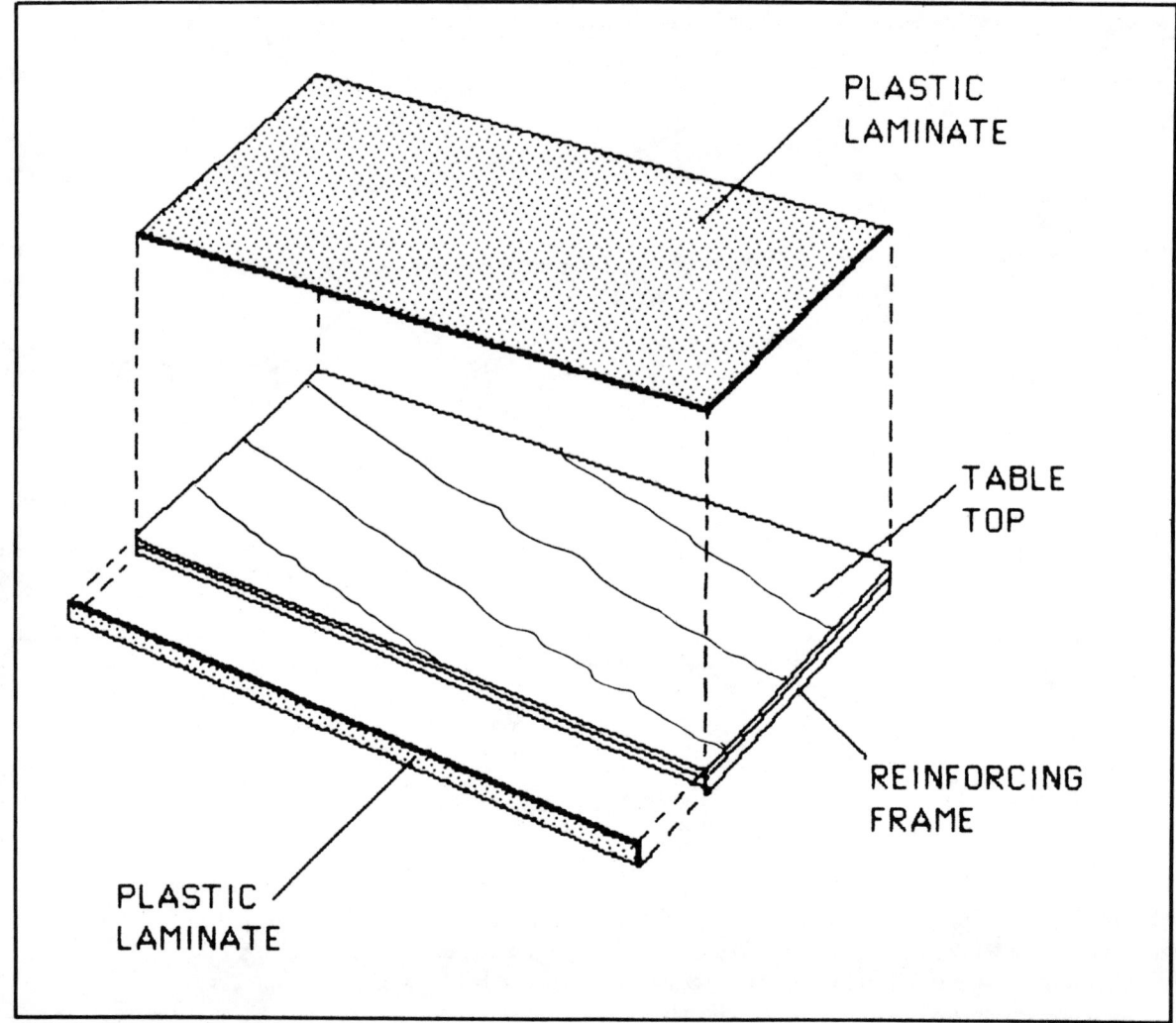

Fig. 3-123. Adding plastic laminate to top and forward edge of table top.

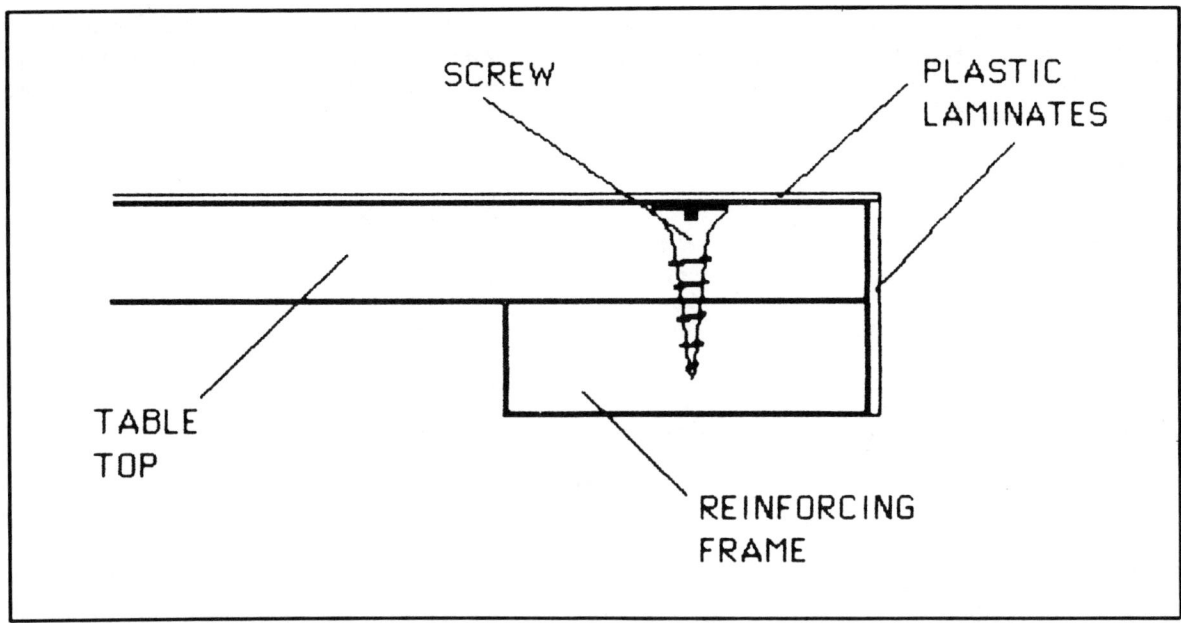

Fig. 3-124. Adding plastic laminates to top.

- Use a file to remove the surplus plastic laminate from the edges, or use a special cutter with a router, which trims off excess plastic laminate to flush with the plywood edges.
- The thinner recommended for the contact cement can be used for cleaning contact cement from wood and plastic laminate and tools.

The next step is to construct the shelves, as detailed in Fig. 3-125. If you purchased pieces of plywood that were already cut to the 13-inch-

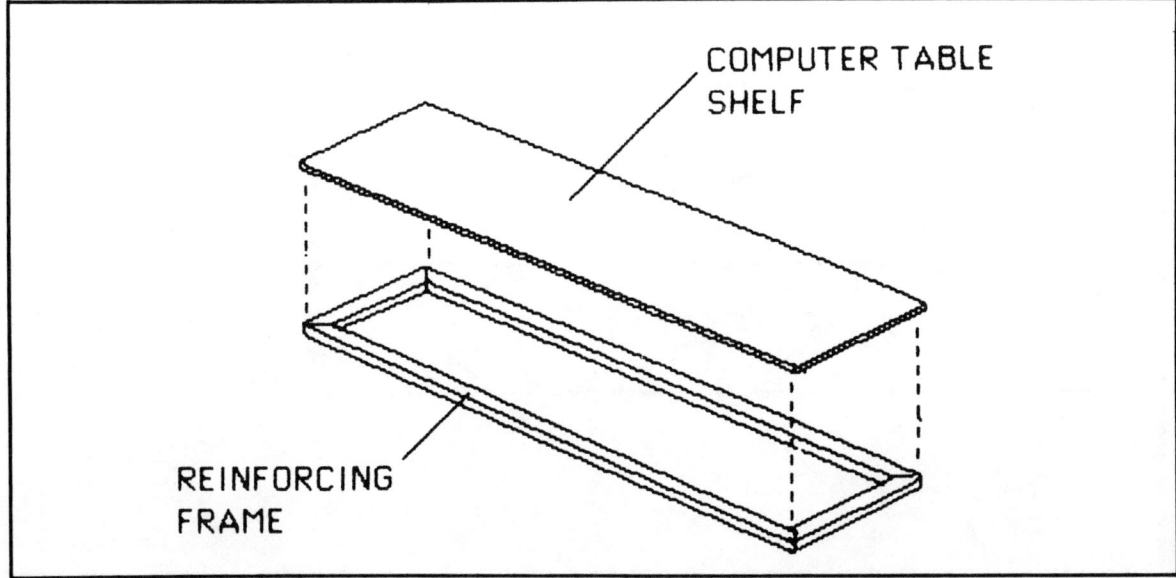

Fig. 3-125. Assembly of shelf top to reinforcing frame.

127

by-4-foot size, no additional cutting of the plywood will be required, assuming that the piece was cut accurately and is a true rectangular form. You might want to check this with a square.

If you purchased a larger piece of plywood, cut out sections for the shelf tops. In most cases, you will want to have the grain of the top layer running lengthwise. This is not essential if you are going to add a plastic laminate. Use two factory cut edges for a shelf top and cut the other two. Use a ruler and square for making the pattern, marking the lines with a sharp pencil or scribing tool. Cut and sand the shelf pieces carefully, following the special procedures described for the table top.

Next, add the reinforcing frame to the shelf plywood, as shown in Fig. 3-125. Using a ruler and a square, draw the patterns on the framing wood with a sharp pencil or other marking device. Then

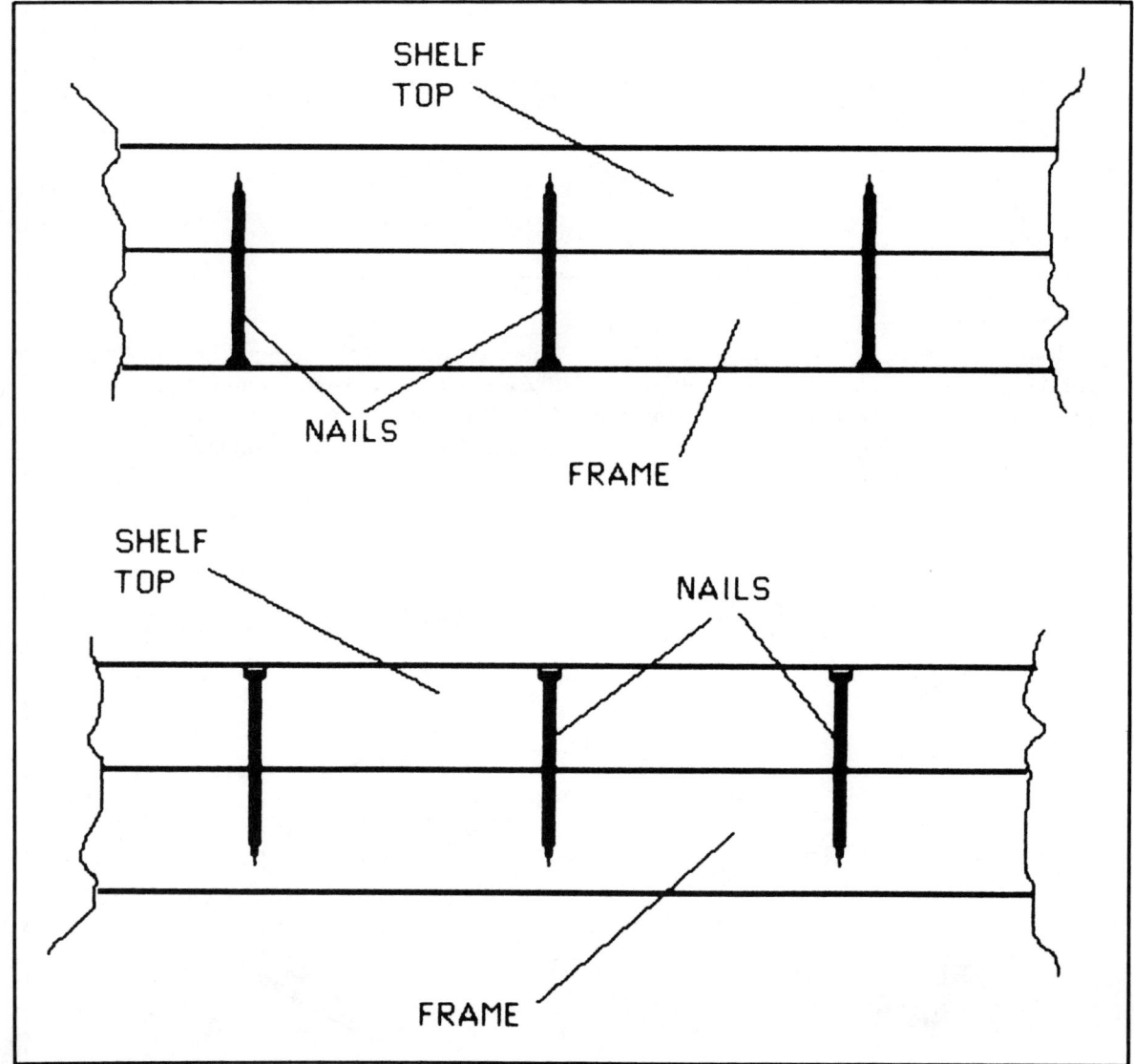

Fig. 3-126. Assembly of shelf top to frame piece with nails and glue.

make the necessary saw cuts. The frame pieces should be glued and nailed or screwed in position (see Figs. 3-126 and 3-127). If the plywood shelf tops will be left natural wood, the fasteners should go through the framing and into the plywood, but care should be taken so that the fasteners do not pass all the way through the plywood or leave a bulge in the upper surface. If using an acrylic or epoxy glue, it alone should give adequate strength.

The fasteners are mainly used as a clamping device for the gluing and will not have much holding power. To give greater holding power, pass the fasteners through the plywood and into the framing (if a plastic laminate is to be added).

The same options are available for finishing off the shelves as for the table top:

- Use the plywood surface as the shelf top and

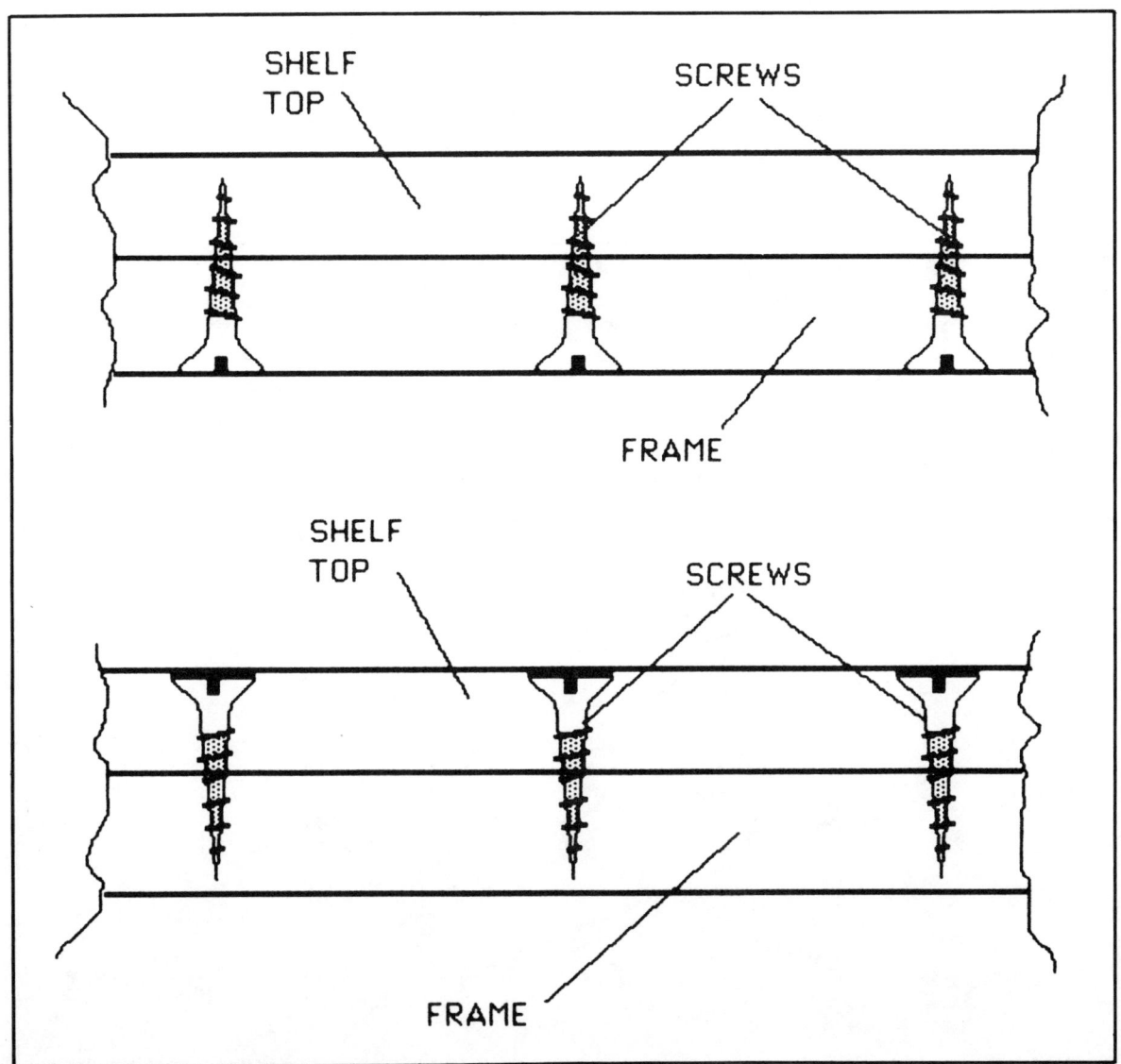

Fig. 3-127. Assembly of shelf top to frame pieces with screws and glue.

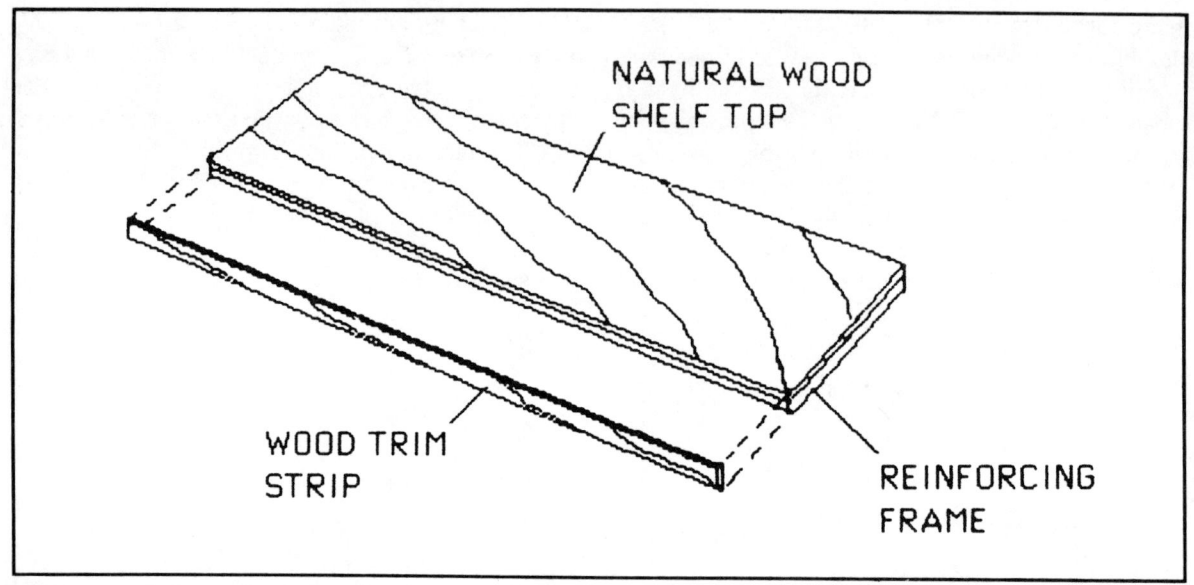

Fig. 3-128. Adding wood trim strip to forward edge of shelf.

add a wood trim strip to the forward edge, as shown in Fig. 3-128. Glue and fasten the trim strip in place with finishing nails. Set the heads below the wood surface and fill holes with wood filler to flush with the wood surface.

• Add a plastic laminate to the forward edge and leave the shelf top natural wood, as detailed in Fig. 3-129.

• Add a plastic laminate to the shelf top and a wood trim strip to the forward edge, as shown in Fig. 3-130.

• Add plastic laminates to both the top and for-

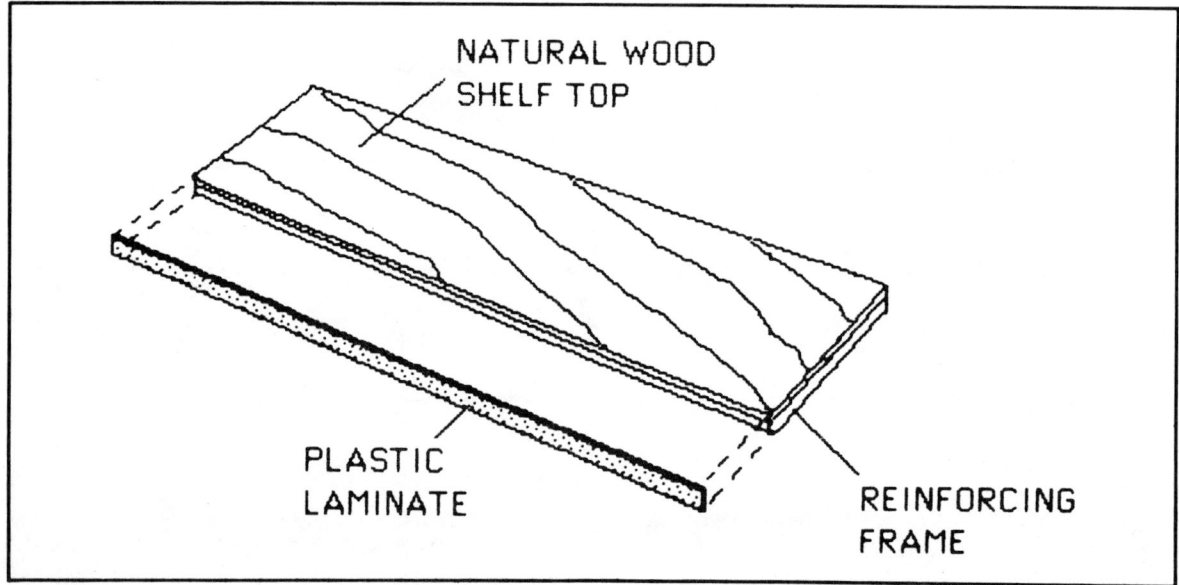

Fig. 3-129. Adding plastic laminate to forward edge of shelf.

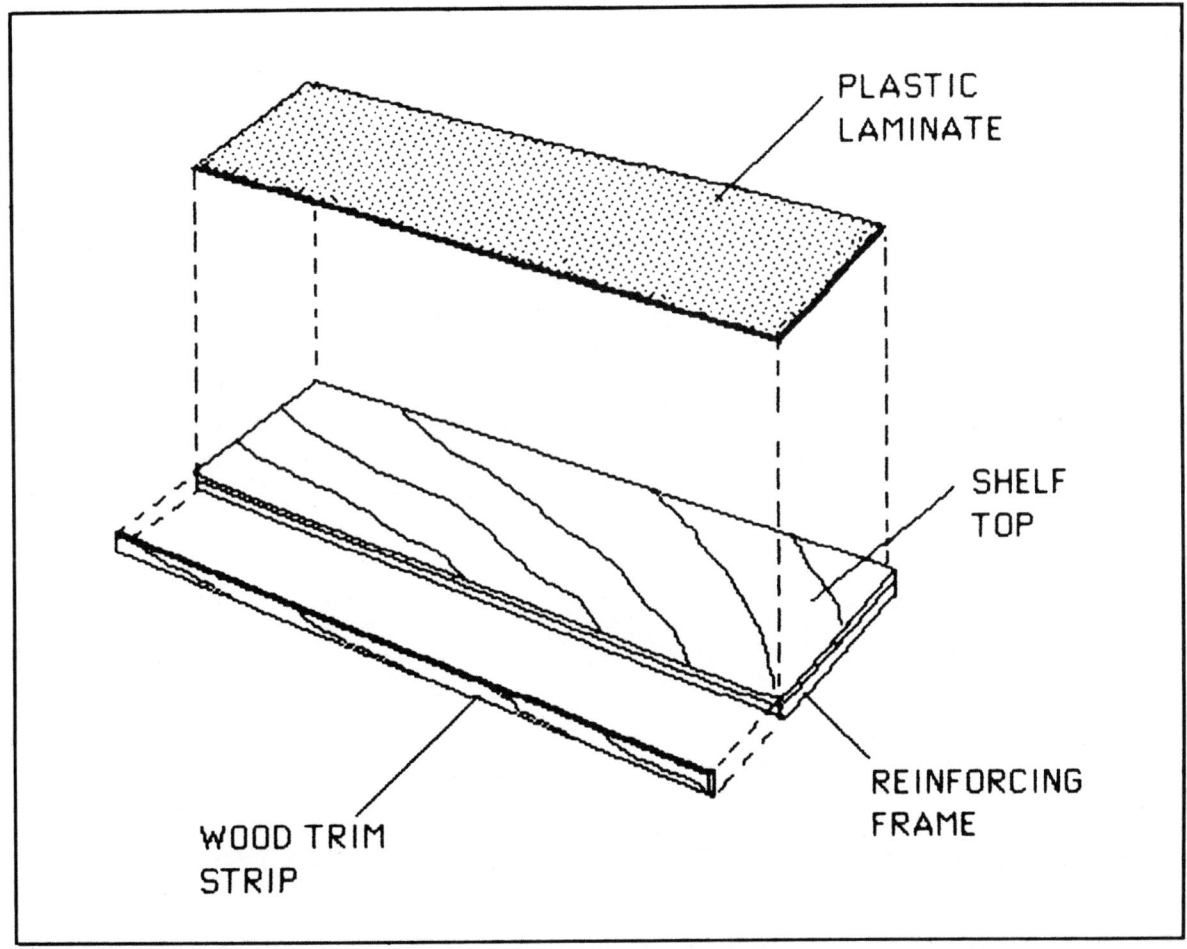

Fig. 3-130. Adding plastic laminate to top and wood trim strip to forward edge of shelf.

ward edge, as shown in Figs. 3-131 and 3-132.

If a plastic laminate is applied to the plywood shelf top and/or the forward edge, install it now. If a plastic laminate is to also be applied to the forward edge of the shelf top, it should be applied first. This is then finished flush with the shelf top. The top laminate is then applied so that the edge overlaps the top edge of the laminate on the forward edge of the shelf, as shown in Fig. 3-132. See the instructions given for applying laminate to the table top.

Next, cut the end pieces to rectangular size and round off the corners, as shown. The curves can be on a 1/2 inch radius or whatever fits a particular molding corner piece. A power circular saw is ideal for making straight cuts, and a saber saw can be used for making the curved corner cuts.

The next step is to add plastic (Fig. 3-133) or wood (Fig. 3-134) trim to the forward and top edges of the end pieces. This will protect the laminated edges of the plywood and produce a neat appearance.

An overview of the remainder of the assembly is shown in Fig. 3-135. Assemble the table top, shelves, and rack to the side pieces, as shown in Fig. 3-136. This is accomplished by both glue and mechanical fasteners. One method is to use finishing nails, passing them through the end pieces and into the framing wood of the top and shelves. Set the heads below the wood surface and fill with

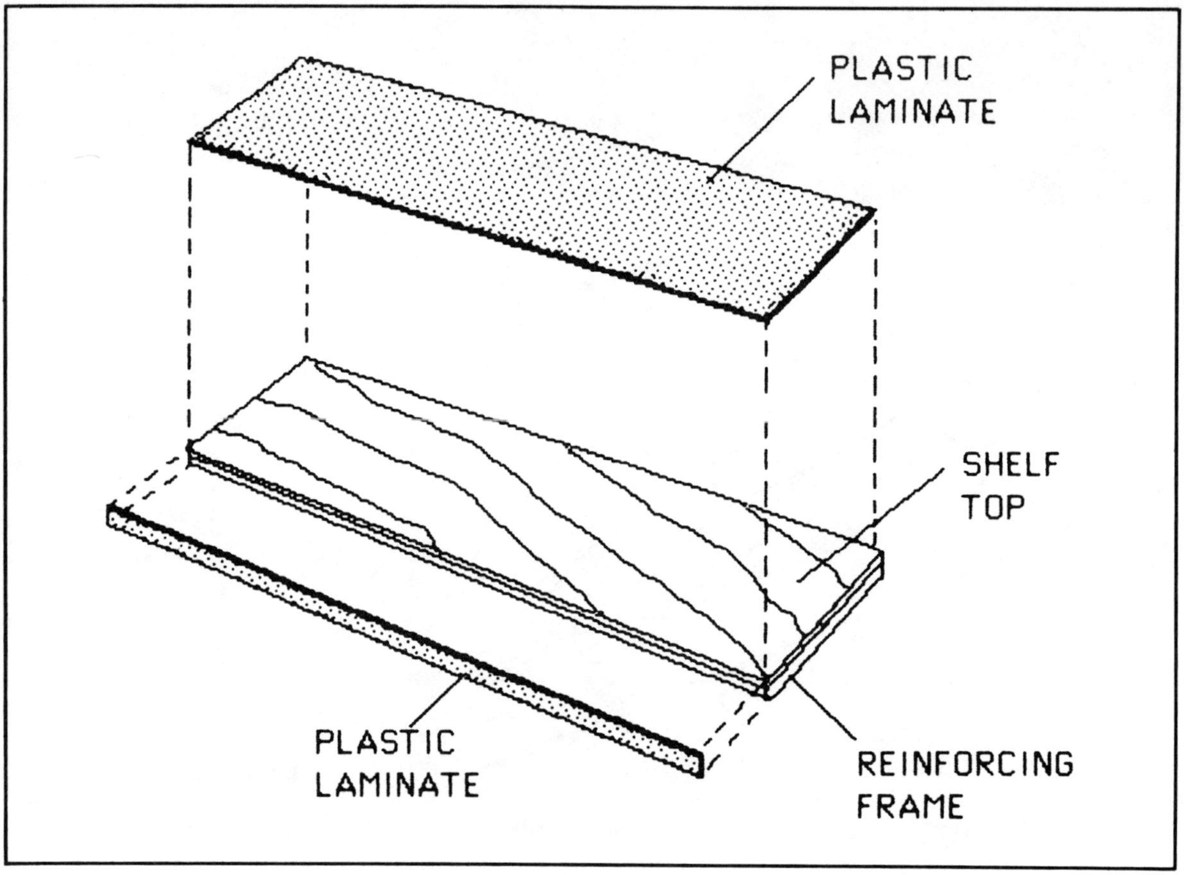

Fig. 3-131. Adding plastic laminate to top and forward edge of shelf.

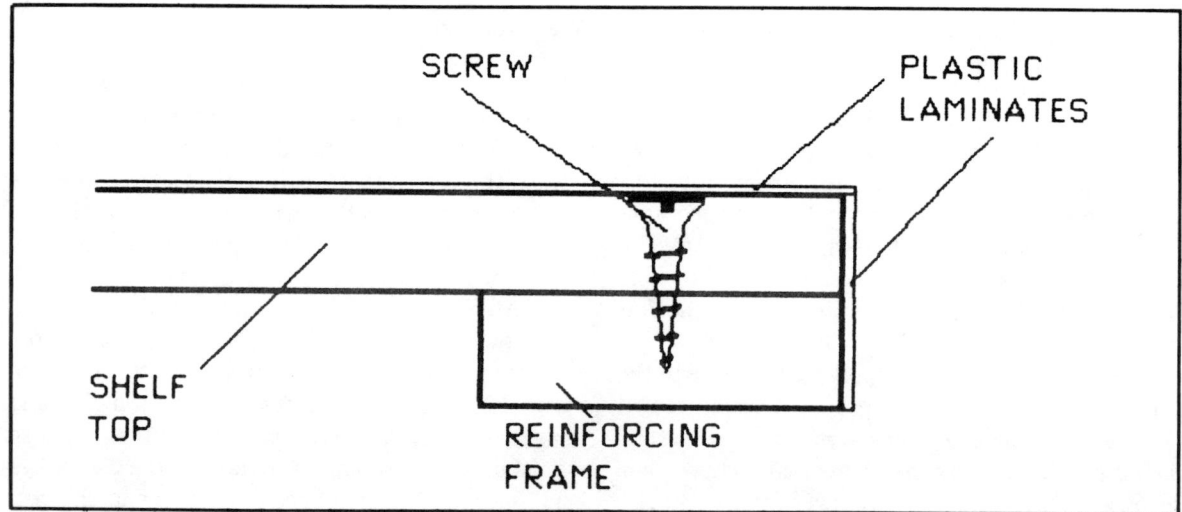

Fig. 3-132. Adding plastic laminate to shelf.

132

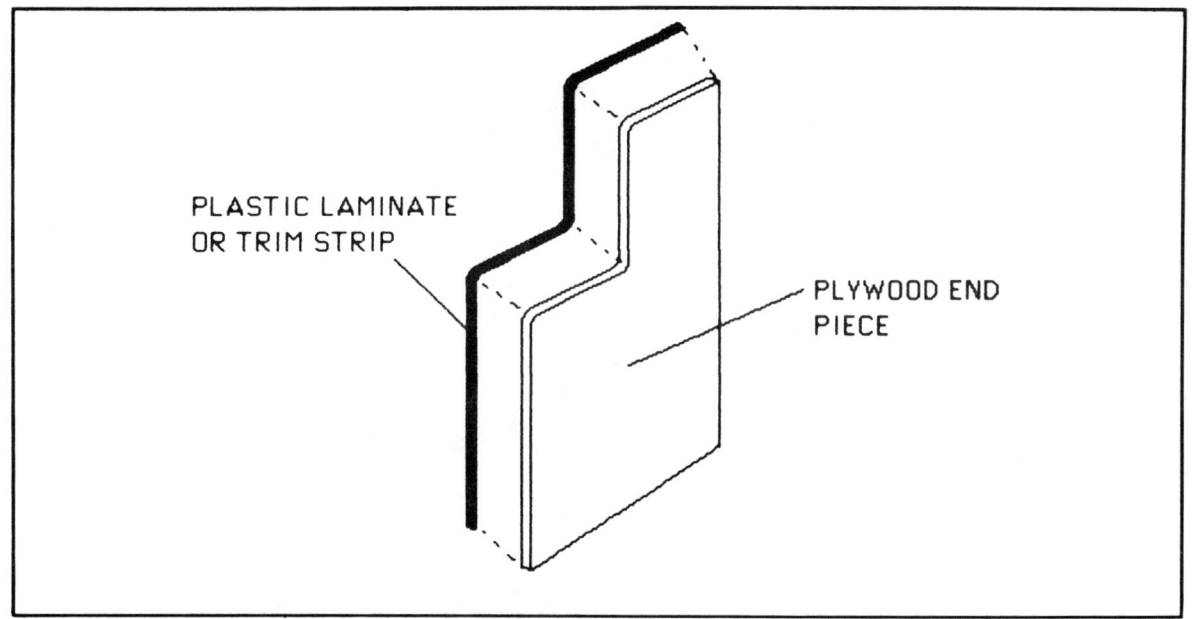

Fig. 3-133. Adding plastic laminate or trim strip to end pieces.

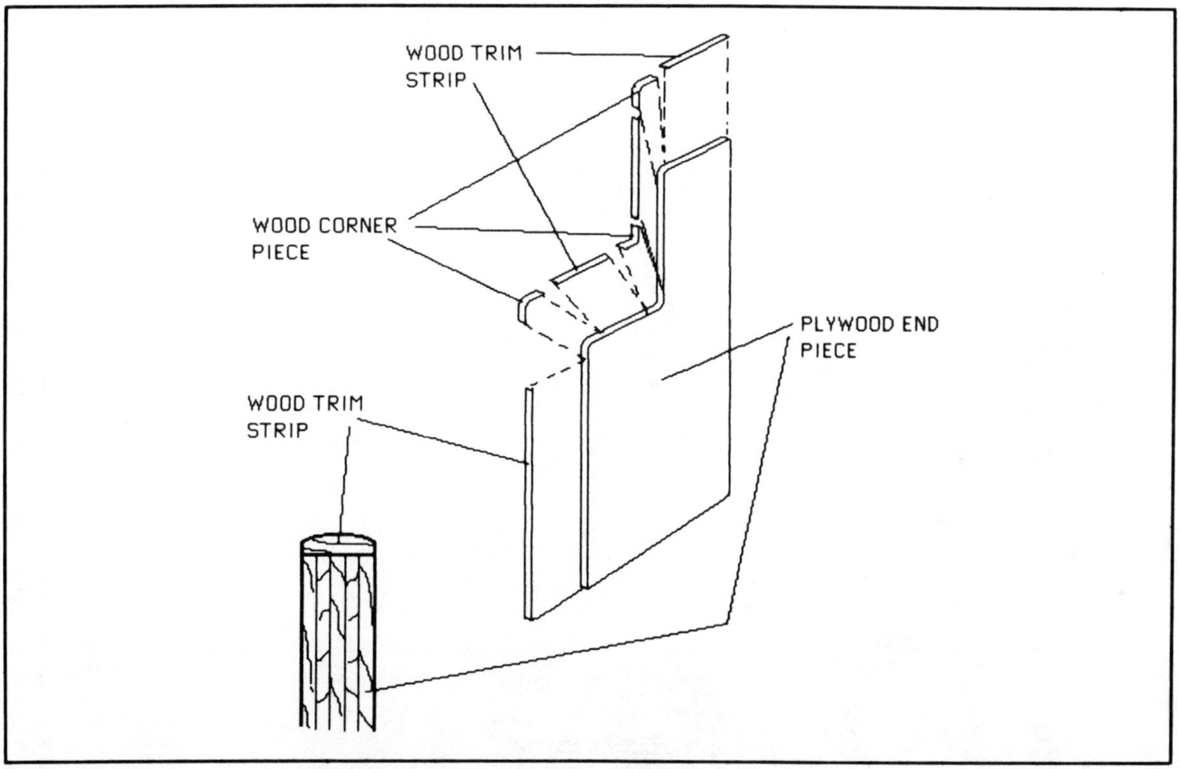

Fig. 3-134. Adding wood trim strips and corner pieces to end pieces.

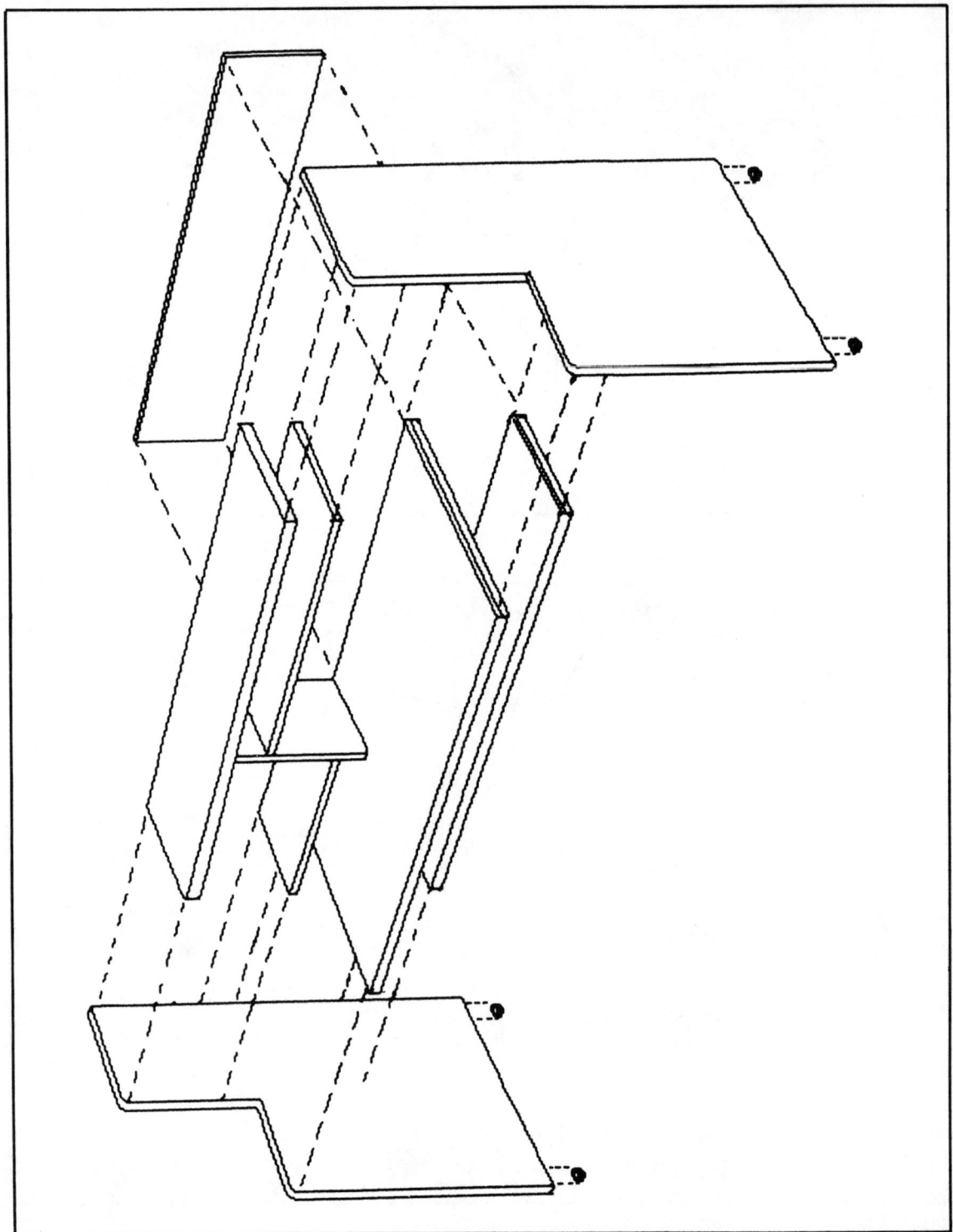

Fig. 3-135. Assembly of basic computer table with full sides and video and storage rack.

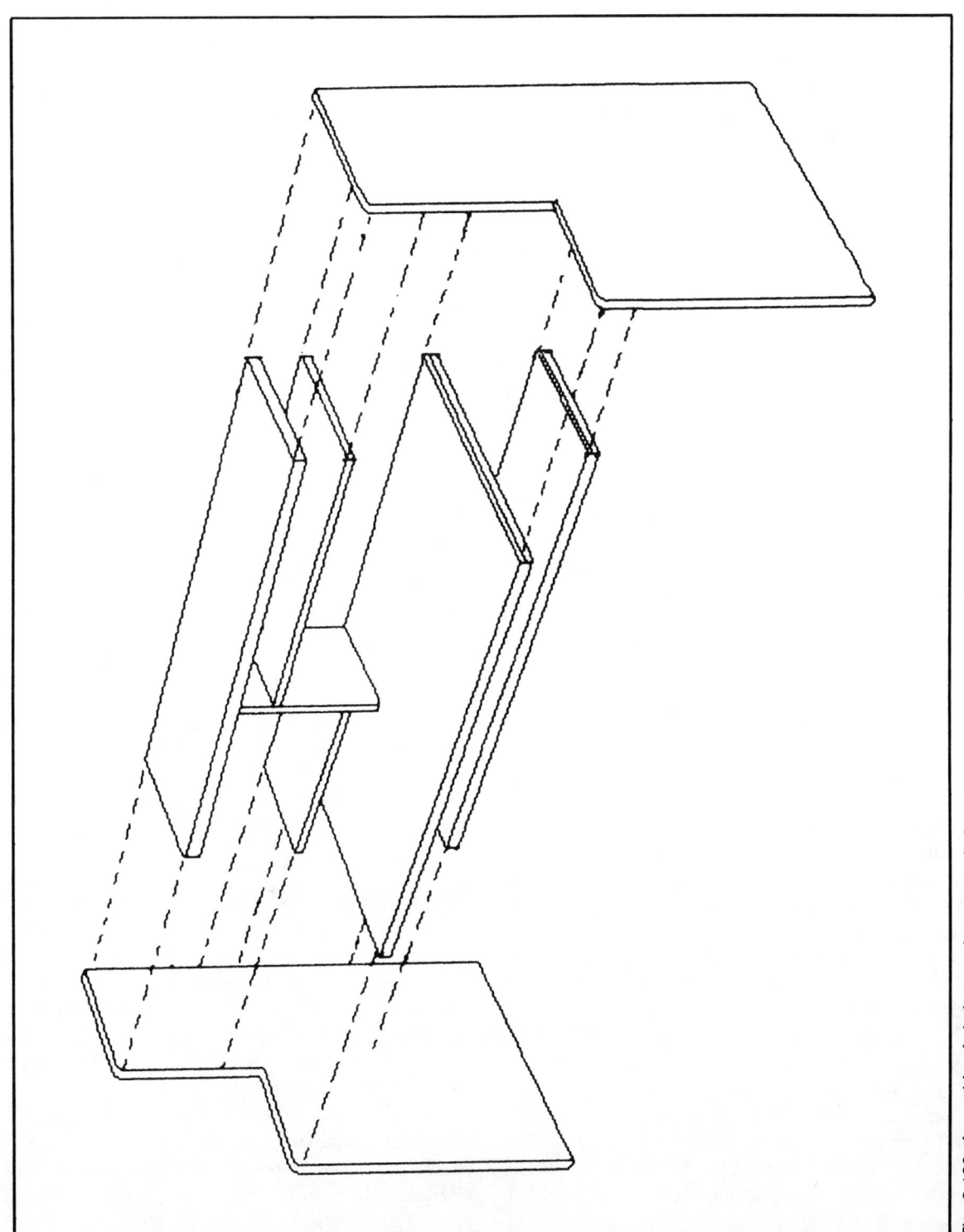

Fig. 3-136. Assembly of shelves and top to end pieces.

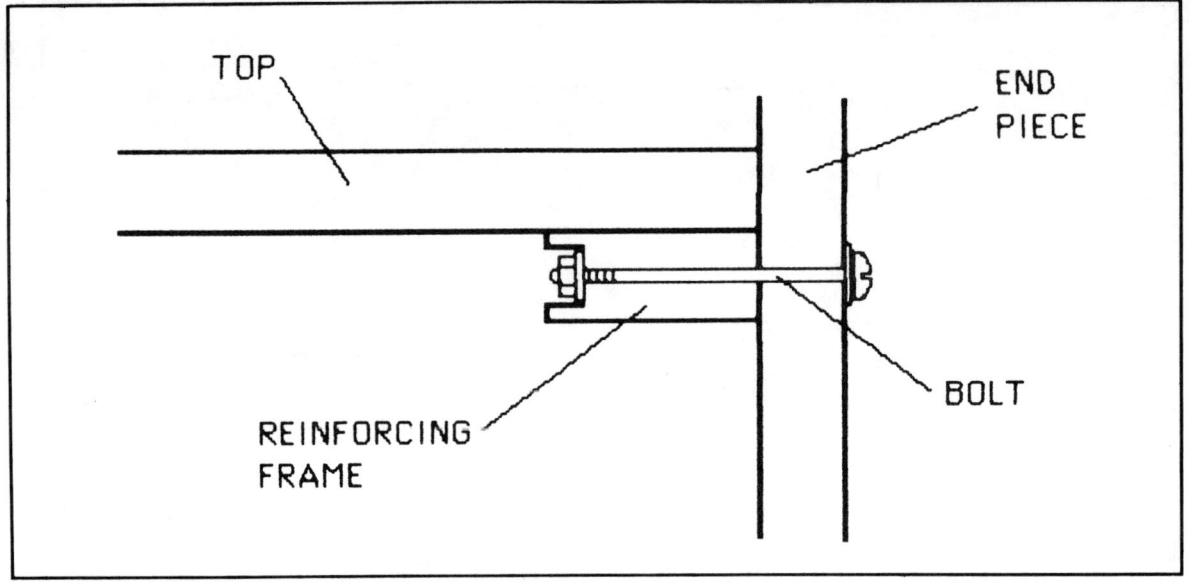

Fig. 3-137. Assembly of top and shelves to side pieces with bolts.

wood filler to flush with the wood surface. Another method is to use through-bolts, as detailed in Fig. 3-137.

The rack parts inside the rack frame can be assembled by using metal L-straps and attaching them with wood screws. Figure 3-138 shows the completed assembly. Plastic laminates or wood trim pieces can be added to exposed edges of the plywood shelves inside the rack frame.

Regardless of the method of fastening, it is extremely important to install the side pieces perpendicular to the table top and shelf in a crosswise direction. Use a square to make pattern lines on the side pieces. It is also important to have exactly the same distance between the top and shelf on both sides. This distance can be as desired, but a minimum of 12 inches is required to give the table adequate strength.

After the lower shelf, table top, and rack have been assembled to the side pieces, the next step is to add the backing piece, as shown in Fig. 3-139. The backing piece forms a box with the top, shelf, and side pieces. It is important that the backing piece be attached securely to the wood members all the way around the edges, both glued and nailed into position. It is extremely important to make certain that the backing piece is a true rectangle and that the side pieces are perpendicular to the table top and shelf before the backing piece is attached and the glue allowed to set. Figure 3-140 shows the backing piece installed.

The floor guides are installed next (see Fig. 3-141). Their installation varies depending on the type of floor guides selected. Some fit in a mounting drilled in the wood beam, others are driven or screwed into the wood and still others have separate screw fasteners to hold them in place.

Sanding and Finishing

Sanding and applying a finish are important last steps in the construction process. Many beginners do a good job constructing the table up to this point, only to give the table a very amateur appearance by sloppy application of a finish. By taking care and a little time, however, even a beginner can give the table a professional finish.

Sanding is an important step in preparing the wood for varnishing or painting. Small holes, checks, and other open defects in the wood should be filled in before sanding. If a clear finish is to be applied, use a wood filler that matches the color of

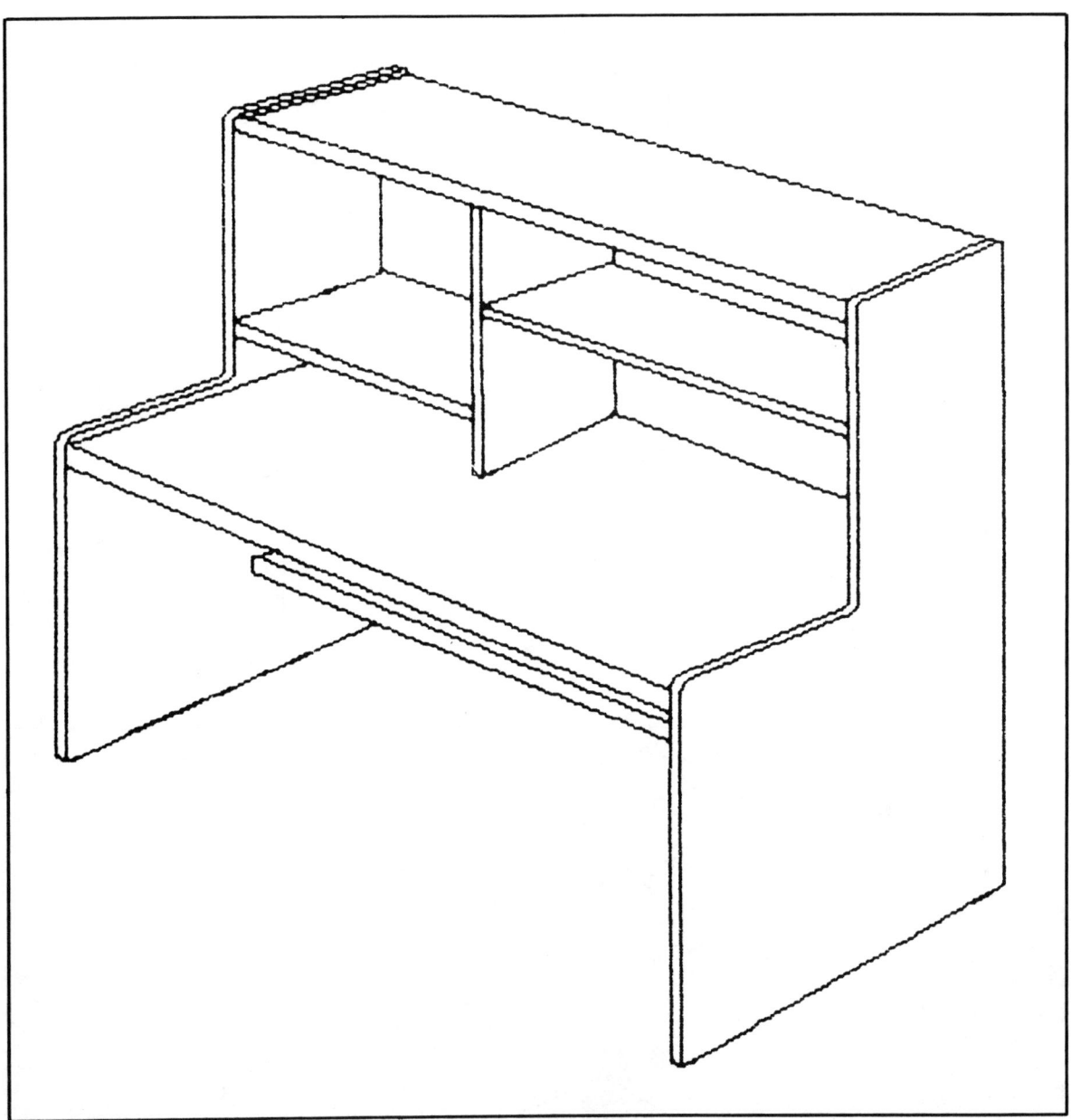

Fig. 3-138. Basic computer table with full sides and video and storage rack with sides installed.

the wood. A sanding sealer should be applied to the plywood before sanding.

The general principle to follow is to work from coarse grits to progressively finer grits. Don't start with a grit that is coarser than necessary for the particular sanding; the condition of the surface might be such that you can start with a medium or even fine grit. Coarser grits tend to leave scratches that need to be sanded away with finer grits.

Sand wood parallel to the grain. Across the grain sanding leaves scratches, tears, and roughens the wood surface, and a scratch free surface is

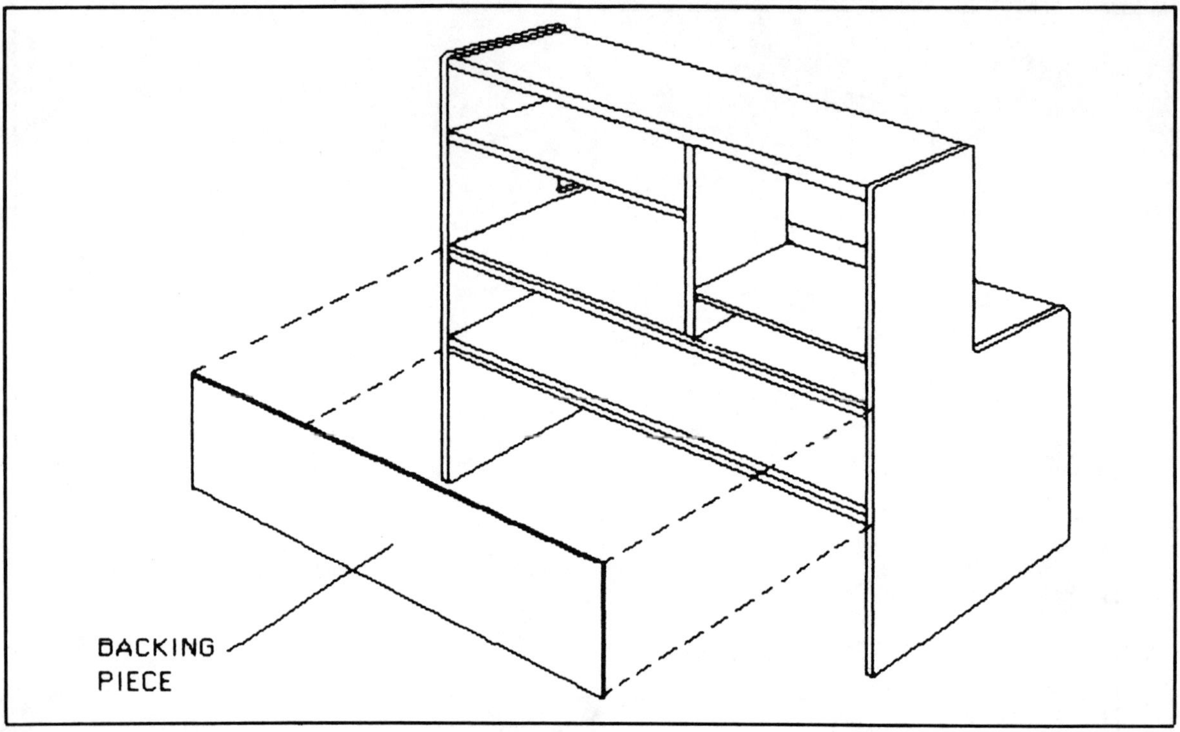

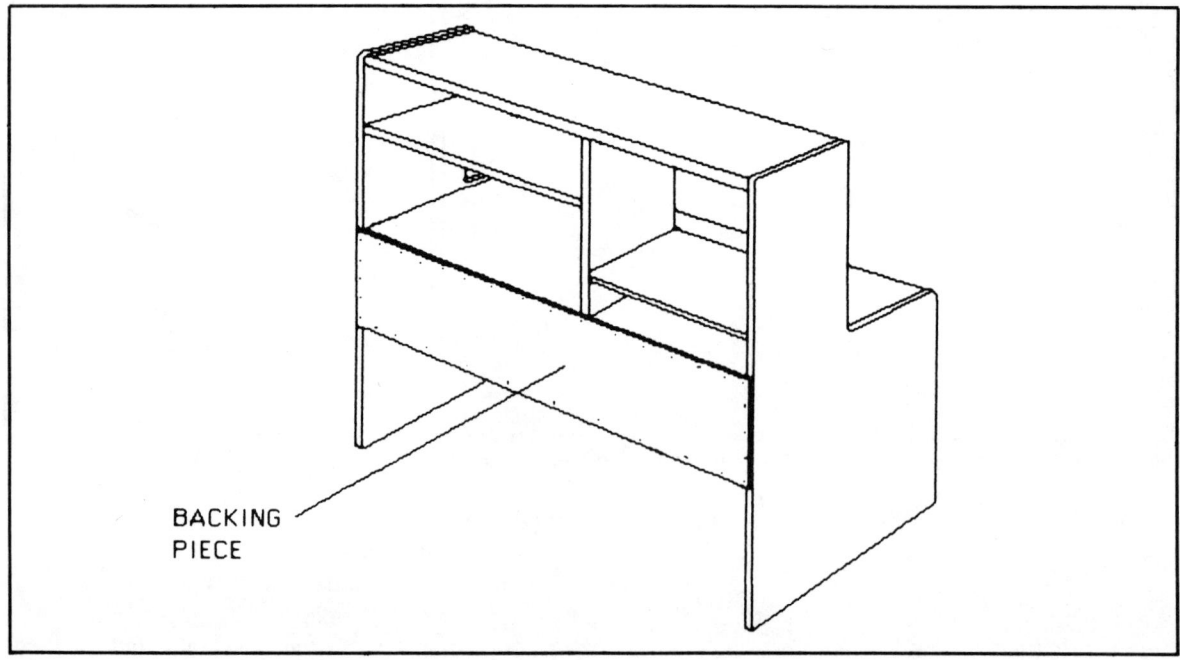

Fig. 3-139. Installing backing piece.

Fig. 3-140. Backing piece installed.

138

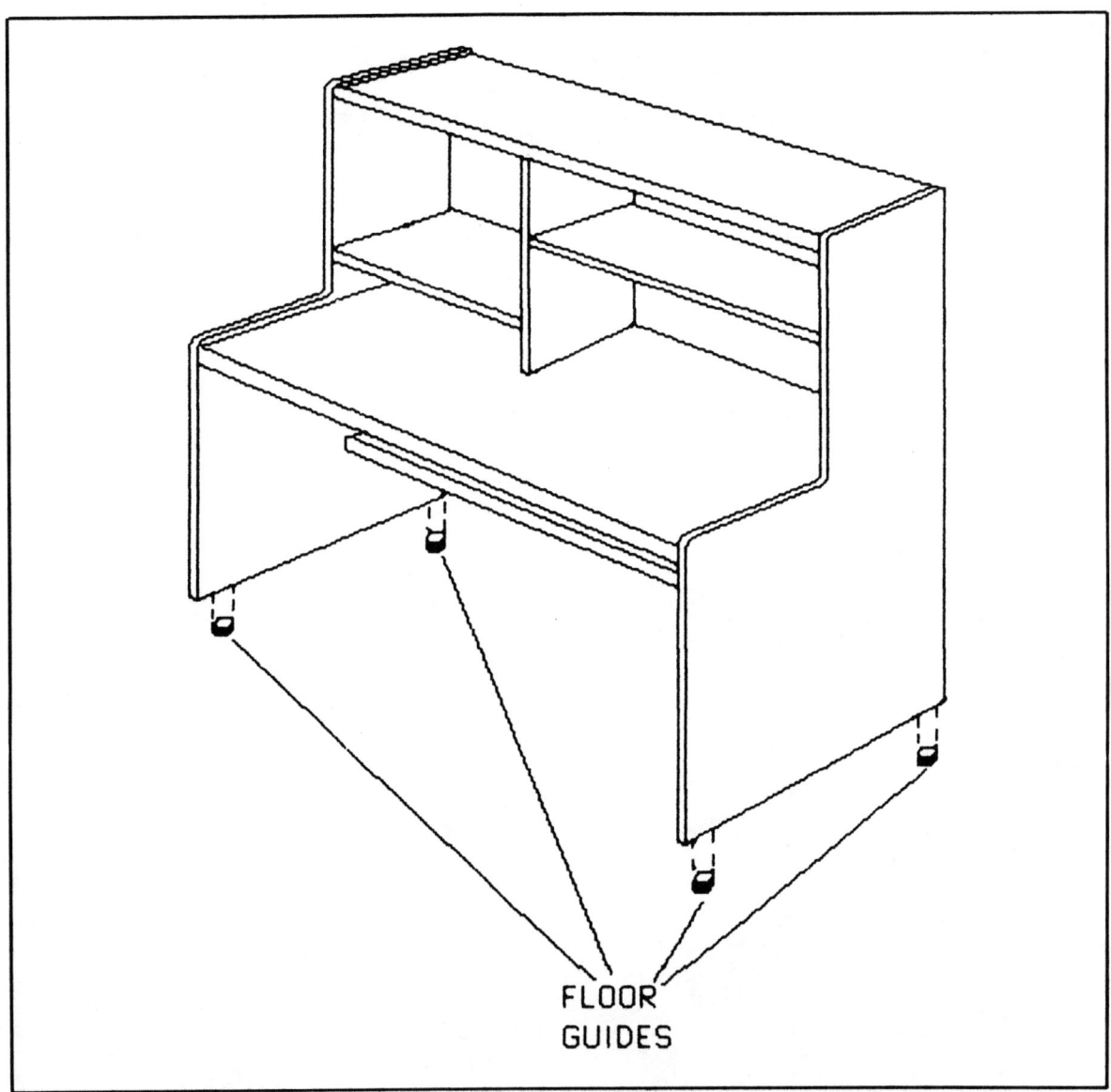

Fig. 3-141. Installing floor guides.

especially important if you are going to finish with oil or varnish.

For most hand sanding, especially on flat surfaces, use a sanding block. Holding the sandpaper in your hand leaves a wavy surface on the wood because of uneven pressure. A carpet or felt pad between the block and the sandpaper also helps.

At the final stages of sanding, use your eyes and fingertips to judge the smoothness of the surface. Careful sanding is an important step toward a fine finish.

If desired, a power sanded can be used. A pad sander is the easiest to use without damaging the wood surface. Belt sanders can be used by experienced operators.

A clear polyurethane plastic finish can be applied directly to natural wood, or you can first stain the wood. Staining can enhance the natural grains of the wood and enrich relatively lifeless woods.

Before applying stain, first test color on a scrap piece of similar wood. Clean the surface area where stain is to be applied, using a tack cloth to eliminate as much dust as possible. The stain can then be applied with a brush, foam brush applicator, or cloth in a smooth, even coat. Allow the stain to penetrate the wood: depending on the humidity, temperature, and particular stain used, this usually takes from 5 to 15 minutes. While the stain is still wet, wipe off the excess stain with a clean cloth, being careful not to remove too much from corners and edges. Wipe across the grain first so that you work the stain into the wood pores. Then give a final wipe with the grain. Allow the stain to dry—at least 8 hours. The finish can then be applied.

It is usually best to apply a series of light, even coats of clear finish rather than one thick coat. This will minimize possible drips and wrinkles as the finish dries.

Apply finish in brush-width strokes in direction of wood grain. Turn table so that finish is applied to wood surface in a horizontal position whenever possible.

A minimum of two coats is recommended. Allow 6 to 8 hours for the first coat to dry before applying second coat. Sand lightly and use a tack cloth to remove sanded finish dust before applying next coat of finish.

Clear or stained finishes are usually applied to natural wood furniture, but if desired color paint finishes can also be applied.

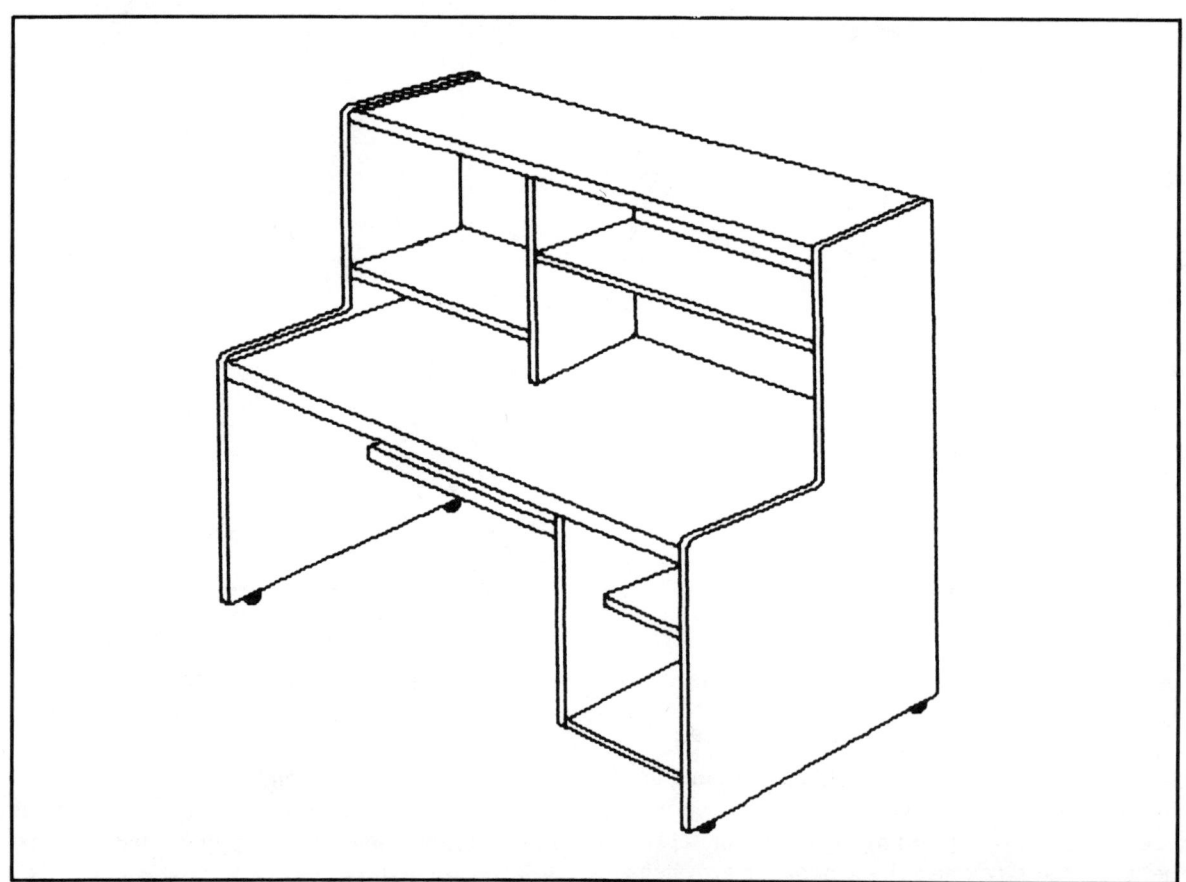

Fig. 3-142. Basic computer table with full sides and video and storage rack with alternate lower storage unit.

Variations

A number of variations are possible on the basic computer table with full sides with video and storage rack. One possibility is to substitute materials, such as particle board instead of plywood for the top and/or other components. Another common variation is to construct the table with a different size of top.

You can also add additional storage shelves below the table and/or a drawer immediately below the table top. A popular shelf and storage arrangement is shown in Figs. 3-142 and 3-143. Additional shelves or an alternate arrangement of shelves can also be used inside the video and storage rack.

The basic computer table with full sides and video and storage rack makes a functional and attractive computer table even when built from inexpensive woods. This design is ideal for anyone who wants to build computer tables to sell to others. The table can be sold either unfinished or with finish applied. By using more expensive woods, such as oak, you can give the table a custom appearance. The plans given here show simple butt joints, but if you have the cabinet-making skills and know-how, you can also use more difficult joints and assembly.

BASIC COMPUTER TABLE WITH HALF SIDES AND VIDEO AND STORAGE RACK

This table is slightly more difficult to construct than the basic budget computer table with video and storage rack and of about equal difficulty to the

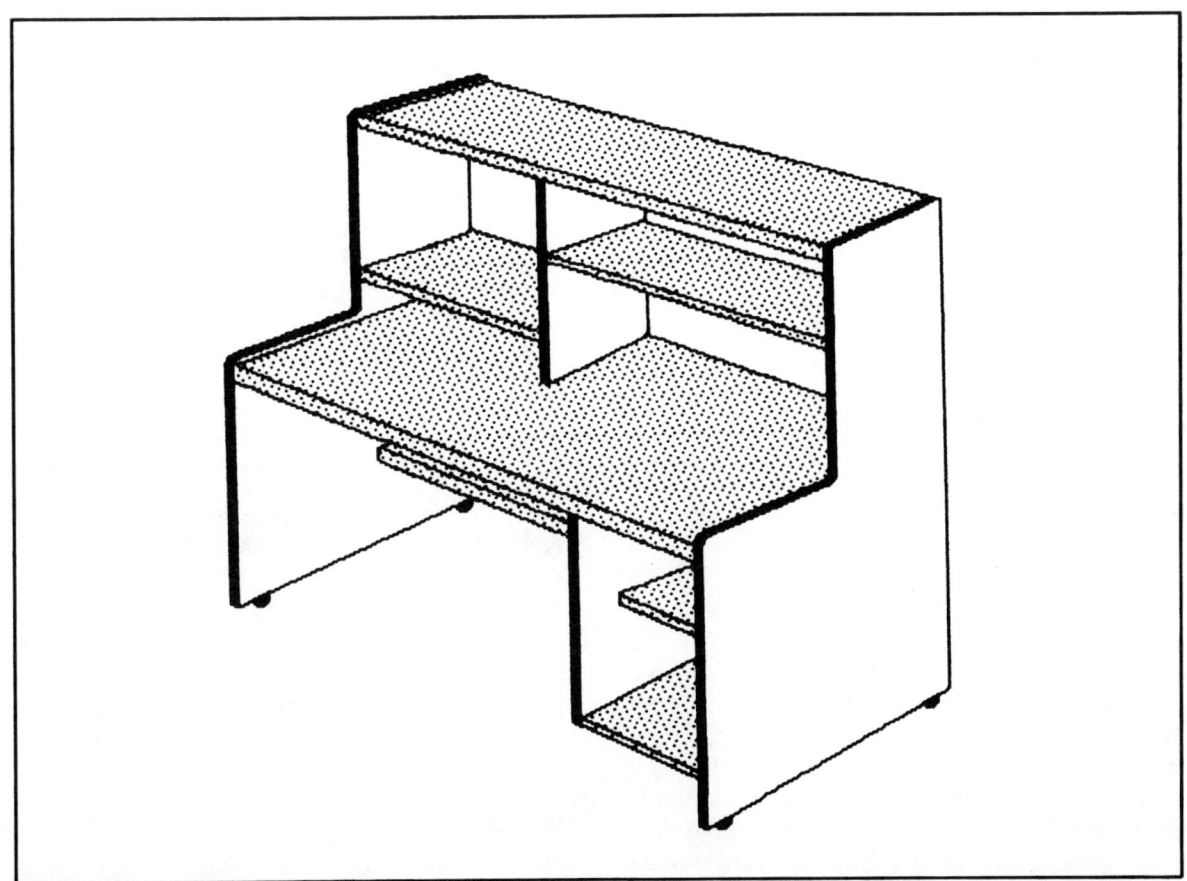

Fig. 3-143. Basic computer table with full sides and video and storage rack with alternate lower storage unit with plastic laminates.

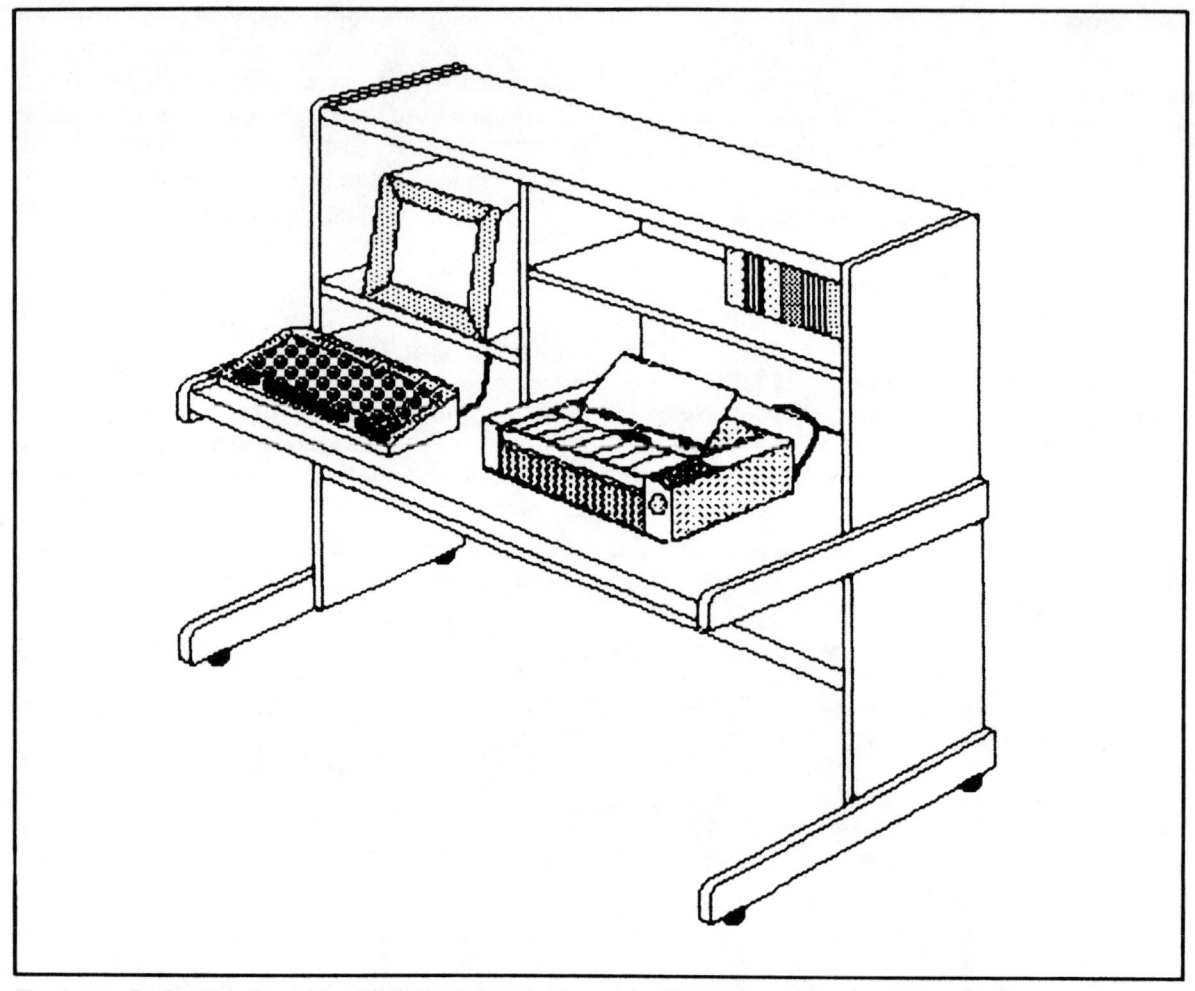

Fig. 3-144. Basic computer table with half sides and video and storage rack, along with a computer and printer.

basic computer table with full sides with video and storage rack described earlier. This table is constructed mainly from plywood. Materials to build this table vary in cost, but would run around $40 (at 1984 prices) using Douglas fir plywood and a plastic laminate top and around $90 using oak-faced plywood. These prices will vary, however, depending on where you purchase your wood, your area, and other factors, but you can save a lot by building your own. This modern, attractive computer table gives a good appearance even when built from standard plywood. You can give it a custom appearance by building the same design from more expensive plywoods faced with oak or other hardwoods.

The basic computer table with half sides with video and storage rack is shown in Figs. 3-144 and 3-145. The top has space for both a computer and printer. The table and shelves can have natural wood tops or be covered with plastic laminates. The table features a shelf underneath that provides storage space and gives the table added strength and an attractive video and storage rack.

Materials

The patterns for the plywood parts are shown in Fig. 3-146. The top of the table is a 26-inch-by-4-foot piece of 3/4-inch thick plywood. If you in-

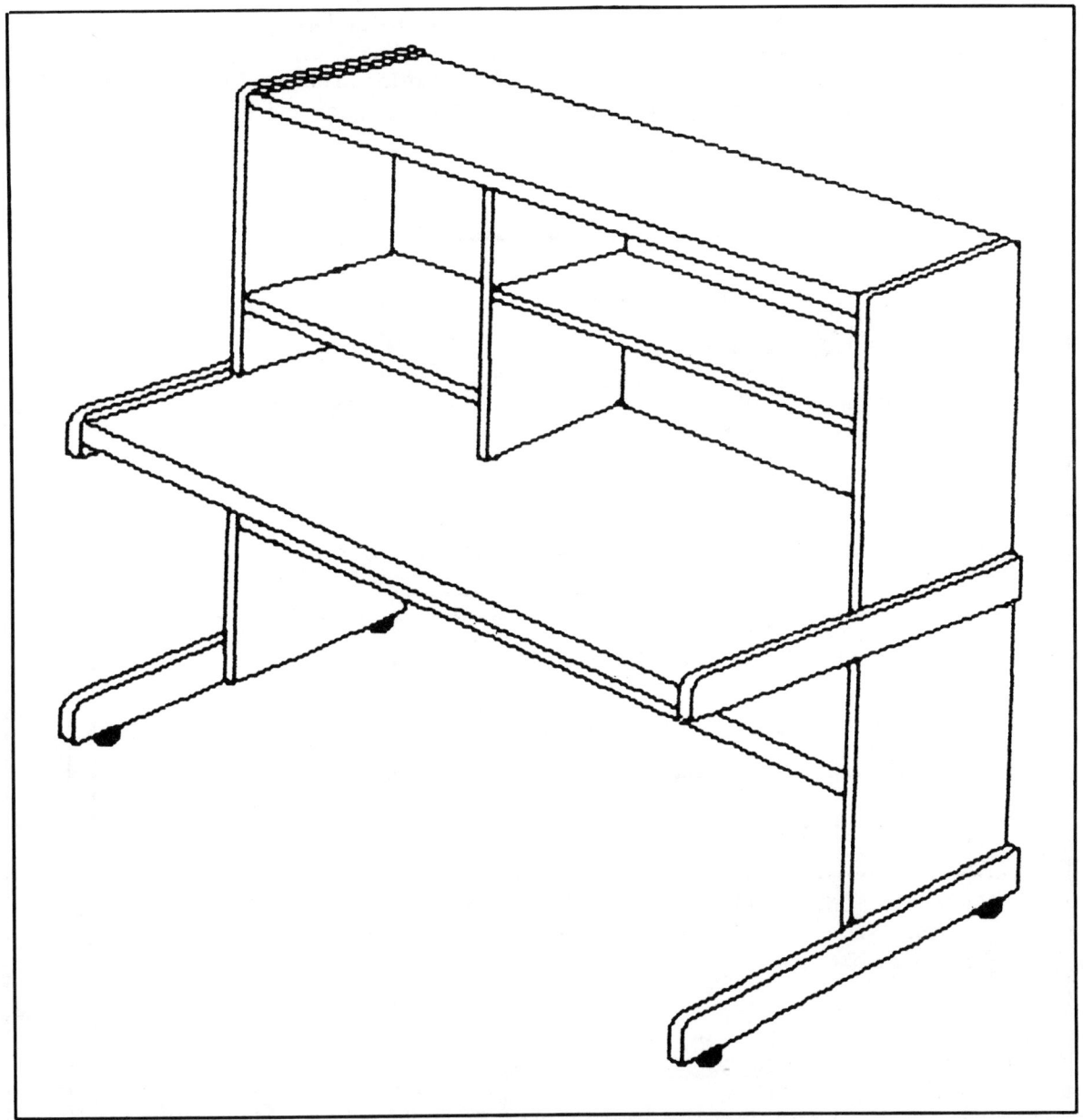

Fig. 3-145. Basic computer table with half sides and video and storage rack.

tend to use the wood surface as the finished table top, without adding a plastic laminate, plywood with the upper layer of a hardwood is recommended. If a laminate is to be added, exterior grade shop plywood will suffice.

The shelves are 3/4-inch thick plywood. The shelves measure 46 1/2 inches by 13 inches.

The end pieces are 3/4-inch thick plywood and measure 13-inch-by-49-inch. The table is 29 inches high, not counting the height added by whatever floor guides are used, so you may want to change the 49-inch dimension if you want your table a dif-

143

ferent height. Two end pieces are required.

The patterns for the shelf parts used inside the rack are shown in Fig. 3-146.

Plywood is normally sold in standard 4-foot-by-8-foot sheets. Lay out the patterns to take advantage of this standard size and arrange them to keep waste to a minimum. You may be able to have the plywood sheets cut for you to desired size,

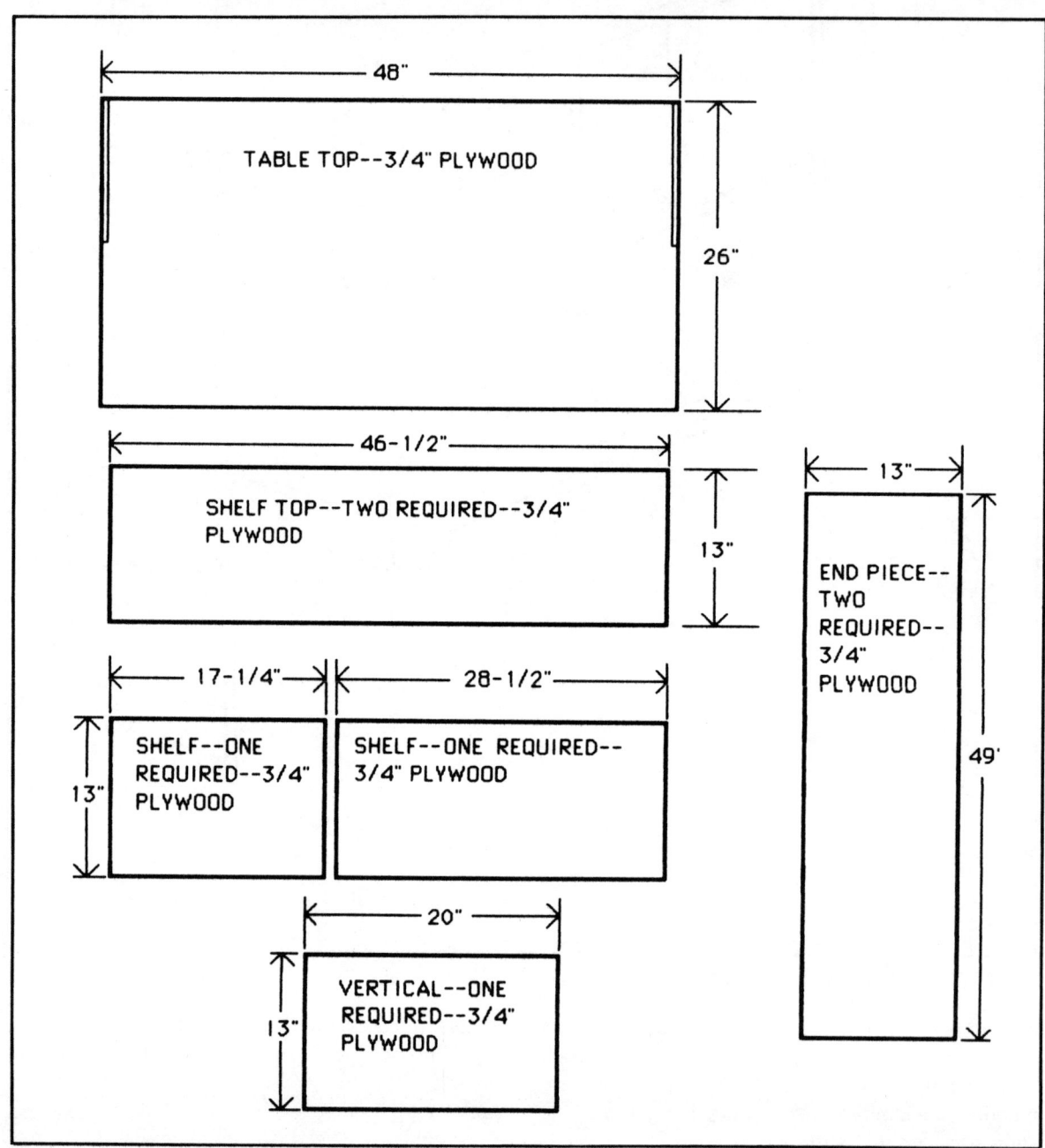

Fig. 3-146. Patterns for plywood parts.

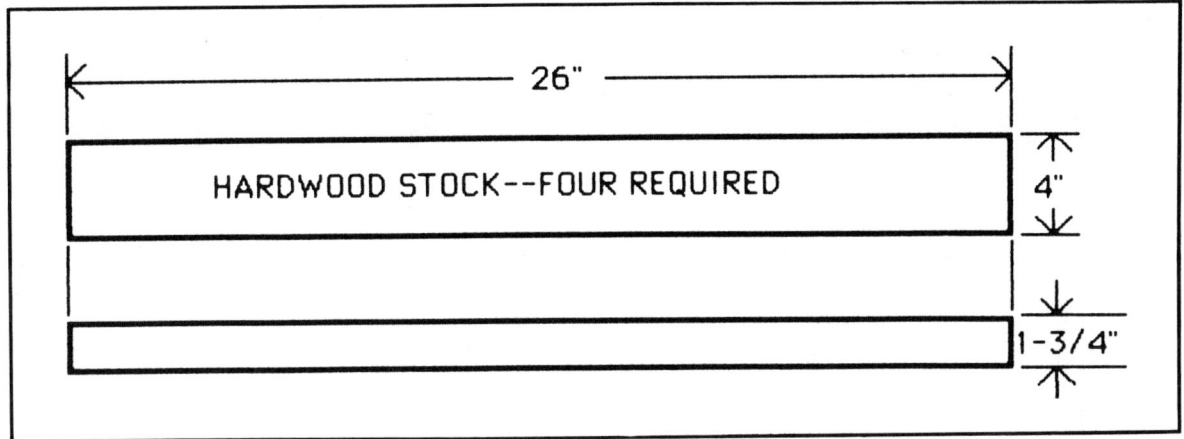

Fig. 3-147. Patterns for side pieces.

usually at additional cost, and this can be worth it if you don't need full sheets, don't have room to carry full sheets in your car, or don't have a saw to accurately cut plywood.

Although 1/2-inch thick plywood could also be used, I don't recommend this. Savings are negligible, and you'll end up with a weaker table. Particle board can be substituted for the plywood if you are on an absolute minimum budget. It can be difficult to work with, however, and it is very difficult to get plastic laminates to bond properly to this material without special equipment.

Four side beam pieces, 26 inches long, of 2-inch-by-4-inch hardwood stock are required (Fig. 3-147).

The backing piece (Fig. 3-148) can be either plywood or fiberboard. The backing piece is used to strengthen the table base and hold the frame in rectangular form. The length of the backing piece is 48 inches. A 13-inch height is shown for the backing piece, which is about the minimum required to give this table adequate strength. The shelf can be installed a greater distance below the top, which will require changing the height of the backing piece. Notice that the top, shelf, backing piece, and side pieces form a box with the forward side open.

You will also need 1-inch-by-2-inch or larger framing stock for use under the plywood table top and the shelves.

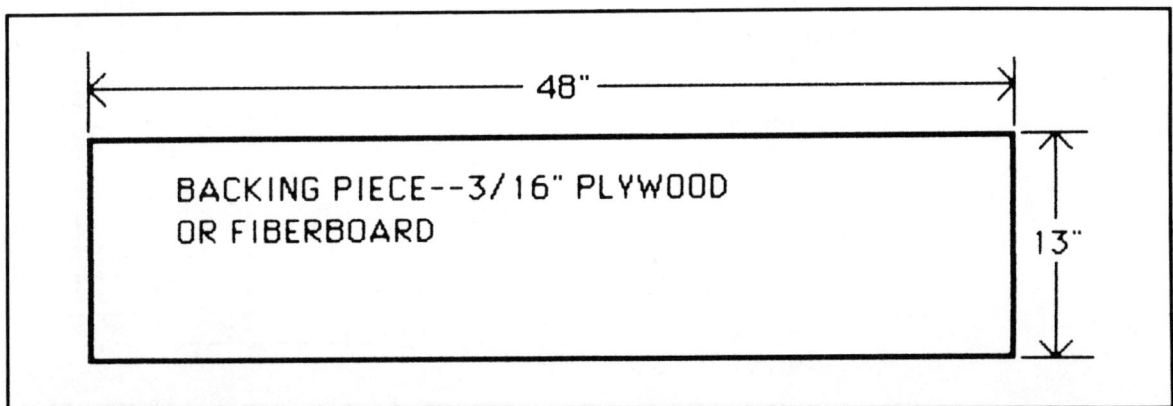

Fig. 3-148. Pattern for backing piece.

Wood or plastic trim strips can be used to cover the forward edges of the table top and shelves. These pieces are 48 inches and 46 1/2 inches long respectively and about 1 3/4 inches wide. The minimum width should be such that it will completely cover the widths of the plywood (3/4 inch for the top plywood) and the framing (approximately 7/8 inch). The trim strips can be slightly wider than this, however.

Four floor pods or guides are used on the floor beams. A variety of suitable fixed or adjustable types are available from hardware stores.

Various fasteners can be used for assembly—nails, screws, etc. You will also need a good wood glue. The finish can be clear urethane or whatever else you like.

The table top can be left natural wood or a plastic laminate can be added. If a plastic laminate is applied, you will need a 26-inch-by-4-foot piece and contact cement to attach it to the plywood. If

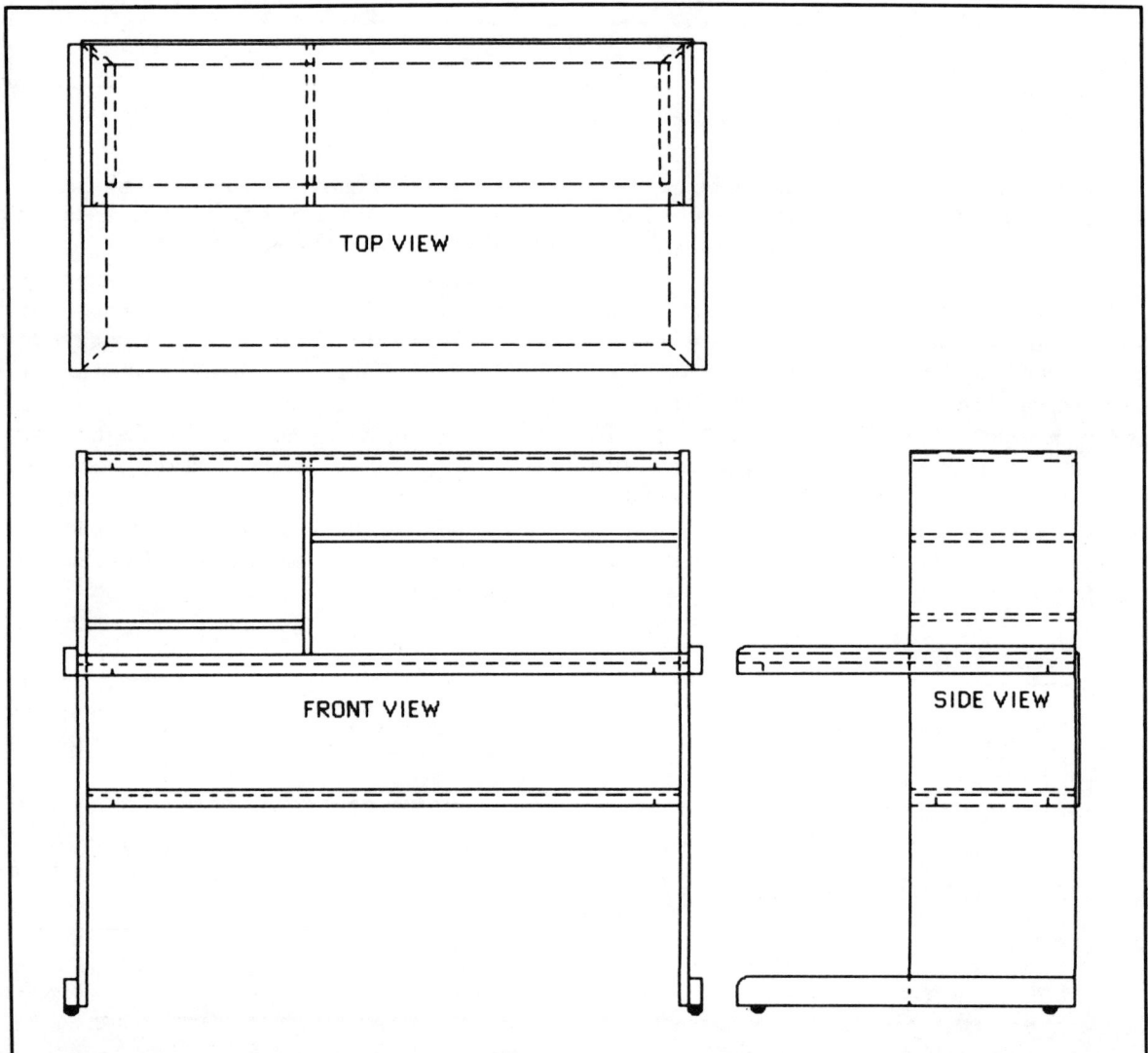

Fig. 3-149. Basic computer table with half sides and video and storage rack.

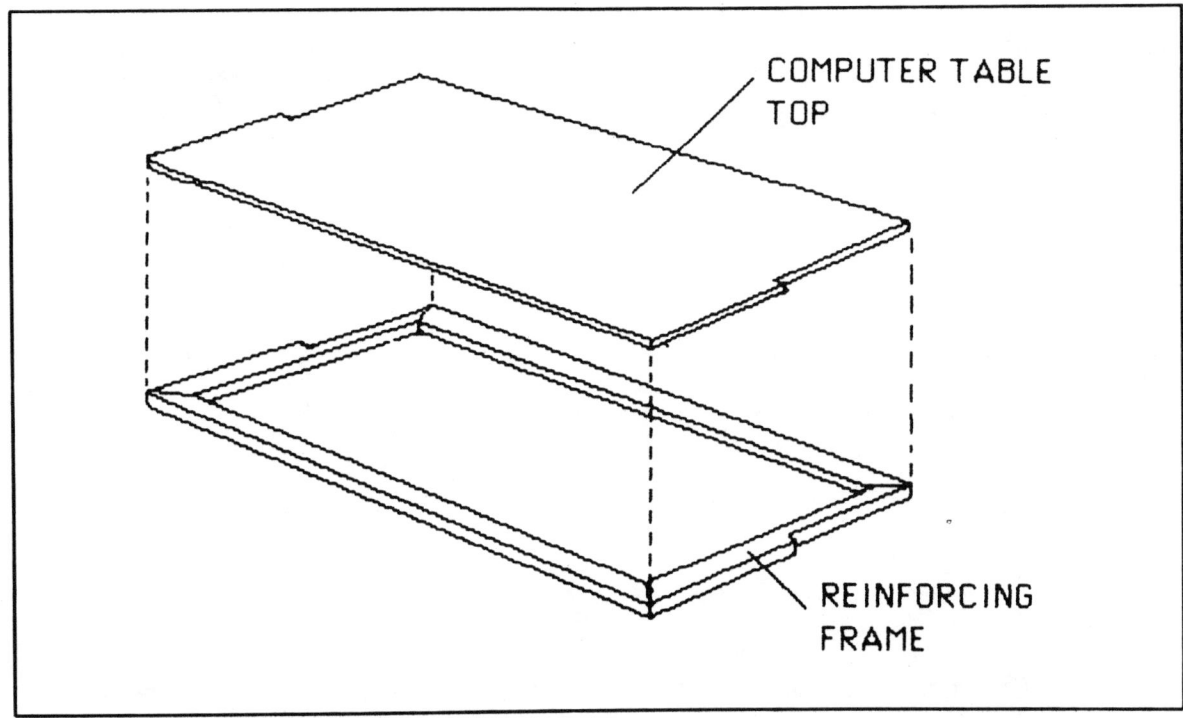

Fig. 3-150. Assembly of top and reinforcing frame.

desired, the shelf tops can also be covered with plastic laminates.

Construction

An overview of the complete assembly is shown in Fig. 3-149. Begin by constructing the table top, as detailed in Fig. 3-150. If you purchased a piece of plywood that was already cut to the 26-inch-by-4-foot size, no additional cutting will be required. This assumes that it was cut accurately and is a true rectangle. Check this with a square.

If you purchased a standard 4-foot-by-8-foot sheet, you will need to cut out a section for the table top. Try to have the grain of the top layer running lengthwise; this is not essential if you are going to apply laminate. To save time, use two factory cut edges for your table top and cut the other two. Use a ruler and square and mark the lines with a sharp pencil or scribing tool.

Sawing plywood requires that special considerations be taken to avoid chipping and splintering along the cut edge. Handsaws or power saws with special fine-toothed or carbide-tipped blades designed especially for plywood should be used. To prevent splintering, apply a strip of masking tape over the area to be cut on both sides of the plywood, especially on the underside, or clamp a solid piece of wood to the underside and make the cut through both the plywood and the piece of wood.

Be extremely careful when sanding plywood edges. Use a sanding block, and avoid sanding the surfaces of plywood until a wood sealer has been applied to prevent snags and chips.

After the table top is finished, add the reinforcing frame, as shown in Fig. 3-150. Use a ruler and a square to make the patterns on the framing wood, drawing the lines with a sharp pencil or scribe. Then make the necessary saw cuts, following procedures detailed in Chapter 2. The frame pieces should be glued and nailed or screwed in position (see Figs. 3-151 and 3-152). If the plywood top will be left natural wood (no plastic laminate added), the fasteners should go through the framing and into

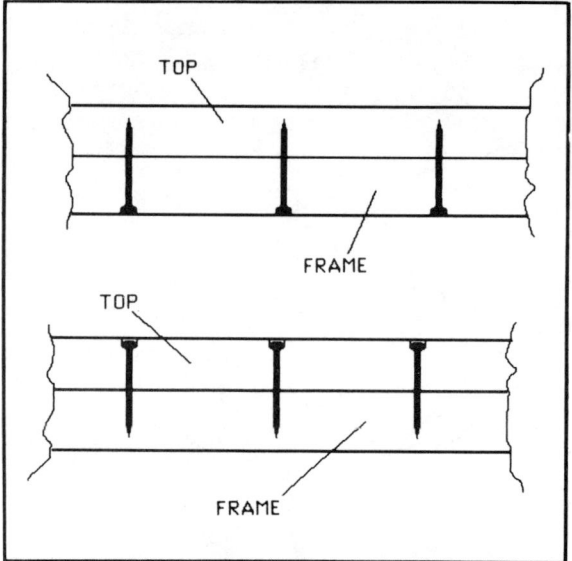

Fig. 3-151. Assembly of table top to frame pieces with nails and glue.

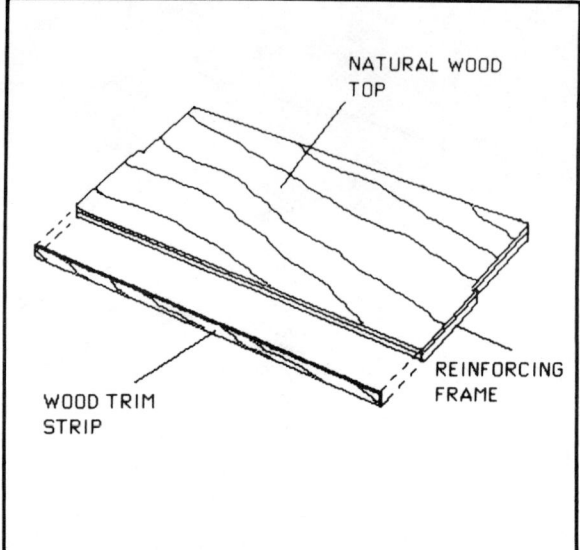

Fig. 3-153. Adding wood trim strip to forward edge of table top.

the plywood. Take care that the fasteners do not pass all the way through the plywood or leave a bulge in the upper surface. If a good acrylic or epoxy glue is used, it alone will give adequate strength. Here, the fasteners are mainly used as clamping devices and will not have much holding power. For greater holding power, pass the fasteners through the plywood and into the framing, but only if a plastic laminate is to be added.

Many options are available to you for finishing off the table top. You can use the natural plywood surface as the top and add a wood trim strip to the

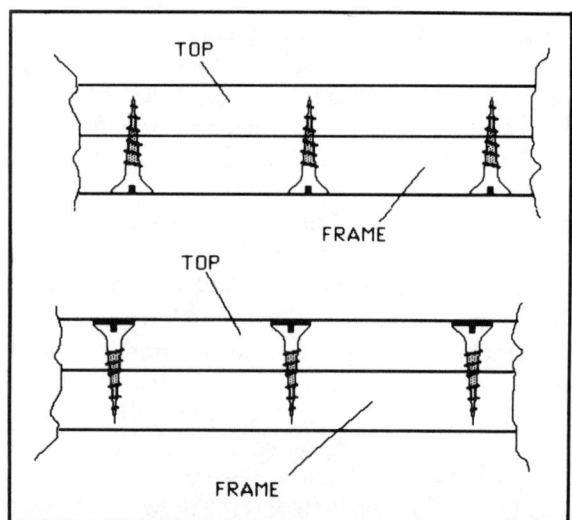

Fig. 3-152. Assembly of table top to frame pieces with screws and glue.

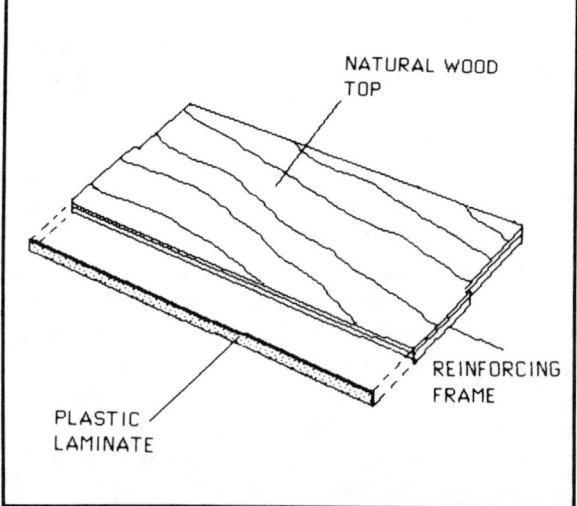

Fig. 3-154. Adding plastic laminate to forward edge of table top.

forward edge, as shown in Fig. 3-153. Glue and fasten the trim strip in place with finishing nails. Set the heads below the wood surface and fill holes with wood filler to flush with the wood surface.

A second possibility is to add a plastic laminate to the forward edge and leave the top natural wood, as detailed in Fig. 3-154.

Another method adds a plastic laminate to the top and a wood trim strip to the forward edge, as shown in Fig. 3-155. Yet another possibility adds plastic laminates to both the top and forward edge, as shown in Figs. 3-156 and 3-157.

If you choose to apply laminate to the plywood table top and/or the forward edge, install it now. Plastic laminates are often applied to plywood to create sturdy computer table tops. A large selection of plastic laminates are on the market, but I suggest using only high quality plastic laminates for computer table tops.

If a plastic laminate will be applied to the forward edge of the table top, it should be applied first. This is then finished flush with the table top. The top laminate is applied so that the edge overlaps the top edge of the laminate on the forward edge

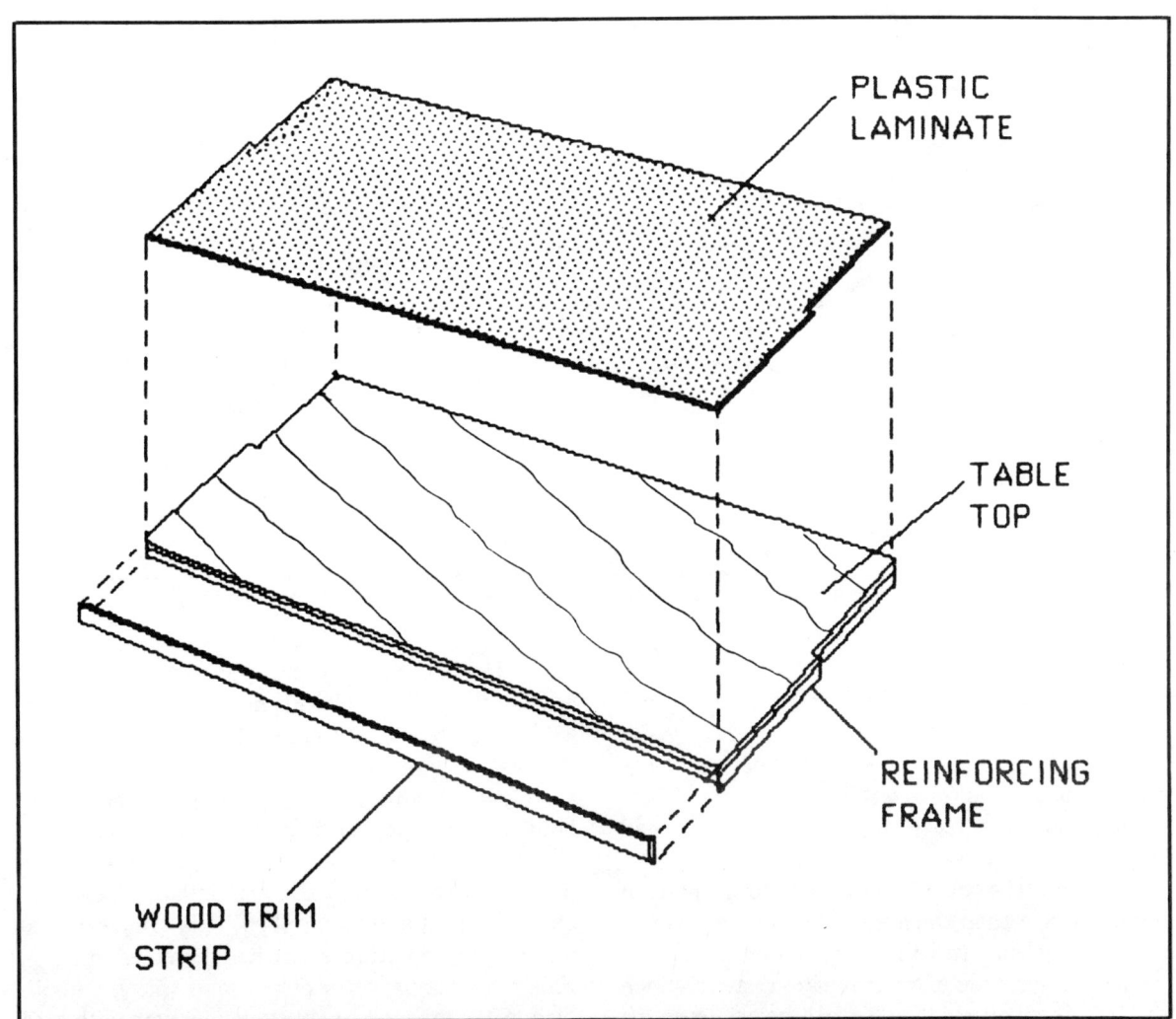

Fig. 3-155. Adding plastic laminate to top and wood trim strip to forward edge of computer table top.

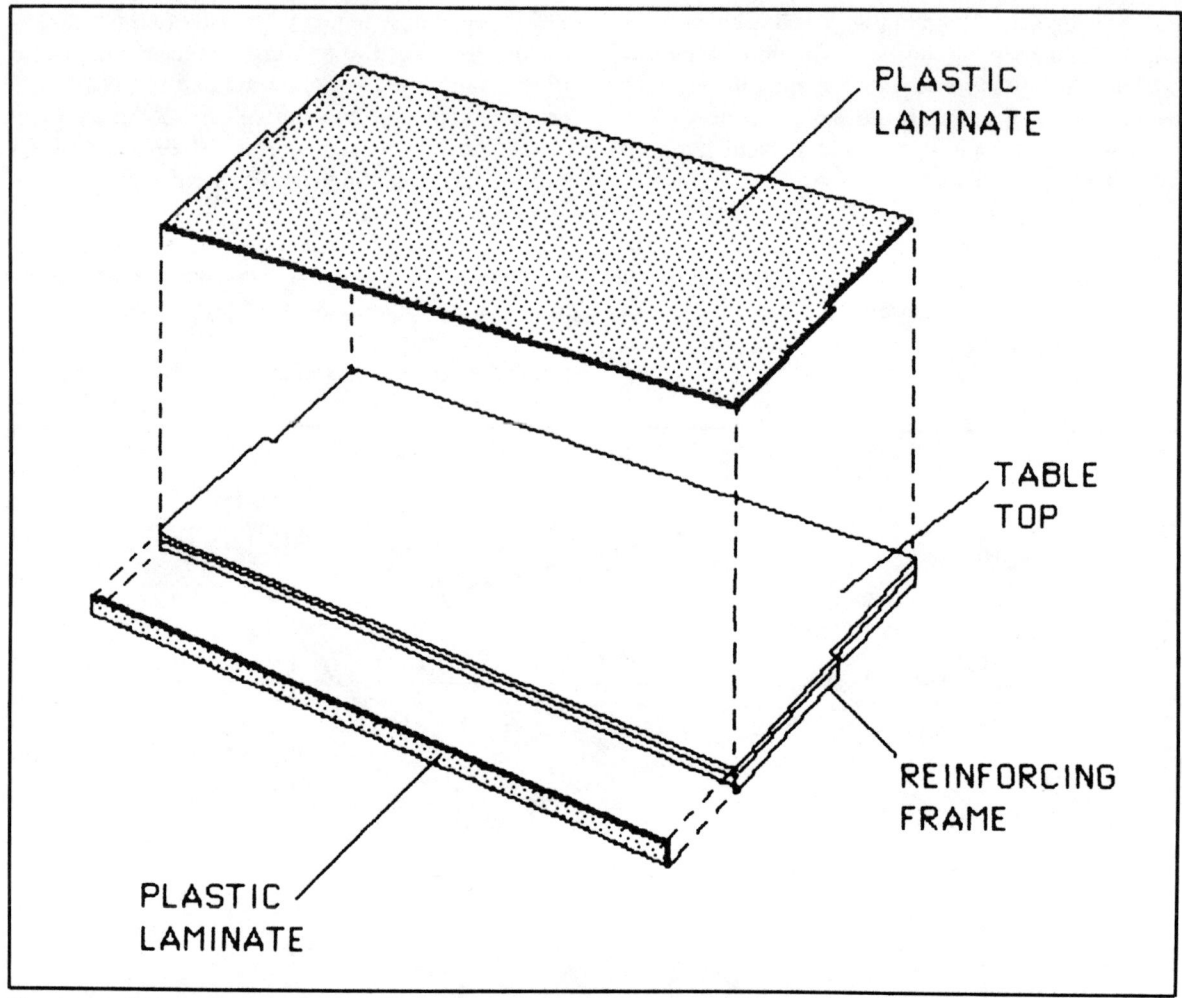

Fig. 3-156. Adding plastic laminates to top and wood trim strip to forward edge of computer table top.

of the table, as shown in Fig. 3-157.

The plastic laminate is installed as follows:

- All holes and defects in the surface of the plywood should be filled with putty or wood filler.
- Sand the surface to be covered. This will help ensure good adhesion.
- Mark the plastic laminate to a pattern slightly larger than the area to be covered. Use a straightedge and draw the pattern lines on the finished or pattern side of the laminate. Leave 1/4 inch to 1/2 inch on all sides. This will be trimmed off later.

- If a laminate is to be applied to the forward edge of the table, apply this first. After installation, as detailed below, trim and file the upper edge of the plastic laminate flush with the upper edge of the plywood table top before installing the plastic laminate to upper surface of the table top.
- Cut the plastic laminate to the pattern marked. Even though the plastic laminate is extremely durable once applied, it is vulnerable to cracking and splitting before it is cemented in place. Fine-tooth handsaws or power saws with fine-tooth blades can be used. A rotary power saw with a 14 to 16 teeth per inch blade is ideal. Place the plastic

laminate face up when cutting. Be careful that the plastic laminate is not chipped or broken. An alternate method is to use a carbide tip knife to score the plastic by drawing the knife point along a metal straightedge. Cut through the decorative surface. The laminate can then be broken by bending it toward the decorative surface side over the edge of a table or workbench.

• Apply contact cement to the surface of the plywood to be covered and the back side of the plastic laminate with a brush, roller, or metal spreader with a serrated edge. A thin, even application is important.

• Follow the manufacturer's instructions regarding drying time. Usually, this takes about 20 to 30 minutes.

• Place a sheet of heavy wrapping paper over the plywood surface to be covered, then position the laminate on the plywood surface with the paper between. The contact cement will not stick to the paper if it has been allowed to dry properly. Make certain that the laminate is positioned correctly: once the two surfaces of contact cement touch, the laminate sheet cannot be moved again.

When everything is lined up properly, pull the paper out from between the plywood and the plastic laminate.

• Using a small block of wood and a hammer, lightly tap the laminate in place, or use a rolling pin to smooth the laminate.

• Use a file to remove the surplus plastic laminate from the edges. Another method is to use a special cutter with a router, which allows you to trim off excess plastic laminate flush with the plywood edges.

• The thinner recommended for the contact cement can be used for cleaning contact cement from wood and plastic laminate and tools.

The next step is to construct the shelves, as detailed in Fig. 3-158. If you purchased pieces of plywood cut to the 13-inch-by-46 1/2-inch sizes, no additional cutting will be required, assuming that they were cut accurately. Check for trueness with a square.

If you purchased a larger piece of plywood, you will need to cut out sections for the shelf tops. Have the grain of the top layer running lengthwise. This is not essential if you are going to add a plastic lam-

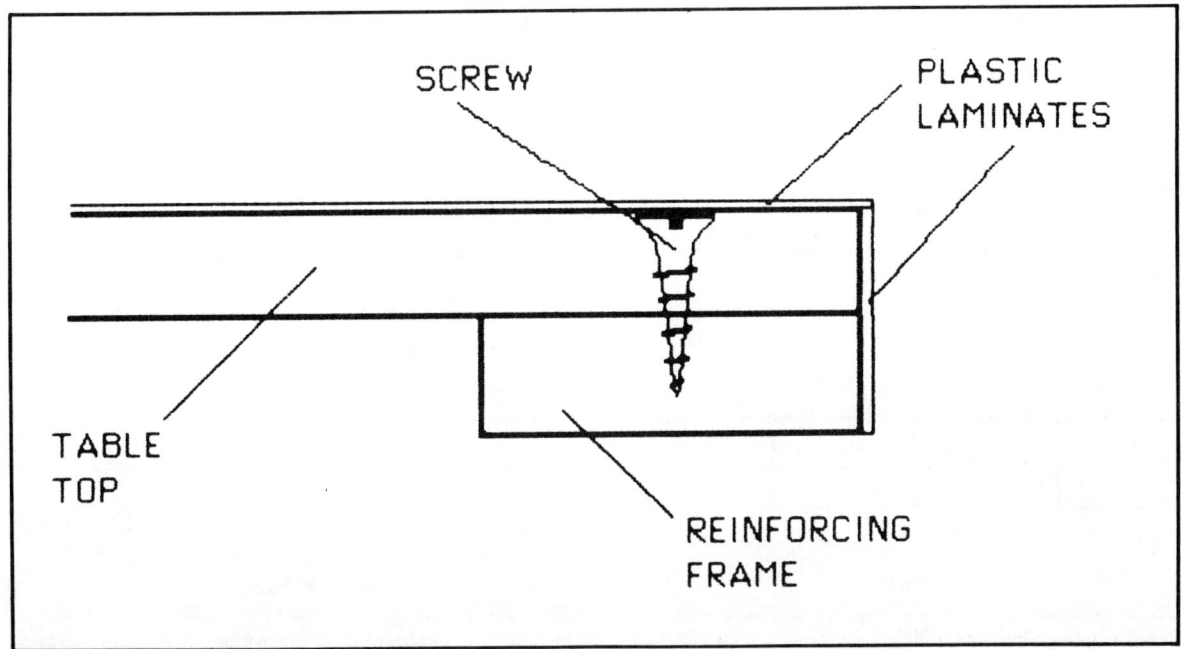

Fig. 3-157. Adding plastic laminates to shelf.

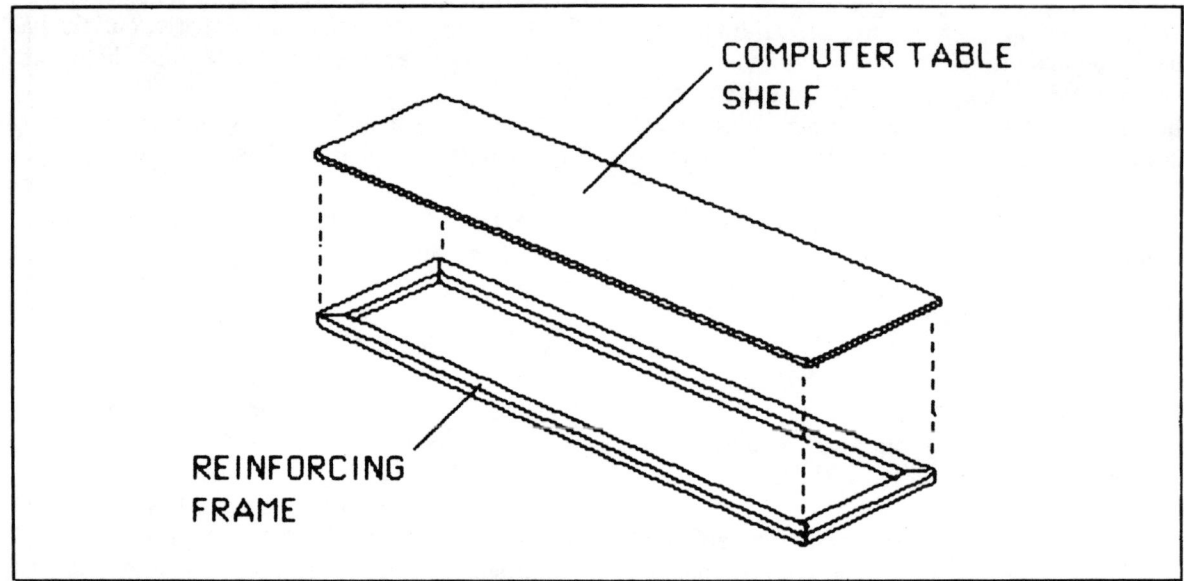

Fig. 3-158. Assembly of shelf top to reinforcing frame.

inate. In most cases, you will use two factory cut edges for a shelf top and cut the other two. Use a ruler and square to mark the pattern with a sharp pencil or scribing tool. Saw and sand carefully.

The next step is to add the reinforcing frames to the shelf pieces, as shown in Fig. 3-158. Draw the patterns on the framing wood with a ruler and square. Then make the necessary saw cuts. The frame pieces should be glued and nailed or screwed in position (see Figs. 3-159 and 3-160). If the plywood shelf tops will have a natural wood finish, the fasteners should go through the framing and

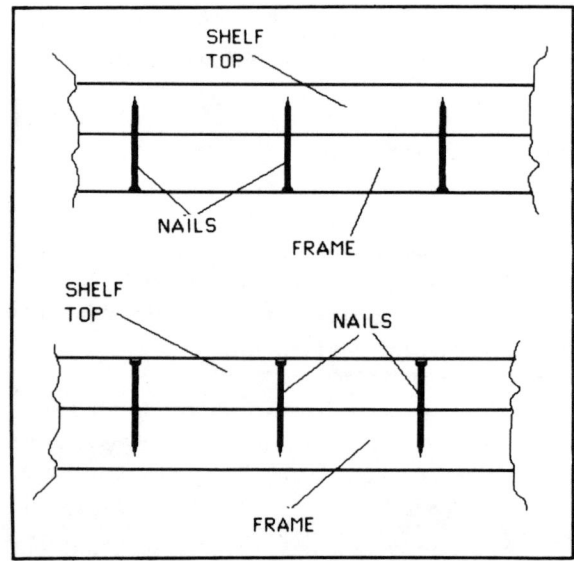

Fig. 3-159. Assembly of shelf top to frame pieces with nails and glue.

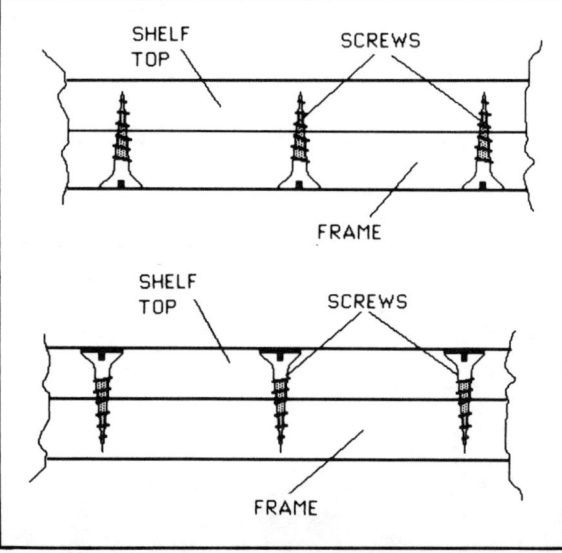

Fig. 3-160. Assembly of shelf top to frame pieces with screws and glue.

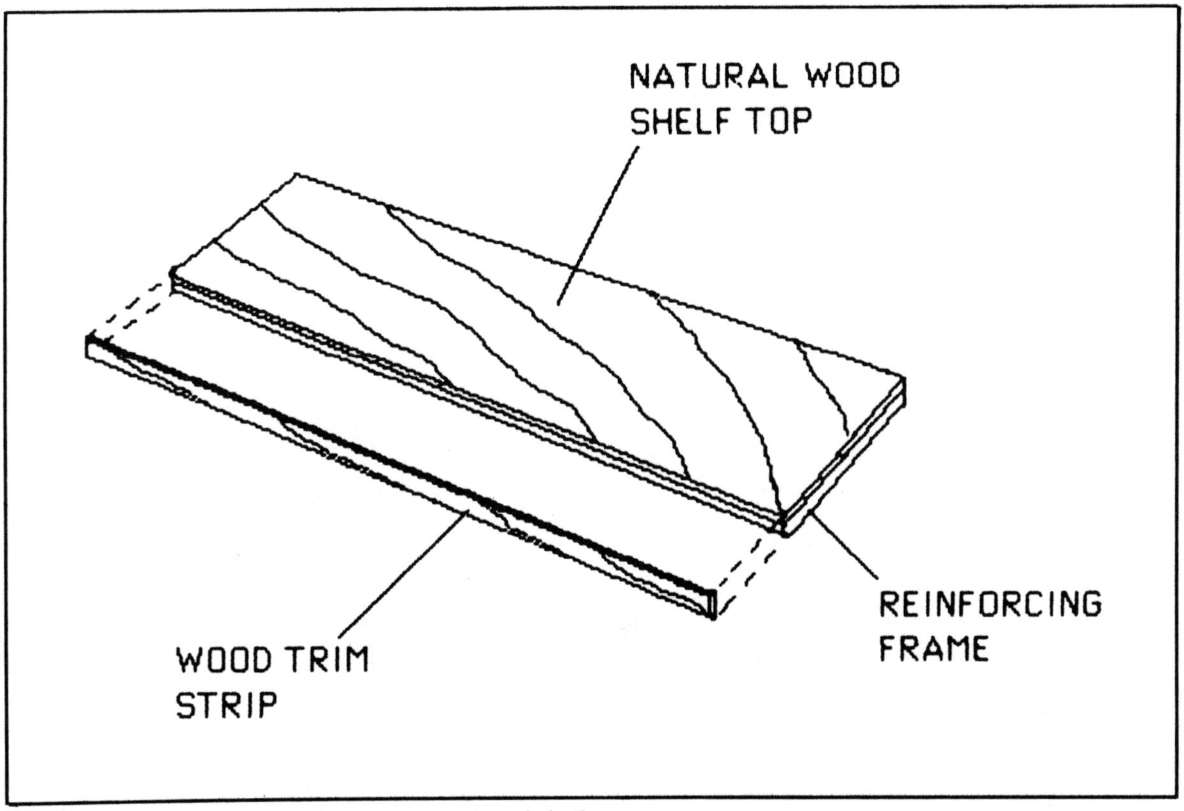

Fig. 3-161. Adding wood trip strip to forward edge of shelf.

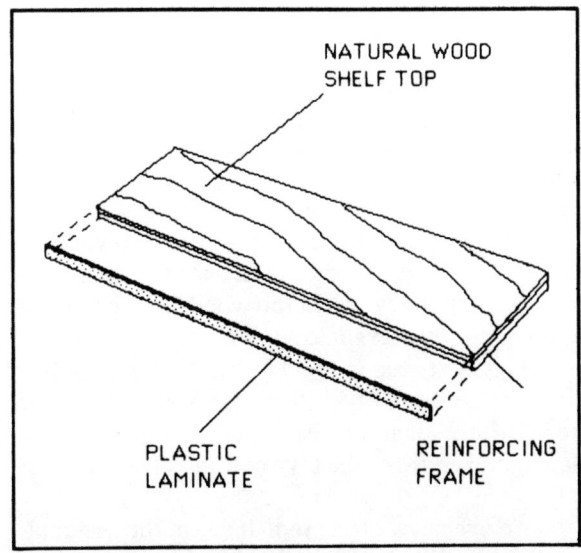

Fig. 3-162. Adding plastic laminate to forward edge of a shelf.

into the plywood, but not all the way through the plywood or that they leave a bulge in the upper surface. If a good glue is used, such as acrylic or epoxy, the glue alone should give adequate strength, with the fasteners used as a clamping device. Fasteners will not have much holding power in plywood. To give greater holding power, the fasteners can be passed through the plywood and into the framing if a plastic laminate is to be added.

The same options are available for finishing off the shelves as for the table top:

• Use the plywood surface as the shelf top and add a wood trim strip to the forward edge, as shown in Fig. 3-161. Glue and fasten the trim strip in place with finishing nails. Set the heads below the wood surface and fill holes with wood filler to flush with the wood surface.

• Add a plastic laminate to the forward edge

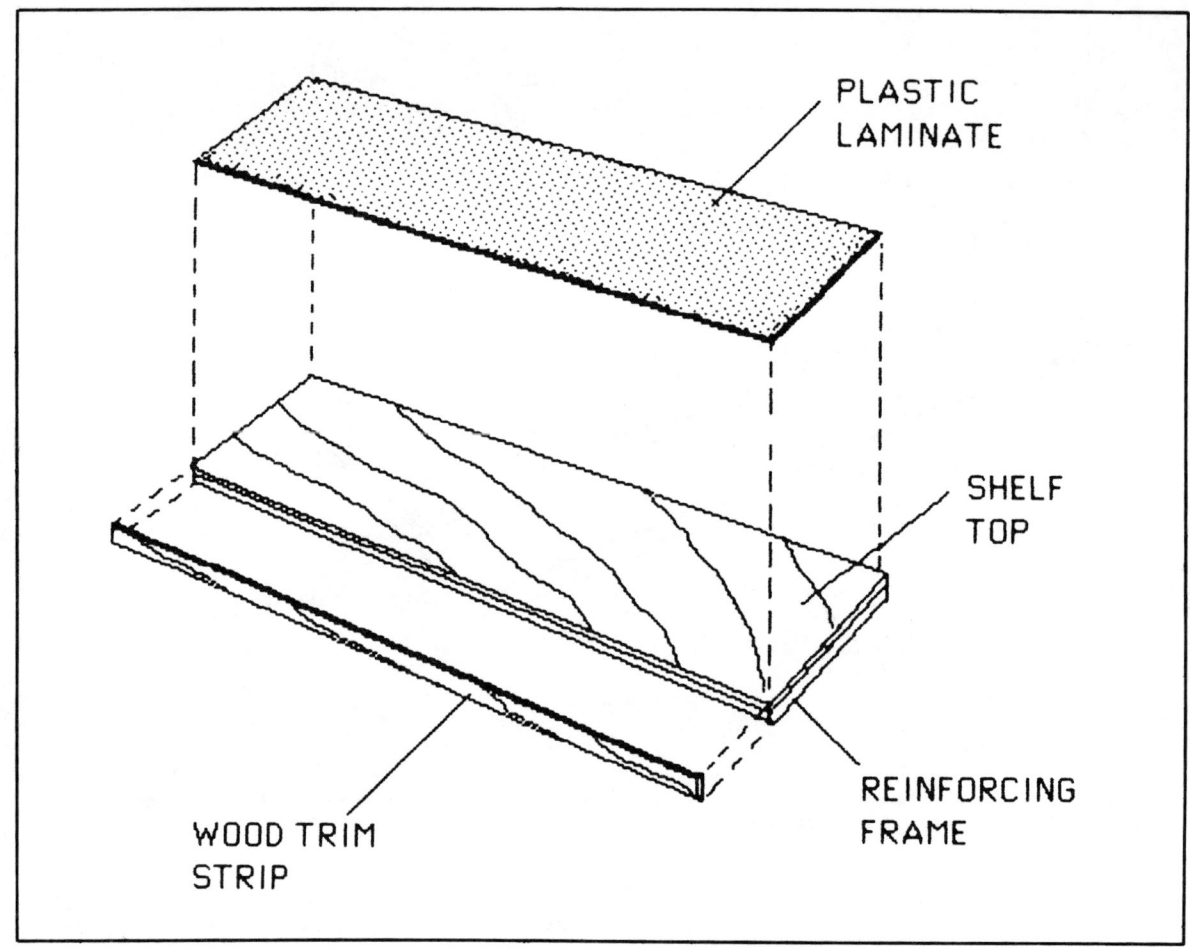

Fig. 3-163. Adding plastic laminate to top and wood trim strip to forward edge of shelf.

and leave the shelf top natural wood, as detailed in Fig. 3-162.

- Add a plastic laminate to the shelf top and a wood trim strip to the forward edge, as shown in Fig. 3-163, or add plastic laminates to both the top and forward edge, as shown in Figs. 3-164 and 3-165.

If laminate is added to the plywood shelf tops and/or the forward edges, these pieces can be installed at this time. If a plastic laminate is to also be applied to the forward edge of the shelf top, it should be applied first, then finished flush with the shelf top. The top laminate is then applied so that the edge overlaps the top edge of the laminate on the forward edge of the shelf, as shown in Fig. 3-165. Follow application instructions given for the table top above.

Next, cut the end pieces to rectangular size. A power circular saw is ideal for making straight cuts. Apply a strip of masking tape over the area to be cut on both sides of the plywood, especially the underside, to prevent chipping.

The next step is to add plastic (Fig. 3-166) or wood (Fig. 3-167) trim to the forward edges and tops of the end pieces. This will protect the laminated edges of the plywood and give a neat appearance.

An overview of the remainder of the assembly is shown in Fig. 3-168. Assemble the table top and shelves to the side pieces, as shown in Fig. 3-169.

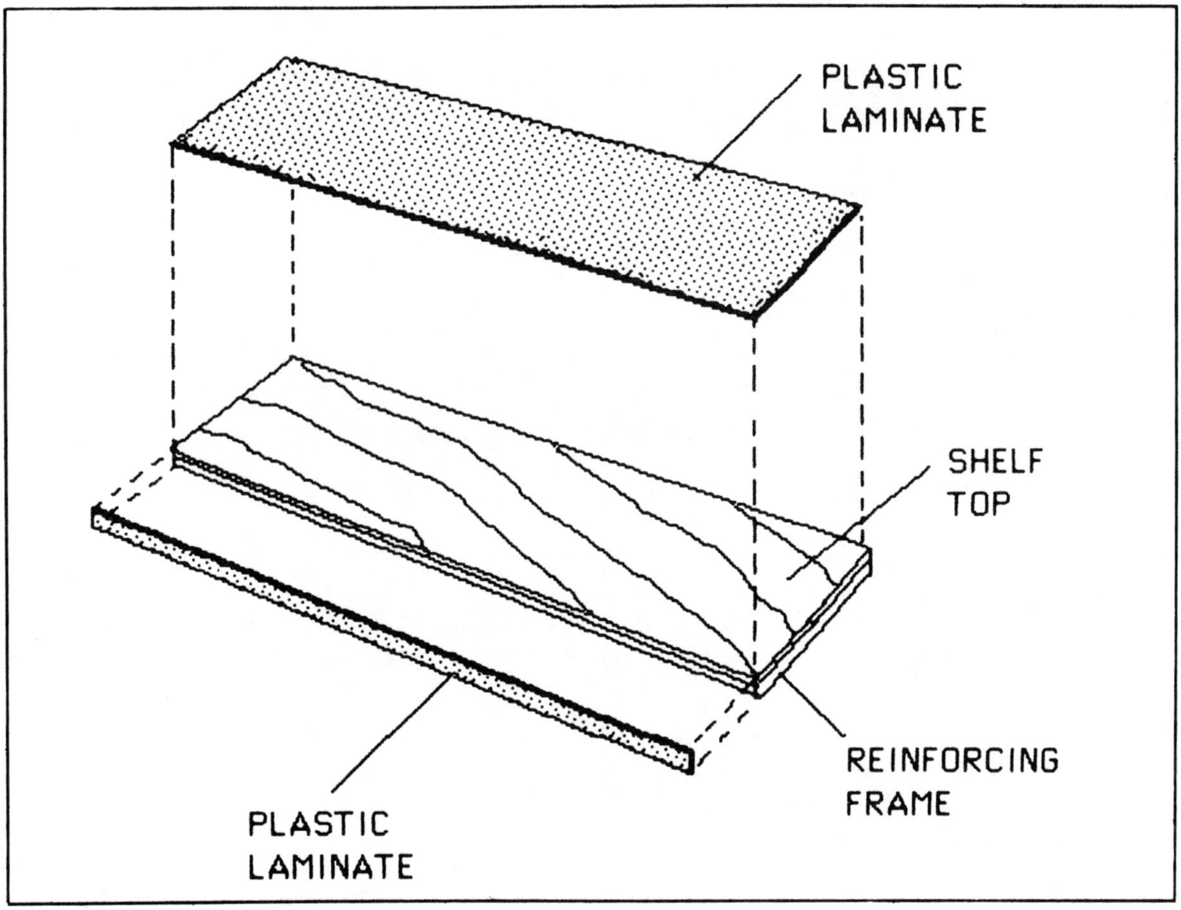

Fig. 3-164. Adding plastic laminates to top and forward edge of shelf.

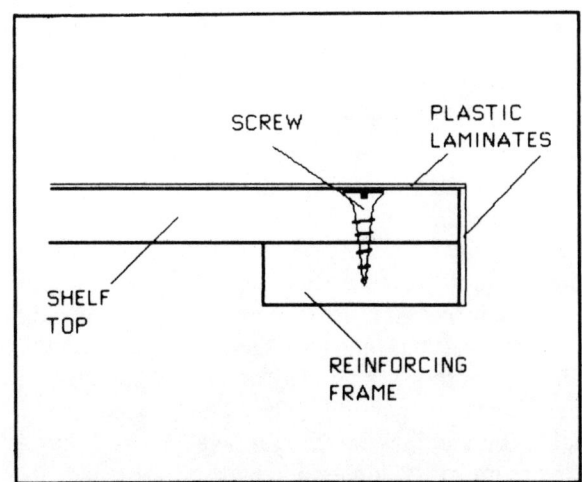

Fig. 3-165. Adding plastic laminate to shelf.

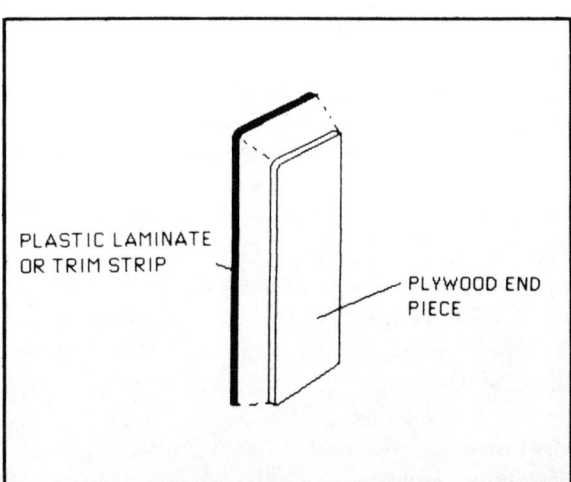

Fig. 3-166. Adding plastic laminate or trim strip to end pieces.

155

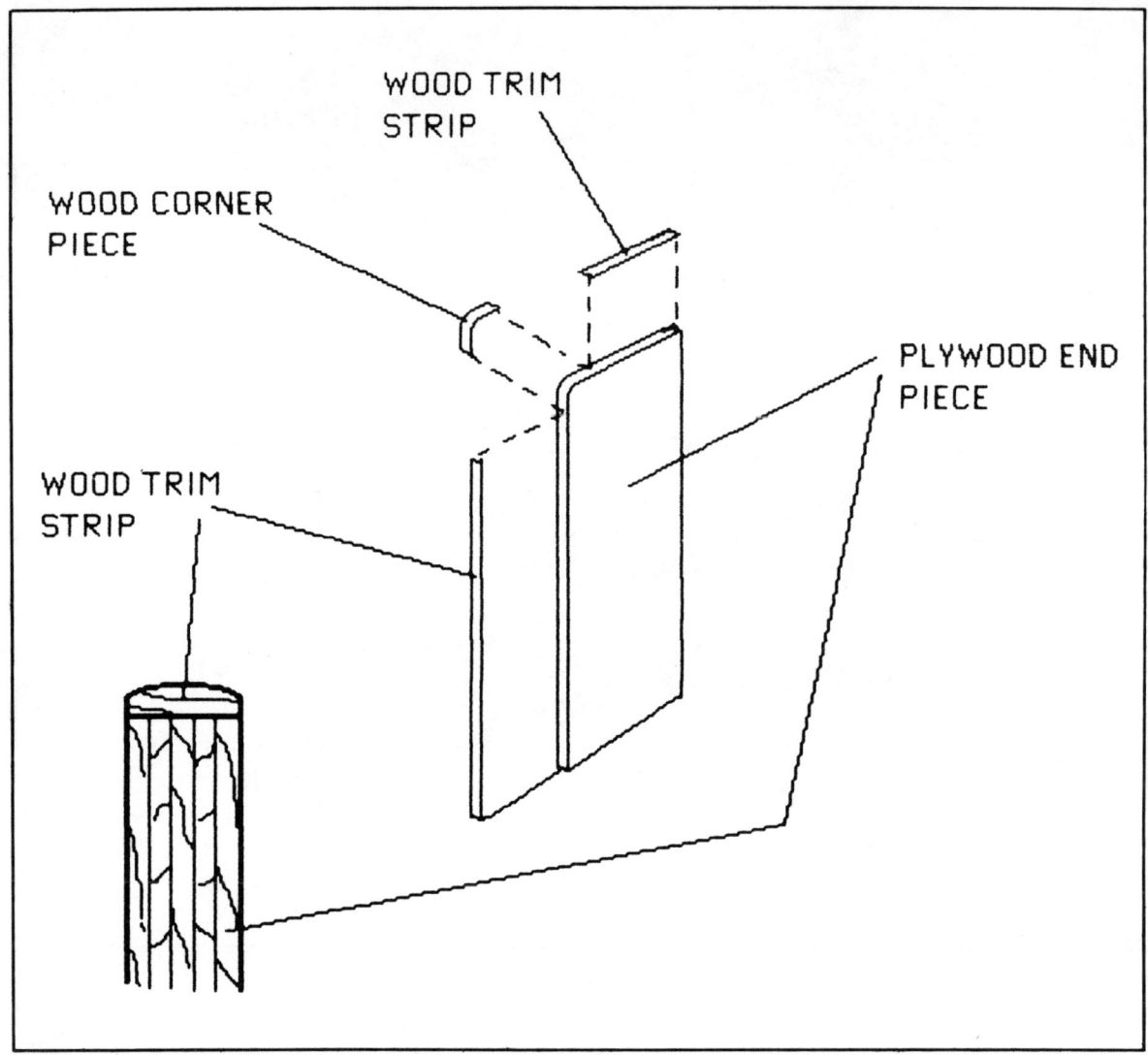

Fig. 3-167. Adding wood trim strips and corner piece to end pieces.

This is accomplished by both glue and mechanical fasteners. One method is to use finishing nails, passing them through the end pieces and into the framing wood of the top and shelf. Set the heads below the wood surface and fill with wood filler to flush with the wood surface. Another method is to use through-bolts, as detailed in Fig. 3-170. The bolts for the top will also pass through the beam pieces, as detailed later.

Regardless of the method of fastening, it is extremely important to install the side pieces perpendicular to the table top and shelves in a crosswise direction, using a square to make pattern lines on the side pieces. It is also important to have exactly the same distance between the table top and lower shelf on both sides and the table top and shelf at top of rack on both sides. The distance between the table top and lower shelf can be as desired, but a minimum of 12 inches is required for adequate strength.

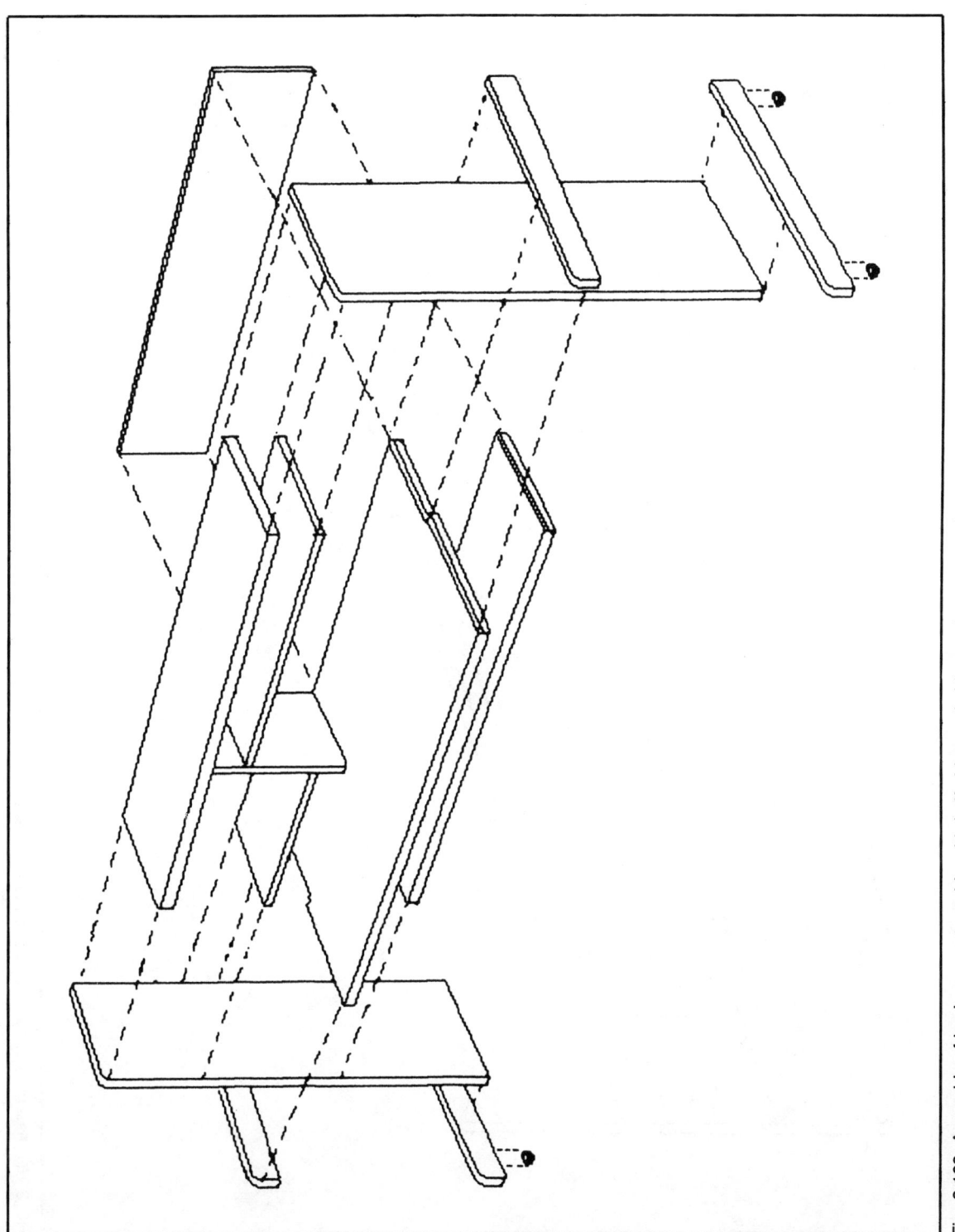

Fig. 3-168. Assembly of basic computer table with half sides and video and storage rack.

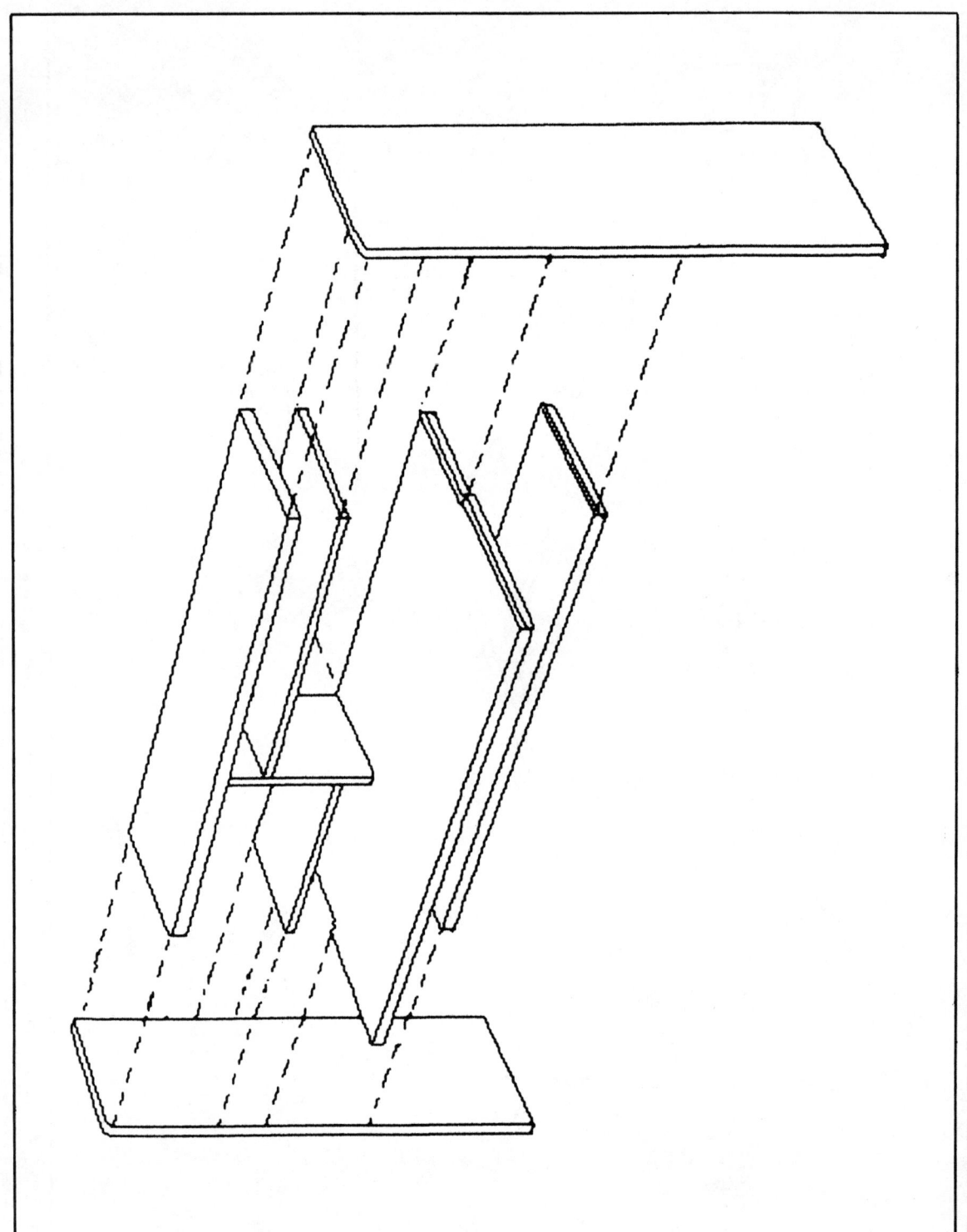

Fig. 3-169. Assembly of shelves and top to end pieces.

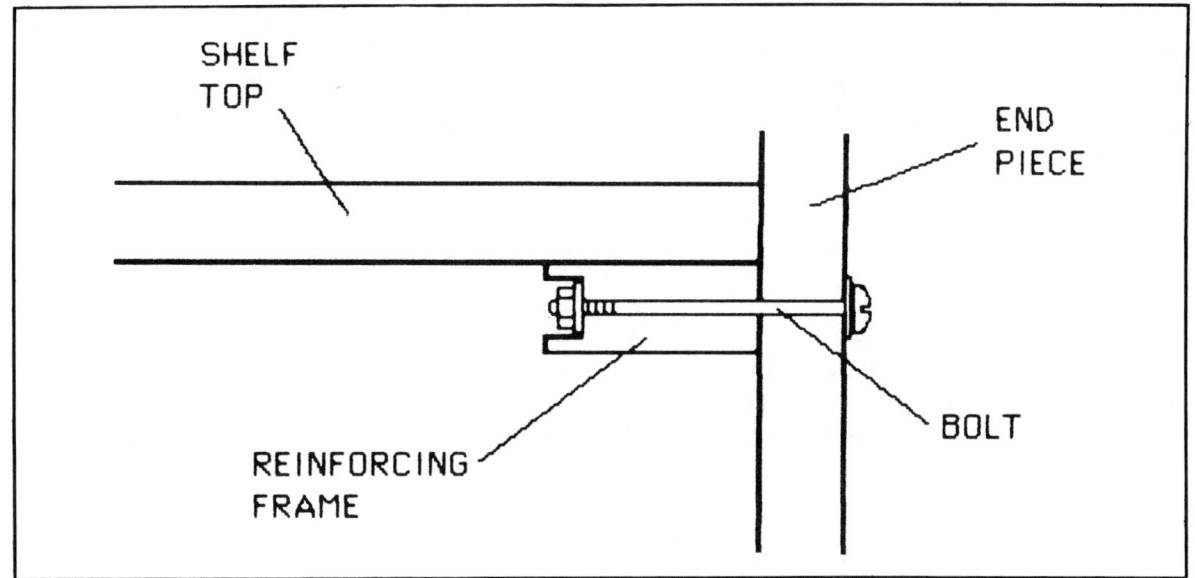

Fig. 3-170. Assembly of shelves to side pieces with bolts.

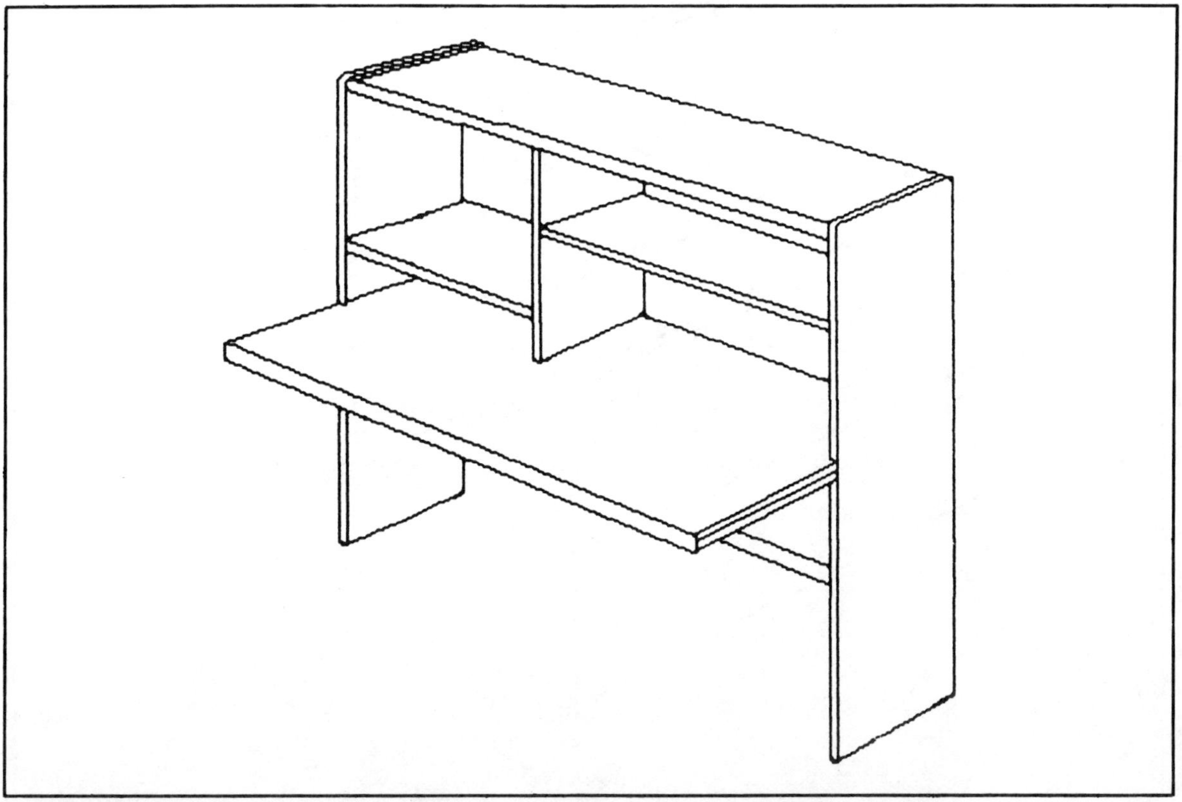

Fig. 3-171. Basic computer table with half sides and video and storage rack with sides installed.

The next step is to assemble and install the shelves inside the rack frame. Attachment can be by means of angle straps fastened with wood screws. Figure 3-171 shows the table top and shelves assembled to the end pieces.

After the shelves and table top have been assembled to the side pieces, add the backing piece, as shown in Fig. 3-172. The backing piece forms a box with the top, lower shelf, and side pieces. It is important that the backing piece be attached securely to the wood members all the way around the edges. The backing piece is glued and nailed into position. It is extremely important to make certain that the backing piece is a true rectangle and that the side pieces are perpendicular to the table top and shelf before the backing piece is attached and the glue allowed to set.

The side and floor beams are added next, as shown in Fig. 3-173. These should be glued and through-bolted, as shown in Figs. 3-174, 3-175, 3-176, and 3-177. Figure 3-178 shows the side and floor beams installed on the table.

The floor guides are installed (see Fig. 3-179). Depending on the type selected: some fit in mounting holes drilled in the wood beams; others are driven or screwed into the wood; still others have separate screw fasteners to hold them in place.

Sanding and Finishing

Proper sanding and finishing are important

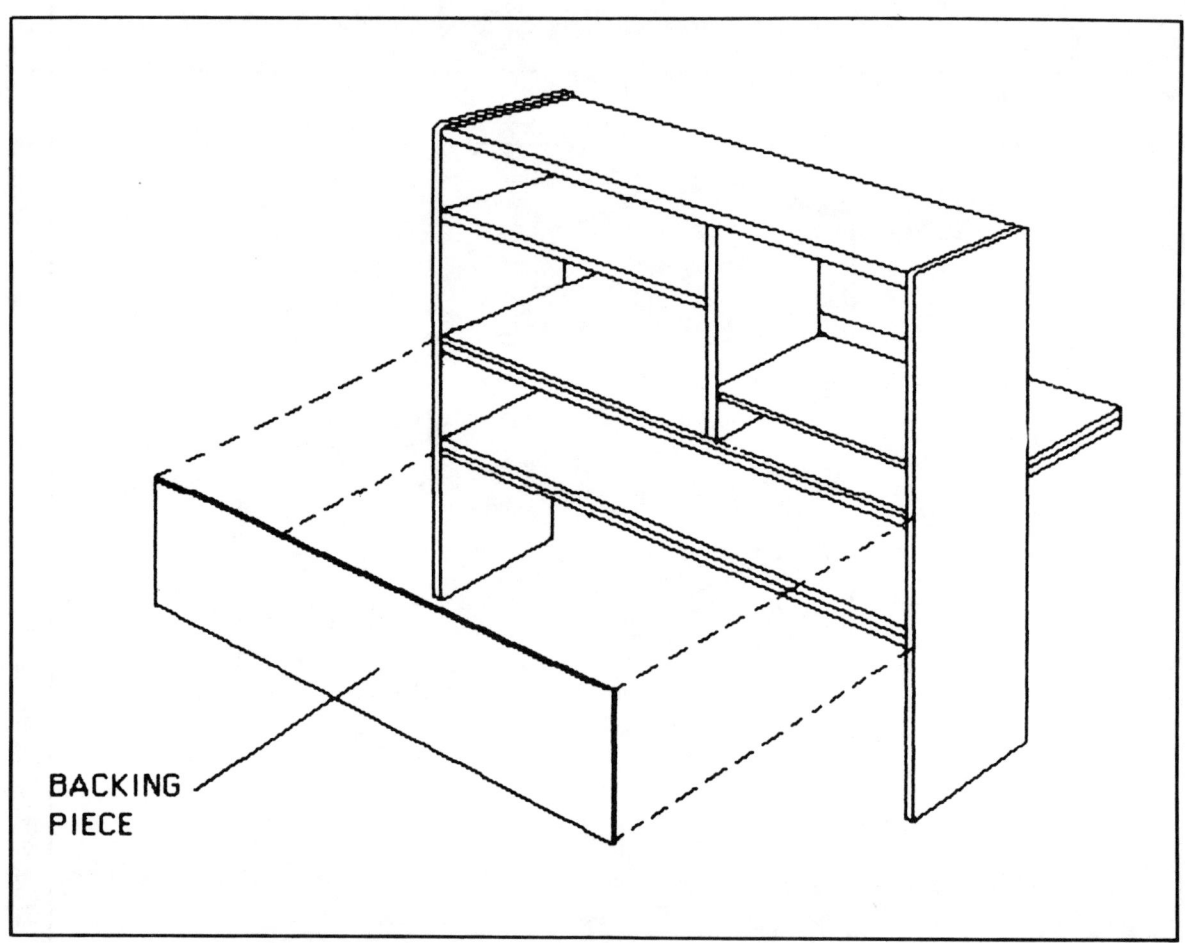

Fig. 3-172. Installing backing piece.

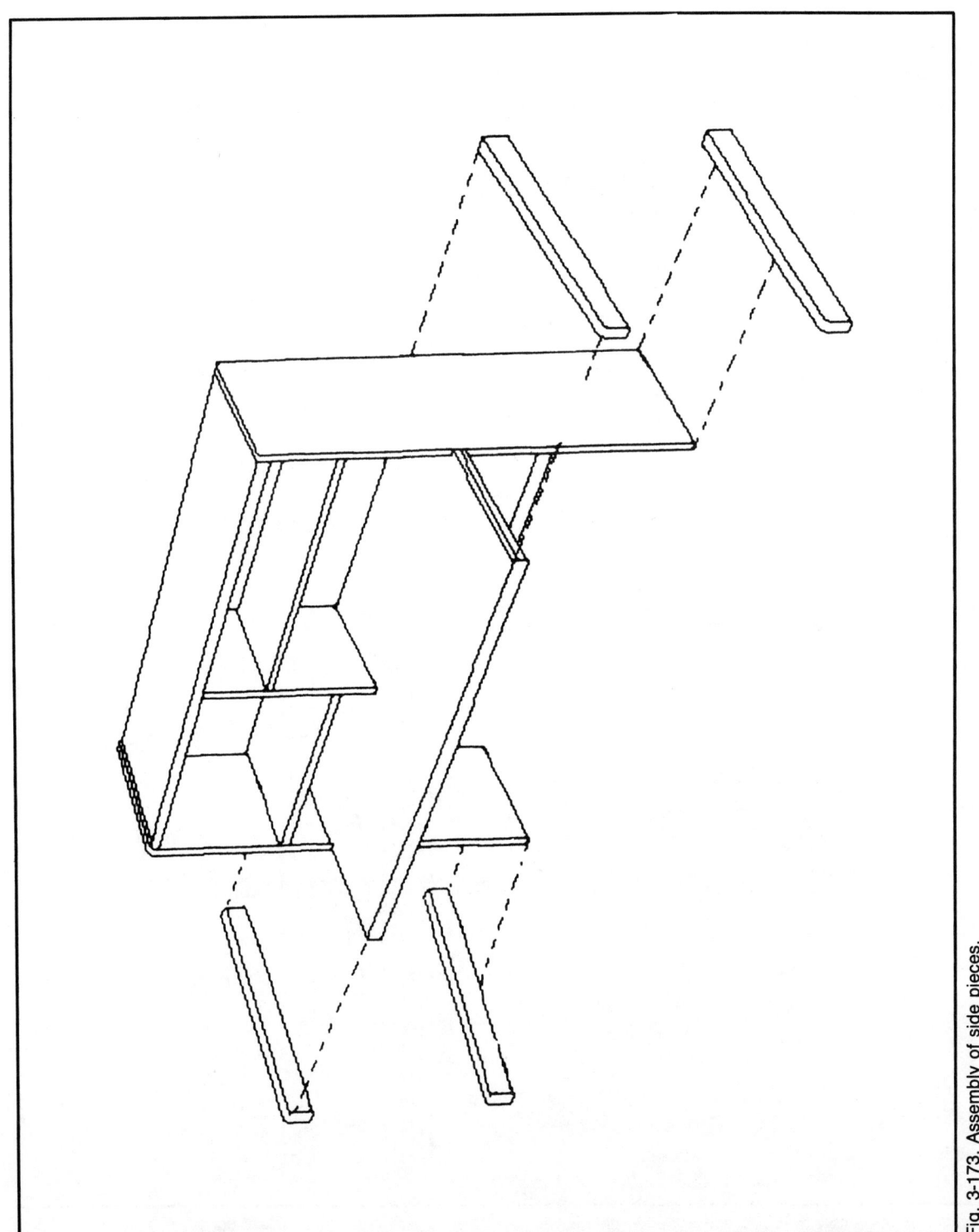

Fig. 3-173. Assembly of side pieces.

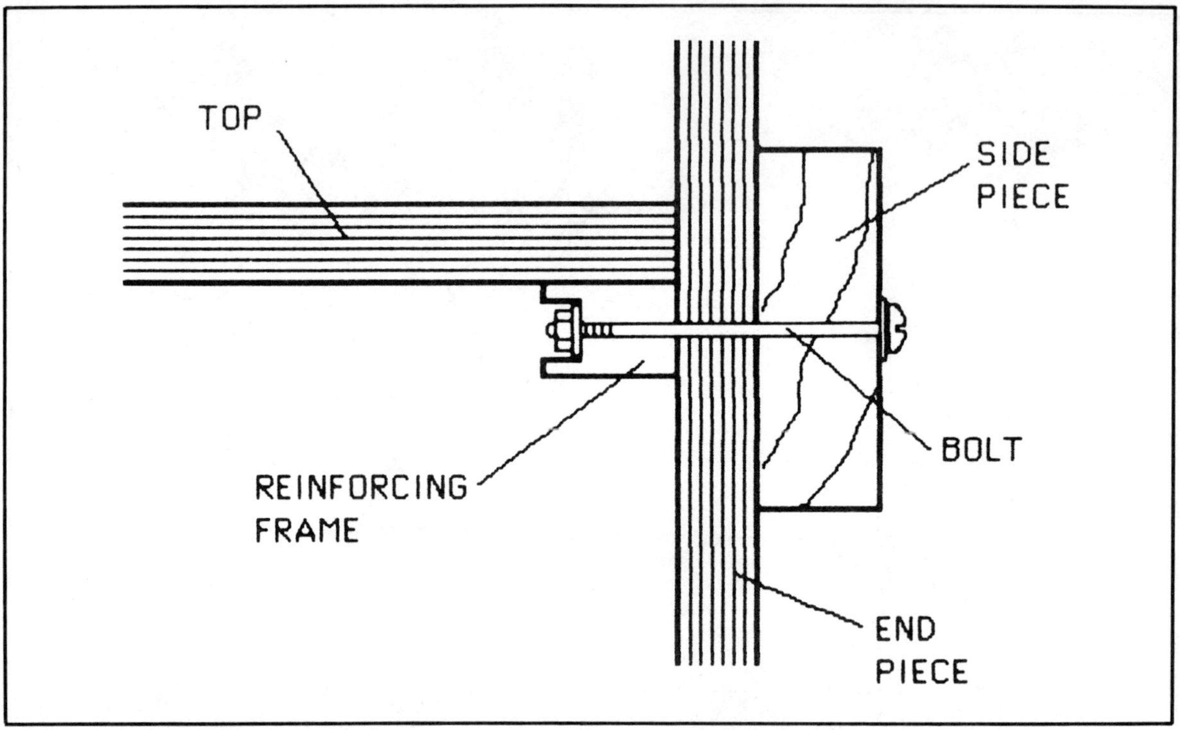

Fig. 3-174. Assembly of top to end and side pieces with bolts.

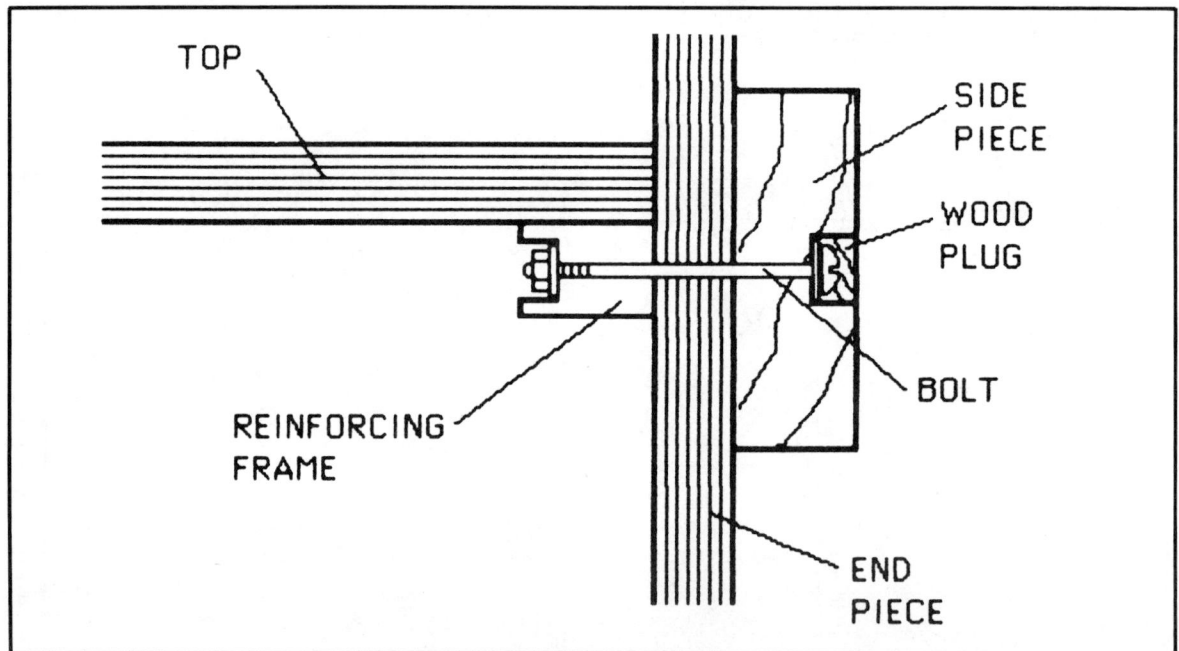

Fig. 3-175. Assembly of top to end and side pieces with bolt head countersunk and hole plugged.

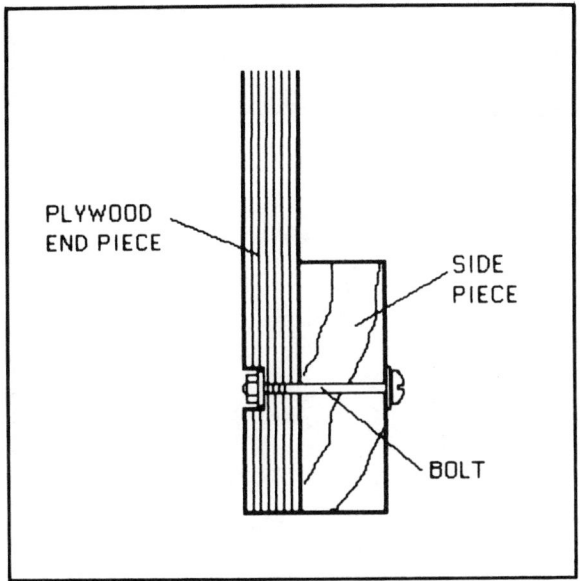

Fig. 3-176. Assembly of end and side pieces with bolts.

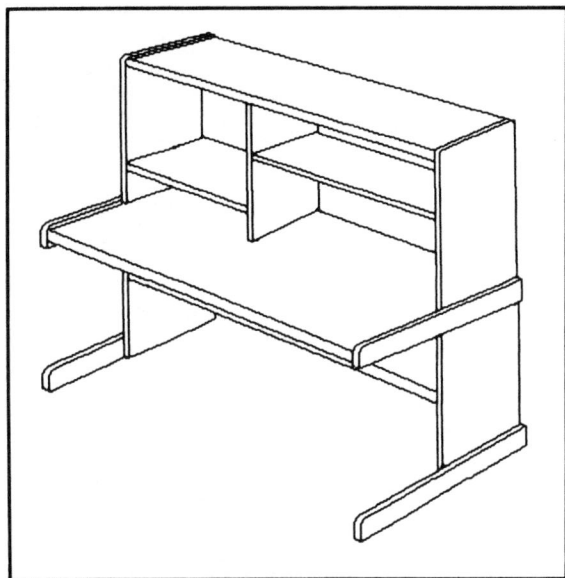

Fig. 3-178. Basic computer table with half sides and video and storage rack with side pieces installed.

steps in the construction process. Many beginners do a good job constructing the table up to this point, only to give the table a very amateur appearance by sloppy application of a finish. By taking care and a little time, however, even a beginner can give the table a professional finish.

Sanding is an important operation in preparing the wood for varnishing or painting. Small holes, checks, and open defects in the wood should be filled in. If a clear finish is to be applied, use a wood filler that matches the color of the wood. Apply a sanding sealer before doing any sanding on the surface.

The general principle to follow for sanding is to work from coarse grits progressively to finer grits, but don't start with a grit that is coarser than necessary for the particular sanding. You may be able to start with a medium or fine grit. Coarser grits tend to leave scratches that need to be sanded away with finer grits.

Wood sanding is done parallel to the grain. Sanding across the grain leaves scratches and tends to tear and roughen the wood surface. A scratch free surface is especially important if you are going to finish with oil or varnish.

For most hand sanding, especially on flat surfaces, use a sanding block rather than hold the sandpaper in your hand. Holding the sandpaper in your hand leaves a wavy surface on the wood because pressure is not applied evenly to all areas. A carpet or felt pad between the block and the sandpaper also helps.

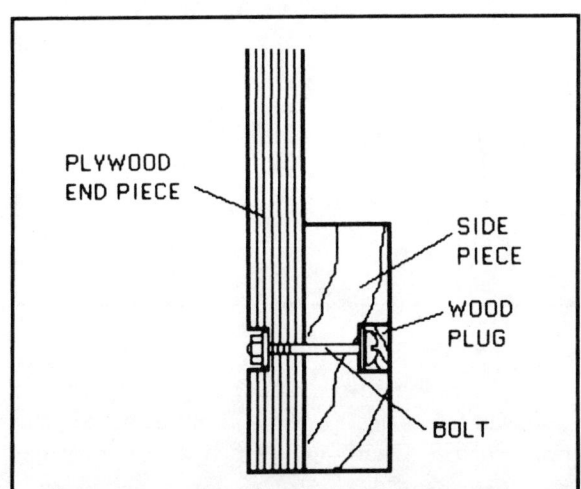

Fig. 3-177. Assembly of end and side pieces with bolt head and countersunk and hole plugged.

163

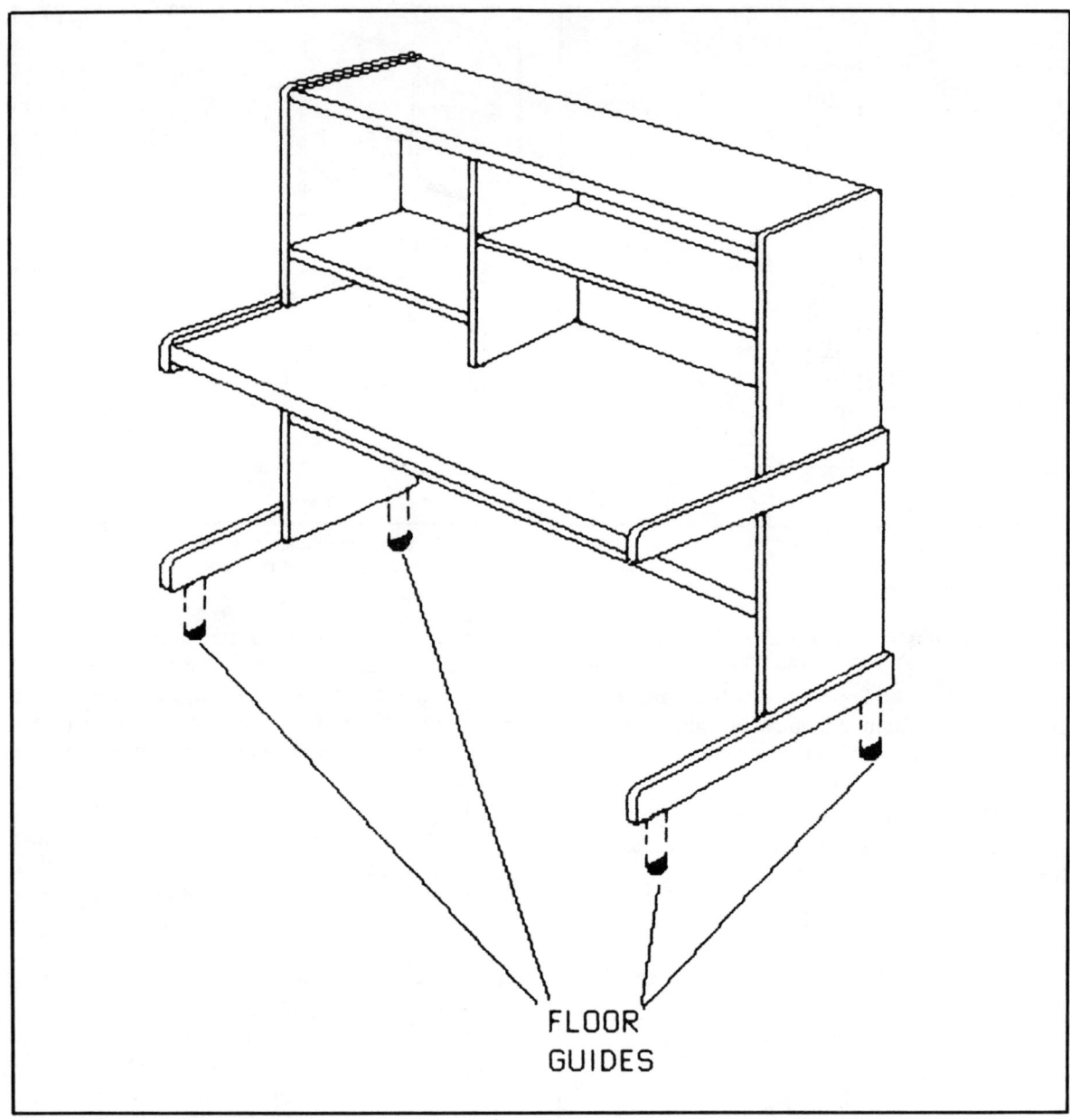

Fig. 3-179. Installing floor guides.

At the final stages of sanding, most craftsmen use their fingertips to judge the smoothness of the surface. You can also judge by looking across the surface at a light held at a low angle to the wood surface. Careful sanding will produce a finish of which you can be proud.

If desired, a power sander can be used; a pad sander is the easiest to use without damaging the wood surface. Belt sanders can be used by experienced operators.

Either stain the wood or apply a clear finish directly to natural wood. Staining enhances the natural grains of the wood and enriches relatively lifeless woods.

Before applying stain, first test color on a scrap of similar wood. clean the surface area where stain is to be applied and use a cloth to eliminate as much dust as possible. The stain can then be applied with a brush, foam brush applicator, or cloth. Apply a smooth, even coat of stain, allowing the stain to penetrate the wood. Depending on the humidity, temperature, and particular stain used, penetration usually takes from 5 to 15 minutes. While the stain is still wet, wipe off the excess stain with a clean

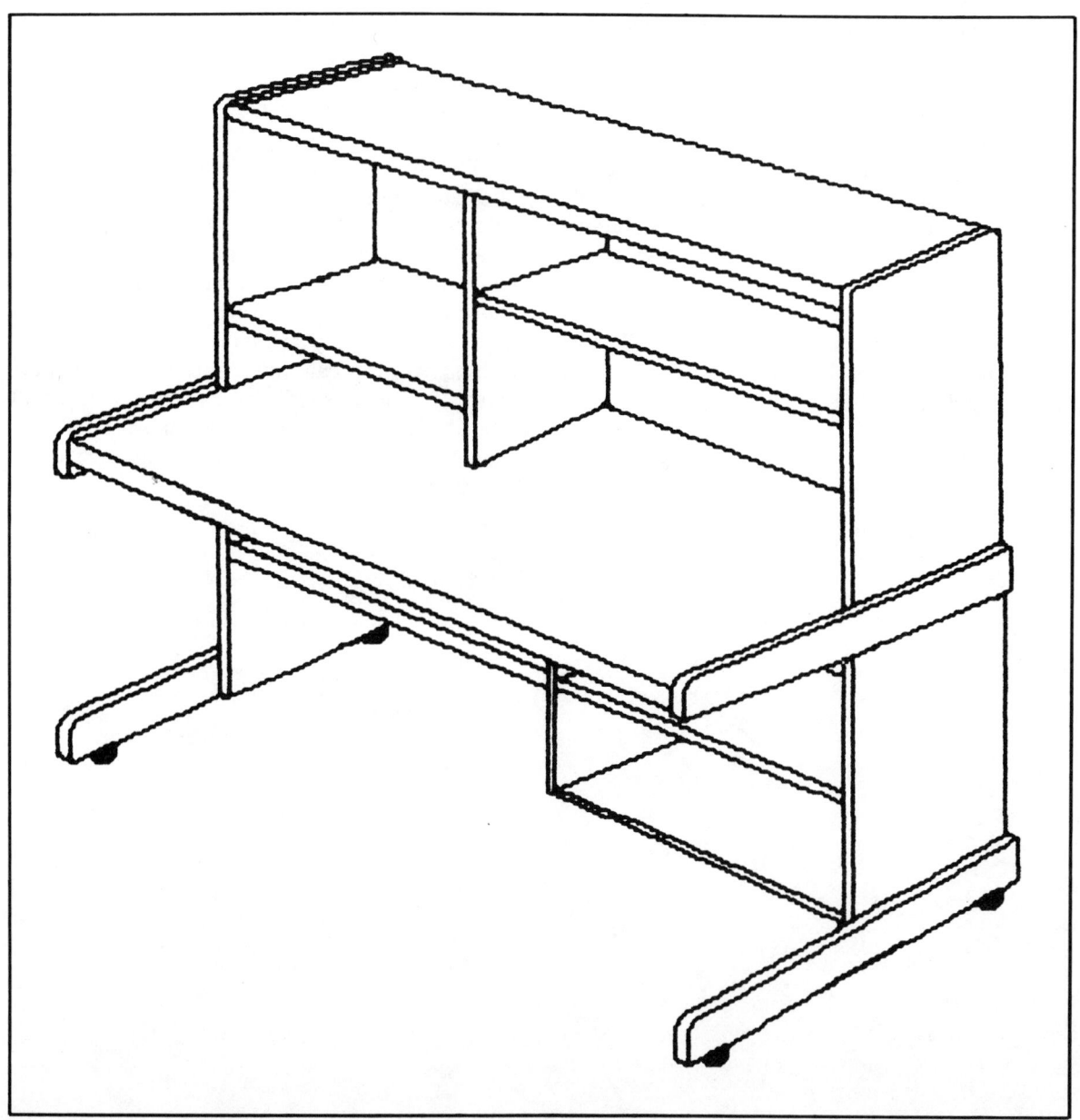

Fig. 3-180. Basic computer table with half sides and video and storage rack with alternate lower shelf arrangement.

cloth, but be careful not to remove too much from corners and edges. Wipe across the grain first so that you work the stain into the wood pores, then give a final wipe with the grain. Allow the stain to dry. This usually takes at least 8 hours. The finish can then be applied.

It is usually best to apply a series of light, even coats of clear finish rather than one thick coat. This will minimize possible drips and wrinkles as the finish dries.

Apply finish in brush-width strokes in direction of wood grain. Turn table so that finish is applied to horizontal wood surfaces whenever possible.

A minimum of two coats is recommended. Allow 6 to 8 hours for the first coat to dry before applying second coat. Sand lightly and use a tack cloth to remove sanded finish dust before applying next coat of finish.

Clear or stained finishes are usually applied to natural wood furniture, but color paint finishes can also be applied.

Variations

Several variations are possible for the basic computer table with half sides with video and storage rack. One possibility is to substitute materials, such as particle board instead of plywood for the top and/or other components. Another common variation is to construct the table with a different size of top.

You can also add additional storage shelves below the table and/or drawer immediately below the table top. A popular shelf and storage arrangement is shown in Fig. 3-180. Additional shelves and/or an alternate arrangement of shelves can be used in the rack.

The basic computer table with half sides with video and storage rack makes a functional and attractive computer table even when built from inexpensive woods. This design is ideal for anyone who wants to build computer tables to sell to others. The table can be sold either unfinished or with finish applied. By using more expensive woods, such as oak, you can give the table a custom appearance. The plans given here show simple butt joints, but if you have the cabinet-making skills and know-how, you can also use more difficult joints, like rabbet or miter joints.

Chapter 4

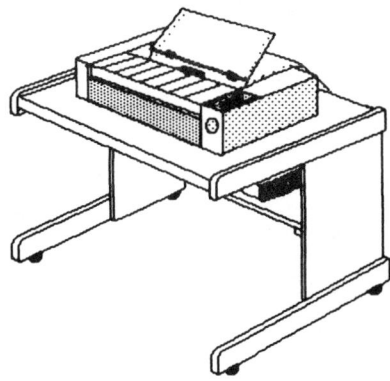

Plans and Patterns for Basic Printer Stands

Printer stands are essentially separate tables for printers. Many computer users like to have the printer on a separate table because some printers vibrate and shake to the point where they could be harmful to the computer if placed on the same table with the computer.

An easy-to-build basic budget printer stand made of lumber and plywood available at discount stores is presented first. This is an ideal starting project. This stand is very functional, and can be built for a very low price. This project is followed by more difficult constructions. In most cases, measurements are given, but you can vary these to fit your special needs. The same applies to construction materials. For most uses, I recommend plywood rather that particle board, but particle board can be used if you want to make the furniture on the lowest possible budget.

BASIC BUDGET PRINTER STAND

I call this a basic budget printer stand because it can be built from standard size pieces of plywood and lumber available from discount home building supply stores for a very low materials cost. This computer printer stand is attractive and modern and gives a good appearance even when built from low cost wood. You can give a custom appearance by making the same design from more expensive woods, such as birch or oak.

The basic budget printer stand is shown in Figs. 4-1 and 4-2. The top has ample space for most computer printers. It can have a natural wood top or plastic laminates can be added. The table features a shelf underneath that can serve as a platform for computer printer paper and gives the table added strength. The half sides give a modern appearance.

Materials

The patterns for the wood parts are shown in Fig. 4-3. The top of the table is a 2-foot-by-2-foot piece of 3/4-inch thick plywood. If you intend to use the wood surface as the finished table top, without adding a plastic laminate, hardwood-faced plywood

167

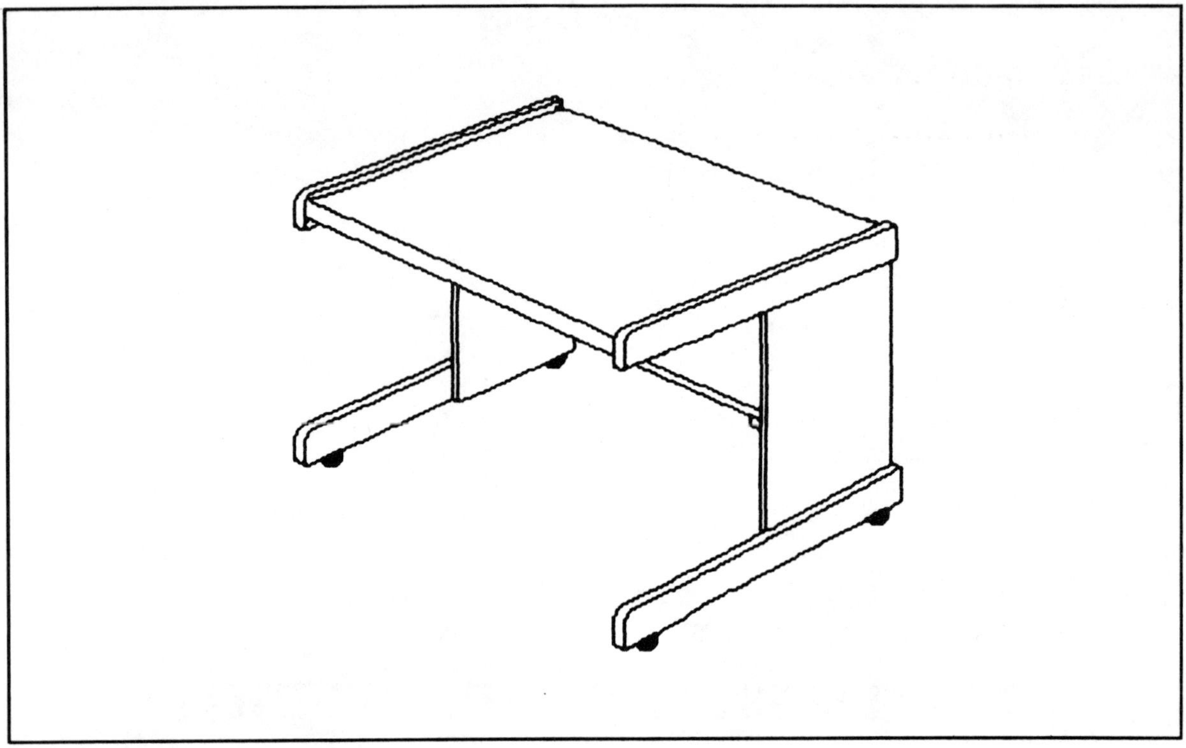

Fig. 4-1. Basic budget printer stand.

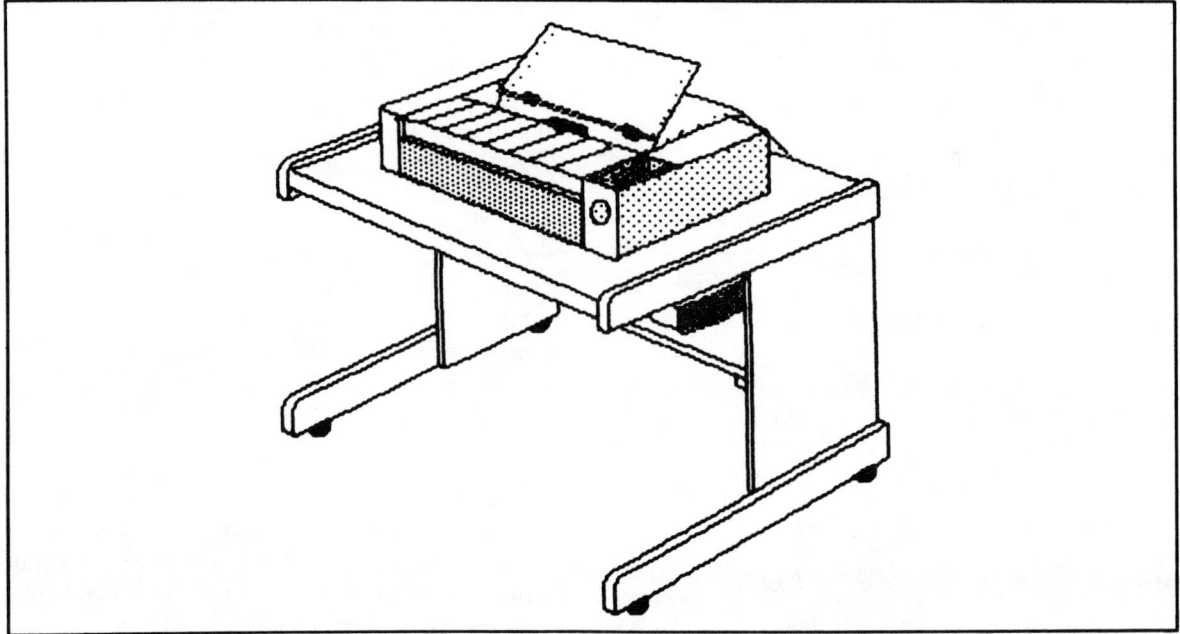

Fig. 4-2. Basic budget printer stand with printer.

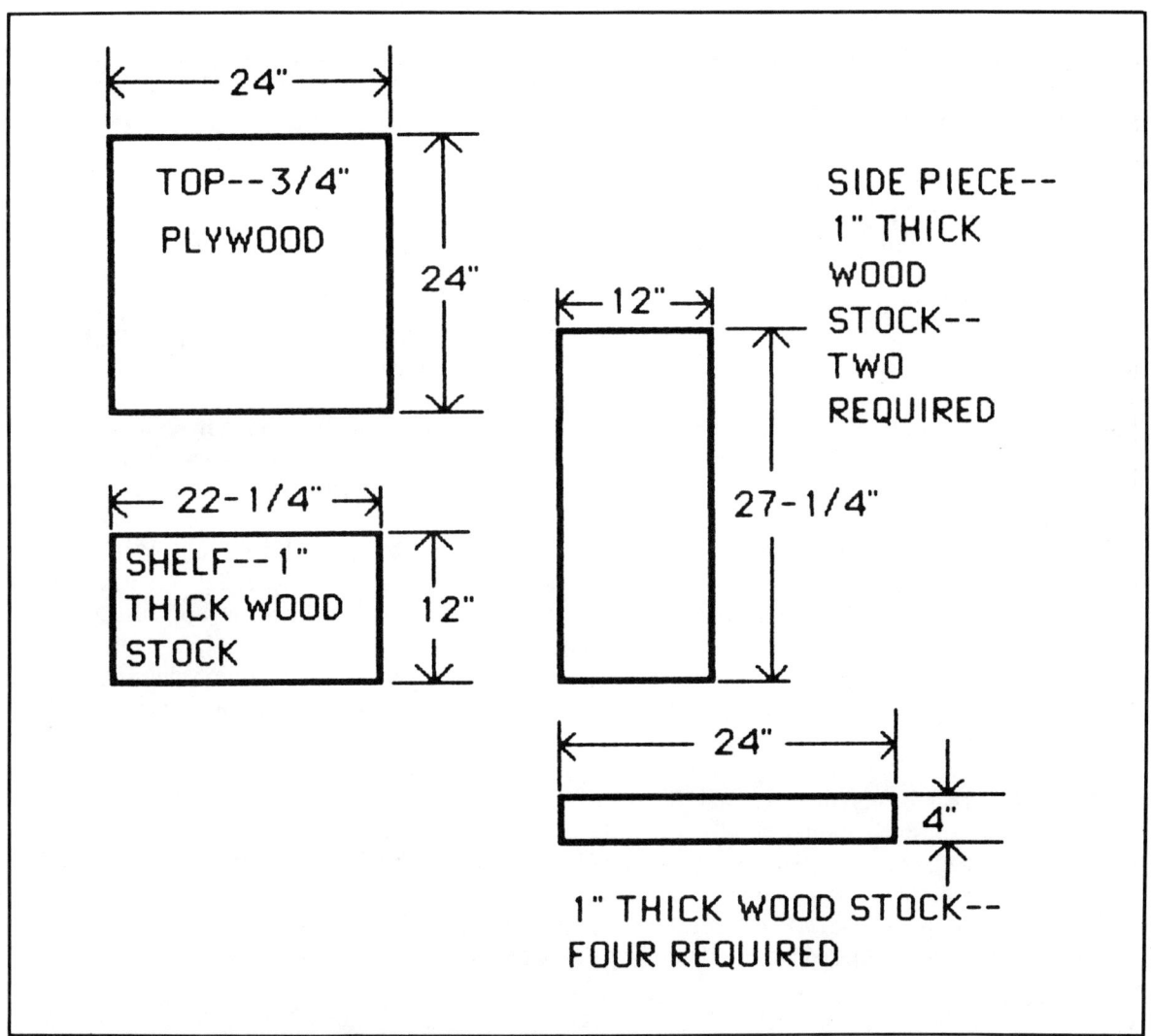

Fig. 4-3. Patterns for wood parts for basic budget printer stand.

is recommended. If a laminate is to be added, even an exterior grade of shop plywood will suffice. Although plywood is normally sold in standard 4-foot-by-8-foot sheets, many home building and discount stores also offer 2-foot-by-4-foot cuts. If this size is purchased, the only required cutting will be to cut the piece in half.

Although 1/2-inch thick plywood could also be used, I don't recommend this. The savings are insignificant, and a less sturdy table will result. Particle board can be substituted fo the plywood if you are on an absolute minimum budget. Considerable amounts of high-priced low-grade manufactured computer furniture are made from particle board covered by plastic laminates. Particle board can be difficult to work with, however, and it is very difficult to get plastic laminates to bond properly to this material without special equipment. (It must be difficult even with special machinery, because laminates on manufactured furniture always seem to come loose at the edges.)

The side pieces and shelf are 1-inch thick by

12-inch wide wood stock. These are the dimensions before the wood was surfaced, so the wood that you purchase will have dimensions of slightly less than these. When fitting parts, make certain that you take this into account. The shelf should be two wood thicknesses (1 3/4 inch) less than 24 inches, which will be about 22 1/4 inches, but you will want to be as exact as possible so that the shelf will fit properly between the end pieces.

A height of 27 1/4 inches is shown for the side pieces. With the addition of the 3/4-inch thick table top, this will give a height of 28 inches before floor guides are added, which will increase the height somewhat, the exact distance depending on the type of floor guides used. You may want to have your table lower than this. Adjustable floor guides are available that allow you to vary the height of the table within a limited range. You may prefer to have your printer stand even lower to the floor. Experiment before you decide on the height to build your printer stand.

When selecting the wood stock, you can use pine, fir, or birch, but try to select wood that is as straight as possible and without cracks or other defects.

The end pieces or beams are 1-inch thick by 4-inch wide wood stock (dimensions before the wood was surfaced; the measurements of the wood you buy will be slightly less). You will need four of these, each 24-inches long. The beams form a base of support for the table, add strength, and give a decorative appearance.

The backing piece (Fig. 4-4) can be either plywood or fiberboard. The backing piece is used to strengthen the table base and hold the frame in rectangular form. The backing piece is 24 inches long. A 14-inch height is shown for the backing piece, but this will vary depending on how far below the top you wish to place the shelf. A minimum distance of 12 inches between the top plywood and the shelf is recommended to give the table base adequate strength. Notice that the top, shelf, backing piece, and side pieces form a box with the forward side open.

You will also need 1-inch-by-2-inch or larger framing stock for use under the plywood table top and as cleats under the ends of the shelf. A wood or plastic trim strip is used to cover the forward edge of the table top. This piece is 24 inches long and about 1 3/4 inches wide. The minimum width should be such that it will completely cover the widths of the plywood top (3/4 inch) and the framing (approximately 7/8 inch), or slightly wider.

Four floor pods or guides are used on the floor beams. Many suitable types are available from hardware stores; these can be of a fixed or adjustable type, as desired.

Finishing nails and other fasteners are required for assembly, as detailed below in this section. You will also need a suitable wood glue. The finish can be clear urethane or any other type.

The top can be left natural or a plastic lami-

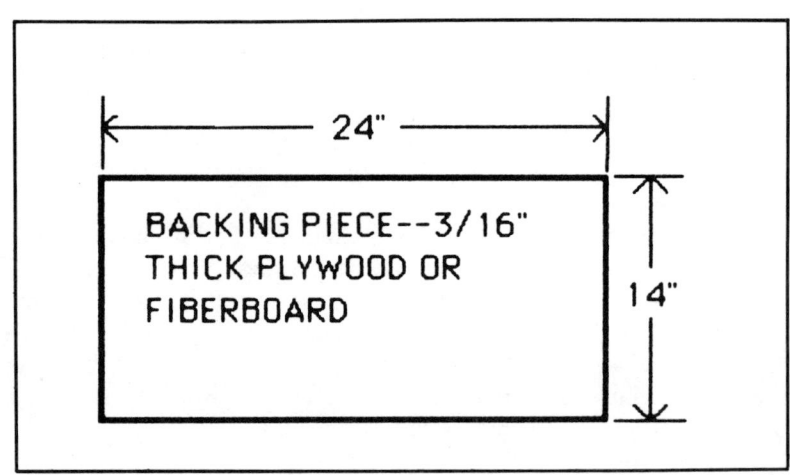

Fig. 4-4. Pattern for backing piece.

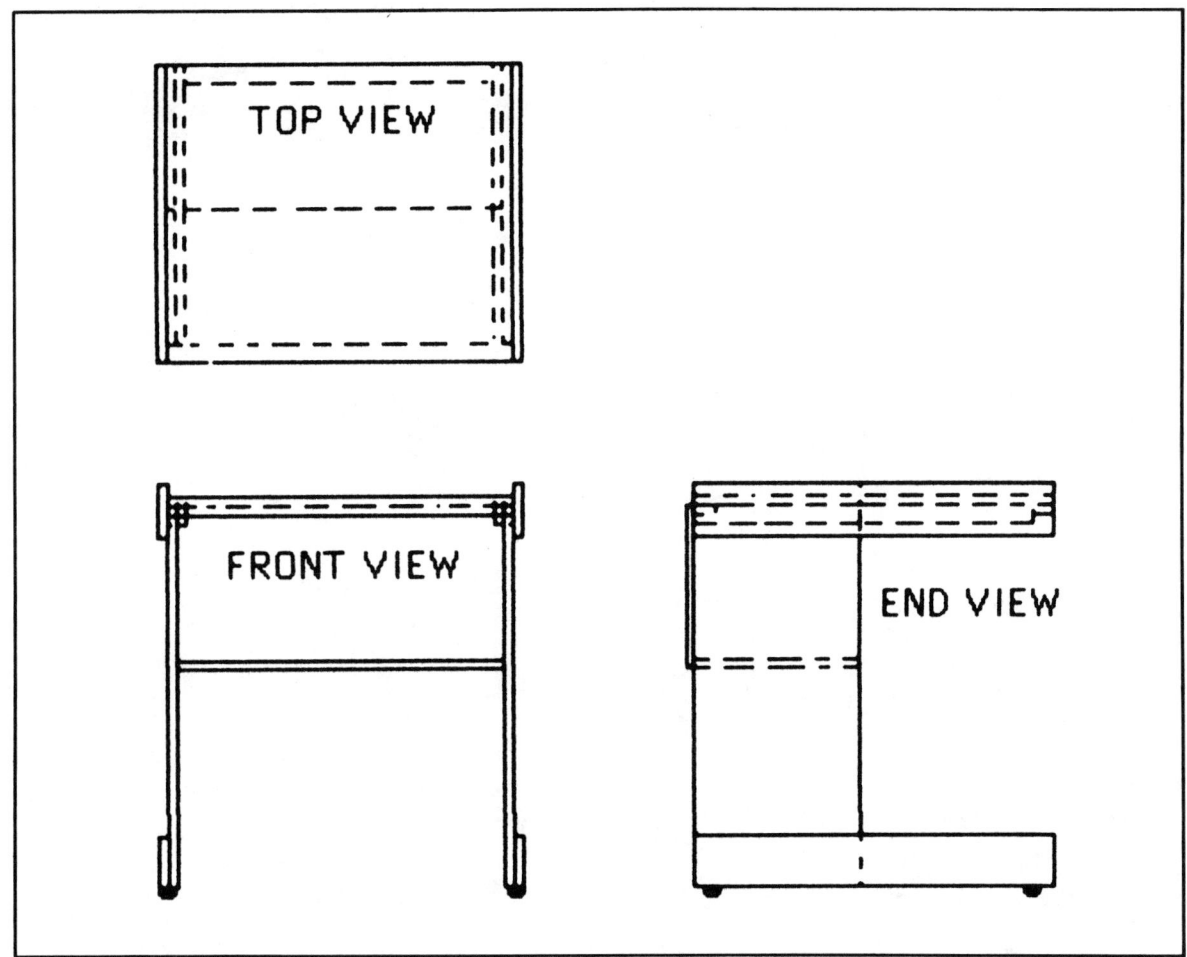

Fig. 4-5. Exploded view of the assembly of basic budget printer stand.

nate can be added. If a plastic laminate is added, you will need a 2-foot-by-2-foot piece of suitable plastic laminate and contact cement for attaching it to the plywood.

Construction

Overviews of the complete assembly are shown in Figs. 4-5 and 4-6. Begin by constructing the table top. If you purchased a piece of plywood that was already cut to the 2-foot-by-2-foot size, no additional cutting will be required, assuming that it was cut accurately and is a true rectangular form. You might want to check this with a square.

If you purchased a larger piece of plywood, such as a standard 4-foot-by-8-foot sheet, you will need to cut out a section for the table top. The grain should run lengthwise, unless you are planning to laminate the top. In most cases, you will use two factory cut edges for your table top and cut the other two. Use a ruler and square to draw the pattern, marking the lines with a sharp pencil or scribing tool.

Sawing plywood requires special considerations. Special care must be taken to avoid chipping and splintering along the cut edge. Handsaws or power saws with special fine-toothed blades designed especially for plywood should be used; special carbide-tipped blades are even better. Ap-

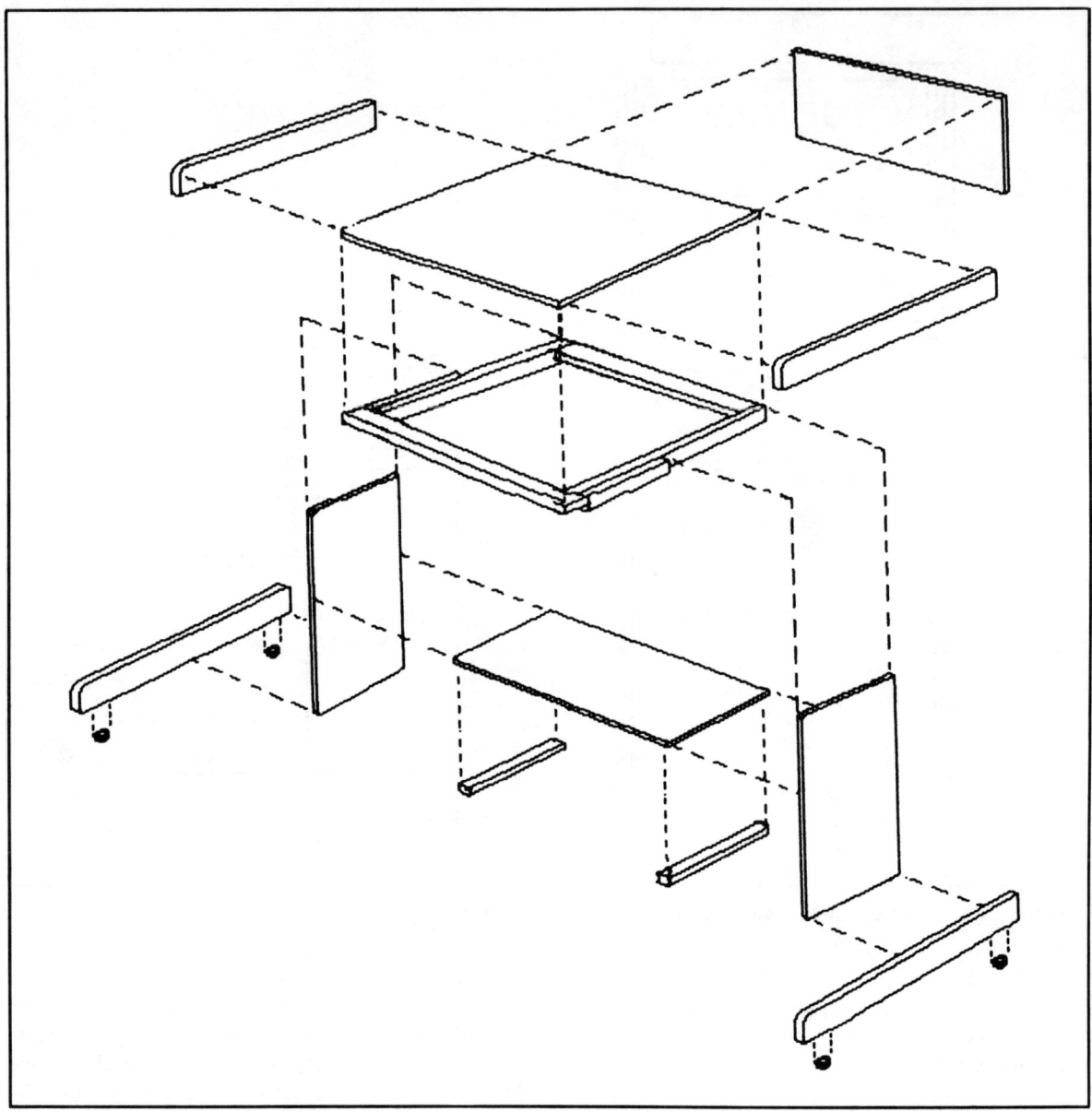

Fig. 4-6. Assembly of basic budget printer stand.

plying a strip of masking tape over the area to be cut on both sides of the plywood, but especially on the side opposite the one you are cutting from, will prevent chipping. Another possibility is to clamp a solid piece of wood to the underside and make the cut through both the plywood and the piece of wood.

Be extremely careful when sanding edges of plywood. Use a sanding block. Avoid sanding the surfaces of plywood until a wood sealer has been applied.

The next step is to add the reinforcing frame to the table top, as shown in Fig. 4-7. Use a ruler and a square to mark the patterns on the framing

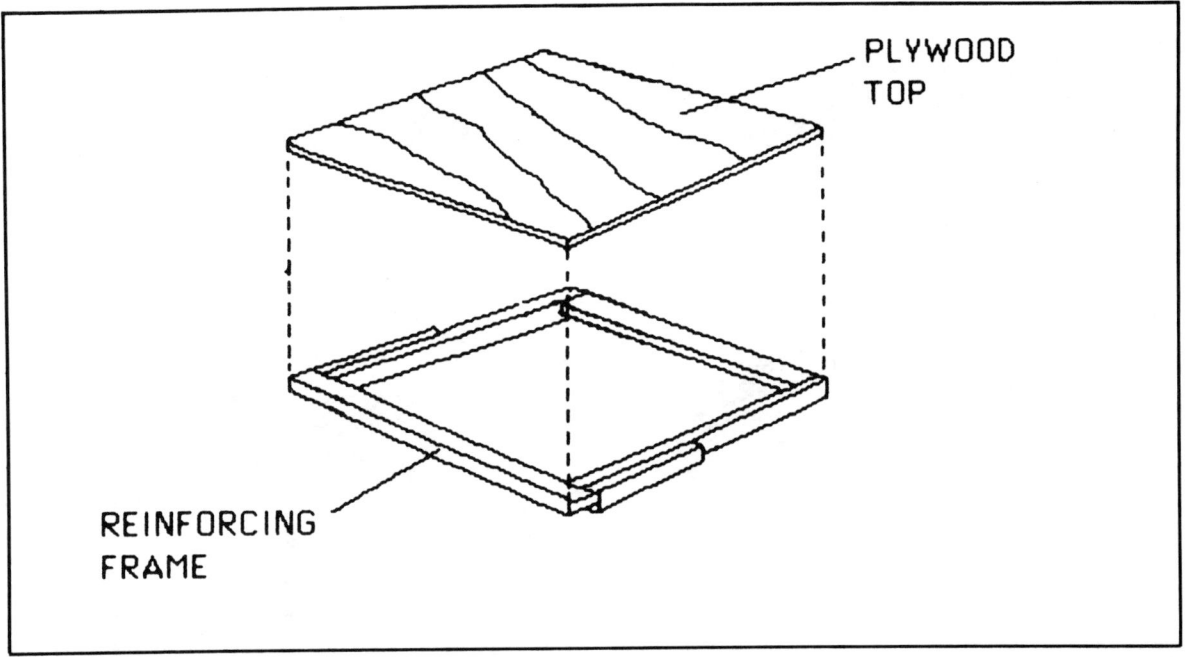

Fig. 4-7. Assembly of top to reinforcing frame.

wood with a sharp pencil or other marking device. Then make the necessary saw cuts, as detailed in Chapter 2. The frame pieces should be glued and nailed or screwed in position. If the plywood top is to be left natural wood (without a plastic laminate being added), the fasteners should go through the framing and into the plywood. Take care that the fasteners do not pass all the way through the plywood or leave a bulge in the upper surface. If a good glue is used, such as acrylic or epoxy, the glue alone will give adequate bonding strength. The fasteners are mainly used as a clamping device for the gluing and will not have much holding power. To give greater holding power, the fasteners can be passed through the plywood and into the framing, if a plastic laminate is to be added.

Next, cut the shelf wood to length. The shelf should be 24 inches long, minus the combined widths of the two side pieces. You will need to measure and cut this accurately so that the side pieces will be exactly perpendicular to the top when the table is assembled. The ends of the shelf should be perpendicular to the sides of the wood. Use a square as a guide for marking pattern lines.

Next, cut 1-inch-by-2-inch wood cleats to length, as shown in Fig. 4-8. These should match the depth of the shelf, as shown. Glue and nail these to the bottom of the shelf.

The table top and shelf are then assembled to

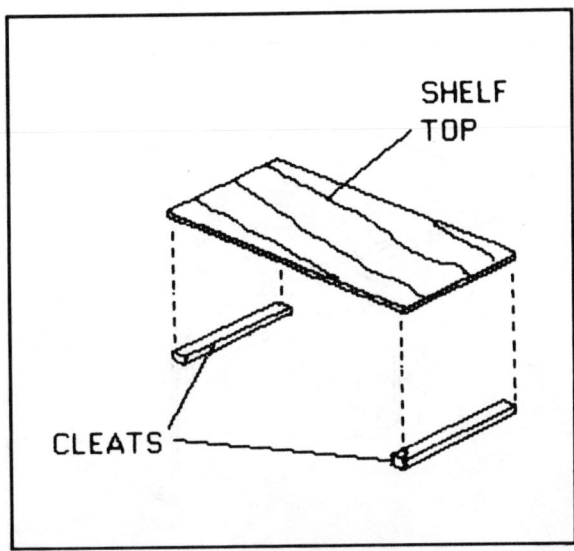

Fig. 4-8. Assembly of cleats to shelf.

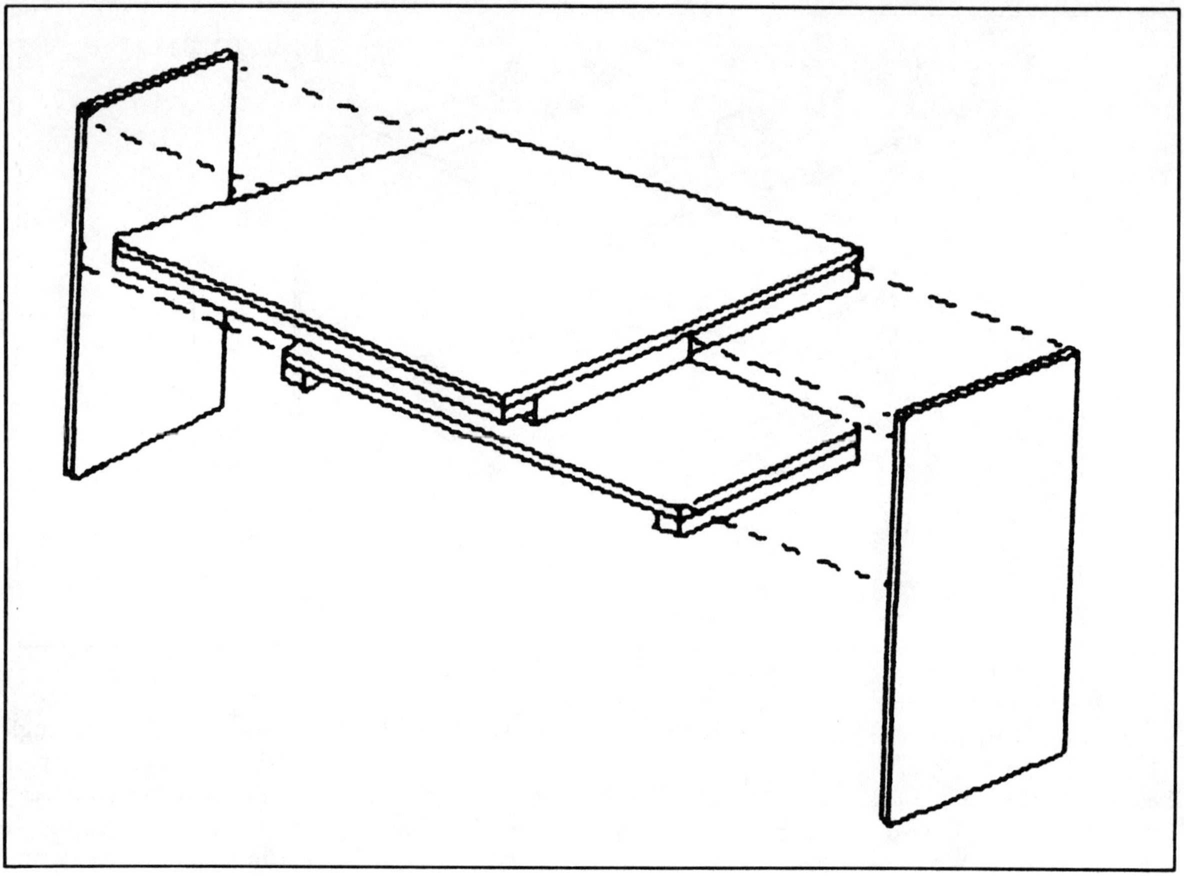

Fig. 4-9. Assembly of top and shelves to end pieces.

the side pieces, as shown in Fig. 4-9. The end pieces should first be cut to desired length, as detailed previously. The side pieces are then glued and fastened to the top and shelf frame members and cleats. A variety of fasteners can be used. Finishing nails can be driven through the side pieces and into the frame members and cleats. These can be set below the wood surface and wood filler used to cover and hide the nail heads. Another possibility is to use screws or bolts; washers can be used and heads and nuts can extend beyond the surface of the wood. Or the heads and/or nuts can be countersunk below the surface of the wood. Wood plugs can be used to cover the holes and hide the fasteners.

Regardless of the method of fastening, it is extremely important to install the side pieces perpen-

Fig. 4-10. Shelf and top assembled to end pieces.

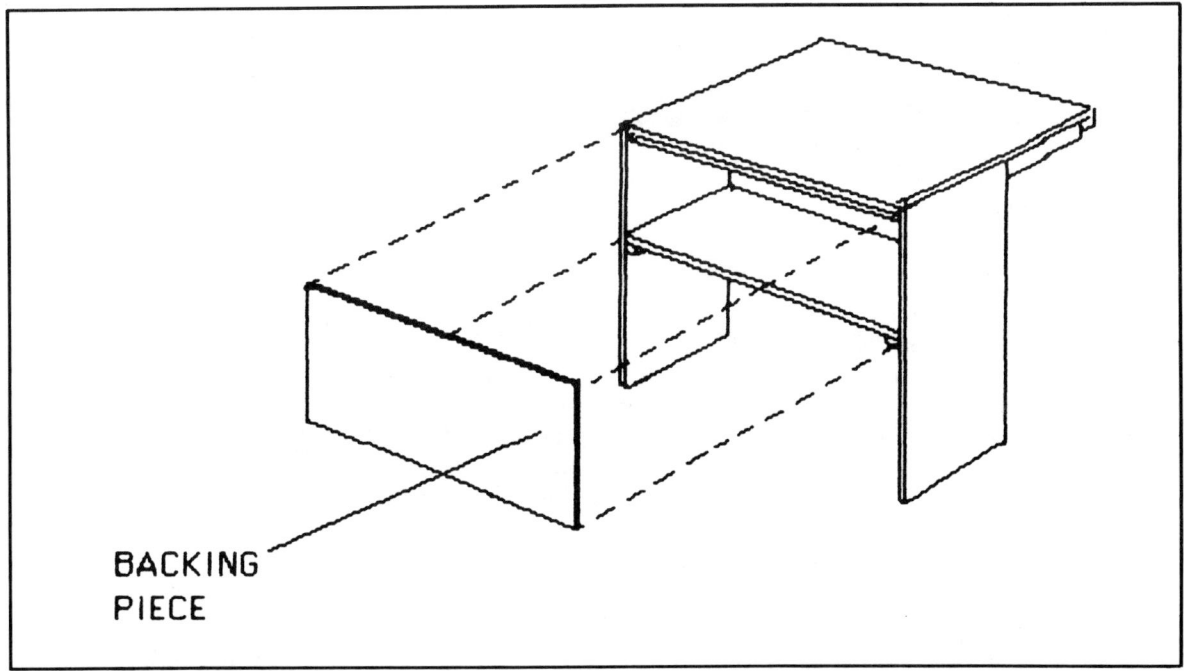

Fig. 4-11. Assembly of backing piece.

dicular to the table top and shelf in a crosswise direction, using a square to make pattern lines on the side pieces. It is also important to have exactly the same distance between the top and shelf on both sides. This distance can be whatever you want, but a minimum of 12 inches is required to give the table adequate strength.

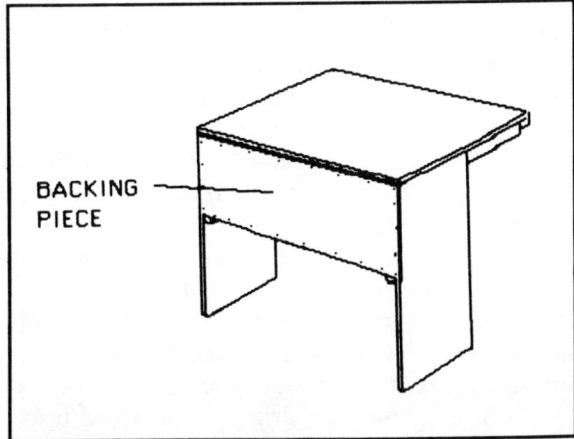

Fig. 4-12. Backing piece installed.

Figure 4-10 shows the shelf and top assembled to the end pieces. The next step is to add the backing piece, as shown in Fig. 4-11. The backing piece forms a box with the top, shelf, and side pieces. It is important that the backing piece be attached securely to the wood members all the way around the edges. The backing piece is glued and nailed into position (Fig. 4-12). It is extremely important to make certain that the backing piece is truly rectangular and that the side pieces are perpendicular to the table top and shelf before the backing piece is attached and the glue allowed to set.

If a plastic laminate is to be added to the plywood table top or shelf, it can be installed at this time. Plastic laminates are often applied to plywood for computer table tops, and a large selection is on the market. I suggest using only high quality plastic laminates for computer table tops.

If a plastic laminate is to also be applied to the forward edge of the table top or shelf, it should be applied first. This is then finished flush with the table top or shelf. The top laminate is then applied so that the edge overlaps the top edge of the laminate on the forward edge of the table.

The plastic laminate is installed as follows:

- All holes and defects in the surface of the plywood should be filled with putty or wood filler.
- Sand the surface to be covered to help ensure good adhesion.
- Mark the plastic laminate to a pattern slightly larger than the area to be covered. Use a straightedge and draw the pattern lines on the finished or pattern side of the laminate. Leave 1/4 inch to 1/2 inch on all sides. This will be trimmed off later.
- If a laminate is to be applied to the forward edge of the table, apply this first. After installation, as detailed below, trim and file the upper edge of the plastic laminate flush with the upper edge of the plywood table top before installing the plastic laminate to upper surface of the table top.
- Cut the plastic laminate to the pattern marked. Even though the plastic laminate is extremely durable once applied, it is vulnerable to cracking and splitting before it is cemented in place. Fine-tooth handsaws or power saws with fine-tooth blades can be used; a rotary power saw with a 14 to 16 teeth per inch blade is ideal. Place the plastic laminate face up when cutting, being careful that the plastic laminate is not chipped or broken. An alternate method is to use a carbide tip knife for scoring the plastic by drawing the knife point along a metal straightedge. Cut through the decorative surface. The laminate can then be broken by bending it toward the decorative surface side over the edge of a table or workbench.
- Apply contact cement to the surface of the plywood to be covered and the back side of the plastic laminate. A brush, roller, or metal spreader with a separated edge can be used to spread the contact cement. A thin, even application is important.
- Follow the manufacturer's instructions regarding drying time. Usually, this takes about 20 to 30 minutes.
- Place a sheet of heavy wrapping paper over the plywood surface to be covered. Then position the laminate on the plywood surface with the paper between. The contact cement will not stick to the paper if it has been allowed to dry properly. Make certain that the laminate is positioned correctly. Once the two surfaces of contact cement touch, the laminate sheet can not be moved again. When everything is lined up properly, pull the paper out from between the plywood and the plastic laminate.
- Using a small block of wood and a hammer, lightly tap the laminate in place. An alternate method is to use a rolling pin.
- Use a file to remove the surplus plastic laminate from the edges. Another method is to use a special cutter with a router, which allows convenient trimming of excess plastic laminate to flush with the plywood edges.
- The thinner recommended for the contact cement can be used for cleaning contact cement from wood and plastic laminate and tools.

If a plastic laminate was not added to the forward edge of the table previously, regardless of whether the top is natural wood or covered with a plastic laminate, the next step is to add a wood or plastic trim strip to the forward edge of the table top (Fig. 4-13). If plastic is used, it can be glued in place and/or installed with fasteners. A wood trim strip can be attached with glue and finishing nails. Set the heads below the wood surface and fill holes in with wood filler to flush with the wood surface.

The wood end pieces or beams are installed next, as shown in Figs. 4-14 and 4-15. Glue and use mechanical fasteners to make the joint. One method is to use finishing nails that first pass through the end pieces and into the side pieces or reinforcing frame. Set the heads below the wood surface and fill holes in with wood filler to flush with the wood surface.

An alternate method is to fasten the end pieces with wood screws or through bolts.

The floor guides are installed to the floor beams as shown in Fig. 4-16. This installation will vary depending on the type of floor guides selected; some fit in a mounting drilled in the wood beam, others are driven or screwed into the wood, and still

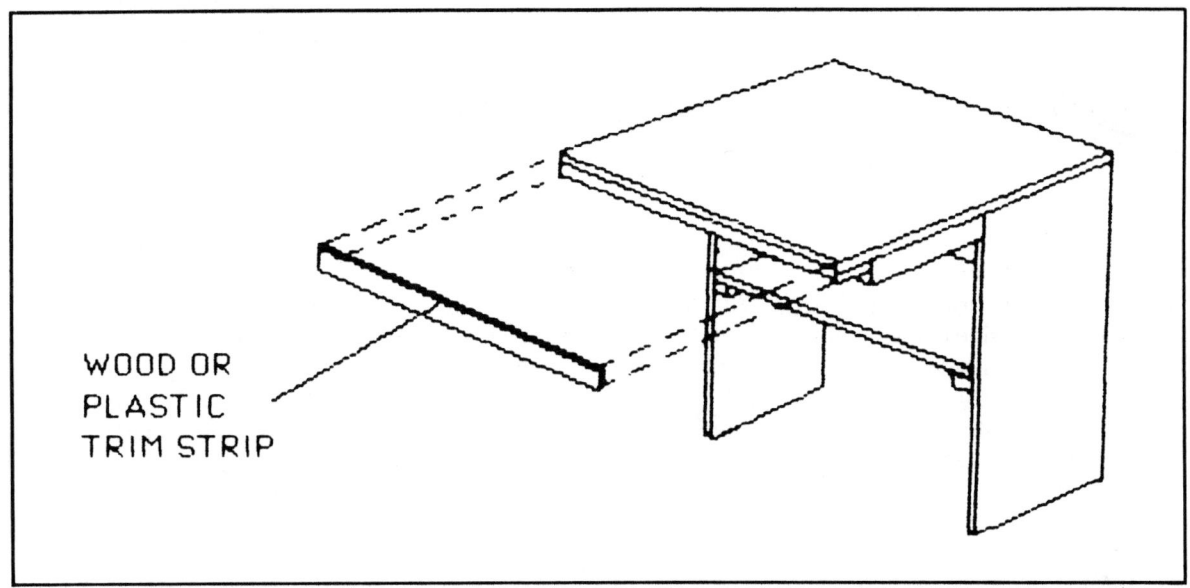

Fig. 4-13. Adding wood or plastic trim strip to front edge of top.

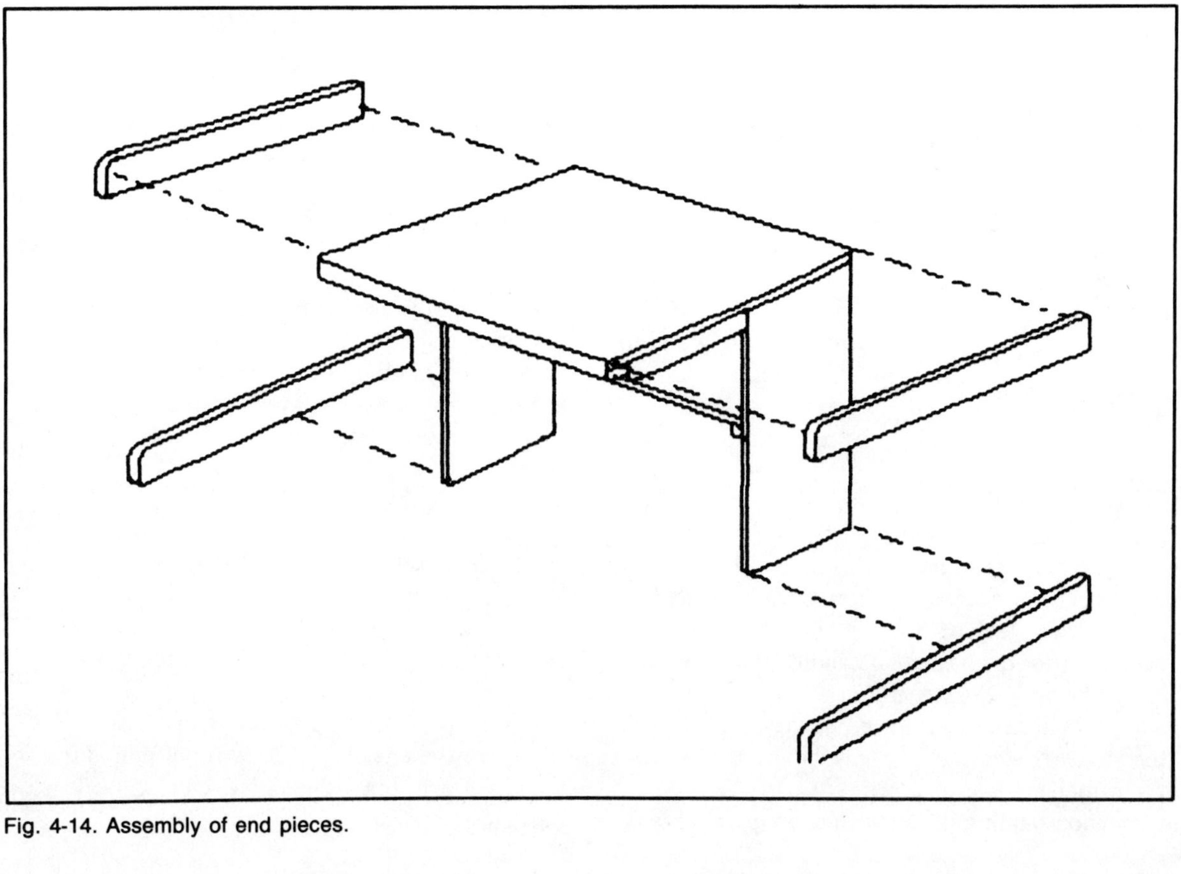

Fig. 4-14. Assembly of end pieces.

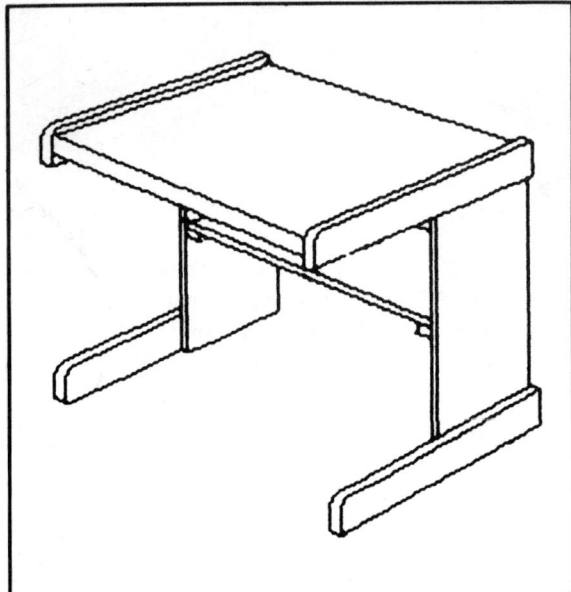

Fig. 4-15. Printer stand with end pieces installed.

others have separate screw fasteners to hold them in place.

Sanding and Finishing

Many beginners do a good job building the table up to this point, but give the table a very amateur appearance by being careless with the finish. By taking care and a little time, however, even a beginner can give the table a professional finish.

Sanding is important to prepare the wood for varnishing or painting. Small holes, checks, and other open defects in the wood should be filled in first. If a clear finish is to be applied, use a wood filler that matches the color of the wood. A sanding sealer should always be applied to the plywood before doing any sanding on the surface.

The general principle to follow for sanding is to work from coarse grits progressively to finer grits. Don't start with a grit that is coarser than necessary for the particular sanding, however. The condition of the surface might be such that you can start with a medium or even fine grit. Coarser grits tend to leave scratches that need to be sanded away with finer grits.

Wood sanding is done primarily parallel to the

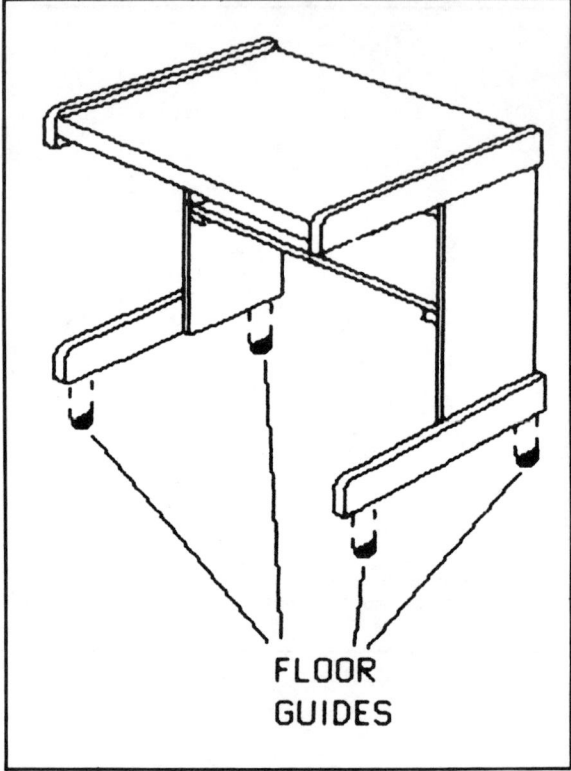

Fig. 4-16. Installing floor guides.

grain. Across the grain sanding leaves scratches and tends to tear and roughen the wood surface. A scratch free surface is especially important if you are going to finish with oil or varnish.

For most hand sanding, especially on flat surfaces, use a sanding block. Holding the sandpaper in your hand leaves a wavy surface on the wood because pressure is not applied evenly to all areas. A carpet or felt pad between the block and the sandpaper also helps.

At the final stages of sanding, most craftsmen use their fingertips to judge the smoothness of the surface. You can also judge by looking at the surface across a light held at a low angle to the wood surface. Careful sanding will produce a fine finish that you will be proud of.

If desired, a power sander can be used. A pad sander is the easiest to use without damaging the wood surface, but belt sanders can be used by experienced operators.

A clear finish (polyurethane plastic is ideal) can be applied directly to natural wood, or you can first stain the wood to give it another color. Staining can enhance the natural grain and enrich relatively lifeless woods.

Before applying stain, first test color on a scrap piece of similar wood. Clean the surface area where stain is to be applied. Use a cloth to eliminate as much dust as possible. The stain can then be applied with a brush, foam brush applicator, or cloth. Apply a smooth, even coat of a stain. Allow the stain to penetrate the wood. Depending on the humidity, temperature, and particular stain used, this usually takes from 5 to 15 minutes. While the stain is still wet, wipe off the excess stain with a clean cloth. Be careful not to remove too much from corners and edges. Wipe across the grain first so that you work the stain into the wood pores. Then give a final wipe with the grain. Allow the stain to dry. This usually takes at least 8 hours. The finish can then be applied.

It is usually best to apply a series of light, even coats of clear finish rather than one thick coat. This will minimize possible drips and wrinkles as the finish dries.

Apply finish in brush-width strokes in direction of wood grain. Turn table so that finish is applied to wood surface in a horizontal position whenever possible.

A minimum of two coats is recommended. Allow 6 to 8 hours for the first coat to dry before applying second coat. Sand lightly and use a tack cloth to remove sanded finish dust before applying next coat of finish.

Clear or stained finishes are usually applied to natural wood furniture, but if desired color paint finishes can also be applied.

Variations

Many variations are possible for the basic budget printer stand. One possibility is to substitute materials, such as particle board instead of plywood for the top, or you can construct the table with a different size top. It is important not to have the width of the top wider than about twice the length of the width of the side boards. Another variation is to cut a slot in the backing board for continuous form computer paper.

The basic budget printer stand makes a functional and attractive table even when built from inexpensive woods. This design is ideal for anyone who wants to build computer furniture to sell to others, because it can be sold either unfinished or with finish applied. By using more expensive woods, such as oak, you can give the table a custom appearance. The plans given here use simple butt joints, but if you have cabinet-making skills and know-how, you can use difficult joints.

BASIC PRINTER STAND WITH FULL SIDES

This printer stand, made of plywood, is slightly more difficult to construct than the basic budget printer stand described above. It presents more difficulties in cutting and covering edges than does the stock wood used on the basic budget printer stand. The materials are also more expensive, but this stand gives more of a custom appearance than the basic budget stand. By using hardwood faced plywood, you can construct an expensive-looking table for a fraction of the cost of making it out of solid hardwood. In any case, large savings are possible by building your own.

The basic printer stand with full sides is shown in Fig. 4-17. The top has ample space for most types of computer printers. The table can have a natural wood plastic laminated (Fig. 4-18) top. The table features a shelf underneath that provides storage space and a platform for continuous form paper.

Materials

The patterns for the wood parts are shown in Fig. 4-19. The top of the table is a 20-inch-by-24-inch piece of 3/4-inch thick plywood. If you intend to use the wood surface as the finished table top, without adding a plastic laminate, I recommend plywood with the upper layer of hardwood. If a laminate is to be added, exterior grade shop plywood will suffice.

The shelves are 3/4-inch thick plywood. Three are required. they measure 16 inches by 24 inches. If desired, you can make the shelves other depths.

The end pieces are 3/4-inch thick plywood and

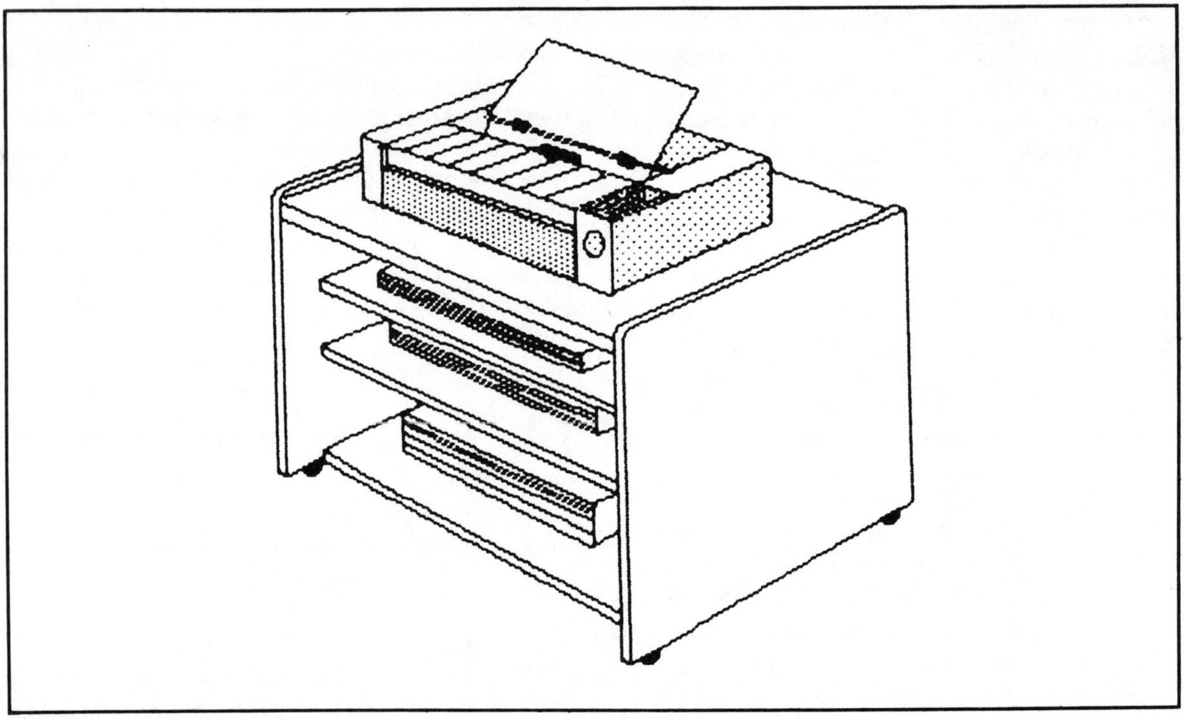

Fig. 4-17. Basic printer stand with full sides.

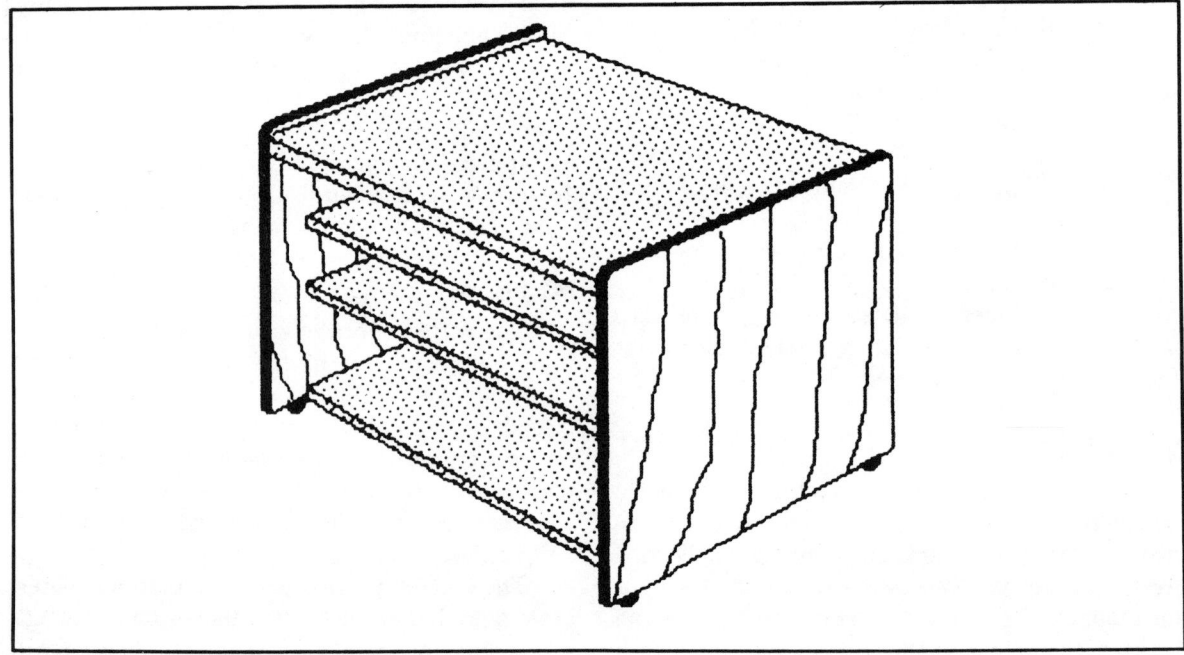

Fig. 4-18. Basic printer stand with plastic laminates.

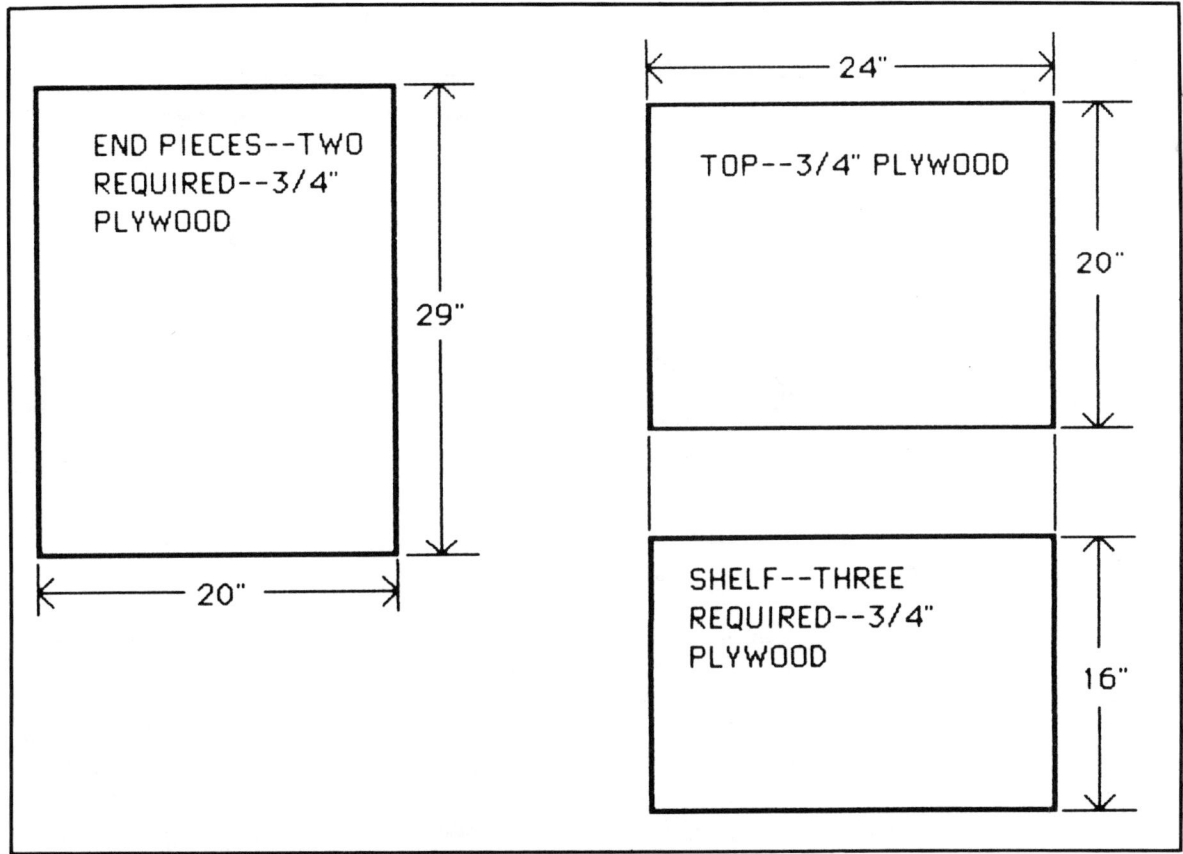

Fig. 4-19. Patterns for plywood parts for basic printer stand with full sides.

measure 20 inches by 29 inches. The 29-inch dimension gives a table that is 28 1/4 inches high, not counting the height added by whatever floor guides are used. You may want to change the 29-inch dimension if you want your table a different height. Two end pieces are required.

Plywood is normally sold in standard 4-foot-by-8-foot sheets. Lay out the patterns to take advantage of this standard size and arrange them to keep waste to a minimum. Some lumberyards and plywood stores will cut plywood sheets for you to size, usually at additional cost. This can be worth the cost if you don't need full sheets, don't have room to carry full sheets in your car, or don't have a saw to accurately cut plywood.

Although 1/2-inch thick plywood could also be used, I don't recommend it because the savings are small, and a less sturdy table will result. Particle board can be substituted for the plywood if you are on an absolute minimum budget, but it can be difficult to work with. It is very difficult to get plastic laminates to bond properly to particle board without special equipment.

The backing piece (Fig. 4-20) can be either plywood or fiberboard. The backing piece is used to strengthen the table base and hold the frame in rectangular form. The length of the backing piece is 25 1/2 inches. A 12-inch height is shown for the backing piece, which is about the minimum required to give this table adequate strength. The upper shelf can be installed a greater distance below the top, which will require changing the height of the backing piece. Notice that the top, upper shelf, backing piece, and side pieces form a box with the

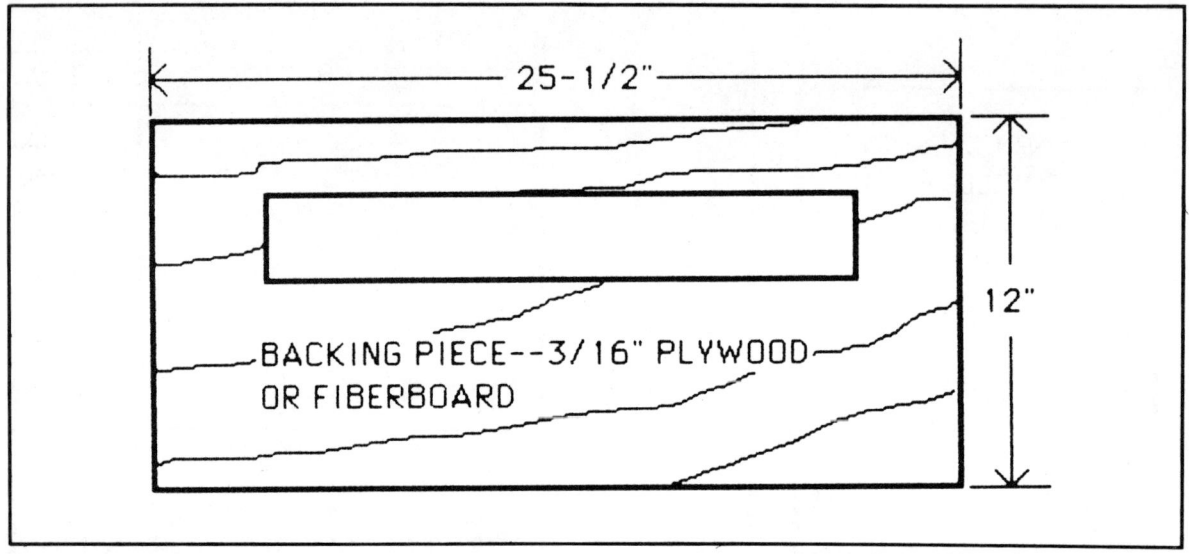

Fig. 4-20. Pattern for backing piece.

forward side open. A slot is cut in the backing piece for continuous form paper to pass through. You will also need 1-inch-by-2-inch or larger framing stock for use under the plywood table top.

Wood and plastic trim strips can be used to cover the exposed edges of the plywood forward edge of the table top. This piece is 24 inches long and about 1 3/4 inches wide. The minimum width should be such that it will completely cover the widths of the plywood (3/4 inch) and the framing (approximately 7/8 inch). The trim strips can be slightly wider than this, however.

Four fixed or adjustable floor pods or guides are used on the floor beams, available from hardware stores.

A variety of fasteners can be used for assembly, as detailed below in this section. You will also need a suitable wood glue and whatever wood finish you choose.

The top can be left natural or a plastic laminate can be added. If a plastic laminate is applied, you will need a 20-inch-by-24-inch piece and the contact cement for attaching it to the plywood.

Construction

Overviews of the complete assembly are shown in Figs. 4-21 and 4-22. Begin by constructing the table top, as detailed in Fig. 4-23. If you purchased a piece of plywood that was already cut to the 20-inch-by-24-inch size, no additional cutting is required, assuming that it was cut accurately. You might want to check for trueness with a square first.

If you purchased a larger piece of plywood, cut out a section for the table top. In most cases, you will want to have the grain of the top layer running lengthwise, although this is not essential if you are going to add a plastic laminate. Use two factory cut edges for your table top and cut the other two. Use a ruler and square to make the pattern, marking the lines with a sharp pencil or scribing tool.

Sawing plywood requires special care to avoid chipping and splintering along the cut edge. Handsaws or power saws with special fine-toothed or carbide-tipped blades designed especially for plywood should be used. Apply a strip of masking tape over the area to be cut on both sides of the plywood, but especially on the underside, to prevent splintering. Another possibility is to clamp a solid piece of wood to the underside and make the cut through both the plywood and the piece of wood.

Be extremely careful when sanding plywood edges. Use a sanding block. Avoid sanding the surfaces of plywood until a wood sealer has been applied.

The next step is to add the reinforcing frame to the table top, as shown in Fig. 4-23. Use a ruler and a square to make the patterns on the framing wood and mark the lines with a sharp pencil. Make the necessary saw cuts. The frame pieces should be glued and nailed or screwed in position (see Figs. 4-24 and 4-25). If the plywood top will be left natu-

ral wood, the fasteners should go through the framing and into the plywood, taking care that the fasteners do not pass all the way through the plywood or leave a bulge in the upper surface. If a good acrylic or epoxy glue is used, it alone should give adequate strength, with the fasteners mainly used as clamping devices. Fasteners will not have much holding power into the plywood: for greater holding power, the fasteners can be passed through

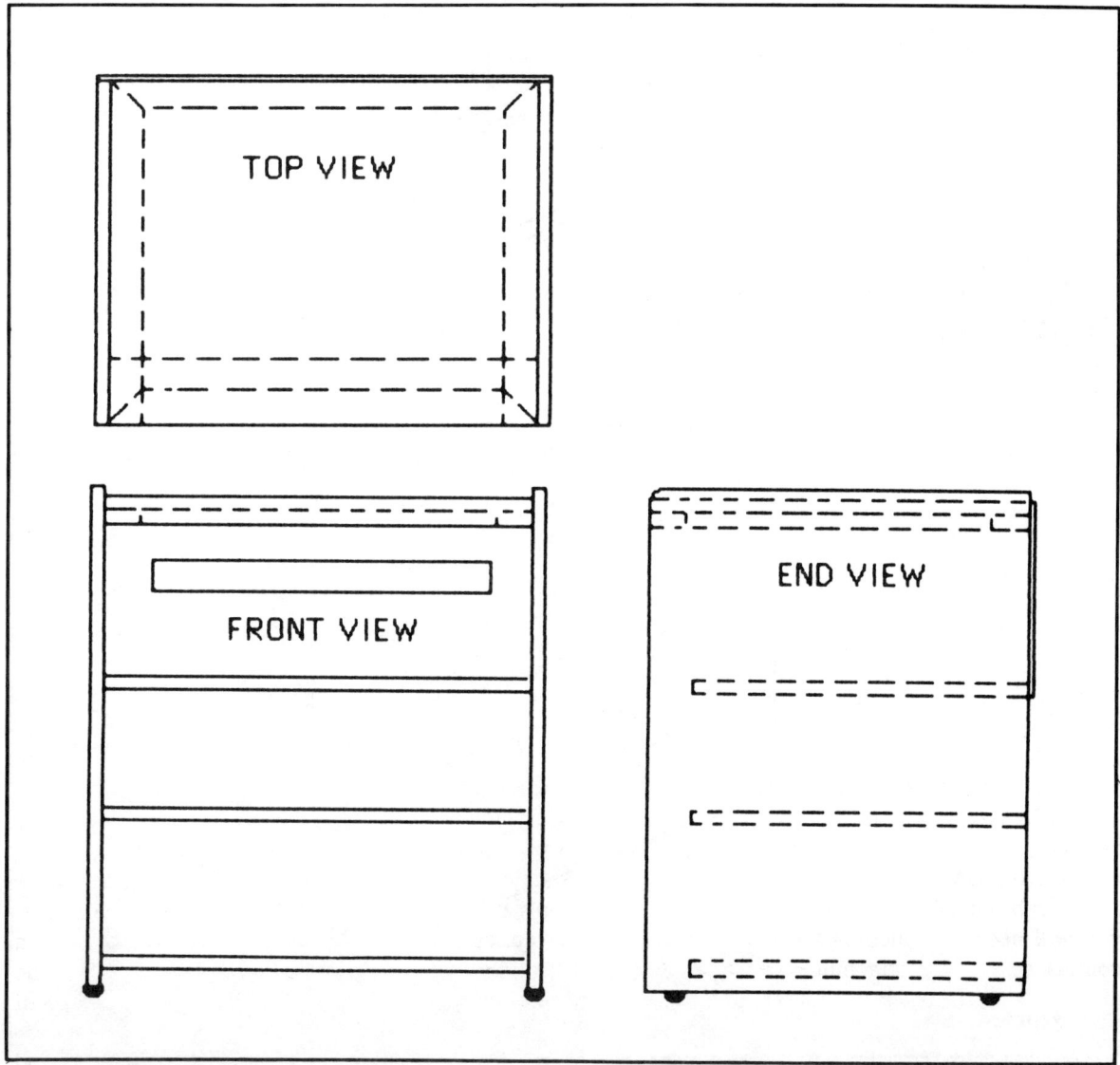

Fig. 4-21. Basic printer stand with full sides.

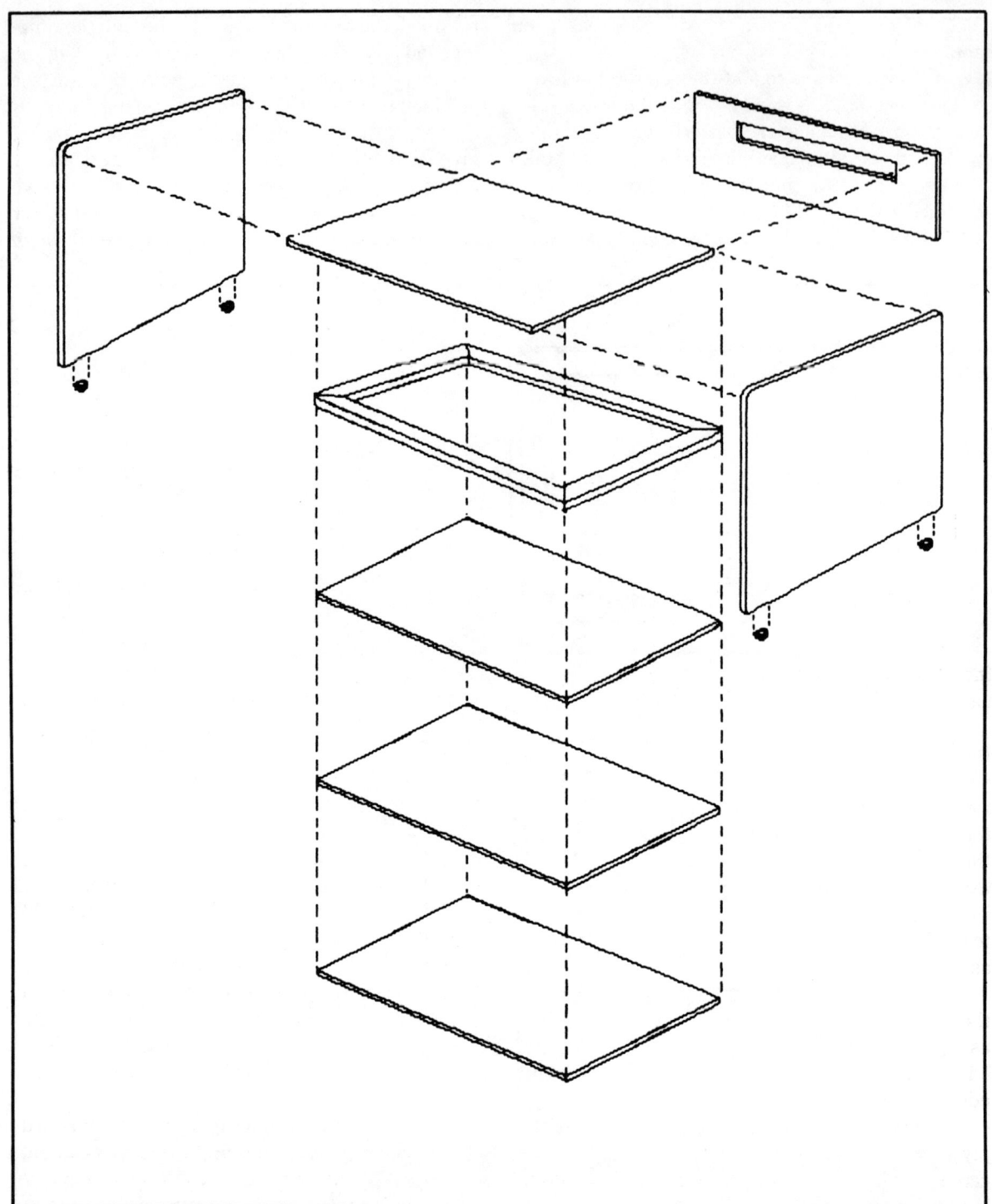

Fig. 4-22. Assembly of basic printer stand with full sides.

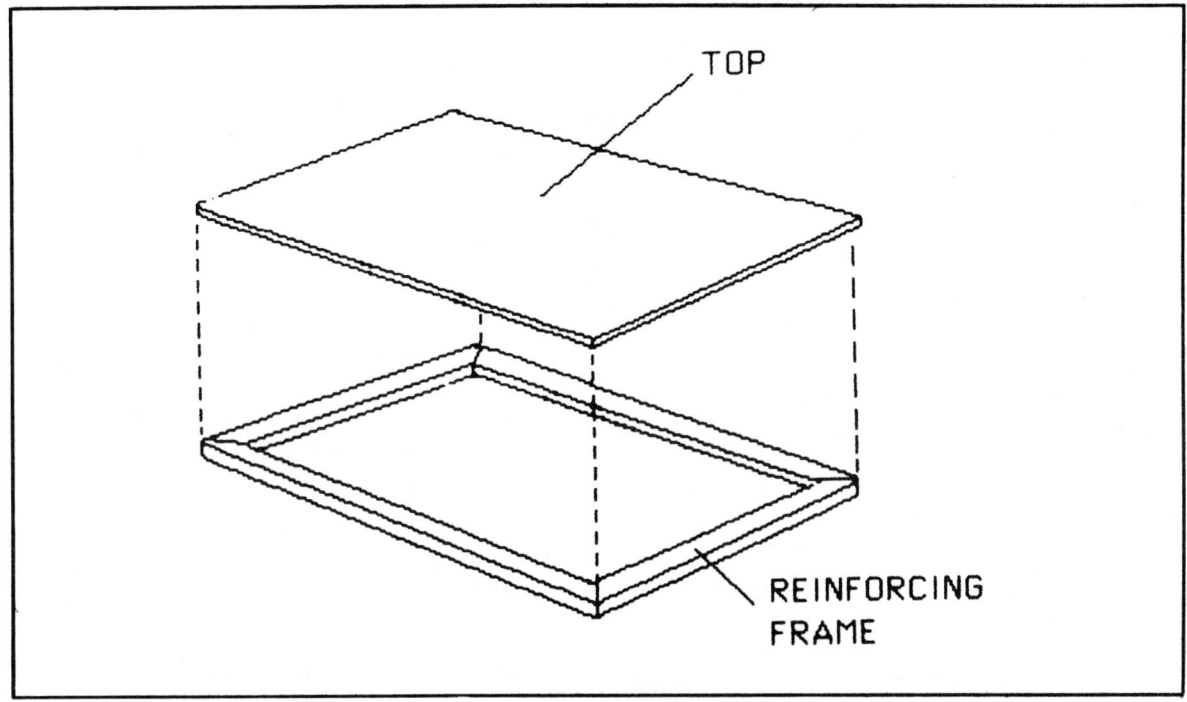

Fig. 4-23. Assembly of printer stand top to reinforcing frame underneath.

the plywood and into the framing (if a plastic laminate is to be added).

Several options are available for finishing off the table top. One possibility is to use the plywood surface as the top and add a wood trim strip to the forward edge, as shown in Fig. 4-26. Glue and fasten the trim strip in place with finishing nails. Set the heads below the wood surface and fill holes with wood filler to flush with the wood surface.

A second possibility is to add a plastic laminate to the forward edge and leave the top natural wood, as detailed in Fig. 4-27.

Another method is to add a plastic laminate to the top and a wood trim strip to the forward edge, as shown in Fig. 4-28. Still another possibility is to add plastic laminates to both the top and forward edge, as shown in Figs. 4-29 and 4-30.

If a plastic laminate is to be added to the plywood table top and/or the forward edge, these can be installed at this time. Use high quality plastic laminates for computer furniture.

If a plastic laminate is to also be applied to the forward edge of the top, it should be applied first. This is then finished flush with the table top. The top laminate is then applied so that the edge overlaps the top edge of the laminate on the forward edge of the table, as shown in Fig. 4-30.

The plastic laminate is installed as follows:

- All holes and defects in the surface of the plywood should be filled with putty or wood filler.
- Sand the surface to be covered. This will help ensure good adhesion.
- Mark the plastic laminate to a pattern slightly larger than the area to be covered. Use a straightedge and draw the pattern lines on the finished or pattern side of the laminate. Leave 1/4 inch to 1/2 inch on all sides. This will be trimmed off later.
- If a laminate is to be applied to the forward edge of the table, apply this first. After installation, as detailed below, trim and file the upper edge of the plastic laminate flush with the upper edge of the plywood table top before installing the plastic

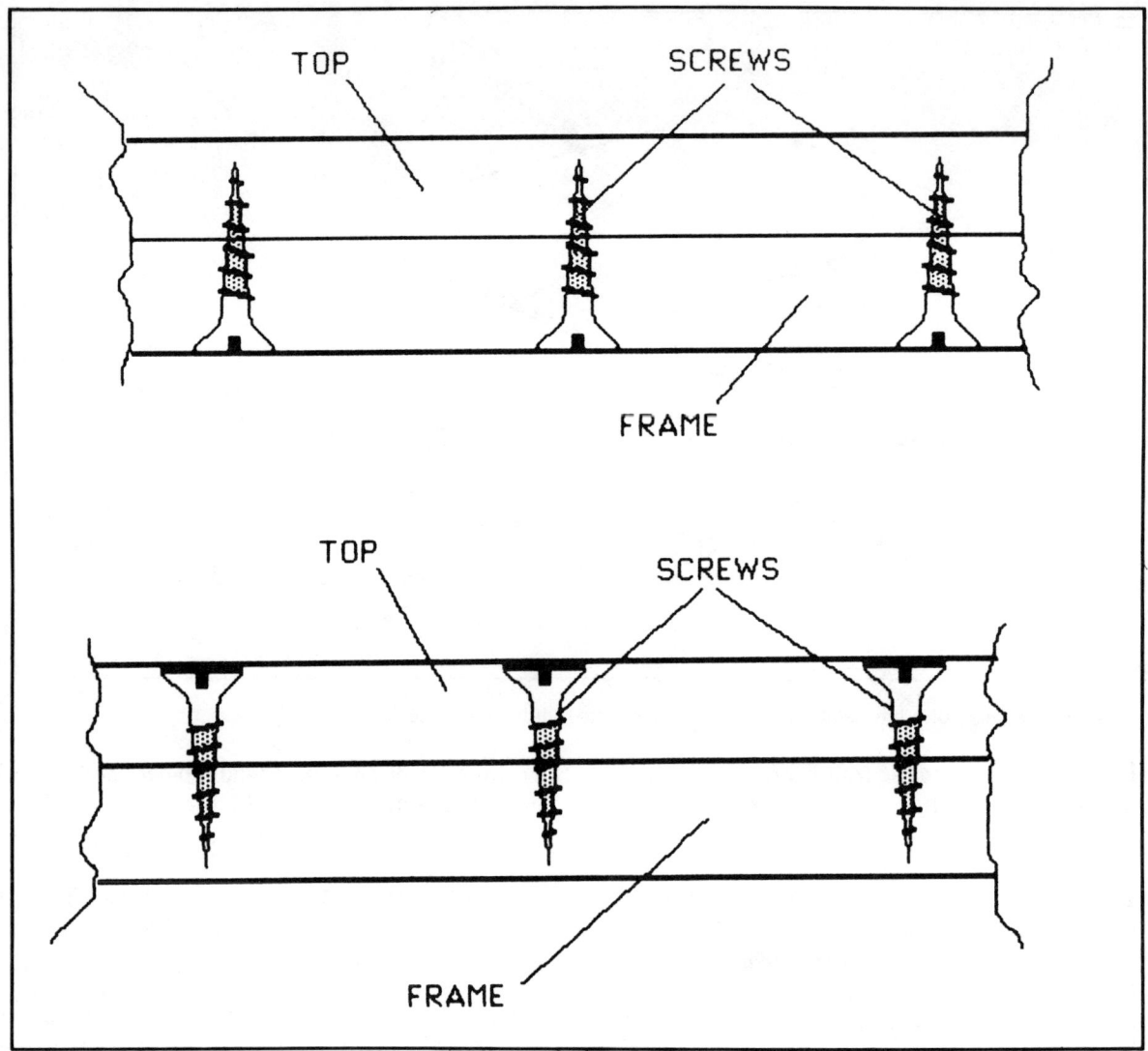

Fig. 4-24. Assembly of top to frame pieces with screws and glue.

laminate to upper surface of the table top.
- Cut the plastic laminate to the pattern marked. Even though the plastic laminate is extremely durable once applied, it is vulnerable to cracking and splitting before it is cemented in place. Fine-tooth handsaws or power saws with fine-tooth blades can be used. A rotary power saw with a 14 to 16 teeth per inch blade is ideal. Place the plastic laminate face up when cutting. Care should be taken so that the plastic laminate is not chipped or broken. An alternate method is to use a carbide tip knife for scoring the plastic by drawing the knife point along a metal straightedge. Cut through the decorative surface. The laminate can then be broken by bending it toward the decorative surface side over the edge of a table or workbench.
- Apply contact cement to the surface of the plywood to be covered and the back side of the plastic laminate. A brush, roller, or metal spreader with a serrated edge can be used to spread the con-

tact cement. A thin, even application is important.

• Follow the manufacturer's instructions regarding drying time. Usually, this takes about 20 to 30 minutes.

• Place a sheet of heavy wrapping paper over the plywood surface to be covered. Then position the laminate on the plywood surface with the paper between. The contact cement will not stick to the paper if it has been allowed to dry properly. Make certain that the laminate is positioned correctly. Once the two surfaces of contact cement touch, the laminate sheet cannot be moved again.

When everything is lined up properly, pull the paper out from between the plywood and the plastic laminate.

• Using a small block of wood and a hammer, lightly tap the laminate in place. An alternate method is to use a rolling pin.

• Use a file to remove the surplus plastic laminate from the edges. Another method is to use a special cutter with a router, which allows convenient trimming of excess plastic laminate to flush with the plywood edges.

• The thinner recommended for the contact ce-

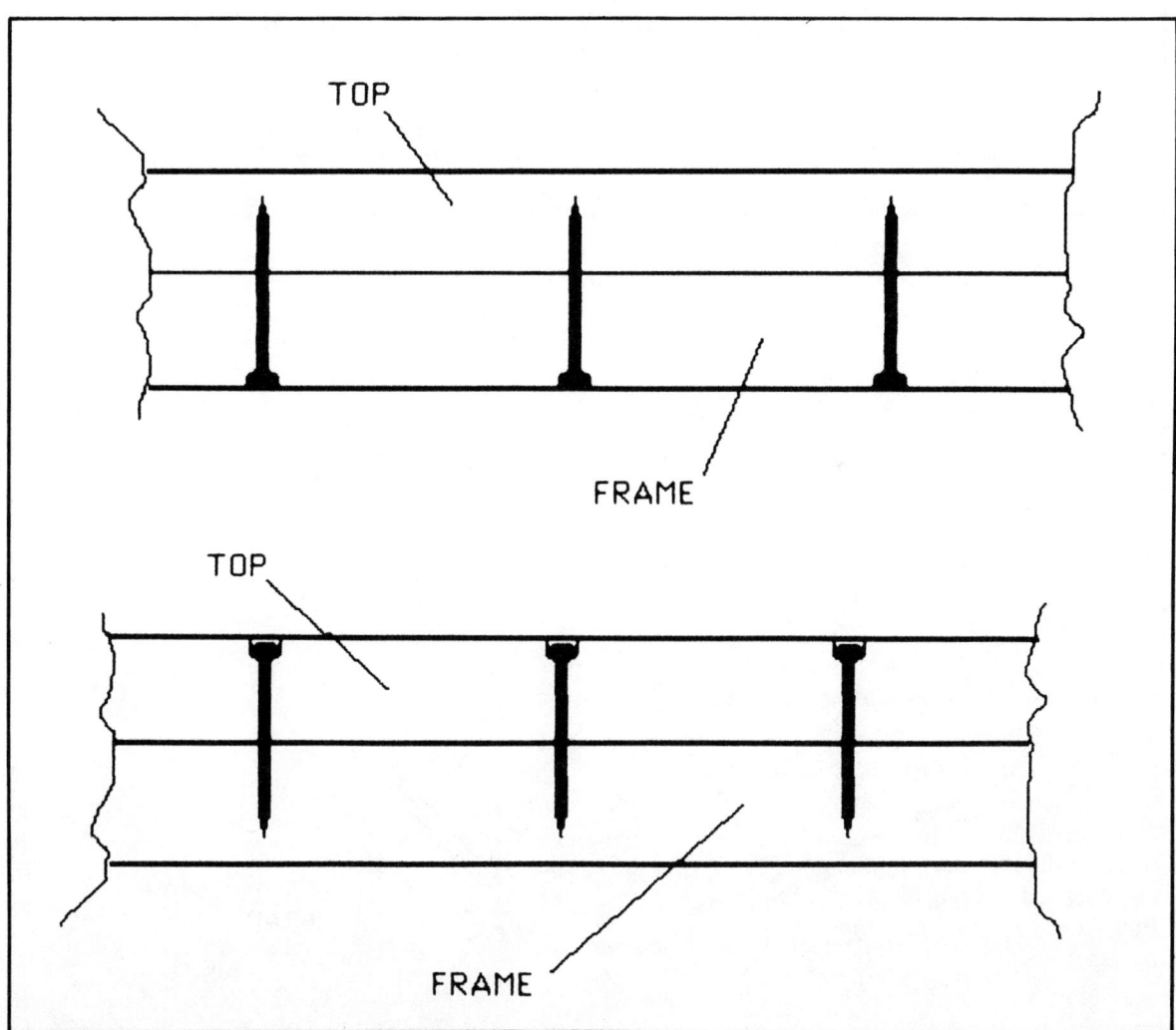

Fig. 4-25. Assembly of top to frame pieces with nails and glue.

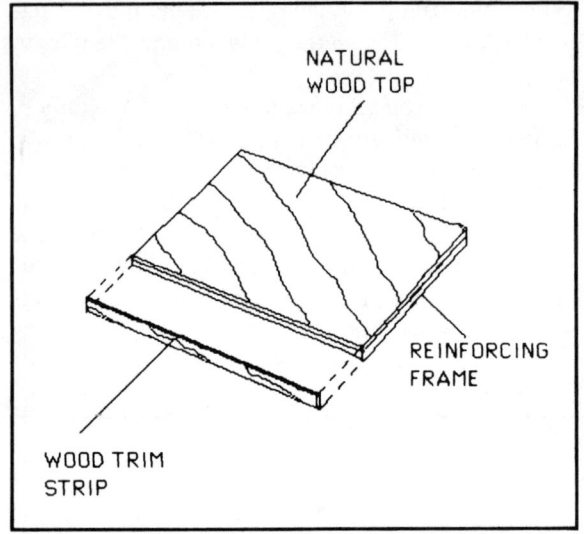

Fig. 4-26. Adding wood trim strip to forward edge of top.

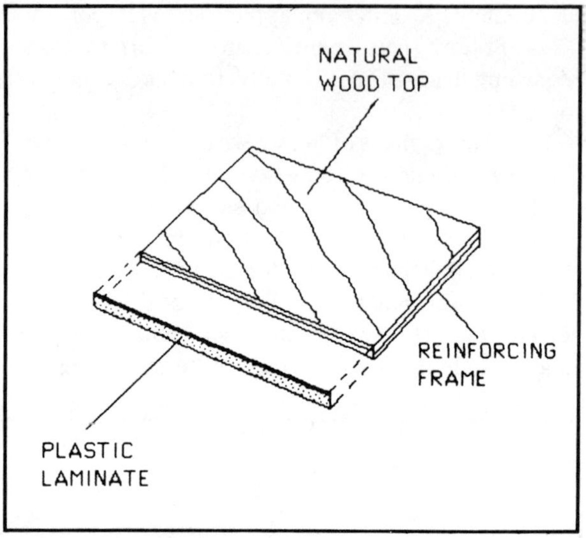

Fig. 4-27. Adding plastic laminate to forward edge of top.

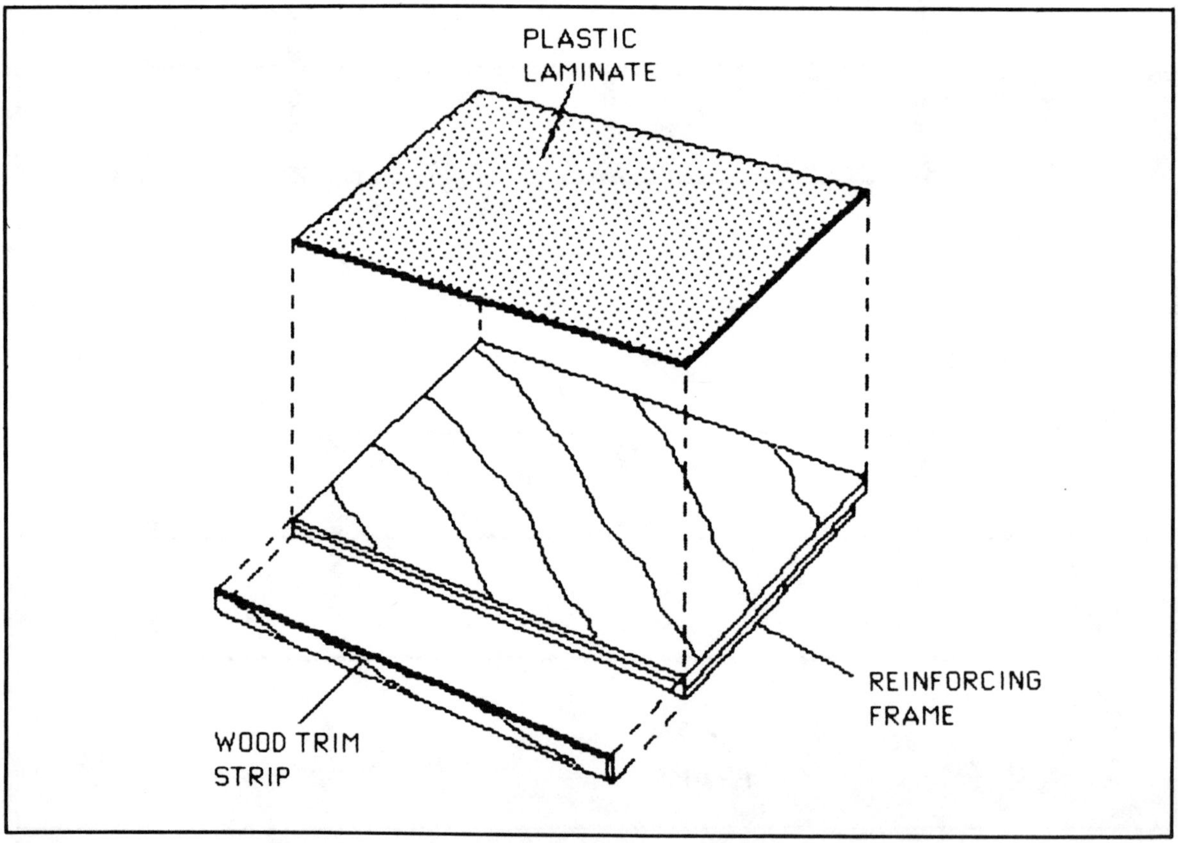

Fig. 4-28. Adding plastic laminate to top and wood trim strip to forward edge.

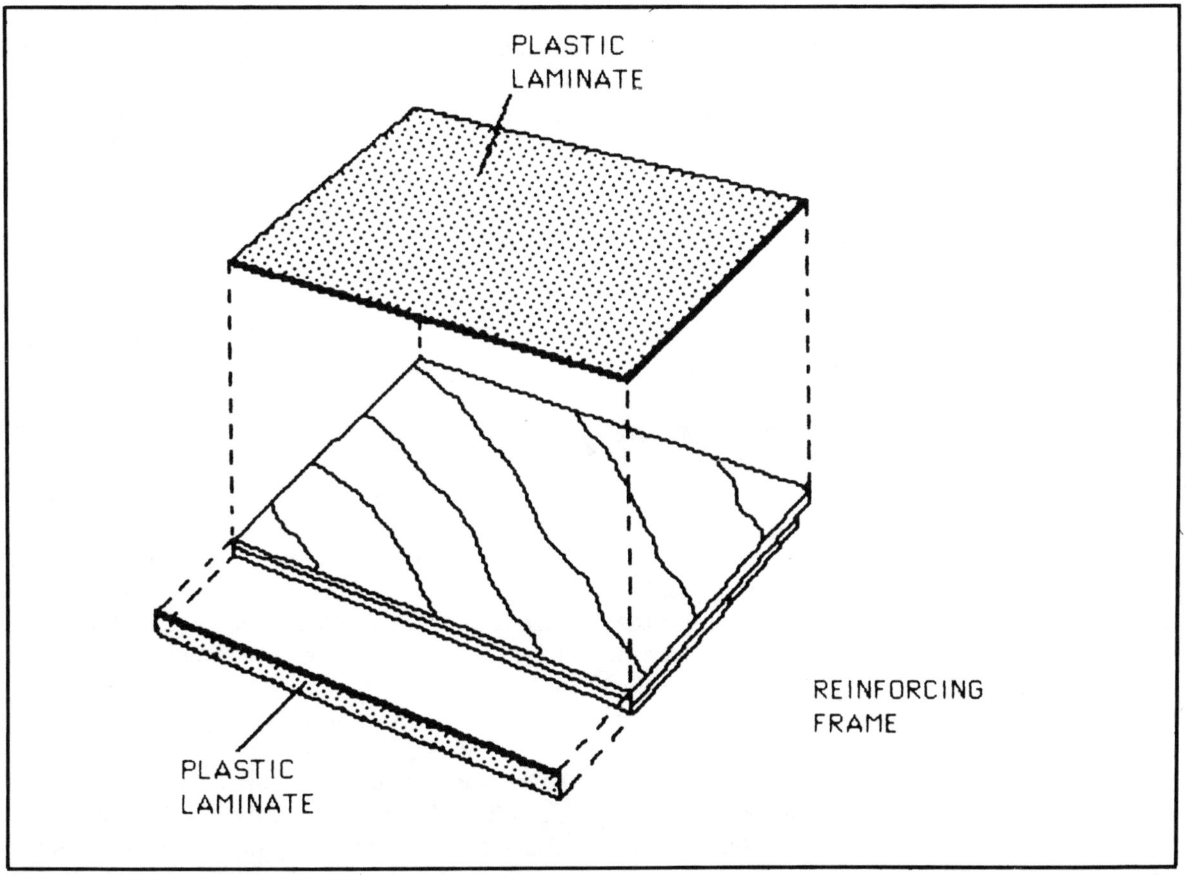

Fig. 4-29. Adding plastic laminate to top and forward edge of top.

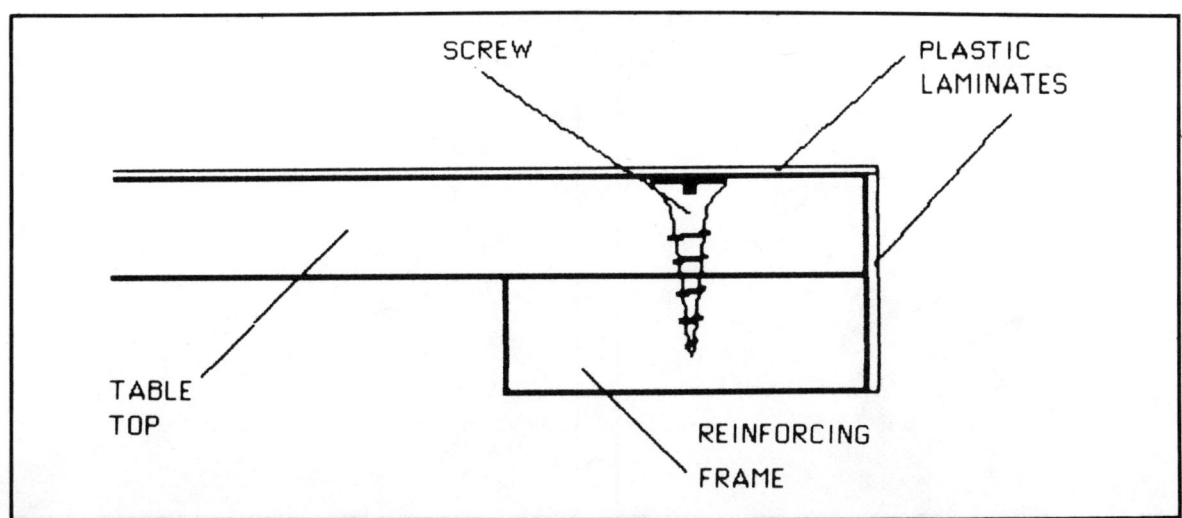

Fig. 4-30. Adding plastic laminate to top.

ment can be used for cleaning contact cement from wood and plastic laminate and tools.

The next step is to construct the shelves. If you purchased pieces of plywood that were already cut to the 16-inch-by-2-foot size, no additional cutting is required, if they are cut accurately and form true rectangles. Check this with a square.

If you purchased a larger piece of plywood, cut out the pieces for the shelves, having the grain of the top layer running lengthwise. This is not essential if you are going to add a plastic laminate. To save time, you will use two factory cut edges for each shelf top and cut the other two. Use a ruler and square to draw the pattern, marking the lines with a sharp pencil or scribing tool. Saw and sand carefully to avoid chipping, splintering, or wavy surface finishes.

You can finish the shelf the same way you finished the table, using the plywood surface as the shelf top and add a wood trim strip to the forward edge, as shown in Fig. 4-31. Glue and fasten the trim strip in place with finishing nails. Set the heads below the wood surface and fill holes with wood filler to flush with the wood surface.

Or, you can add a plastic laminate to the forward edge and leave the shelf top natural wood, as detailed in Fig. 4-32.

Another method is to add a plastic laminate to the shelf top and a wood trim strip to the forward edge, as shown in Fig. 4-33; still another possibility is to add plastic laminates to both the top and forward edge, as shown in Figs. 4-34 and 4-35.

If a plastic laminate is to be added to the plywood shelf top and/or the forward edges, these can be installed now. When plastic laminate is to also be applied to the forward edge of the shelf top, it should be applied first, then finished flush with the shelf top. The top laminate is then applied so that the edge overlaps the top edge of the laminate on the forward edge of the shelf, as shown in Fig. 4-35.

Next, cut the end pieces to rectangular size and round off the upper forward corners. The curve can be on a 1/2-inch radius or as desired to fit a particular molding corner piece. A power circular saw is ideal for making straight cuts. A saber saw can be used for making the curved corner cuts.

The next step is to add plastic (Fig. 4-36) or wood (Fig. 4-37) trim to the forward and top edges of the end pieces to protect the laminated edges of the plywood and give a neat appearance.

An overview of the remainder of the assembly is shown in Fig. 4-38. The next step is to assemble the top and shelves to the side pieces, as shown in Fig. 4-39. This is accomplished by both glue and mechanical fasteners. If you use finishing nails, pass them through the end pieces and into the framing wood of the top. Set the heads below the wood surface and fill with wood filler to flush with the

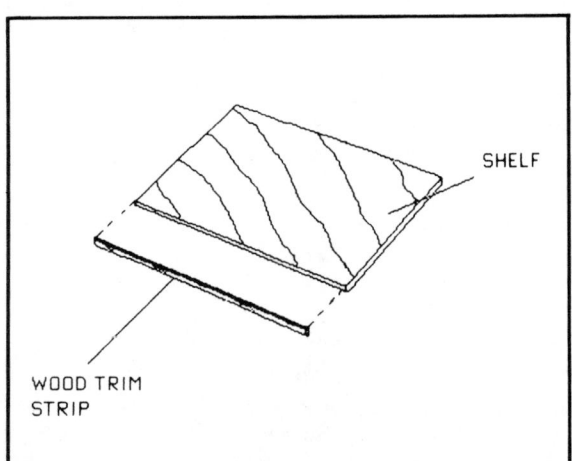

Fig. 4-31. Adding wood trim strip to forward edge of shelf.

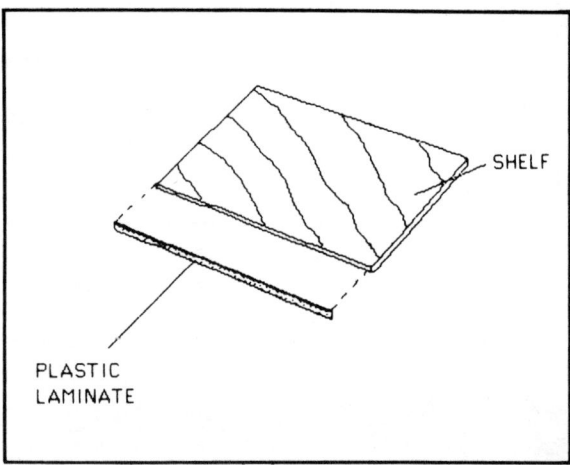

Fig. 4-32. Adding plastic laminate to forward edge of shelf.

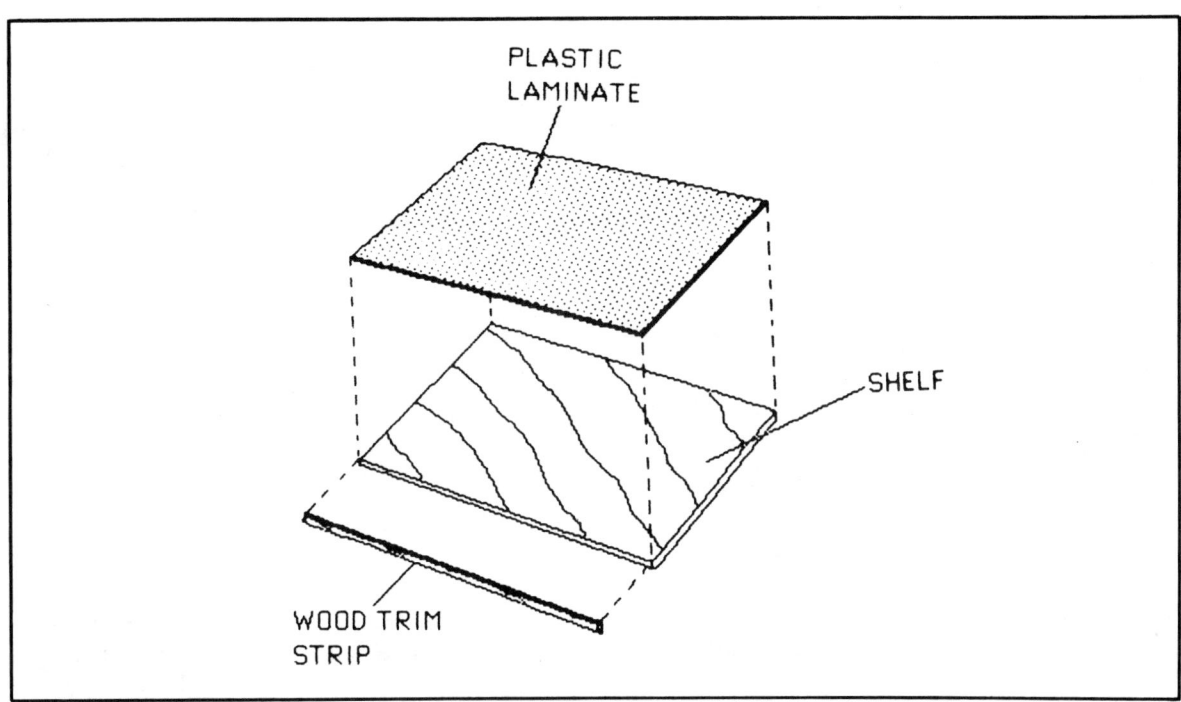

Fig. 4-33. Adding wood trim strip to forward edge of shelf and plastic laminate to top.

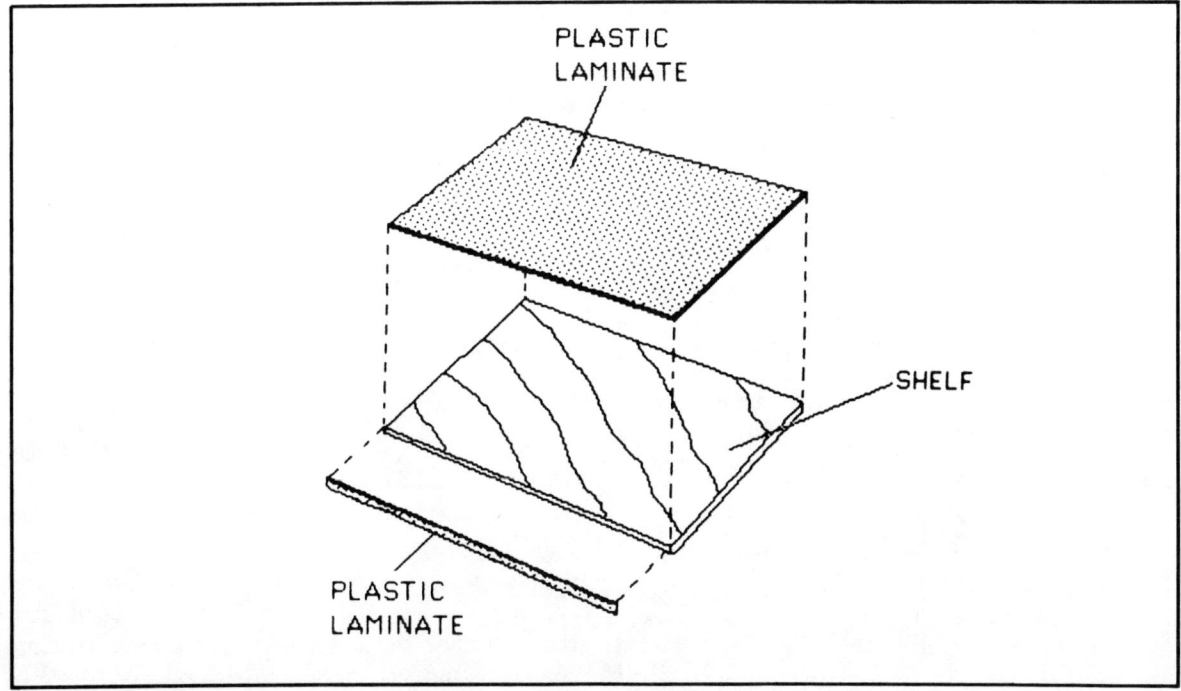

Fig. 4-34. Adding plastic laminates to forward edge and top or shelf.

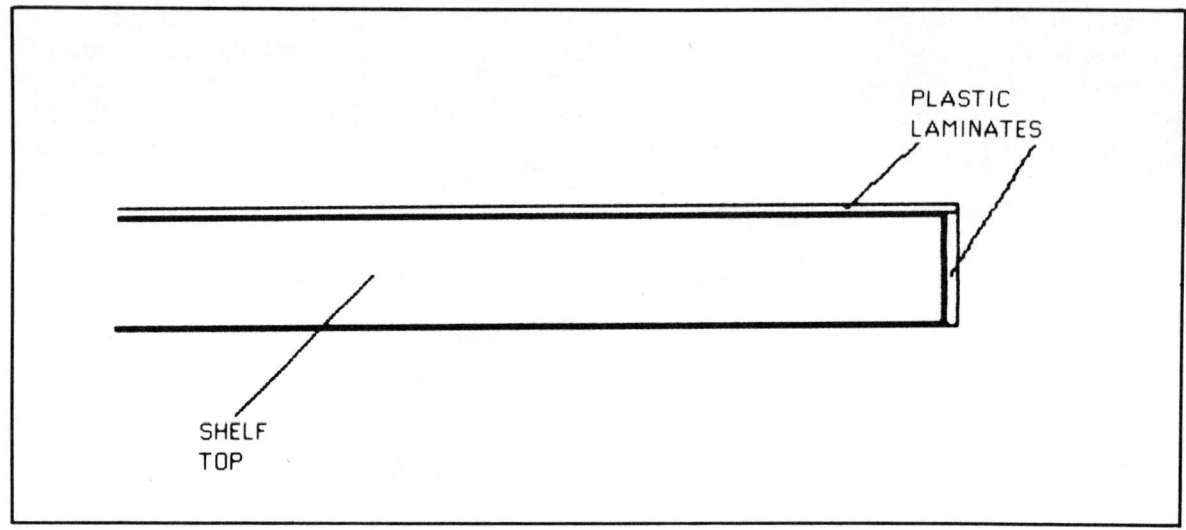

Fig. 4-35. Adding plastic laminates to shelf.

wood surface. Or, use through-bolts, as detailed in Fig. 4-40. The shelves can be attached with metal angle straps or aluminum angle pieces, as detailed in Fig. 4-41.

Regardless of the method of fastening, it is extremely important to install the side pieces perpendicular to the table top and shelves in a crosswise direction. Use a square to make pattern lines on the side pieces. It is also important to have exactly the same distance between the top and upper shelf on both sides and the three shelves parallel to each other.

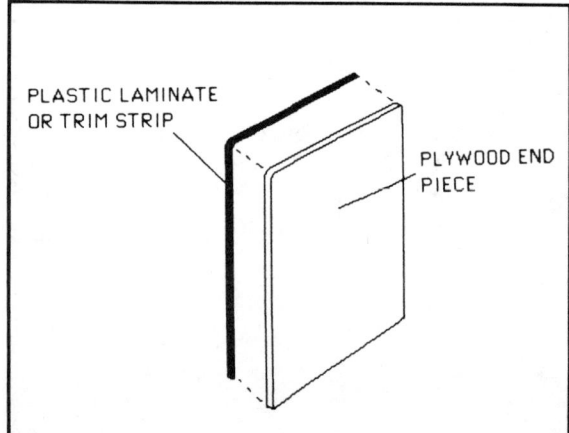

Fig. 4-36. Adding plastic laminate or trim strip to end pieces.

After the shelves and top have been assembled to the side pieces, add the backing piece, as shown in Fig. 4-42. The backing piece forms a box with the top, shelf, and side pieces, and it is important that the backing piece be attached securely to the wood members all the way around the edges. Glue and nail it into position. It is extremely important to make certain that the backing piece is a true rectangular form and that the side pieces are perpendicular to the table top and upper shelf before the backing piece is attached and the glue allowed to set. Figure 4-43 shows the backing piece installed.

The floor guides are installed next (see Fig. 4-44), depending on the type selected. Follow manufacturer's directions.

Sanding and Finishing

Sanding and applying a finish are important steps in the construction process. By taking care and a little time, even a beginner can give the table a professional finish.

Sanding prepares the wood for varnishing or painting. Small holes, checks, and other open defects in the wood should be filled in before sanding. If a clear finish is applied, use a wood filler that matches the color of the wood. A sanding sealer should be applied to the plywood before doing any sanding on the surface.

When sanding wood, work from coarse grits to progressively finer grits, but don't start with a grit coarser than necessary for the particular sanding. You may be able to start with a medium or even fine grit, because coarser grits tend to leave scratches that need to be sanded away with finer grits.

Wood sanding is done primarily parallel to the grain. Sanding across the grain leaves scratches and tears and roughens the wood surface. A scratch free surface is especially important if you are going to finish with oil or varnish.

For most hand sanding, especially on flat surfaces, use a sanding block. Holding the sandpaper in your hand leaves a wavy surface on the wood because of uneven pressure. A carpet or felt pad between the block and the sandpaper also helps.

At the final stages of sanding, use your eyes and fingertips to judge the smoothness of the surface. Taking special care with the sanding is an important step if a fine finish that you will be proud of is to be achieved.

If desired, a power sander can be used; a pad

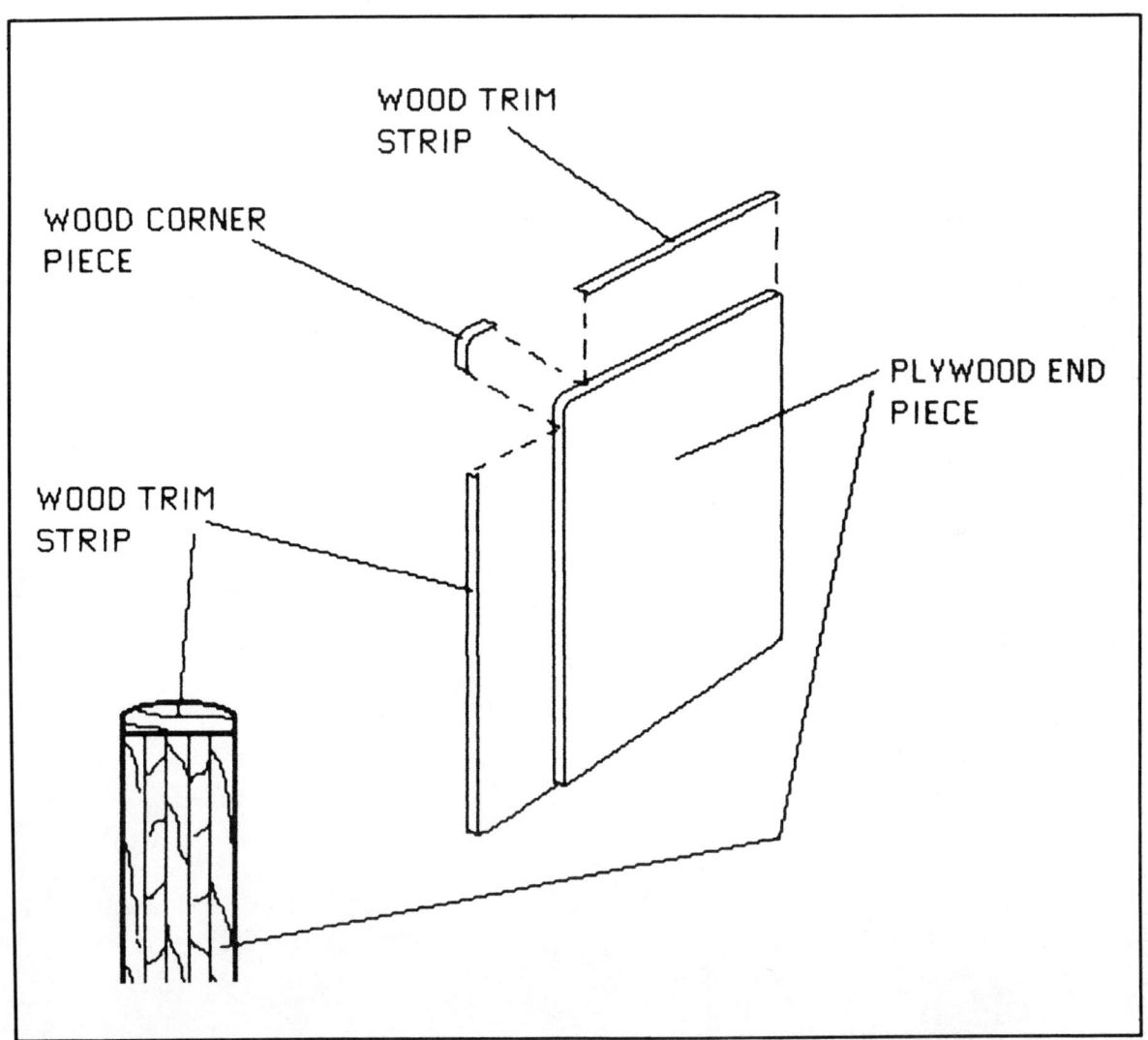

Fig. 4-37. Adding wood trim strips and corner piece to end pieces.

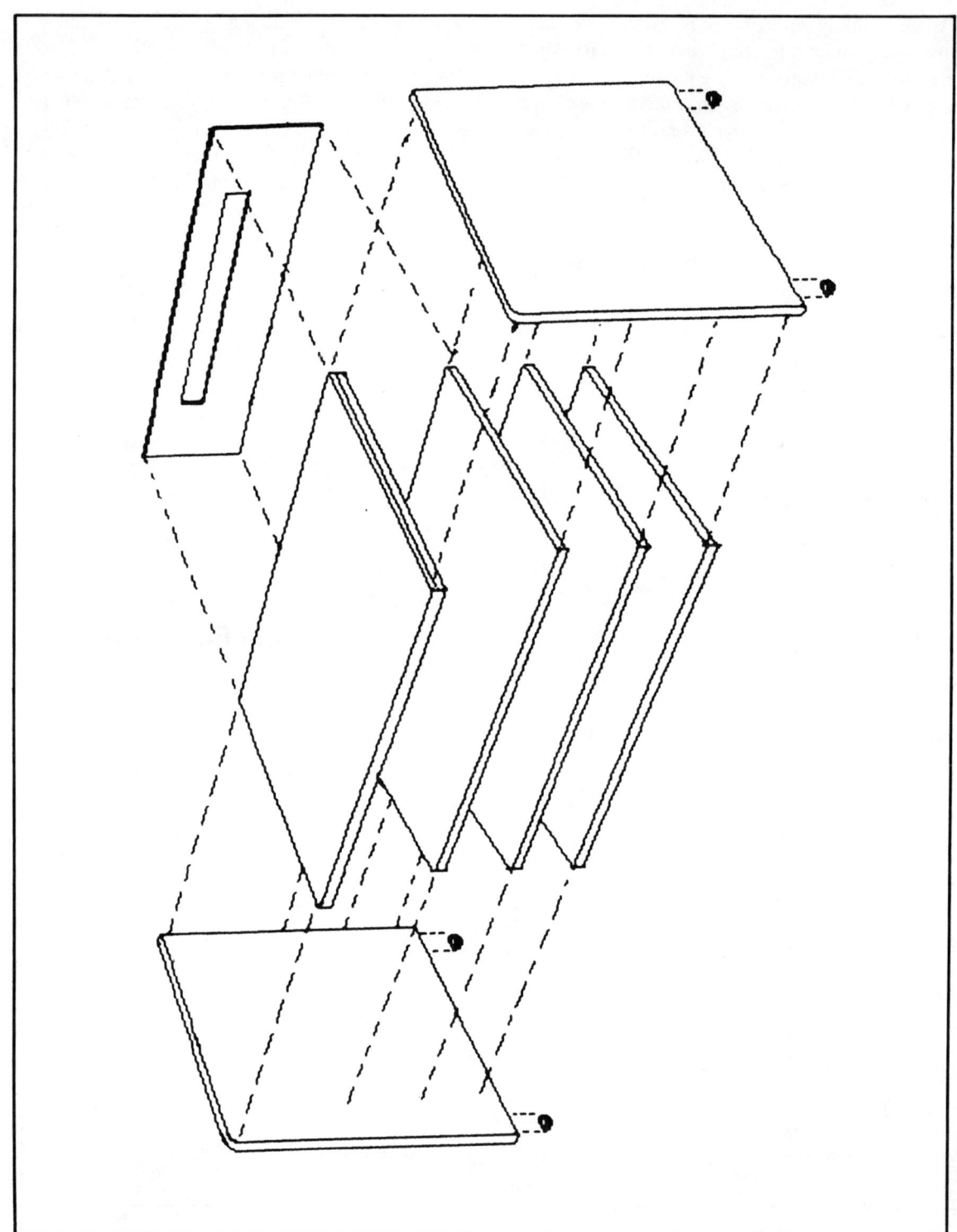

Fig. 4-38. Assembly of basic printer stand with full sides.

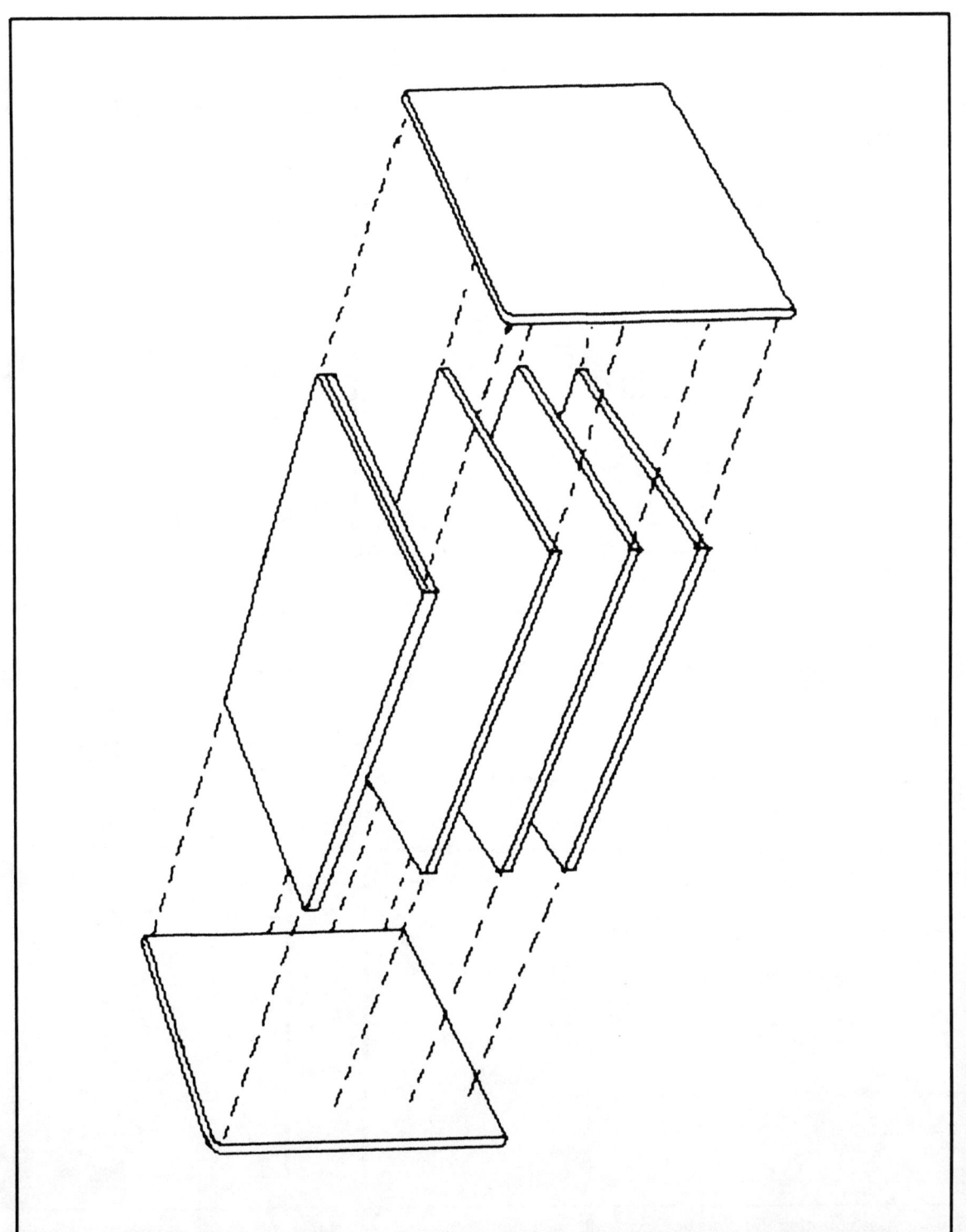

Fig. 4-39. Assembly of shelves and top to end pieces.

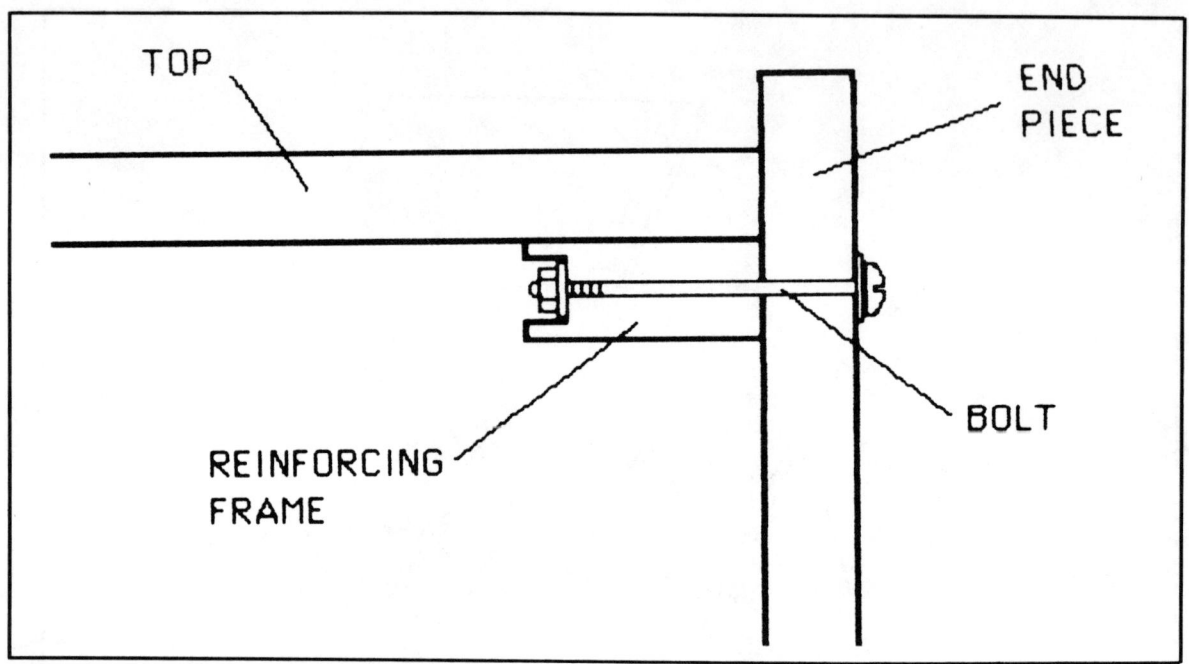

Fig. 4-40. Assembly of top to side pieces with bolts.

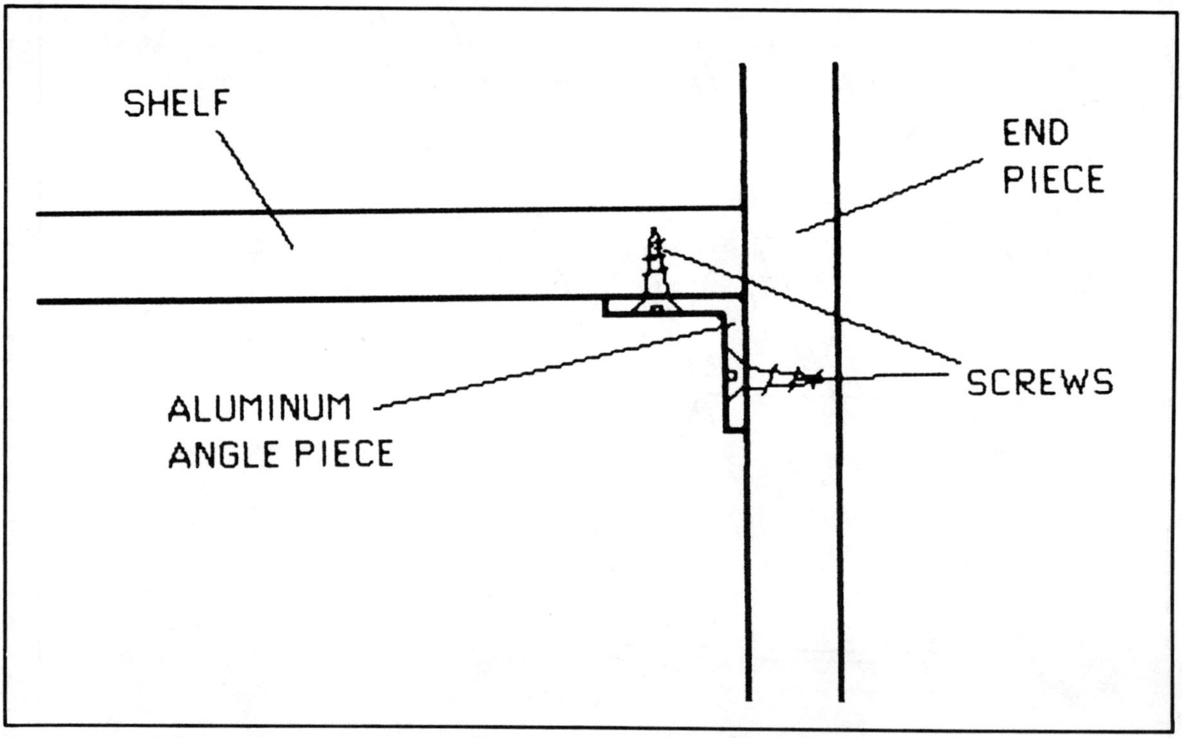

Fig. 4-41. Assembly of shelves to side pieces with aluminum angle strips and screws.

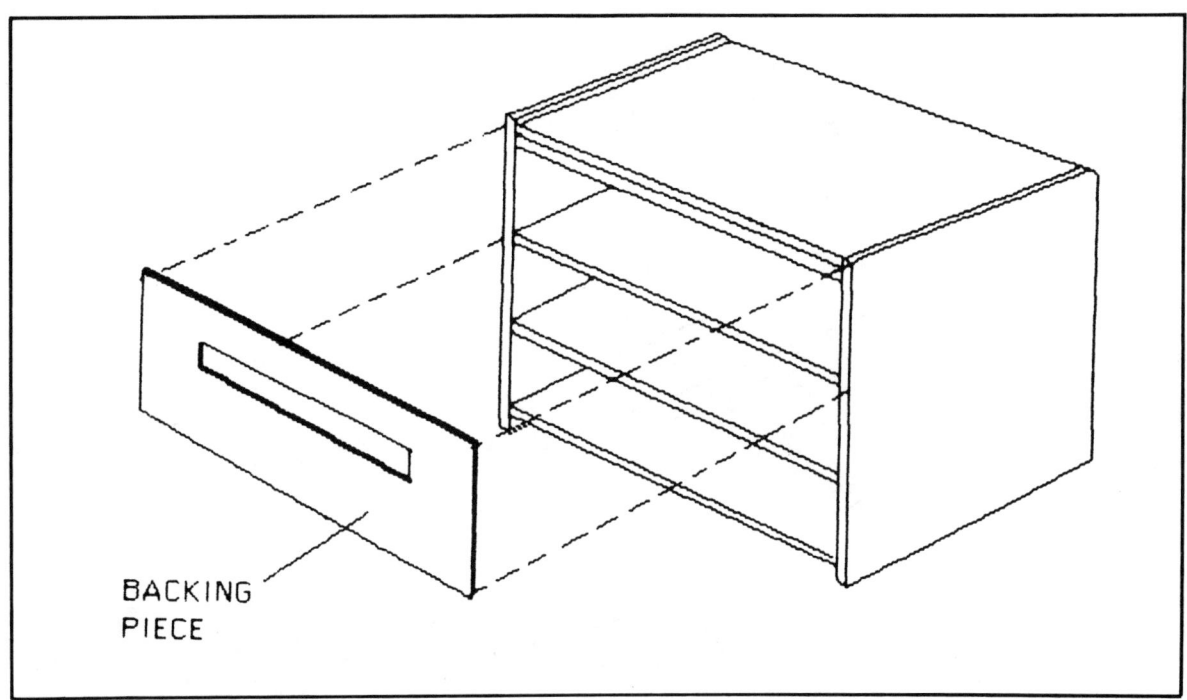

Fig. 4-42. Installing backing piece to printer stand.

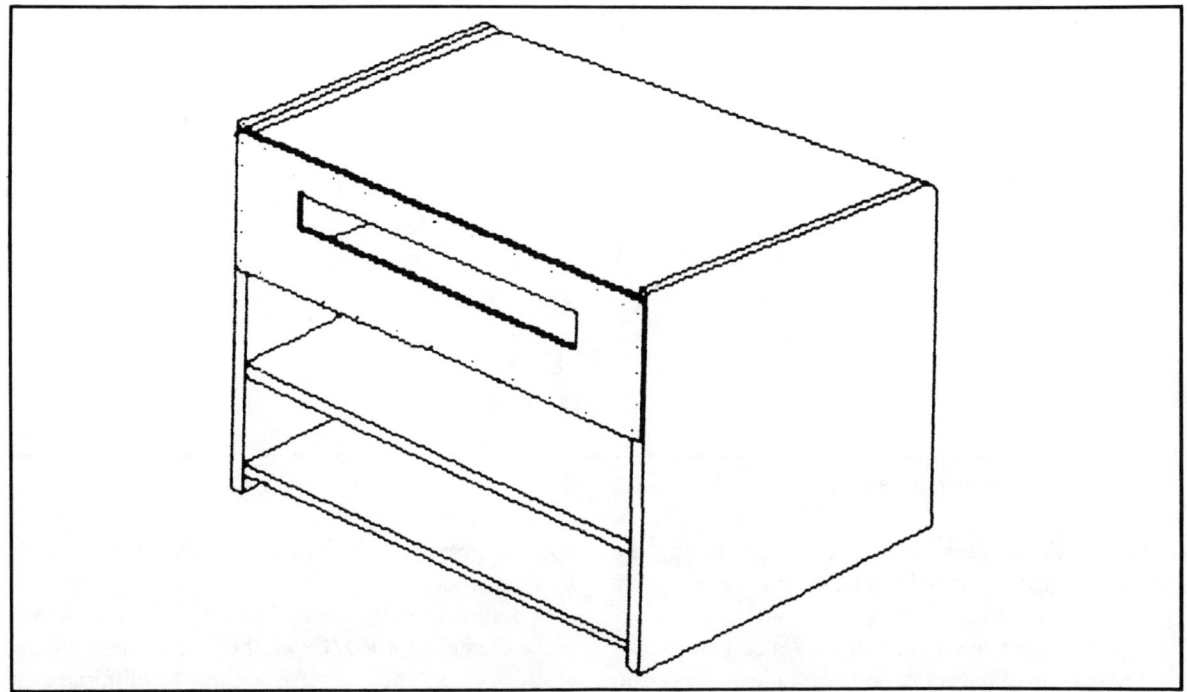

Fig. 4-43. Backing piece installed to basic printer stand.

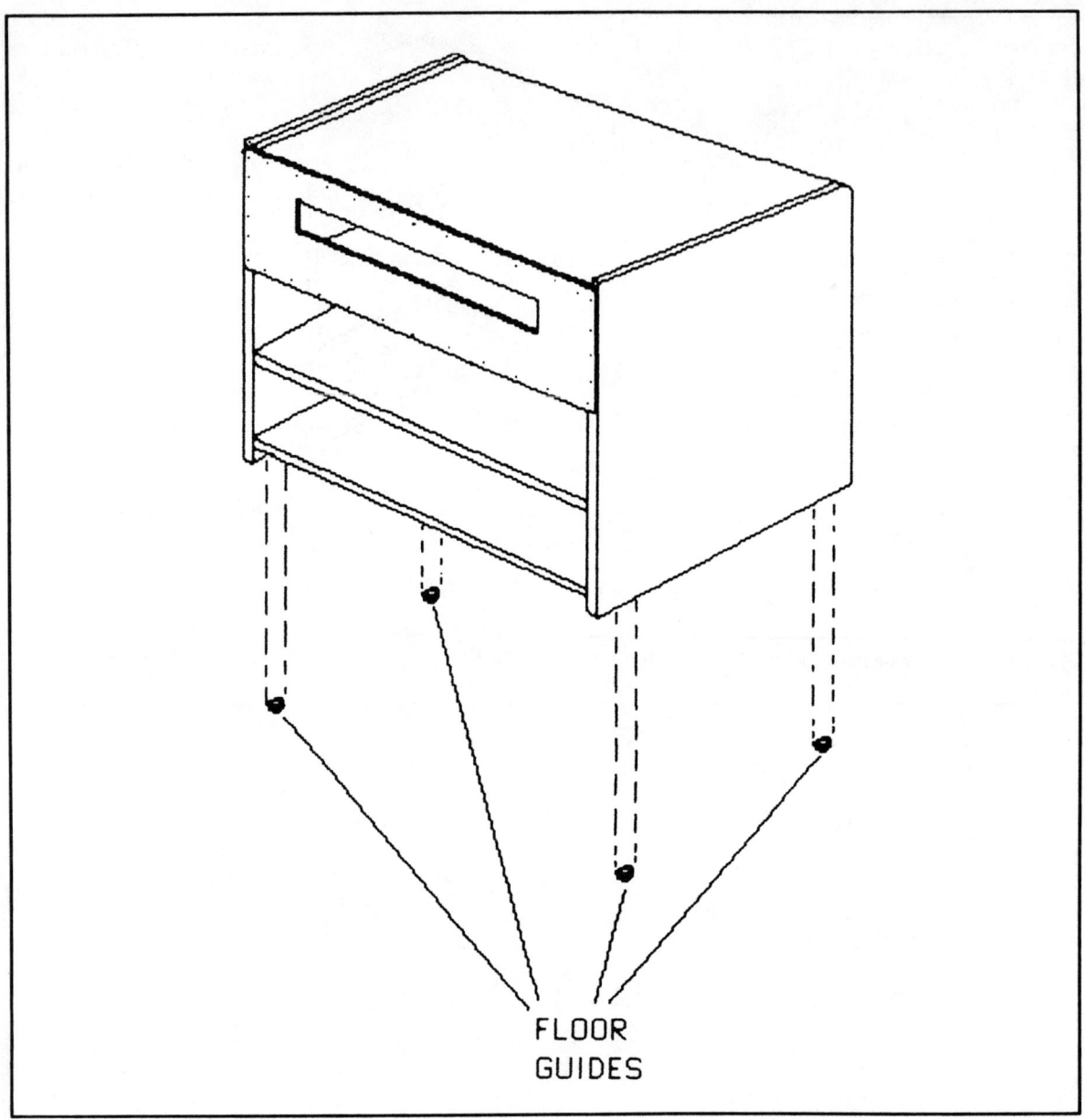

Fig. 4-44. Installing floor guides.

sander is the easiest to use without damaging the wood surface. Belt sanders can be used by experienced operators.

A clear polyurethane plastic finish can be applied directly to natural wood, or you can first stain the wood to another color. Staining can enhance the natural grains of the wood and enrich relatively lifeless woods.

Before applying stain, first test color on a scrap piece of similar wood. Clean the surface area where stain is to be applied. Use a cloth to eliminate as much dust as possible. The stain can then be applied with a brush, foam brush applicator, or cloth. Apply a smooth, even coat of stain. Allow the stain to penetrate the wood. Depending on the humidity, temperature, and particular stain used, this usually takes from 5 to 15 minutes. While the stain is still wet, wipe off the excess stain with a clean cloth. Be careful not to remove too much from corners and edges. Wipe across the grain first so that you work the stain into the wood pores. Then give a final wipe with the grain. Allow the stain to dry. This usually takes at least 8 hours. The finish can then be applied.

It is usually best to apply a series of light of light, even coats of clear finish rather than one thick coat. This will minimize possible drips and wrinkles as the finish dries.

Apply finish in brush-width strokes in direction of wood grain. Turn table so that finish is applied to wood surface in a horizontal position whenever possible.

A minimum of two coats is recommended. Allow 6 to 8 hours for the first coat to dry before applying second coat. Sand lightly and use a tack cloth to remove sanded finish dust before applying

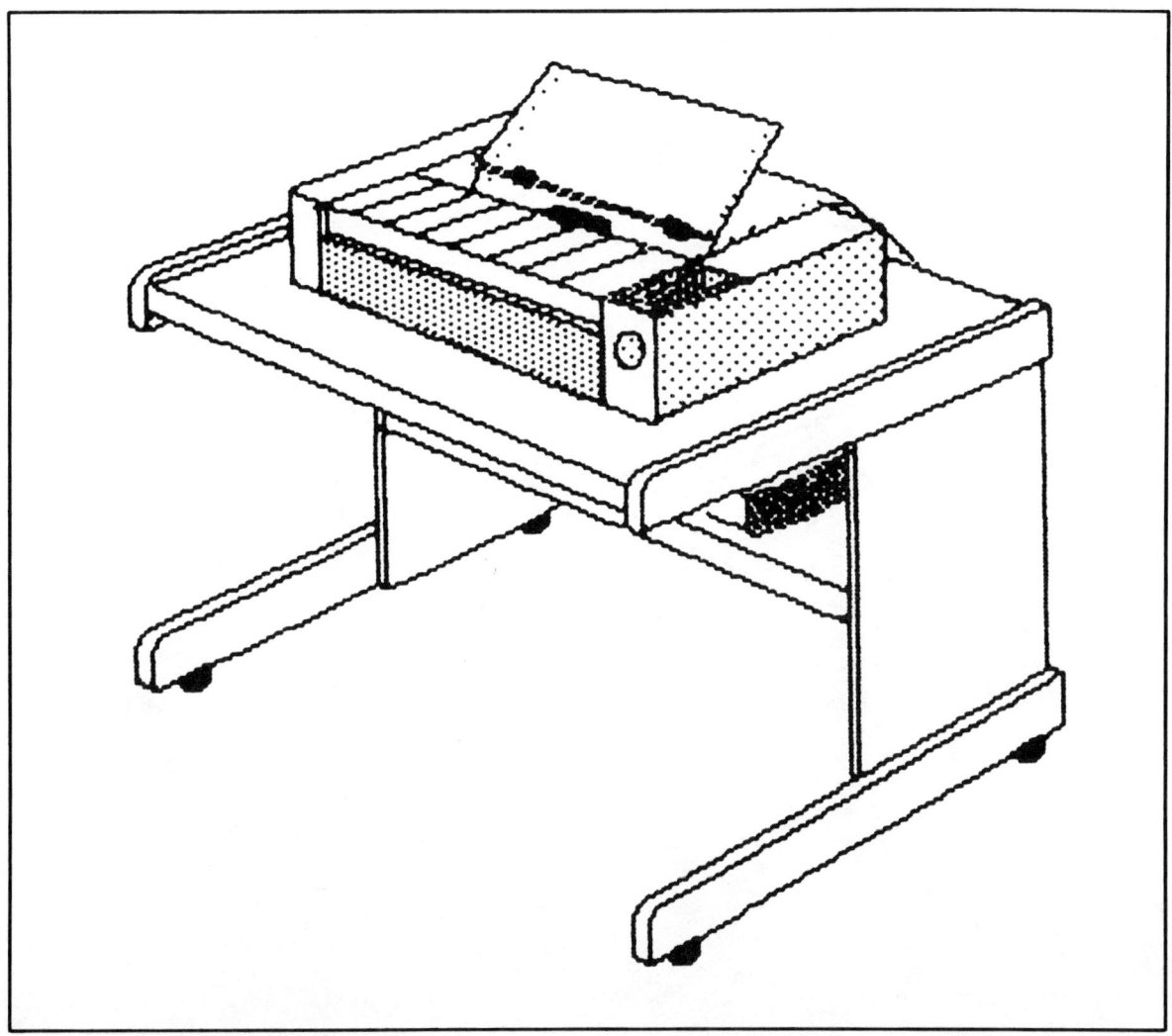

Fig. 4-45. Basic printer stand with half sides.

next coat of finish.

Clear or stained finishes are usually applied to natural wood furniture, but if desired color paint finishes can also be applied.

Variations

Many variations are possible for the basic printer stand with full sides. One possibility is to substitute particle board instead of plywood for the top and/or other components or make the printer stand with a different size of top. You can also modify the shelf arrangements, and there are many possibilities here.

The basic printer stand with full sides is functional and attractive even when built from inexpensive woods—ideal for anyone who wants to build computer furniture to sell. It can be sold either unfinished or with finish applied. More expensive woods, such as oak, can give the table a custom appearance. The plans given here show simple butt joints, but more difficult cabinetry joints can be used.

BASIC PRINTER STAND WITH HALF SIDES

This printer stand is slightly more difficult to construct than the basic budget printer stand and of about equal difficulty to the basic printer stand with full sides described above. Constructed mainly

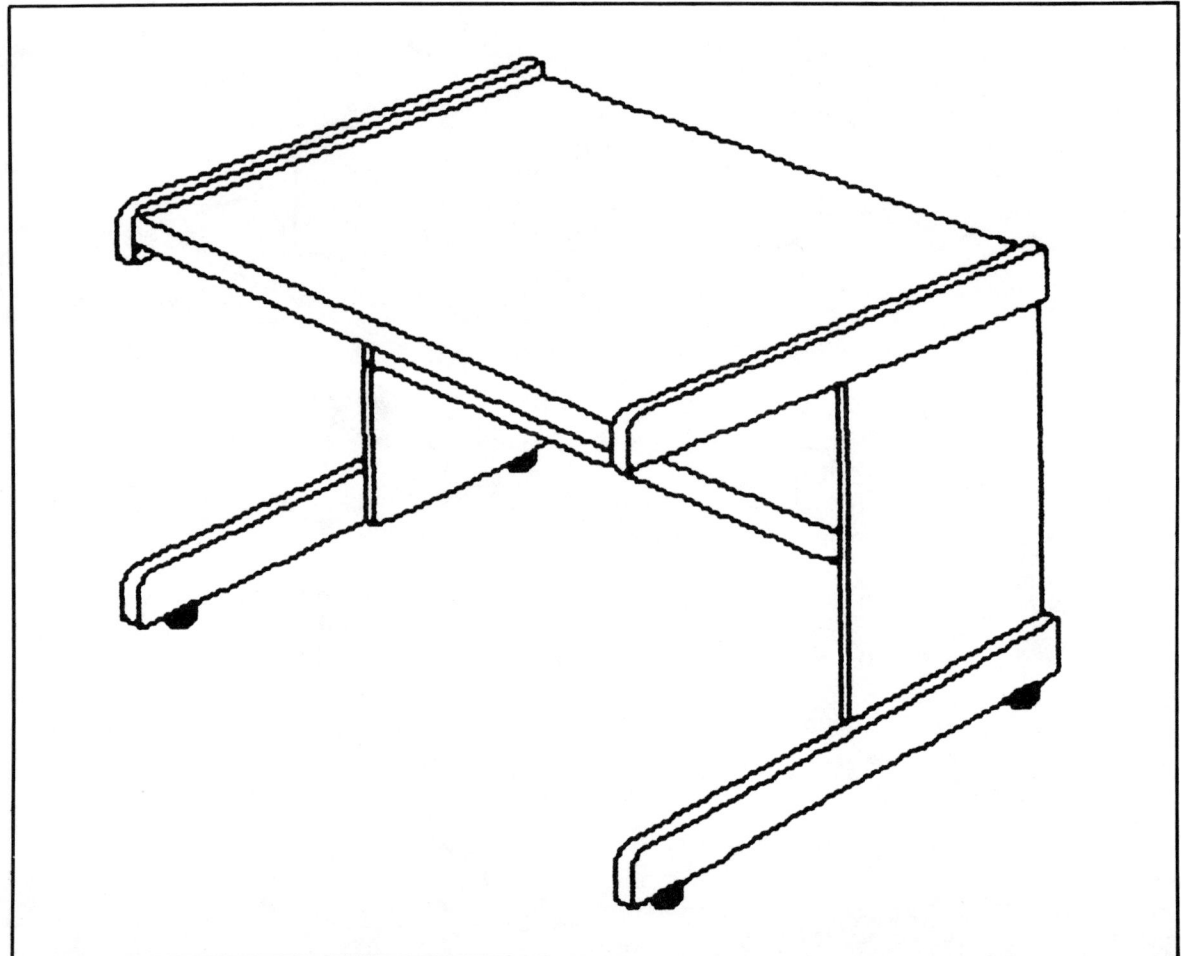

Fig. 4-46. Basic printer stand with half sides.

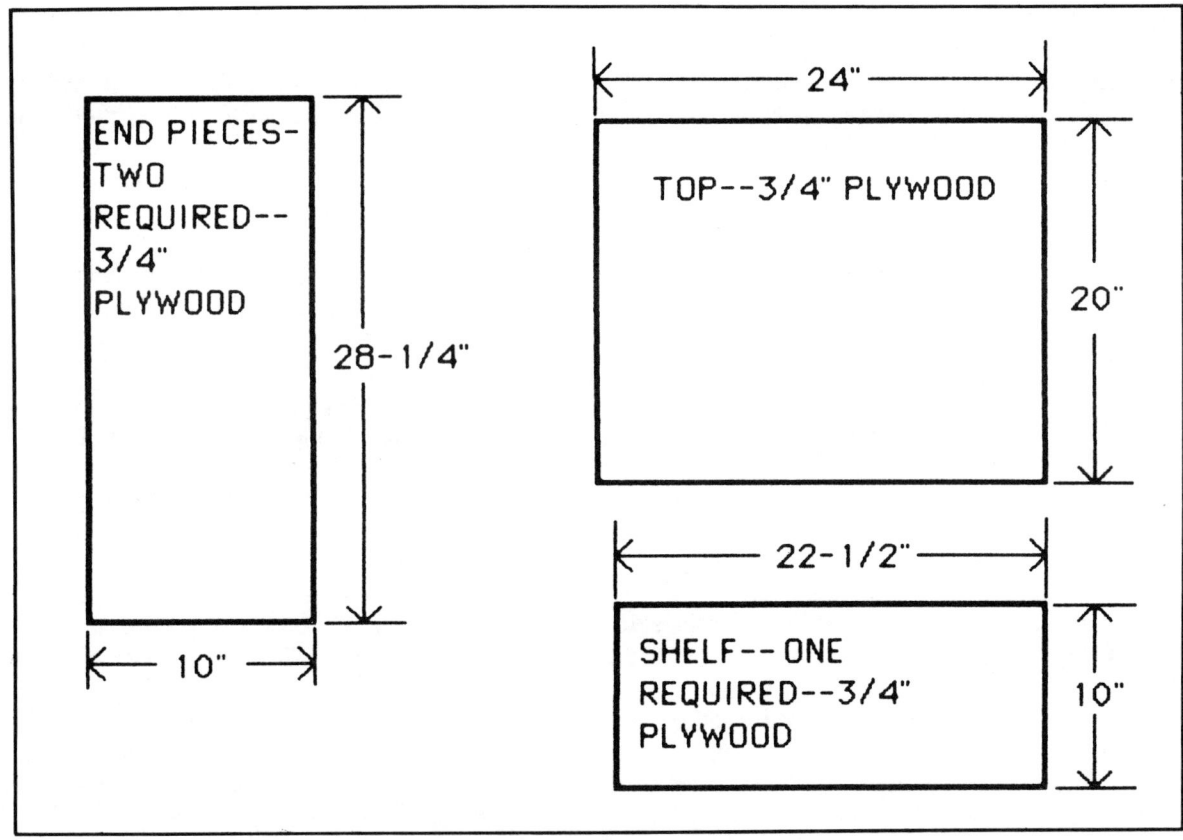

Fig. 4-47. Patterns for plywood parts for basic printer stand with half sides.

from plywood, it is of attractive and modern design and gives a good appearance even when built from standard plywood. You can give a custom appearance by making the same design from more expensive plywoods, such as those faced with oak or other hardwoods.

The basic printer stand with half sides is shown in Figs. 4-45 and 4-46. The top has ample space for most computer printers. The printer stand can have a natural wood top or plastic laminates can be applied. The printer stand features a shelf underneath that provides storage space and gives the table added strength.

Materials

The wooden parts' patterns are shown in Fig. 4-47. The top of the printer stand is a 20-inch-by-2-foot piece of 3/4-inch thick plywood. If you intend to use the wood surface as the finished table top, without adding a plastic laminate, plywood with the upper layer of a hardwood, is recommended. If a laminate is added, even an exterior grade of shop plywood will suffice.

The shelf is 3/4-inch thick plywood; it measures 10 inches by 22 1/2 inches.

The two end pieces are 3/4-inch thick plywood and measure 10 inches by 28 1/4 inches, for a printer stand that is 29 inches high, not counting the height added by floor guides. You may want to change the 29-inch dimension if you want your printer stand a different height.

Plywood is usually sold in standard 4-foot-by-8-foot sheets. Lay out the patterns to take advantage of this standard size, arranging them to keep waste to a minimum. Some lumberyards and plywood stores will cut the sheets for you to desired size, usually at additional cost. The minimal extra cost is worth it if you don't need full sheets, don't have room to carry full sheets in your car, or don't have a saw to accurately cut plywood.

Half-inch thick plywood can be used, but I don't recommend it. The savings are negligible, and you end up with a less sturdy table. Particle board can be substituted for the plywood if you are on an absolute minimum budget. A lot of low-grade manufactured computer furniture, but often high priced, is made from particle board covered by plastic laminates. Particle board can be difficult to work with, however, and it is very difficult to get plastic laminates to bond properly to this material without special equipment. (Even with special machinery, there are difficulties, because manufactured furniture often come loose at the edges.)

Four end pieces, 20 inches long, of 2-inch-by-4-inch hardwood stock are required for the side pieces (Fig. 4-48).

The backing piece (Fig. 4-49) can be either plywood or fiberboard. It is used to strengthen the table base and hold the frame in rectangular form. The length of the backing piece is 24 inches. A 13-inch height is shown for the backing piece, which is about the minimum required to give this table adequate strength. The shelf can, if desired, be installed a greater distance below the top. This will require you to change the height of the backing piece. Notice that the top, shelf, backing piece, and side pieces form a box with the forward side open. You will also need 1-inch-by-2-inch or larger framing stock to use under the plywood top and the shelf.

Different wood and plastic trim strips can be used to cover the exposed edges of the plywood, as detailed later in this section. A wood or plastic trim strip is used to cover the forward edge of the table top and shelf. These pieces are 24 inches and 22 1/2 inches long respectively, and about 1 3/4 inches wide. The minimum width should completely cover the widths of the plywood (3/4 inch) and the framing (approximately 7/8 inch). The trim strips can be slightly wider than this, however.

Four floor pods or guides are used on the floor beams. A variety of suitable types are available from hardware stores. These can be of a fixed or adjustable type, as desired.

Nails, screws, or bolts can be used for assembly, as detailed below in this section. You will also need a suitable wood glue. The finish can be clear urethane or other type, as desired.

The top can be left natural or a plastic lami-

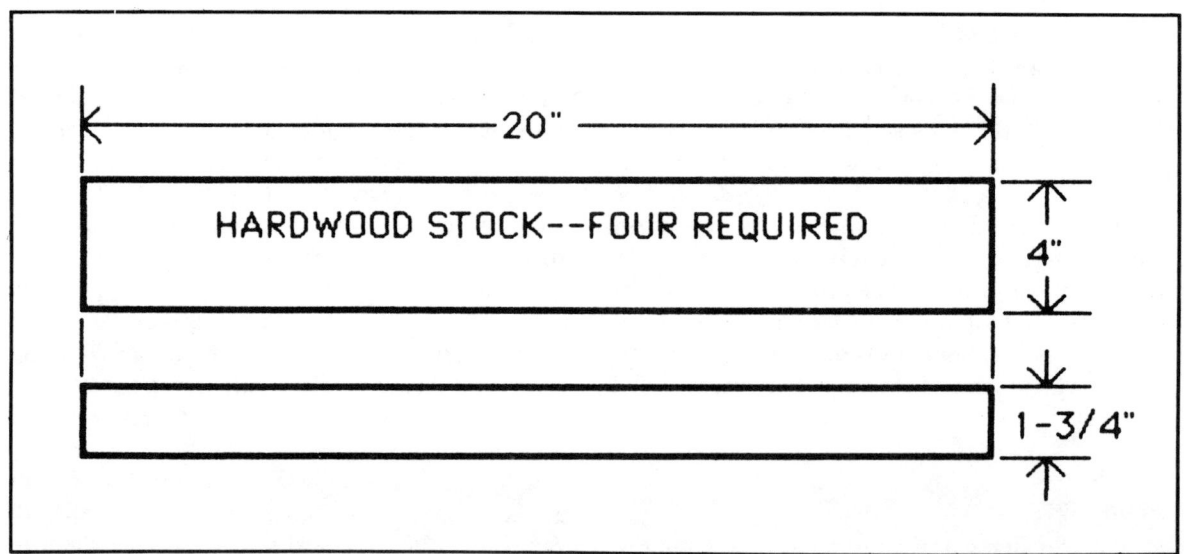

Fig. 4-48. Pattern for side pieces.

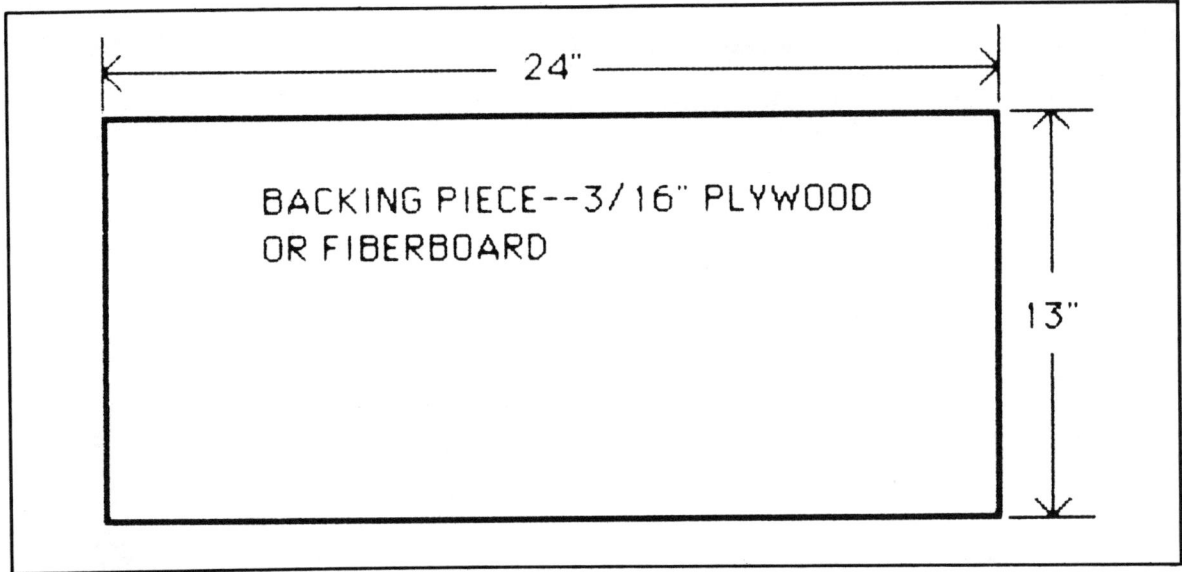

Fig. 4-49. Pattern for backing piece.

nate can be added. If a plastic laminate is to be added, you will need a 20-inch-by-2-foot piece of suitable laminate and contact cement for attaching it to the plywood.

Construction

Overviews of the complete assembly are shown in Figs. 4-50 and 4-51. Begin by constructing the printer stand top, as detailed in Fig. 4-52. If you purchased a piece of plywood that was already cut to the 20-inch-by-2-foot size, no additional cutting is necessary if it was cut accurately and is a true rectangle. You might want to check this with a square.

If you purchased a standard 4-foot-by-8-foot sheet, you will need to cut out a section for the printer stand top. In most cases, you will want to have the grain of the top layer running lengthwise, although this is not essential if you are going to add a plastic laminate. Use two factory cut edges for your table top and cut the other two. Use a ruler and square to draw the pattern, marking the lines with a sharp pencil or scribing tool.

Sawing plywood requires special care to avoid chipping and splintering along the cut edge. Handsaws or power saws with special fine-toothed or carbide-tipped blades designed especially for plywood should be used. Applying a strip of masking tape over the area to be cut on both sides of the plywood, but especially on the side opposite the one you are cutting, is also helpful. Or, clamp a solid piece of wood to the underside and make the cut through both the plywood and the piece of wood.

Be extremely careful when sanding edges, also because of possible splintering. Use a sanding block and avoid sanding the surfaces of plywood until a wood sealer has been applied.

The next step is to add the reinforcing frame to the top plywood, as shown in Fig. 4-52. Use a ruler and a square to make the patterns on the framing wood, marking the lines with a sharp marking device. Then make the necessary saw cuts, as detailed in Chapter 2. The frame pieces should be glued and nailed or screwed in position (see Figs. 4-53 and 4-54). If the plywood top is to be left without a plastic laminate covering, the fasteners should go through the framing and into the plywood, but care should be taken so that they do not pass all the way through the plywood or leave a bulge in the upper surface. If a good glue is used, such as acrylic or epoxy, the glue alone should give ade-

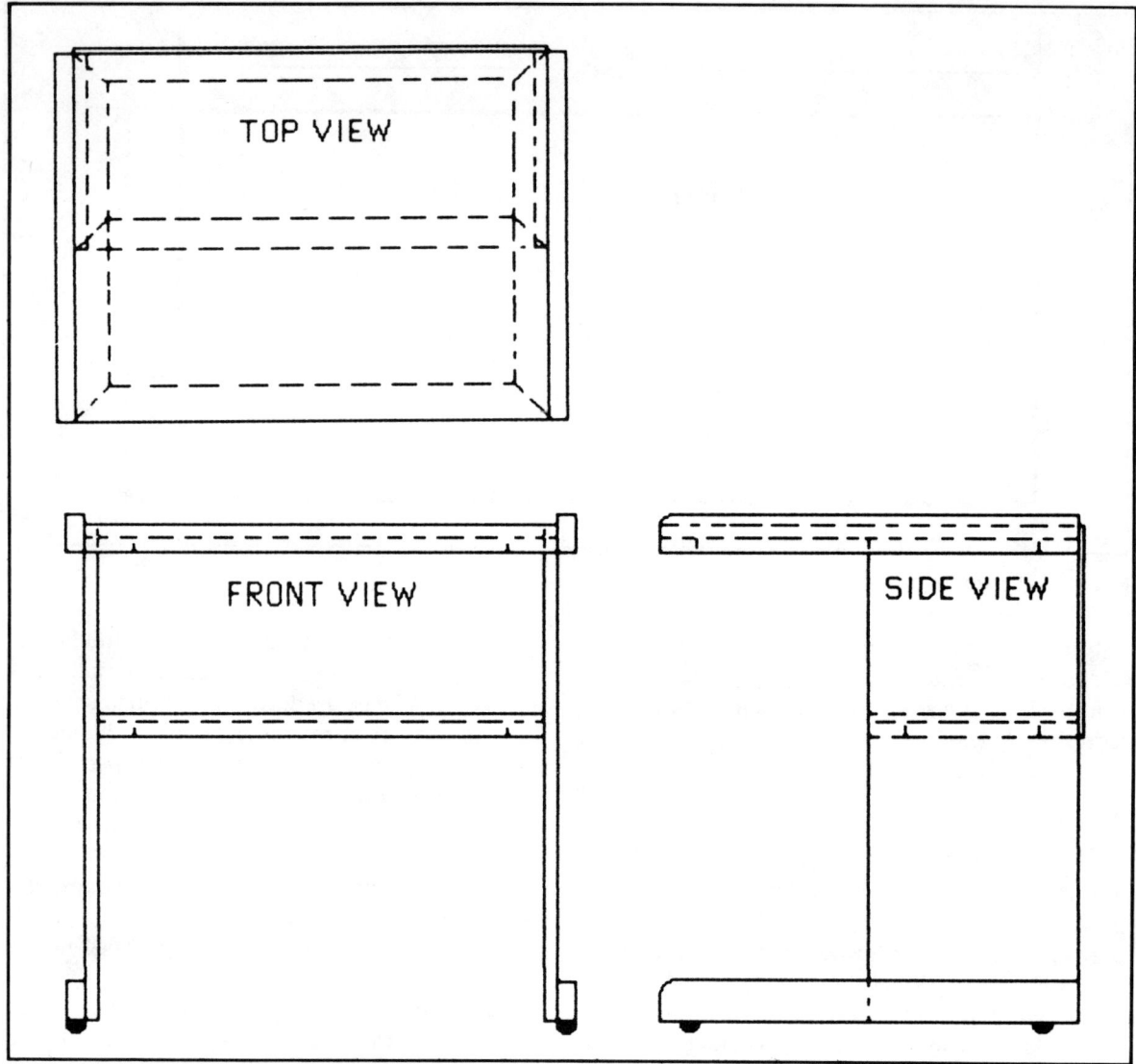

Fig. 4-50. Basic printer stand with half sides.

quate strength. The fasteners are mainly used as a clamping device for the gluing; they will not have much holding power into the plywood. For greater holding power, the fasteners can be passed through the plywood and into the framing, if a plastic laminate is to be added.

A variety of options are available for finishing off the printer stand top. One possibility is to use the plywood surface as the top and add a wood trim strip to the forward edge, as shown in Fig. 4-55. Glue fasten the trim strip in place with finishing nails. Set the heads below the wood surface and fill holes with wood filler to flush with the wood surface.

You may also choose to add a plastic laminate to the forward edge and leave the top natural wood, as detailed in Fig. 4-56.

Another method is to add a plastic laminate to

the top and a wood trim strip to the forward edge, as shown in Fig. 4-57. Yet another possibility is to add plastic laminates to both the top and forward edge, as shown in Figs. 4-58 and 4-59.

If a plastic laminate is to be added to the plywood top and/or the forward edge, install these new. Plastic laminates are often applied to plywood for computer furniture tops, but I suggest using a high quality laminate for computer furniture.

If a plastic laminate is to also be applied to the forward edge of the printer stand top, it should be applied first. This is then finished flush with the table top. The top laminate is then applied so that the edge overlaps the top edge of the laminate on

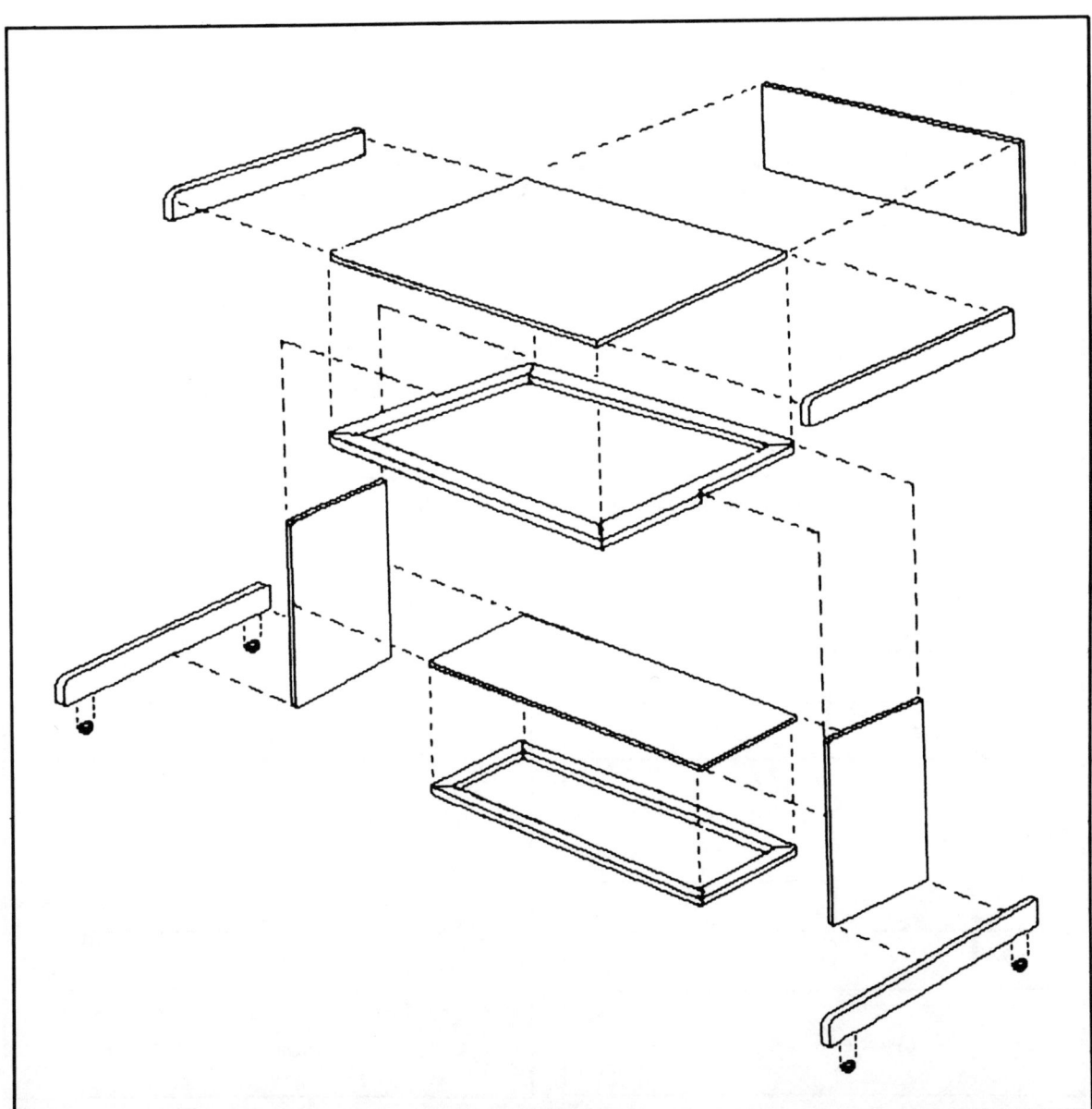

Fig. 4-51. Assembly of basic printer stand with half sides.

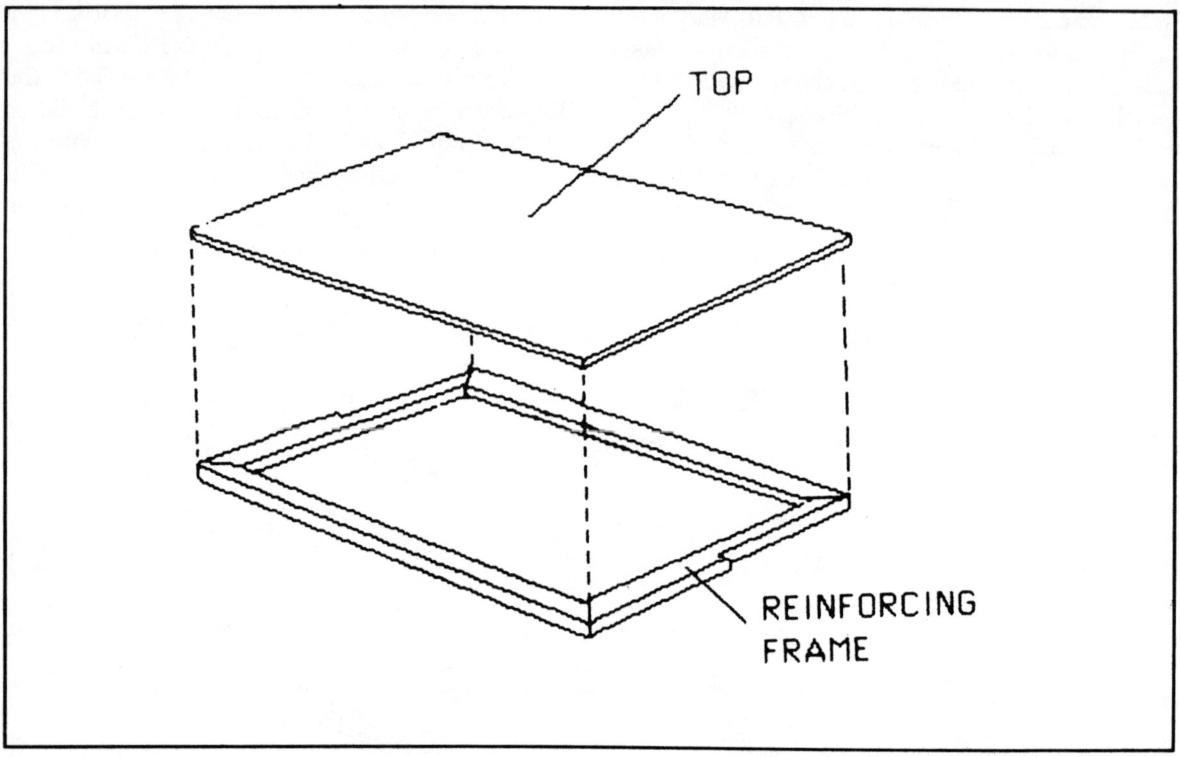

Fig. 4-52. Assembly of printer stand top to reinforcing frame.

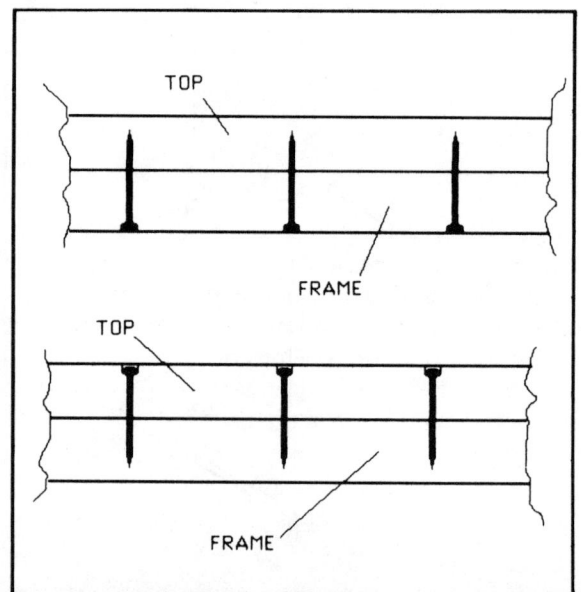

Fig. 4-53. Assembly of top to frame pieces with nails and glue.

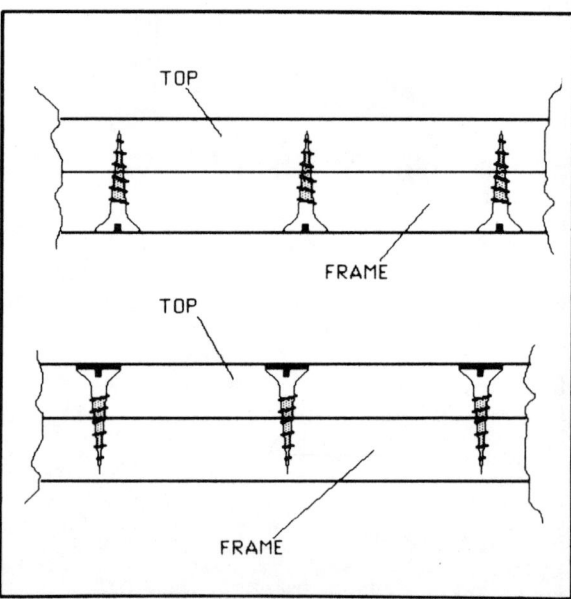

Fig. 4-54. Assembly of top to frame pieces with screws and glue.

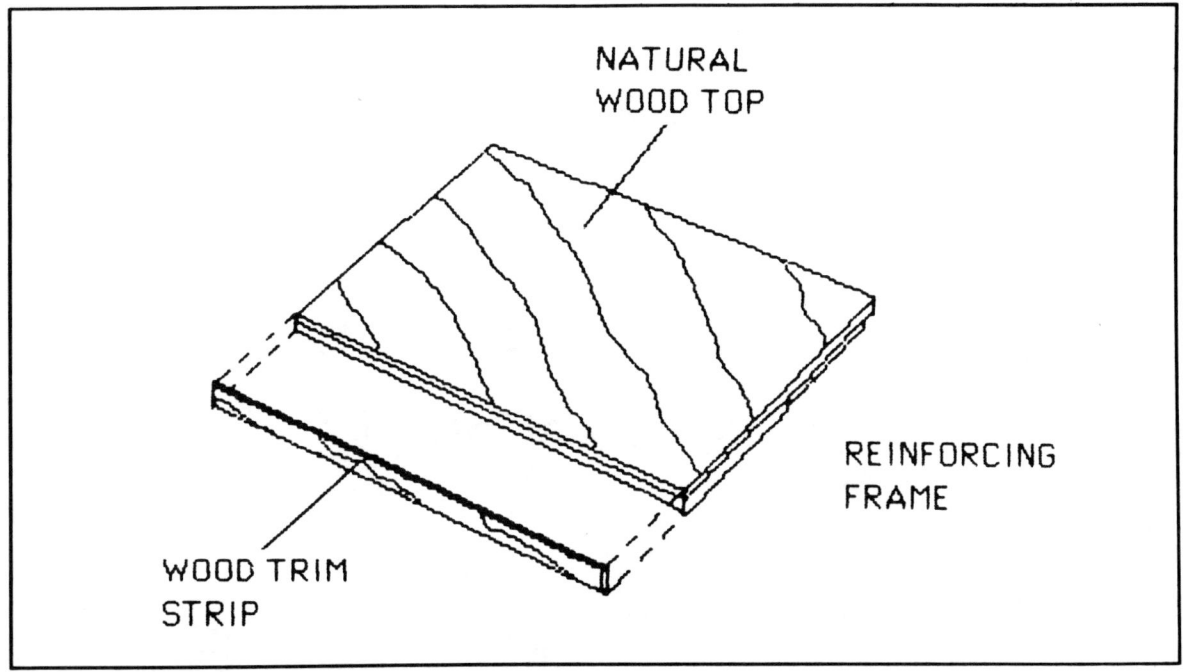

Fig. 4-55. Adding wood trim strip to forward edge of top.

the forward edge of the table, as shown in Fig. 4-59. The plastic laminate is installed as follows:

- All holes and defects in the surface of the plywood should be filled with putty or wood filler.
- Sand the surface to be covered. This will help ensure good adhesion.
- Mark the plastic laminate to a pattern slightly larger than the area to be covered. Use a straightedge and draw the pattern lines on the finished or pattern side of the laminate. Leave 1/4 inch to 1/2 inch on all sides. This will be trimmed off later.
- If a laminate is to be applied to the forward edge of the table, apply this first. After installation, as detailed below, trim and file the upper edge of the plastic laminate flush with the upper edge of the plywood table top before installing.
- Cut the plastic laminate to the pattern marked. Even though the plastic laminate is extremely durable once applied, it is vulnerable to cracking and splitting before it is cemented in place. Fine-tooth handsaws or power saws with fine-tooth blades can be used. A rotary power saw with a 14 to 16 teeth per inch blade is ideal. Place the plastic laminate face up when cutting. Care should be taken so that the plastic laminate is not chipped or

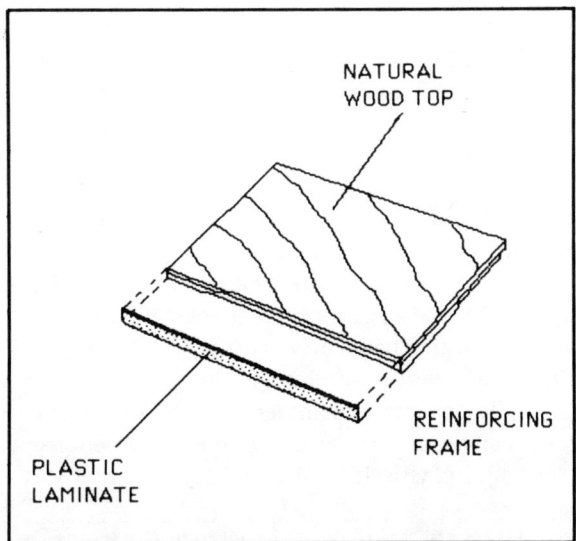

Fig. 4-56. Adding plastic laminate to forward edge of top.

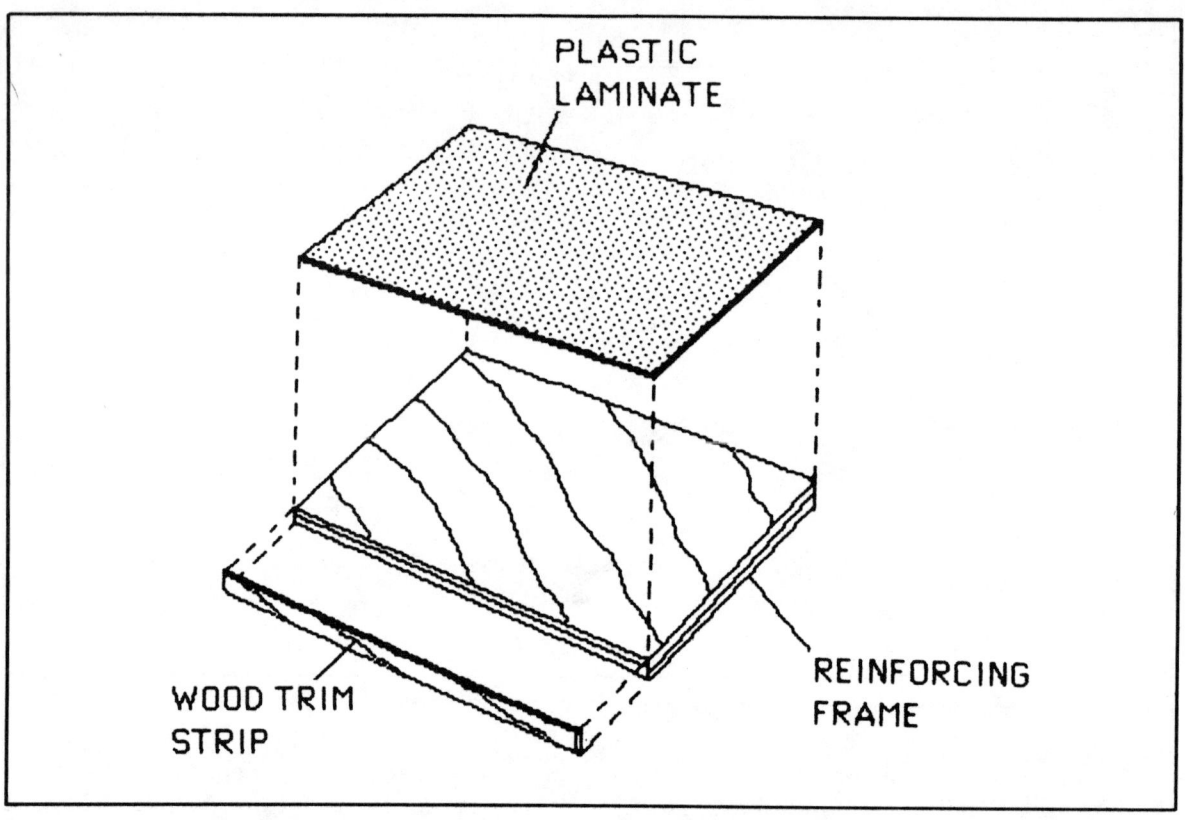

Fig. 4-57. Adding plastic laminate to top and wood trim strip to forward edge.

broken. An alternate method is to use a carbide tip knife for scoring the plastic by drawing the knife point along a metal straight edge. Cut through the decorative surface. The laminate can then be broken by bending it toward the decorative surface side over the edge of a table or workbench.

• Apply contact cement to the surface of the plywood to be covered and the back side of the plastic laminate with a brush, roller, or metal spreader with a serrated edge. A thin, even application is important.

• Follow the manufacturer's instructions regarding drying time. Usually, this takes about 20 to 30 minutes.

• Place a sheet of heavy wrapping paper over the plywood surface to be covered. Then position the laminate on the plywood surface with the paper between. The contact cement will not stick to the paper if it has been allowed to dry properly.

Make certain that the laminate is positioned correctly. Once the two surfaces of contact cement touch, the laminate sheet cannot be moved again. When everything is lined up properly, pull the paper out from between the plywood and the plastic laminate.

• Using a small block of wood and a hammer, lightly tap the laminate in place. An alternate method is to use a rolling pin.

• Use a file to remove the surplus plastic laminate from the edges, or use a special cutter with a router, which trims off excess plastic laminate to flush with the plywood edges.

• The thinner recommended for the contact cement can be used for cleaning contact cement from wood and plastic laminate and tools.

The next step is to construct the shelf, as detailed in Fig. 4-60. If you purchased a piece of

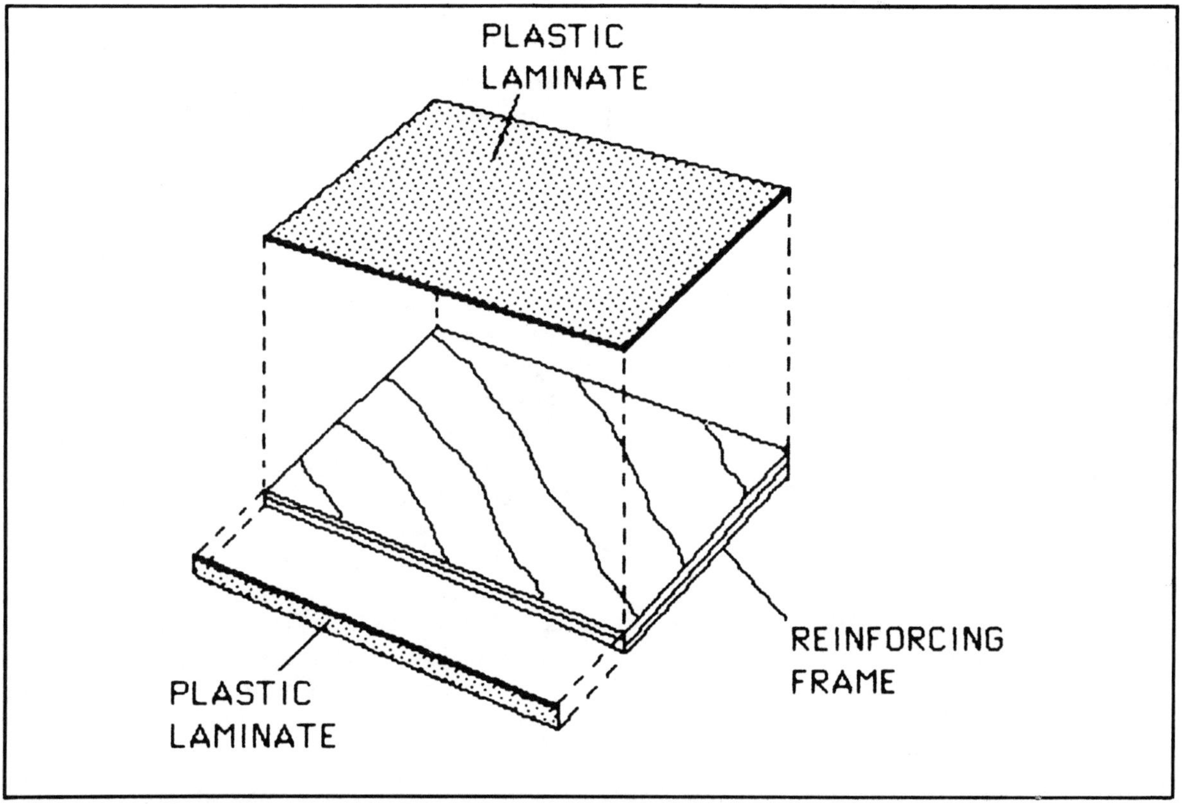

Fig. 4-58. Adding plastic laminate to top and forward edge of top.

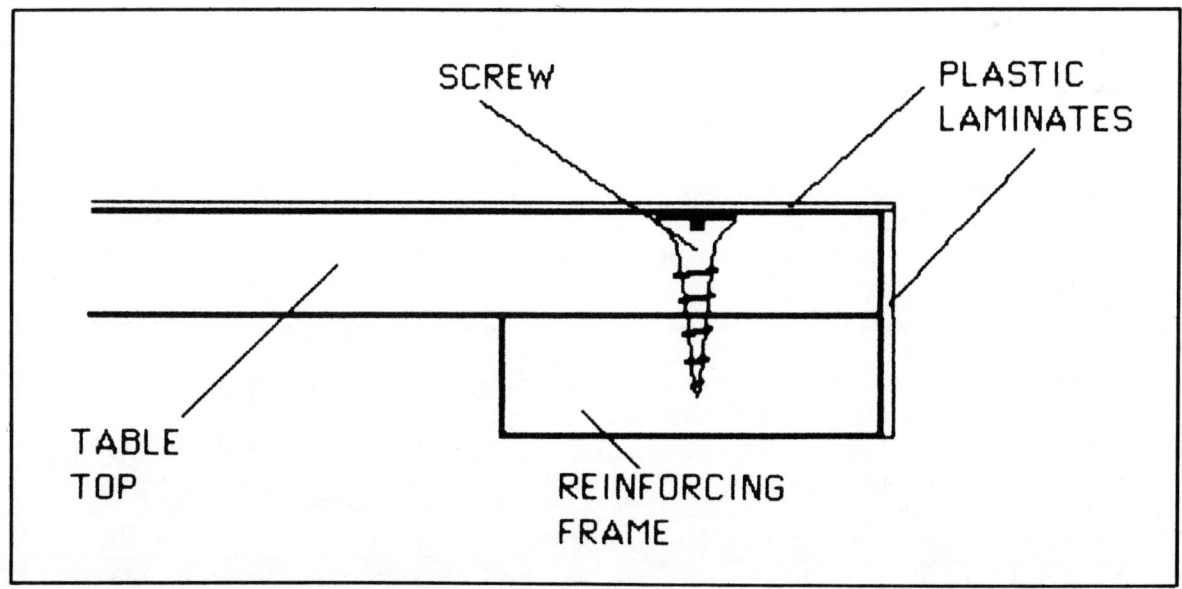

Fig. 4-59. Adding plastic laminate to top.

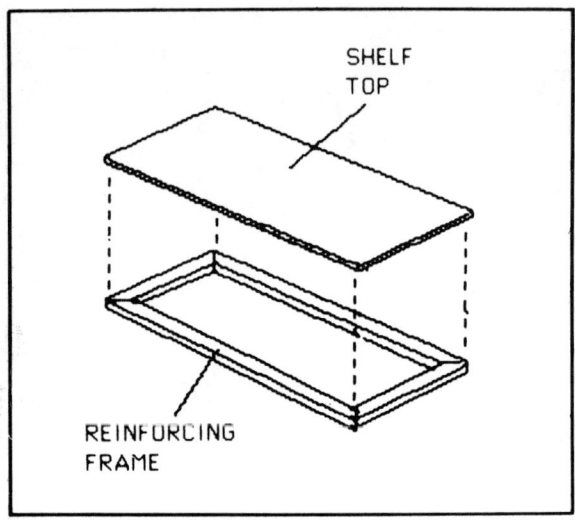

Fig. 4-60. Assembly of shelf top to reinforcing frame.

the top layer running lengthwise. This is not essential if you are going to add a plastic laminate. In most cases, you will use two factory cut edges for your shelf top and cut the other two. Use a ruler and square to draw the pattern lines with a sharp pencil or scribing tool. Saw and sand carefully.

Next, add the reinforcing frame of the shelf, as shown in Fig. 4-60. Using a ruler and a square, mark the lines with a sharp pencil or other marking device. Then make the necessary saw cuts. The frame pieces should be glued and nailed or screwed in position (see Figs. 4-61 and 4-62). If the plywood shelf top will be left natural wood, the fasteners should go through the framing and into the plywood, but care should be taken so that the fasteners do not pass all the way through the plywood or leave a bulge in the upper surface. If a good acrylic or epoxy glue is used, it should give adequate strength. The fasteners are mainly used as a clamping device for the gluing and will not have much holding power. To give greater holding power, the fasteners can be passed through the plywood and into the framing (if a plastic laminate is to be added).

plywood that was already cut to the 10-inch-by-22 1/2-inch size, no additional cutting is needed. Use a square to double-check for trueness and accuracy.

If you purchased a larger piece of plywood, cut out a section for the shelf top. Have the grain of

Fig. 4-61. Assembly of shelf top to frame pieces with nails and glue.

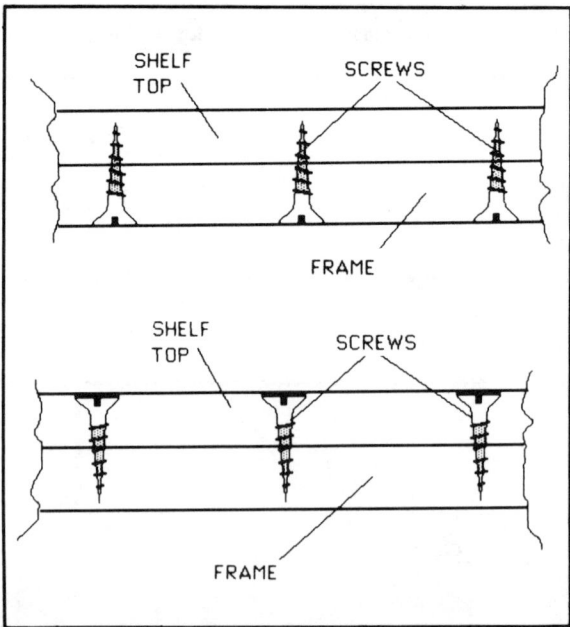

Fig. 4-62. Assembly of shelf to frame pieces with screws and glue.

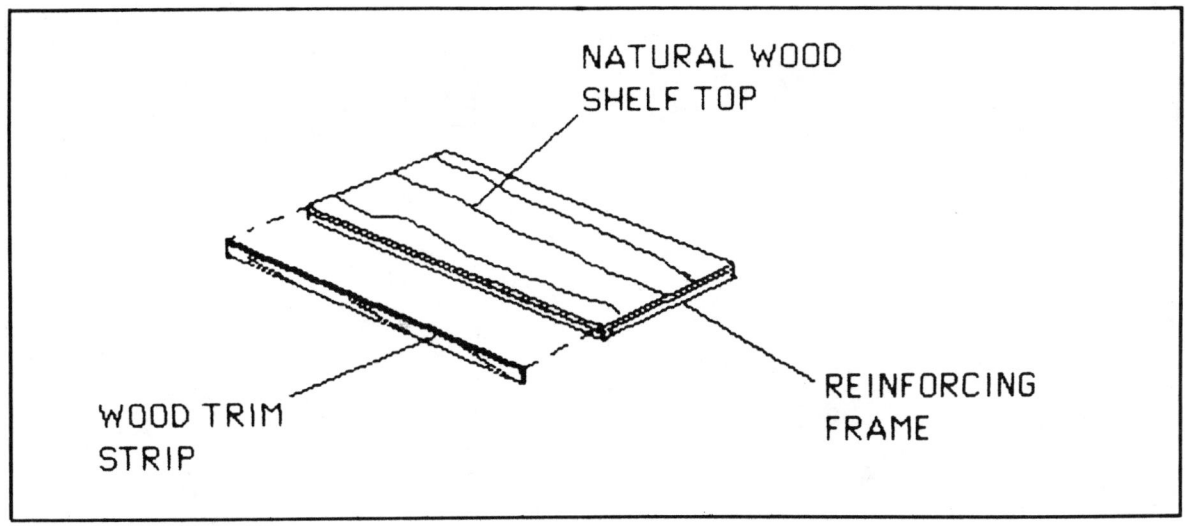

Fig. 4-63. Adding wood trim to forward edge of shelf.

The same variety of options is available for finishing off the shelf:

• Use the plywood surface as the shelf top and add a wood trim strip to the forward edge, as shown in Fig. 4-63. Glue and fasten the trim strip in place with finishing nails. Set the heads below the wood surface and fill holes with wood filler to flush with the wood surface.

• Add a plastic laminate to the forward edge and leave the shelf top natural wood, as detailed in Fig. 4-64.

• Add a plastic laminate to the shelf top and wood trim strip to the forward edge, as shown in Fig. 4-65.

• Add plastic laminates to both the top and forward edge, as shown in Figs. 4-66 and 4-67.

If a plastic laminate is installed on the plywood shelf top and/or the forward edge, do it now. If a

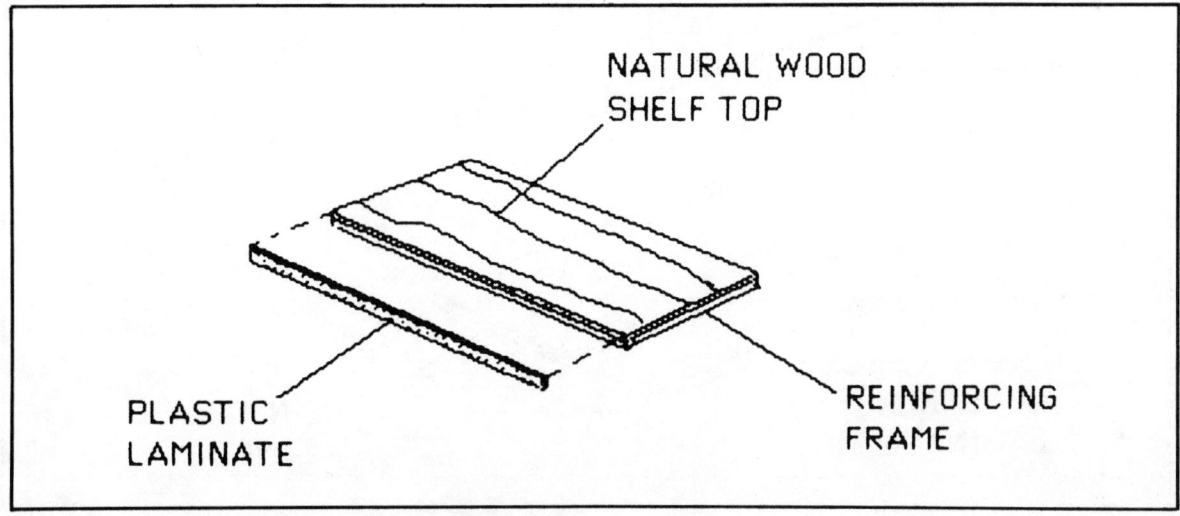

Fig. 4-64. Adding plastic laminate to forward edge of shelf.

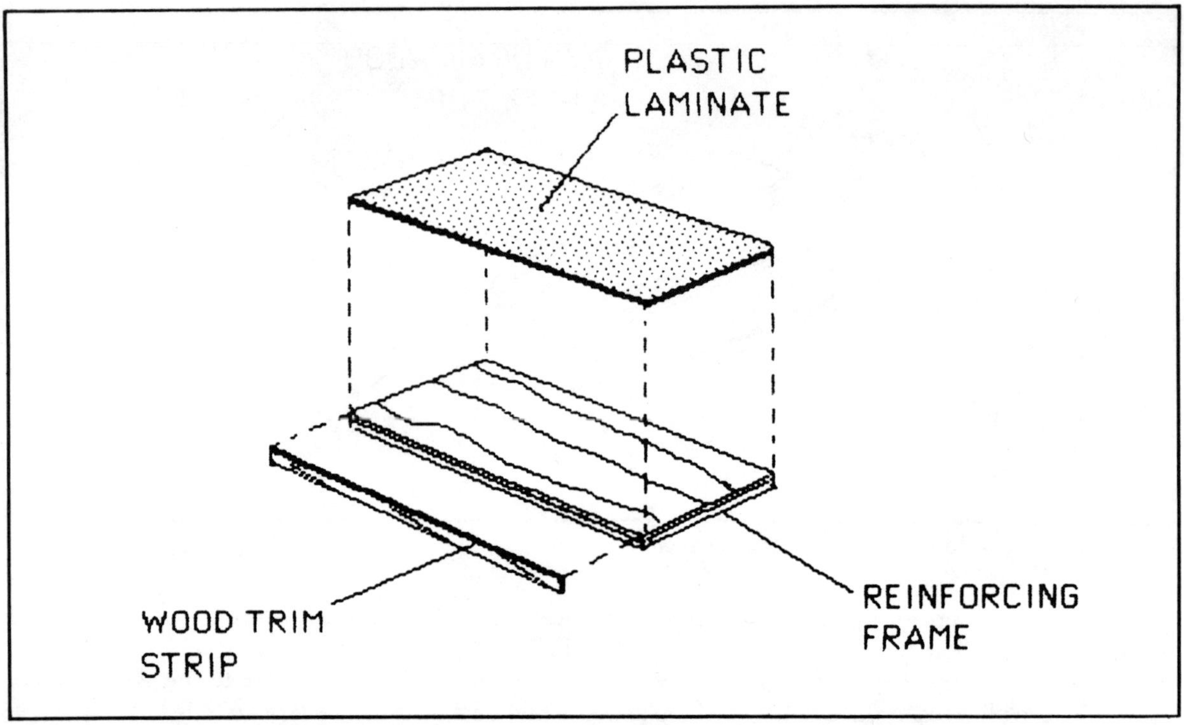

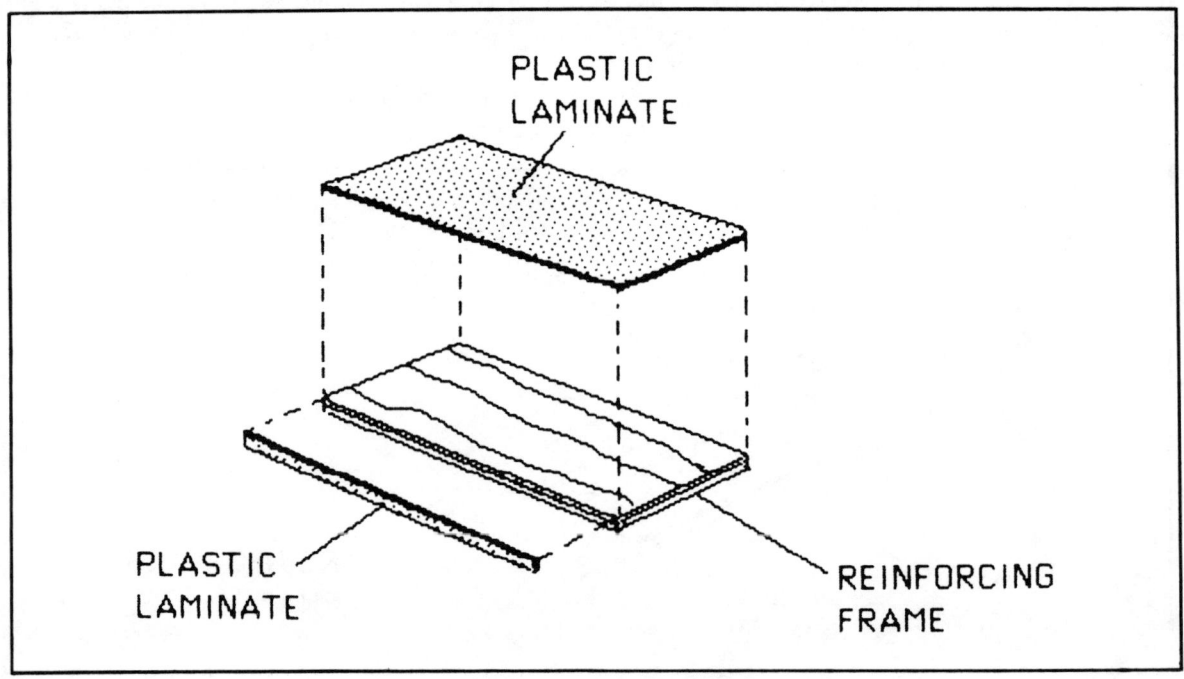

Fig. 4-65. Adding plastic laminate to top section and wood trim strip to forward edge of shelf.

Fig. 4-66. Adding plastic laminates to top section and forward edge of shelf.

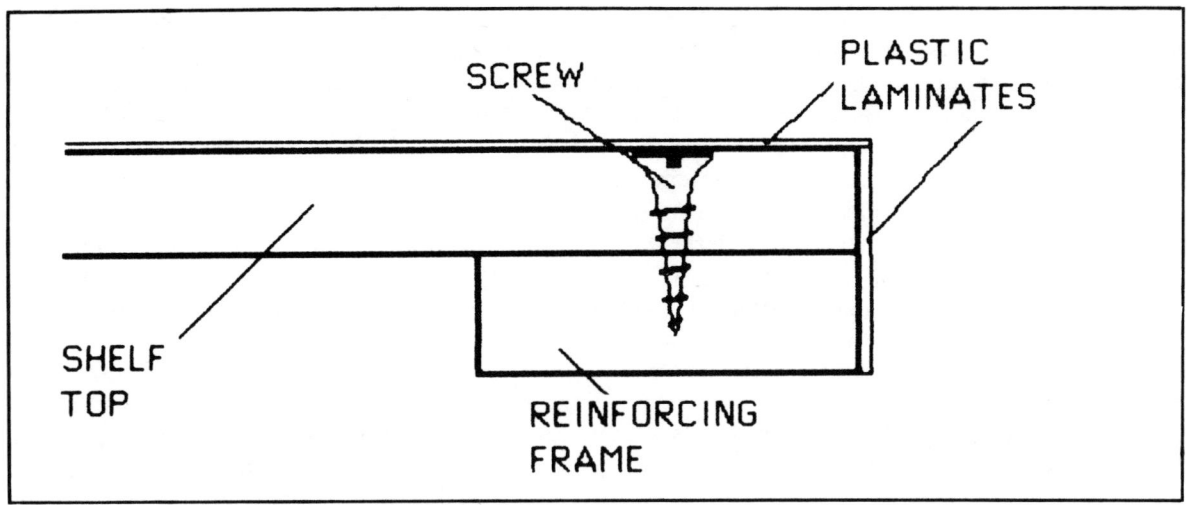

Fig. 4-67. Adding plastic laminates to shelf.

plastic laminate is to also be applied to the forward edge of the shelf top, it should be applied first. This is then finished flush with the shelf top. The top laminate is then applied so that the edge overlaps the top edge of the laminate on the forward edge of the shelf, as shown in Fig. 4-67.

Next, cut the end pieces to rectangular size. A power circular saw is ideal for making straight cuts.

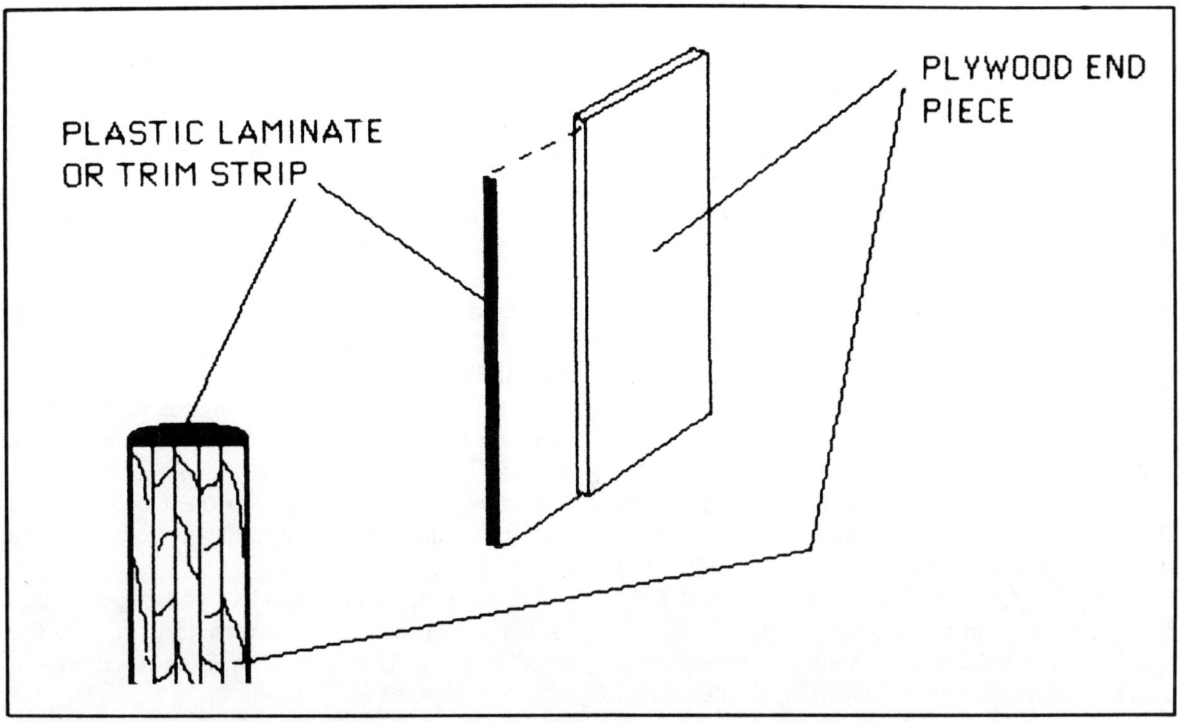

Fig. 4-68. Adding plastic laminate or trim strip to forward edge of plywood end piece.

The next step is to add plastic (Fig. 4-68) or wood trim to the forward edges of the end pieces. This will protect the laminated edges of the plywood and give a neat appearance.

An overview of the remainder of the assembly is shown in Fig. 4-69. The next step is to assemble the top and shelf to the side pieces, as shown in Fig. 4-70, by both glue and mechanical fasteners. One method is to use finishing nails, passing them through the end pieces and into the framing wood of the top and shelf. Set the heads below the wood surface and fill with wood filler to flush with the wood surface. Another method is to use through-bolts, as detailed in Fig. 4-71. The bolts for the top will also pass through the beam pieces, as detailed in this section.

Regardless of the method of fastening, it is extremely important to install the side pieces perpendicular to the printer stand top and shelf in a crosswise direction. Use a square to make pattern lines on the side pieces. It is also important to have exactly the same distance between the top and shelf on both sides. Figure 4-72 shows the top and shelf assembled to the end pieces.

After the shelf and top have been assembled to the side pieces, the next step is to add the backing piece, as shown in Fig. 4-73. The backing piece forms a box with the top, shelf, and side pieces. It is important that the backing piece be attached securely to the wood members all the way around the edges, being both glued and nailed into position. It is extremely important to make certain that the backing piece is a true rectangle to make certain that the backing piece is true rectangle and that the side pieces are perpendicular to the table top and shelf before the backing piece is attached and the glue allowed to set. Figure 4-74 shows the backing piece installed.

The side and floor beams are added next, as shown in Fig. 4-75. These should be glued and through-bolted, as shown in Figs. 4-76, 4-77, 4-78, and 4-79. Figure 4-80 shows the side and floor beams installed on the printer stand.

The floor guides are installed next (see Fig. 4-81). Attachment varies depending on the type of floor guides selected; either in a mounting drilled in the wood beam, driven or screwed into the wood, or with screw fasteners to hold them in place.

Sanding and Finishing

Many beginners do a good job constructing the printer up to this point, only to give the table a very amateur appearance by sloppy application of a finish. By taking care and a little time, however, even a beginner can give the table a professional finish.

Sanding is an important operation in preparing the wood for varnishing or painting. Small holes, checks, and other open defects in the wood should be filled in first. If a clear finish is to be applied, use a wood filler that matches the color of the wood. Apply a sanding sealer to the surfaces before sanding.

Work from coarse to progressively finer grits, but don't start with a grit that is coarser than necessary for the particular sanding. The condition of the surface might be such that you can start with a medium or even fine grit. Coarse grits leave scratches that must be sanded away with finer grits.

Wood sanding is done primarily parallel to the grain. Across the grain sanding leaves scratches and tends to tear and roughen the wood surface. A scratch free surface is especially important if you are going to finish with oil or varnish.

For most hand sanding, especially on flat surfaces, use a sanding block. Holding the sandpaper in your hand tends to leave a wavy surface on the wood since pressure is not applied evenly to all areas. A carpet or felt pad between the block and the sandpaper also helps.

At the final stages of sanding, most craftsmen use their fingertips to judge the smoothness of the surface. You can also judge by looking if you use a light held at a low angle to the wood surface. Careful sanding is an important step toward a fine finish.

If desired, a power sander can be used; a pad sander is the easiest to use without damaging the wood surface. Belt sanders can be used by experienced operators.

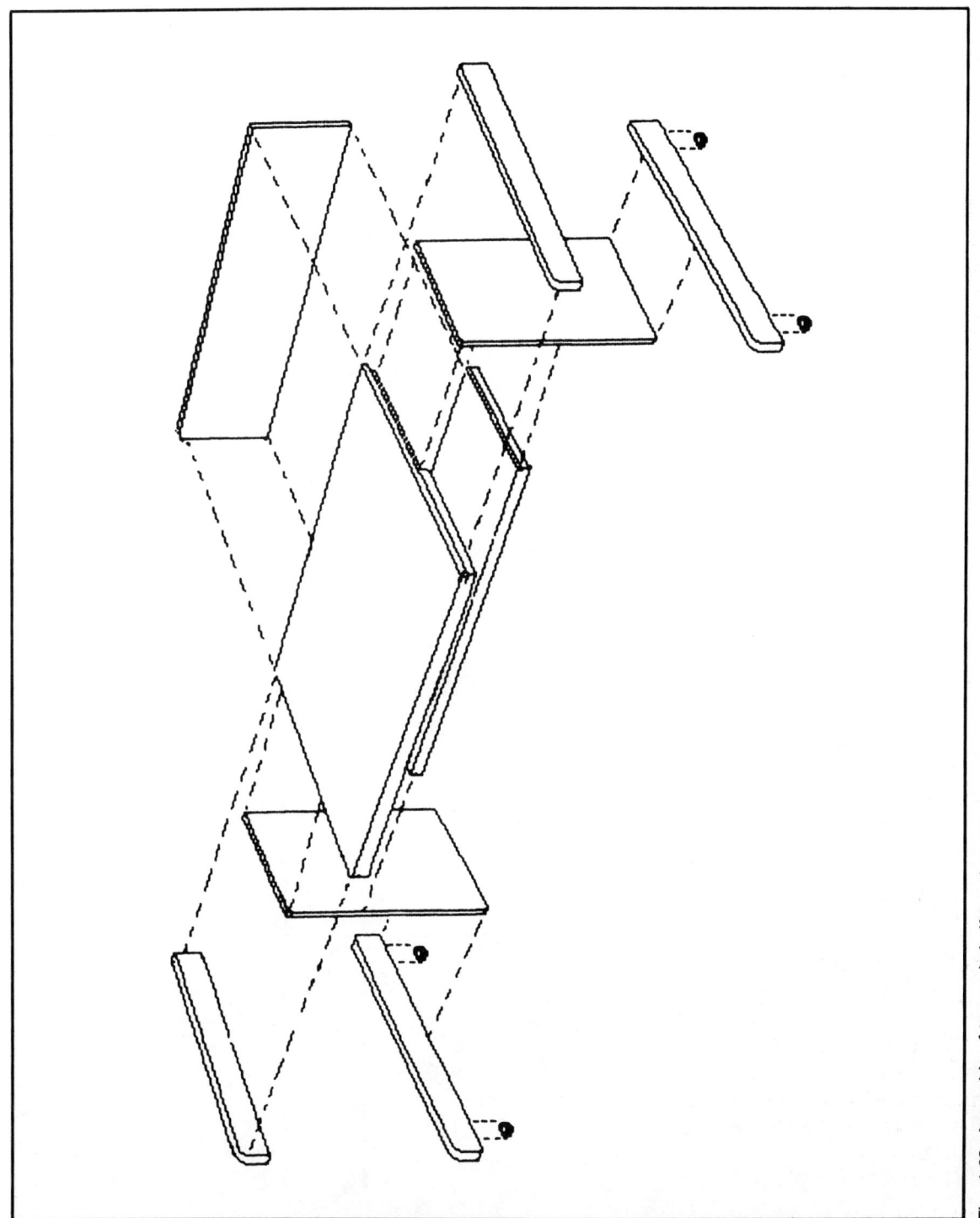

Fig. 4-69. Assembly of top and shelf to other components.

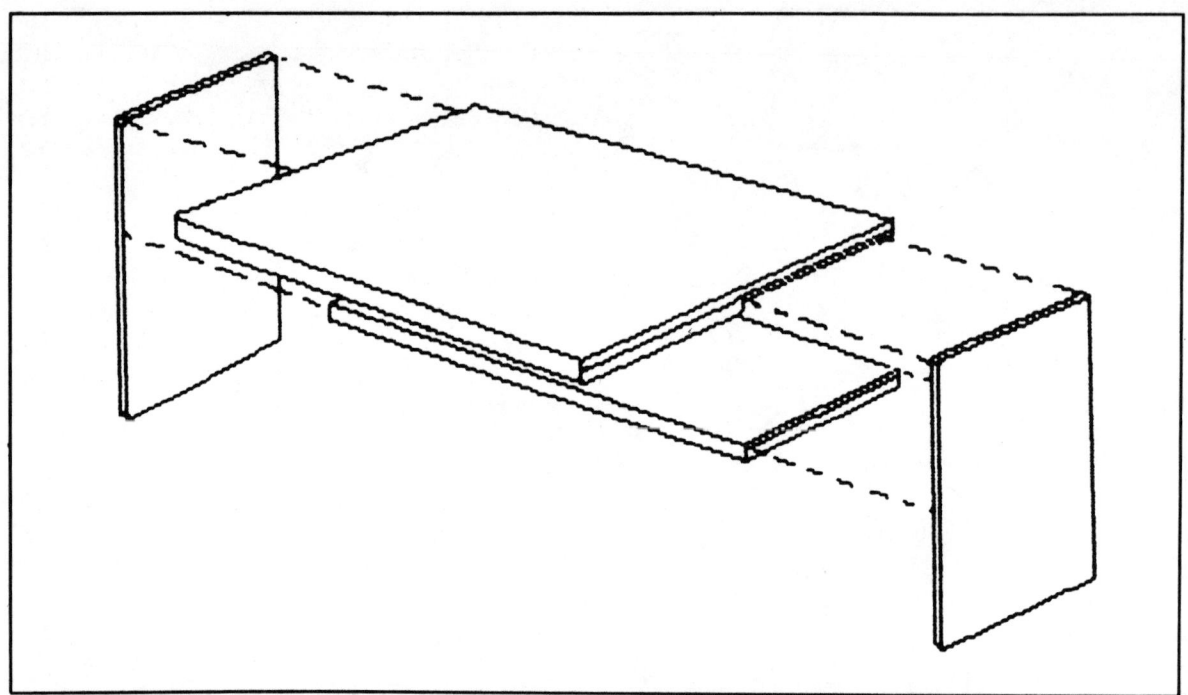

Fig. 4-70. Assembly of top and shelf to end pieces.

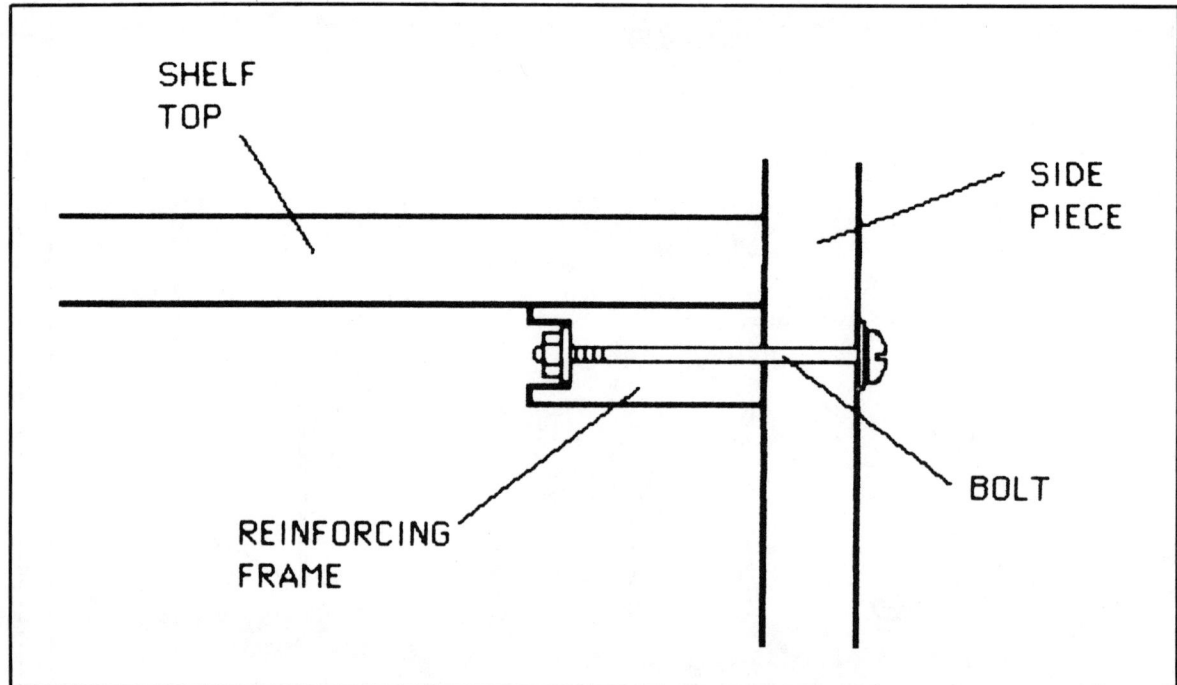

Fig. 4-71. Assembly of shelf to side pieces with bolts.

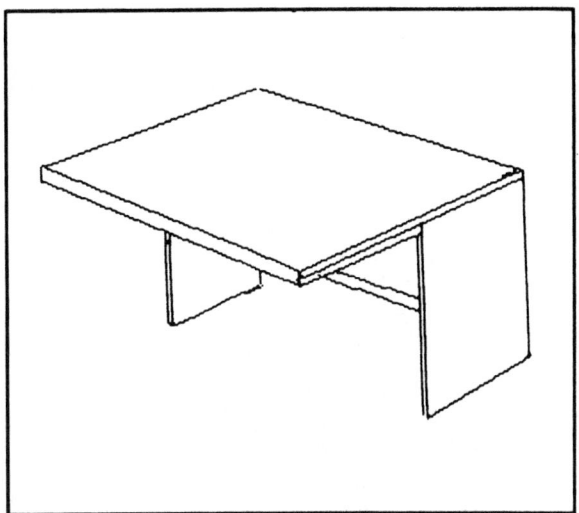

Fig. 4-72. Top and shelf assembled to end pieces.

A clear finish (polyurethane plastic is ideal) can be applied directly to natural wood, or you can first stain the wood to give it another color. Staining can enhance the natural grains of the wood and enrich relatively lifeless woods.

Before applying stain, first test color on a scrap piece of the wood. Clean the surface to eliminate as much dust as possible. The stain can then be applied with a brush, foam brush applicator, or cloth in a smooth, even coat. Allow the stain to penetrate the wood; depending on the humidity, temperature, and particular stain used, this usually takes from 5 to 15 minutes. While the stain is still wet, wipe off the excess stain with a clean cloth. Be careful not to remove too much from the corners and edges. Wipe across the grain first so that you work the stain into the wood pores, then give a final wipe with the grain. Allow the stain to dry. This usually takes at least 8 hours. The finish can then be applied.

It is usually best to apply a series of light, even coats of clear finish, rather than one thick coat, to minimize possible drips and wrinkles as the finish dries. Apply finish in brush-width strokes in direction of wood grain. Position the table so that finish is applied to horizontal wood surface whenever possible.

A minimum of two coats is recommended, allowing 6 to 8 hours for the first coat to dry before applying second coat. Sand lightly and use a tack cloth to remove sanded finish dust before applying next coat of finish.

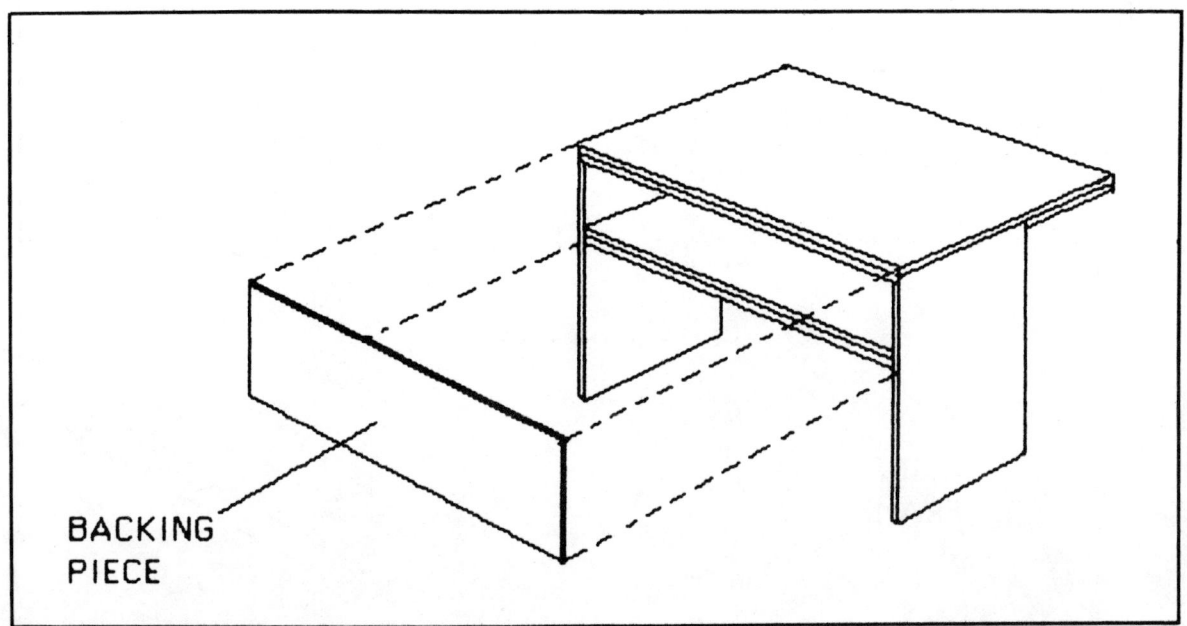

Fig. 4-73. Assembly of backing piece.

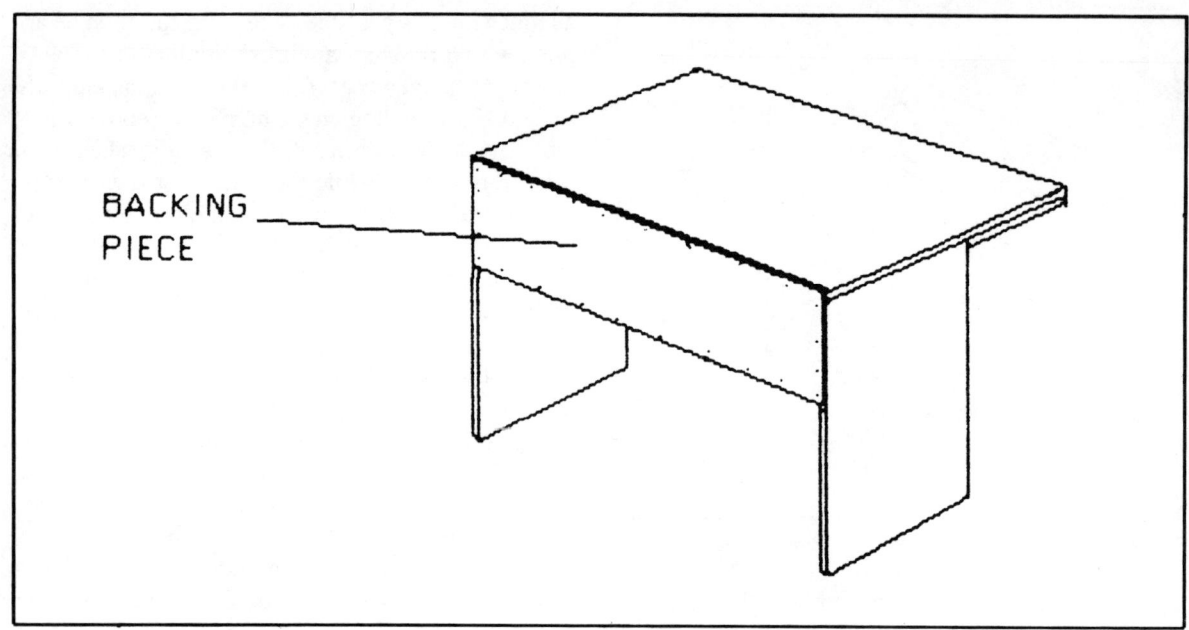

Fig. 4-74. Backing piece installed.

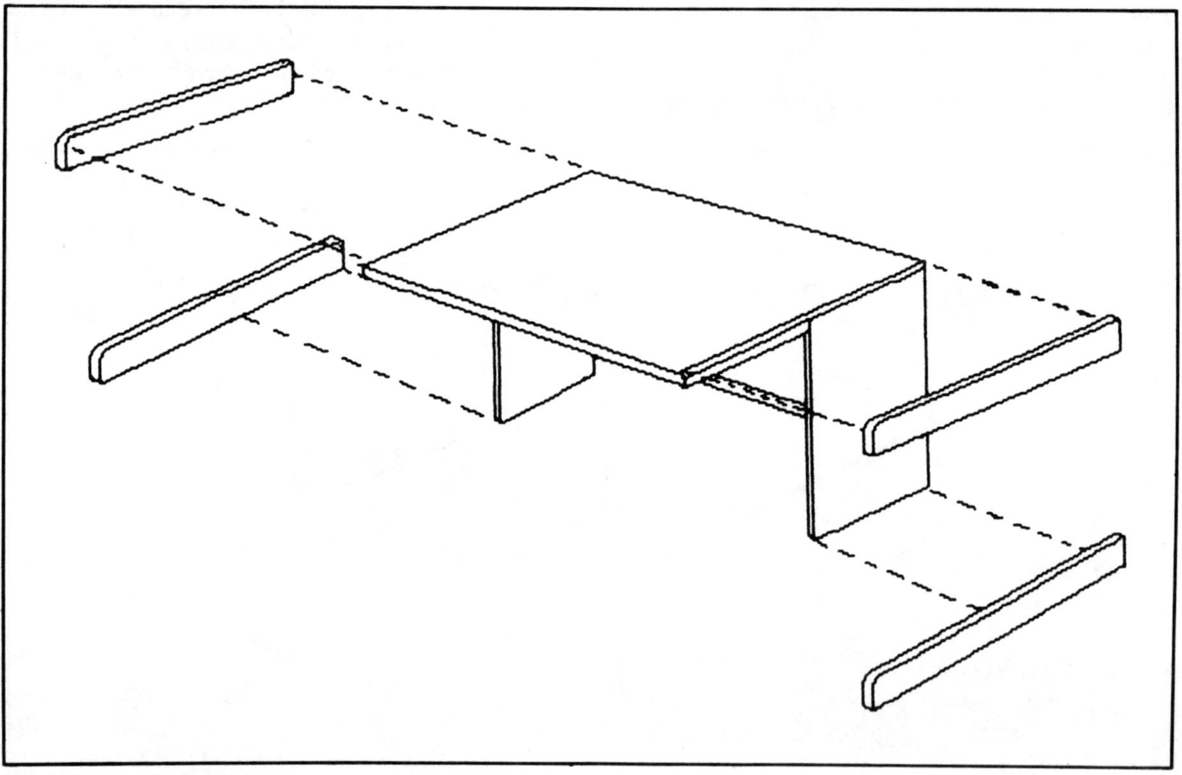

Fig. 4-75. Assembly of side pieces.

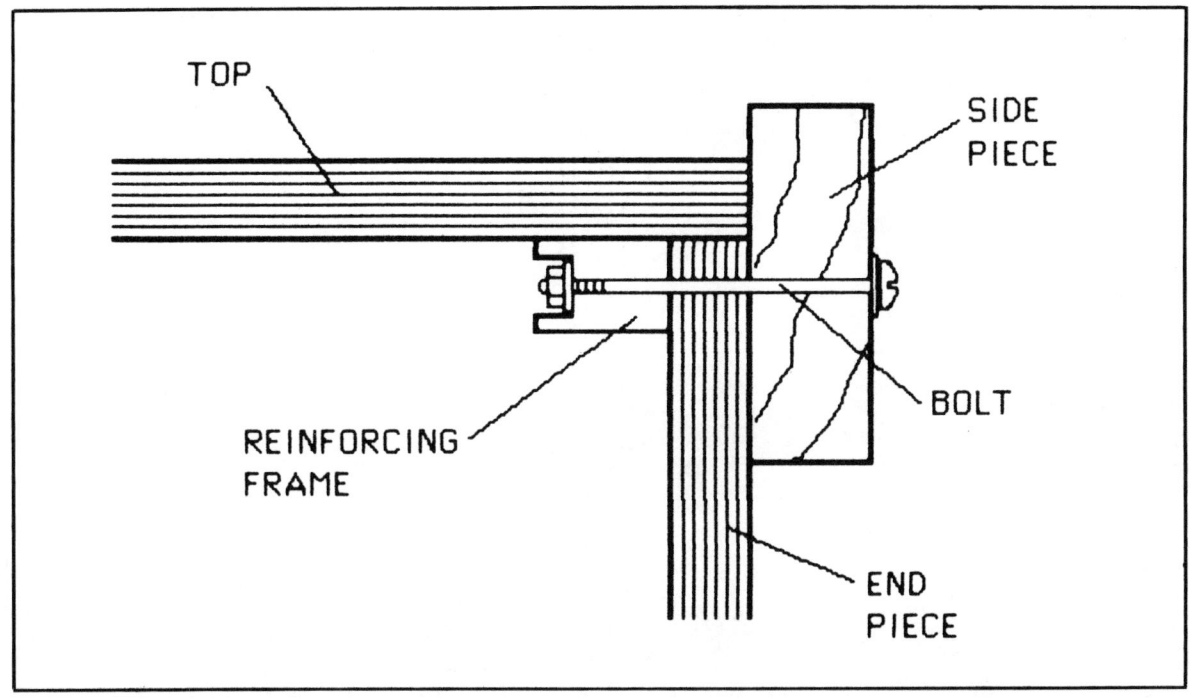

Fig. 4-76. Assembly of top to end and side pieces with bolts.

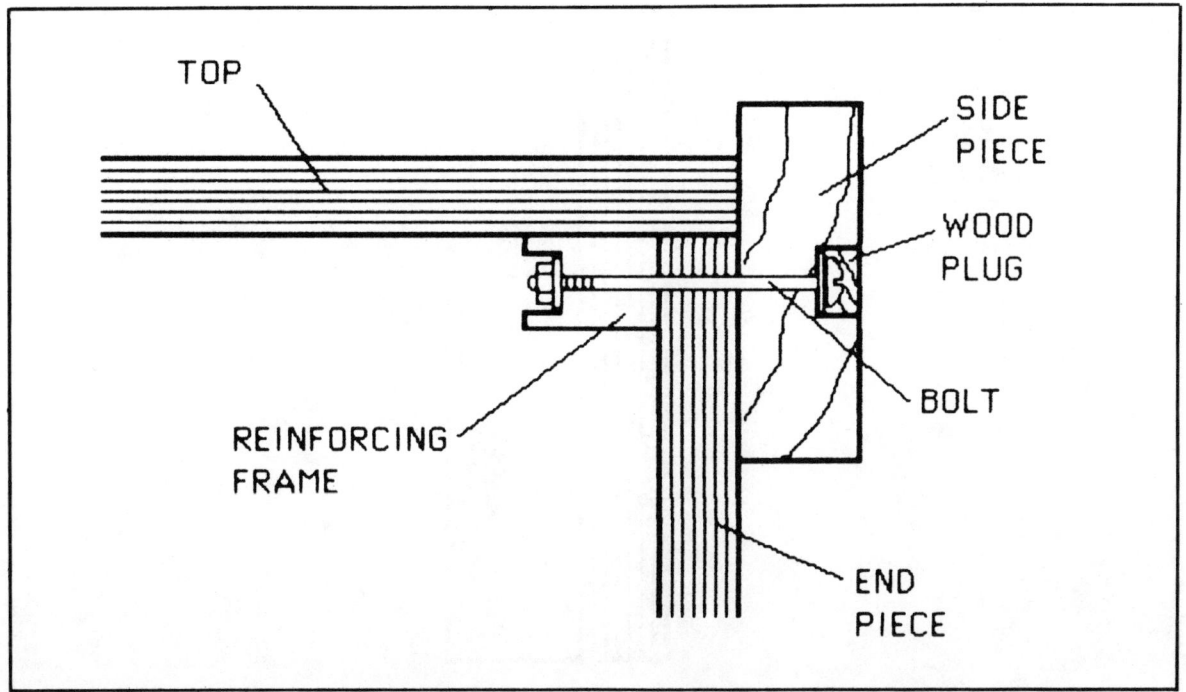

Fig. 4-77. Assembly of top to end and side pieces with bolt head countersunk and hole plugged.

219

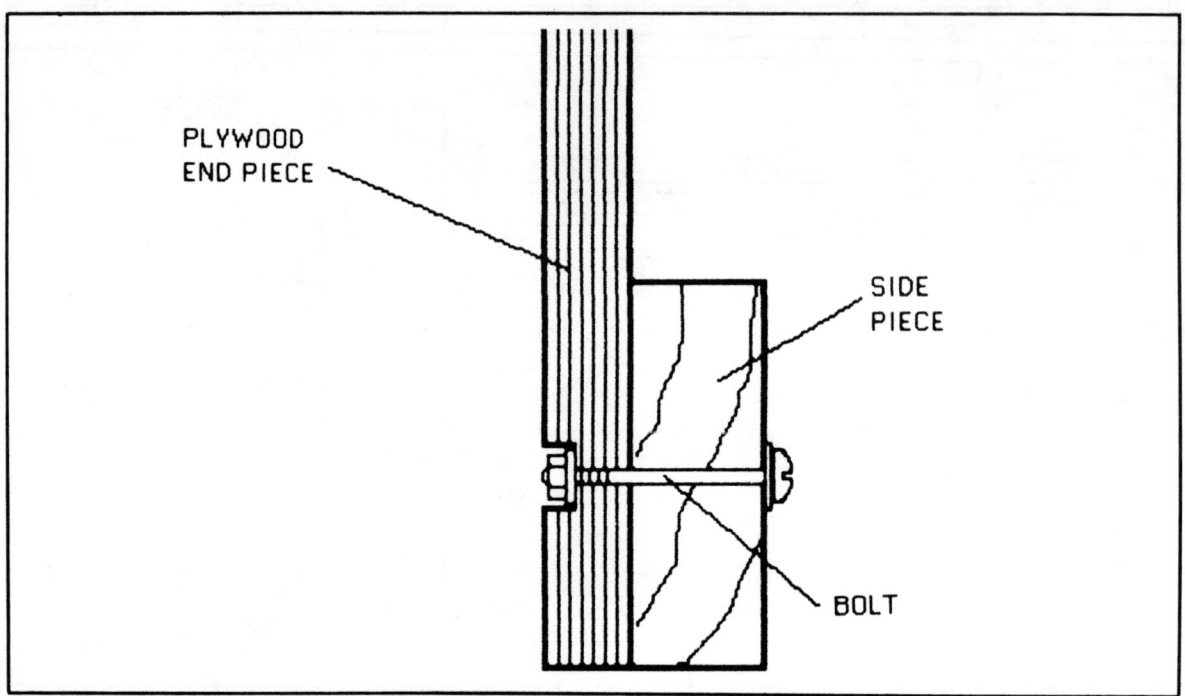

Fig. 4-78. Assembly of end and side pieces with bolts.

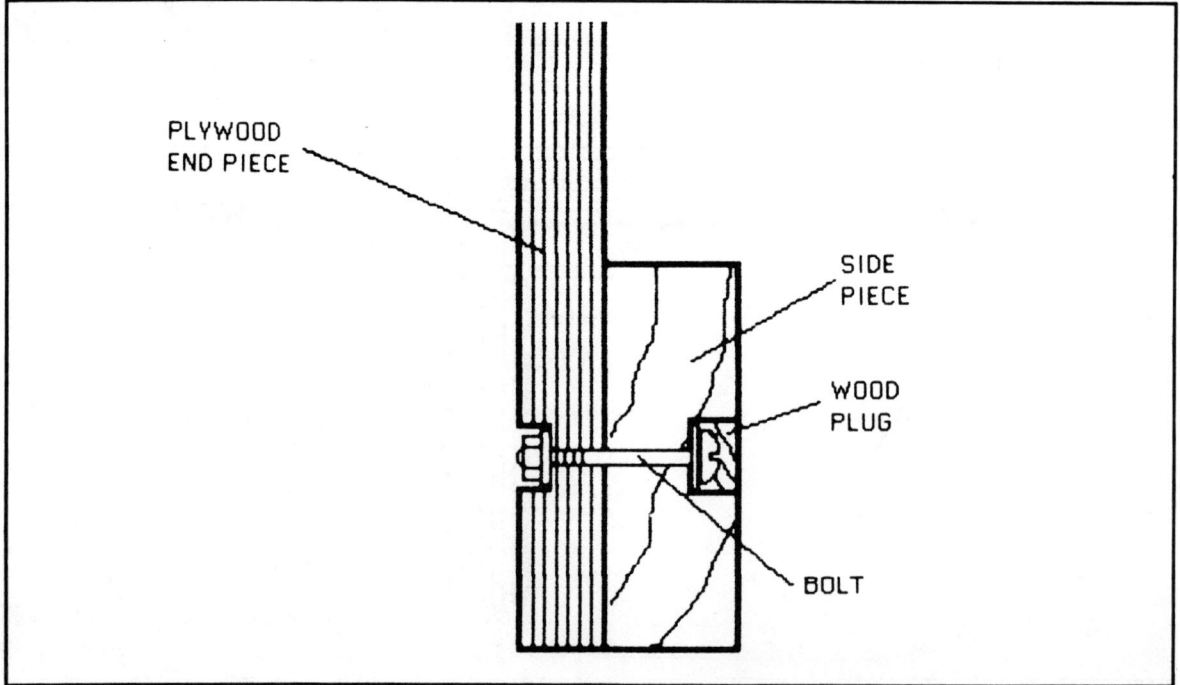

Fig. 4-79. Assembly of end and side pieces with bolt head countersunk and hole plugged.

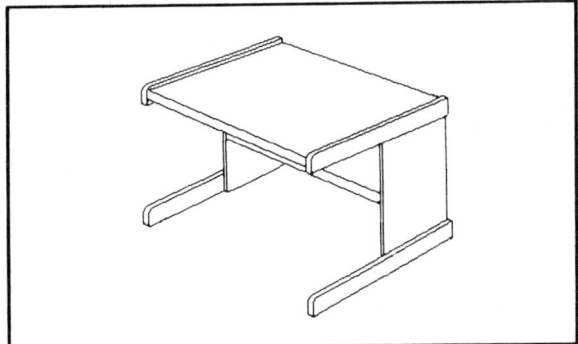

Fig. 4-80. Side pieces installed.

Clear or stained finishes are usually applied to natural wood furniture, but if desired color paint finishes can also be applied.

Variations

You can vary the basic printer table with half sides by substituting materials, such as using particle board instead of plywood for the top and/or other components. Another common variation is to construct the printer stand with a different size of top.

You can also add additional storage shelves below the table and/or use a different shelving arrangement. A slot can be cut from the backing piece so that continuous form computer paper can be fed to the printer from the shelf.

The basic printer stand with half sides makes a functional and attractive printer table even when built from inexpensive woods and is ideal to sell to others. The printer stand can be sold either unfinished or with finish applied. By using more expensive woods, such as oak, you can give the table a custom appearance. These plans show simple butt joints, but if you have the cabinet-making skills and know-how, you can also use more difficult joints.

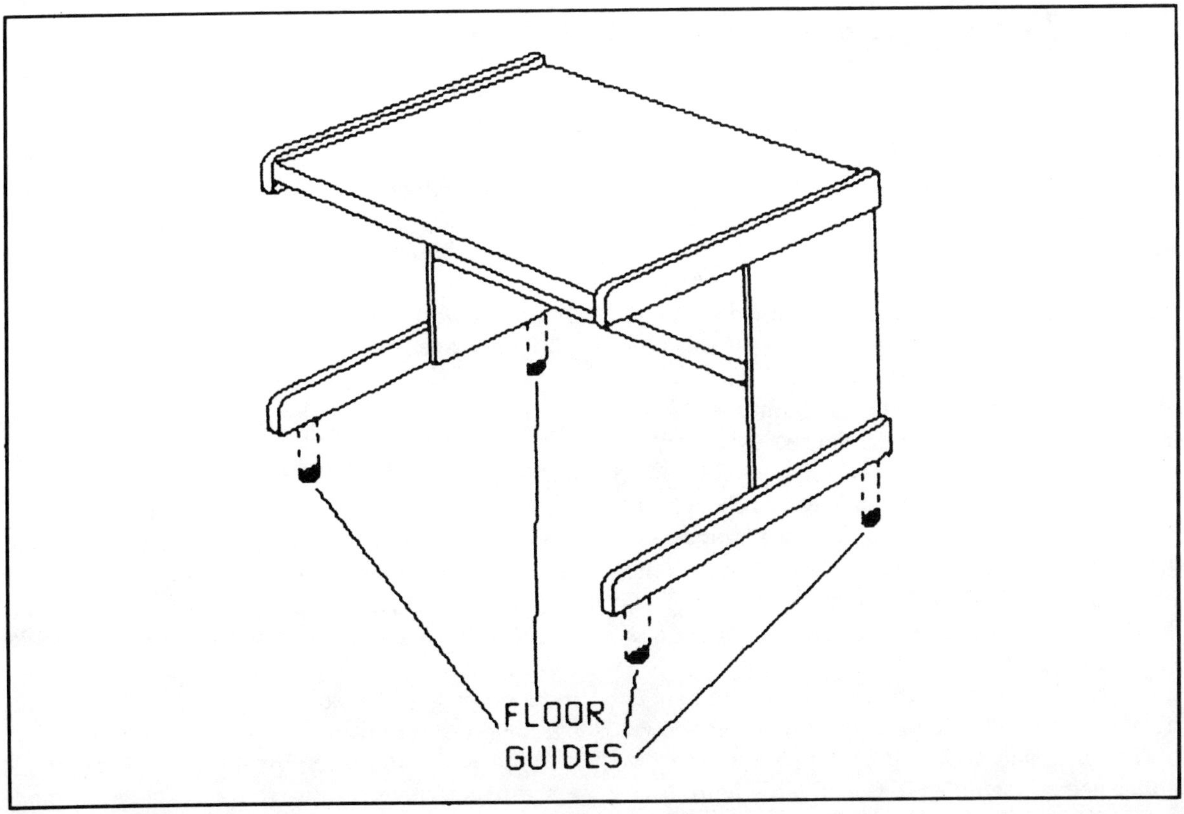

Fig. 4-81. Installing floor guides.

Chapter 5

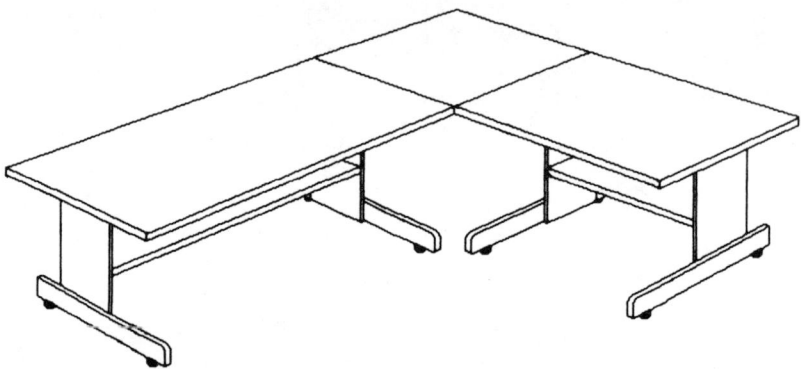

Plans and Patterns for Modular Units

Modular units can be assembled in a variety of ways into computer work stations. A basic computer table for a modular unit is shown in Figs. 5-1 and 5-2. A shorter version of the table is shown in Fig. 5-3.

With a 90-degree extender, a long and short table can be assembled in the L-shaped arrangement shown in Fig. 5-4. Figure 5-5 shows this unit with computer and printers, and Fig. 5-6 shows the tables and extender with plastic laminates. A U-shaped arrangement with 90-degree extenders is shown in Fig. 5-7.

With a square extender, a long and short table can be assembled in the L-shaped arrangement shown in Figs. 5-8 and 5-9. Figure 5-10 shows the tables and extender with plastic laminates. A U-shaped arrangement with square extenders is shown in Fig. 5-11.

With a 60-degree extender, a long and short table can be assembled in the arrangement shown in Figs. 5-12 and 5-13. Figure 5-14 shows the extender being assembled to the tables. Figure 5-15 shows this unit with a computer and printer, and

Fig. 5-16 shows the tables and extender with plastic laminates. An arrangement with one long table, two 60-degree extenders, and two short tables is shown in Fig. 5-17.

The modular units can be assembled in many other forms and are ideal for both home and office computer work stations, where individual tables are no longer adequate.

BASIC COMPUTER TABLE FOR MODULAR UNITS

The assembly of a basic computer table for modular units is shown in Figs. 5-18 and 5-19. The table is constructed mainly from plywood, is attractive and modern, and gives a good appearance even when built from standard plywood. A custom look can be achieved by making the same design from more expensive plywoods, such as those faced with oak or other hardwoods.

The basic table is shown in Fig. 5-1. It features a shelf underneath to provide storage space and give the table added strength. Figure 5-2 shows the

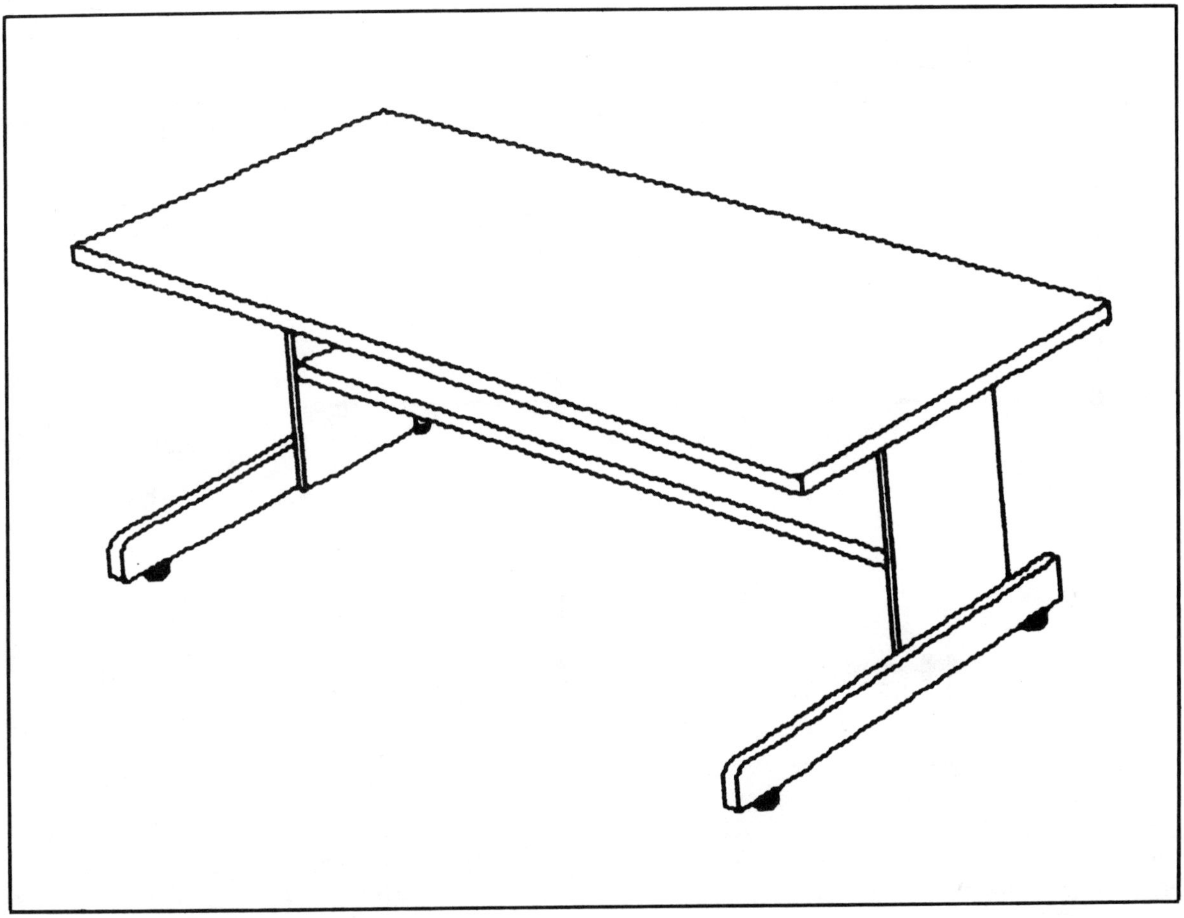

Fig. 5-1. Basic computer table for modular units.

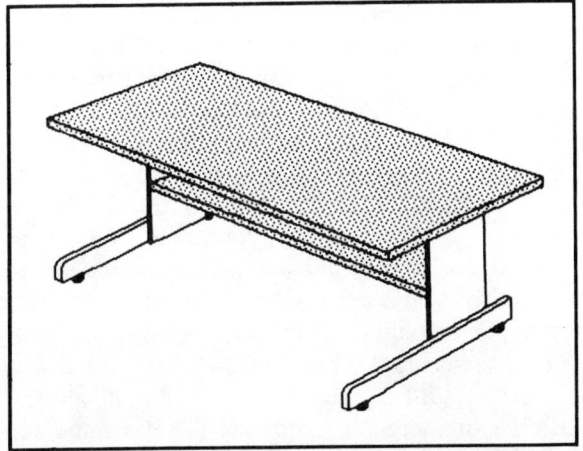

Fig. 5-2. Basic computer table for modular units with plastic laminate.

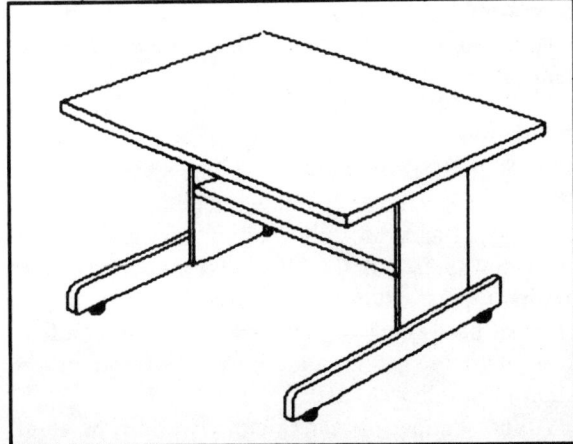

Fig. 5-3. Shorter version of basic computer table for modular units.

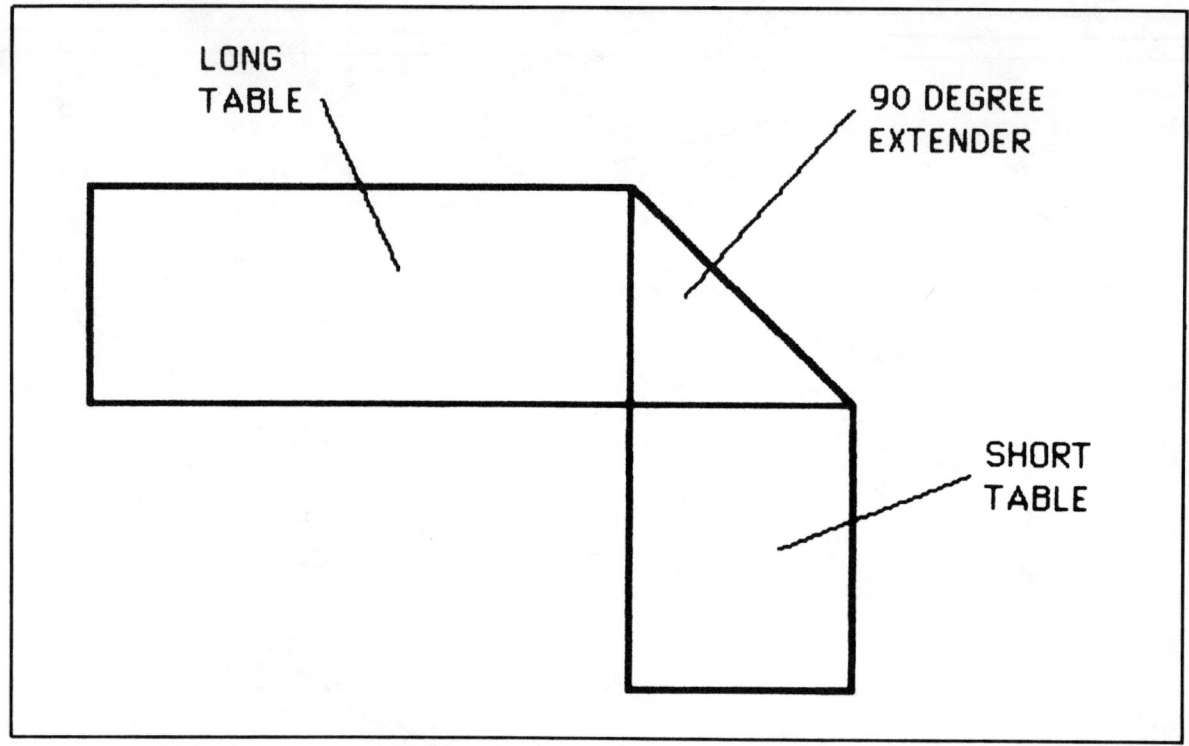

Fig. 5-4. L-shaped arrangement with 90 degree extender.

table with plastic laminate facing. The patterns that follow are for this long version of the table with a 60-inch long top, but shorter tables, as shown in Fig. 5-3, are constructed similarly with the subtraction of the same length from all longitudinal members. For a modular unit, you will need to construct two or more tables of the same or different lengths.

Materials

The patterns for the wood parts are shown in Fig. 5-20. The top of the table is a 30-inch-by-5-foot piece of 3/4-inch thick plywood. If you intend to use the wood surface as the finished table top, without adding a plastic laminate, plywood with an upper layer of hardwood, such as oak, is recommended. If a laminate is to be added, even exterior grade shop plywood will suffice.

The shelf is 3/4-inch thick plywood. The shelf measures 14 1/2 inches by 46 1/2 inches.

The end pieces are 3/4-inch thick plywood and measure 15 inches by 27 1/4 inches. This produces a table that is 28 inches high, not counting the height added by whatever floor guides are used, so you may want to change the 27 1/4 inch dimension if you want your table a different height. Two end pieces are required.

The backing piece is 1/2-inch thick plywood and measures 15 inches by 46 1/2 inches.

Plywood is normally sold in standard 4-foot-by-8-foot sheets. Lay out the patterns to take advantage of this standard size and arrange them to keep waste to a minimum. Some lumberyards and plywood stores will cut plywood sheets for you to desired size, usually at additional cost. This can be worth it if you don't need full sheets, don't have room to carry full sheets in your car, or don't have a saw to accurately cut plywood.

Although 1/2-inch thick plywood could also be used, I don't recommend this. The savings are small, and a less sturdy table will result. Particle board can be substituted for the plywood if you are

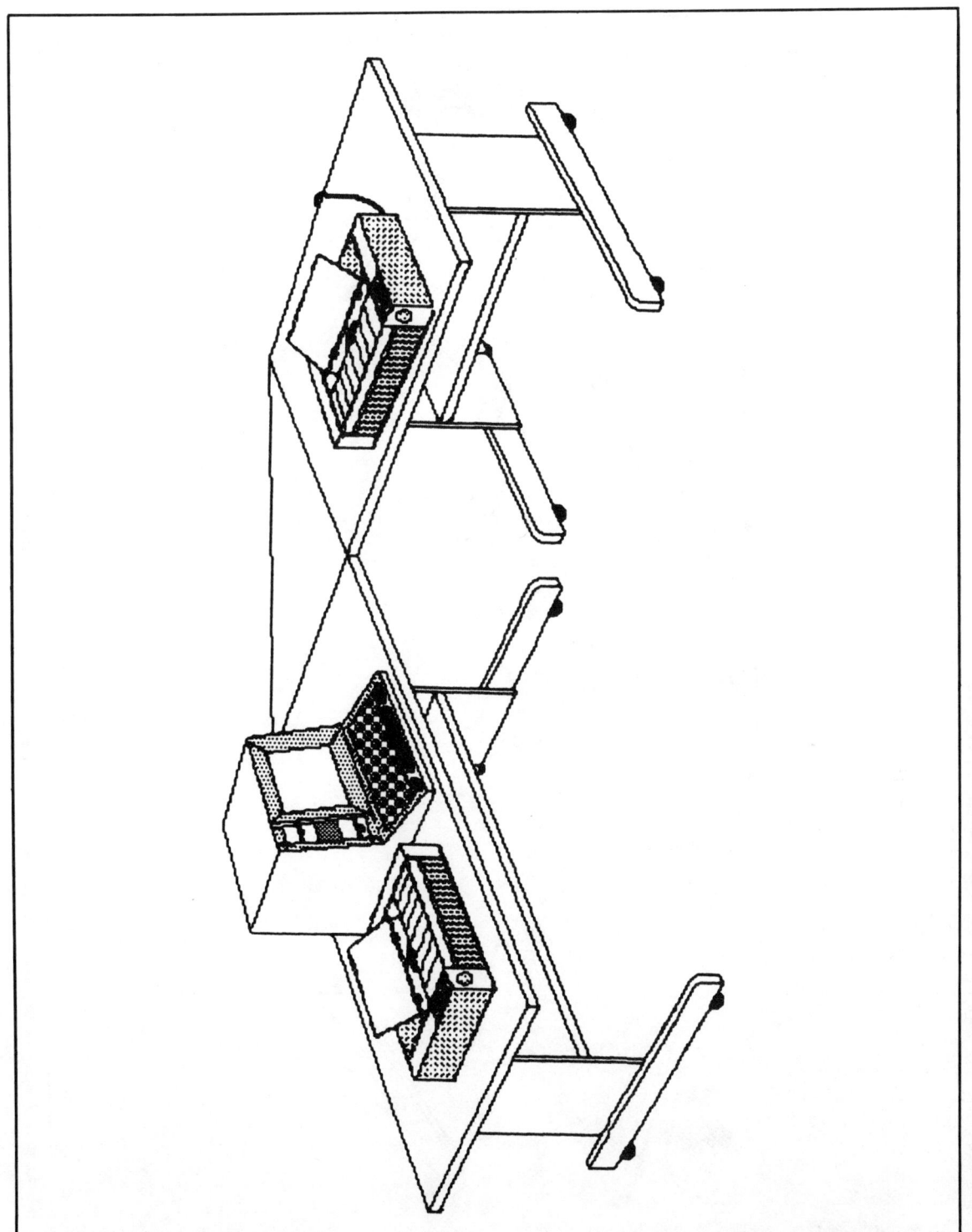

Fig. 5-5. Long and short tables connected with 90 degree extender.

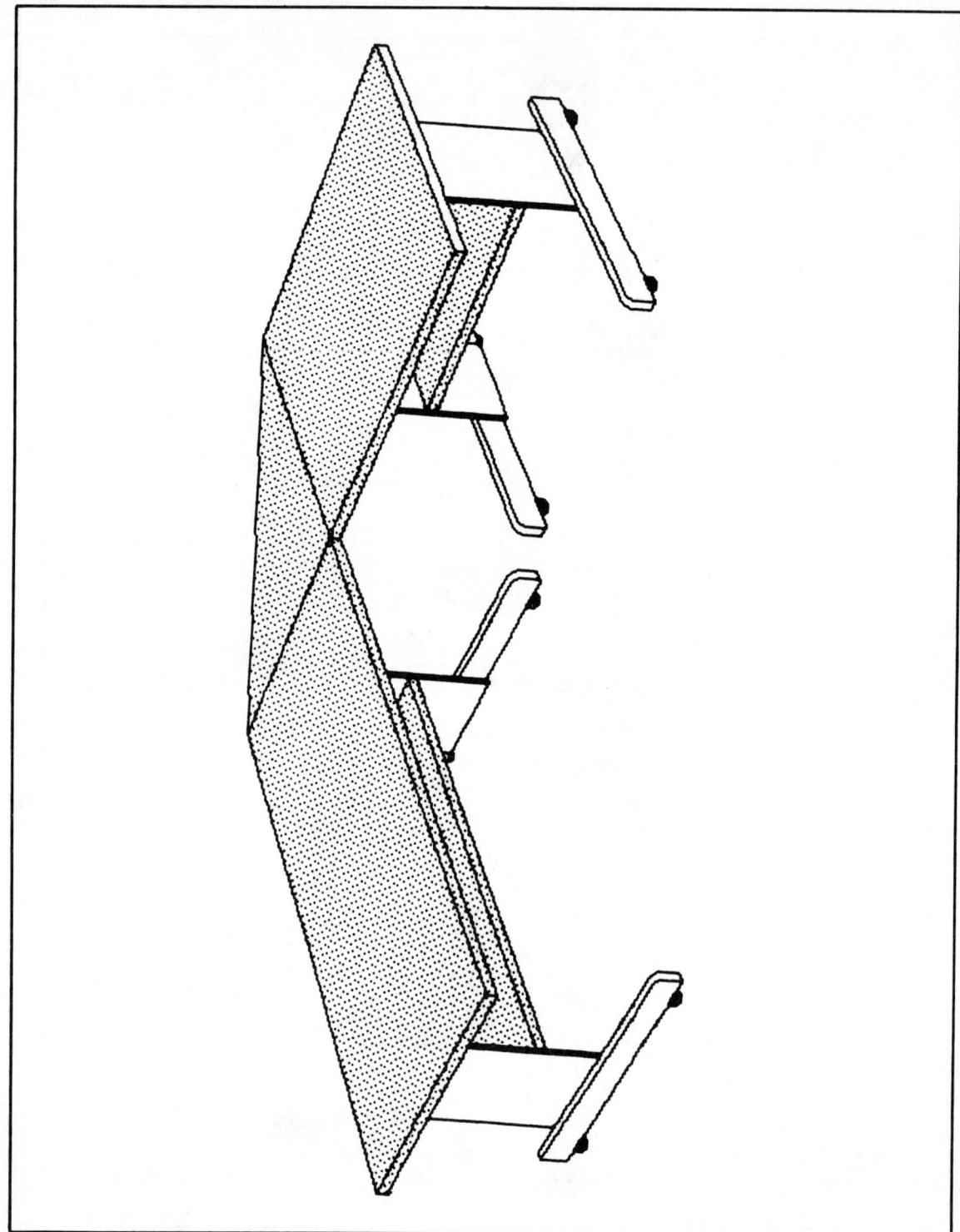

Fig. 5-6. Long and short tables connected with 90 degree extender with plastic laminate.

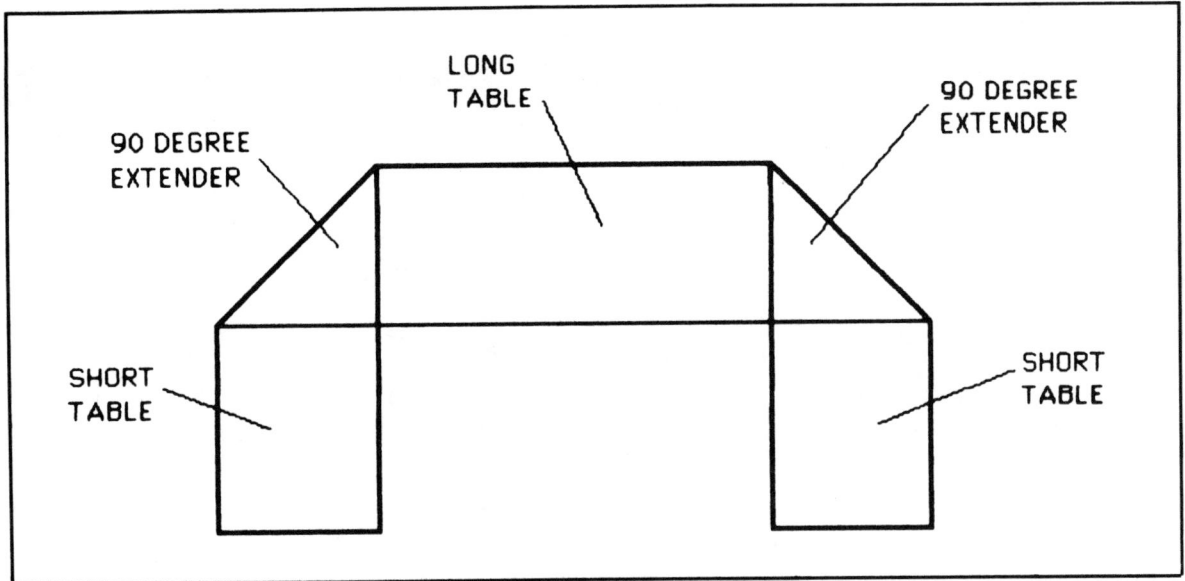

Fig. 5-7. U-shaped arrangement with 90 degree extenders.

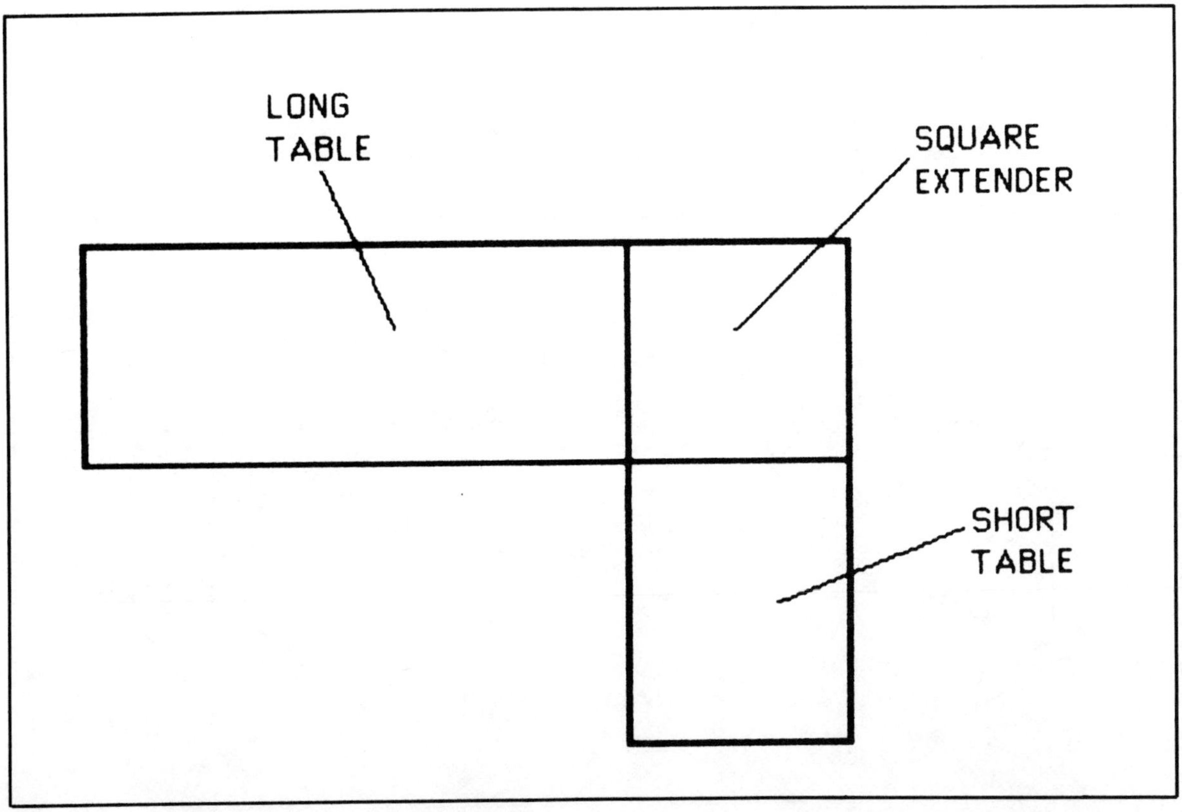

Fig. 5-8. L-shaped arrangement with square extender.

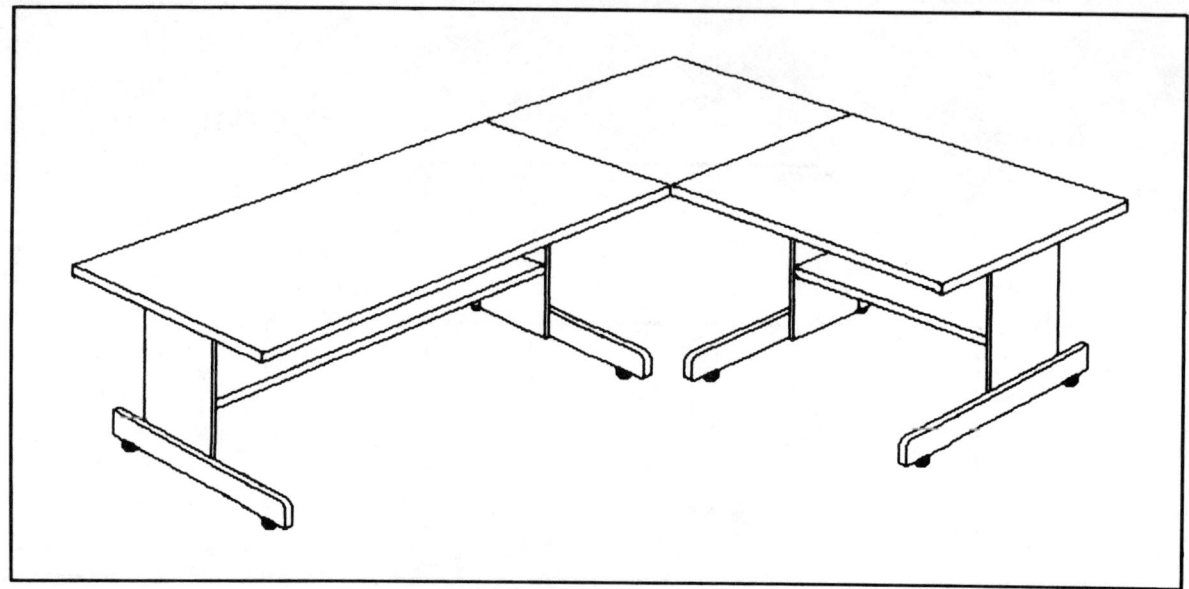

Fig. 5-9. Long and short tables connected with square extender.

on an absolute minimum budget. There is low-grade high-priced manufactured computer furniture made from particle board covered by plastic laminates, but it can be difficult to work with. It is very difficult to get plastic laminates to bond properly to this material without special equipment. Even laminate on manufactured furniture comes loose at the edges.

Four beam side pieces of 2-inch-by-4-inch hardwood stock are required (Fig. 5-21). Two of these

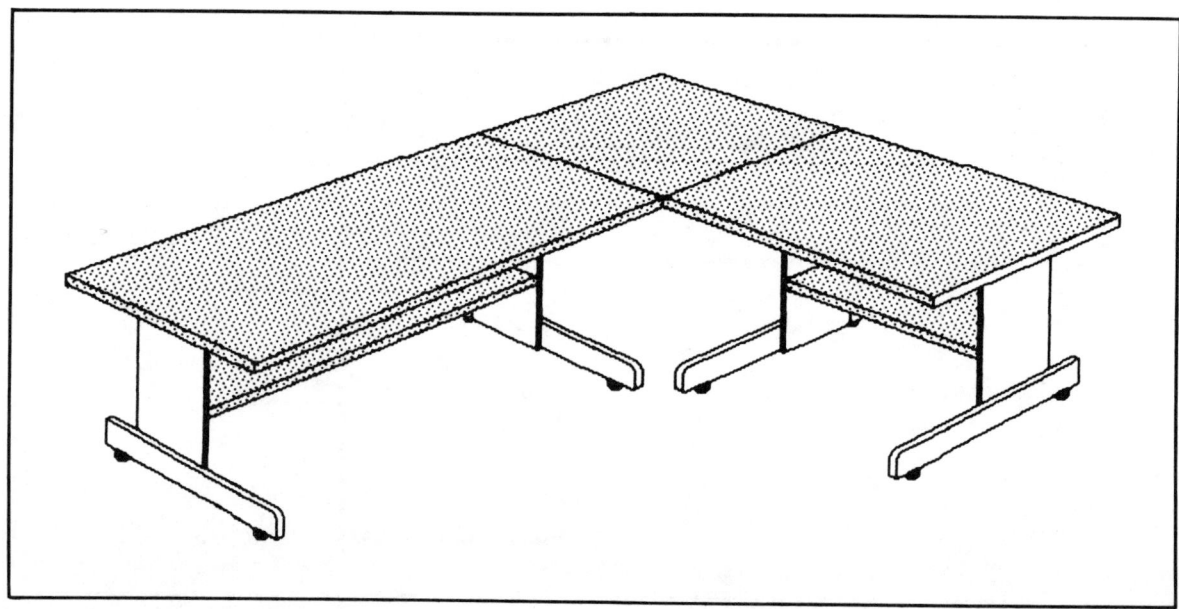

Fig. 5-10. Long and short tables connected with square extender with plastic laminates.

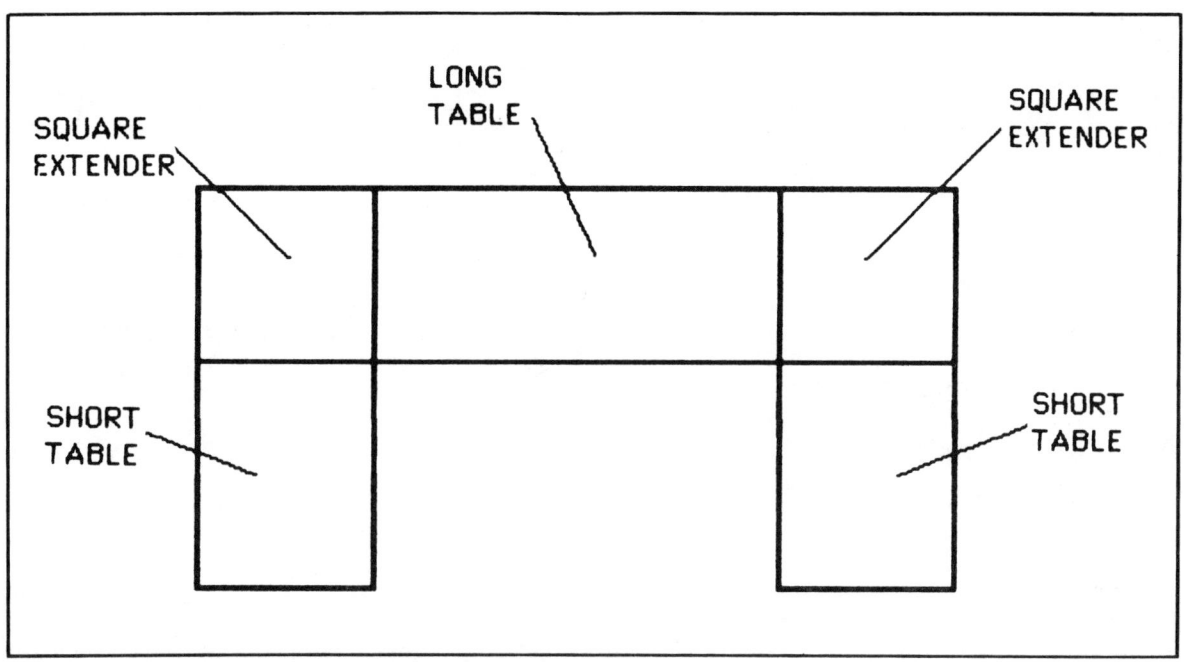

Fig. 5-11. U-shaped arrangement with square extenders.

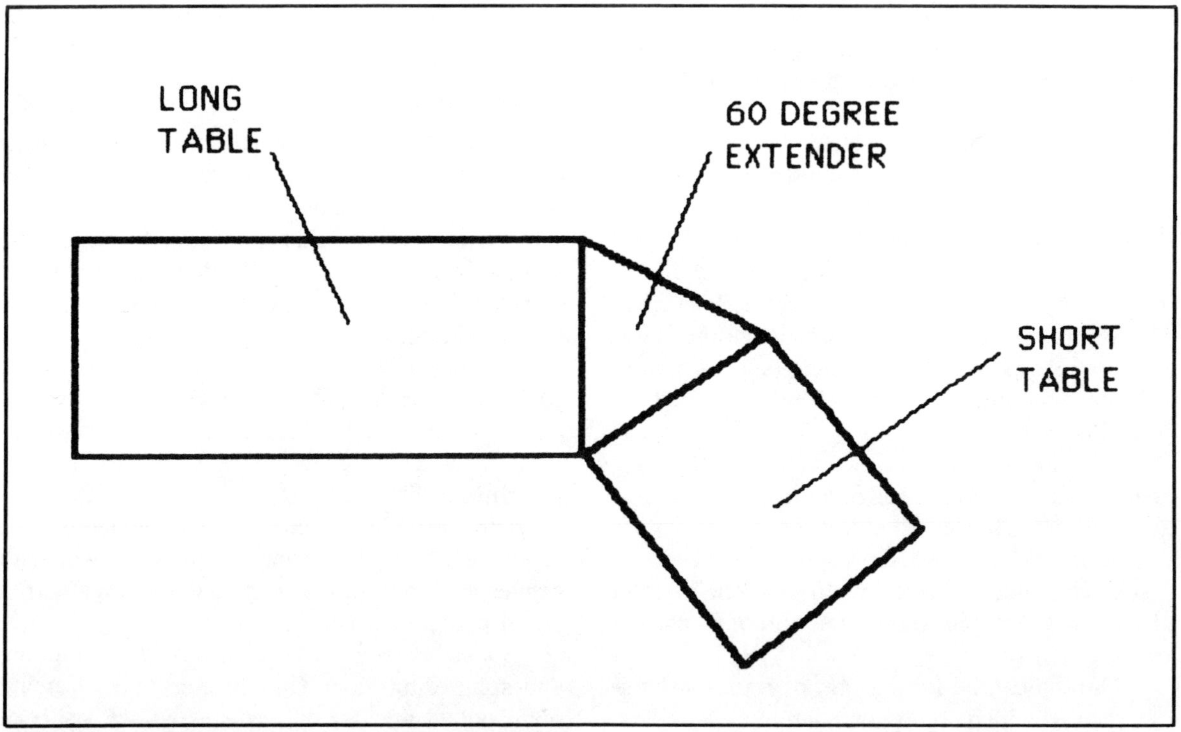

Fig. 5-12. Arrangement with one 60 degree extender.

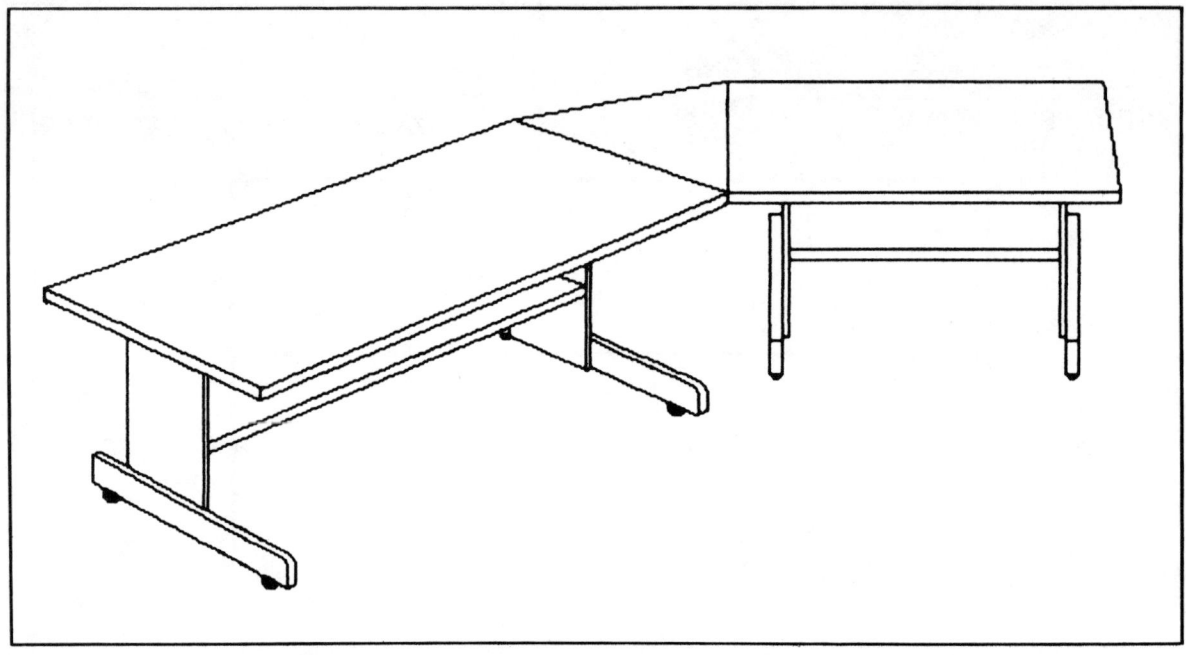

Fig. 5-13. Long and short tables connected with 60 degree extender.

are 26 inches long and two are 30 inches long.

You will also need 1-inch-by-2-inch or larger framing stock for use under the plywood top and the shelf.

Wood and plastic trim strips can be used to cover the exposed edges of the plywood, as detailed later in this section. A wood or plastic trim strip is used to cover the forward edge of the table top and shelf. These pieces are 60 inches and 46 1/2 inches long respectively, and about 1 3/4 inches wide. This will completely cover the widths of the plywood (3/4 inch) and the framing (approximately 7/8 inch). The trim strips can be slightly wider than this, however.

Four floor pods or guides are used on the floor beams. Many suitable fixed or adjustable types are available from hardware stores.

Your choice of fasteners can be used for assembly, as detailed below in this section. You will also need a suitable wood glue, and your chosen finish product.

The top can be left natural or a plastic laminate can be added. If a plastic laminate is added, you will need a 30-inch-by-5-foot piece of suitable plastic laminate and contact cement to attach it to the plywood.

Construction

Overviews of the complete assembly are shown in Figs. 5-18 and 5-19. Begin by constructing the table top, as detailed in Fig. 5-20. If you purchased a piece of plywood that was already cut to the 30-inch-by-5-foot size, no additional cutting is required, if it was cut accurately and true. Check this with a square.

If you purchased a larger piece of plywood, such as a standard 4-foot-by-8-foot sheet, cut out a section for the table top. In most cases, you will want to have the grain of the top layer running lengthwise, although this is not essential if you are going to add a plastic laminate. Use two factory cut edges for your table top and cut the other two. With a ruler and square, mark the pattern lines with a sharp pencil or scribing tool.

Special care must be taken to avoid chipping and splintering along the cut edge when sawing plywood. Handsaws or power saws with special fine-toothed blades designed especially for plywood

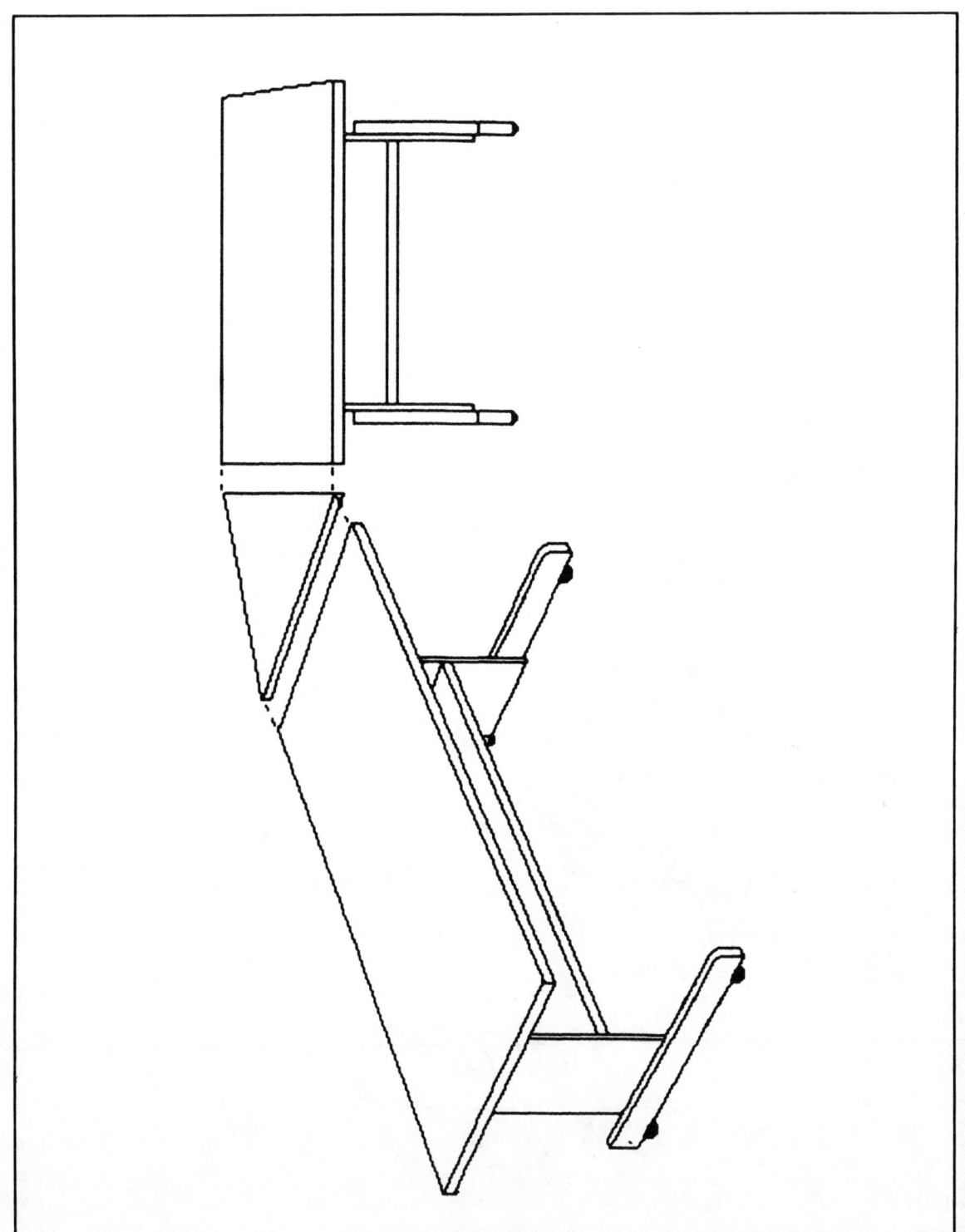

Fig. 5-14. Connecting long and short tables with 60 degree extender.

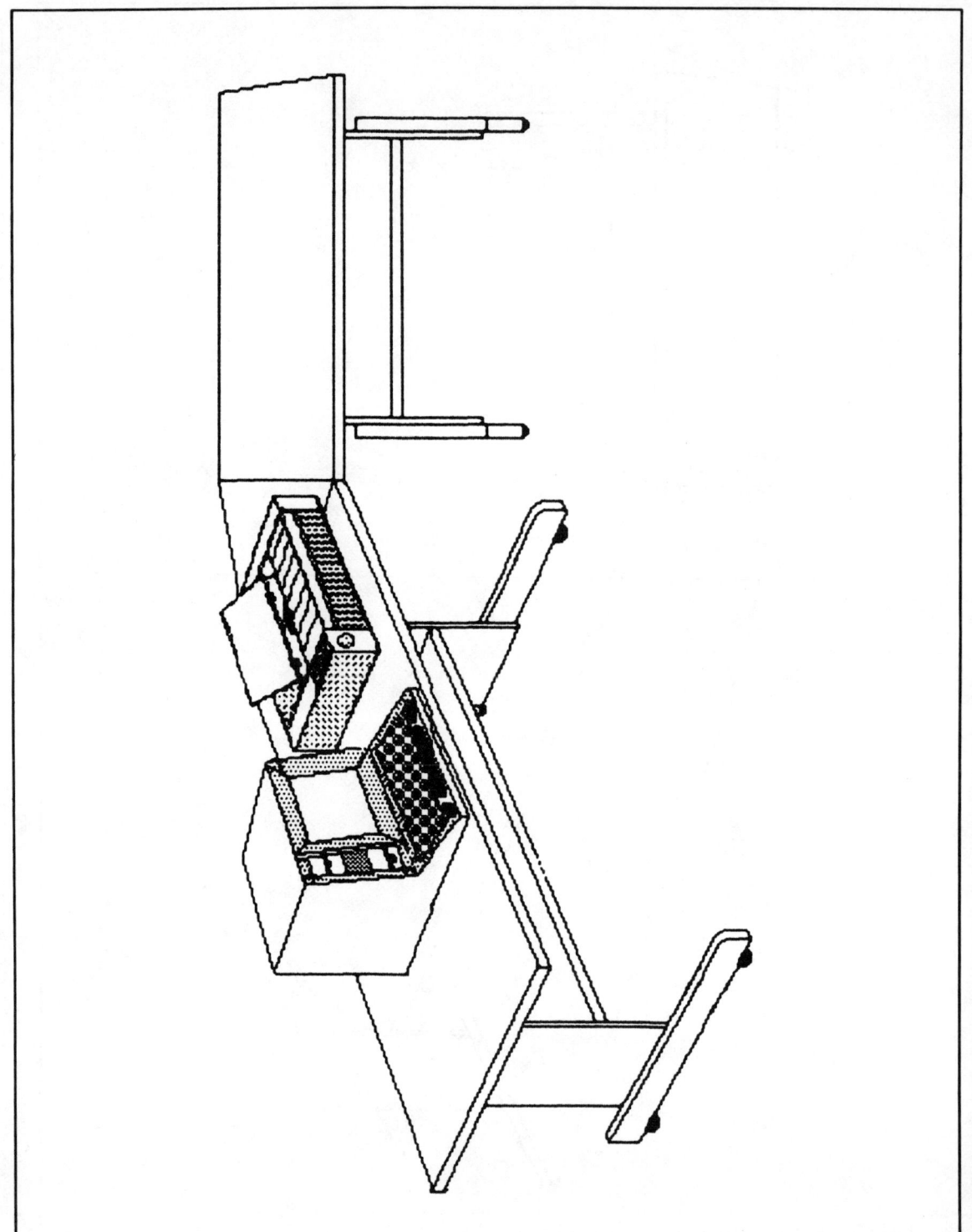

Fig. 5-15. Long and short tables connected with 60 degree extender.

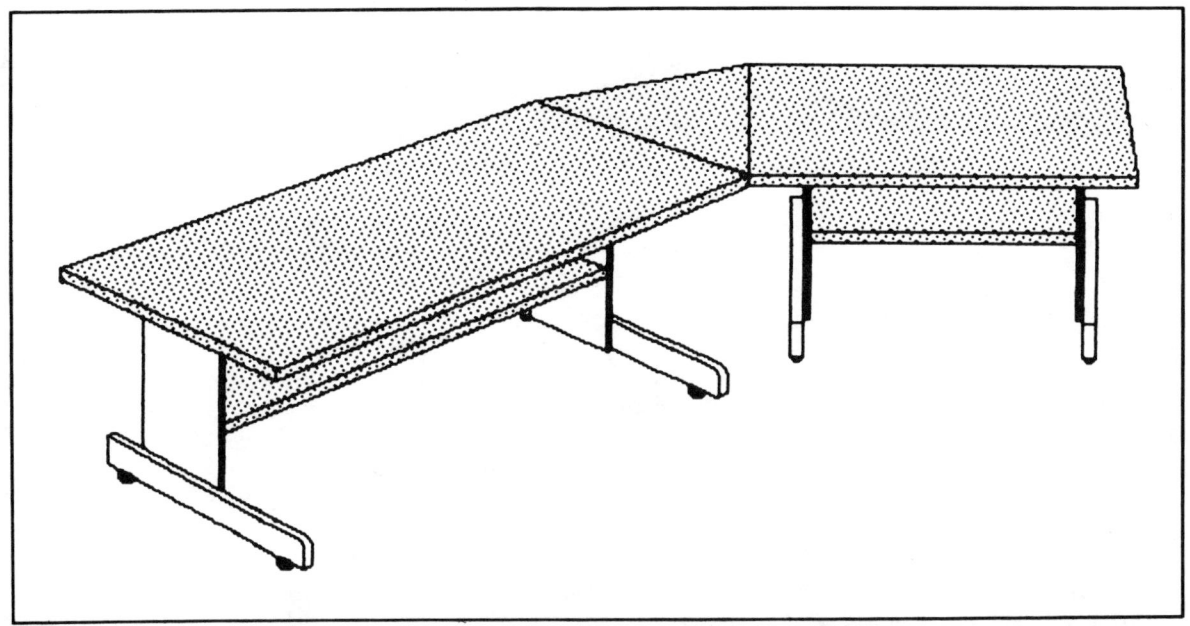

Fig. 5-16. Long and short tables connected with 60 degree extender with plastic laminates.

should be used; even better are special carbide-tipped blades. Apply a strip of masking tape over the area to be cut on both sides of the plywood, especially the underside. Or, clamp a solid piece of wood to the underside and make the cut through both the plywood and the piece of wood.

Be extremely careful when sanding edges of plywood. Use a sanding block. Avoid sanding the surfaces of plywood until a wood sealer has been applied.

The next step is to add the reinforcing frame to the table top, as shown in Fig. 5-22. Use a ruler

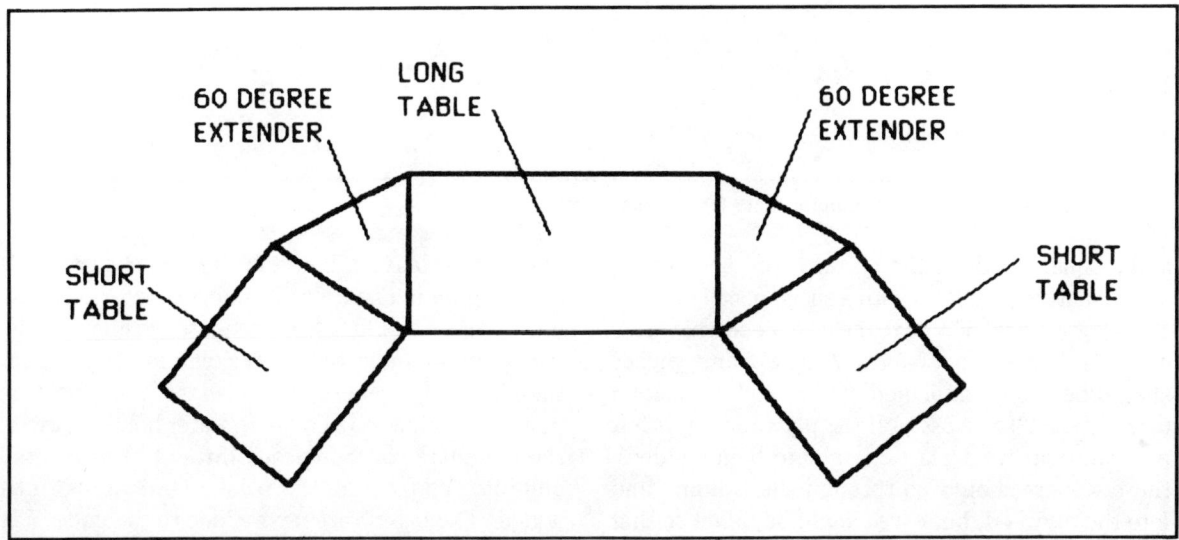

Fig. 5-17. Arrangement with two 60 degree extenders.

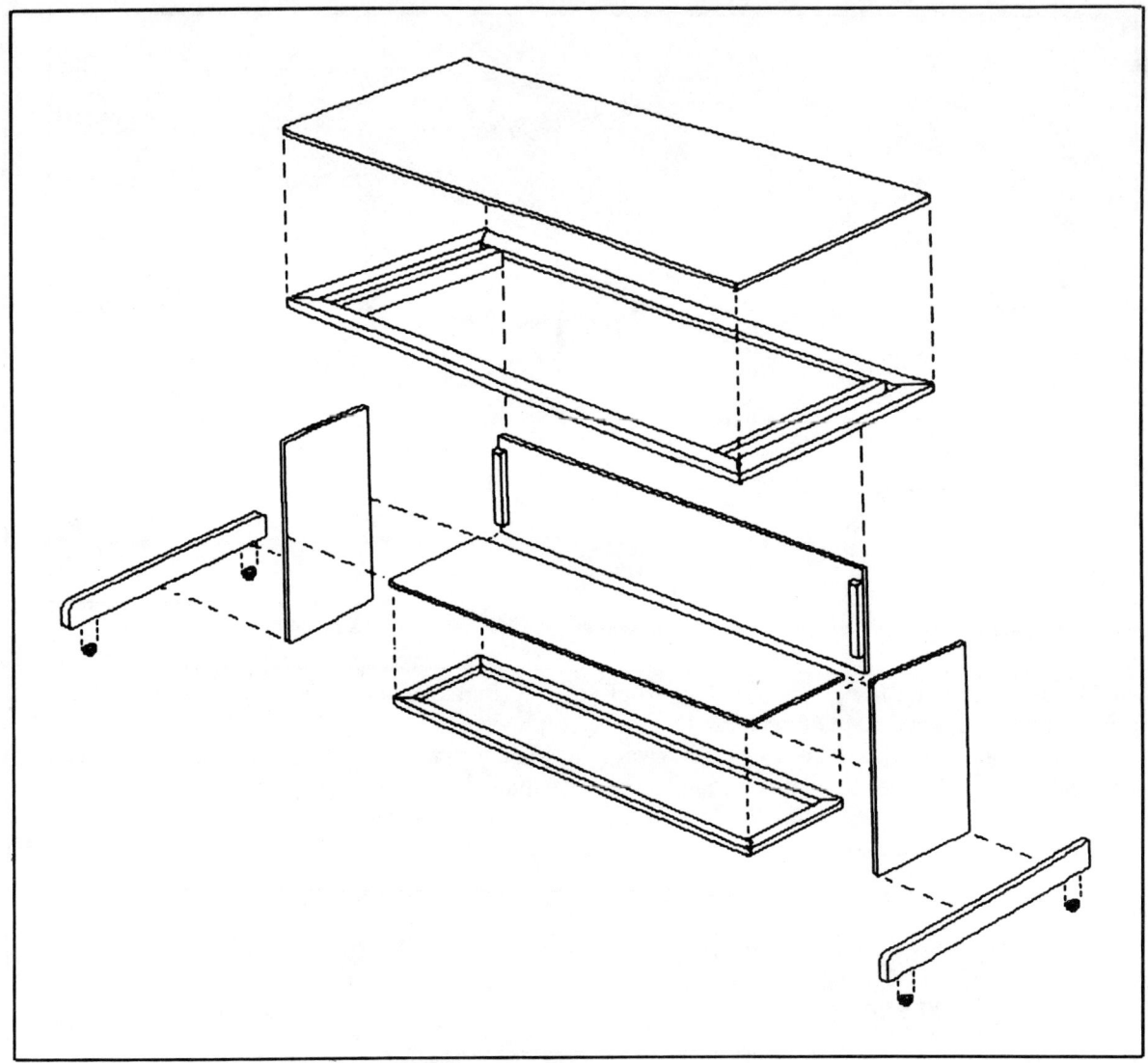

Fig. 5-18. Assembly of basic computer table for modular units.

and a square to draw the patterns on the framing wood, marking the lines with a sharp pencil or other marking device. Then make the necessary saw cuts, as detailed in Chapter 2. The frame pieces should be glued and nailed or screwed in position (see Figs. 5-23 and 5-24.) If the plywood top is left natural, (without a plastic laminate being added), the fasteners should go through the framing and into the plywood, but care should be taken so that the fasteners do not pass all the way through the plywood or leave a bulge in the upper surface. If a good glue is used, such as acrylic or epoxy, the glue alone should give adequate strength. The fasteners are mainly used as a clamping device for the gluing. Fasteners will not have much holding power into plywood. To give greater holding power, the fasteners can be passed through the plywood and into the framing if a plastic laminate is to be added. The beams are next added to the underside of the table top, as shown.

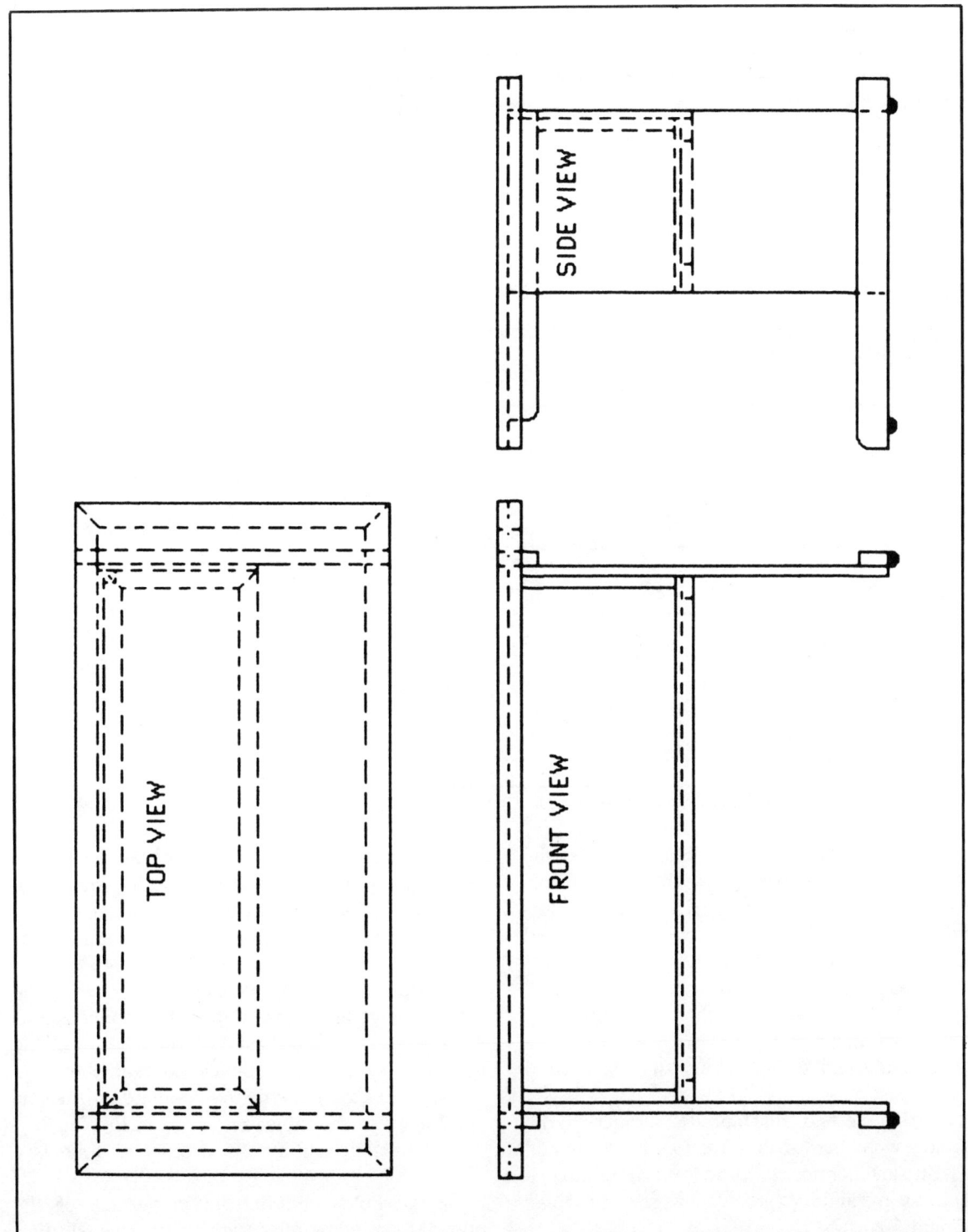

Fig. 5-19. Basic computer table for modular units.

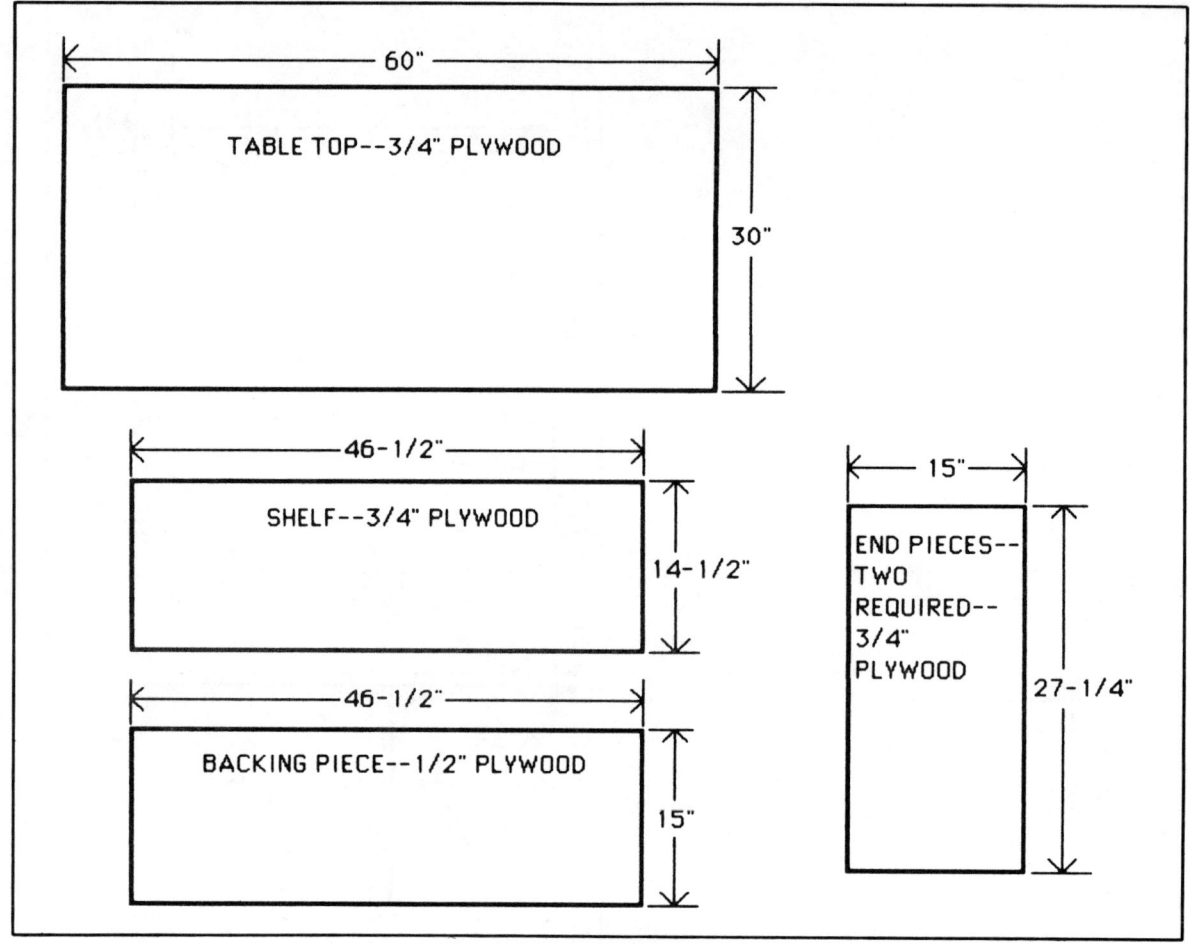

Fig. 5-20. Patterns for plywood parts of basic table for modular units.

Several options are available for finishing the table top. You may choose to use the plywood surface as the top and add a wood trim strip to the forward edge and ends of the table top. Glue and fasten the trim strip in place with finishing nails. Set the heads below the wood surface and fill holes with wood filler to flush with the wood surface. A second possibility is to add a plastic laminate to the forward edge and ends, leaving the top natural wood.

Another method adds a plastic laminate to the top and a wood trim strip to the forward edge and ends. Still another possibility adds plastic laminates to both the top and forward edge, as shown in Figs. 5-25 and 5-26.

If a plastic laminate is to be added to the plywood top and/or the forward edge and ends, these can be installed at this time. I suggest using high quality plastic laminates for computer furniture.

If a plastic laminate is to also be applied to the forward edge and ends, it should be applied first. This is then finished flush with the table top. The top laminate is then applied so that the edge overlaps the top edge of the laminate on the forward edge of the table, as shown in Fig. 5-26.

The plastic laminate is installed as follows:

• All holes and defects in surface of the plywood should be filled with putty or wood filler.

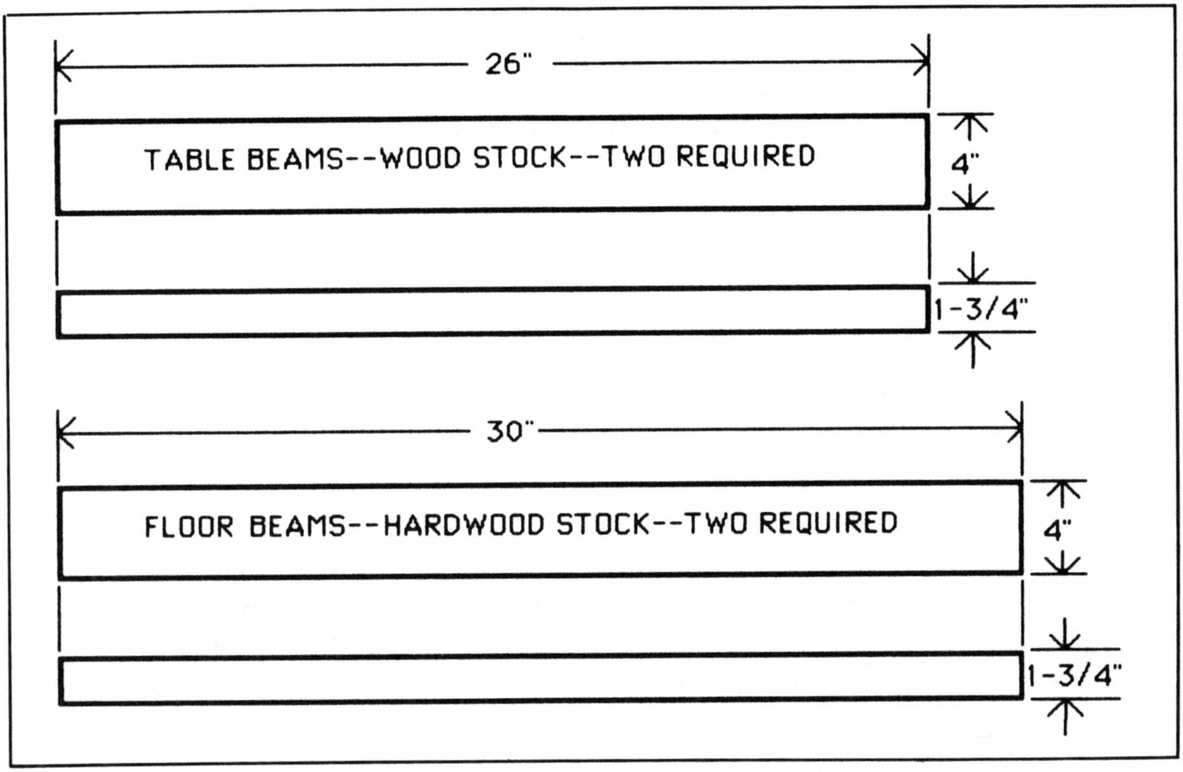

Pattern for wood beams

- TABLE BEAMS -- WOOD STOCK -- TWO REQUIRED — 26" × 4" × 1-3/4"
- FLOOR BEAMS -- HARDWOOD STOCK -- TWO REQUIRED — 30" × 4" × 1-3/4"

Fig. 5-21. Pattern for wood beams.

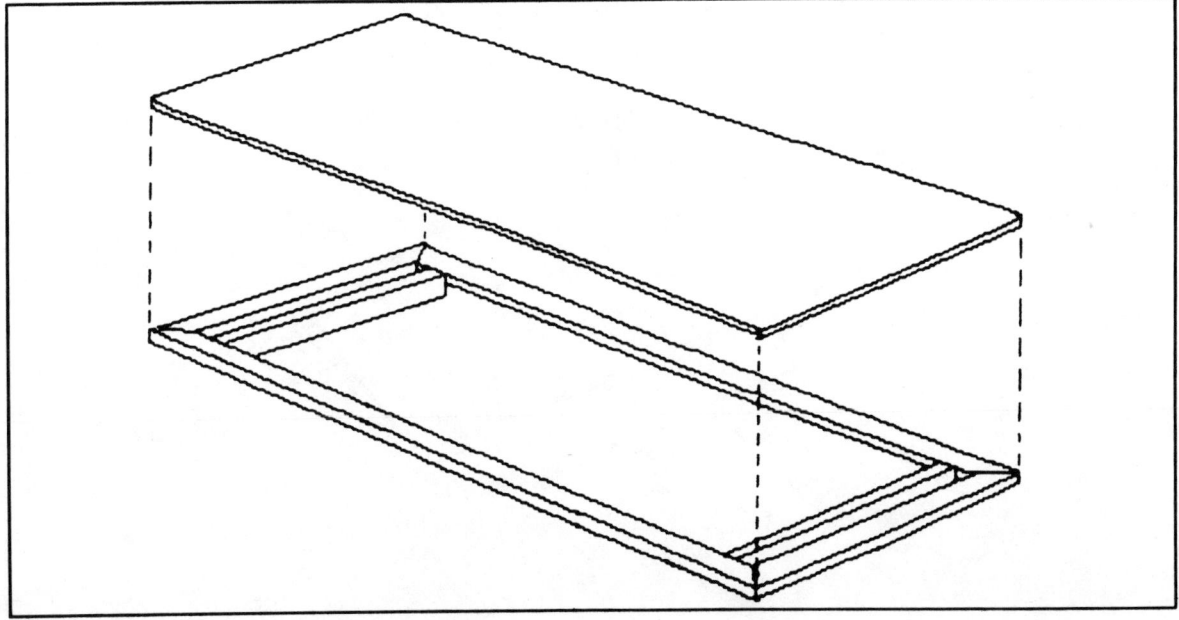

Fig. 5-22. Assembly of top and reinforcing frame.

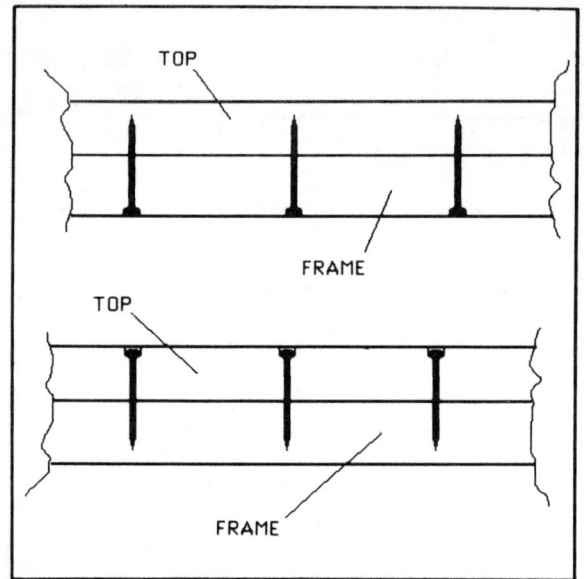

Fig. 5-23. Assembly of table top to frame pieces with nails and glue.

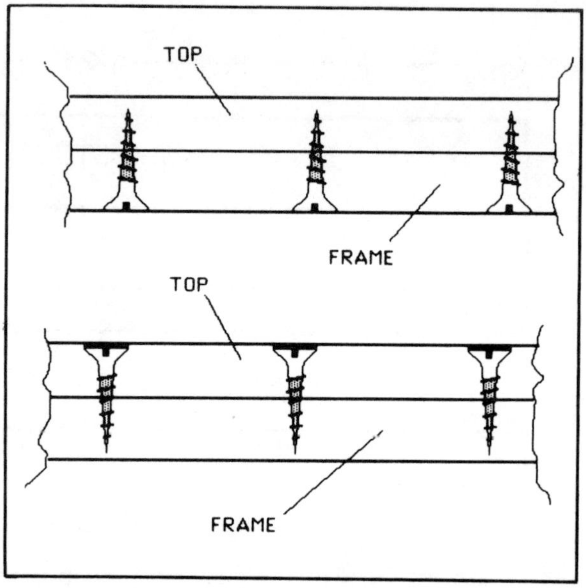

Fig. 5-24. Assembly of table to frame pieces with screws and glue.

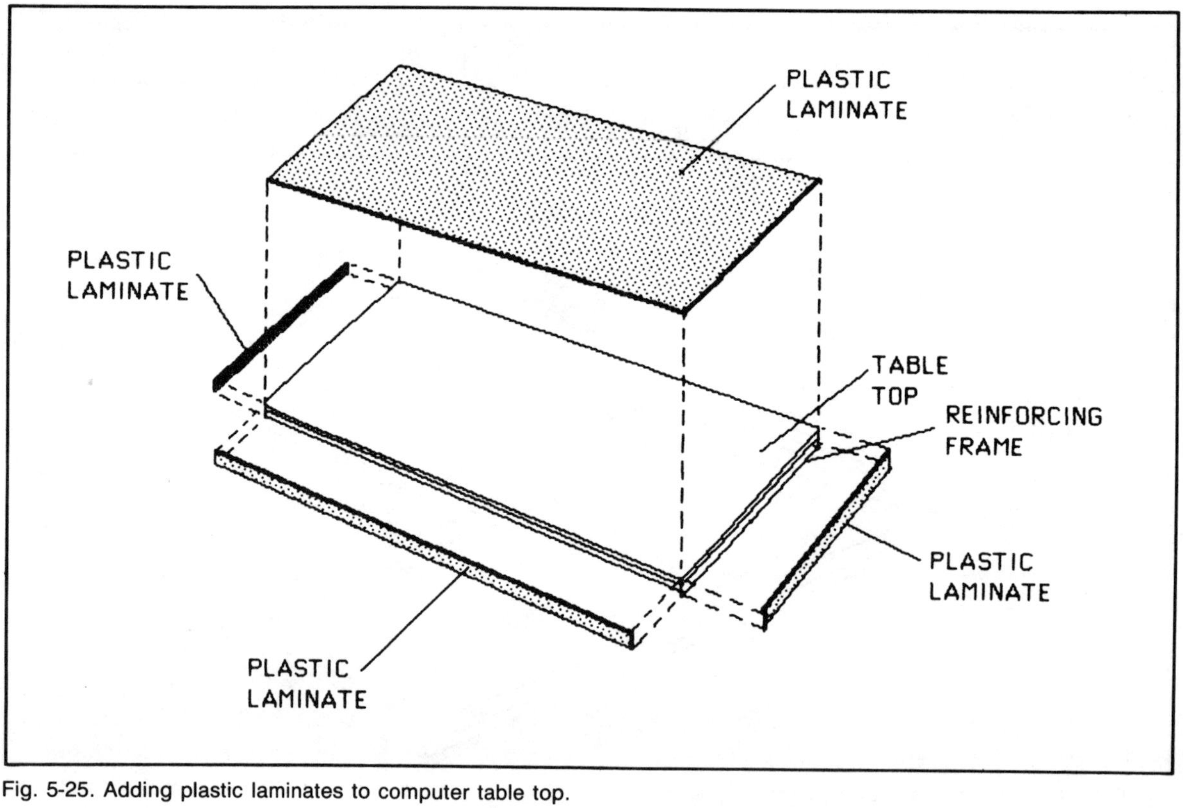

Fig. 5-25. Adding plastic laminates to computer table top.

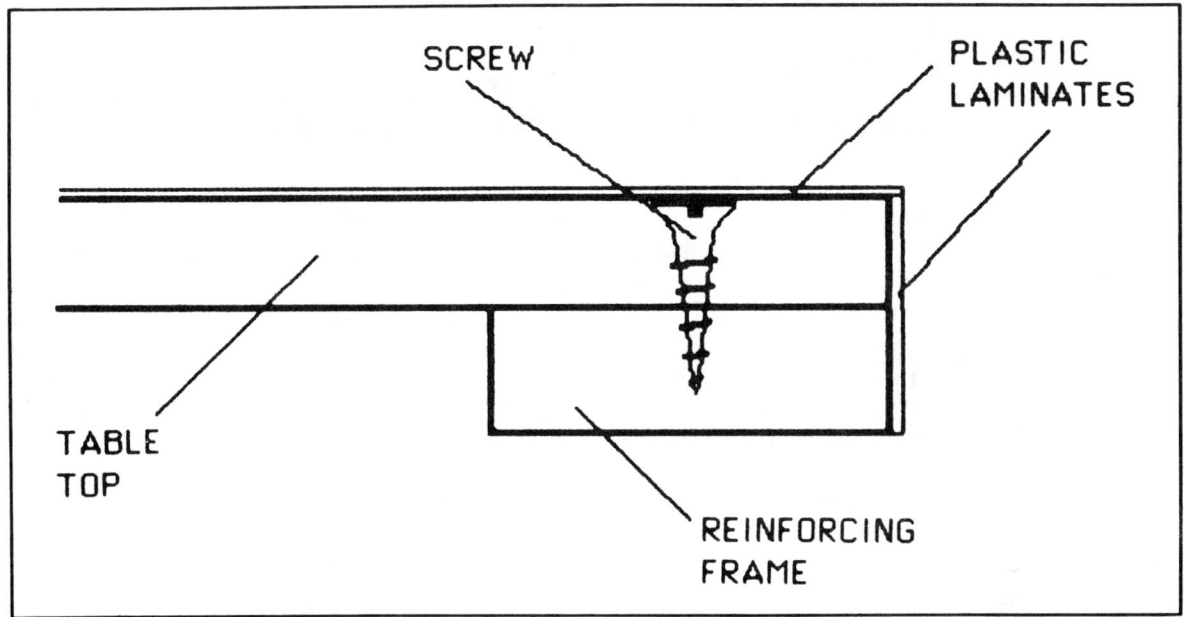

Fig. 5-26. Adding plastic laminates to table top.

• Sand the surface to be covered. This will help ensure good adhesion.

• Mark the plastic laminate to a pattern slightly larger than the area to be covered. Use a straightedge and draw the pattern lines on the finished or pattern side of the laminate. Leave 1/4 inch to 1/2 inch on all sides. This will be trimmed off later.

• If a laminate is to be applied to the forward edge and ends of the table top, apply these first. After installation, as detailed below, trim and file the upper edge of the plastic laminates flush with the upper edge of the plywood table top before installing the plastic laminate to upper surface of the table top.

• Cut the plastic laminate to the pattern marked. Even though the plastic laminate is extremely durable one applied, it is vulnerable to cracking and splitting before it is cemented in place. Fine-tooth handsaws or power saws with fine-tooth blades can be used. A rotary power saw with a 14 to 16 teeth per inch blade is ideal. Place the plastic laminate face up when cutting. Care should be taken so that the plastic laminate is not chipped or broken. An alternate method is to use a carbide tip knife for scoring the plastic by drawing the knife point along a metal straight edge. Cut through the decorative surface. The laminate can then be broken by bending it toward the decorative surface side over the edge of a table or workbench.

• Apply contact cement to the surface of the plywood to be covered and the back side of the plastic laminate. A brush, roller, or metal spreader with a serrated edge can be used to spread the contact cement. A thin even application is important.

• Follow the manufacturer's instructions regarding drying time. Usually, this takes about 20 to 30 minutes.

• Place a sheet of heavy wrapping paper over the plywood surface to be covered. Then position the laminate on the plywood surface with the paper between. The contact cement will not stick to the paper if it has been allowed to dry properly. Make certain that the laminate is positioned correctly. Once the two surfaces of contact cement touch, the laminate sheet cannot be moved again. When everything is lined up properly, pull the paper out from between the plywood and the plastic laminate.

• Using a small block of wood and a hammer,

lightly tap the laminate in place. An alternate method is to use a rolling pin.

- Use a file to remove the surplus plastic laminate from the edges. Another method is to use a special cutter with a router, which allows convenient trimming of excess plastic laminate to flush with the plywood edges.
- The thinner recommended for the contact cement can be used for cleaning contact cement from wood and plastic laminate and tools.

The next step is to construct the shelf, as detailed in Fig. 5-27. If you purchased a piece of plywood that was already cut to the 14-1/2-inch-by-46-1/2 inch size, no additional cutting of the plywood will be required, assuming that it was cut accurately and is a true rectangular form. Check with a square.

If you purchased a larger piece of plywood, you will need to cut out a section for the shelf top. The grain of the top layer should run lengthwise. This is not essential if you are going to add a plastic laminate. To save time, you will use two factory cut edges for your shelf top and cut the other two. Use a ruler and square for making the pattern, marking the lines with a sharp pencil or scribing tool. Saw and sand carefully, following instructions given for making the table top.

Next, add the reinforcing frame to the shelf, as shown in Fig. 5-27. Use a ruler and a square to make the patterns on the framing wood, marking the lines with a sharp pencil or other marking device, then make the necessary saw cuts. The frame pieces should be glued and nailed or screwed in position (see Figs. 5-28 and 5-29). If the plywood shelf top is to be left without a plastic laminate finish, the fasteners should go through the framing and into the plywood. Take care that the fasteners do not pass all the way through the plywood or leave a bulge in the upper surface. If a good glue is used, such as acrylic or epoxy, the glue alone should give adequate strength, and the

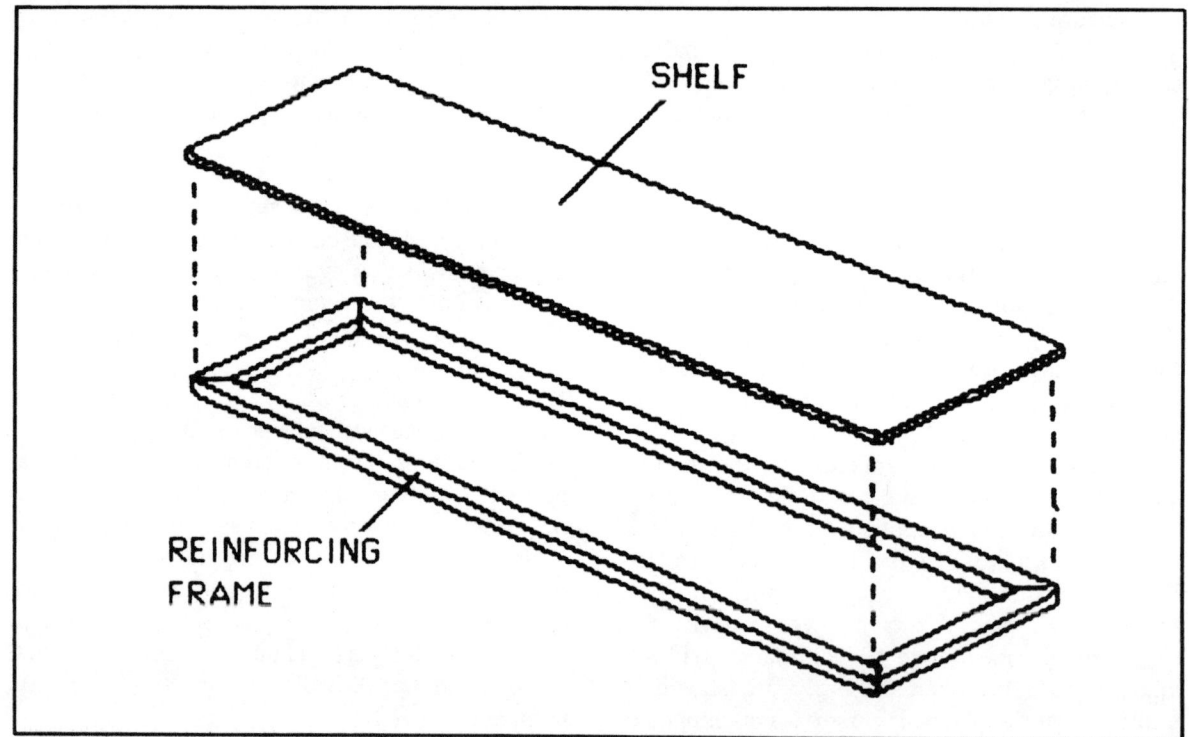

Fig. 5-27. Assembly of shelf top to reinforcing frame.

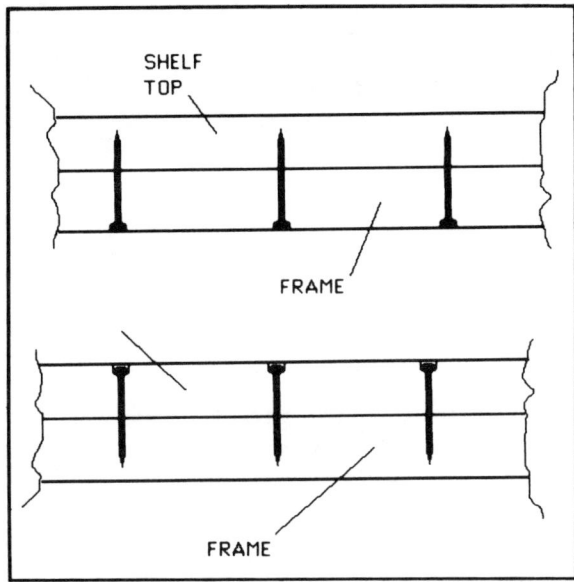

Fig. 5-28. Assembly of shelf top to frame pieces with nails and glue.

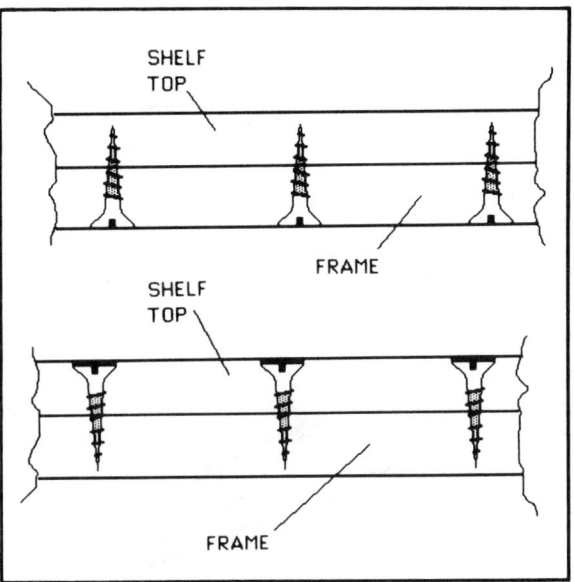

Fig. 5-29. Assembly of shelf top to frame pieces with screws and glue.

fasteners are mainly used as clamps. Fasteners will not have much holding power into the plywood; for greater holding power, the fasteners can be passed through the plywood and into the framing if a plastic laminate is to be added.

The same options are available to finishing the shelf top as for the table: Use the plywood surface as the shelf top and add a wood trim strip to the forward edge. Glue and fasten the trim strip in place with finishing nails. Set the heads below the wood surface and fill holes with wood filler to flush with wood surface.

• Add a plastic laminate to the forward edge, leaving the top natural wood.
• Add a plastic laminate to the top and a wood trim strip to the forward edge.
• Add plastic laminates to both the top and forward edge, as shown in Figs. 5-30 and 5-31.

If a plastic laminate is to be added to the plywood top and/or the forward edge and ends, these can be installed now. If a plastic laminate is to also be applied to the forward edge and ends, it should be applied first. This is then finished flush with the table top. The top laminate is then applied so that the edge overlaps the top edge of the laminate on the forward edge of the table, as shown in Fig. 5-31.

Next, cut the end pieces to rectangular size. A power circular saw is ideal for making straight cuts. Use the suggestions given earlier to prevent chips and splinters.

The next step is to add plastic (Fig. 5-32) or wood (Fig. 5-33) trim to the forward edges of the end pieces. This protects the laminated edges of the plywood and gives a neat appearance.

The assembly of the bottom section is shown in Fig. 5-34. The shelf and backing piece are assembled to the side pieces by both glue and mechanical fasteners. One method is to use finishing nails, passing them through the end pieces and into the framing wood of the shelf and backing piece. Set the heads below the wood surface. Another method is to use through-bolts, as detailed in Fig. 5-35. The floor beams are through-bolted (see Fig. 5-36).

Regardless of the method used, it is extremely important to install the side pieces perpendicular to the shelf in a crosswise direction. Use a square

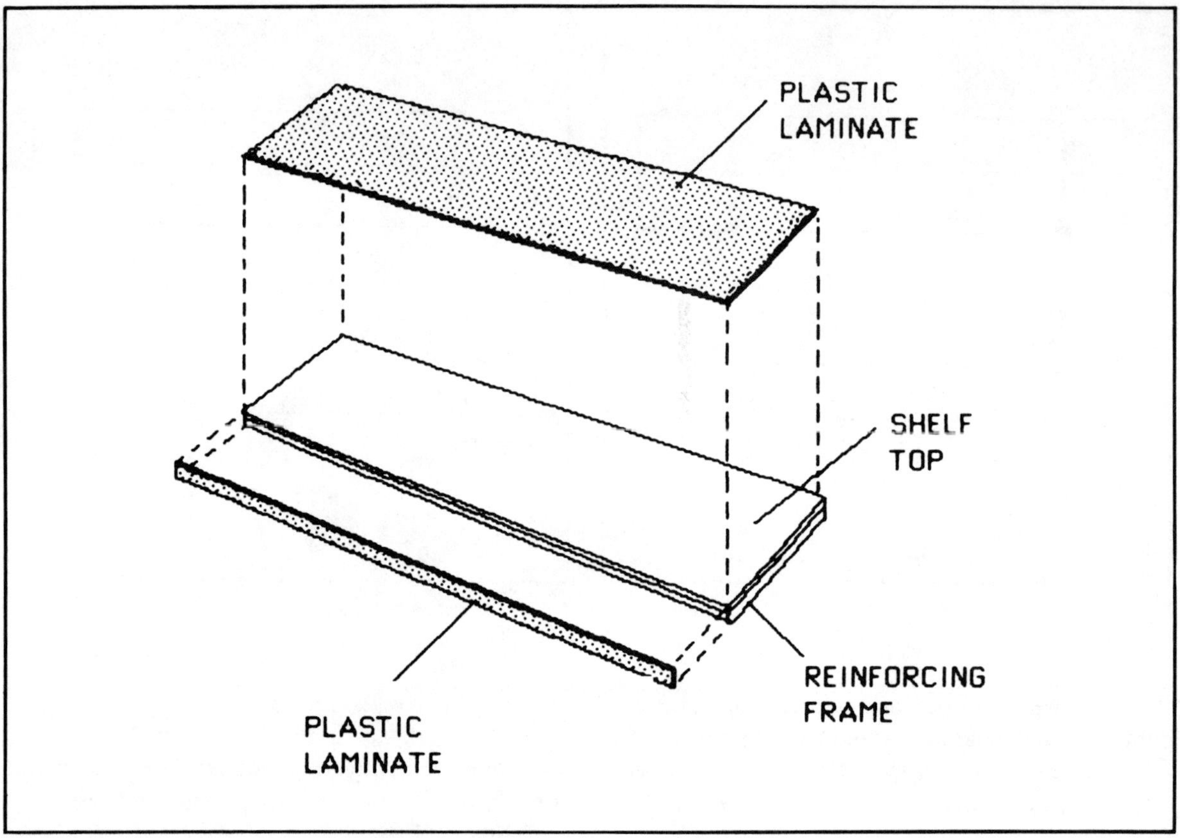

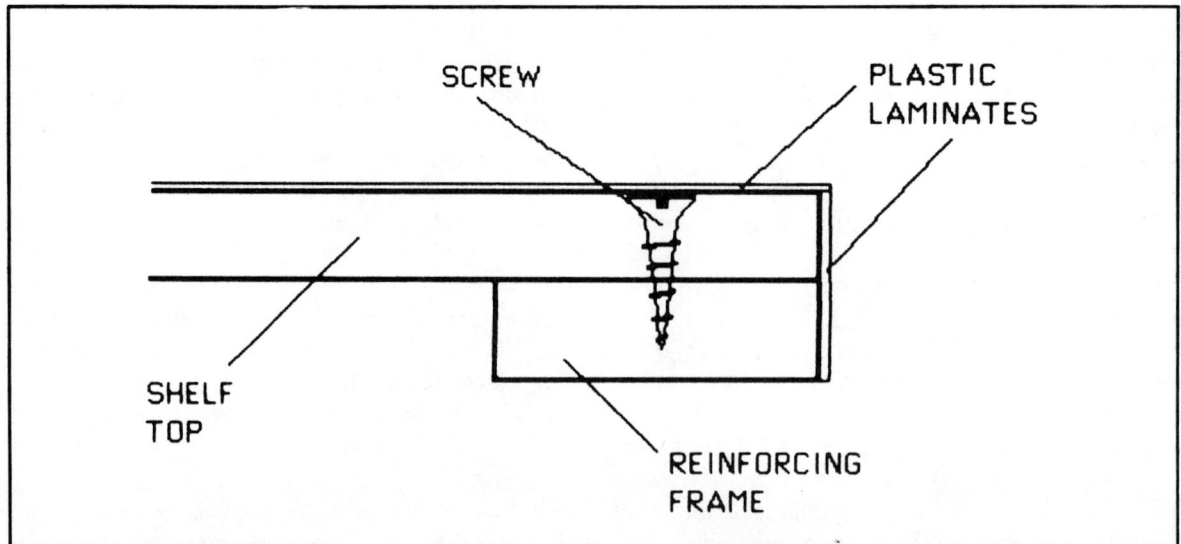

Fig. 5-30. Adding plastic laminate to top and forward edge of shelf.

Fig. 5-31. Adding plastic laminate to shelf top.

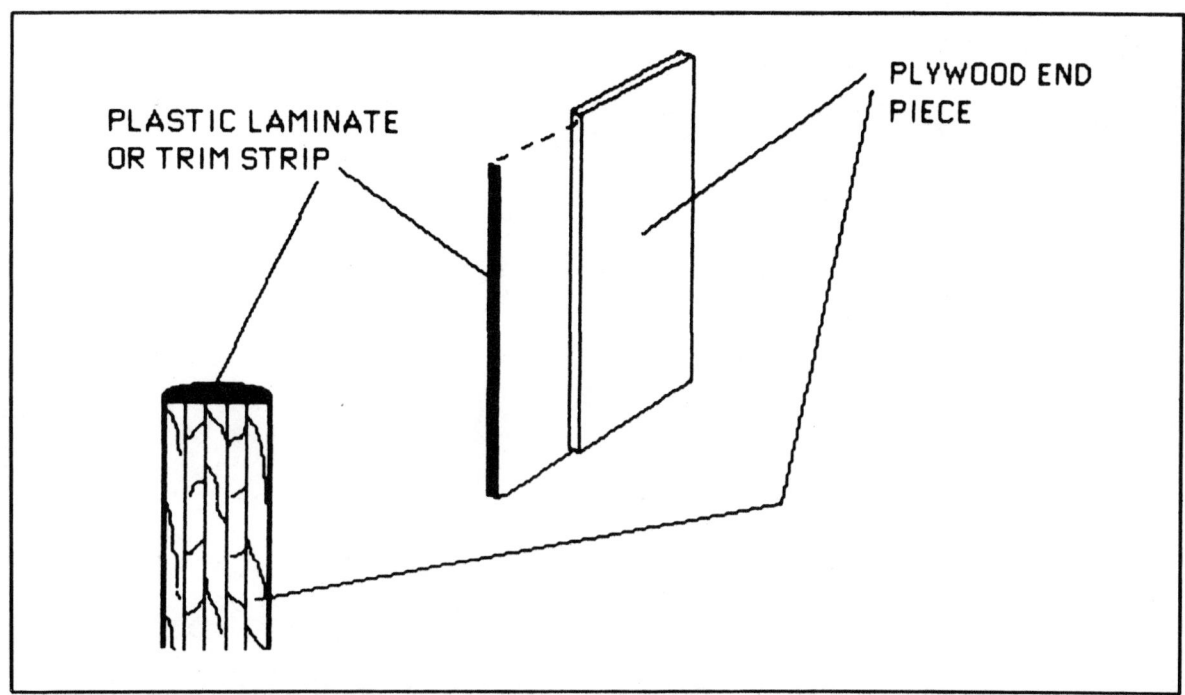

Fig. 5-32. Adding plastic laminate or trim strip to forward edge of plywood end piece.

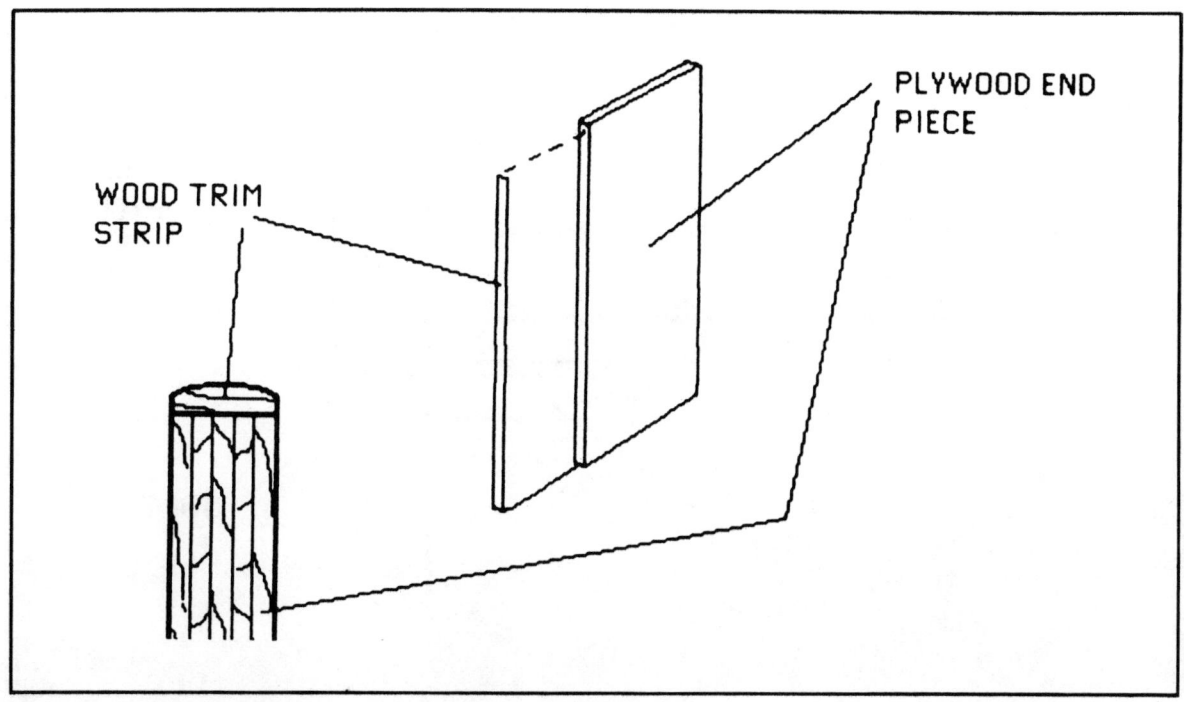

Fig. 5-33. Adding wood trim strip to forward edge of end piece.

243

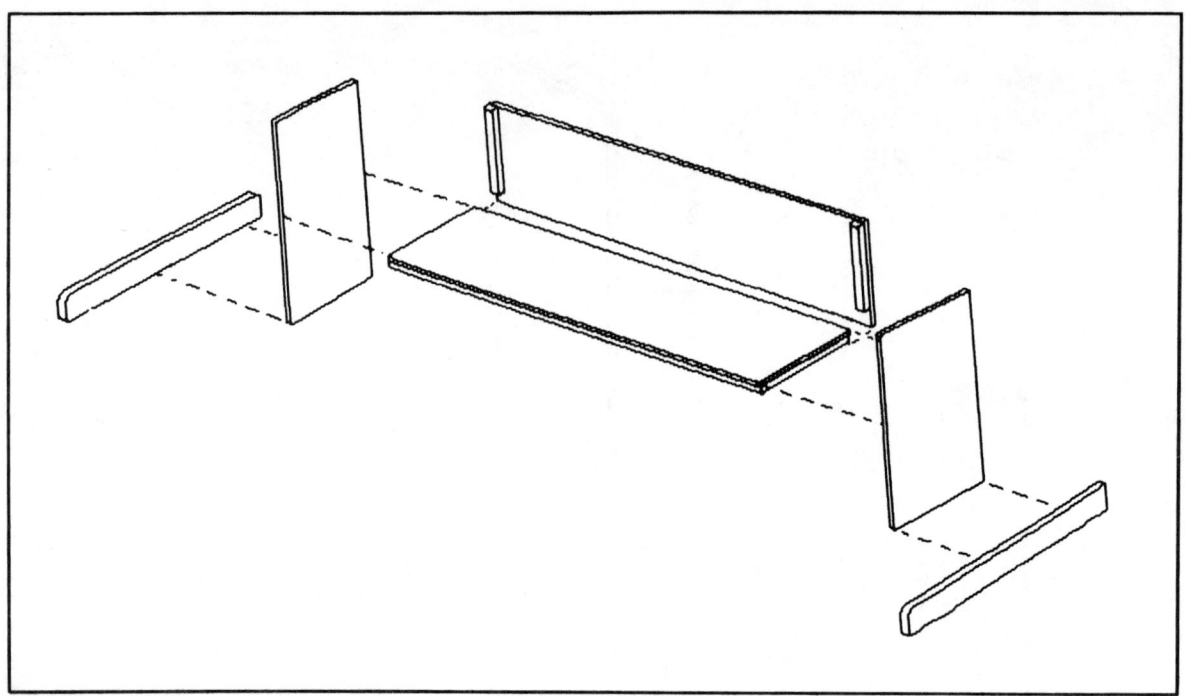

Fig. 5-34. Assembly of bottom section.

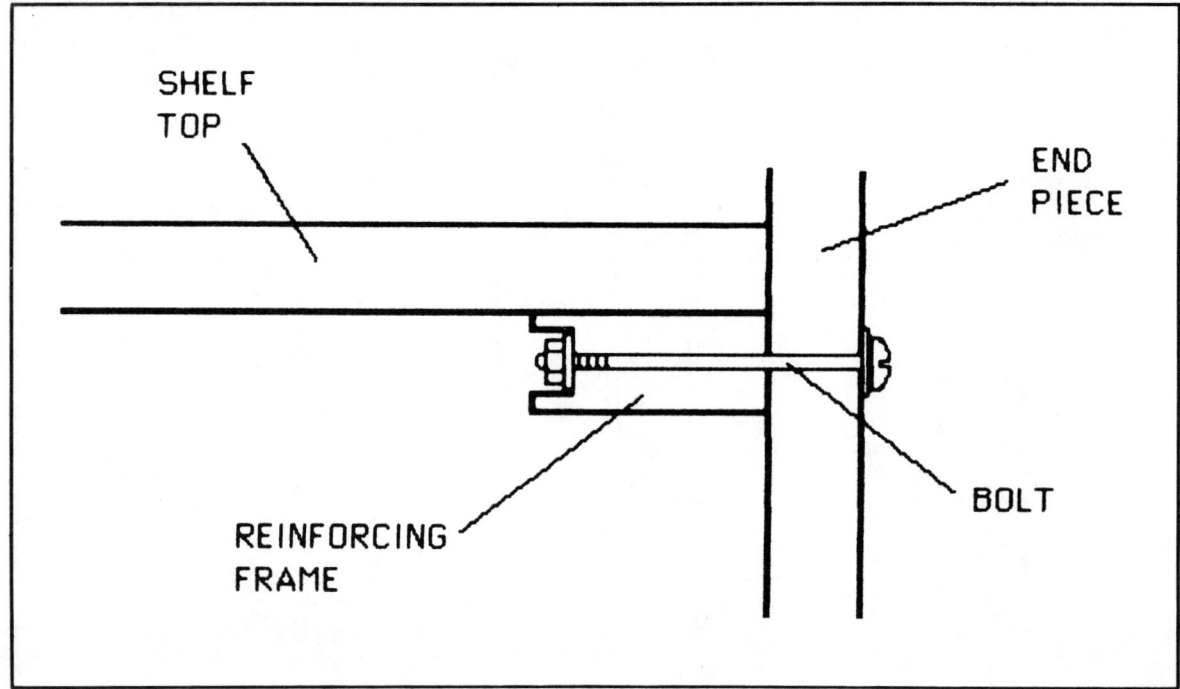

Fig. 5-35. Assembly of shelf to side pieces with bolts.

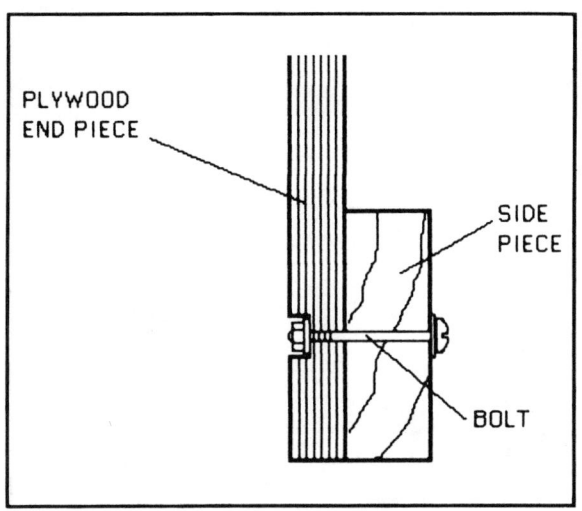

Fig. 5-36. Assembly of end and side pieces with bolts.

to make pattern lines on the side pieces. It is also important to have exactly the same distance between the top of the shelf and the top of the side pieces on both ends.

Figure 5-37 shows the assembled bottom section. The next step is to assemble the table top to the bottom section, as shown in Fig. 5-38. Attachment is by means of bolts that pass through the end pieces and the table beams, as shown in Fig. 5-39.

The floor guides are installed next (see Fig. 5-40). Attachment varies depending on whether they fit in a mounting drilled in the wood beam, are driven or screwed into the wood, or have separate screw fasteners to hold them in place.

Sanding and Finishing

Sanding and applying a finish are important

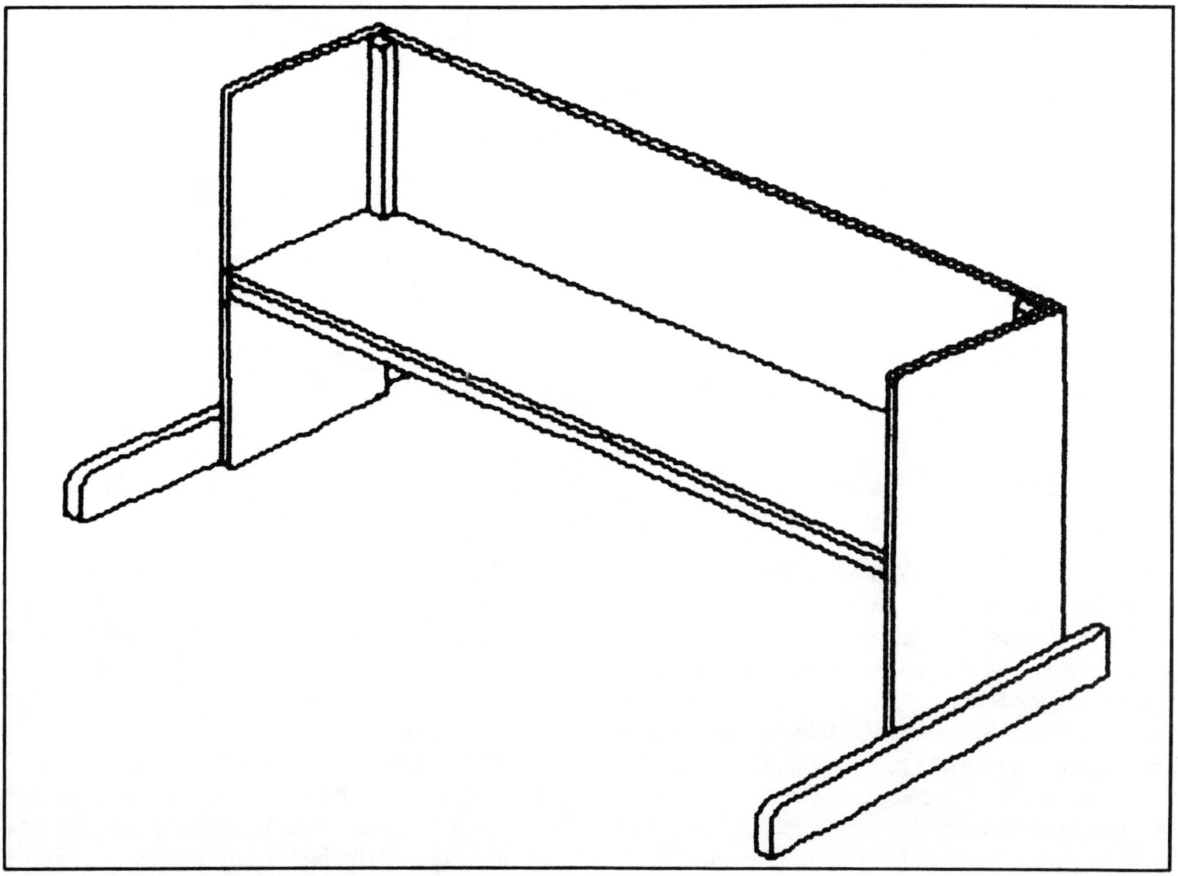

Fig. 5-37. Assembled bottom section.

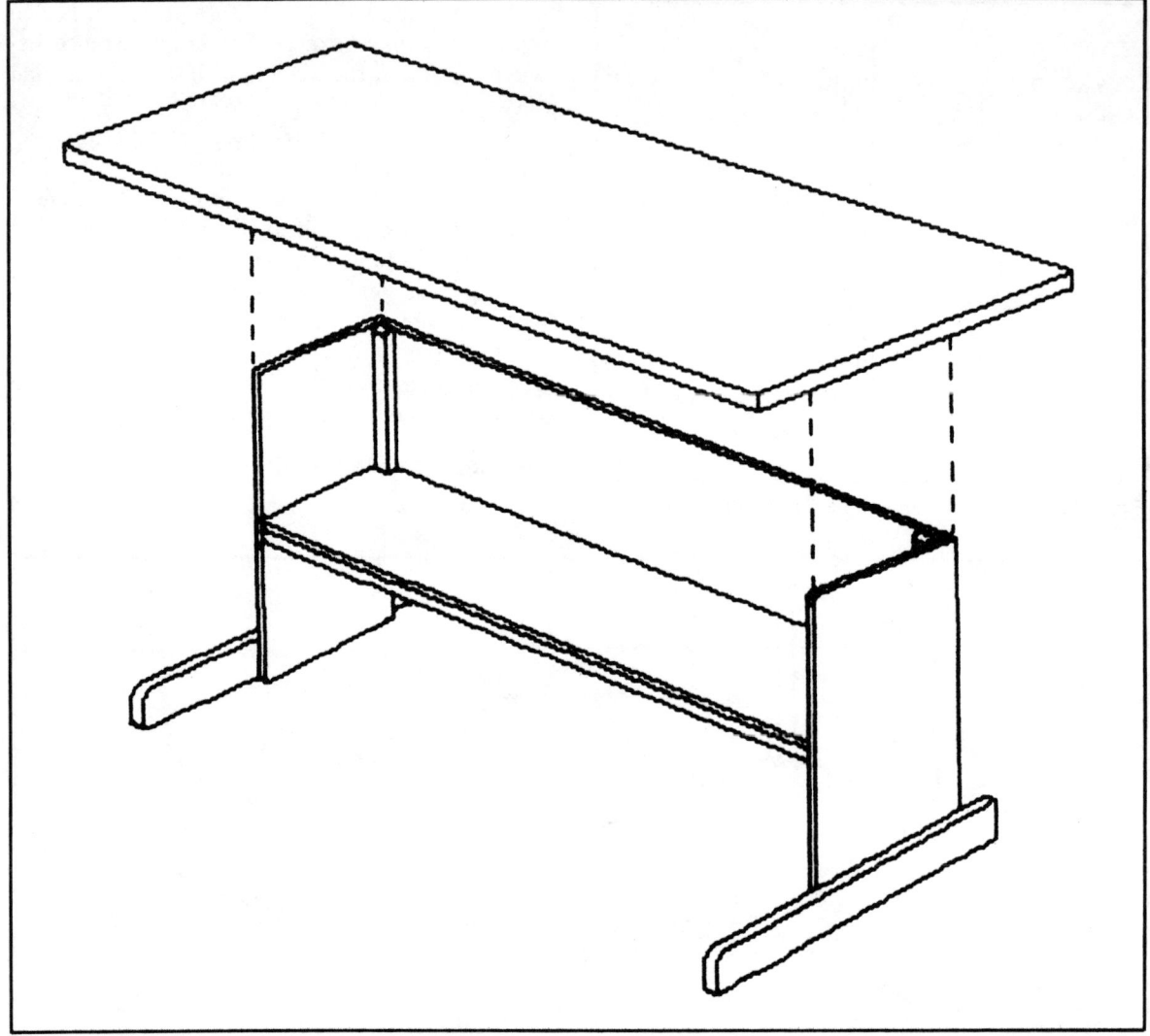

Fig. 5-38. Assembly of table top to bottom section.

steps in the construction process. By taking care and a little time, however, even a beginner can give a table a professional finish.

Sanding prepares the wood for varnishing or painting. Small holes, checks, and other open defects in the wood should be filled in before sanding. If a clear finish is to be applied, use a wood filler that matches the color of the wood. A sanding sealer should be applied before doing any sanding.

The general principle to follow for sanding is to work from coarse grits progressively to finer grits. Don't start with a grit that is coarser than necessary for the particular sanding job, however. The condition of the surface might be such that you can start with a medium or even fine grit; coarse grits leave scratches that need to be sanded away with finer grits.

Sand wood primarily parallel to the grain. Sanding across the grain leaves scratches and tends to tear and roughen the wood surface. A scratch free surface is especially important if you are going to finish with oil or varnish.

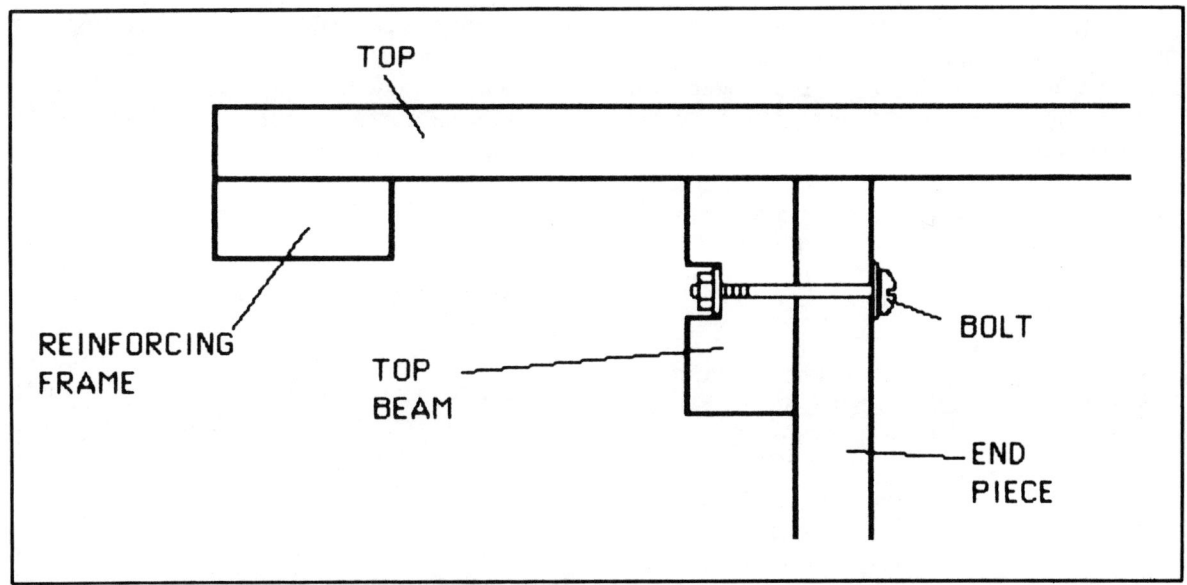

Fig. 5-39. Assembly of top beams to side pieces with bolts.

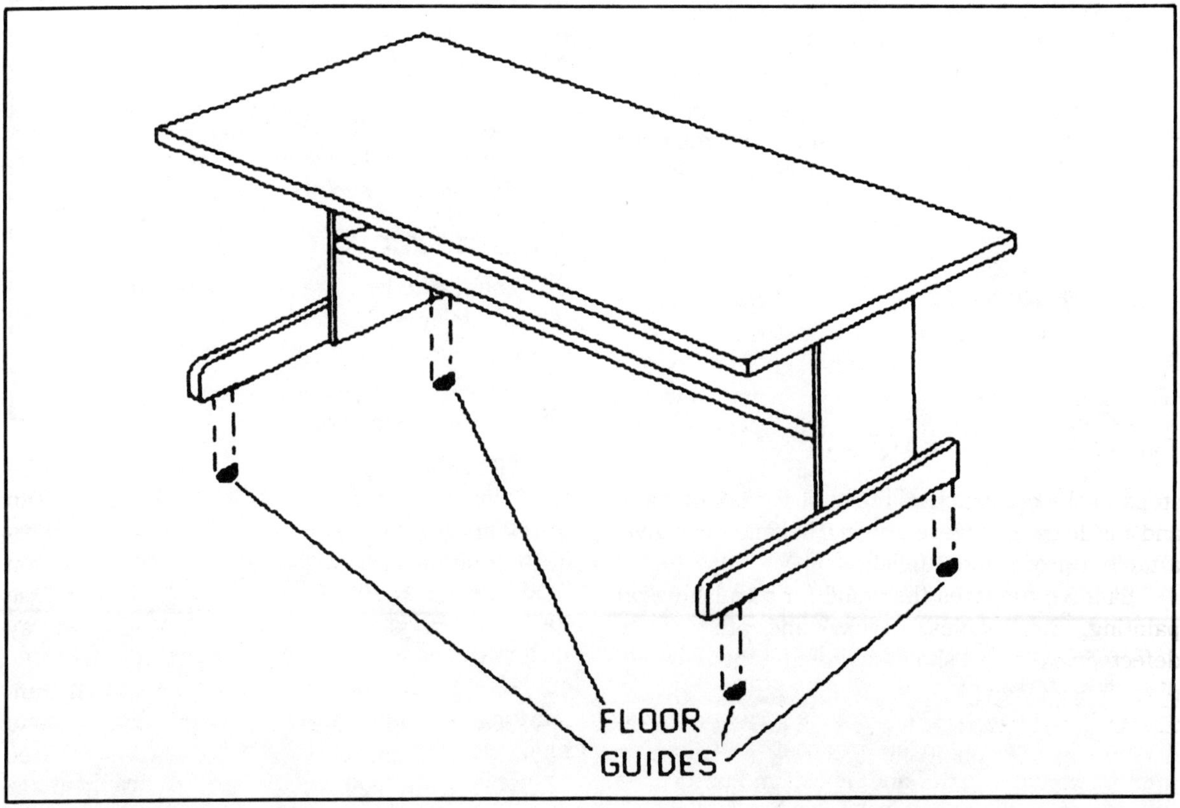

Fig. 5-40. Installing floor guides.

247

For most hand sanding, especially on flat surfaces, use a sanding block rather than holding the sandpaper in your hand. Holding the sandpaper in your hand tends to leave a wavy surface on the wood because pressure is not applied evenly to all areas. A carpet or felt pad between the block and the sandpaper also helps. If desired, a power sander can be used. A pad sander is the easiest to use without damaging the wood surface. Belt sanders can be used by experienced operators.

At the final stages of sanding, use your eyes and fingertips to judge the smoothness of the surface. Taking special care with the sanding is an important step if a fine finish that you will be proud of is to be achieved.

A clear finish (polyurethane plastic is ideal) can be applied directly to natural wood, or you can first stain the wood to give it another color, enhance the natural grain or enrich relatively lifeless woods.

Before applying stain, first test color on a scrap piece of similar wood. Clean the surface area where stain is to be applied, using a cloth to eliminate as much dust as possible. The stain can then be applied with a brush, foam brush applicator, or cloth. Apply a smooth, even coat of stain, allowing the stain to penetrate the wood. Depending on the humidity, temperature, and particular stain used, this usually takes from 5 to 15 minutes. While the stain is still wet, wipe off the excess stain with a clean cloth, but be careful not to remove too much from corners and edges. Wipe across the grain first so that you work the stain into the wood pores. Then give a final wipe with the grain and allow the stain to dry. This usually takes at least 8 hours. The finish can then be applied.

It is usually best to apply a series of light, even coats of clear finish rather than one thick coat. This will minimize possible drips and wrinkles as the finish dries. Apply finish in brush-width strokes in direction of wood grain. Turn table so that finish is applied to wood surface in a horizontal position whenever possible.

A minimum of two coats is recommended. Allow 6 to 8 hours for the first coat to dry before applying second coat. Sand lightly and use a tack cloth to remove sanded finish dust before applying next coat of finish.

Clear or stained finishes are usually applied to natural wood furniture, but if desired color paint finishes can also be applied.

Variations

Variations are possible for the basic modular table. One possibility is to substitute materials, such as using particle board instead of plywood for the top and/or other components. Another common variation is to construct the table with a different size of top. You can also add additional storage shelves below the table and/or use a different shelving arrangement.

The basic modular table makes a functional and attractive table for modular units (it can also be used by itself) even when built from inexpensive woods. This design is ideal for anyone who wants to build computer furniture to sell to others, because the table can be sold either unfinished or with finish applied. More expensive woods, such as oak, can give the table a custom appearance. The plans given here use simple butt joints, but if you have the skill and know-how, you can also use more difficult cabinetry joints.

CONSTRUCTION OF EXTENDERS

The extenders are used for connecting the tables into modular units. There are three basic designs: 90-degree, square, and 60-degree.

90-Degree Extender

The pattern for the top section of the 90-degree extender, which is made from 3/4-inch thick plywood, is shown in Fig. 5-41. If you purchased a larger piece of plywood, such as a standard 4-foot-by-8-foot sheet, you will need to cut out a section for the extender. In most cases, you will use two factory cut edges for your extender and make one cut. Use a ruler and square to draw the pattern, marking the lines with a sharp pencil or scribing tool.

Sawing plywood requires special considerations

to avoid chipping and splintering along the cut edge. Handsaws or power saws with special fine-toothed blades designed especially for plywood should be used; special carbide-tipped blades are best. Applying a strip of masking tape over the area to be cut on both sides of the plywood, but especially on the side opposite the one you are cutting from, is also helpful. Or, clamp a solid piece of wood to the underside and make the cut through both the plywood and the pieces of wood.

Be extremely careful when sanding edges of plywood. Use a sanding block. Avoid sanding the surfaces of plywood until a wood sealer has been applied.

The next step is to add the reinforcing frame to the extender plywood, as shown in Fig. 5-42. Use a ruler and a square to draw the patterns on the framing wood with a sharp marking tool. Make the necessary saw cuts. The frame pieces should be glued and nailed or screwed in position. If the plywood extender top is to be left natural wood (without a plastic laminate being added), the fasteners should go through the framing and into the plywood, but care should be taken so that the fasteners do not pass all the way through the plywood or leave a bulge in the upper surface. If a good glue is used, such as acrylic or epoxy, the glue alone should give adequate strength. The fasteners are mainly used as a clamping device for the gluing. Fasteners will not have much holding power into the plywood. To give greater holding power, the fasteners can be passed through the plywood and into the framing if a plastic laminate is to be added.

A plastic laminate is installed as follows:

• All holes and defects in the surface of the plywood should be filled with putty or wood filler.

• Sand the surface to be covered. This will help ensure good adhesion.

• Mark the plastic laminate to a pattern slightly larger than the area to be covered. Use a straightedge and draw the pattern lines on the finished or pattern side of the laminate. Leave 1/4 inch to 1/2 inch on all sides. This will be trimmed off later.

• Cut the plastic laminate to the pattern marked. Even though the plastic laminate is extremely durable once applied, it is vulnerable to cracking and splitting before it is cemented in place.

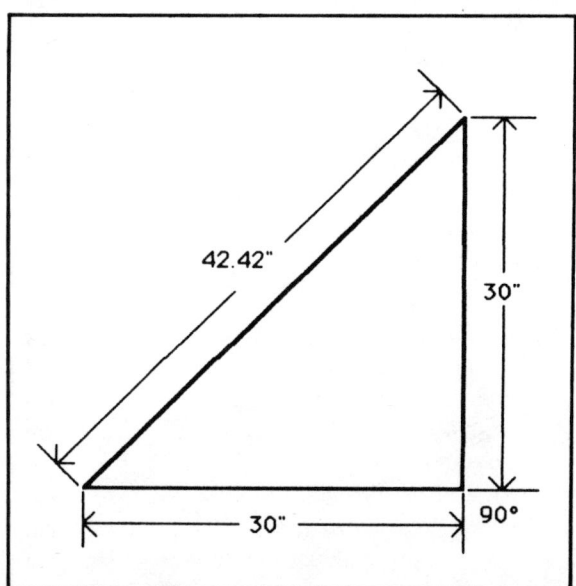

Fig. 5-41. Pattern for 90 degree extender.

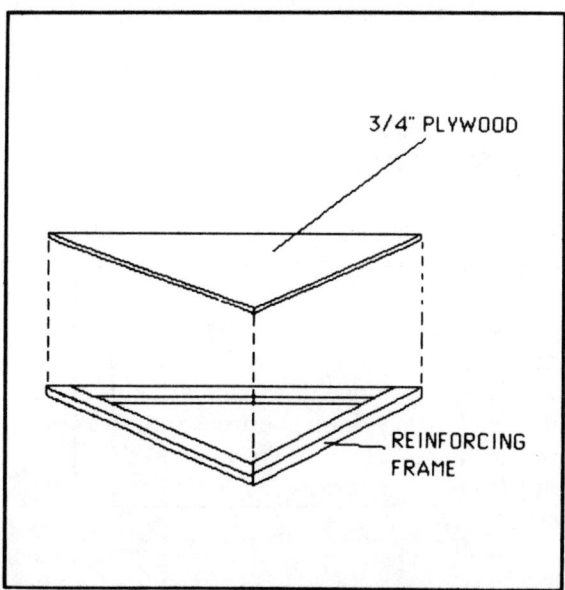

Fig. 5-42. Assembly of 90 degree extender.

Fine-tooth handsaws or power saws with fine-tooth blades can be used; a rotary power saw with a 14 to 16 teeth per inch blade is ideal. Place the plastic laminate face up when cutting and be careful that the plastic laminate is not chipped or broken. You can use a carbide tip knife to score the plastic by drawing the knife point along a metal straightedge. Cut through the decorative surface side over the edge of a table or workbench.

• Apply contact cement to the surface of the plywood to be covered and the back side of the plastic laminate. A brush, roller, or metal spreader with a serrated edge can be used to spread the contact cement. A thin even application is important.

• Follow the manufacturer's instructions regarding drying time. Usually, this takes about 20 to 30 minutes.

• Place a sheet of heavy wrapping paper over the plywood surface to be covered. Then position the laminate on the plywood surface with the paper between. The contact cement will not stick to the paper if it has been allowed to dry properly. Make certain that the laminate is positioned correctly. Once the two surfaces of contact cement touch, the laminate sheet cannot be moved again. When everything is lined up properly, pull the paper out from between the plywood and the plastic laminate.

• Using a small block of wood and a hammer, lightly tap the laminate in place. An alternate method is to use a rolling pin.

• Use a file to remove the surplus plastic laminate from the edges. Another method is to use a special cutter with a router, which allows convenient trimming of excess plastic laminate to flush with the plywood edges.

• The thinner recommended for the contact cement can be used for cleaning contact cement from wood and plastic laminate and tools.

This completes the construction of the 90-degree extender. The extender can be attached to the table tops by using metal straps with screws fastening it to the extender and table top frames. You may also choose to use special table fasteners available at hardware stores.

Square Extender

The pattern for the tops section of the square extender, which is made from 3/4-inch thick plywood, is shown in Fig. 5-43. If you purchase a larger piece of plywood, cut out a section for the

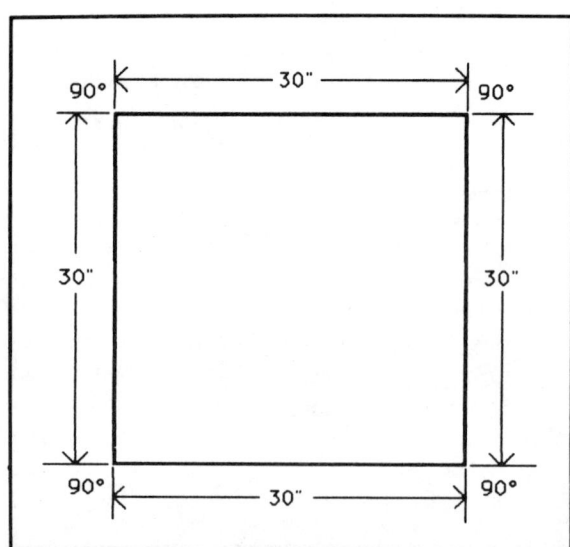

Fig. 5-43. Pattern for square extender.

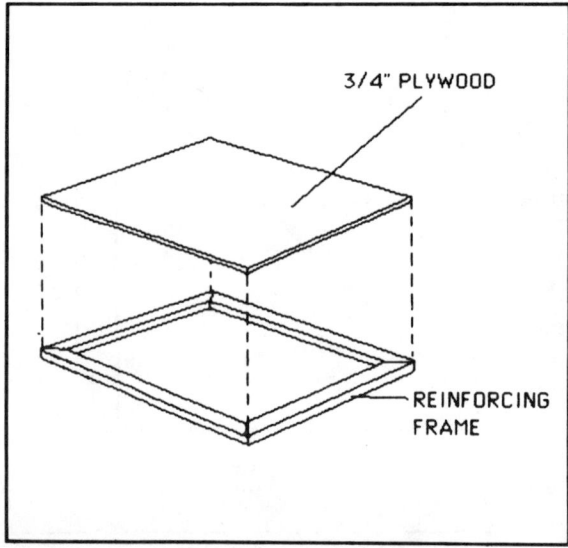

Fig. 5-44. Assembly of square extender.

extender. Use two factory cut edges for your extender and make two cuts. Use a ruler and square and mark the lines with a sharp pencil or scribing tool.

When sawing plywood, special care must be taken to avoid splintering and chipping along the cut edge. Handsaws or power saws with special fine-toothed or carbide-tipped blades designed especially for plywood should be used. A strip of masking tape applied over the cutting line on both sides of the plywood, but especially on the side opposite you, is also helpful. You may also choose to clamp a solid piece of wood to the underside and make the cut through both the plywood and the piece of wood.

Be extremely careful when sanding edges of plywood. Use a sanding block. Avoid sanding the surfaces of plywood until a wood sealer has been applied.

The next step is to add the reinforcing frame to the plywood, as shown in Fig. 5-44. Use a ruler and a square for making the patterns on the framing wood, marking the lines with a sharp pencil or other marking device. Then make the necessary saw cuts, as detailed in Chapter 2. The frame pieces should be glued and nailed or screwed in position. If the plywood extender top will be left without a plastic laminate covering, the fasteners should go through the framing and into the plywood, but they should not pass all the way through the plywood or leave a bulge in the upper surface. If a good acrylic or epoxy glue is used, the glue alone should give adequate strength and the fasteners are mainly used as a clamping device. They will not have much holding power in the plywood. To give greater holding power, the fasteners can be passed through the plywood and into the framing if a plastic laminate is to be added.

A plastic laminate is installed according to directions given for the 90-degree extender above.

This completes the construction of the square extender. The extender can be attached to the table top frames by using metal straps with screw fasteners, or special table fasteners, available at hardware stores, can be used.

60-Degree Extender

The pattern for the top section of the 60-degree extender, which is made from 3/4-inch thick plywood, is shown in Fig. 5-45. If you purchased a large, standard sheet of plywood, you will need to cut out a section for the extender. In most cases, you will use one factory cut edge for your extender and make two cuts. Use a ruler and square to scribe the pattern lines onto the wood.

Sawing plywood requires special considerations. Special care must be taken to avoid chipping and splintering along the cut edge. Handsaws or power saws with special fine-toothed blades designed especially for plywood should be used. Even better are special carbide-tipped blades. Applying a strip of masking tape over the area to be cut on both sides of the plywood, but especially on the side opposite the one you are cutting from, is also helpful. Another possibility is to clamp a solid piece of wood to the underside and make the cut through both the plywood and the piece of wood.

Be extremely careful when sanding edges of plywood. Use a sanding block. Avoid sanding the surfaces of plywood until a wood sealer has been applied.

The next step is to add the reinforcing frame to the plywood, as shown in Fig. 5-46. Use a ruler and a square to make the patterns on the framing wood, marking the lines with a sharp pencil or other marking device. Then make the necessary saw cuts. The frame pieces should be glued and nailed or screwed in position. If the plywood extender top will be left with a natural wood finish, the fasteners should go through the framing and into the plywood, being careful that they do not pass all the way through the plywood or leave a bulge in the upper surface. If a good glue is used, such as acrylic or epoxy, the glue alone should give adequate strength. The fasteners are mainly used as a clamping device for the gluing. Fasteners will not have much holding power into the plywood. To give greater holding power, the fasteners can be passed through the plywood and into the framing if a plastic laminate is to be added.

A plastic laminate is installed according to the

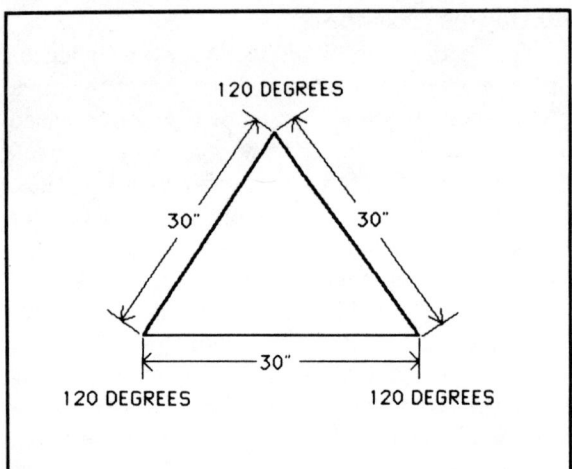

Fig. 5-45. Pattern for 60 degree extender.

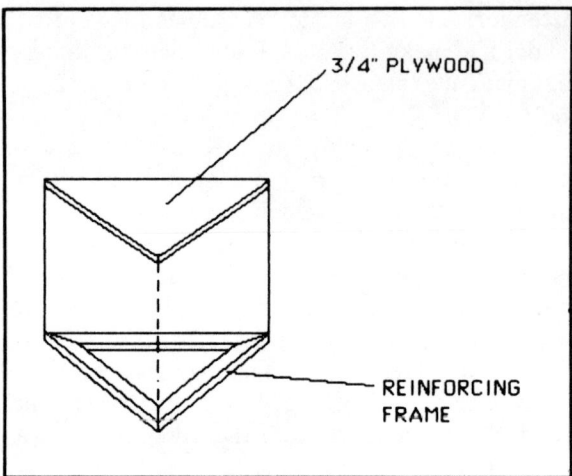

Fig. 5-46. Assembly of 60 degree extender.

instructions given for the 90-degree extender above.

This completes the construction of the 60-degree extender. It can be joined to the table tops with metal straps and screw fasteners attached to the extender and table top frames or special table fasteners, available at hardware stores, can be used.

Chapter 6

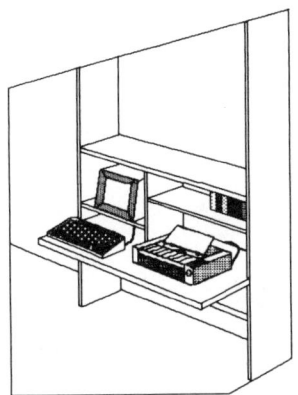

Built-In Wall Units

There are many possibilities for built-in computer furniture; this chapter details a basic built in wall unit that includes a storage shelf below the table and an overhead rack. This unit can be built to the plans given below or modified to fit your particular needs.

The construction is mainly from plywood. This unit is of attractive and modern design and gives a good appearance even when built from standard plywood. You can give it a custom appearance by making the same design from more expensive plywoods, such as those faced with oak or other hardwoods.

The built-in wall unit is shown in Fig. 6-1. The top has space for both a computer and printer. The table and shelves can have a natural wood tops or be covered with plastic laminates (Fig. 6-2). The table features a shelf underneath that provides storage space and an attractive video and storage rack.

CONSTRUCTION

The construction is based on two vertical side pieces, which should be firmly attached to the wall and floor and ceiling.

Materials

The patterns for the wood parts are shown in Fig. 6-3. The top of the table is a 30-inch-by-4-foot piece of 3/4-inch thick plywood. If you intend to use the wood surface as the finished table top, without adding a plastic laminate, hardwood-faced plywood is recommended. If a laminate is to be added, even an exterior grade of shop plywood will suffice.

The shelves are 3/4-inch thick plywood. The upper and lower shelves measures 46 1/2 inches by 15 inches. The other shelf pieces are detailed in Fig. 6-3. The wall mounted end pieces can be of any desired wood stock of 15-inch depth from the wall when attached.

Plywood is normally sold in standard 4-foot-by-8-foot sheets. Lay out the patterns to take advantage of this standard size and arrange them to keep waste to a minimum. Some lumberyards and plywood stores will cut plywood sheets for you to

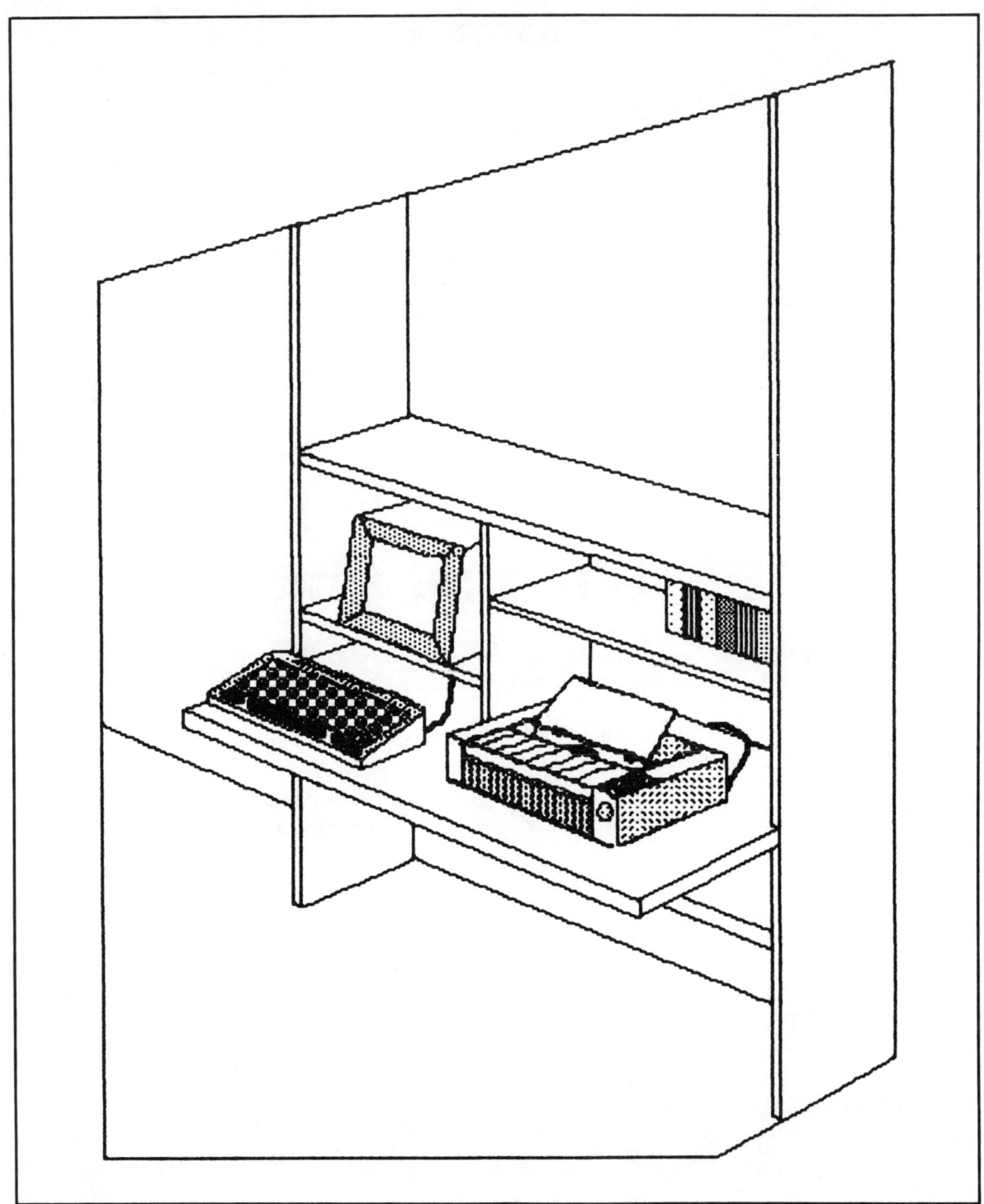

Fig. 6-1. Built-in wall unit.

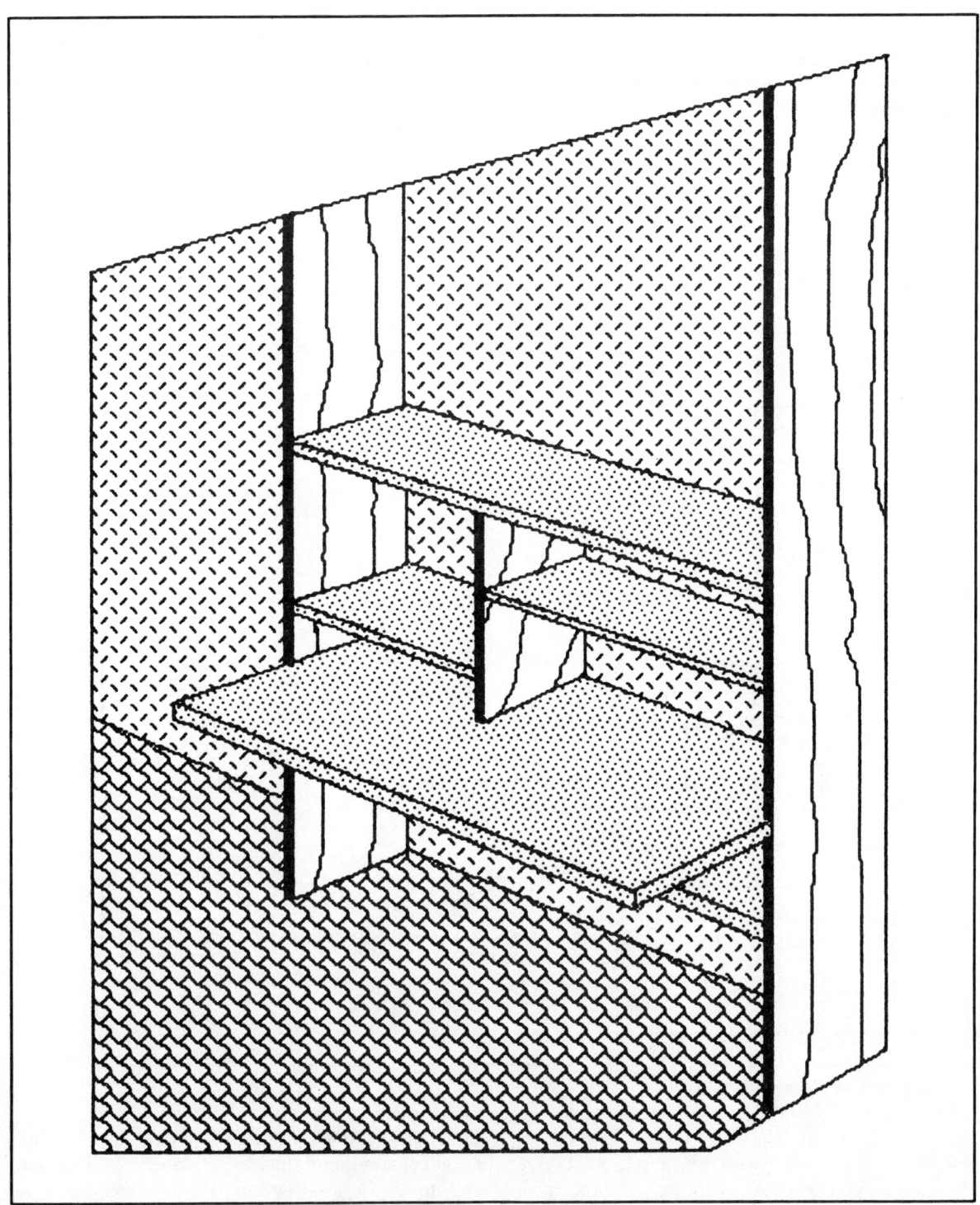
Fig. 6-2. Built-in wall unit with plastic laminates.

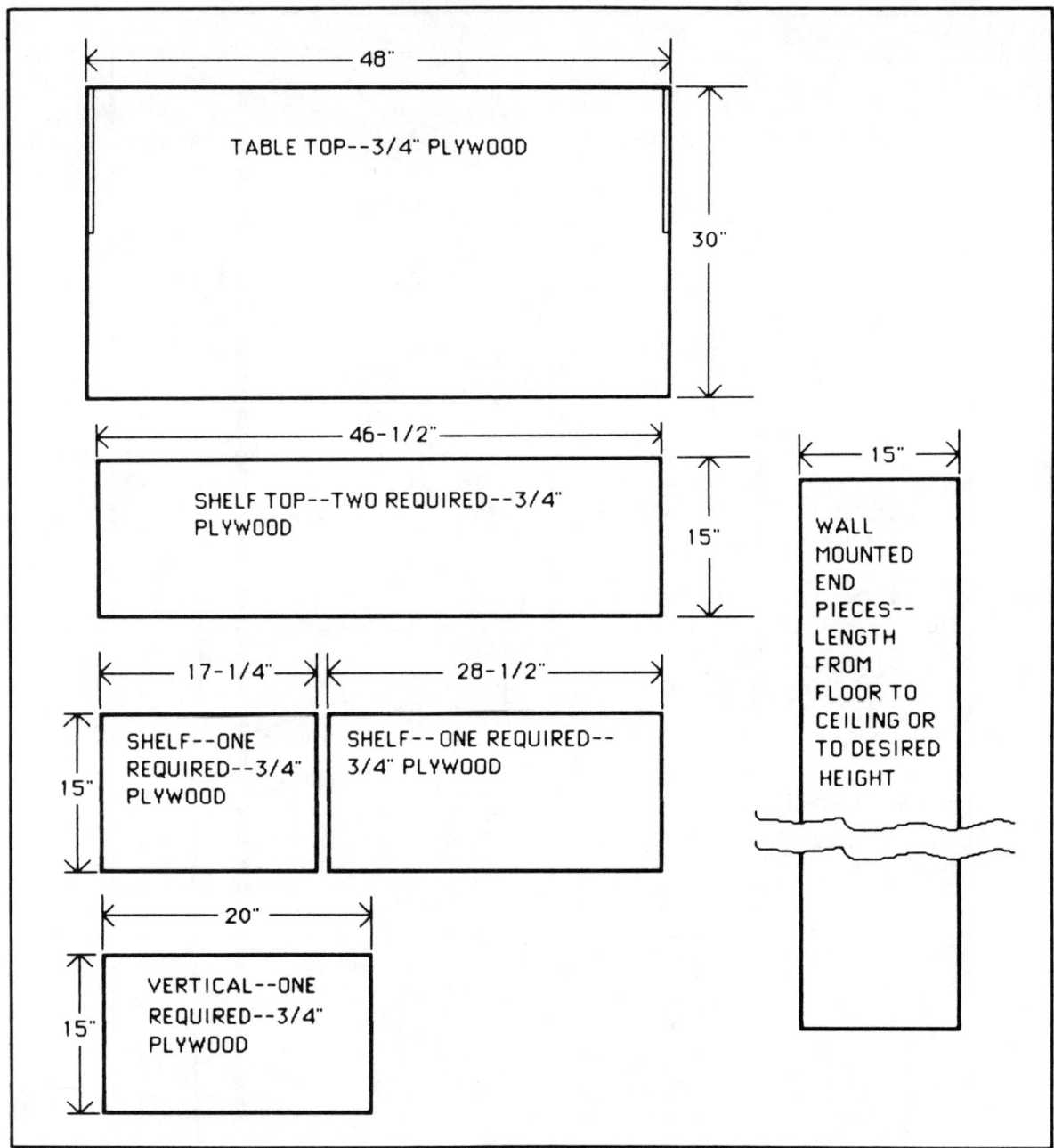

Fig. 6-3. Patterns for wood parts.

desired size, usually at additional cost. This can be worthwhile if you don't need full sheets, don't have room to carry full sheets in your car, or don't have a saw to accurately cut plywood.

Half-inch thick plywood could also be used, but I don't recommend this. You'll save very little and end up with a weaker unit. Particle board can be substituted for the plywood if you are on an absolute minimum budget and a lot of cheaply made high priced manufactured computer furniture is made from particle board covered by plastic laminates. It can be difficult to work with, however, and it is very difficult to get plastic laminates to bond properly to this material without special equipment. (It must be difficult even with special machinery, because laminates on manufactured furniture often seem to come loose at the edges.)

Two beams, 26 inches long, of 2-inch-by-4-inch wood stock are used as beams under the table. You will also need 1-inch-by-2-inch or larger framing stock for use under the plywood table top and the lower shelf.

A variety of wood and plastic trim strips can be used to cover the exposed edges of the plywood, as detailed later in this section. A wood or plastic trim strip is used to cover the forward edges of the table top and lower shelf. These pieces are 48 inches and 46 1/2 inches long, respectively, and about 1 3/4 inches wide. Minimum width should be such that it will completely cover the widths of the plywood (3/4 inch) and the framing approximately 7/8 inch. The trim strips can be slightly wider than this.

Nails, screws, or bolts can be used for assembly, as detailed below in this section. You will also need a suitable wood glue. And a quantity of the finish of your choice.

The table top can be left natural or a plastic laminate top can be added. If a plastic laminate is to be added, you will need a 30-inch-by-4-foot piece and suitable contact cement for attaching it to the plywood. If desired, the shelf tops can also be covered with plastic laminates.

Assembly

An overview of the complete assembly is shown in Fig. 6-4. Begin by constructing the table top, as detailed in Fig. 6-5. If you purchased a piece of plywood that was already cut to the 30-inch-by-4-foot size, no additional cuts will be required, assuming that it was cut accurately and is a truly rectangular form. You might want to check this with a square.

If you purchased a larger piece of plywood, such as a standard sheet, you will need to cut out a section for the table top. Try to have the grain of the top layer running lengthwise. This is not essential if you are going to add a plastic laminate. Use two factory cut edges for your table top and cut the other two. Use a ruler and square to make the pattern, marking the lines with a sharp pencil or scribing tool.

Sawing plywood requires special considerations to avoid chipping and splintering along the cut edge. Power saws or handsaws with special fine-toothed or carbide-tipped blades designed especially for plywood should be used. A strip of masking tape applied over the area to be cut on both sides of the plywood, but especially on the side opposite the one you are cutting from, is also helpful. You can also clamp a solid piece of wood to the underside and make the cut through both the plywood and the piece of wood.

Be extremely careful when sanding edges of plywood. Use a sanding block. Avoid sanding the surfaces of plywood until a wood sealer has been applied.

The next step is to add the reinforcing frame to the plywood, as shown in Fig. 6-5. Use a ruler and a square to mark the pattern lines on the framing wood with a sharp pencil or other marking device. Then make the necessary saw cuts, as detailed in Chapter 2. The frame pieces should be glued and nailed or screwed in position (see Figs. 6-6 and 6-7). If the plywood top is to be left natural wood (without a plastic laminate being added), the fasteners should go through the framing and into the plywood, but care should be taken so that the fasteners do not pass all the way through the plywood or leave a bulge in the upper surface. A good acrylic or epoxy glue alone should give adequate strength, and the fasteners are mainly used as a clamping device for the gluing. Fasteners will not have much holding power into the plywood. To give greater holding power, the fasteners can be passed through the plywood and into the framing if a plastic laminate is to be added.

Various options are available for finishing off the table top. One possibility is to use the plywood surface as the top and add wood trim strips to the

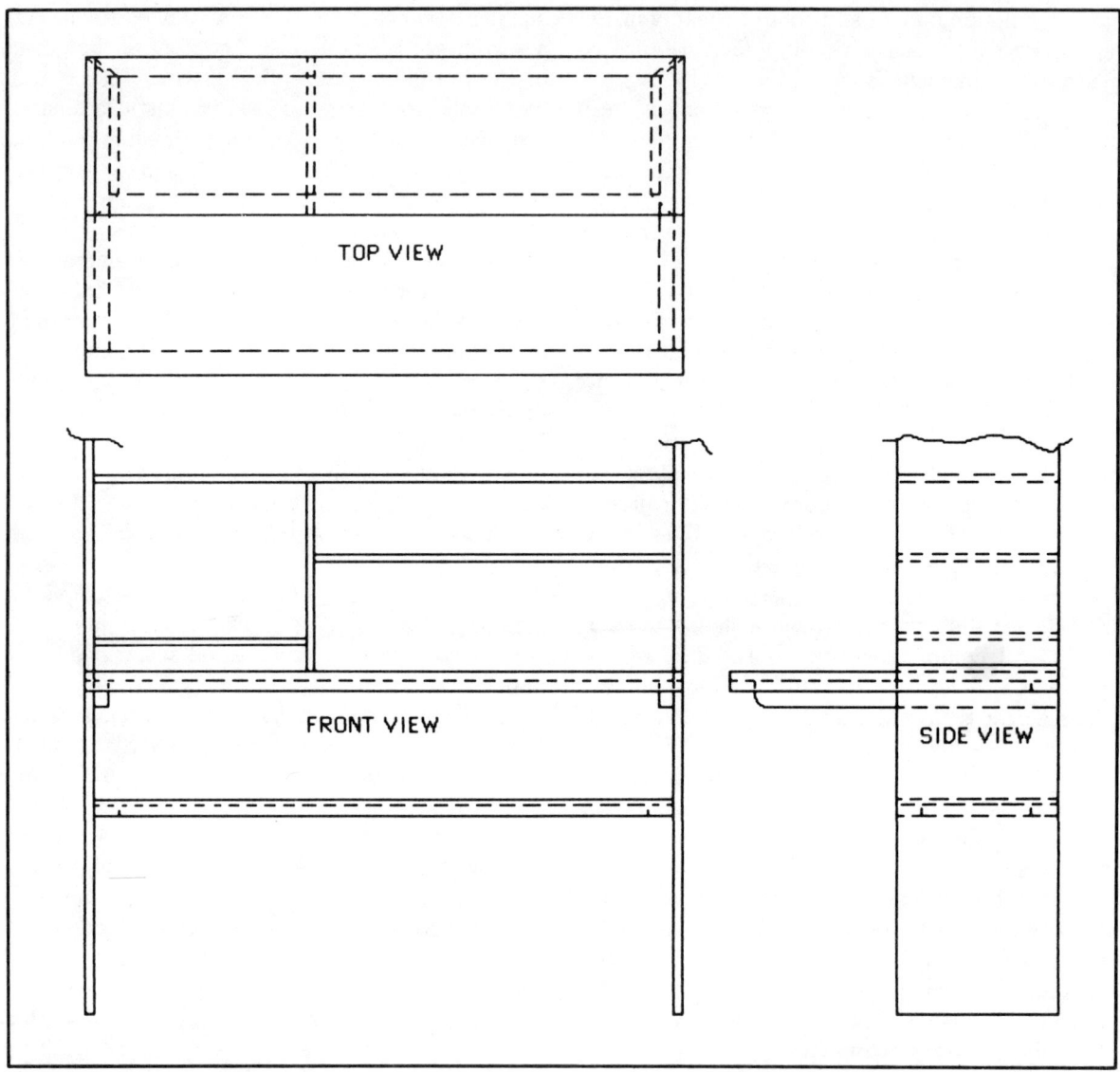

Fig. 6-4. Built-in wall unit.

forward edge and ends, as shown in Fig. 6-8. Glue and fasten the trim strips in place with finishing nails. Set the heads below the wood surface and fill holes with wood filler to flush with the wood surface.

A second possibility is to add plastic laminates to the forward edge and ends of the table top and leave the top natural wood, as detailed in Fig. 6-9.

Another method is to add a plaster laminate to the top and a wood trim strips to the forward edge and ends of the table top, as shown in Fig. 6-10. Still another possibility is to add plastic laminates to both the top and edges, as shown in Figs. 6-11 and 6-12.

If a plastic laminate is to be added to the plywood table top and/or edges, these can be installed at this time. Plastic laminates are often applied to plywood for computer table tops. A large

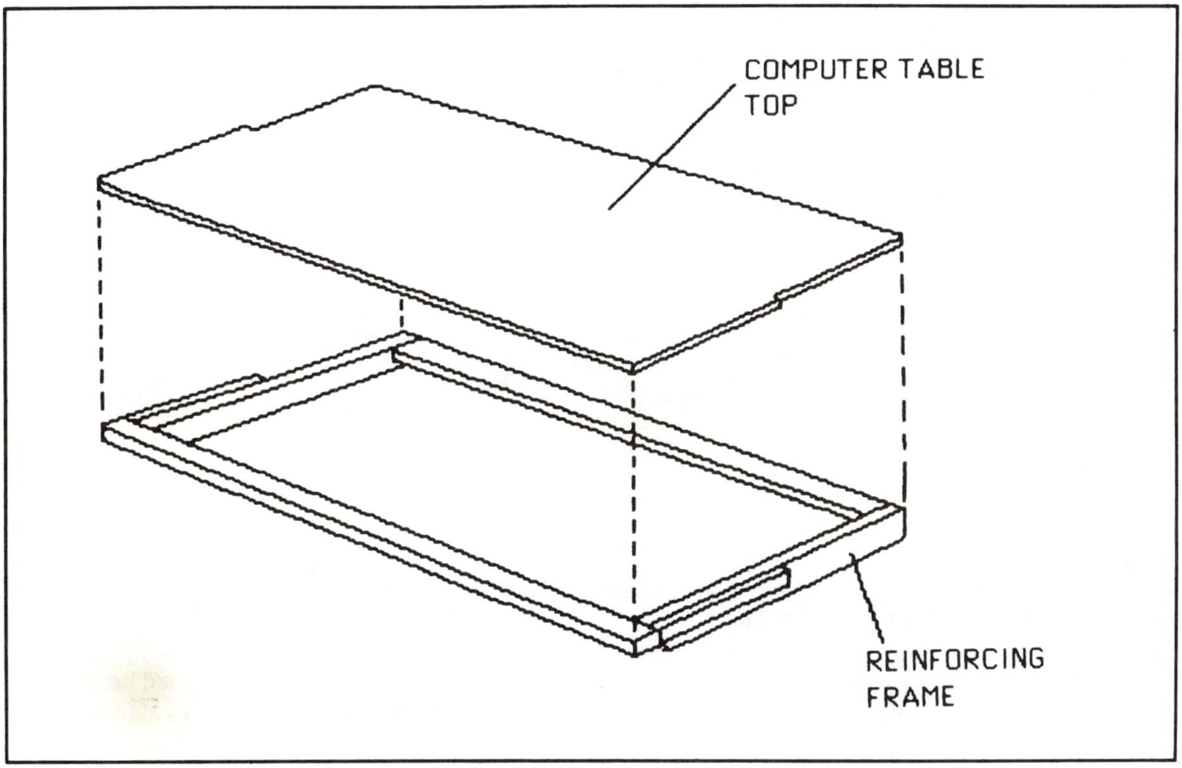

Fig. 6-5. Assembly of table top and reinforcing frame.

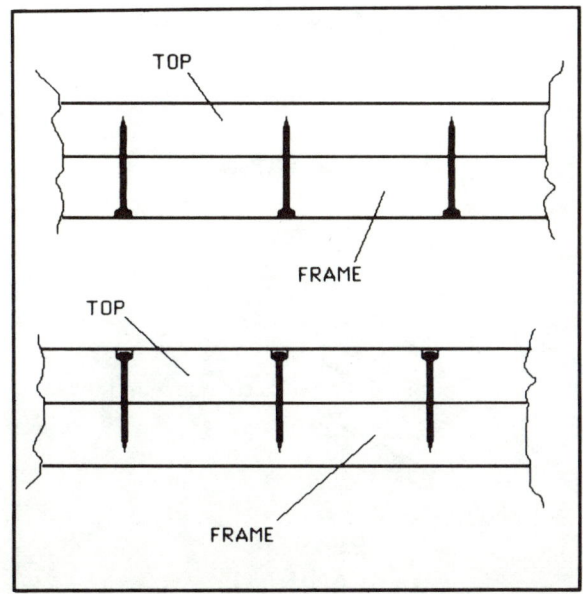

Fig. 6-6. Assembly of table top to frame pieces with nails and glue.

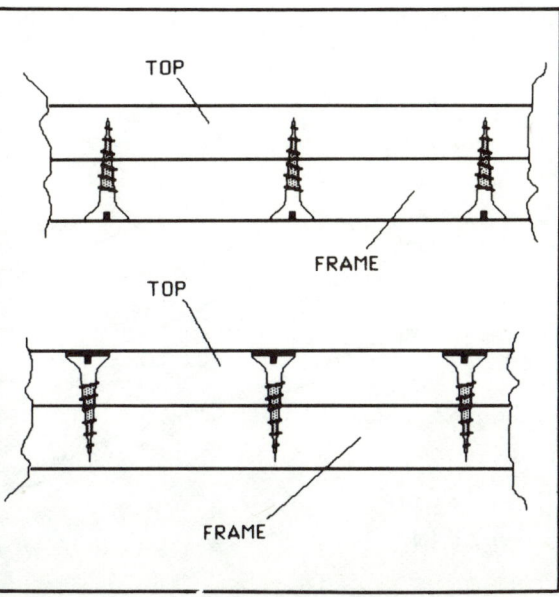

Fig. 6-7. Assembly of table top to frame pieces with screws and glue.

259

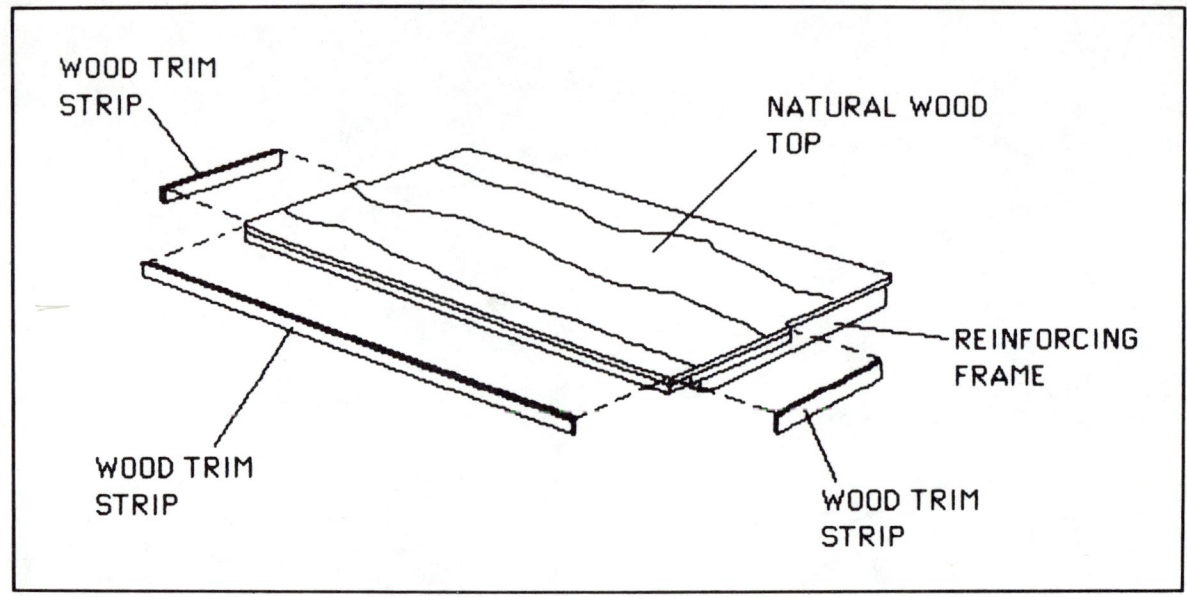

Fig. 6-8. Adding wood trim strips to table top.

selection of plastic laminates are on the market, but I suggest using high quality plastic laminates for computer table tops.

If plastic laminate is to also be applied to the edges of the table top, the pieces should be applied first. These are then finished flush with the table top. The top laminate is then applied so that the edge overlaps the edge laminates, as shown in Fig. 6-12.

The plastic laminate is installed as follows:

- All holes and defects in the surface of the

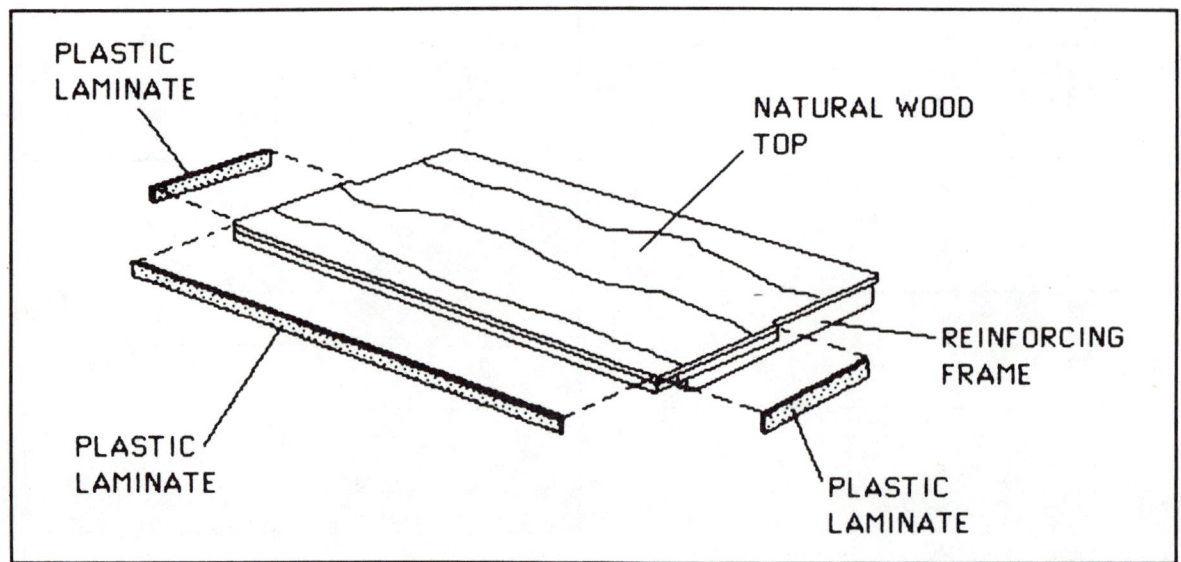

Fig. 6-9. Adding plastic laminates to edges of table top.

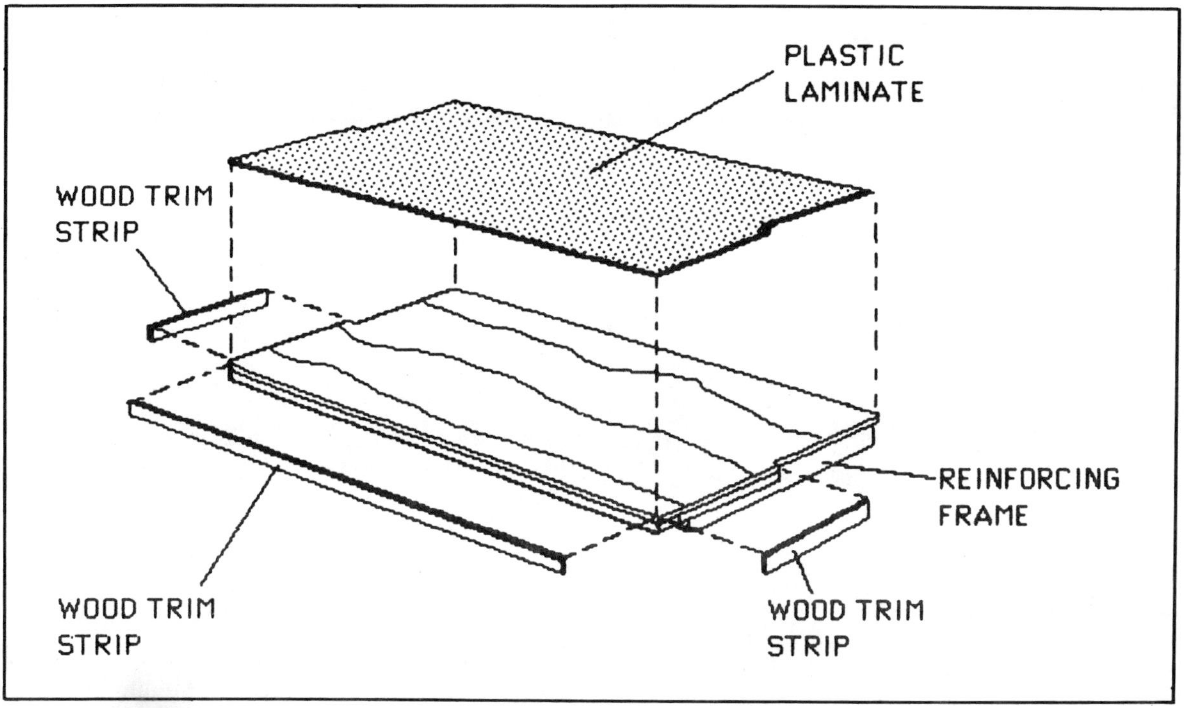

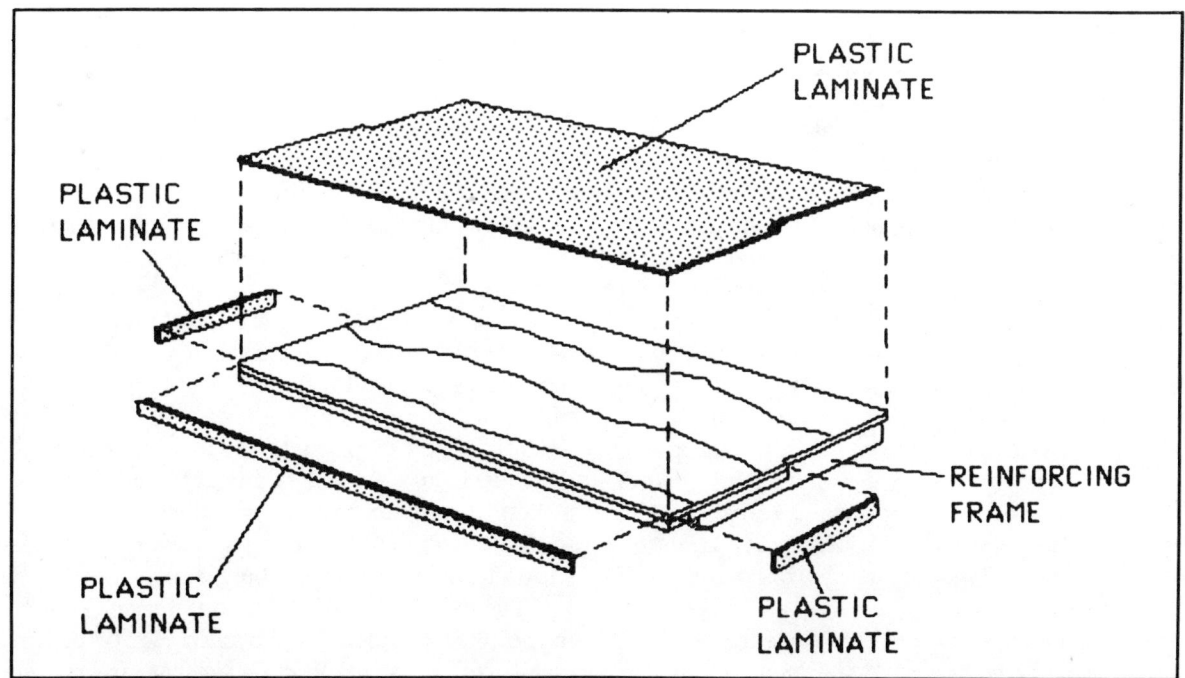

Fig. 6-10. Adding plastic laminate and wood trim pieces.

Fig. 6-11. Adding plastic laminates.

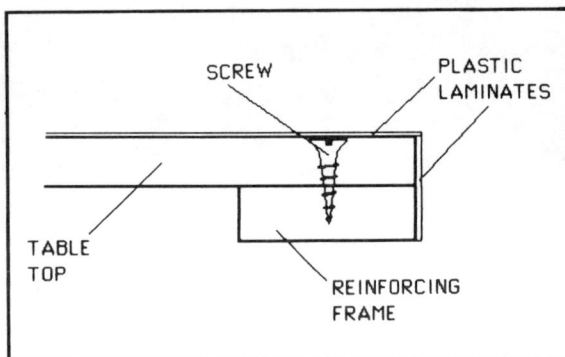

Fig. 6-12. Adding plastic laminates to table top.

plywood should be filled with putty or wood filler.
• Sand the surface to be covered. This will help ensure good adhesion.
• Mark the plastic laminate to a pattern slightly larger than the area to be covered. Use a straightedge and draw the pattern lines on the finished or pattern side of the laminate. Leave 1/4 inch to 1/2 inch on all sides. This will be trimmed off later.
• If a laminate is to be applied to the edges of the table, apply these first. After installation, as detailed below, trim and file the upper edge of the plastic laminate flush with the upper edges of the plywood table top before installing the plastic laminate to upper surface of the table top.
• Cut the plastic laminate to the pattern marked. Even though the plastic laminate is extremely durable once applied, it is vulnerable to cracking and splitting before it is cemented in place. Fine-tooth handsaws or power saws with fine-tooth blades can be used. A rotary power saw with a 14 to 16 teeth per inch blade is ideal. Place the plastic laminate face up when cutting. Care should be taken so that the plastic laminate is not chipped or broken. You can use a carbide tip knife to score the plastic by drawing the knife point along a metal straight-edge. Cut through the decorative surface. The laminate can then be broken by bending it toward the decorative surface side over the edge of a table or workbench.
• Apply contact cement to the surface of the plywood to be covered and the back side of the plastic laminate with a brush, roller, or metal spreader with a serrated edge. A thin even application is important.
• Follow the manufacturer's instructions regarding drying time. Usually, this takes about 20 to 30 minutes.
• Place a sheet of heavy wrapping paper over the plywood surface to be covered. Then position the laminate on the plywood surface with the paper between. The contact cement will not stick to the paper if it has been allowed to dry properly. Make certain that the laminate is positioned correctly. Once the two surfaces of contact cement touch, the laminate sheet cannot be moved again. When everything is lined up properly, pull the paper out from between the plywood and the plastic laminate.
• Using a small block of wood and a hammer, lightly tap the laminate in place. An alternate method is to use a rolling pin.
• Use a file to remove the surplus plastic laminate from the edges. Another method is to use a special cutter with a router, which allows convenient trimming of excess plastic laminate to flush with the plywood edges.
• The thinner recommended for the contact cement can be used for cleaning contact cement from wood and plastic laminate and tools.

The next step is to construct the lower shelf, as detailed in Fig. 6-13. If you purchased pieces of plywood that cut to the 15-inch-by-46 1/2-inch sizes, no additional cutting is necessary if they were cut accurately and in true rectangular form. Check with a square.

If you purchased a larger piece of plywood, you will need to cut out a section for the shelf top. In most cases, you will want to have the grain of the top layer running lengthwise, although this is not essential if you are going to add a plastic laminate. Whenever possible, use two factory cut edges for a shelf top and cut the other two. Use a ruler and square for making the pattern, marking the lines with a sharp pencil or scribing tool.

The next step is to add the reinforcing frames to the plywood shelf, as shown in Fig. 6-13. Use a ruler and a square to draw the patterns on the framing wood, marking the lines with a sharp mark-

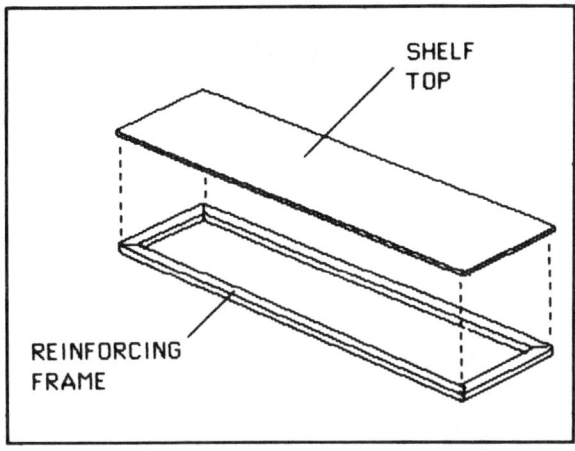

Fig. 6-13. Assembly of shelf top to reinforcing frame.

ing device. Make the necessary saw cuts. The frame pieces should be glued and nailed or screwed in position (see Figs. 6-14 and 6-15). If the plywood shelf top is to be left without a plastic laminate, the fasteners should go through the framing and into the plywood, being careful that the fasteners do not pass all the way through the plywood or leave a bulge in the upper surface. If a good glue is used, such as acrylic or epoxy, the glue alone should give adequate strength. The fasteners are mainly used as a clamping device for the gluing; they will not have much holding power into the plywood. To give greater holding power, the fasteners can be passed through the plywood and into the framing if a plastic laminate is to be added.

You can choose to finish the shelf in a number of ways. You could use the plywood surface as the shelf top and add a wood trim strip to the forward edge, as shown in Fig. 6-16. Glue and fasten the trim strip in place with finishing nails. Set the heads below the wood surface, filling holes with wood filler flush with the surface.

A second possibility is to add a plastic laminate to the forward edge and leave the shelf top natural wood, as detailed in Fig. 6-17.

Or, you may add a plastic laminate to the shelf top and a wood trim strip to the forward edge, as shown in Fig. 6-18. Still another possibility is to add plastic laminates to both the top and forward edge, as shown in Figs. 6-19 and 6-20.

If a plastic laminate is to be added to the plywood shelf top and/or forward edge, these can be installed now. If a plastic laminate is to also be applied to the forward edge of the shelf top, it

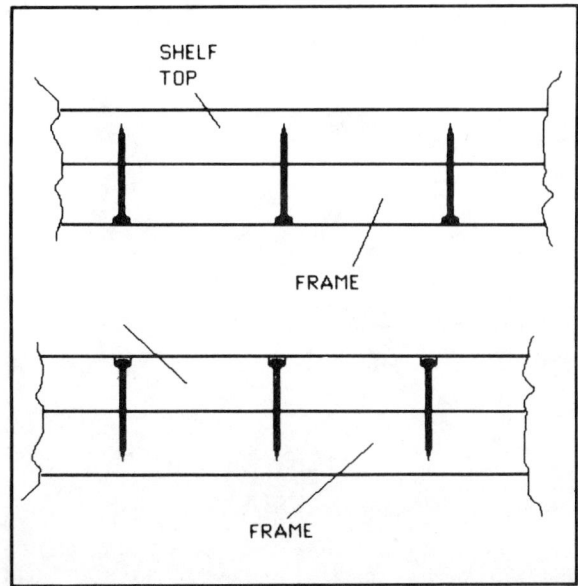

Fig. 6-14. Assembly of shelf top to frame pieces with nails and glue.

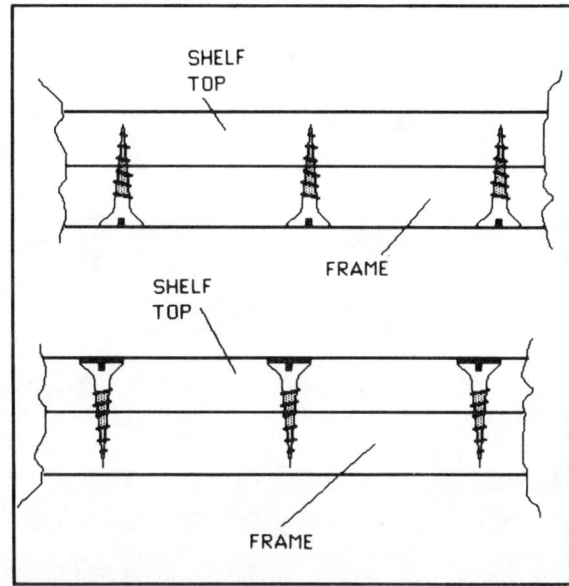

Fig. 6-15. Assembly of shelf top to frame pieces with screws and glue.

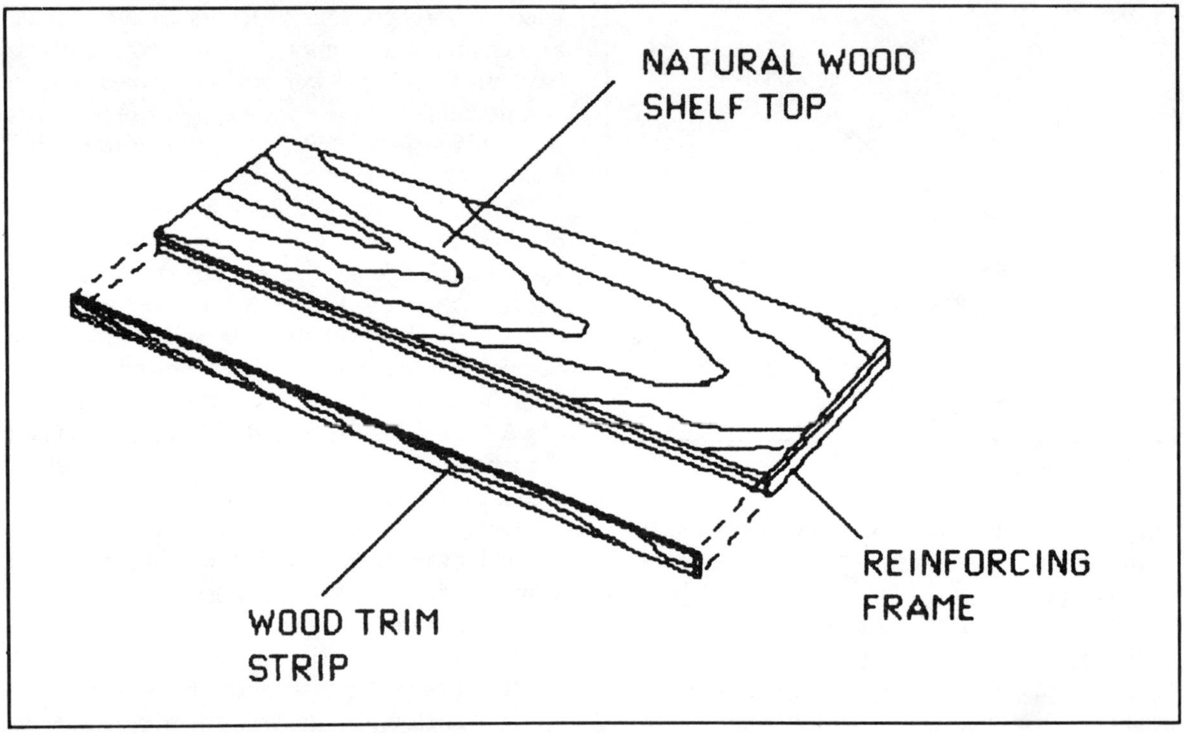

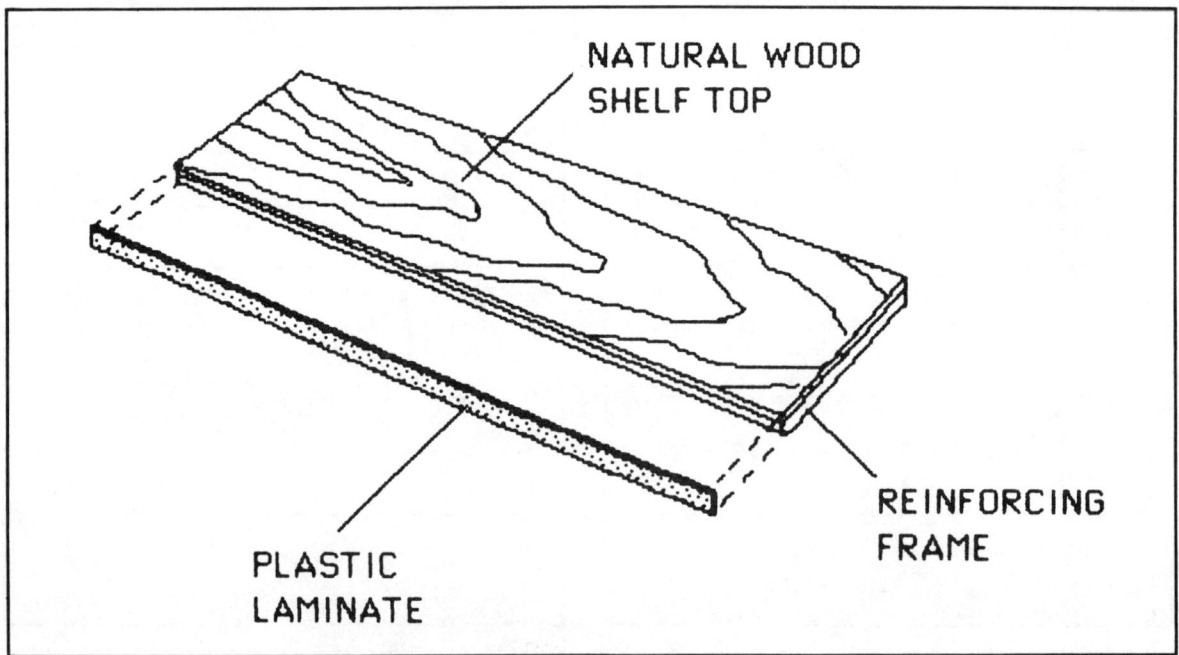

Fig. 6-16. Adding wood trim strip to forward edge of shelf.

Fig. 6-17. Adding plastic laminate to forward edge of shelf.

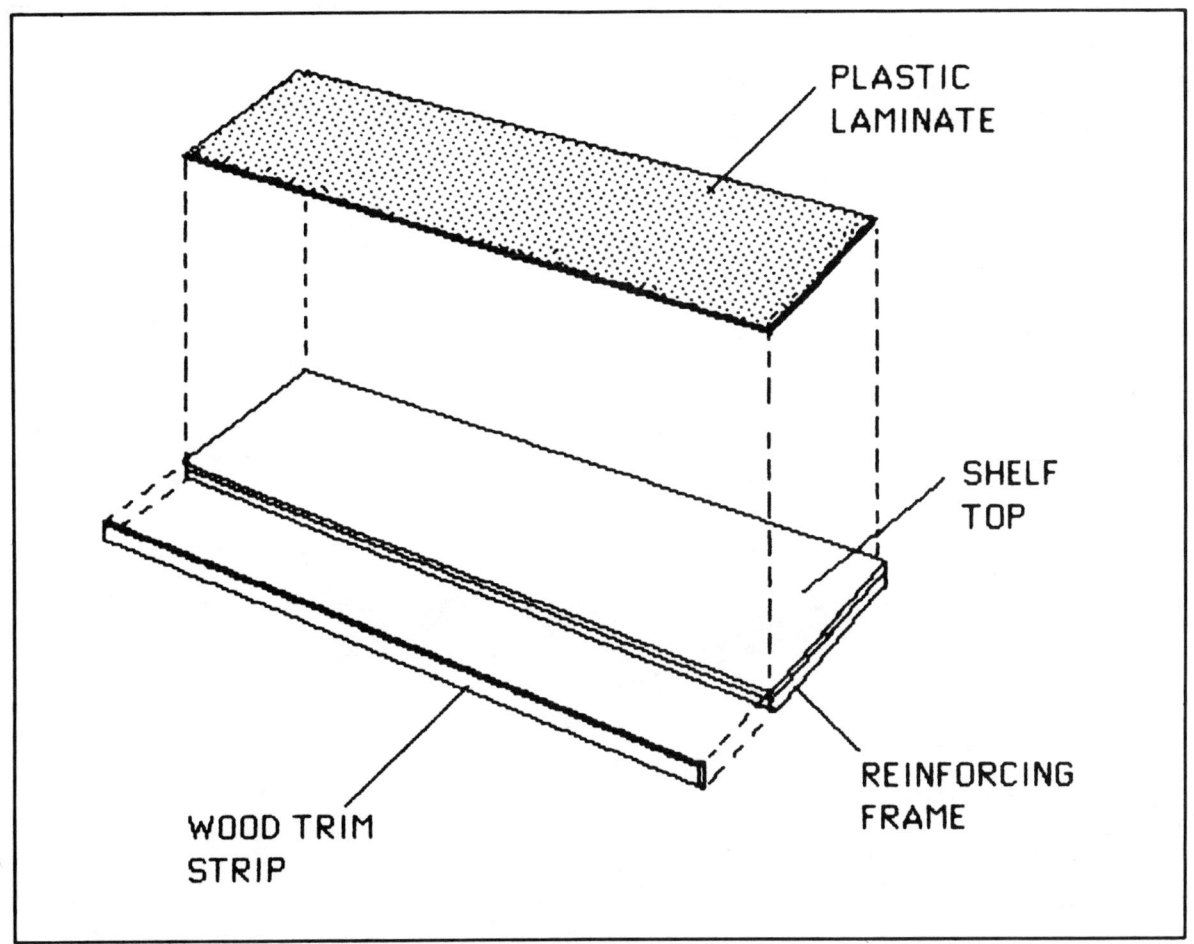

Fig. 6-18. Adding plastic laminate and wood trim strips to shelf.

should be applied first. This is then finished flush with the shelf top. The top laminate is then applied so that the edge overlaps the top edge of the laminate on the forward edge of the shelf, as shown in Fig. 6-20.

Next, cut the end pieces to rectangular size, following the special cutting steps outlined above. A power circular saw is ideal for making straight cuts.

Plastic laminates or wood trim strips can also be added to the forward edges of the shelves above the table top. This will protect the laminated edges of the plywood and give a neat appearance. The shelf tops can be left natural wood or covered with plastic laminates, as desired.

An overview of the remainder of the assembly is shown in Fig. 6-21. Assemble with the table top and shelves to the side pieces with both glue and mechanical fasteners. One method is to use finishing nails, passing them through the end pieces and into the wood beams mounted under the ends of the top and the framing wood under the lower shelf top. Set the heads below the wood surface and fill the holes with wood filler to flush with the wood surface. Another method is to use through-bolts: the bolts for the top will pass through the side pieces and beam pieces that are mounted to the ends of the table. The bolts for the lower shelf will pass through the side pieces and the frame pieces of the shelf.

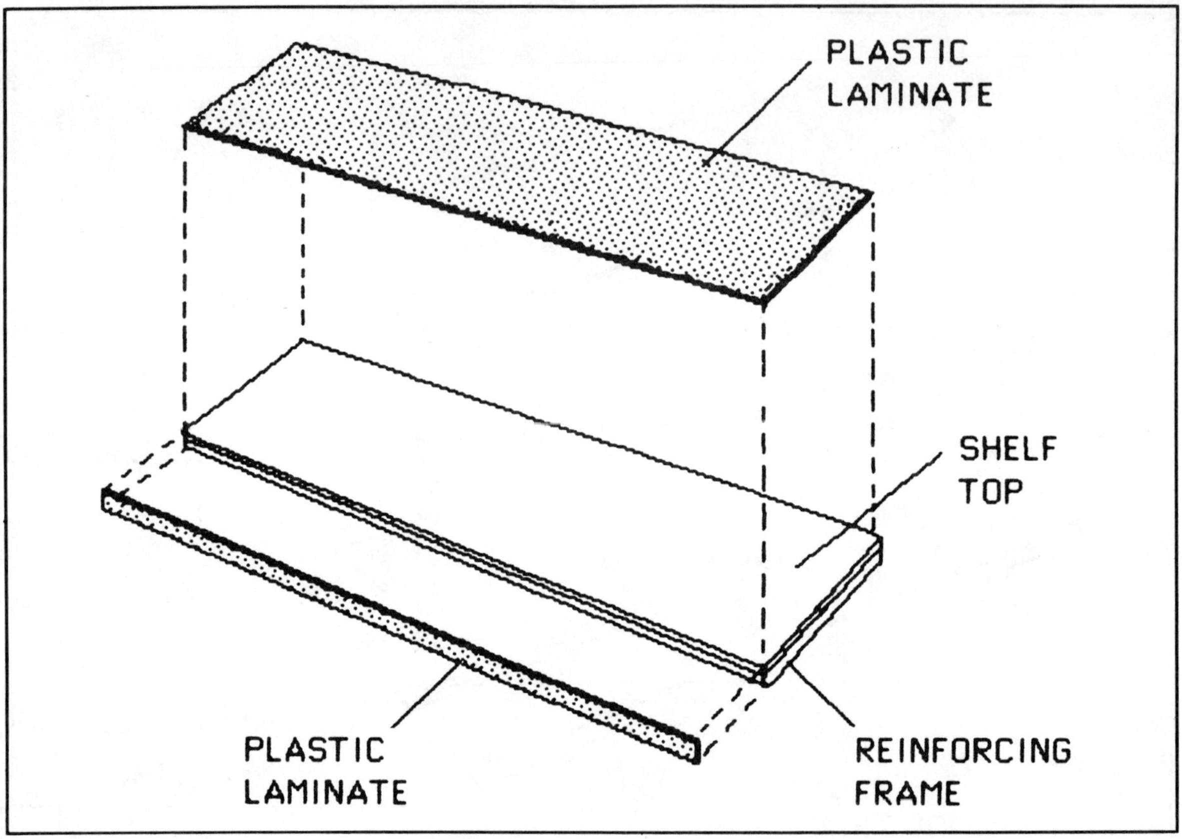

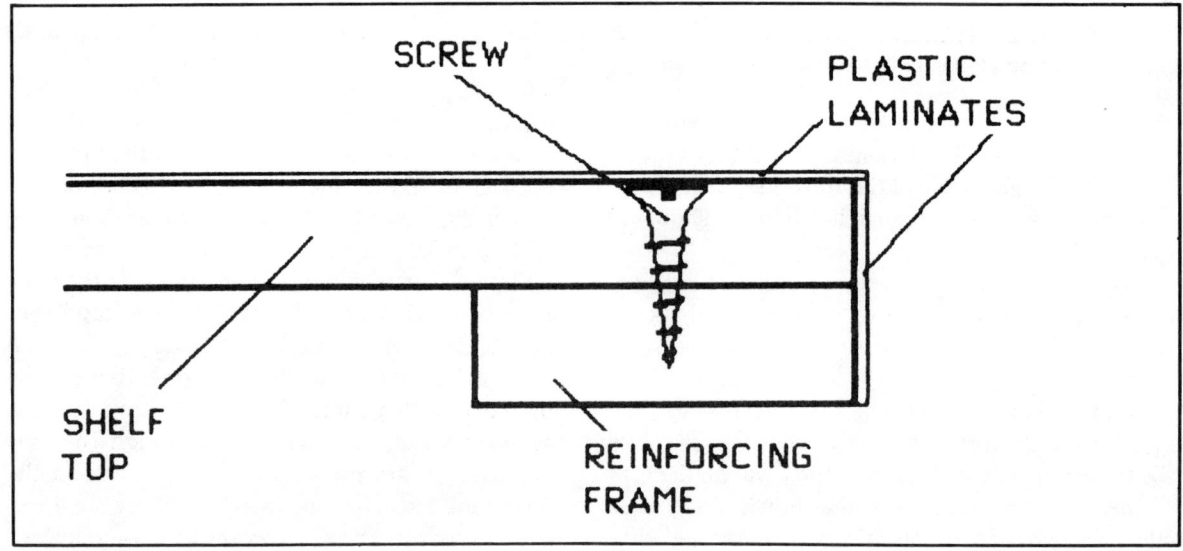

Fig. 6-19. Adding plastic laminate to top and forward edge of shelf.

Fig. 6-20. Adding plastic laminates to shelf top.

266

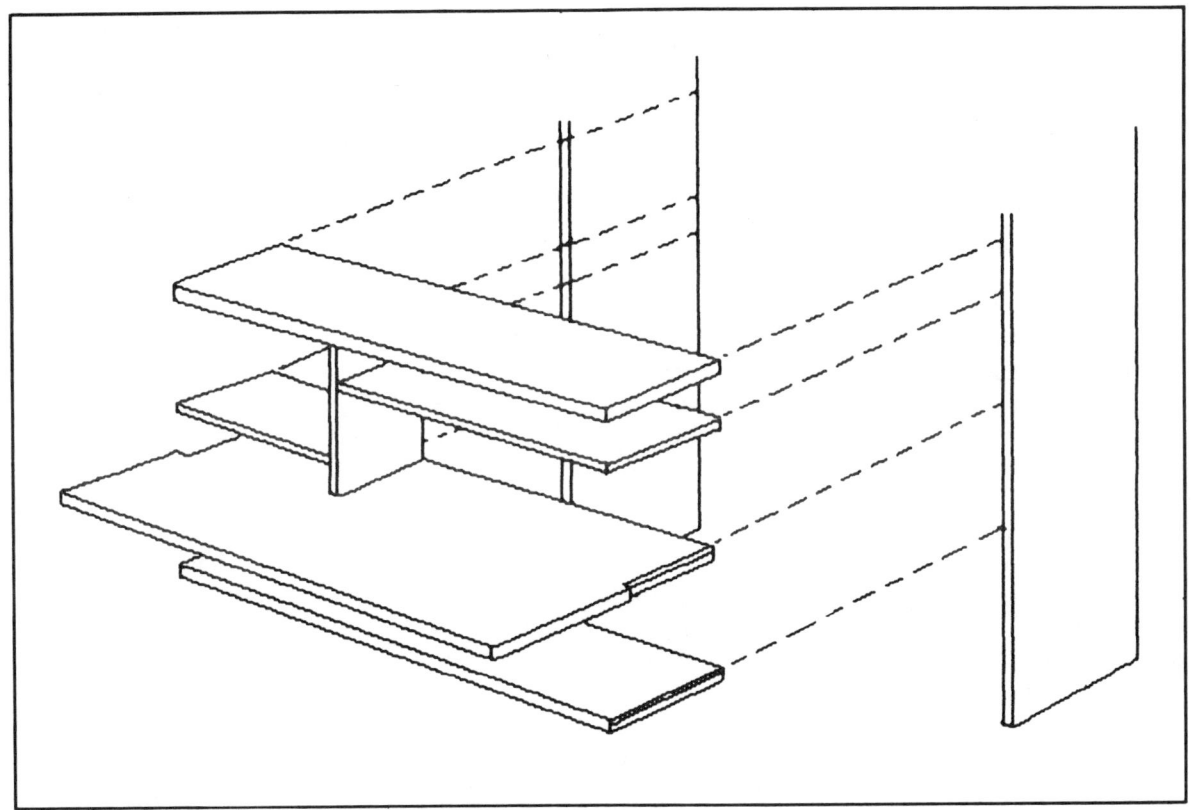

Fig. 6-21. Assembly of shelves and top to end pieces for built-in unit.

No matter what fasteners you use, it is extremely important to install the table top and lower shelf perpendicular to the side pieces. Use a square to make pattern lines on the side pieces. It is also important to have exactly the same distance between the table top and lower shelf on both sides.

The next step is to install the shelf at the top of the rack. This can be attached to the side pieces by using metal angle straps and fastening them to the wood members with wood screws or by using wood cleats mounted below the ends of the shelf plywood.

Next, assemble and install the shelves inside the rack frame. Attachment can be by means of angle straps fastened with wood screws.

Sanding and Finishing

Many beginners do a good job constructing the wall unit up to this point, only to give the unit a very amateur appearance by applying a sloppy finish. By taking care and a little time, however, even a beginner can give the table a professional finish.

Sanding is an important operation in preparing the wood for varnishing or painting. Small holes, checks, and other open defects in the wood should be filled in before sanding. If a clear finish is to be applied, use a wood filler that matches the color of the wood. A sander sealer should be applied to the plywood before doing any sanding on the surface.

Generally, you should work from coarse grits to progressively to finer grits, but don't start with a grit that is coarser than necessary for the particular sanding. The condition of the surface might be such that you can start with a medium or even fine grit. Coarser grits tend to leave scratches that need to be sanded away with finer grits.

Wood sanding is done primarily parallel to the grain. Across the grain sanding leaves scratches and tears and roughens the wood surface. A scratch free surface is especially important if you are going to finish with oil or varnish.

For most hand sanding, especially on flat surfaces, use a sanding block. Holding the sandpaper in your hand tends to leave a wavy surface on the wood since pressure is not applied evenly to all areas. A carpet or felt pad between the block and the sandpaper also helps.

At the final stages of sanding, most craftsmen use their fingertips to judge the smoothness of the surface. You can also judge by looking across the wood at a light held at a low angle to the surface. Taking special care with the sanding is an important step toward a fine finish.

If desired, a power sander can be used; a pad sander is the easiest to use without damaging the wood surface. Belt sanders can be used by experienced operators.

A clear finish (polyurethane plastic is ideal) can be applied directly to natural wood, or you can first stain the wood another color. Staining can enhance the natural grains of the wood and enrich relatively lifeless woods.

Before applying stain, first test color on a scrap piece of similar wood. Clean the surface area where stain is to be applied. Use a cloth to eliminate as much dust as possible. The stain can then be applied with a brush, foam brush applicator, or cloth in a smooth, even coat. Allow the stain to penetrate the wood. Depending on the humidity, temperature, and particular stain used, this usually takes from 5 to 15 minutes. While the stain is still wet, wipe off the excess stain with a clean cloth. Be careful not to remove too much from corners and edges. Wipe across the grain first so that you work the stain into the wood pores. Then give a final wipe with the grain. Allow the stain to dry. This usually takes at least 8 hours. The finish can then be applied.

It is usually best to apply a series of light, even coats of clear finish rather than one thick coat. This will minimize possible drips and wrinkles as the finish dries. Apply finish in brush-width strokes in direction of wood grain. Turn table so that finish is applied to wood surfaces in a horizontal position whenever possible.

A minimum of two coats is recommended. Allow 6 to 8 hours for the first coat to dry before applying second coat. Sand lightly and use a tack cloth to remove sanded finish dust before applying next coat of finish. Clear or stained finishes are usually applied to natural wood furniture, but you can paint the wall unit any color.

VARIATIONS

Many variations are possible for the built-in wall unit by substituting other materials for the top and/or other components or by constructing the table with a different size of top. You can also add additional storage shelves above and/or below the table top or arrange them differently. There are hundreds of possibilities.

The built-in wall unit makes a functional and attractive computer work station even when built from inexpensive woods. By using more expensive woods, such as oak, you can give the table a custom appearance. The plans given here show simple butt joints, but if you have cabinet-making skills, you can also use rabbet, T-rabbet, or miter joints.

Chapter 7

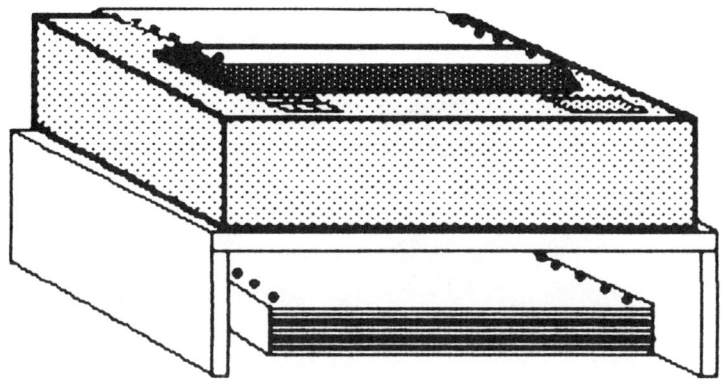

Plans and Patterns for Miscellaneous Projects

In this chapter some miscellaneous projects are detailed. These projects are generally less difficult than the computer furniture described in previous chapters.

PRINTER PLATFORM

The printer platform shown in Fig. 7-1 is easy to construct. The platform is used on a computer table top and allows the use of computer form paper (see Fig. 7-2). The printer platform can be left natural wood or covered with plastic laminates.

Materials

The patterns for the wood parts are shown in Fig. 7-3. The top of the platform is a 14-inch-by-14-inch piece of 3/4-inch thick plywood. If you intend to use the wood surface as the finished table top, without adding a plastic laminate, plywood with the upper layer of a hardwood, such as oak, is recommended. If a laminate is to be added, exterior grade shop plywood will suffice.

Although 1/2-inch thick plywood could also be used, I don't recommend this. The savings are small, and a less sturdy platform will result. Particle board can be substituted for the plywood if you are on an absolute minimum budget. Particle board can be difficult to work with, however, and it is very difficult to get plastic laminates to bond properly to this material without special equipment.

The side pieces and shelf are 1-inch thick by 4-inch wide wood stock. These are the dimensions before the wood was surfaced, so the wood that you purchase will have dimensions slightly less than these. The end pieces are 14 inches long. When selecting the wood stock, you can use a variety of woods, including pine, fir, and birch, but try to select wood that is as straight as possible and without cracks or other defects.

Finishing nails and/or other fasteners are required for assembly, detailed below in this section. You will also need a suitable wood glue. The finish can be clear urethane or other type, as desired. Or plastic laminates can be added. If plastic laminates

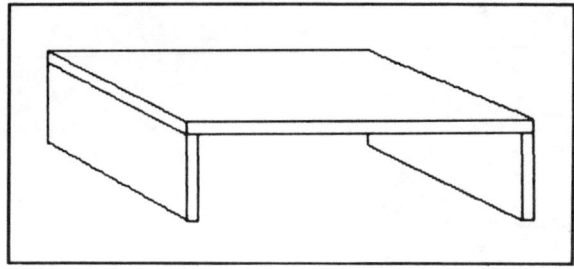

Fig. 7-1. Printer platform.

are to be added, you will need suitable plastic laminate and contact cement for attaching it to the wood.

Construction

Overviews of the complete assembly are shown in Figs. 7-4 and 7-5. Begin by constructing the top. If you purchased a piece of plywood that was already cut to the 14-inch-by-14-inch size, no additional cutting will be required. This assumes that it was cut accurately and is a truly rectangular form. You might want to check it with a square.

If you purchased a larger piece of plywood, such as a standard 4-foot-by-8-foot sheet, you will need to cut out a section for the table top. Try to have the grain of the top layer running lengthwise, although this is not essential if you are going to add a plastic laminate. In most cases, you will use two factory cut edges for your table top and cut the other two. Use a ruler and square to make the pattern, marking the lines with a sharp pencil or scribing tool.

Sawing plywood requires attention because special care must be taken to avoid chipping and splintering along the cut edge. Handsaws or power saws with special fine-toothed blades designed especially for plywood should be used; even better are special carbide-tipped blades. Applying a strip of masking tape over the area to be cut on both sides of the plywood, but especially on the side opposite the one you are cutting from, is also helpful. Another possibility is to clamp a solid piece of wood to the underside and make the cut through both the plywood and the piece of wood.

Be extremely careful when sanding edges of

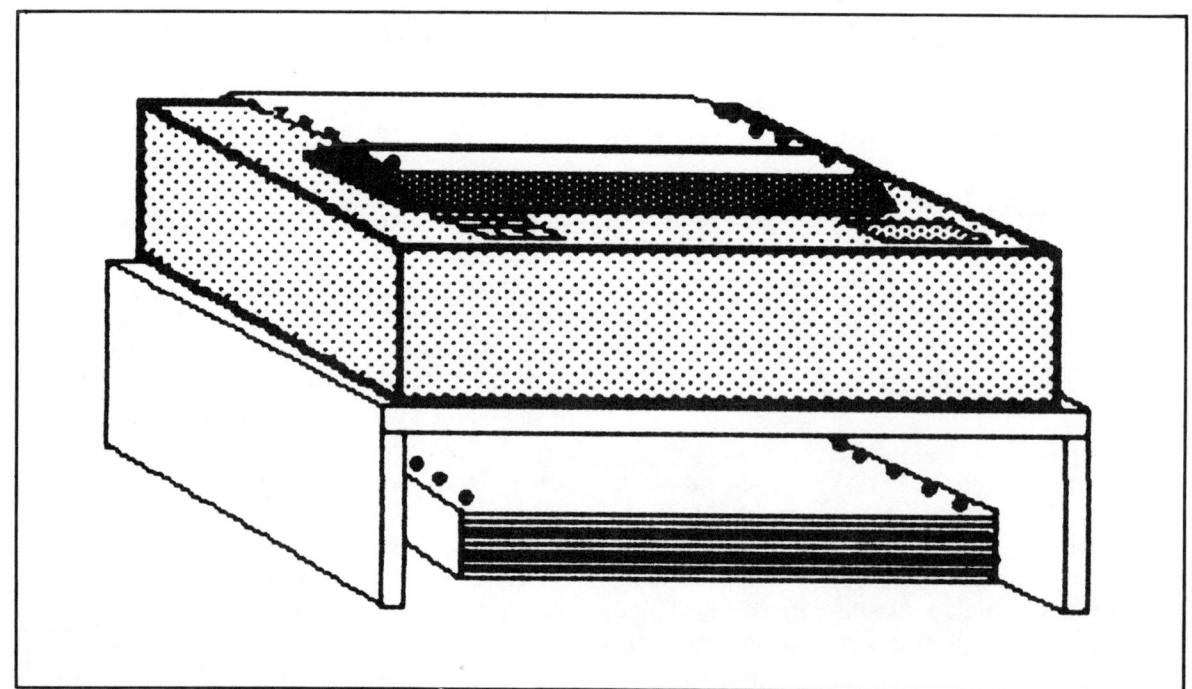

Fig. 7-2. Printer platform and printer.

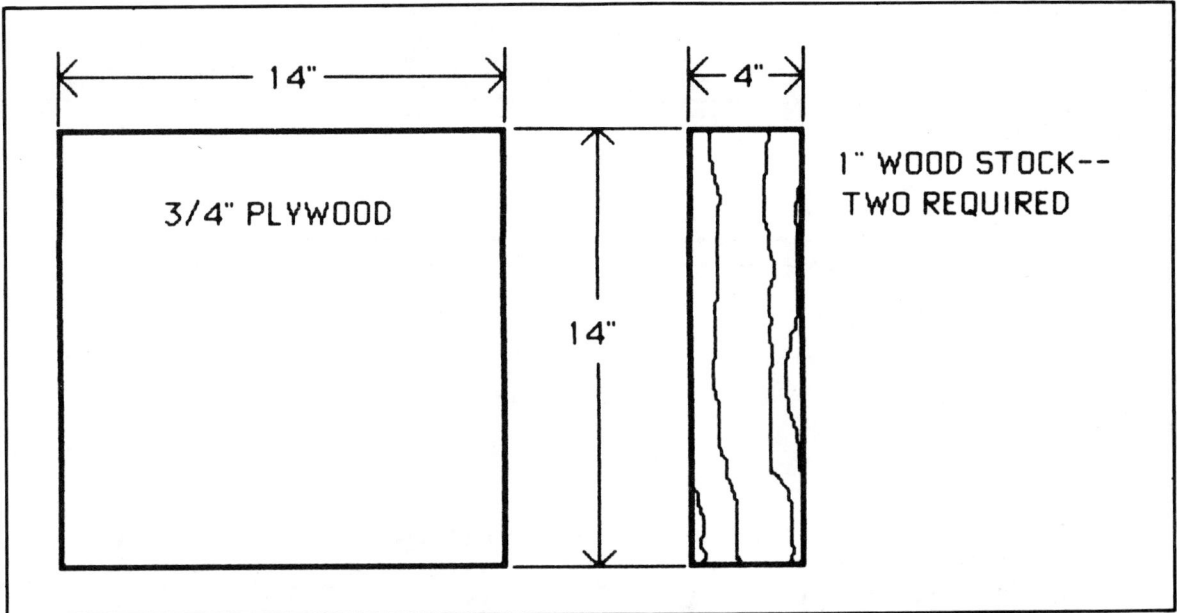

Fig. 7-3. Pattern for printer platform.

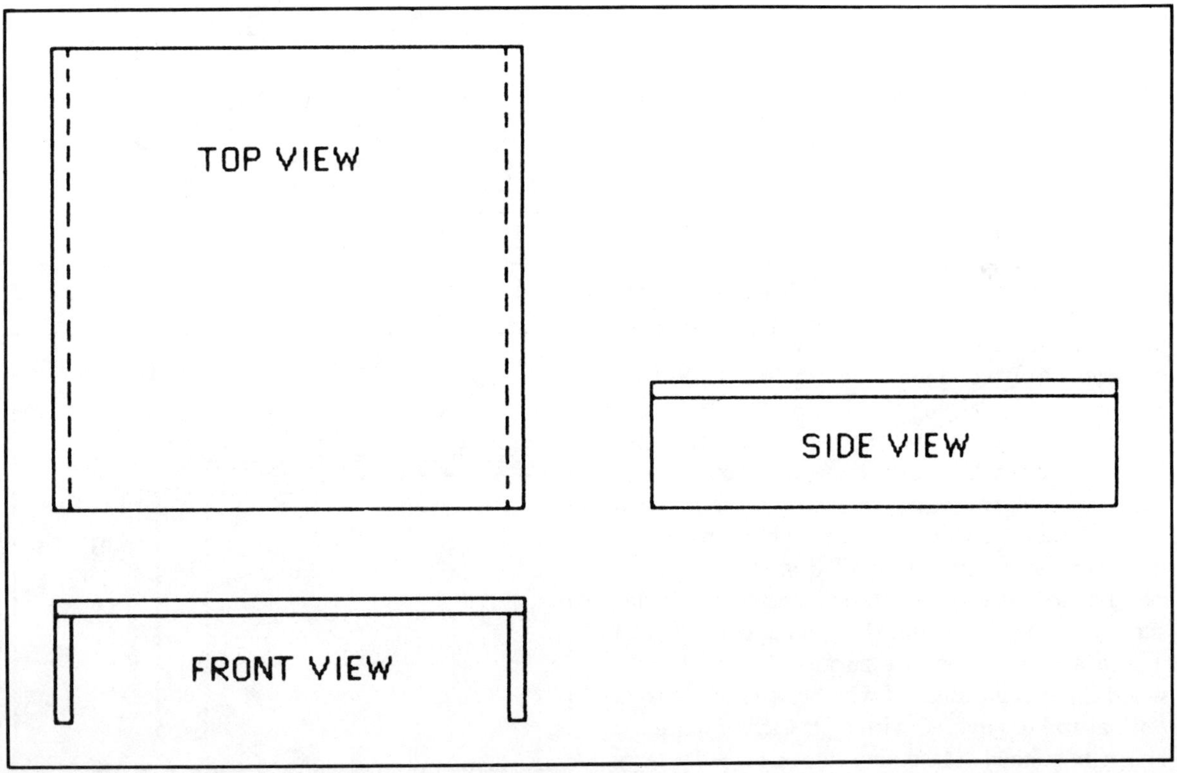

Fig. 7-4. Assembly of printer platform (top, front, and side views).

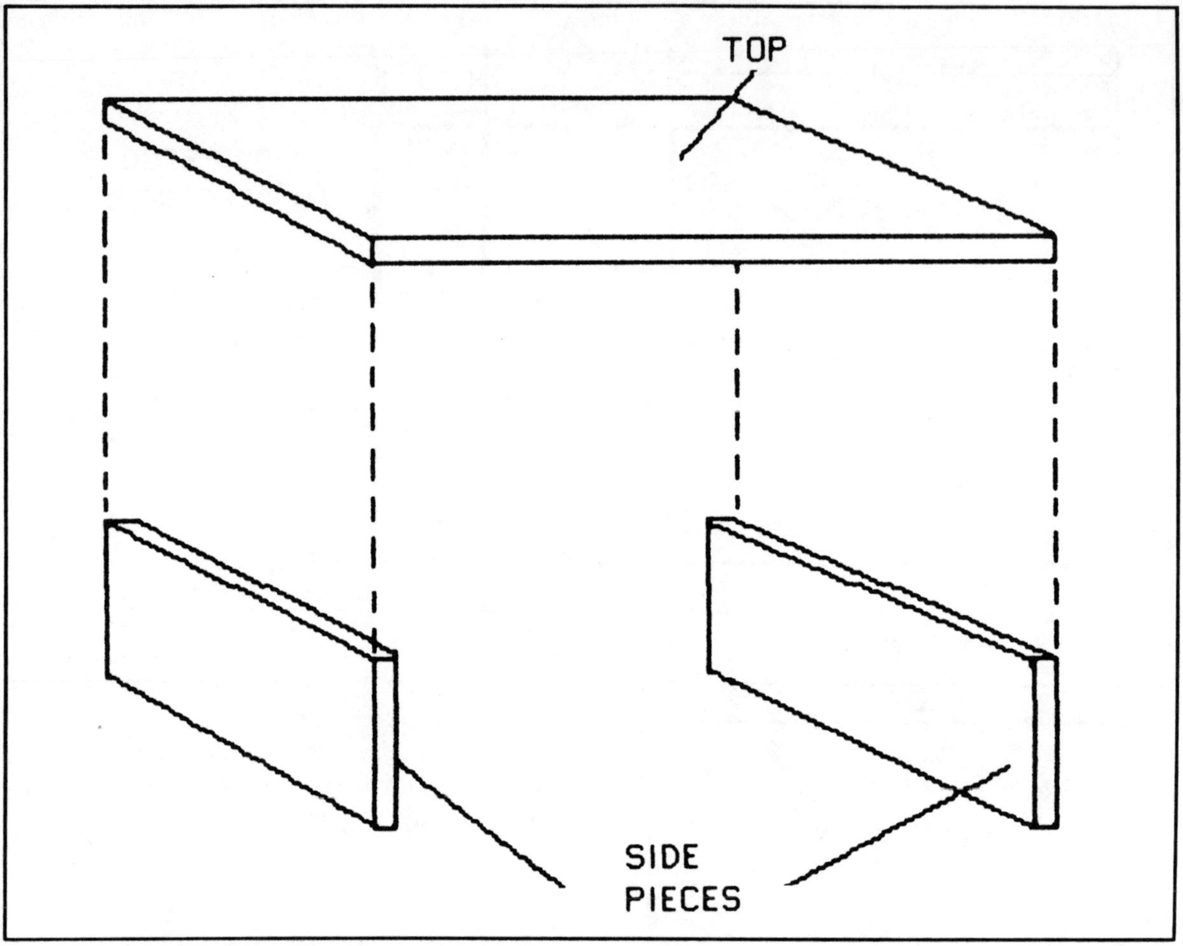

Fig. 7-5. Assembly of printer platform (top and side pieces).

plywood. Use a sanding block. Avoid sanding the surfaces of plywood until a wood sealer has been applied.

This next step is to cut the side pieces to length. Use a ruler and a square to draw the patterns on the wood stock, marking the lines with a sharp pencil or other marking device. Then make the necessary saw cuts, as detailed in Chapter 2.

The side pieces should be glued and nailed or screwed in position. Finishing nails can be used. These are set below the surface and filled with wood filler, regardless of whether the top is to be left natural or covered with a plastic laminate. An alternate method of fastening is to use wood screws, as shown in Fig. 7-6.

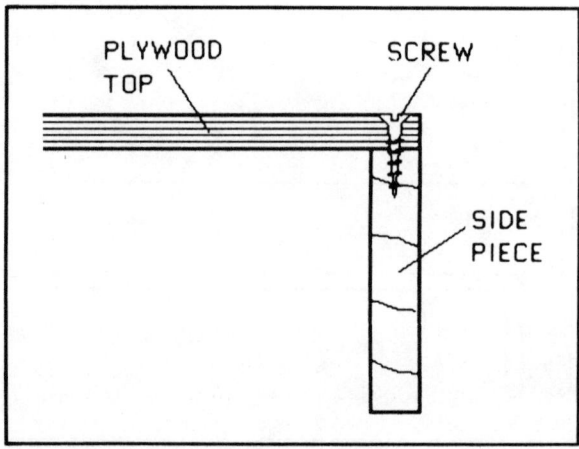

Fig. 7-6. Assembly of printer platform.

If a plastic laminate is to be added, it can be installed at this time. The top only can be covered, the sides only, or the forward edges only, or all of these or any combination.

If a plastic laminate is to also be applied to the sides and/or edges, they should be applied first. The laminates are then finished flush with the top plywood. The top laminate is then applied so that the edge overlaps the top edge of the laminate on the sides.

The plastic laminate is installed as follows:

- All holes and defects in the surface of the wood should be filled with putty or wood filler.
- Sand the surface to be covered. This will help ensure good adhesion.
- Mark the plastic laminate to a pattern slightly larger than the area to be covered. Use a straightedge and draw the pattern lines on the finished or pattern side of the laminate. Leave 1/4 inch to 1/2 inch on all sides. This will be trimmed off later.
- If a laminate is to be applied to the forward edge or sides of the platform, apply these first. After installation, as detailed below, trim and file the upper edge of the plastic laminate flush with the upper edge of the plywood top before installing the plastic laminate to upper surface of the top.
- Cut the plastic laminate to the pattern marked. Even though the plastic laminate is extremely durable once applied, it is vulnerable to cracking and splitting before it is cemented in place. Fine-tooth handsaws or power saws with fine-tooth blades can be used. A rotary power saw with a 14 to 16 teeth per inch blade is ideal. Place the plastic laminate face up when cutting. Care should be taken so that the plastic laminate is not chipped or broken. An alternate method is to use a carbide tip knife for scoring the plastic by drawing the knife point along a metal straightedge. Cut through the decorative surface. The laminate can then be broken by bending it toward the decorative surface side over the edge of a table or workbench.
- Apply contact cement to the surface of the wood to be covered and the back side of the plastic laminate. A brush, roller, or metal spreader with a serrated edge can be used to spread the contact cement. A thin, even application is important.
- Follow the manufacturer's instructions regarding drying time. Usually, this takes about 20 to 30 minutes.
- Place a sheet of heavy wrapping paper over the wood surface to be covered. Then position the laminate on the wood surface with the paper between. The contact cement will not stick to the paper if it has been allowed to dry properly. Make certain that the laminate is positioned correctly. Once the two surfaces of contact cement touch, the laminate sheet cannot be moved again. When everything is lined up properly, pull the paper out from between the wood and the plastic laminate.
- Using a small block of wood and a hammer, lightly tap the laminate in place. An alternate method is to use a rolling pin.
- Use a file to remove the surplus plastic laminate from the edges. Another method is to use a special cutter with a router, which allows convenient trimming of excess plastic laminate to flush with the wood edges.
- The thinner recommended for the contact cement can be used for cleaning contact cement from wood and plastic laminate and tools.

Sanding and Finishing

If the wood is not covered with a plastic laminate, or only part of it is covered, sanding and applying a finish are important steps in the construction process. Many beginners do a good job constructing the printer platform up to this point, only to give it a very amateur appearance by sloppy application of a finish. By taking care and a little time, however, even a beginner can give the printer stand a professional finish.

Sanding is an important operation. Small holes, checks, and other open defects in the wood should be filled in before sanding. If a clear finish is to be applied, use a wood filler that matches the color of the wood. A sanding sealer should be applied to the plywood before doing any sanding on the surface.

The general principle to follow for sanding is to work from coarse grits to progressively finer grits. Don't start with a grit that is coarser than necessary for the particular sanding; the condition of the surface might be such that you can start with a medium or even fine grit. Coarser grits tend to leave scratches that need to be sanded away with finer grits.

Wood sanding is done primarily parallel to the grain. Sanding across the grain leaves scratches and tends to tear and roughen the wood surface. A scratch free surface is especially important if you are going to finish with oil or varnish.

For most hand sanding, especially on flat surfaces, use a sanding block. Holding the sandpaper in your hand tends to leave a wavy surface on the wood since pressure is not applied evenly to all areas. A carpet or felt pad between the block and the sandpaper also helps.

At the final stages of sanding, use your eyes and fingertips to judge the smoothness of the surface. Taking special care with the sanding is an important step toward a finish that you will be proud of.

If you like, a power sander can be used. A pad sander is the easiest to use without damaging the wood surface. Belt sanders can be used by experienced operators.

A clear finish (polyurethane plastic is ideal) can be applied directly to natural wood, or you can first stain the wood to give it another color. Staining can enhance the natural grains of the wood and enrich relatively lifeless woods.

Before applying stain, first test color on a scrap piece of similar wood. Clean the surface area where stain is to be applied. Use a cloth to eliminate as much dust as possible. The stain can then be applied with a brush, foam brush applicator, or cloth. Apply a smooth, even coat of stain. Allow the stain to penetrate the wood. Depending on the humidity, temperature, and particular stain used, this usually takes from 5 to 15 minutes. While the stain is still wet, wipe off the excess stain with a clean cloth. Be careful not to remove too much from corners and edges. Wipe across the grain first so that you work the stain into the wood pores. Then give a final wipe with the grain. Allow the stain to dry. This usually takes at least 8 hours. The finish can then be applied.

It is usually best to apply a series of light, even coats of clear finish rather than one thick coat. This will minimize possible drips and wrinkles as the finish dries. Apply it in brush-width strokes in direction of wood grain. Turn table so that finish is applied to horizontal wood surfaces whenever possible.

A minimum of two coats is recommended. Allow 6 to 8 hours for the first coat to dry before applying second coat. Sand lightly and use a tack cloth to remove sanded finish dust before applying next coat of finish.

Clear or stained finishes are usually applied to natural wood furniture but, if desired, color paint finishes can also be applied.

Variations

A number of variations are possible for the printer platform. One possibility is to substitute materials, such as particle board instead of plywood, for the top. Another common variation is to construct the platform with a different size of top or a different height of side pieces.

The printer platform makes a functional and attractive table top stand for a printer when built from inexpensive woods. By using more expensive woods, such as oak, you can give the printer platform a custom appearance. The plans given here show simple butt joints, but if you have the cabinetmaking skills and know-how, you can also use more difficult joints.

STORAGE RACK

The storage rack shown in Fig. 7-7 is attractive and functional. It can be used with a computer table without a rack or a regular table to give storage space for your computer needs. The storage rack can be left natural wood or covered with plastic laminates. This rack presents a good appearance even when built from low cost wood, but you can make the same design from more expensive woods, such as birch or even better, oak.

Specific dimensions are given for the storage rack, but you can vary these to fit your particular needs.

Materials

The patterns for the wood parts are shown in

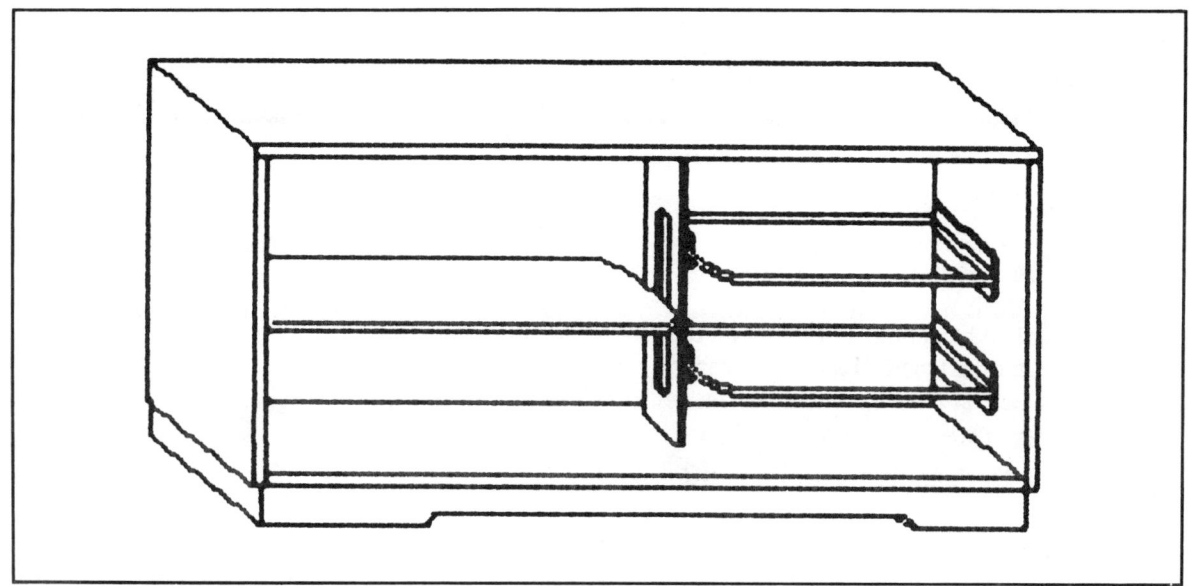

Fig. 7-7. Storage rack.

Fig. 7-8. The top piece for the rack is a 12-inch-by-36-inch piece of 1/2-inch thick plywood. The bottom piece is a 12-inch-by-35-inch piece of 1/2-inch thick plywood. The end pieces (two are required) are 12-inch-by-16-inch pieces of 1/2-inch thick plywood. If you intend to use the wood surfaces as the finished storage rack, without adding plastic laminates, plywood with the upper layer of a hardwood, is recommended. If a laminate is to be added, an exterior grade of shop plywood will suffice. Plywood is normally sold in standard 4-foot-by-8-foot sheets, but many home building and discount stores also offer 2-foot-by-4-foot cuts, which may be easier to handle for a small project like this.

Particle board can be substituted if you are on an absolute minimum budget. Some manufactured computer furniture is made from particle board covered by plastic laminates. Particle board can be difficult to work with, however, and it is very difficult to get plastic laminates to bond properly without special equipment.

The base pieces are of 1-inch-by-2-inch wood stock (dimensions before the wood was surfaced—the wood that you purchase will have dimensions slightly less than these), cut to the patterns shown in Fig. 7-8.

You will also need suitable wood for a shelf and rack vertical, shelf cleats, and two glass shelves. There are many possibilities here.

When selecting the wood stock, you can use many woods, including pine, fir, and birch, but try to select wood that is straight and without cracks or other defects.

Finishing nails and other fasteners are required for assembly, as detailed below in this section. You will also need a suitable wood glue. The finish can be clear urethane, paint, varnish, or whatever you like.

An alternate method is to add plastic laminates to the wood surfaces. If plastic laminates are to be added, you will need contact cement for attaching it to the wood.

Construction

An overview of the assembly is shown in Fig. 7-9. Begin by cutting out the plywood parts. If you purchased the pieces of plywood already cut to the required sizes, no additional cutting will be necessary if the pieces were cut accurately and are a true rectangular form. Check them with a square.

If you purchased a larger piece of plywood, cut out the required sections for the rack parts. In many

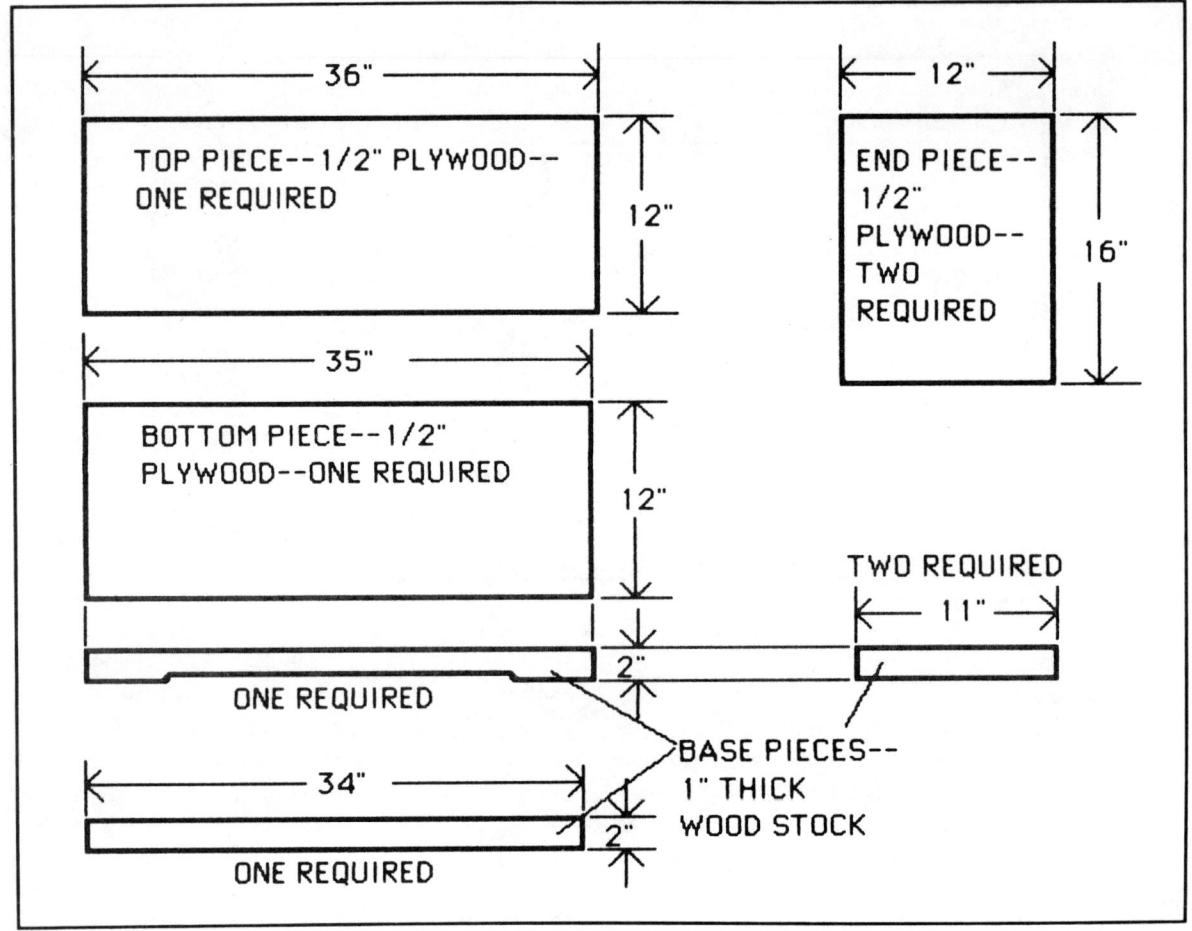

Fig. 7-8. Pattern for storage rack.

cases, you will use two factory cut edges for the parts and cut the other two. Use a ruler and square to draw the pattern lines with a sharp pencil or scribing tool.

When sawing plywood, special care must be taken to avoid chipping and splintering along the cut edge. Handsaws or power saws with special fine-toothed or carbide-tipped blades designed especially for plywood should be used. A strip of masking tape applied over the area to be cut on both sides of the plywood, especially the underside, is also helpful. Another possibility is to clamp the solid piece of wood to the underside and make the cut through both the plywood and the piece of wood.

Be extremely careful when sanding edges of plywood. Use a sanding block and avoid sanding the surfaces of plywood until a wood sealer has been applied.

The next step is to cut the base parts from 1-inch-by-2-inch wood stock to the patterns shown in Fig. 7-8. Use a ruler and a square to make the patterns on the wood, marking the lines with a sharp marking device. Then make the necessary saw cuts.

Next, assemble the rack frame and base, using both glue and mechanical fasteners. One possibility is to use finishing nails, setting the heads below the surface of the wood and filling the holes with wood filler to flush with the surface of the wood. Most of the strength is provided by the glue.

The fasteners are mainly used as a clamping device for the gluing and will not have much holding power into the plywood. An alternate method of assembly is to use metal angle straps, attaching them to the wood with wood screws.

If a plastic laminate is to be added to the rack (to all or part of the surfaces), it can be installed at this time. Use only high quality plastic laminates for computer furniture.

The plastic laminate is installed according to instructions given for the printer platform above.

The next step is to add the vertical member and shelves inside the rack frame, as shown in Fig. 7-9.

Sanding and Finishing

Sanding and applying a finish are important steps in the construction process if surfaces were left natural wood. By taking care and a little time, however, even a beginner can give the storage rack a professional finish.

Sanding is an important operation in preparing the wood to accept varnish or paint. Small holes, checks, and other open defects in the wood should be filled in before sanding. If a clear finish is to be applied, use a wood filler that matches the color of the wood. A sanding sealer should be applied to the plywood before doing any sanding on the surface.

Work from coarse grits progressively to finer grits, but don't start with a grit that is coarser than necessary for the particular sanding. The condition of the surface might be such that you can start with a medium or even fine grit. Coarser grits tend to leave scratches that need to be sanded away with finer grits.

Wood sanding is done parallel to the grain. Across the grain sanding leaves scratches and tears and roughens the wood surface. A scratch free surface is especially important if you are going to finish with oil or varnish.

For most hand sanding, especially on flat surfaces, use a sanding block rather than holding the sandpaper in your hand. Holding the sandpaper in your hand tends to leave a wavy surface on the wood since pressure is not applied evenly to all areas. A carpet or felt pad between the block and the sandpaper also helps.

At the final stages of sanding, craftsmen use their fingertips and eyes to judge the smoothness

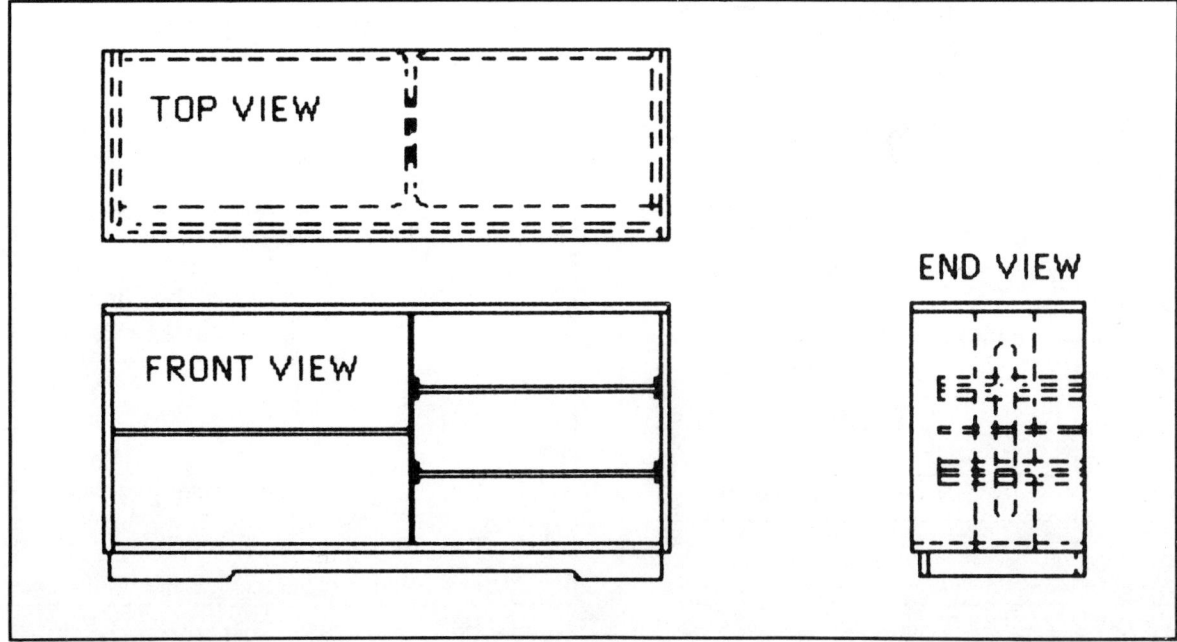

Fig. 7-9. Assembly of storage rack.

of the surface. Careful sanding will produce a finish that you will be proud of.

If desired, a power sander can be used. A pad sander is the easiest to use without damaging the wood surface. Belt sanders can be used by experienced operators.

A clear polyurethane plastic finish can be applied directly to natural wood, or you can first stain the wood another color to enhance the natural grains of the wood and enrich relatively lifeless woods.

Before applying stain, first test color on a scrap piece of similar wood. Clean the surface area where stain is to be applied. Use a cloth to eliminate as much dust as possible. The stain can then be applied with a brush, foam brush applicator, or cloth. Apply a smooth, even coat of stain, allowing the stain to penetrate the wood. Depending on the humidity, temperature, and particular stain used, this usually takes from 5 to 15 minutes. While the stain is still wet, wipe off the excess stain with a clean cloth, but be careful not to remove too much from corners and edges. Wipe across the grain first so that you work the stain into the wood pores. Then give a final wipe with the grain. Allow the stain to dry. This usually takes at least 8 hours. The finish can then be applied.

It is usually best to apply a series of light, even coats of clear finish rather than one thick coat. This will minimize possible drips and wrinkles as the finish dries.

Apply finish in brush-width strokes in direction of wood grain. Turn rack so that finish is applied to horizontal wood surfaces whenever possible.

A minimum of two coats is recommended. Allow 6 to 8 hours for the first coat to dry before applying second coat. Sand lightly and use a tack cloth to remove sanded finish dust before applying next coat of finish.

Clear or stained finishes are usually applied to natural wood furniture, but if desired color paint finishes can also be applied.

Variations

Variations are possible for the storage rack. You may want to substitute materials, such as particle board, instead of plywood. Another common variation is to construct the storage rack to different dimensions. Alternate arrangements of shelves, such as shown in Figs. 7-10 and 7-11, are another possibility.

The storage rack is functional and attractive when built from inexpensive woods, but by using more expensive woods, it can take on an expensive custom appearance. The plans given here show simple butt joints, but if you have the cabinet-making skills and know-how, you can also use more difficult joints.

KNEELING CHAIR

The kneeling chair shown in Fig. 7-12 is a con-

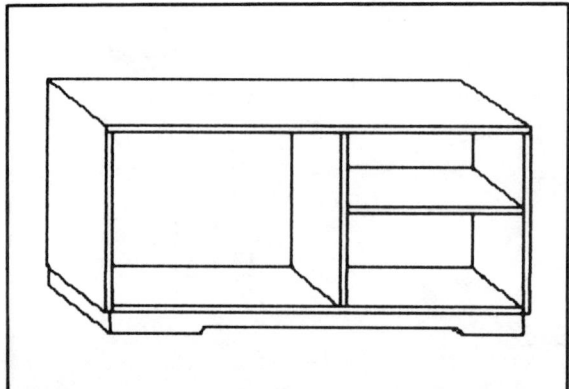

Fig. 7-10. Storage rack with alternate shelf arrangement.

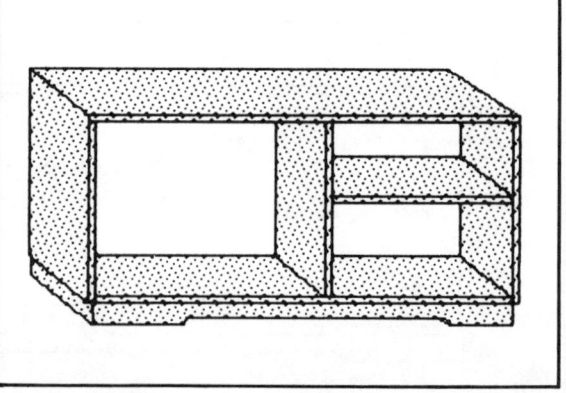

Fig. 7-11. Storage rack with alternate shelf arrangement with plastic laminates.

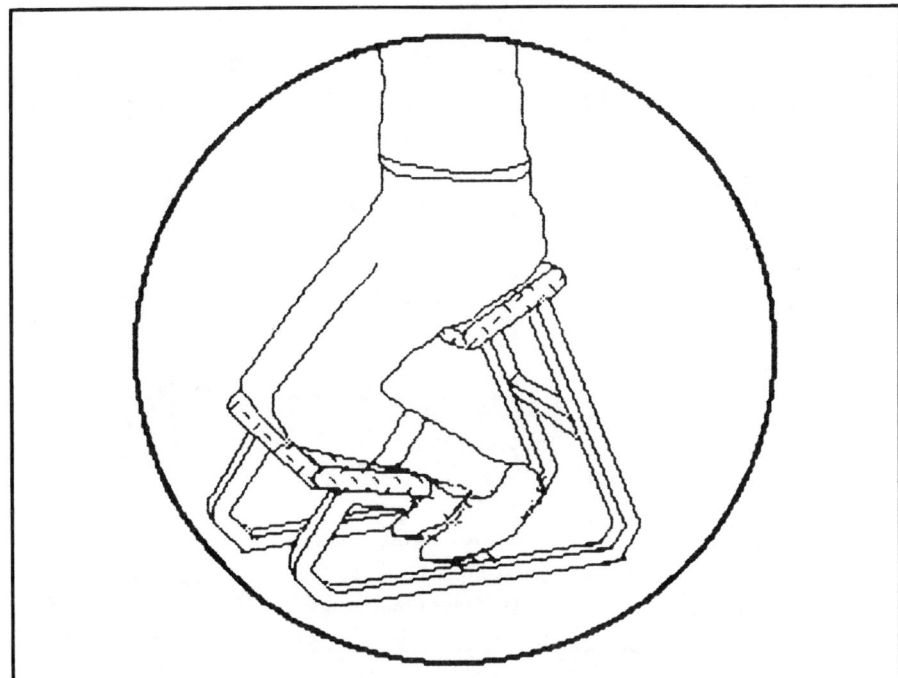

Fig. 7-12. Kneeling chair.

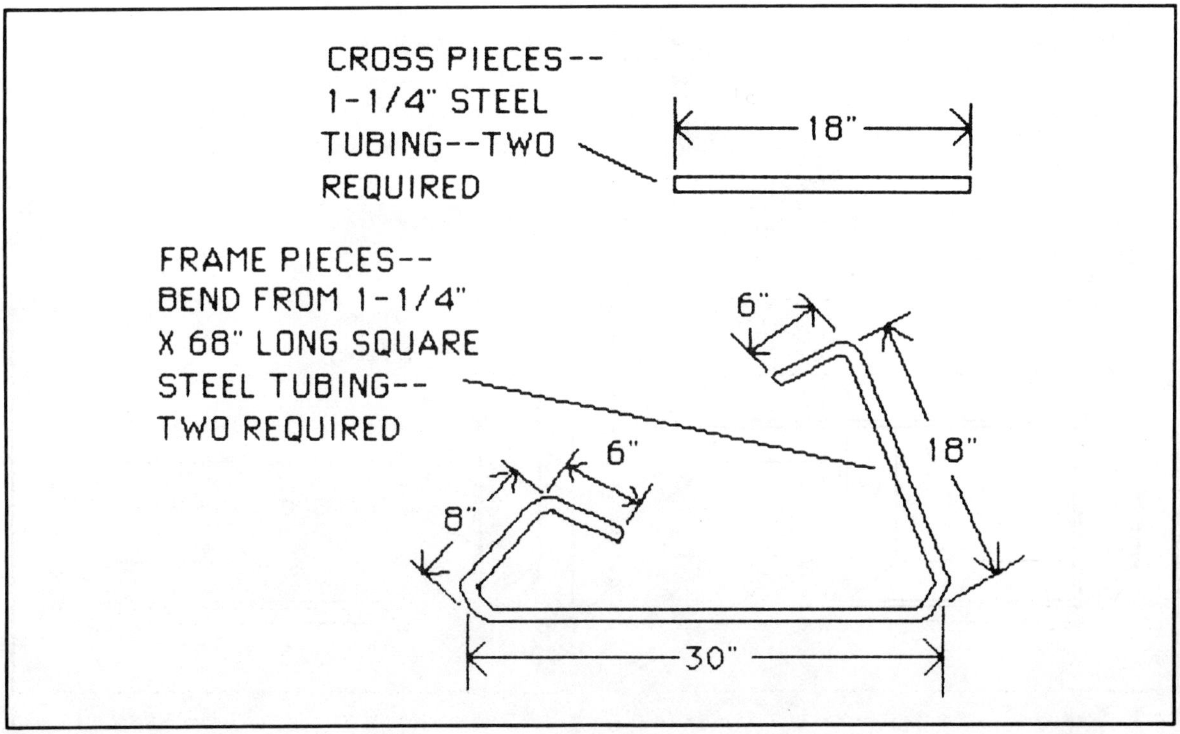

Fig. 7-13. Frame pattern for kneeling chair.

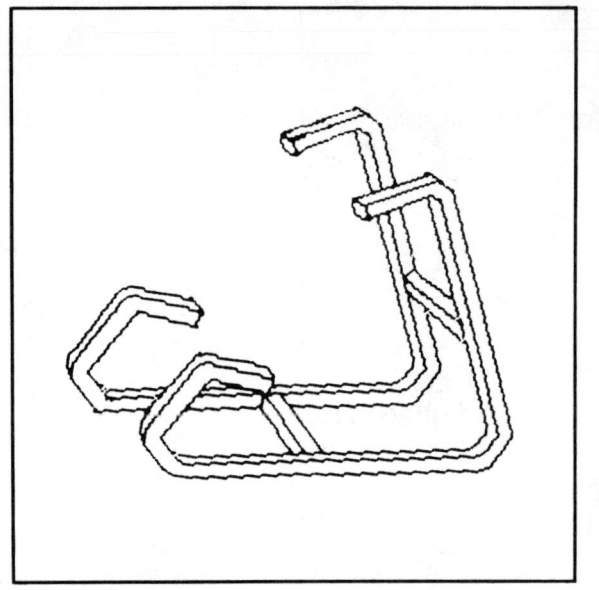

Fig. 7-14. Kneeling chair frame pieces are welded together.

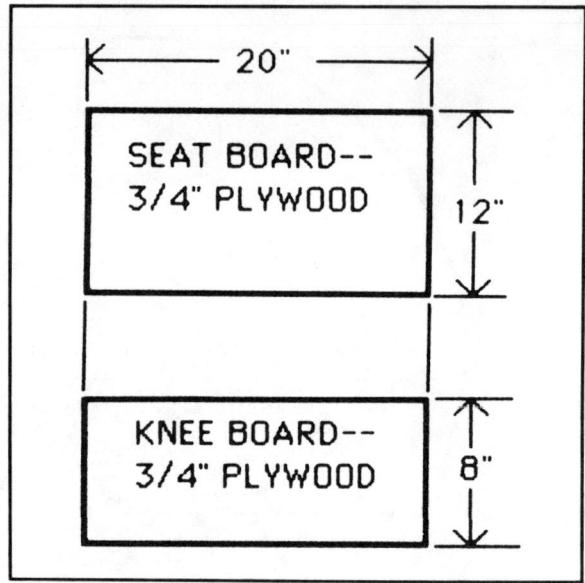

Fig. 7-15. Pattern for cushion boards.

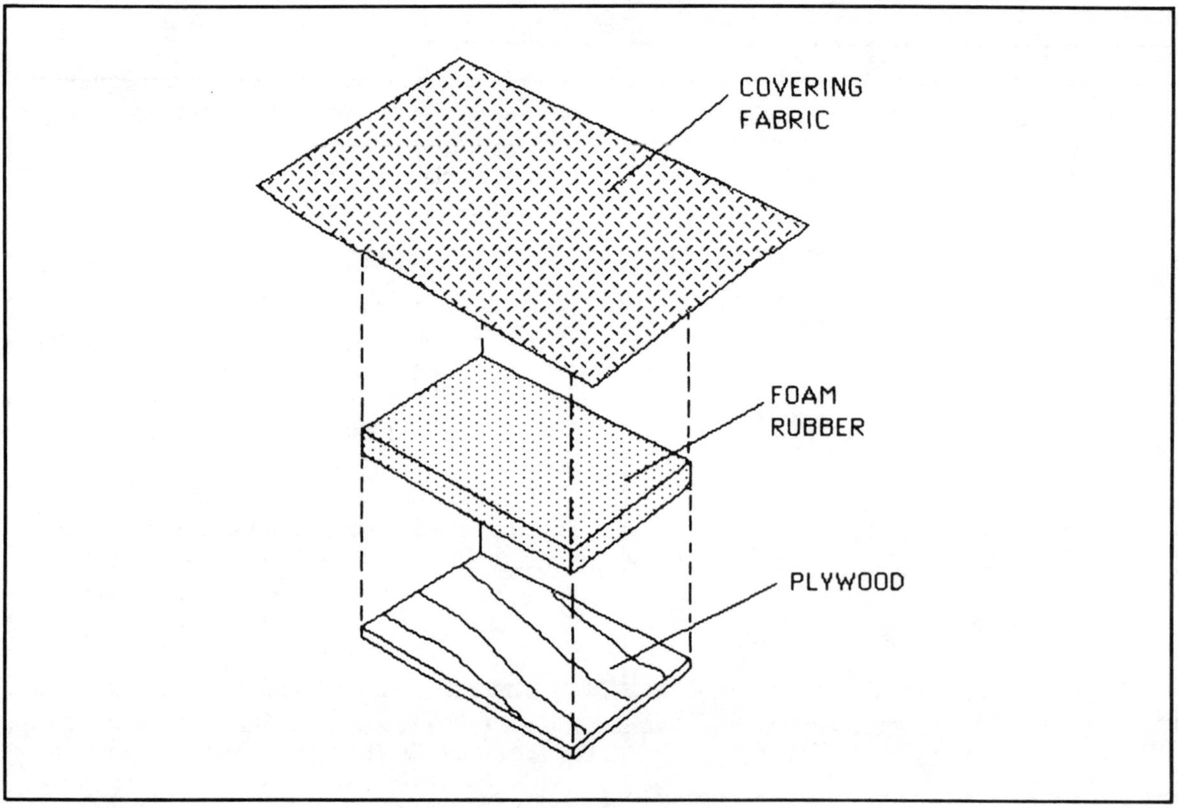

Fig. 7-16. Assembly of cushions (covering fabric, foam rubber, and plywood).

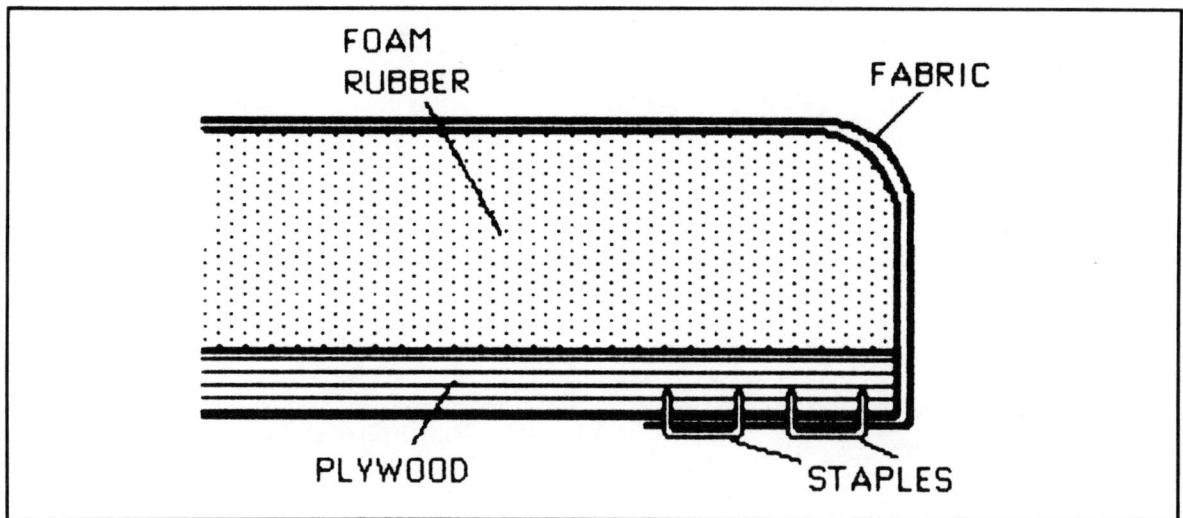

Fig. 7-17. Assembly of cushions.

troversial piece of computer furniture. Some people seem to think they are comfortable to use; others think they are ridiculous. Try a manufactured version out before building your own.

The frame for the kneeling chair is shown in Fig. 7-13. The square steel tubing is heated and bent to the pattern shown. The cross pieces are then welded to the side frame pieces, as shown in Fig. 7-14.

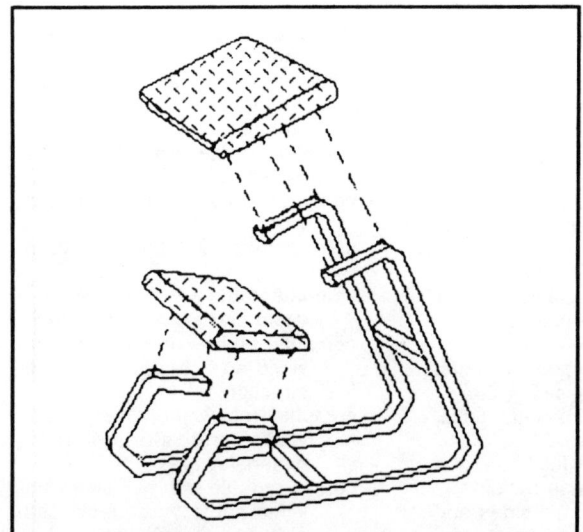

Fig. 7-18. Assembly of kneeling chair.

The patterns for the plywood seat base and knee cushion base are shown in Fig. 7-15. Both pieces are 3/4-inch thick. The seat board measures 12 inches by 20 inches. The knee board measures 8 inches by 20 inches. Use a ruler and square to make the pattern, marking the lines with a sharp pencil or scribing tool.

Use special care when sawing plywood to avoid chipping and splintering along the cut edge. Handsaws or power saws with special fine-toothed or carbide blades designed especially for plywood should be used. Masking tape applied to both sides of the cutting line, especially on the side opposite the one you are cutting from, is also helpful. Or, clamp a solid piece of wood to the underside and make the cut through both the plywood and the piece of wood.

The next step is to add the foam rubber padding and covering fabric to the seat board and knee board, as shown in Figs. 7-16 and 7-17. The fabric covering material can be attached to the undersides of the base boards with staples or tacks.

Holes are drilled through the metal frame parts for attaching the seat and knee boards. The assembly is shown in Fig. 7-18. Wood screws pass through the holes in the metal frame and into, but not all the way through, the plywood bases. Finish by painting the metal frame as desired.

Index

A
angle butt joint, 26
auger bit, 17

B
backsaw, 16
ball-peen hammers, 18
band saw, 16
basic budget computer table, 38
basic budget computer table, construction, 42
basic budget computer table, materials, 38
basic budget computer table, sanding and finishing, 52
basic budget computer table, variations, 54
basic budget printer stand, 167
basic budget printer stand, construction, 171
basic budget printer stand, materials, 167
basic budget printer stand, sanding and finishing, 178
basic budget printer stand, variations, 179
belt sanders, 17
board foot, 22
bolts, 29
brace, 16

built-in wall units, 253
built-in wall units, assembly, 257
built-in wall units, construction, 253
built-in wall units, materials, 253
built-in wall units, sanding and finishing, 267
built-in wall units, variations, 268

C
chisels, 17
circular saw, 16
clamps, 18
claw hammers, 18
compass saw, 16
computer furniture, basic concepts, 1-14
computer furniture, design, 1-14
computer furniture, planning, 1-14
computer table for modular units, 222
computer table for modular units, sanding and finishing, 245
computer table for modular units, variations, 248
computer table with full sides and video and storage rack, 116
computer table with full sides and video and storage rack, construction, 120

computer table with full sides and video and storage rack, materials, 116
computer table with full sides and video and storage rack, sanding and finishing, 136
computer table with full sides and video and storage rack, variations, 141
computer table with full sides, 55
computer table with full sides, construction, 59
computer table with full sides, materials, 56
computer table with full sides, sanding and finishing, 69
computer table with full sides, variations, 71
computer table with half sides and video and storage rack, 141
computer table with half sides and video and storage rack, construction, 147
computer table with half sides and video and storage rack, materials, 142
computer table with half sides and video and storage rack, sanding and finishing, 160
computer table with half sides and

video and storage rack, variations, 166
computer table with half sides, 74
computer table with half sides, construction, 79
computer table with half sides, materials, 75
computer table with half sides, sanding and finishing, 93
computer table with half sides, variations, 94
computer table with modular units, construction, 230
computer table with modular units, materials, 224
computer table with video and storage rack, 97
computer table with video and storage rack, construction, 103
computer table with video and storage rack, materials, 97
computer table with video and storage rack, sanding and finishing, 111
computer table with video and storage rack, variations, 116
computer table, basic budget, 38
computer tables, plans and patterns for, 38-166
construction techniques, 15-37
coping saw, 16
counterbore section, 26
countersink bit, 26
crosscut saw, 15

D
disk sanders, 17
Douglas fir, 19
dovetail saw, 16
drawknife, 17
drill presses, 17
drills, push, 17
drills, twist, 17

E
epoxy glue, 67
extender, 60-degree, 251
extender, 90-degree, 248
extender, square, 250
extenders, 248
extenders, construction of, 248

F
fastening, 26
fiberboard, 78
files, 17
finishing, 35
fly cutters, 26

folding rule, 18

G
gluing, 26

H
hammers, 18
hammers, ball-peen, 18
hammers, claw, 18
holes, boring, 25
holes, drilling, 25

J
jigsaw, 16
joining, 26
joint, angle butt, 26
joint, miter, 27
joint, rabbet, 27
joint, T-butt, 26
joint, T-rabbet, 27

K
keyhole saw, 16
kneeling chair, 278

M
mallets, 18
measuring and marking tools, 17
miter joint, 27
modular concept, 3
modular units, plans and patterns for, 222-252

P
pad sanders, 17
pine, white, 19
pine, yellow, 19
planes, 17
planing, 25
plastic laminates, 30
plastic laminates, adding to wood, 30
plug cutter, 26
plywood, 20
polyurethane plastic finish, 53
printer platform, 269
printer platform, construction, 270
printer platform, materials, 269
printer platform, sanding and finishing, 273
printer platform, variations, 274
printer stand with full sides, 179
printer stand with full sides, construction, 182
printer stand with full sides, materials, 179
printer stand with full sides, sanding and finishing, 192

printer stand with full sides, variations, 200
printer stand with half sides, 200
printer stand with half sides, construction, 203
printer stand with half sides, materials, 201
printer stand with half sides, sanding and finishing, 214
printer stand with half sides, variations, 221
printer stand, basic budget, 167
printer stands, plans and patterns for, 167-221
projects, plans and patterns for, 269
protractors, 18
putty, 49

R
rabbet joint, 27
radial arm saw, 16
rasps, 17
ripsaw, 15
rotary power saw, 125
router, 65

S
saber saw, 16
sanding papers, 17
sawing, 24
saws, 15
screwdrivers, 18
steel rule, 18
storage rack, 274
storage rack, construction, 275
storage rack, materials, 274
storage rack, sanding and finishing, 277
storage rack, variations, 278
surfacing, 25
Surform tools, 17

T
T-butt joint, 26
T-rabbet joint, 27
tape rule, 18
tools, 15
tools, hole making, 16
tools, measuring and marking, 17
tools, surform, 17

V
vises, 18

W
wall units, built-in, 253-268
wood filler, 49
wood parts, shaping, 21
wood, 19

OTHER POPULAR TAB BOOKS OF INTEREST

44 Terrific Woodworking Plans & Projects (No. 1762—$12.50 paper; $21.95 hard)

How to Repair Briggs & Stratton Engines—2nd Edition (No. 1687—$8.95 paper; $15.95 hard)

Security for You and Your Home . . . A Complete Handbook (No. 1680—$17.50 paper; $29.95 hard)

46 Step-by-Step Wooden Toy Projects (No. 1675—$9.95 paper; $17.95 hard)

The Kite Building & Kite Flying Handbook, with 42 Kite Plans (No. 1669—$15.50 paper)

Building Better Beds (No. 1664—$14.50 paper; $19.95 hard)

Organic Vegetable Gardening (No. 1660—$16.50 paper; $25.95 hard)

The Woodturning Handbook, with Projects (No. 1655—$14.50 paper; $21.95 hard)

Clock Making for the Woodworker (No. 1648—$11.50 paper; $16.95 hard)

Steel Homes (No. 1641—$15.50 paper; $21.95 hard)

The Homeowner's Illustrated Guide to Concrete (No. 1626—$15.50 paper; $24.95 hard)

Kerosene Heaters (No. 1598—$10.25 paper; $16.95 hard)

Clocks—Construction, Maintenance and Repair (No. 1569—$13.50 paper; $18.95 hard)

The Underground Home Answer Book (No. 1562—$11.50 paper; $16.95 hard)

Airbrushing (No. 1555—$20.50 paper)

Basic Blueprint Reading for Practical Applications (No. 1546—$13.50 paper; $18.95 hard)

Central Heating and Air Conditioning Repair Guide—2nd Edition (No. 1520—$13.50 paper; $18.95 hard)

The Complete Book of Fences (No. 1508—$12.95 paper; $19.95 hard)

How to Sharpen Anything (No. 1463—$12.95 paper; $19.95 hard)

Building a Log Home from Scratch or Kit (No. 1458—$12.50 paper; $17.95 hard)

Build It with Plywood: 88 Furniture Projects (No. 1430—$13.50 paper; $18.95 hard)

The GIANT Book of Metalworking Projects (No. 1357—$12.95 paper; $19.95 hard)

The Welder's Bible (No. 1244—$13.95 paper)

The GIANT Handbook of Food-Preserving Basics (No. 1727—$13.50 paper; $17.95 hard)

Ventilation: Your Secret Key to an Energy-Efficient Home (No. 1681—$8.95 paper; $15.95 hard)

Tuning and Repairing Your Own Piano (No. 1678—$12.50 paper)

Superinsulated, Truss-Frame House Construction (No. 1674—$15.50 paper; $21.95 hard)

Raising Animals for Fun and Profit (No. 1666—$13.50 paper; $18.95 hard)

Practical Herb Gardening . . . with Recipes (No. 1661—$11.95 paper; $15.95 hard)

Effective Lighting for Home and Business (No. 1658—$13.50 paper; $18.95 hard)

Constructing and Maintaining Your Well and Septic System (No. 1654—$12.50 paper; $17.95 hard)

Maps and Compasses: A User's Handbook (No. 1644—$9.25 paper; $15.95 hard)

Woodcarving, with Projects (No. 1639—$11.50 paper; $16.95 hard)

Sign Carving (No. 1601—$13.50 paper; $19.95 hard)

Mastering Household Electrical Wiring (No. 1587—$13.50 paper; $19.95 hard)

Cave Exploring (No. 1566—$10.25 paper; $16.95 hard)

The Radio Control Hobbyist's Handbook (No. 1561—$19.50 paper)

Be Your Own Contractor: The Affordable Way to Home Ownership (No. 1554—$12.50 paper; $17.95 hard)

Beekeeping—An Illustrated Handbook (No. 1524—$10.95 paper; $15.95 hard)

101 Model Railroad Layouts (No. 1514—$11.50 paper; $17.95 hard)

53 Space-Saving, Built-In Furniture Projects (No. 1504—$17.50 paper)

The Home Brewer's Handbook (No. 1461—$10.25 paper; $16.95 hard)

Constructing Outdoor Furniture, with 99 Projects (No. 1454—$15.50 paper)

Draw Your Own House Plans (No. 1381—$14.50 paper; $19.95 hard)

The Fiberglass Repair & Construction Handbook (No. 1297—$11.50 paper; $17.95 hard)

TAB   TAB BOOKS Inc.

Blue Ridge Summit, Pa. 17214

Send for FREE TAB Catalog describing over 750 current titles in print.